The Wiley Blackwell Handbook of Sche

The Wiley Blackwell Handbook of Schema Therapy

Theory, Research, and Practice

Edited by

Michiel van Vreeswijk
G-kracht, Psychomedisch Centrum Delft, The Netherlands

Jenny Broersen
GGZ Delfland, Delft, and G-kracht, Psychomedisch Centrum Amsterdam, Delft, The Netherlands

Marjon Nadort
VU Medical Center, and G-kracht, Psychomedisch Centrum Amsterdam, The Netherlands

WILEY Blackwell

This paperback edition first published 2015
© 2012 John Wiley & Sons, Ltd.

Edition history: The Wiley-Blackwell Handbook of Schema Therapy, edited by Michiel van Vreeswijk, Jenny Broersen, and Marjon Nadort, John Wiley & Sons, Ltd (hardback, 2012)

Registered Office
John Wiley & Sons, Ltd, The Atrium, Southern Gate, Chichester, West Sussex, PO19 8SQ, UK

Editorial Offices
350 Main Street, Malden, MA 02148-5020, USA
9600 Garsington Road, Oxford, OX4 2DQ, UK
The Atrium, Southern Gate, Chichester, West Sussex, PO19 8SQ, UK

For details of our global editorial offices, for customer services, and for information about how to apply for permission to reuse the copyright material in this book please see our website at www.wiley.com/wiley-blackwell.

The right of Michiel van Vreeswijk, Jenny Broersen, and Marjon Nadort to be identified as the authors of the editorial material in this work has been asserted in accordance with the UK Copyright, Designs and Patents Act 1988.

All rights reserved. No part of this publication may be reproduced, stored in a retrieval system, or transmitted, in any form or by any means, electronic, mechanical, photocopying, recording or otherwise, except as permitted by the UK Copyright, Designs and Patents Act 1988, without the prior permission of the publisher.

Wiley also publishes its books in a variety of electronic formats. Some content that appears in print may not be available in electronic books.

Designations used by companies to distinguish their products are often claimed as trademarks. All brand names and product names used in this book are trade names, service marks, trademarks or registered trademarks of their respective owners. The publisher is not associated with any product or vendor mentioned in this book.

Limit of Liability/Disclaimer of Warranty: While the publisher and authors have used their best efforts in preparing this book, they make no representations or warranties with respect to the accuracy or completeness of the contents of this book and specifically disclaim any implied warranties of merchantability or fitness for a particular purpose. It is sold on the understanding that the publisher is not engaged in rendering professional services and neither the publisher nor the author shall be liable for damages arising herefrom. If professional advice or other expert assistance is required, the services of a competent professional should be sought.

Library of Congress Cataloging-in-Publication Data

The Wiley Blackwell handbook of schema therapy: theory, research, and practice / edited by Michiel van Vreeswijk, Jenny Broersen, Marjon Nadort.
   p. cm.
   Includes index.
   ISBN 978-0-470-97561-9 (cloth) ISBN 978-1-119-05729-1 (paper)
1. Schema-focused–Handbooks, manuals, etc. I. Vreeswijk, Michiel van. II. Broersen, Jenny.
III. Nadort, Marjon. IV. Title: Handbook of schema therapy.
   RC455.4.S36W55 2012
   616.89′1425–dc23
                                        2011035197

A catalogue record for this book is available from the British Library.

Cover image: © Mikadun / Shutterstock

Set in 10/12.5 Galliard by SPi Global, Pondicherry, India
Printed and bound in Malaysia by Vivar Printing Sdn Bhd

1   2015

Contents

List of Contributors		ix
Foreword		xxiii
Jeffrey Young		
Acknowledgments		xxv
Part I	**An Introduction to Schema Therapy**	1
	Chapter 1: Schema Therapy in Historical Perspective *David Edwards and Arnoud Arntz*	3
	Chapter 2: Theoretical Model: Schemas, Coping Styles, and Modes *Hannie van Genderen, Marleen Rijkeboer, and Arnoud Arntz*	27
	Chapter 3: A New Look at Core Emotional Needs *George Lockwood and Poul Perris*	41
Part II	**The Indication Process in Schema Therapy**	67
	Chapter 1: The Case Formulation Process in Schema Therapy of Chronic Axis I Disorder (Affective/Anxiety Disorder) *Asle Hoffart*	69
	Chapter 2: Schema Therapy for Narcissism – A Case Study *Wendy Behary*	81
	Chapter 3: Assessment for Schema Therapy *Anoek Weertman and Hilde de Saeger*	91
	Chapter 4: The Use of Experiential Techniques for Diagnostics *Anoek Weertman*	101
	Chapter 5: Clinical Use of Schema Inventories *Alexandra Sheffield and Glenn Waller*	111
	Chapter 6: Case Conceptualization in Schema Therapy *Hannie van Genderen*	125

Part III	Schema Therapy Techniques	143
	Chapter 1: Schema Therapy for Eating Disorders: A Case Study Illustration of the Mode Approach *Susan Simpson*	145
	Chapter 2: Treating OCD with the Schema Mode Model *Ellen Gross, Nicola Stelzer, and Gitta Jacob*	173
	Chapter 3: Techniques within Schema Therapy *Michiel van Vreeswijk, Jenny Broersen, Josephine Bloo, and Suzanne Haeyen*	185
	Chapter 4: On Speaking One's Mind: Using ChairWork Dialogues in Schema Therapy *Scott Kellogg*	197
	Chapter 5: Schema Therapy and the Role of Joy and Play *George Lockwood and Ida Shaw*	209
	Chapter 6: Schema Therapy, Mindfulness, and ACT – Differences and Points of Contact *Erwin Parfy*	229
	Chapter 7: Why Are Mindfulness and Acceptance Central Elements for Therapeutic Change in Schema Therapy Too?: An Integrative Perspective *Eckhard Roediger*	239
	Chapter 8: Mindfulness and ACT as Strategies to Enhance the Healthy Adult Mode: The Use of the Mindfulness Flash Card as an Example *Pierre Cousineau*	249
	Chapter 9: Teaching Mindfulness Meditation within a Schema Therapy Framework *David Bricker and Miriam Labin*	259
	Chapter 10: Schema-Focused Mindfulness: an Eight-Session Protocol *Michiel van Vreeswijk and Jenny Broersen*	271
	Chapter 11: The Impact of Measuring: Therapy Results and Therapeutic Alliance *Michiel van Vreeswijk, Jenny Broersen, and Philip Spinhoven*	283
Part IV	Schema Therapy Settings and Patient Populations	299
	Chapter 1: Inpatient Schema Therapy for Patients with Borderline Personality Disorder – a Case Study *Neele Reiss, Gitta Jacob, and Joan Farrell*	301
	Chapter 2: Individual Schema Therapy: Practical Experience with Adults *Pien van den Kieboom and Daan Jonker*	311

Chapter 3:	Schema Therapy for Couples: Healing Partners in a Relationship *Travis Atkinson*	323
Chapter 4:	Introduction to Group Schema Therapy *Joan Farrell*	337
Chapter 5:	Group Schema Therapy for Borderline Personality Disorder Patients: Catalyzing Schema and Mode Change *Joan Farrell, Ida Shaw, and Neele Reiss*	341
Chapter 6:	Implementation of Schema Therapy in an Inpatient and Day Treatment Group Setting *Eelco Muste*	359
Chapter 7:	Schema Therapy in Groups: A Short-Term Schema CBT Protocol *Jenny Broersen and Michiel van Vreeswijk*	373
Chapter 8:	Schema Therapy in a Psychodynamic Group *Helga Aalders and Janie van Dijk*	383
Chapter 9:	Schema Therapy in Adolescents *Maryke Geerdink, Erik Jongman, and Agnes Scholing*	391
Chapter 10:	Schema Therapy for Cluster C Personality Disorders *Arnoud Arntz*	397
Chapter 11:	Schema Therapy for Personality Disorders and Addiction *Truus Kersten*	415
Chapter 12:	Schema Therapy in Forensic Settings *David Bernstein, Marije Keulen-de Vos, Philip Jonkers, Ellen de Jonge, and Arnoud Arntz*	425

Part V The Therapist: Training, Supervision, and Self-Care in Schema Therapy — 439

Chapter 1:	Training for and Registrations of Schema Therapists *Marjon Nadort, Hannie van Genderen, and Wendy Behary*	441
Chapter 2:	Training and Supervision in Schema Therapy *Marjon Nadort, Hannie van Genderen, and Wendy Behary*	453
Chapter 3:	The Schema Mode Model in Personal Therapy *Gitta Jacob*	463
Chapter 4:	Therapist Self-Care in the Context of Limited Reparenting *Poul Perris, Heather Fretwell, and Ida Shaw*	473

Part VI	Research in Schema Therapy	493
	Chapter 1: Effectiveness Studies *Lotte Bamelis, Josephine Bloo,* *David Bernstein, and Arnoud Arntz*	495
	Chapter 2: Experimental Studies of Schema Modes *Jill Lobbestael*	511
	Chapter 3: Experimental Studies for Schemas *Simkje Sieswerda*	519
	Chapter 4: Validation of the Young Schema Questionnaire *Marleen Rijkeboer*	531
	Chapter 5: Validation of the Schema Mode Inventory *Jill Lobbestael*	541
Part VII	Implementation and Public Relations in Schema Therapy	553
	Chapter 1: Implementation of Schema Therapy in General Mental Healthcare Institutes *Marjon Nadort*	555
	Chapter 2: Using ST Principles to Increase the Therapeutic Efficacy of the Forensic Care Team's Interactions with Personality Disordered Clients *Naomi Murphy, Des McVey, and Geoff Hopping*	569
	Chapter 3: Implementation of Schema Therapy in de Rooyse Wissel Forensic Psychiatric Center *Truus Kersten and Lieda van de Vis*	579
	Chapter 4: Cost-Effectiveness of Schema Therapy *Thea van Asselt and Josephine Bloo*	585
	Chapter 5: Public Relations for Schema Therapy *Michiel van Vreeswijk, Marjon Nadort,* *and Jenny Broersen*	599
	Chapter 6: Concluding Thoughts *Michiel van Vreeswijk, Jenny Broersen,* *and Marjon Nadort*	609

Author Index   611

Subject Index – Schema Therapy   627

List of Contributors

Helga Aalders is a Clinical Psychologist/Psychotherapist and works both at the Altrecht Outpatient Clinic, Utrecht and in private practice in Zeist, the Netherlands. She was trained in various fields (CBT/Schema Therapy/psychoanalytical and group dynamic therapy) and she is part of the Care Program Personality Disorders at the Altrecht outpatients' clinic. She is also a teacher, supervisor, and coach within the P&A training institute.

Arnoud Arntz is a professor of Clinical Psychology and Experimental Psychopathology at Maastricht University, the Netherlands. He studies both fundamental psychological processes in and treatment of anxiety and personality disorders. He is also active as a therapist. Together with professor Marcel van den Hout he is editor of the Journal of Behavior Therapy and Experimental Psychiatry. Arnoud Arntz was and is project leader of various multicenter randomized controlled trials into the effectiveness and cost-effectiveness of Schema Therapy. Together with Hannie van Genderen he published a book describing a Schema Therapy protocol for borderline personality disorder published by Wiley. That protocol was the basis of the version of Schema Therapy which was successfully tested in Giesen-Bloo and colleagues' study (2006), published in the *Archives of General Psychiatry*.

Thea van Asselt is a senior researcher at Maastricht University Medical Center, the Netherlands. She studied economics at Groningen State University, the Netherlands, and has been working as a health economist since 1998. Her PhD (awarded in 2008) was on the economic aspects of treatment, including Schema Therapy, for borderline personality disorders. Her cost-effectiveness research covers not only psychiatry, but other clinical areas as well, such as cardiovascular diseases and surgical infections.

Travis Atkinson LCSW is the Clinical Director of Advanced Cognitive Therapy of New York. He is a highly experienced, compassionate therapist working in Manhattan for many years, and is affiliated with the Cognitive Therapy Center of New York and the Schema Therapy Institute. Travis presented with Jeffrey Young, the founder of Schema Therapy, at the prestigious New England Educational Institute, training other couples therapists in the latest Schema Therapy techniques for couples therapy. He has completed advanced training with Susan Johnson, the founder of the top-rated Emotionally Focused Couples Therapy (EFT). He also has completed years of extensive training in couples therapy with the Gottman Institute, headed by the founder, John Gottman, and was awarded the distinguished title of Certified Gottman Therapist.

Lotte Bamelis is a PhD student at the Department of Clinical Psychological Science, Maastricht University, the Netherlands. Since 2006, she has been conducting a large, multi-center, randomized controlled trial on the clinical and cost-effectiveness of Schema Therapy for Cluster C, paranoid, histrionic, and narcissistic personality disorders. More than 300 patients are being treated in 12 mental health centers throughout the Netherlands.

Wendy Behary is with 25 years' postgraduate training and advanced level certifications, the founder and director of The Cognitive Therapy Center of New Jersey and the New Jersey Institute for Schema Therapy. She has been treating clients, training professionals, and supervising psychotherapists for more than 20 years. Wendy is also on the faculty of the Cognitive Therapy Center and Schema Therapy Institute of New York, where she has trained and worked with Jeffrey Young since 1989. She is a founding fellow of the Academy of Cognitive Therapy (Aaron T. Beck). Wendy is also the President of the Executive Board of the International Society of Schema Therapy (ISST).

Wendy has co-authored several chapters and articles on Schema Therapy and cognitive therapy. She is the author of *Disarming the Narcissist . . . Surviving and Thriving with the Self-Absorbed."* Wendy has a specialty in treating narcissists and the people who live with and deal with them. She has lectured both nationally and internationally to professional and general audiences on the subject of narcissism and how to deal with difficult people. Her work with industry has included speaking engagements focused on interpersonal conflict resolution.

Wendy's private practice is primarily devoted to treating narcissists, partners/people dealing with them, and couples experiencing relationship problems. She is also an expert in coaching individuals in interviewing, public speaking, and interpersonal skills enhancement.

David Bernstein is Professor of Forensic Psychotherapy (endowed chair) at Maastricht University and the de Rooyse Wissel forensic psychiatric center. He received his doctoral degree from New York University in 1990. He joined the faculty of Maastricht University in 2004, where he now serves as Chair of the Forensic Psychology Section in the Faculty of Psychology and Neuroscience. He is currently Vice-President of the International Society for Schema Therapy and is past President of the Association for Research on Personality Disorders. His research spans a wide range of areas, including forensic psychology, psychotherapy, personality disorders, childhood trauma, and addictions. He is an internationally acknowledged expert on Schema Therapy, an integrative psychotherapy for personality disorders. He is the author or co-author of more than 90 publications, including *Schema Therapy: Distinctive Features* and the forthcoming *Treating Aggression, Addiction, and Personality Disorder: A Schema-Focused Approach to Complex, Antisocial Patients*. His current research focuses on developing, testing, and implementing innovative forms of therapy for forensic patients with personality disorders.

Josephine Bloo was awarded a PhD for her thesis "Crossing Borders: theory, assessment and treatment in borderline personality disorder" at Maastricht University, in cooperation with the Leiden University and the VU Medical Center, Amsterdam in 2006. Her most important publications are on the subject of the efficacy of schema-focused therapy vs. transference-focused psychotherapy. Since 2008, she has worked as a therapist at LavOri BV, a department of the academic related RIAGG in Maastricht.

David Bricker is a psychologist in private practice in New York City. He received his PhD in psychology from the State University of New York at Albany. He is a member of the graduate faculty of the Ferkauf Graduate School of Yeshiva University. He is also an affiliate of the Schema Therapy Institute in New York and is a certified Schema Therapist. He splits his practice between individuals and couples and is also a certified Gottman Method Therapist. His main research interest has been the integration of various systems of psychotherapy.

Jenny Broersen is Mental Healthcare Psychologist and Psychotherapist. She is a Certified supervisor Supervisor Schema Therapist (ISST, Dutch register ST). In the last 15 years she has worked in outpatient and day treatment centers. She has a vast wealth of experience in the treatment of personality disorders working as site director of G-kracht Psychomedisch Centrum BV in Amsterdam, The Netherlands, together with her colleague Marjon Nadort. Jenny works in the Mental Healthcare Institute in GGZ Delfland in Delft (the Netherlands). She is co-author/editor of several schema books, chapters and articles and gives post doctorate courses in Schema Therapy and Cognitive Behavioral Therapy.

Pierre Cousineau is psychotherapist and supervisor in Montreal, Canada. He gives workshops to French-speaking psychotherapists in Quebec, Francophone European countries, and Morocco. He studied psychology in Montreal (Quebec) and in Waterloo (Ontario). He gained his PhD at the University of Waterloo in 1980. He wrote papers and was co-author of a textbook in the French language. He has a specific interest for the integration of mindfulness and ACT strategies into Schema Therapy.

Janie van Dijk works as a Clinical Psychologist/Psychotherapist in private practice and at Altrecht Cura, Utrecht, the Netherlands. She specializes in the treatment of personality problems, anxiety disorders, and couples therapy. She is a supervisor for Schema Therapy and couples therapy. She also teaches in both these specialist areas. Among other publications, she has written on the subject of trauma treatment for war victims.

David Edwards is a Professor at Rhodes University, South Africa. He was fortunate to be connected to the beginnings of Schema Therapy when, in 1984, he attended seminars with Jeffrey Young while training in cognitive therapy at the University of Pennsylvania. He has a long-standing interest in psychotherapy integration and has experience with expressive approaches to psychotherapy through drama, dance, sculpture, painting, and drawing, particularly within the humanistic and transpersonal traditions. He has promoted the role of case-study methodology in the development of applied clinical science and used case studies to provide a contextualized evidence base for the treatment of post-traumatic stress disorder in South Africa. His interest in historical perspectives on psychotherapy arose from reflection on his own experience and from writing an article and a book chapter on the history of imagery in psychotherapy.

Joan Farrell was awarded a PhD in Clinical Psychology in 1978. She is Program Director and founder of the Center for BPD Treatment and Research at Indiana University School of Medicine and has been a faculty member in psychiatry there for 25 years. She holds faculty appointments in the psychology departments of Purdue University and the University of Indianapolis. With Ida Shaw, she developed a group ST treatment for borderline personality disorder (BPD), which was tested in a successful randomized-controlled trial (RCT). Together, they developed an inpatient ST program and a dedicated unit for patients with severe BPD, which was awarded a Governor's Showcase award. Farrell is co-PI with Arntz on a four-country, 14-site RCT of group ST for BPD. Her research focus is the evaluation of group ST and she consults in this area internationally. She is co-director of the Schema Therapy Institute Midwest–Indianapolis. Farrell is the co-author of *Group Schema Therapy for BPD* and has written book chapters and articles in research journals on BPD treatment. Farrell and Shaw give workshops and master classes internationally in the GST model they developed. She is an advanced-level Schema Therapist and Trainer certified by ISST.

Heather Fretwell is an Assistant Professor of Clinical Psychiatry at the Indiana University School of Medicine. She graduated magna cum laude with an Honors BS from Ball State University, and then earned her MD at the Indiana University School of Medicine in 2002, and completed her residency training in psychiatry there in 2006. She is the director of the IU Center for Borderline Personality Disorder Treatment and Research. Clinically, she directs the outpatient ST treatment program for borderline PD at Midtown Community Mental Health, the largest CMHC in Indiana, and supervises the psychiatry residency training site there. She is an associate of the Schema Therapy Institute Midwest. Her research interests are in the psychotherapeutic and pharmaceutical treatments of borderline personality disorder. She is a co-investigator on the multi-site international trial of group and individual ST with the co-PIs Arnoud Arntz and Joan Farrell. She has co-authored several articles on ST for various presentations and media and is a contributor to the *Group Schema Therapy Treatment Manual* (Wiley, 2012).

Maryke Geerdink is a forensic Psychologist working for De Waag Amsterdam, Centre for Outpatient Forensic Psychiatry, since 2003. She has many years of experience giving individual and group therapy to youths (12+) and adults with severe personality disorders. As a cognitive and behavioral therapist she specializes in relapse prevention with adult males with problematic sexual behavior and youths and adults with aggression and emotional regulation disorders. She is also a teacher, experienced in teaching post-graduate training for mental health professionals.

Hannie van Genderen is employed at the Mental Health Center, Maastricht and is a Clinical Psychologist and senior consultant on research. She was trained in Schema Therapy by Jeffrey Young in 1995. She closely collaborates with Arnoud Arntz at Maastricht University, with whom she wrote *Schema Therapy for the Borderline Personality Disorder*. She is a trainer and supervisor in Schema Therapy and cognitive behavioral therapy in the Netherlands. She is a member of the board of the International Society of Schema Therapy and the Dutch Schema Therapy Association. For both boards, she is the coordinator of Training and Certification.

Suzanne Haeyen is an Art Therapist and Master of Art Therapies, and is chairman for Art Therapy at Scelta, Expert Center for Personality Disorders, at GGNet, a mental healthcare institution in the Netherlands. She is the coordinator of content and lecturer of the Part Time Study Arts Therapy of HAN University. She has authored and co-authored several publications about art therapy and personality disorders, including *Don't Act Out but Live Through*. She co-edited the *Dutch Handbook for Art Therapy*. In 2010, she carried out research focused on the effects of art therapy which resulted in her book *The connecting quality of Art Therapy* in 2011. Besides her specialization in borderline and Cluster B and C personality disorders, includes working with clients with traumas, eating disorders, and mood disorders, and with adolescents.

Asle Hoffart is Senior Researcher at the Research Institute, Modum Bad (a psychiatric hospital in Norway), Professor at the Department of Psychology, University of Oslo. He has written two books on social phobia and has published over 80 scientific articles in international journals, is a specialist in clinical psychology, and is an approved supervisor in cognitive therapy and Schema Therapy. His research interests are psychotherapy research, process and outcome in cognitive therapy, anxiety disorders including PTSD, the relationship between theories and clinical practice, and the philosophical basis of psychotherapy.

Geoff Hopping is a Consultant Psychotherapist in a prison unit for people with severe personality disorder who are at risk of harming others. He is qualified in psychoanalytic psychotherapy and is a Teaching and Supervising Transactional Analyst. He studied at the Metanoia Institute in London, where he works as a visiting lecturer. He previously worked for 20 years in private practice as a psychotherapist, trainer, and supervisor. His current interest is in relational group psychotherapy and the ways that this can have a reparative impact on destructive behaviors. He recently co-authored a chapter on group work, published in *Relational Transactional Analysis: Theory and Practice*.

Gitta Jacob is a Clinical Psychologist, Cognitive and Schema Therapist in the Department of Clinical Psychology and Psychotherapy, Freiburg, Germany. She is a founding board member of the International Society for Schema Therapy and was Chair of the Working Group on Borderline Personality Disorders at the Department of Psychiatry and Psychotherapy, University Hospital Freiburg. Her main research interests are borderline personality disorder and emotion-focused interventions. She is co-author of more than 40 publications in clinical psychology, psychotherapy, and borderline personality disorder.

Ellen de Jonge currently works as a psychologist for forensic outpatients at GGZ Noord-Holland Noord in the Netherlands. She studied clinical psychology at Utrecht University and received her MSc in 2006. Subsequently she did postgraduate research and treatment at FPC de Oostvaarderskliniek forensic psychiatric hospital to become a fully licensed psychologist. She is an associate member of the Dutch Association of Cognitive Behavioral Therapy.

Erik Jongman is a manager and therapist of adolescents (12–23 years old) with forensic and psychiatric problems. Most of these adolescents come from MPG (Multi Family Problems) families and have completed at least three treatments. He works mainly with family systems, and also uses individual treatments: EMDR, CBT, and Schema Therapy.

Daan Jonker works as a coach for the postdoctoral program of Clinical Psychology, Health Care Psychologist, and Psychotherapist. He is also coordinator of the Care Program Personality Problems at the GGZ Zoetermeer, Rivierduinen, the Netherlands). He has made a name for himself for his research into treatment of suicidal behavior, and has worked as a supervisor and trainer in family treatment, hypnosis, and schema-focused treatments for a long period. His work is particularly characterized by the integrative approach, partly as a result of his prior training in hypnosis, directive therapy, family therapy, psychoanalytical and group dynamic treatments, cognitive therapy, and Young's Schema Therapy. In addition to his involvement in several professional associations in the Netherlands and Switzerland, he is a board member of the Dutch Register of Schema Therapy.

Philip Jonkers currently works as a psychologist-psychotherapist in private practice and in the Oostvaarderskliniek forensic psychiatry center, Almere, the Netherlands. In this clinic he participates in a multi-centre study initiated by David Bernstein, entitled: "Efficacy of Schema-Focused Therapy versus Treatment as Usual in Forensic Patients with Antisocial, Narcissistic, Borderline, or Paranoid Personality Disorder." He has an MSc and studied psychology and family studies at the University of Amsterdam. He spent a year in Paris studying and working in a psychological institute, a school based on the ideas of Jacques Lacan. His postdoctoral studies in psychotherapy and sexuology were completed in Amsterdam at RINO, a regional institute for postdoctoral studies in psychotherapy. His specialisation is Schema Therapy, and Pesso-Boyden psychotherapy (a psychomotor system). He is a supervisor in Schema Therapy and cognitive behavioral psychotherapy.

Scott Kellogg is a Clinical Assistant Professor in the Department of Psychology at New York University; previously, he was on the faculties of The Rockefeller

University, the Yale University School of Medicine, and the Program in Counseling and Clinical Psychology at Teachers College/Columbia University. Having trained in both Schema Therapy and Gestalt Therapy, he is currently a psychotherapist and a supervisor at the Schema Therapy Institute in New York City. Kellogg has created the Transformational Chairwork Training program and he is currently teaching this method of psychotherapeutic dialogue to practitioners in both the US and Europe.

Kellogg is the current and past President of the Division on Addictions of the New York State Psychological Association (2011, 2005, 2001), and a co-director of the Harm Reduction and Mental Health Project at New York University. He is also a leading advocate for gradualism, a vision of healing that seeks to utilize and integrate the best aspects of the harm reduction, scientific, and traditional treatment approaches. He has written on Schema Therapy, borderline personality disorder, and the integration of gestalt techniques in cognitive behavioral treatment. He has addressed such topics as addiction treatment, identity theory, trauma and violence, contingency management, harm reduction, and assessment.

Truus Kersten is a Psychotherapist at the de Rooyse Wissel Forensic Psychiatric Center, Venray. She also works as a self-employed consultant and trainer since gaining her PhD in 1998 on matching patients to addiction treatment. She specializes in projects that focus on developing, training, and implementing evidence-based treatments in addiction and forensic care. In the Rooyse Wissel, she is implementation leader in a project aimed at tailoring and teaching evidence-based addiction treatments and Schema Therapy in the treatment units. Participates as a Schema Therapist in the randomized clinical trial of Schema Therapy for forensic patients. She is a supervisor and trainer in Schema Therapy and also in cognitive behavior therapy. She trains psychologists and other professionals (e.g., nurses) in Schema Therapy and has developed manuals and protocols for implementing addiction treatment and Schema Therapy in a forensic setting. She has written national publications on the treatment of addictions and on treatment of personality disorders with Schema Therapy. In the study set up by David Bernstein and Elsa van den Broek she is currently writing a book on Schema Therapy for personality disorders, aggression, and addiction.

She is co-author of the fortcoming *Treating Agression, Addiction, and Personality Disorder: A Schema-Focused approach to complex, Antisocial patients.*

Marije Keulen-de Vos works as a researcher at the De Rooyse Wissel Forensic Psychiatric Center, Venray. She studied Health Sciences at Maastricht University. Her PhD research focuses on patterns and predictors in the treatment response of forensic patients with personality disorders. She is particularly interested in the effective aspects of Schema Therapy.

Pien van den Kieboom is a cognitive behavioral therapist and a supervisor at the Dutch association of CBT (VGCt). She is also a supervisor of the Dutch Register of Schema Therapy and the ISST, a trainer in mindfulness MBSR and MBCT, and a member of VMBN.

She works as a cognitive behavioral therapist, supervisor, learning therapist, and mindfulness trainer at the GGZ, Stichting Rivierduinen, GGZ Leiden en omstreken.

She is affiliated to the RINO, Utrecht, as a Schema Therapy instructor, and she also offers supervision and personal therapy to people who would like to become a member of the Dutch association of CBT (VGCt), or subscribe to the Dutch Register of Schema Therapy.

Ellen Gross works as a resident in Psychiatry at the University Hospital, Department of Psychiatry and Psychotherapy, in Freiburg, Germany. She studied medicine in Heidelberg, Germany, where she received her doctor's degree for research in Child and Adolescent Psychiatry. Her current research is concerned with psychotherapy of severe personality disorders, mainly borderline personality disorder, as well as psychotherapy of chronic obsessive-compulsive disorder. Much of her work is aimed at identifying the mechanisms of non-response to standard cognitive and behavioral techniques and developing new approaches. Ellen N. Gross is a certified schema therapist (ISST) since 2009 and supervisor in Schema Therapy since 2011. She is also well trained in dialectic behavioral therapy.

Miriam Labin is a Clinical Psychologist who currently works in private practice in Hertzelia, Israel. She gained her PsyD at Yeshiva University in 2006 and her BA as a psychology major at Bar-Ilan University, Israel. She recently worked at the Cognitive Behavioral Therapy unit for anxiety disorders at Geha Hospital, Israel. She is conducting lectures on the CBT for social anxiety for students and social workers in the Israeli Ministry of Defense and in Tel-Aviv University. Her clinical work focuses on people who suffer from anxiety disorders and depression while integrating CBT and Schema Therapy.

Jill Lobbestael is an assistant professor in the Department of Clinical Psychological Science, Maastricht University, the Netherlands. She was a postdoctoral fellow at Florida State University, Tallahassee, and at Harvard University, Cambridge, MA. She also coordinates the research track of the postdoctoral clinical psychology track at Rino Zuid. Her research interests are personality disorders – Cluster B disorders in particular – aggression, emotion regulation, trauma, Schema Therapy, and self-control. Recently, she received several grants for her work from the renewal impulse of the Dutch Research Organization, Brain and Cognition program, and the Niels Stensen organization.

George Lockwood is the Director of the Schema Therapy Institute Midwest, Kalamazoo, Michigan, US. He is a Founding Fellow of the Academy of Cognitive Therapy. He completed a postdoctoral fellowship in cognitive therapy under the supervision of Aaron T. Beck in 1982, and has training in psychoanalytic psychotherapy and object-relations approaches. He has Advanced International Certification in Schema Therapy, has written a number of articles on cognitive and Schema Therapy, and has maintained a private practice for the past 29 years.

Des McVey is a consultant nurse and psychotherapist with over 25 years' experience of working within and developing forensic services across the full range of settings. He is a visiting lecturer at York University and regularly teaches on nursing and clinical psychology courses. Des has a particular interest in developing strategies that maintain treatment integrity and developing models of care for psychiatric nursing. He is co-editor of *Treating Personality Disorder: Creating Robust Services for People with Complex Mental Health Problems* and has co-authored several articles on using schema-focused principles to create a therapeutic milieu. Much of his clinical practice has been devoted to facilitating a strong role for psychiatric nurses in treatment and developing services that are embracing of psychological treatment principles.

Naomi Murphy is a consultant Clinical and Forensic Psychologist with over 15 years' experience of working with clients presenting with complex psychopathology. Naomi has been instrumental in developing services for people with personality disorder in the community, secure services, and prisons. Naomi has a particular interest in the development of transdisciplinary teams and enabling non-psychologists to use psychological concepts to enhance their own role. She is co-editor of *Treating Personality Disorder: Creating Robust Services for People with Complex Mental Health Problems* and has co-authored several articles on using schema-focused principles to create a therapeutic milieu. Much of her clinical practice has been dedicated to enabling non-psychologists to use psychological principles to enhance their own role through the medium of schema-focused therapy.

Eelco Muste is a Clinical Psychologist and Psychotherapist. He works as a clinic director and team manager of the Department Schema Therapy at the De Viersprong psychotherapeutic center, a Dutch institute that specializes in the treatment of personality disorders. Following his psychology studies in Leiden, the Netherlands, he undertook postgraduate work in clinical psychology and psychotherapy, and he worked for different institutes, in several settings. Since 1996, he has worked at the de Viersprong psychotherapeutic center, where Schema Therapy was introduced in 1998. Since then, he has further specialized in Schema Therapy and he has initiated his own treatment program. Based on his clinical practice, he has written several articles and chapters on Schema Therapy and was the chief editor of the *Handboek en Werkboek Klinische schematherapie*. He runs several training programs and workshops and lectures in the field of Schema Therapy and is actively involved in the Register for Schema Therapists, both as a board member and as treasurer.

Marjon Nadort is a Mental Healthcare Psychologist and Psychotherapist. She is a Certified Cognitive Behavioral Therapist (VGCt) and Certified Supervisor Schema Therapist (ISST, Dutch register ST). She is site director of the private practice G-kracht Psychomedisch Centrum BV in Amsterdam, The Netherlands, together with her colleague Jenny Broersen. She also works at the Mental Health Institute GGZ in Geest - VU University Amsterdam.

She is also an Internationally Certified Schema Therapist and Supervisor. Having been trained by Jeffrey Young, she is one of the Dutch researchers/trainers on the successful randomized controlled trial of Schema Therapy for borderline personality disorder. In 2012 she will finalize her thesis on the implementation of Schema Therapy for Borderline Patients in regular mental healthcare in the Netherlands. She has given many presentations in Europe and America. She has also given workshops in the Netherlands, Oxford, Cambridge, Berlin and Australia. She is (co-) author/editor of several schema books/chapters/articles.

Erwin Parfy works in private practice in Vienna, where he studied psychology and was certified to practice as a behavioral and cognitive-behavioral therapist. He gained his PhD for his investigations into concrete forms of psychotherapy integration between behavioral case conceptualization and the psychoanalytic concept of defense mechanisms, which were subsequently published by the university. Further books dealt with attachment theory and interaction in psychotherapy and with behavioral therapy and modern approaches in theory and practice. As a psychotherapist he worked for many years in a forensic hospital, specializing in personality disorders; as a teacher and supervisor he gave many workshops within different training programs. As board member and currently vice-president of the Austrian Society of Behavioral Therapy he continues to support the integration of all new treatment approaches (e.g., ST, DBT, ACT) in the behavioral tradition.

Poul Perris is the Director of the Swedish Institute for CBT and Schema Therapy and a licensed Psychotherapist with an advanced international certification in Schema Therapy, trained and supervised by Jeffrey Young. He is the Founding President of the International Society for Schema Therapy and the current President of the Swedish Association for Cognitive & Behavioral Therapies. He was trained in group ST by J. Farrell and I. Shaw and is a member of the protocol board in the international multisite study on group ST for patients with BPD. He offers international Schema Therapy workshops and supervision. He is part of a research group that focuses on the concepts of core emotional needs and limited reparenting.

Neele Reiss currently works as a Research Fellow at the University Medical Center, Department of Psychiatry and Psychotherapy in Mainz and as a Clinical Psychotherapist. She is a founding member of the Institute for Psychotherapy in Mainz, Germany and a member of the training faculty of the Schema Therapy Institute Midwest – Indianapolis Center. She is collaborating on the development of group ST and outcome studies to evaluate this model. She studied psychology in Marburg, Germany and State College, Pennsylvania. Her research focuses on intensive ST for patients with BPD in settings where a combination of group ST and individual Schema Therapy is applied. She also conducts research in ST-related psychological assessment. She has published in international journals and contributed chapters to books on Schema Therapy.

Marleen Rijkeboer is a Psychotherapist and Clinical Psychologist and is affiliated to the department Clinical and Health Psychology at Utrecht University as associate professor. In this position she heads the Academisch Angstcentrum Altrecht and is the chief trainer of postgraduate education for Clinical Psychologists. In addition, she works for the Ambulatorium, the psychotherapeutic center of the Department of Social Sciences, Utrecht University, as a practitioner. Marleen researches into and provides training on Schema Therapy, and is a board member of the ISST and the Dutch Register of Schema Therapy.

Eckhard Roediger is the Director of Schema Therapy Institute in Frankfurt, Germany and ISST secretary since its foundation in 2008. He studied medicine in Frankfurt and gained his MD in 1986. He is a Neurologist and Psychiatrist and went through a psychodynamic and cognitive-behavior therapy training. After running an addiction treatment clinic near Frankfurt for more than eight years he became director of a psychosomatic department of a clinic in Berlin. Since 2007 he is working in private practice, is training Schema Therapy in Germany, Switzerland, and Austria and published several books about Schema Therapy and self-help books.

Hilde de Saeger works as a Clinical Psychologist and Psychotherapist at the Psychotherapeutic Center De Viersprong in Halsteren, the Netherlands, a diagnostic and therapeutic center for clients with severe personality pathology. In addition, Hilde is researching the effects of therapeutic assessment at the University of Amsterdam. In 1992, Hilde graduated from the Catholic University Leuven, Belgium.

Agnes Scholing is Program Manager for Adult Treatments at De Waag, Ambulatory Forensic Mental Health Center. In addition, she is an associate professor at the University of Amsterdam, Department of Clinical Psychology. She is also a Clinical Psychologist/Psychotherapist and cognitive behavior therapist. In 1993, she gained her PhD at Groningen University on the assessment and treatment of social phobia. Following this, she worked at the University of Amsterdam, mainly on anxiety disorders in children and adolescents. In 2000, she started work at De Waag. Her current research is mainly on the assessment and treatment of domestic violence and substance use disorders, and on risk assessment.

Ida Shaw holds an MA in developmental psychology and has extensive training in experiential therapies. Her professional focus is training and supervision in ST and the group ST model that she developed with Farrell. Together, they developed an inpatient ST program and a dedicated unit for patients with severe BPD, which was awarded a Governor's Showcase award. Shaw is the co-director of the Schema Therapy Institute Midwest-Indianapolis and an ISST certified advanced-level Schema Therapist and Trainer. She is co-author of *Group Schema Therapy for BPD* and has published book chapters and articles in research journals on BPD treatment. Shaw is the main clinical supervisor for the multi-site trial of GST underway in four countries and provides supervision and master classes in ST internationally.

Alex Sheffield is a Clinical Psychologist with a particular interest in Schema Therapy for eating disorders. Alex gained a BSc in Psychology and a Doctorate in Clinical Psychology from the University of Surrey, England. She worked in the field of adult eating disorders for a number of years before making the transition to working with adolescents. Alex currently works for The South London and Maudsley NHS Trust in an inpatient unit for adolescents with mental health problems. Most of Alex's published work has focused on validating some of the schema inventories and using them to aid our understanding of the development of the eating disorders.

Simkje Sieswerda currently works as an assistant professor and licensed psychotherapist at Heidelberg University, Germany. She studied Psychology in Amsterdam and gained a PhD at Maastricht University in 2009. Her research seeks to understand specific underlying cognitive mechanisms in borderline personality disorder, using experimental studies. In particular, she is interested in the role of hypervigilance, extreme evaluations, negativistic evaluations, and emotion recognition in this disorder. She has published in *Behaviour Research and Therapy*, *Journal of Behaviour Therapy and Experimental Psychiatry* and *Behavioural and Cognitive Psychotherapy*.

Susan Simpson currently works at the University of South Australia as Clinic Director for the postgraduate clinical psychology programme. She trained as a clinical psychologist at Flinders University, Australia, and completed her clinical doctorate at the University of Newcastle upon Tyne, England. She practised as a Clinical Psychologist in the Scottish National Health Service (NHS) for 16 years, specializing in the treatment of complex eating disorders. Her research focuses on Schema Therapy for complex or chronic eating disorders and personality disorders. Her other research interest is the provision of clinical psychology services to remote and rural areas via videoconferencing.

Philip Spinhoven is Professor of Clinical Psychology and Dean of the Faculty of Social and Behavioral Sciences at Leiden University. His research focuses on how distant, recent, and current stressors interact with cognitive processes (e.g., attention, memory, thought, reasoning), behavioral processes (e.g., approach and avoidance), and biological processes (e.g., HPA axis) in anxiety disorders, mood disorders, somatoform disorders, and personality disorders. He has received several grants for his research and has supervised more than 30 PhD students since 1994. His publications total more than 350.

Nicola Stelzer currently works as a Psychologist in the Department of Psychiatry and Psychotherapy, University Hospital of Freiburg, Germany and as a Clinical Psychotherapist at the Freiburger Ausbildungsinstitut für Verhaltenstherapie, Germany. She studied psychology in Freiburg and Cologne. Her research focuses on intensive ST for patients with so far non-responding obsessive-compulsive disorder in an inpatient setting where a combination of individual schema therapy and exposure and response prevention is applied. Furthermore she participates in the professional training in Schema Therapy.

Lieda van de Vis is a Healthcare Psychologist and she has had several management roles in mental healthcare for 15 years. Until October 2010, she worked in the Forensic Psychiatric Hospital, de Rooyse Wissel, Venray and Maastricht, the Netherlands, as a Cluster Manager Treatment, Care and Daytime Programming, in which innovation and development were the main focus and was the project manager for several major development counselling programs, for example, projects of implementation of care and treatment of drug addicts and implementation of Schema Therapy, in cooperation with field experts. She currently works as a Content Manager of Clinical Care at the Dr. Leo Kannerhuis, a center for autism in Oosterbeek, the Netherlands.

Michiel van Vreeswijk is Clinical Psychologist and CEO of the private practice G-kracht Psychomedisch Centrum BV, The Netherlands. He is a Certified Cognitive Behavioral Therapist (VGCt) and Certified Supervisor Schema Therapist (ISST, Dutch register ST) and specializes in Schema Group Therapy. He is member of the board of the Dutch Schema Therapy register, study board member and protocol board member of the International RCT on group ST (Arntz and Farrell, 2010). He gives regular workshops and supervision in Schema (group) Therapy in the Netherlands and across Europe. He is (co-) author and editor of several schema books, chapters and articles.

Glenn Waller is a Consultant Clinical Psychologist with the Vincent Square Eating Disorders Service, Central and North West London NHS Foundation Trust. He is also Visiting Professor of Psychology at the Institute of Psychiatry, King's College London. He has published widely in the field of the psychology of the eating disorders, focusing particularly on cognitive-behavioral models and therapy. He has also published a number of papers about the clinical and psychometric properties of schema measures. He has served on the editorial boards of the *International Journal of Eating Disorders* and other journals.

Anoek Weertman is a Psychotherapist and currently works in private practice in psychotherapy, supervision, and education. She studied psychotherapy in Maastricht and during this period, she wrote her thesis on personality disorders under the supervision of Arnoud Arntz. Until recently, she worked at the Psychotherapeutic Center De Viersprong in Halsteren, the Netherlands, a diagnostic and therapeutic center for clients with severe personality pathology. During the last few years, she has mainly specialized in Schema Therapy for personality problems in adults and trauma treatment. She has been active within the Dutch Register of Schema Therapy for several years and is currently Chairman of this Register.

Foreword

I'm excited to have an opportunity to write the foreword for this outstanding handbook on Schema Therapy. This volume represents an important step in going well beyond the books that have already been published on the Schema Therapy approach.

Until now, readers have had access to textbooks on Schema Therapy that lay out basic schema theory and clinical strategies for treating personality disorders; self-help books written for the general public; and a detailed protocol for treating borderline personality disorder. But this is the first volume that extends the basic model beyond BPD and narcissism to a wide range of client populations and disorders, as well as addressing theoretical and research considerations that have not been discussed before in one book. This book represents the next logical step in the development of Schema Therapy: a state-of-the-art extension of the schema approach to new areas of theory, research, and clinical practice.

The three editors, all of whom are highly respected in the field, have done a remarkable job of enlisting the top schema therapists from around the world to contribute chapters across an extremely wide range of topics in their own areas of expertise. Each chapter is written from theoretical, research, and practical perspectives.

I want to mention how the book is organized, and mention some of the highlights, to give readers a sense of the breadth of topics covered. The first part provides an introduction to Schema Therapy that reviews its history and the basic schema conceptual model, along with a chapter by Lockwood and Perris that significantly extends the concept of core emotional needs that has only been touched upon in earlier books.

Part II focuses on diagnostic considerations. This includes chapters on the indications for utilizing ST, the relationship between chronic Axis I disorders and ST, experiential and questionnaire approaches to assessment, case conceptualization, and a case study on diagnosing narcissism from a schema perspective.

Parts III and IV will be of special interest to clinicians. These chapters include case studies and protocols that illustrate how Schema Therapy has been successfully applied to specific clinical groups, including important new techniques that have not been discussed previously. Two questions that I'm frequently asked at workshops are whether ST has been integrated with mindfulness techniques, and whether the approach has been applied to specific populations such as adolescents. There are several intriguing chapters on the integration of ST with mindfulness-based techniques and with ACT. Another chapter addresses the use of ST with an extremely difficult population – dual-diagnosis patients who suffer from both addiction problems and personality disorders. Other chapters focus on ST with eating disorders, OCD, gestalt "chair work," "playful" techniques (such as puppets and games), adapting ST to adolescents, and working with Cluster C personality disorders. Another chapter is a valuable contribution by Travis Atkinson on the application of Schema Therapy to couples work, which integrates ST with both Gottman's work and emotion-focused therapy.

I also want to highlight two important topics in this handbook that represent major expansions of Schema Therapy. The first is a series of excellent chapters on Schema Therapy in groups. I consider this one of the most promising advances in ST thus far, since the group format may allow clinicians and institutions to deliver schema treatment at a significantly lower cost, yet with equivalent or perhaps superior results, than individual approaches. Initial studies by Farrell, Shaw, Arntz, and others show great promise in terms of efficacy with BPD clients.

A second especially exciting new development is the application of ST to forensic patients, led by David Bernstein and his group in the Netherlands. Their preliminary work suggests that this adaptation of ST may prove to be a highly efficacious treatment for a population that is generally considered almost untreatable. Their chapter summarizes the protocol they have developed.

Part V deals with the training and supervision of Schema Therapists. This should be of particular interest to clinicians who are interested in becoming certified Schema Therapists themselves.

Part VI is written for readers interested in research on Schema Therapy. This is the first book I'm aware of that reviews the research across a wide range of ST topics, including: efficacy studies across several clinical disorders; experimental research on the schema and mode constructs; and validation studies of both the Young Schema Questionnaire and the Schema Mode Inventory.

The final part deals with an often neglected topic in psychotherapy handbooks: public policy considerations related to the implementation of ST in a variety of mental-health settings, including cost-effectiveness. These chapters will be of particular interest to mental health administrators and policy planners.

As the founder of Schema Therapy, it is difficult to express how gratifying it is for me to see how the field of Schema Therapy has expanded since its beginnings in the 1980s and 1990s. There is no better way for readers to grasp the extent of the new theoretical, research, and clinical work that has been done in recent years than to study the chapters in this handbook. This volume will provide clinicians, theoreticians, researchers, and mental health administrators with a roadmap for future directions in Schema Therapy. I believe that this handbook should be required reading for anyone interested in the field.

Congratulations to Michiel, Jenny, and Marjon for this outstanding contribution!

Jeffrey Young
Columbia University, Department of Psychiatry
Schema Therapy Institute of New York

Acknowledgments

Writing a book like this with dear friends like Jenny and Marjon has been one of the most wonderful journeys. The two of you have become more and more like sisters to me. Jenny, your inquiring and methodological way of working proved to be a strong backbone for me to rely on. Marjon, your enthusiasm for new ideas and your willpower have made it easy for me to come up with fresh ideas and to continue working.

I dedicate this book to my father, mother, and wife, Aglaia. Of my father (†1988), who died while still young, I hold fond memories of a warm, patient, loving, and nurturing man. You taught me to see nature and human beings in an open mind. You inspired me to go forward in science. You will always be with me. To my mother, you raised me with all your love and kindness, always being there when I needed you. A true, good-enough mother. Both of you are in my mind and heart when I work with my patients in their struggle with life. To Aglaia, from the start of our relationship you showed patience and interest in all the work I was doing. You have been an enormous support to me. I love you with all my heart and want to share my life with you.

Michiel van Vreeswijk, Utrecht, (The Netherlands) January 2012

Writing a book with Michiel and Marjon was an enormously enjoyable experience. In the past years both of you have become very good friends. I want to thank you for the collaboration and the warm friendship. I want to express my respect for my partner, Jeroen, in particular. I deeply appreciate your patience, love, safety, and humor; it helped me to prepare this book. In recent years I have had less time for my family and friends, so I look forward to seeing you more often.

I dedicate this book to my parents and sister, Inge. We have shared a lot. I am profoundly grateful that you are in my life. I dedicate this book to Anneke, who unfortunately died too young. She was like a mother and a good friend to me. She made me feel valued and inspired me to become a psychotherapist.

Jenny Broersen, Amsterdam, The Netherlands, January 2012

I would like to gratefully acknowledge the following people whose love, patience, guidance, and support carried me through the past years. I could not have co edited this book without you, Michiel and Jenny – both of you are such warm, loving people. You are the two people that made me believe that unconditional love and friendship really do exist. Thank you for your love, friendship, and support during all these years. I hope that there will be an infinite future for the three of us.

Mama, you have always supported and helped me with your love, doing all the housework and childcare of Fimme and Lorenzo. Without you I would not be the person I am today, and I could not have co edited this book and at the same time finished my thesis! I thank you for your love and practical help every day. Lorenzo and Fimme, my two beautiful sons, you are the lights of my life. Lorenzo, now 21 years old, you have become such a beautiful, strong young adult with such a warm, loving character: "your eyes, it's a day's work just looking into them" (Laurie Anderson). Fimme, my 16-year-old son, living with you makes me so happy, our daily life is pleasant and warm and full of excitement, sometimes a bit too much. But luckily, over the last year you have become stable and well balanced. "Your smiling eyes are just a mirror to the sun" (Red Hot Chili Peppers).

Papa (†1990), without your genes, your sense of humor, and your optimism, I probably would not have started this project. Thank you for being who you are.

To the rest of my family and friends, thank you for your support, patience, love, and warmth. I am so blessed to have the many fortunes of your love.

Marjon Nadort, Amsterdam, The Netherlands, January 2012

We would like to thank all the patients on whom our experience is based. Names and other details in case examples in this book have been changed to maintain patient confidentiality.

Michiel, Jenny and Marjon

Part I
An Introduction to Schema Therapy

1
Schema Therapy in Historical Perspective

David Edwards and Arnoud Arntz

Schema Therapy (ST) evolved as a treatment for complex psychological problems over a period of some 20 years. In due course, it became sufficiently defined and operationalized that it could be manualized and evaluated in a randomized controlled trial (RCT) (Giesen-Bloo et al., 2006). As suggested by Young (2010), its recent development can be divided into three phases. The first was a period in which Young's reflection on his own cases led to the formulation of the key concepts. He then put these to work and tested them in new cases, not only on his own, but increasingly in consultation with clinicians working closely with him. In the second phase, a group of Dutch researchers conducted the RCT and in the process large numbers of Dutch psychologists contributed to the ongoing theoretical and clinical development of the model. In the third, Farrell and Shaw published a study of a group therapy model that added yet another dimension to ST treatment.

ST is an integrative therapy that draws on many concepts and methods that had existed before it evolved with its own identity. In this chapter we will look back at developments in cognitive behavior therapy and other psychotherapies, particularly between 1960 and about 1995, that have directly influenced the theories and techniques of ST. We will also look farther back within the history of psychotherapy and point to parallels that may or may not have had a direct or traceable influence. Readers will see how ST as developed by Young is part of a broader trend in cognitive therapy of attending to information processing that is not readily accessible to conscious awareness. It will become clear how it draws on schema models and theories and incorporates methods and techniques developed within other psychotherapy traditions. Next, we will examine each of the three phases. Lastly, we will reflect on the relationship between ST and science.

The Wiley Blackwell Handbook of Schema Therapy: Theory, Research, and Practice, First Edition.
Edited by Michiel van Vreeswijk, Jenny Broersen, and Marjon Nadort.
© 2012 John Wiley & Sons, Ltd. Published 2015 by John Wiley & Sons, Ltd.

Beyond Beck's Cognitive Therapy

The movement towards integration in psychotherapy

In the 1970s and 1980s, at most universities in the US psychology departments involved in training clinicians were associated with one of two paradigms: the older psychoanalytic and psychodynamic tradition and the emerging cognitive behavior therapy (CBT). Those associated with CBT argued that theirs was the only approach founded in experimental science and began to underline the credibility of their approach by demonstrating the efficacy of CBT treatments in RCTs. They were often dismissive not only of psychodynamic approaches but also of the humanistic and experiential therapies that had only a limited influence in most universities but were a growing force outside. However, once qualified, many practitioners found the academic models too limited to address the range of clients and client problems they were presented with in practice and a chronic rift developed between university-based researchers and clinicians (Dattilio, Edwards and Fishman, 2010). In due course, some university-based clinicians and researchers experimented with the humanistic and experiential approaches. As those trained in CBT explored psychodynamic approaches more carefully (and vice versa), they began to integrate them into more comprehensive treatment models. This was reflected in the founding of the *Journal of Psychotherapy Integration* in 1990 and the publication of the *Handbook of Psychotherapy Integration* (Norcross and Goldfried, 1992). The development of ST was part of this wider process.

ST is a theoretical and technical integration that is largely the work of Jeffrey Young. He developed the approach on the basis of his own clinical observations, his reflection on cases he found difficult and challenging, and in collaboration with colleagues who worked with him using the model on their own cases as it evolved. Many of these original collaborators are acknowledged by Young, Klosko, and Weishaar (2003, p. ix). As a graduate trained in clinical psychology in the US during the 1970s, Young would have had a broad theoretical grounding. After qualifying, he did postdoctoral training in Beck's cognitive therapy (CT) in Philadelphia and subsequently was clinical director of the Center for Cognitive Therapy in the early 1980s. At that time the basic treatment model for depression had already been developed (Beck *et al.*, 1979) and work was underway to adapt the model for anxiety disorders as well as to test the models in clinical trials. Like many clinicians trained in treatment models designed for fewer than 20 sessions, Young found himself preoccupied with those clients who did not respond to short-term approaches. He set about identifying the characteristics of these clients and finding treatment strategies that would address the difficulties they presented. In 1984, the first author was given a seminar handout by Young entitled "Cognitive therapy for personality disorders and difficult patients," which summarized his analysis of the problems posed by these clients. This would later be incorporated into Young's (1990) first publication on ST and into Young *et al.*'s (2003) ST manual. In the process of finding ways to address the needs of these clients, Young added to the already rich array of cognitive and behavioral techniques in which he had been trained by incorporating relational perspectives, experiential techniques, and the recognition that the self is not a unity, but functionally divided into parts that can be in conflict with each other.

Beck's cognitive therapy

Beck's CT is often thought of as a brief, manualized, and highly technical approach designed for short-term interventions, like other therapies within the broad family of CBT. This is at least in part because of the constraints of outcome research that require psychotherapies to be packaged in this way. However, CT as developed by Beck and colleagues from the 1970s was never just a set of CBT techniques. Beck had been trained in psychoanalysis. Although he quickly became disillusioned with working with clients who were free-associating on a couch and began to experiment with a more pragmatic and practical approach, he did not entirely jettison his former training. By the time Young was training with Beck, CT was already an integrative therapy. This is acknowledged in the introduction to the landmark book on CT for depression (Beck, Rush, Shaw and Emery, 1979) which listed a diverse range of forerunners whose influence had been incorporated into the new approach (see also Mahoney and Freeman, 1985).

This included cognitive approaches such as George Kelly's (1905–67) Personal Construct Theory and the work of Albert Ellis (1913–2007), whose main focus was the development of a cognitive therapy based on the classic Stoic maxim that it is not events that distress us but the meaning we give to them. Identifying distorted or exaggerated personal meanings and actively challenging them was central to Ellis's therapy – which changed its name over the years from Rational Therapy to Rational Emotive Therapy to Rational Emotive Behavior Therapy as Ellis integrated new aspects. Behavior therapy was another important component. Joseph Wolpe (1915–97), who had developed systematic desensitization (Wolpe, Salter and Reyna, 1964), was a professor at the same university as Beck and CT was being put together at a time when many behavior therapists were taking a pragmatic approach to behavior change (London, 1972) and linking cognitive and behavioral methods into what would soon be called cognitive behavior therapy (CBT). Another important influence came from Carl Rogers' (1902–87) client-centered therapy and from phenomenological and existential writers who emphasized understanding the lived experience of clients and the idiosyncratic nature of each individual's patterns of thought and feeling.

Beck's approach to intervention was very different from traditional psychodynamic practice. However, concepts from several psychodynamic theories were used as a basis for case formulation and treatment planning, provided they were grounded in evidence from the data of the case. Humorously, in 2000, during a dialogue with Albert Ellis, Beck acknowledged this when he referred to himself as "a closet psychoanalyst" (Beck and Ellis, 2000). Alfred Adler (1870–1937) was one of these influences. His break with Sigmund Freud (1856–1939) had come about because of his own cognitive emphasis and an approach to therapy that had many parallels with the pragmatic, action-oriented methods that would come to be called CBT. Another was Karen Horney (1885–1952). Her model included an understanding of the way early experiences could lead to negative experiences of self and the world, and compensatory processes that might get set up to neutralize these. This became an important feature of case conceptualization in cognitive therapy and later, ST. Beck would regularly appeal to Horney's phrase, "the tyranny of the shoulds" (which Ellis, in his robust manner, had rebranded "musterbation"), a precursor to ST's "demanding parent."

Two other important influences are discussed later in this chapter. Franz Alexander (1891–1964) introduced the concept of the corrective emotional experience and Harry Stack Sullivan (1892–1949) pioneered the understanding of interpersonal schemas and the way they interact in relationships. Beck et al. (1979) also acknowledged being influenced by Eric Berne (1910–70), the founder of Transactional Analysis (TA), and Jerome Frank (1909–2005), who had identified common factors contributing to effectiveness in all psychotherapies.

What distinguished the emerging cognitive and behavioral therapies was a focus on and careful analysis of factors currently maintaining clients' problems. These included clients' negative beliefs and assumptions and vicious cycles of thought and behavior, and the way in which these impacted within the contexts of their lives and personal concerns. Despite this emphasis, developmental analysis of factors likely to predispose clients to current difficulties has always been part of case formulation in CBT (e.g., Hawton, Salkovskis, Kirk and Clark, 1989) and case conceptualization in CT always took into account the client's history. Emery, who worked closely with Beck (Beck and Emery, 1984; Beck et al., 1979), pointed out that clients would be more motivated to change beliefs and behaviors if they recognized how they had developed:

> Discover where your beliefs come from . . . by going back and seeing where you adopted your beliefs you can often make them clearer to you . . . Many beliefs are passed down for generations. We traced one patient's fear of going broke back three generations to immigrants from Russia who were very poor. (Emery, 1982, pp. 186–7)

Nevertheless, pressure to manualize the therapy for treatment trials meant that there was more emphasis on immediate maintaining factors than developmental analysis of clients' problems.

The Integration of Attachment, Interpersonal, and Object Relations Theories

The limits of the collaborative relationship

An important aspect of the collaborative relationship in CT is the therapist's empathic understanding of clients. This is directed more broadly toward appreciating what clients were struggling with in their lives and more specifically toward what they were experiencing moment by moment in the therapy session. This was the hallmark of Rogers' client-centered approach in which the therapist offered the client a relationship characterized by unconditional positive regard, empathy, and congruence (genuineness). It had been Otto Rank (1884–1939) who, in 1935, had introduced Rogers to what at that time seemed a revolutionary approach to the therapeutic relationship. Until then he had worked in a traditional psychoanalytic model (Kramer, 1995).

In addition, however, the collaborative relationship is one in which therapists encourage clients to identify goals for therapy and to work on them together. Many clients who seek psychological help can respond quickly to this kind of collaborative, empathic, and action-oriented approach. But this does not work for a significant proportion of clients. Some don't seem to take naturally to collaboration, but act passively and helplessly, expecting the therapist to do all the work. Others become hostile or withdrawn and unmotivated. Yet others work to change their thoughts and experiment with new behaviors but do not experience meaningful change (Young, 1984). Cognitive therapists have to find a balance between being empathic and attending to clients' experience on the one hand, and working actively for change on the other. For some clients this balance is difficult to maintain. Some feel misunderstood when therapists encourage them to change their thoughts or try out new behaviors. Some simply won't do homework and in other ways appear to be uncooperative. Yet if therapists merely focus on empathically attuning to them, they do not seem to make much progress in actually changing their lives (Edwards, 1990b).

The integration of relational perspectives

These aspects of the therapeutic process had been the focus of relational theories for several decades. Sullivan's (1950, 1953) interpersonal theory, object relations theories (Cashdan, 1988), and Bowlby's (1979) attachment theory all proposed that each individual's engagement in human relationships was governed by cognitive representations of self and other, and the nature of the relationship between them. Trained as a psychoanalyst, John Bowlby (1907–90) was influenced by ethological research based on close observations of animals and their relationships to their young. In his theory, which was psychodynamic and developmental, but conceptualized in cognitive terms, he drew on metaphors from information processing and described how individuals develop "one or more working models, representing principal features of the world" (1979, p. 117). These underlying cognitive structures formed by early experiences encode representations of self and other and shape experience and emotions in later life. This was a cognitive theory with strong similarities to Beck's theoretical model where such internal representations were conceptualized in terms of schemas. By the mid-1980s and early 1990s the relationship between disturbed attachment and personality disorders was an increasing focus of clinical theory and research (Brennan and Shaver, 1998; Perris, 1999; Liotti *et al.*, 2000) and became a central feature of case formulation in ST.

All these theorists recognized the significance of interpersonal or relationship schemas that encoded representations of self and other in relationship and guided interpersonal behavior. They understood that relationship schemas would develop in a healthy and adaptive manner provided certain conditions were met in the social environment, particularly with respect to the quality of relationship offered by those who were primary caretakers. However, they would become disturbed or dysfunctional if the relationship with the mother or other primary caretaker(s) was characterized by emotional coldness, unpredictability, or hostility and abuse. In such cases, individuals would develop problems with affect regulation, becoming either overly restricted in their experience or expression of emotions, failing to develop adequate self-control, or swinging between over-control and lack of control. Their interpersonal schemas would become the source of severe difficulties in interpersonal relationships, especially intimate ones, and would not only lead to difficulties in their lives, but would also impact on the relationship with the therapist from whom they sought help. As a result, such clients would fail to respond constructively to the therapist's offer of empathic collaboration. Their interpersonal schemas would generate beliefs and assumptions about their therapists – not all of which were easily accessible to awareness – that reflected their earlier experience with neglectful, unpredictable, or abusive caretakers. These would lead to disruption of the collaboration, leaving therapists bewildered and frustrated that the well-meaning help they were offering was not being received in the spirit in which it was intended.

In the early 1980s, cognitive therapists were recognizing these problems and drawing on interpersonal and relational theories to address them (Arnkoff, 1981). Safran's (1984) work on integrating Sullivan's interpersonal theory with cognitive therapy was already underway, His 1984 article was a precursor to what would become a research project spanning over two decades (Safran, Muran, Samstag and Winston, 2005). However, the most important influence on Young was the work of the Italians Guidano and Liotti (1983), who integrated the developmental concepts of Jean Piaget (1896–1980) with Beck's cognitive therapy and Bowlby's attachment theory and spelled out the implications of this approach for working with patients with such problems as depression, eating disorders, and agoraphobia.

Limited reparenting

Attachment theory was an effective tool for formulating the difficulties of many clients who could not form a collaborative relationship. In mode terms, these are clients who have limited development of the Healthy Adult (HA) and whose interpersonal schemas became stuck in dysfunctional childhood patterns. Young (1990) reasoned that technically the theory meant that the therapist had to offer not only a collaborative adult relationship, as in standard cognitive therapy, but also a parenting relationship to the client's child side. This was needed to help to correct the dysfunctional schemas and to allow healthy new schemas to form in the same way that they would have had clients had a better experience with their own parents. This would involve "find[ing] out what needs of the child did not get met and try[ing] to meet them to a reasonable degree" (p. 39).

The importance of therapists offering a parenting relationship had been recognized within psychoanalysis by Ferenczi (1873–1933). He stressed the importance of accessing these child states, engaging in dialogue with them – he called it an "infantile conversation" – and responding in a manner that provided what the client needed and did not receive as a child – what he called "the advantages of a normal nursery" (Ferenczi, 1929). Ferenczi's view was developed by Alexander between 1946 and 1956, who advocated that therapists should behave toward clients not just neutrally, but in a way that provided them with a completely different experience from that which they had had with critical and punitive parents. They should

> assume intentionally a kind of attitude that is conducive to provoking the kind of emotional experience in the patient which is suited to undo the pathogenic effect of the original parental attitude. (Alexander, 1956, cited by Wallerstein, 1995, p. 53)

This would provide clients with a "corrective emotional experience" that would change their underlying relational schemas. Within psychoanalysis, this view was roundly rejected in favor of the traditional neutrality of the therapist. However, as the object relations therapies grew in influence, for example through the work of Michael Balint (1896–1970) and Donald Winnicott (1896–1971), there was increasing emphasis on clients changing as a result of experiencing security and care within the evolving relationship with the therapist (Wallerstein, 1995).

The most explicit experimentation with Ferenczi's principle occurred during the 1970s among TA therapists where the term "reparenting" began to be explicitly used. Initially, this referred to a very radical application of the principle of corrective emotional experience when Schiff (1970, 1977) and colleagues experimented with providing disturbed clients with 24-hour care in a simulated family situation. They allowed them to regress to infantile and childhood states and would meet their needs even to the extent of putting them in nappies and changing them. Although a number of remarkable case studies provided evidence for the therapeutic impact of this approach, the high degree of commitment and organization required to deliver such an intervention meant that it was impractical in most settings. Furthermore, the intensity of interaction and physical contact between therapists and clients made it very controversial.

Nevertheless, a more limited approach to reparenting was adopted by several TA therapists who emphasized the importance of providing a corrective experience. Woollams (1977, p. 365), for example, used it in describing a group therapy approach that integrated TA and gestalt methods. He recommends that therapists should respond to "the cathected little person in a way that is appropriate to her age." The term "cathected little person" is equivalent to activating the Vulnerable Child (VC) mode in ST. So the term "reparenting" came to encompass both therapists' caring attitude toward their clients and their dealing with whatever came up in the relationship in the same way as a good parent would. It was also used to refer to psychodramatic enactments of parenting by the therapist toward the client's VC in imagery and dialogue work. Thus Wallas (1991), working with clients from families with an alcoholic parent, used the term reparenting to refer to a method of presenting healing narratives under hypnosis. In TA, the term "self-reparenting" was also used for the process by which individuals who had been poorly parented learned to become healthy parents themselves (James, 1977). Within ST this would be part of building the Healthy Adult, and would not be conceptualized as reparenting since it did not include the activation and rebuilding of childhood schemas. The history of psychotherapy has provided growing evidence that many clients can reconstruct their basic relationship schemas while carrying on with their lives. Seeing a therapist once or twice a week can be enough to establish a relationship that can provide the kind of corrective experience envisaged by Ferenczi and Alexander, and this can be supported by explicit reparenting in imagery and chair work. So, large numbers of clients can benefit from limited reparenting and it has become an important component of ST.

Empathic confrontation

Beck's concept of the collaborative relationship assumed that therapist and client worked together as a rational team. The therapist's main tool for confronting irrational thoughts or dysfunctional behaviors was through gently evoking cognitive dissonance through Socratic questioning or drawing clients' attention to the self-defeating nature of some of their behaviors. However Young (1990, p. 41) realized that there are many clients who do not respond to such a rational or gentle approach, and "a more confrontational style" was needed if the processes maintaining the schema were to be changed. The challenge for the therapist is to confront while conveying empathy for the pain clients feel, and their fears of letting go of avoidances and compensations. This means that "the therapist is continually working to find a balance" in providing "empathic confrontation" (Young et al., 2003, p. 93).

This dilemma has been recognized within many approaches to psychotherapy. Within the Rogerian tradition, confrontation is an essential therapist skill:

> Failure to confront, when confrontation is needed, permits the continuation of self-defeating or unreasonable behavior and inadvertently implies support for such behavior. (Tamminen and Smaby, 1981, p. 42)

Leaman (1978, p. 631) emphasized the importance of "empathy in confrontation" since "confrontation is an act of caring." He gave examples of non-empathic and empathic confrontation. Adler and Myerson (1973) collected similar discussions within the psychodynamic tradition, including one is which Welpton (1973) contrasted "empathic confrontation" (p. 266) with "angry confrontation" (p. 263). Cashdan (1988) devotes a chapter to managing confrontation therapeutically in object relations therapy. Within TA, Weiss and Weiss (1977, p. 128) observe that when clients

> identify what they need and ask us directly to meet that need, we will usually agree to do so, or at least problem-solve with them about how to get that need met . . . At the same time we will confront substitute behaviors and do our best to minimize their getting any rewards from them.

Thus these principles have been widely recognized for a long time. However, the term "empathic confrontation" has achieved new prominence since it featured as part of ST and appears in more recent literature on working with child abuse survivors (Chu, 1992) and dissociative personality (Schwartz, 1994).

The Integration of Experiential Techniques

Two levels of encoding meaning

Within ST, one of the major innovations compared to CBT was the central place given to experiential techniques. These addressed one of the problems that Young had identified as interfering with response to cognitive therapy in clients who, in spite of working with rational analysis, changing negative thoughts, and even experimenting with new behaviors, failed to achieve change at the emotional level. Models of cognitive encoding recognized that there is not just one system of meaning. Zajonc (1980, 1984) reviewed experimental studies that showed the disjunction between conscious experience and rationality on the one hand, and people's pre-reflective experience on the other. Greenberg and Safran (1984) provided evidence that rational, language-based cognitive systems were independent of systems associated with emotion. This became part of Teasdale's (1993) Interacting Cognitive Subsystems (ICS) model that distinguished between *propositional* encoding of meaning, which was language based, and *implicational* encoding of meaning, which was not. There was evidence that only implicational schemas were connected directly to emotional systems, which meant that they needed to be activated and changed if significant change in distressing emotions associated with these schemas was to be achieved.

Within CT, Beck (1985) also pointed out that schemas based on early childhood experiences were not easily accessible to verbal introspection and could be changed only if they were activated. Behavioral exposure was one way to do this – for example, having agoraphobics go out to avoided places and then helping them re-evaluate the cognitions associated with the intense emotions evoked (Coleman, 1981). Imagery provided another route. In an early paper, Beck (1970) recognized that images and fantasies could give access to this level of meaning. He described how repeated rehearsal of a distressing fantasy could result in the fantasy changing to become less distorted and more realistic. Freeman (1981) had also written about how dreams and images could provide access to these levels of cognition. However, the potential of imagery and psychodrama to connect directly with the emotional level had barely been explored, although Arnkoff (1981) described experiments in this direction and Beck and Emery (1985) included some methods, including use of metaphoric imagery and imagery replacement methods, in their account of cognitive therapy for anxiety disorders. By contrast, in several other approaches to psychotherapy, there was already a rich literature on imagery techniques in behavior therapy, hypnotherapy, Jungian therapy, and some psychodynamic approaches (Singer, 1974; Samuels and Samuels, 1975; Singer and Pope, 1978; Shorr, 1983; Sheikh, 1984).

The influence of Gestalt Therapy

In 1984, Young consulted a gestalt therapist who used mainly imagery techniques. Their personal impact on him was immediate. As he later commented, "in about ten sessions of Gestalt Therapy, I learned more about myself than I had learned in a year with the cognitive therapist" (Roediger and Young, 2009). He immediately saw how these experiential methods were a missing piece that could address many of the problems of patients who did not respond to standard CT interventions and began experimenting with using them with his own clients. Others were also experimenting with these methods at Beck's Center for Cognitive Therapy in the mid-1980s. Edwards (2007) had been exposed to them in the United Kingdom and described some of his work with guided imagery during a postdoctoral fellowship, in two widely influential publications that included clinical descriptions and a rationale for the incorporation of these methods into CT (Edwards, 1989, 1990a). Smucker, who was there at the same time, receiving supervision from Young, also had a formative experience with a gestalt therapist and this led to his development of imagery rescripting for PTSD (described by Smucker, Dancu, Foa and Niederee, 1995). Layden also integrated imagery rescripting into a CT approach to the treatment of borderline personality disorder (BPD) (Layden, Newman, Freeman and Morse, 1993). Outside the immediate circle of Beck CT therapists, Lazarus described how gestalt methods such as the empty chair technique could be integrated in multimodal therapy (Lazarus,

1985) and Greenberg and Safran (1987) were providing in-depth accounts of the processes of emotional change set in motion by imagery/dialogue methods. A decade later, Arntz and Weertman (1999) described how to use imagery rescripting and psychodrama techniques in the treatment of current problems that had their roots in personality characteristics related to emotionally charged childhood memories.

An historical perspective on experiential techniques

However, these experiential techniques have a much longer history (Edwards, 2011). Already in the 19th century, Pierre Janet (1859–1947) treated patients with "imagery replacement." He cured his client Marie of psychogenic blindness that had begun when she shared a bed with a child whose face was disfigured by impetigo by having her relive the events but imagining that the child's face was normal and that she was friendly and that she stroked her hair and face (Edwards, 2007). For a long time, Janet's work was sidelined by the dominance of Freud, but in the last few years has been reexamined and re-appreciated (van der Hart, Brown and van der Kolk, 1989; van der Hart and Horst, 1989; van der Hart and Friedman, 1989; Oulahabib, 2009). Carl Jung (1875–1961) developed the method of active imagination in which clients would connect with a feeling and allow images to emerge (Jung, 1960). In contrast to ST's focus on memories of real events, these tended to be symbolic and could give rise to dramatic journeys or dialogues with mythic figures (Hannah, 1981). However, imagery work of the kind pioneered by Janet continued to be used by hypnotherapists throughout the twentieth century (Edwards, 2011).

Fritz Perls' (1893–1970) Gestalt Therapy has been particularly influential in its impact on contemporary psychotherapy. Born in Vienna, Perls gradually moved away from the Freudian psychoanalysis in which he had been trained. In this process he was influenced by Wilhelm Reich (1897–1957), who observed the rigidity in posture and the muscles of the body, which he called "character armor." Reich believed that this was there to prevent the expression of emotions and led to chronic blocking of the flow of energy in the body. His aim was to get the energy flowing freely and he used muscle relaxation, deep breathing, and other body-focused methods to induce emotional release. Alexander Lowen (1910–2008), who developed Reich's approach, called it *bioenergetics* (Lowen, 1976). Although this often triggered childhood and infantile memories, Reich himself did not pay much attention to working with the memories themselves. Another important influence on Perls was a lifelong interest in the theater (Madewell and Shaughnessy, 2009). He was actively involved with Max Rheinhart's active drama methods. He must also have known Jacob Moreno (1889–1974), based in Berlin, who experimented with drama methods from as early as 1911 and went on to develop psychodrama and apply it in clinical settings (Moreno, 1939). The use of the term "script" in psychotherapy comes from these connections with the theater and Moreno is reported to have said, "Throw away your old script and write a new one" (Jacobs, 1977), a theme that Berne would develop further.

Perls was also strongly influenced by Ferenczi's work with the traumatized but split-off "inner child" of adult patients. Ferenczi had recognized that it was important to heal this and, as a therapist, took a role that we now recognize as reparenting

(Edwards, 2007). Perls developed a therapy with a strong emphasis on feelings, needs, and impulses. Imagery and empty-chair dialogues were central techniques in bringing these to awareness, allowing them full expression, and promoting resolution. Transcripts of Perls' demonstrations of these methods in workshops, mostly published posthumously, were particularly influential (Perls, 1973). Many TA therapists also integrated these imagery and psychodrama methods with their concepts of ego states and scripts, often in a group therapy environment. The concept of scripts was central to TA and treatment focused on analyzing them as a means of understanding the rigid, repetitive, and compulsive patterns that perpetuated unhappiness (Steiner, 1974). As Berne (1961, p. 118) had put it: "The object of script analysis is to close the show and put a better one on the road." There was an appreciation of the importance of unmet needs and the expression of suppressed emotions. It was also recognized that the experience of the child, often alone, frightened, confused, and angry, needed to be reactivated and rescripted (Goulding and Goulding, 1979; Erskine, 1980; Erskine and Moursund, 1988).

Perls' methods were particularly influential in the human potential movement, where humanistic therapists were focusing on personal growth. They often did this through offering group experiences not only to clients with significant psychological problems, but also to those generally interested in self-exploration and development. However, this kind of format meant that often participants' schemas would be triggered but there was insufficient follow-up to ensure that the next stage of therapy was embarked on. For this reason many clinicians saw these methods as dangerous and did not appreciate their potential within a systematic therapy. Young himself had this experience. As a graduate student he attended several gestalt marathon weekends but found them painful and distressing as there was no follow-up on what had been evoked. However, in 1984, having trained in cognitive therapy, and challenged by his own difficult cases, he saw these experiential methods in a new light as a result of his positive experience of individual Gestalt Therapy. He then recognized how they could be usefully integrated into a systematic and structured therapy.

The evolution of schema mode work

Since ancient times, conflict between incompatible impulses, desires, or beliefs has been recognized as part of human nature. An Egyptian papyrus from 2200 BC describes a disillusioned and suicidal man conversing with his "Ba," a deity who encourages him to find courage and hope despite the selfishness and cruelty that surround him (Lindorff, 2001). During the 19th century such conflicts were explored in depth in fiction (Edwards and Jacobs, 2000) as well as in philosophy, psychiatry, and psychology (once it emerged as a separate discipline). Widespread investigations of hypnotic phenomena and dissociated states at the end of the 19th century provided extensive observations on which new theories were based. In France, as early as 1868, Durand, a hypnotherapist, used the term "polypsychism." Beneath our "ego-in-chief," he argued, is a multiplicity of sub-egos, each of which

> had a consciousness of its own, was able to perceive and to keep memories and to elaborate complex psychic operations. The sum total of these subegos constituted our unconscious life. (Ellenberger, 1970, p. 146)

Most theories of psychotherapy address this multiplicity in one way or another. At the turn of the 20th century, Freud used the concept of "splitting" and explored the conflicts between ego, superego, and id. According to Adler, we each have several sets of inconsistent beliefs and attitudes and in order to create an illusion of consistency, at any time one set of beliefs dominates and others are pushed out of awareness (Edwards and Jacobs, 2000). Jung referred to "feeling toned complexes" as well as to "subconscious personalities" and "subpersonalities" (Redfearn, 1994), and work with sub-personalities was an important aspect of psychosynthesis (Assagioli, 1965), developed by the Italian Roberto Assagioli (1888–1974). By the time ST was emerging, the concept of sub-personalities was being widely used in object relations psychology (Redfearn, 1994) and in the humanistic movement (Rowan, 1990).

Several psychotherapy traditions that recognized the importance of healing the inner child have influenced this aspect of ST. These include the work of Ferenczi and the TA/gestalt therapists already mentioned, as well as the work of Alice Miller and Jungian psychotherapy, where there was an emphasis on the inner child as a source of creativity and guidance (Abrams, 1990). Stone and Winkelman (1985) gave detailed descriptions of their voice dialogue method, which includes a great deal of work with the inner child. Bradshaw (1988) drew many of these traditions together in his *Healing the Shame that Binds You*, a book that particularly influenced Young. Several other explorations of the healing impact of working directly with childhood memories and fragmented and dissociated child parts of the self were published in the years that followed. For example, Bradshaw (1990) presented further accounts of his work in the area, Capacchione (1991) explored the use of art materials (drawing and painting), while Ingerman (1991) described and explored the potential of the therapist's intuition in guiding this kind of work.

What makes this approach so compelling is the way in which identifying parts of the self clarifies the nature of underlying conflicts. In the development of TA, Berne had emphasized this, adopting the term "ego states" to refer to the Parent, Adult, and Child that were central to his model. As he observed, "Parent, adult and child are not just concepts but "phenomenological realities" (Berne, 1961, p. 4). Indeed, quite independently, Theodor Reik (1888–1969) had observed,

> there are three persons in the consultation room. . . . The analyst, the patient as he is now, and the child who continues his existence within the patient. (Reik, 1948, p. 306)

John Watkins, a hypnotherapist, also used the term "ego states," incorporating it into the name of the therapy that he developed – ego state therapy (Watkins and Johnson, 1982).

Beck addressed this multiplicity by means of a "schema mode model," which he used during a workshop in Oxford during the 1980s to help a borderline patient understand her different and confusing emotional states. Young developed the concept of schema modes further as he increasingly experimented with imagery and chair dialogues which bring contrasting parts of the self into focus (see Arntz, 2004). As Young observed those that could be seen again and again across cases, he began a systematic identification of schema modes. By the time of the publication of Young *et al.* (2003) a dozen or so important ones were identified and described. As the model was extended to address a wider range of personality disorders, so more modes were separated out and soon 21 modes would be described by Lobbestael, van Vreeswijk, and Arntz (2007). Humanistic therapists often used colorful terms for these parts of the self. Roth (1989, p. 155), for example, gives a vivid list that includes "Priscilla Perfect . . . Norma Nobody . . . Tommy Tuneout . . . Tara Tuff . . . Captain Control." Most of these can easily be mapped onto the modes used in ST, and schema therapists are free to use personalized names for modes, often ones suggested by clients themselves.

Three Phases in the Development of Young's Schema Therapy

As we have seen, integration of concepts and formulations across different traditions of psychotherapy has been ongoing for at least a quarter of a century; the development of ST has been part of this wider process. Young (2010) has suggested that there have been three major phases in the evolution of the ST that we are familiar with today.

Phase 1: ST as a strategic, formulation-driven approach to treatment

The first phase of the development of ST was driven by the challenge of the kinds of difficult cases that so easily led to treatment failure with brief or one-dimensional treatment approaches. This led to the development of increasingly refined methods of case formulation and treatment selection that could address a wider and wider range of difficult clinical problems. Although many clinical problems respond to quite brief interventions, difficult cases, particularly those where clients have personality disorders, call for more a strategic approach within which clinicians can draw on a range of technical interventions. What Young (1990) initially called schema-focused therapy developed as an adapted version of CT. The main technical differences were the greater focus on early schemas and the integration of relational and experiential approaches. These provided for greater flexibility on the part of therapists in responding to the needs of clients. As ST evolved, there was an increasing focus on addressing the difficulties presented by particular kinds of challenging cases. Thus publications in the early to mid-1990s addressed "personality disorders" or "characterological problems" (Young, 1990; Young and Lindemann, 1992; Bricker, Young, and Flanagan, 1993). A little later, formulations appeared addressing specific disorders such as narcissistic personality (Young and Flanagan, 1998), substance dependence (Ball and Young, 2000), bipolar disorder (Ball, Mitchell, Mahi, Skillecorn, and Smith, 2003), BPD (Kellogg and Young, 2006), and eating disorders (Waller, Kennerley, and Ohanian, 2007).

By the end of the 1990s Young's approach had achieved a distinct identity, with a particular model for case formulation and intervention planning. At any phase of the therapy, the choice of interventions is based on an understanding of: 1) the client's early maladaptive schemas; 2) dysfunctional schema coping methods; 3) the developmental factors that led to their formation; 4) the manner in which they play out in terms of modes; 5) how these patterns affect the client's current life in work, leisure, and relationships; and 6) the impact they have on the relationship with the therapist. The mode approach provides the ST therapist with a clear guideline with respect to goals of therapy: to build the HA, to heal the VC, and to reduce the power of self-defeating modes such as the Critical/Punitive Parent, the Overcontroller, and Protector modes. This was now called "schema therapy," a term first used in Ball and Young's (2000) article on substance abuse and then for the comprehensive manual which was in preparation and soon to appear (Young et al., 2003).

Phase 2: The impact of the Dutch research

Young's ideas attracted considerable interest in Europe, where the pre-CBT paradigm that personality has an influence on psychopathology remained stronger than in the US. However, the scientific recognition of Young's ST lagged behind. It was research on ST in the Netherlands that was to change this. This was initiated by Arnoud Arntz, who had accidently discovered that some of the patients he treated early in his training and who responded poorly to regular CBT were labeled by others as "borderline" and considered to be untreatable. Resisting this kind of therapeutic nihilism toward BPD, Arntz set out to understand borderline pathology from a ST point of view and integrated new techniques designed to help these patients better incorporate corrective information at the schema level. Reading the work of Edwards (1990a, 1990b) he felt supported in his belief that experiential techniques would be helpful and invited Padesky and Beck to offer workshops in Maastricht. This led to his developing an expanded form of CT for BPD based on the view that these clients should partly be viewed as experiencing the world like little frightened children who felt abandoned in a dangerous world where nobody could be trusted. His approach incorporated childhood trauma processing using experiential techniques like drama therapy and imagery rescripting (Arntz, 1994; Arntz and Weertman, 1999).

Arntz wanted to develop this into a model that could be used in a clinical trial. He approached Beck, who recommended the work of Young, which he regarded as the most promising CT model for this disorder. This resulted in a fruitful collaboration between Arntz and Young, as both soon realized how well their ideas and models matched. The next step was the planning of a RCT conducted in the Netherlands over three years. The results were published in the leading journal in the field, the *Archives of General Psychiatry* (Giesen-Bloo et al., 2006). The finding that ST was superior to a specialized highly regarded psychodynamic treatment for BPD and the recognition of the methodological quality of the trial led to an enormous increase in interest in both the clinical and scientific community. Suddenly, the position of ST had changed: it was now an evidence-based treatment. A by-product of the trial was that many of the therapists started to train new therapists in ST, initially in the Netherlands, but soon elsewhere in Europe, notably in Germany and the UK, speeding up dissemination. The term ST soon became institutionalized in the organization founded to provide networking, training, and certification of this therapy model: the International Society of Schema Therapy (ISST). Despite this, the term "schema-focused therapy" continued to be used in influential research studies – including the Dutch RCT (Giesen-Bloo et al., 2006; Bernstein, Arntz, and de Vos, 2007; Gude and Hoffart, 2008; Farrell, Shaw, and Webber, 2009) and Waller et al. (2007) even used the term "schema focused cognitive-behavior therapy."

The influence of the Dutch research was not restricted to this RCT. Other studies were published, notably on the schema mode model and on imagery rescripting (e.g.,

Weertman and Arntz, 2007); and applications of ST and the mode model to other personality disorders were developed and rigorous empirical tests set up, e.g., for Cluster C, paranoid, narcissistic, histrionic, and anti-social PDs, including in forensic patients (Bernstein et al., 2007). Another Dutch RCT demonstrated that ST could be successfully disseminated in clinical practice and that telephone availability of therapists outside office hours was not essential for its success (Nadort et al., 2009).

Phase 3: Group schema therapy

Meanwhile, a parallel development was the work of Joan Farrell and Ida Shaw on a group therapy format for ST (see Farrell, Shaw, and Reiss, this volume, Part 4, Chapter 5). Experiential therapy played a significant part in the development of both of them. Farrell, who trained in the US at the same time as Young, had personal therapy with a bioenergetics therapist. Shaw was trained in Canada in developmental psychology and experiential therapy. They recognized the need to adapt traditional psychotherapy to deal with deficits in early emotional learning and failed attachment in BPD patients. Their collaboration led to the development of an integrative model for group therapy of BPD. This incorporated a reparenting focus from the beginning and was described using the phrase "emotional awareness training" in the first issue of *Cognitive and Behavioral Practice* (Farrell and Shaw, 1994). At this time they recognized the similarities between their approach and the schema-focused model described by Young (1990), and when, in 2002, one of Farrell's supervisees attended a workshop with Young and was exposed to the new mode model, they immediately incorporated it into their group work. By the time they met Young in 2004 they recognized that what they had developed was a group version of ST that integrated interpersonal-process, person-centered, and educational group models, always with the therapists as active directors or "good parents" (Farrell and Shaw, 2010).

Unlike most CBT or dialectical behavior therapy (DBT) models, the Farrell–Shaw model is not individual therapy done while a group watches. Capitalizing on the strengths of group therapy, it adds three valuable features to the individual ST approach. First, the therapeutic factors of group psychotherapy identified by Yalom (1985) directly impact on the main schemas of BPD patients. These include *universality* (members learn that their problems are shared by others), *cohesiveness* (members experience a sense of belonging and acceptance), and *corrective recapitulation of the primary family experience* which catalyzes the reparenting and experiential learning components of ST. Second, two therapists run the group. One focuses on maintaining emotional connection and attending to the process of the group, and will be alert for identifying and challenging interfering coping modes. This increases access to the HA and VC modes and allows the other therapist to focus on implementing ST interventions to build the HA and address the needs of the VC. Third, having a group of participants allows for several members to contribute when using techniques like imagery rescripting and mode role plays and this enhances mutual support and learning (see Farrell et al., this volume, Part 4, Chapter 5).

The value of this integration of the principles of group therapy with the principles of ST was evidenced in the results of an RCT with BPD patients (Farrell, Shaw, and Webber, 2009). Participants were in regular individual therapy; some received no additional intervention (treatment as usual: TAU) while others attended 30 sessions of group ST over eight months. There was no change in symptoms in the TAU group, whereas the ST group showed clinically significant change. This means that the group model shows promise for one of the public health challenges of our time – making an evidence-based treatment widely available for BPD. Furthermore, like individual ST, the group model can be adapted for other PDs and Axis I disorders. This third phase is not only an innovation with respect to ST content, but has also become a major impetus for international collaboration in further development and dissemination of ST. There have been promising results from pilot studies of the group model in the Netherlands and of an intensive version for inpatient or day hospital use in the US. A large international RCT is evaluating the efficacy and cost-effectiveness of the model by comparing it to TAU at the participating sites (Joan Farrell, personal communication, November 2010).

Schema Therapy and Its Relationship to Other Schema-based Models

Psychotherapy integration and the focus on schemas

The use of the term "schema" to refer to cognitive mechanisms for abstracting and generalizing from experience has a long history in psychology. The idea that an individual's underlying schematic model of reality is different from reality itself was set out clearly by Vaihinger in 1911 and drawn on by Adler (1870–1937) in his theories of personality and psychotherapy (Ansbacher and Ansbacher, 1958). It was also central to Bartlett's (1886–1969) (1932) theory of memory in cognitive psychology, and to Piaget's (1896–1980) developmental psychology. From the 1970s, the concept of schema became a point of convergence for cognitive and psychodynamic approaches to therapy. For psychodynamic therapists, it had always been their business to identify and change problematic patterns of response developed in infancy and early childhood (Wallerstein, 1995). Discussing this in terms of schemas was put firmly on the map by Horowitz's (1988) cognitive reformulation of psychodynamic theories. For therapists with a cognitive orientation, it was natural to draw on such a well-established concept in explanatory models and the concept of a schema was central to Beck's work from the beginning. For many cognitive therapists interested in taking developmental factors into account and addressing longstanding patterns with their roots in the early years, Young's (1990) schema-focused approach provided a persuasive set of concepts that became increasingly influential.

However, as previously discussed, this was taking place against the background of widespread moves toward integration across approaches to psychotherapy. Today there is a proliferation of integrative psychotherapies, within which cognitive, behavioral, relational, and experiential techniques are used, including, for example, Cognitive Analytic Therapy (Ryle, 1997; Ryle and Kerr, 2002) and Compassion-Focused Therapy (Gilbert, 2005). Within the broad family of CBT, there is widespread recognition of the significance of paying attention to the therapeutic relationship (Leahy and Gilbert, 2007). Within CT, Beck and colleagues' (1990) *Cognitive Therapy of Personality Disorders* showed how a focus on underlying schemas is an important feature of the treatment of personality disorders. There is also an increasing integration of methods and techniques from other traditions within the overall cognitive framework. Further development of this trend is evident in the second edition (Beck *et al.*, 1990, 2004).

Meanwhile, the literature on experiential techniques has expanded, led by Greenberg's (2004) research on Emotion-Focused Therapy, which has now spanned a quarter of a century. Subsequently, an emotion-focused treatment for complex trauma was developed (Paivio and Pascual-Leone, 2010), which has many parallels with ST. Increasingly, imagery restructuring and rescripting methods have been applied to the treatment of PTSD (Grey, Young and Holmes, 2002; Ehlers, Hackmann, and Michael, 2004) and imagery rescripting of distressing childhood memories is being incorporated into CBT treatments for a wide range of Axis I disorders, including social phobia, depression, eating disorders, and obsessive compulsive disorder (OCD) (Edwards, 2007). These developments are reflected in a comprehensive practical manual of imagery methods used in CT (Hackmann, Bennett-Levy, and Holmes, 2011).

Within psychotherapy there has been a long history of using experiential techniques, including rescripting of childhood memories, to address persistent psychological problems (Edwards, 2011). However, it is only recently that these methods have received recognition in the scientific world. Three factors have contributed to this. First, the recognition of the limitations of narrow approaches fostered the widespread move toward psychotherapy integration. Second, the broadening of theory within cognitive science made it possible to better understand these methods and make them the subject of research (Teasdale, 1993; Holmes and Mathews, 2010). Third, a range of scientific studies has supported the effectiveness of these methods (Giesen-Bloo *et al.*, 2006; Weertman and Arntz, 2007), including collections of articles in two journal special issues: *Memory* (Hackmann and Holmes, 2004) and *Journal of Behavior Therapy and Experimental Psychiatry* (Holmes, Arntz and Smucker, 2007).

Schema Therapy in the age of integration

So is ST just another integrative system or does it have particular strengths and features that make it distinctive? The answers to these questions have already been touched on in this chapter; others will be found in the chapters that follow. Young himself emphasizes the distinctiveness of CT, particularly from its parent, the CT in which he was trained. He told an interviewer:

> ... both are very active therapies, but CT is typically entirely "rational," and in fact tries to teach patients to suppress or get rid of their negative emotions. When we work with longer term patients in ST, we try to evoke affect in the sessions, and try to understand where it comes from. ST also goes much deeper: what is called a core belief in CT is not nearly as "core" as what we call schemas. Our whole emphasis on childhood needs comes from attachment theory and is very much different from any concept in CT. ST has a developmental model, and CT doesn't, in my view. (Roediger and Young, 2009)

Although this may be a fair critique of some CBT approaches it is not universally accurate. As shown above, for many CT/CBT practitioners a developmental analysis of clients' problems, attention to relational aspects, focus on connecting with emotions, and use of imagery methods to effect schema level change are now routine.

Nevertheless, Young's work has had an unquestionable influence. There are four reasons for this. First, ST is based on far more than technical eclecticism and offers a deep integration of insights from various schools into a system of therapy with a coherent, conceptually economic model that translates into a workable practice at practitioner level. Second, the emphasis on limited reparenting in repairing early deficits in the basic needs of the patient is (though not uncontroversial) a feature that intuitively appeals to many therapists. Third, many practitioners have been personally influenced by Young's clinical acumen and personal dedication to sharing his work as a trainer. Fourth, recent research has provided evidence for the efficacy of ST (Giesen-Bloo *et al.*, 2006; Farrell *et al.*, 2009; Nadort *et al.*, 2009).

In addition, Young's work has been so influential that many practitioners use techniques that are important in ST without calling themselves Schema Therapists, and perhaps not even fully aware of the influence of ST in putting these methods on the map. This means that therapists who apply for accreditation as Schema Therapists will receive a very distinctive training with the model summarized by Young and colleagues (2003) at its core, enriched by the technical experience of the Dutch researchers (Arntz and van Genderen, 2009) and the growing clinical experience within the broader ST community. The model for training is still evolving, and with the founding of the ISST and the active involvement of ST practitioners from several countries, ST training is likely to reflect the experience of an ever-wider circle of contributors.

References

Abrams, J. (ed.) (1990) *Reclaiming the Inner Child*. Los Angeles, CA: Jeremy Tarcher.

Adler, G. and Myerson, P.G. (eds) (1973) *Confrontation in Psychotherapy*. New York: Science House.

Ansbacher, H.L. and Ansbacher, R.R. (1958) In Ansbacher R.R. (ed.), *The Individual Psychology of Alfred Adler: a Systematic Presentation in Selections from His Writings*. London: George Allen & Unwin.

Arnkoff, D.B. (1981) Flexibility in practicing cognitive therapy, in *New Directions in Cognitive Therapy* (ed. R.C. Bedrosian). New York: Guilford Press, pp. 203–222.

Arntz, A. (1994) Treatment of borderline personality disorder: a challenge for cognitive-behavioural therapy. *Behaviour Research and Therapy*, 32, 419–430.

Arntz, A. (2004) Borderline personality disorder, in *Cognitive Therapy of Personality Disorders*, 2nd edition (eds. A.T. Beck, A. Freeman, D.D. Davis *et al.*). New York: Guilford Press, pp. 187–215.

Arntz, A. and van Genderen, H. (2009) *Schema Therapy for Borderline Personality Disorder*. Oxford: Wiley-Blackwell.

Arntz, A. and Weertman, A. (1999) Treatment of childhood memories: theory and practice. *Behaviour Research and Therapy*, 37, 715–740.

Assagioli, R. (1965) *Psychosynthesis*. London: Turnstone.

Ball, J., Mitchell, P., Malhi, G., Skillecorn, A. and Smith, M. (2003) Schema-focused cognitive therapy for bipolar disorder: reducing vulnerability to relapse through attitudinal change. *Australian and New Zealand Journal of Psychiatry*, 37, 41–48.

Ball, S.A. and Young, J.E. (2000) Dual focus schema therapy for personality disorders and substance dependence: case study results. *Cognitive and Behavioral Practice*, 7(3), 270–281.

Barnes, G. (ed.) (1977) *Transactional Analysis after Eric Berne*. New York: Harper & Row.
Bartlett, F.C. (1932) *Remembering*. London: Cambridge University Press.
Beck, A.T. (1970) Role of fantasies in psychotherapy and psychopathology. *Journal of Nervous and Mental Disease*, 150(1), 3–17.
Beck, A.T. (1985) Cognitive therapy, behavior therapy, psychoanalysis, and pharmacology: a cognitive continuum, in *Cognition and Psychotherapy* (ed. A. Freeman). New York: Plenum Press, pp. 325–349.
Beck, A.T. and Ellis, A. (2000) New concepts in practice: on therapy – a dialogue with Aaron T. Beck and Albert Ellis. 108th Convention of the American Psychological Association, Washington, DC (August) www.fenichel.com/Beck-Ellis.shtml (accessed July 24, 2010).
Beck, A.T. and Emery, G. (1985) *Anxiety Disorders and Phobias: a Cognitive Approach*. New York: Basic Books.
Beck, A.T., Freeman, A. and Associates (1990) *Cognitive Therapy of Personality Disorders*. New York: Guilford Press.
Beck, A.T., Freeman, A., Davis, D.D. *et al.* (2004) *Cognitive Therapy of Personality Disorders*, 2nd edition. New York: Guilford Press.
Beck, A.T., Rush, A.J., Shaw, B.F. and Emery, G. (1979) *Cognitive Therapy of Depression*. New York: John Wiley.
Berne, E. (1961) *Transactional Analysis in Psychotherapy*. New York: Grove Press.
Bernstein, D.P., Arntz, A. and de Vos, M. (2007) Schema-focused therapy in forensic settings: theoretical model and recommendations for best clinical practice. *International Journal of Forensic Mental Health*, 6(2), 169–183.
Bowlby, J. (1979) *The Making and Breaking of Affectional Bonds*. London: Tavistock.
Bradshaw, J. (1988) *Healing the Shame that Binds You*. Pompano Beach, FL: Health Communications.
Bradshaw, J. (1990) *Home Coming: Reclaiming and Championing Your Inner Child*. New York: Bantam.
Brennan, K.A. and Shaver, P.R. (1998) Attachment styles and personality disorders: their relationship to each other and to parental divorce, parental death and perceptions of parental caregiving. *Journal of Personality*, 66(5), 835–878.
Bricker, D.C., Young, J.E. and Flanagan, C.M. (1993) Schema-focused cognitive therapy: a comprehensive framework for characterological problems, in *Cognitive Therapies in Action* (ed. H. Rosen). San Francisco, CA: Jossey-Bass, pp. 88–125.
Capacchione, L. (1991) *Recovery of Your Inner Child*. New York: Fireside Books.
Cashdan, S. (1988) *Object Relations Theory: Using the Relationship*. New York: W.W. Norton.
Chu, J.A. (1992) Empathic confrontation in the treatment of childhood abuse survivors, including a tribute to the legacy of Dr. David Caul. *Dissociation*, 5(2), 98–103.
Coleman, R.E. (1981) Cognitive-behavioral treatment of agoraphobia. In R. Bedrosian (ed.), *New Directions in Cognitive Therapy: a Casebook* (pp. 101–119). New York: Guilford Press.
Dattilio, F.M., Edwards, D.J.A. and Fishman, D.B. (2010) Case studies within a mixed methods paradigm: towards a resolution of the alienation between researcher and practitioner in psychotherapy research. *Psychotherapy: Theory, Research, Practice and Training*, 47, 427–441.
Edwards, D. (2011) Invited essay. From ancient shamanic healing to 21st century psychotherapy: the central role of imagery methods in effecting psychological change, in *Oxford Guide to Imagery in Cognitive Therapy* (eds A. Hackmann, J. Bennett-Levy and E. Holmes). Oxford: Oxford University Press, pp. xxxiii–xlii.

Edwards, D.J.A. (1989) Cognitive restructuring through guided imagery, in *Comprehensive Handbook of Cognitive Therapy* (eds A. Freeman, K.S. Simon, H. Arkowitz and L. Beutler). New York: Plenum Press, pp. 283–297.

Edwards, D.J.A. (1990a) Cognitive therapy and the restructuring of early memories through guided imagery. *Journal of Cognitive Psychotherapy*, *4*, 33–51.

Edwards, D.J.A. (1990b) Cognitive-behavioral and existential-phenomenological approaches to therapy: complementary or conflicting paradigms? *Journal of Cognitive Psychotherapy*, *4*, 107–123.

Edwards, D.J.A. (2007) Restructuring implicational meaning through memory based imagery: some historical notes. *Journal of Behavior Therapy and Experimental Psychiatry*, *38*, 306–316.

Edwards, D.J.A. and Jacobs, M.D. (2003) *Conscious and Unconscious*. Maidenhead: Open University Press/McGraw-Hill.

Ehlers, A., Hackmann, A. and Michael, T. (2004) Intrusive re-experiencing in post-traumatic stress disorder: phenomenology, theory and therapy. *Memory*, *12*(4), 403–415.

Ellenberger, H.F. (1970) *The Discovery of the Unconscious: the History and Evolution of Dynamic Psychiatry*. New York: Basic Books.

Emery, G. (1982) *Own Your Own Life*. New York: New American Library.

Erskine, R. (1980) Script cure: behavioral, interpsychic and physiological. *Transactional Analysis Journal*, *10*(2), 102–106.

Erskine, R. and Moursund, J. (1988) *Integrative Psychotherapy in Action*. Newbury Park, CA: Sage.

Farrell, J.M. and Shaw, I.A. (1994) Emotional awareness training: a prerequisite to effective cognitive-behavioral treatment of borderline personality disorder. *Cognitive and Behavioral Practice*, *1*(1), 72–92.

Farrell, J.M. and Shaw, I.A. (2010) Schema therapy groups for borderline personality disorder patients: the best of both worlds of group psychotherapy, in *Fortschritte der Schematherapie [Advances in Schema Therapy]* (eds E. Roediger and G. Jacobs), Göttingen: Hogrefe.

Farrell, J.M., Shaw, I.A. and Webber, M.A. (2009) A schema-focused approach to group psychotherapy for outpatients with borderline personality disorder: a randomized controlled trial. *Journal of Behavior Therapy and Experimental Psychiatry*, *40*(2), 317–328.

Ferenczi, S. (1929) The principle of relaxation and neocatharsis, in *Final Contributions to the Problems and Methods of Psycho-Analysis* (ed. M. Balint, transl. E. Mosbacher *et al.*). New York: Brunner/Mazel, pp. 108–125.

Freeman, A. (1981) Dreams and images in cognitive therapy, in *New Directions in Cognitive Therapy* (ed. R.C. Bedrosian). New York: Guilford Press, pp. 224–237.

Giesen-Bloo, J., Van Dyck, R., Spinhoven, P. *et al.* (2006) Outpatient psychotherapy for borderline personality disorder: randomized controlled trial of schema-focused therapy vs. transference-focused psychotherapy. *Archives of General Psychiatry*, *63*, 649–658.

Gilbert, P. (ed.) (2005) *Compassion: Conceptualisations, Research and Use in Psychotherapy*. New York: Routledge.

Goulding, M.M. and Goulding, R.L. (1979) *Changing Lives through Redecision Therapy*. New York: Brunner/Mazel.

Greenberg, L.S. (2004) Emotion-focused therapy. *Clinical Psychology and Psychotherapy*, *11*, 3–16.

Greenberg, L.S. and Safran, J.D. (1984) Integrating affect and cognition: a perspective on the process of therapeutic change. *Cognitive Therapy and Research*, *8*(6), 559–578.

Greenberg, L.S. and Safran, J.D. (1987) *Emotion in Psychotherapy*. New York: Guilford Press.

Grey, N., Young, K. and Holmes, E. (2002) Cognitive restructuring within reliving a treatment for peritraumatic emotional "hotspots" in posttraumatic stress disorder. *Behavioral and Cognitive Psychotherapy*, *30*(1), 37–56.

Gude, T. and Hoffart, A. (2008) Change in interpersonal problems after cognitive agoraphobia and schema-focused therapy versus psychodynamic treatment as usual of inpatients with agoraphobia and cluster C personality disorders. *Scandinavian Journal of Psychology*, 49, 195–199.

Guidano, V.F. and Liotti, G. (1983) *Cognitive Processes and Emotional Disorders*. New York: Guilford Press.

Hackmann, A. and Holmes, E. (2004) Reflecting on imagery: a clinical perspective and overview of the special issue of *Memory* on mental imagery and memory in psychopathology. *Memory*, 12(4), 389–402.

Hackmann, A., Bennett-Levy, J. and Holmes, E. (2011) *Oxford Guide to Imagery in Cognitive Therapy*. Oxford: Oxford University Press.

Hannah, B. (1981) *Encounters with the Soul: Active Imagination*. Boston, MA: Sigo Press.

Hawton, K., Salkovskis, P.M., Kirk, J. and Clark, D.M. (eds) (1989) *Cognitive Behaviour Therapy for Psychiatric Problems: a Practical Guide*. Oxford: Oxford University Press.

Holmes, E.A., Arntz, A. and Smucker, M.R. (2007) Imagery rescripting in cognitive behavior therapy: images, treatment techniques and outcomes. *Journal of Behavior Therapy and Experimental Psychiatry*, 38, 297–305.

Holmes, E.A. and Mathews, A. (2010) Mental imagery in emotion and emotional disorders. *Clinical Psychology Review*, 30, 349–362.

Horowitz, M. (1988) *Introduction to Psychodynamics: a New Synthesis*. London: Routledge.

Ingerman, S. (1991) *Soul Retrieval: Mending the Fragmented Self*. New York: HarperSanFrancisco.

Jacobs, A. (1977) Psychodrama and TA, in *Techniques in Transactional Analysis for Psychotherapists and Counselors*, 1st edition (ed. M. James). Philippines: Addison-Wesley, pp. 239–249.

James, M. (1977) Self-reparenting: theory and process, in *Techniques in Transactional Analysis for Psychotherapists and Counselors* (ed. M. James). Reading, MA: Addison-Wesley, pp. 486–496.

Jung, C.G. (1960) The transcendent function. *The Collected Works of C.G. Jung*, 2nd edition. Volume 8: *The Structure and Dynamics of the Psyche*. London: Routledge & Kegan Paul, pp. 67–91.

Kellogg, S.H. and Young, J.E. (2006) Schema therapy for borderline personality disorder. *Journal of Clinical Psychology*, 62(4), 445–458.

Kramer, R. (1995) The birth of client-centred psychotherapy: Carl Rogers, Otto Rank and "The Beyond." *Journal of Humanistic Psychology*, 35(4), 54–110.

Layden, M.A., Newman, C.F., Freeman, A. and Morse, S.B. (1993) *Cognitive Therapy of Borderline Personality Disorder*. Boston, MA: Allyn & Bacon.

Lazarus, A. (1985) *Casebook of Multimodal Therapy*. New York: Guilford Press.

Leahy, R. and Gilbert, P. (eds) (2007) *The Therapeutic Relationship in the Cognitive-Behavioral Psychotherapies*. London: Routledge.

Leaman, D.R. (1978) Confrontation in counseling. *Personnel and Guidance Journal*, 56, 630–633.

Lindorff, D. (2001) A lecture by Barbara Hannah. *The Society of Analytical Psychology*, 46, 371–373.

Liotti, G., Pasquini, P. and the Italian Group for the Study of Dissociation. (2000) Predictive factors for borderline personality disorder: patients' early traumatic experiences and losses suffered by the attachment figure. *Acta Psychiatrica Scandanavica*, 102, 282–289.

Lobbestael, J., van Vreeswijk, M. and Arntz, A. (2007) Shedding light on schema modes: a clarification of the mode concept and its current research status. *Netherlands Journal of Psychology*, 63, 76–85.

London, P. (1972) The end of ideology in behavior modification. *American Psychologist*, 27, 913–919.

Lowen, A. (1976) *Bioenergetics*. Harmondsworth: Penguin.
Madewell, J. and Shaughnessy, M.F. (2009) An interview with John Wymore: current practice of Gestalt Therapy. *North American Journal of Psychology*. findarticles.com/p/articles/mi_6894/is_3_11/ai_n42379454 (accessed August 13, 2009).
Mahoney, M.J. and Freeman, A. (eds) (1985) *Cognition and Psychotherapy*. New York: Plenum Press.
Moreno, J.L. (1939) Psychodramatic shock therapy: a sociometric approach to the problem of mental disorder. *Sociometry*, 2(1), 1–30.
Nadort, M., Arntz, A., Smit, J.H. et al. (2009) Implementation of outpatient schema therapy for borderline personality disorder with versus without crisis support by the therapist outside office hours: a randomized trial. *Behaviour Research and Therapy*, 47, 961–973.
Norcross, J.C. and Goldfried, M.R. (eds) (1992) *Handbook of Psychotherapy Integration*. New York: Basic Books.
Oulahabib, L.S. (2009) Et si Janet était plus actuel que Freud? [What if Janet were more up-to-date than Freud?] *Psychiatrie, Sciences Humaines, Neurosciences*, 7, 1–14.
Paivio, S.C. and Pascual-Leone, A. (2010) *Emotion-focused Therapy for Complex Trauma: an Integrative Approach*. Washington, DC: American Psychological Association.
Perls, F.S. (1973) *The Gestalt Approach and Eye-Witness to Therapy*. New York: Bantam Books.
Perris, C. (1999) A conceptualization of personality-related disorders of interpersonal behavior with implications for treatment. *Clinical Psychology and Psychotherapy*, 6, 239–260.
Redfearn, J.W. (1994) Introducing subpersonality theory: a clarification of object relations and of complexes, with special reference to the I/not-I gateway. *Journal of Analytical Psychology*, 39, 283–309.
Reik, T. (1948) *Listening with the Third Ear: the Inner Experience of a Psychoanalyst*. New York: Grove Press.
Roediger, E. and Young, J.E. (2009) An interview with Jeffrey Young. www.schematherapie-frankfurt.de/down/Interview.pdf (accessed November 29, 2010).
Roth, G. (1989) *Maps to ecstasy: teachings of an urban shaman*. San Rafael, CA: New World Library.
Rowan, J. (1990) *Subpersonalities*. London: Routledge.
Ryle, A. (1997) *Cognitive Analytic Therapy and Borderline Personality Disorder: the Model and the Method*. Chichester: Wiley.
Ryle, A. and Kerr, I. (2002) *Introducing Cognitive Analytic Therapy: Principles and Practice*. Chichester: Wiley.
Safran, J.D. (1984) Assessing the cognitive interpersonal cycle. *Cognitive Therapy and Research*, 8, 333–348.
Safran, J.D., Muran, J.C., Samstag, L.W. and Winston. A. (2005) Evaluating alliance-focused intervention for potential treatment failures: a feasibility study and descriptive analysis. *Psychotherapy: Theory, Research, Practice, Training*, 42(4), 512–531.
Samuels, M. and Samuels, N. (1975) *Seeing with the Mind's Eye: the History, Techniques, and Uses of Visualization*. New York: Random House.
Schiff, J.L. (1970) *All My Children*. New York: Evans.
Schiff, J.L. (1977) One hundred children generate a lot of TA: history, development, and activities if the Schiff family, in *Transactional Analysis after Eric Berne* (ed. G. Barnes). New York: Harper & Row, pp. 53–76.
Schwartz, H.L. (1994) From dissociation to negotiation: a relational psychoanalytic perspective on multiple personality disorder. *Psychoanalytic Psychology*, 11(2), 189–231.
Sheikh, A. (ed.) (1984) *Imagination and Healing*. Amityville, NY: Baywood.
Shorr, J.E. (1983) *Psychotherapy through Imagery*, 2nd edition. New York: Thieme-Stratton.

Singer, J.L. (1974) *Imagery and Daydream Methods in Psychotherapy and Behavior Modification.* New York: Academic Press.

Singer, J.L. and Pope, K.S. (eds) (1978) *The Power of the Human Imagination: New Methods in Psychotherapy.* New York: Plenum Press.

Smucker, M.R., Dancu, V.C., Foa, E.B. and Niederee, L.J. (1995) Imagery rescripting: a new treatment for survivors of childhood sexual abuse suffering from posttraumatic stress. *Journal of Cognitive Psychotherapy, 9,* 3–17.

Steiner, C.M. (1974) *Scripts People Live.* New York: Bantam Books.

Stone, H. and Winkelman, S. (1985) *Embracing Our Selves.* Marina del Rey CA: de Vorss.

Sullivan, H.S. (1950) The illusion of personal individuality. *Psychiatry, 13,* 317–332.

Sullivan, H.S. (1953) *The Interpersonal Theory of Psychiatry.* New York: W.W. Norton.

Tamminen, A.W. and Smaby, M.H. (1981) Helping counselors learn to confront. *Personnel and Guidance Journal, 60*(1), 41–45.

Teasdale, J.D. (1993) Emotion and two kinds of meaning: cognitive therapy and cognitive science. *Behaviour Research and Therapy, 31,* 339–354.

van der Hart, O., Brown, P. and van der Kolk, B.A. (1989) Pierre Janet's treatment of post-traumatic stress. *Journal of Traumatic Stress, 2,* 379–395.

van der Hart, O. and Friedman, B. (1989) A reader's guide to Pierre Janet: a neglected intellectual heritage. *Dissociation, 2*(1), 3–16.

van der Hart, O. and Horst, R. (1989) The dissociation theory of Pierre Janet. *Journal of Traumatic Stress, 2,* 397–412.

Wallas, L. (1991) *Stories that Heal: Reparenting Adult Children of Dysfunctional Families Using Hypnotic Stories in Psychotherapy.* New York: W.W. Norton.

Waller, G., Kennerley, H. and Ohanian, V. (2007) Schema-focused cognitive-behavioral therapy for eating disorders, in *Cognitive Schemas and Core Beliefs in Psychological Problems: a Scientist–Practitioner Guide* (eds L.P. Riso, P.L. du Toit, D.J. Stein and J.E. Young). Washington, DC: American Psychological Association, pp. 139–175.

Wallerstein, R.S. (1995) *The Talking Cures: the Psychoanalyses and the Psychotherapies.* New Haven, CT: Yale University Press.

Watkins, J.G. and Johnson, R.J. (1982) *We, the Divided Self.* New York: Irvington.

Weertman, A. and Arntz, A. (2007) Effectiveness of treatment of childhood memories in cognitive therapy of personality disorders: a controlled study contrasting methods focusing on the present and methods focusing on childhood memories. *Behaviour Research and Therapy, 45,* 2133–2143.

Weiss, J. and Weiss, L. (1977) Corrective parenting in practice, in *Transactional Analysis after Eric Berne* (ed. G. Barnes). New York: Harper & Row, pp. 114–133.

Welpton, D.F. (1973) Confrontation in the therapeutic process, in *Confrontation in Psychotherapy* (eds G. Adler and P.G. Myerson). New York: Science House, pp. 249–269.

Wolpe, J., Salter, A. and Reyna, L.J. (1964) *The Conditioning Therapies: the Challenge in Psychotherapy.* New York: Holt, Rinehart & Winston.

Woollams, S.J. (1977) From 21 to 43, in *Transactional analysis after Eric Berne* (ed. G. Barnes). New York: Harper & Row, pp. 351–379.

Yalom, I.D. (1985) *The Theory and Practice of Group Psychotherapy,* 3rd edition. New York: Basic Books.

Young, J.E. (1984) *Cognitive Therapy for Personality Disorders and Difficult Patients.* Unpublished: Center for Cognitive Therapy, University of Pennsylvania, Philadelphia.

Young, J.E. (1990) *Cognitive Therapy for Personality Disorders: a Schema-focused Approach.* Sarasota, FL: Professional Resource Press.

Young, J.E. (2010) Schema therapy, past, present and future. Keynote address to the Conference of the International Society for Schema Therapy, Berlin, Germany (July).

Young, J.E. and Flanagan, C. (1998) Schema-focused therapy for narcissistic patients, in *Disorders of Narcissism: Diagnostic, Clinical, and Empirical Implications* (ed. E.F. Ronningstam). Washington, DC: American Psychiatric Press, pp. 239–268.

Young, J.E., Klosko, J. and Weishaar, M.E. (2003) *Schema Therapy: a Practitioner's Guide*. New York: Guilford Press.

Young, J.E. and Lindemann, M.D. (1992) An integrative schema-focused model for personality disorders. *Journal of Cognitive Psychotherapy*, 6, 11–24.

Zajonc, R.B. (1980) Feeling and thinking: preferences need no inferences. *American Psychologist*, 35(2), 151–175.

Zajonc, R.B. (1984) On the primacy of affect. *American Psychologist*, 39, 117–123.

2

Theoretical Model
Schemas, Coping Styles, and Modes

Hannie van Genderen, Marleen Rijkeboer and Arnoud Arntz

Schemas hold a prominent position in modern psychotherapies, especially those in which there is attention to chronic personality-related disorders. There is a long history behind the concept of a schema. The definitions that are used within the current cognitive therapies were created in the 1980s, influenced by constructivism (see Rijkeboer, van Genderen and Arntz, 2007).

Well-known clinic-oriented scientists, such as Beck, Segal, and Young, developed explanatory models for psychopathology, with schemas and related concepts such as schema processes, coping styles, and schema modes as central parameters. In the meantime, use of the term "schema" has become widespread within the psychotherapy world and is growing. Across the diverse schema theories, many definitions are used, resulting in just as much obfuscation (see James, Southam and Blackburn, 2004). The terms "coping style" and "mode" also have several definitions. This chapter will explain these concepts, as defined by Young, Klosko, and Weishaar (2003, 2005). However, Young's schema approach continues to develop. In a forum of therapists and researchers, the discussion now is about the nature of the different concepts and their mutual relationships. This chapter will therefore conclude with a short summary of the main issues.

In Practice

Early maladaptive schemas

The term schema comes from data processing theory, which states that information is ordered in our memory thematically (Williams, Watts, MacLeod and Mathews, 1997; Vonk, 1999). The idea is that experiences are saved in our autobiographic memory by way of schemas from the first years of life (Conway and Pleydell-Pearce,

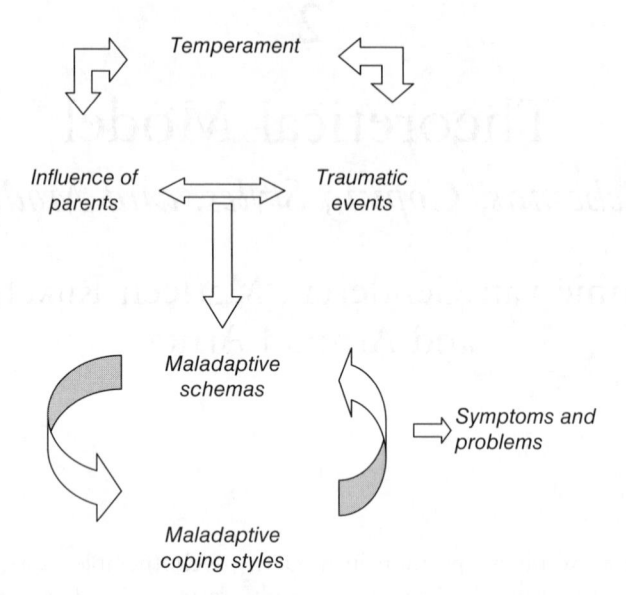

Figure 2.1 Origin of maladaptive schemas

2000). Schemas consist of sensory perceptions, experienced emotions and actions, and the meaning given to them, such that early childhood experiences are memorized non-verbally (Young et al., 2005; Arntz, van Genderen and Wijts, 2006; Rijkeboer et al., 2007). In addition, schemas function as filters through which people order, interpret, and predict the world. Most people have developed schemas that help them to better understand themselves, the behavior of others, and events in the world. This enables them to develop a positive self-image and a differentiated image of others, and to solve problems adequately. People with personality problems have developed maladaptive schemas and therefore handle life less well. According to Young et al. (2005), these maladaptive schemas are developed at an early age as a result of the interactions between factors such as the temperament of the child, the parenting style of the parents, and any significant (sometimes traumatic) experiences (see Figure 2.1). With this hypothesis, Young et al. (2005) proposed a development model of personality and psychopathology in which Bowlby's attachment theory (1988) plays an important role. They hypothesize that maladaptive schemas reflect the unfulfilled yet important emotional needs of the child and represent adaptations to negative experiences, for example, family quarrels, rejection, hostility, or even aggression from parents/educators and peers, lack of love and warmth, and inadequate parental care and support. Research has shown that influences from relationships are important for the emotional development of the child, and disturbances can lead to a deregulation of emotions (Maughan and Cicchetti, 2002; Cohen, Crawford, Johnson and Kasen, 2005). The development of a personality pathology is often linked to traumatic events (e.g., violence or abuse; Grover, Carpenter, Price, Gagne, Mello and Tyrka, 2007), but a constant pattern of negative or inadequate reactions toward a child can also lead to the development of pathology (Johnson, Cohen, Kasen, Smailes and Brook, 2001). Although maladaptive schemas are normally adaptive in early childhood, and endorsed by the circumstances, it is assumed that they also interfere to a considerable extent with completing the developmental tasks well. This can lead to continuous negative experiences, which means that the schema becomes more and more worn and rigid. Whilst the influence of the temperament of the child should not be exaggerated, one child can be more "bothered" by a certain education than another (Gallagher, 2002). Furthermore, temperament itself appears to be influenced by factors such as the environment and the regulation styles that the child develops.

The more someone has problems in a certain area, and the more severe the experienced traumatic events are, the more rigid and strong certain beliefs will be, and the more the subject will be troubled by it in his current life. Schemas are more or less active or influential at any one time. When circumstances show similarities with situations that have led to the development of the schema, then that schema will come to the fore. A subject with the Defectiveness/Shame schema may be troubled very little by this schema in a situation in which he is surrounded by good friends and his work is relatively stable. But as soon as he starts to have difficulties with his friends, or when there is a lot of uncertainty at work (e.g., in the event of company restructuring), the dormant schema will become active and the subject may start to have, for example, symptoms of depression. This may complicate the search for schemas, especially if the patient has also developed ways of avoiding being disturbed by his schemas. A patient with the Defectiveness/Shame schema can, for instance, avoid this by choosing a job in which he runs little risk of criticism and by building a circle of friends who are non-judgmental. In other words, a person not only has schemas, but also strategies to avoid being bothered by them (see coping styles).

Describing the Schemas

In the original version of the Young Schema Questionnaire (YSQ) (Young and Brown, 1994; Dutch translation and adaption: Sterk and Rijkeboer, 1997), 16 schemas were defined. In Young *et al.* (2005), 18 schemas were described, and the Social Undesirability schema had been dropped (see Part V, Chapter 3). For pragmatic reasons, all 19 schemas are described here (see Table 2.1, Part VI Chapter 4), even though some (indicated by an asterisk) must still be investigated with regard to their psychometrical qualities.

Coping Styles

Maladaptive schemas are often maintained because the patient avoids situations that could correct them, or because he is looking for people who will confirm his schemas, and/or because he has no eye for information that would nuance his schemas. The patient learned to behave like this in childhood, in order to survive difficult or threatening situations. At the time that may have been the best way to deal with these kinds of situations, but in the patient's current life, this behavior may be far from optimal and it serves to maintain the schemas. There are three ways in which one can deal with schemas, or coping styles: Surrender, Avoidance, and

Table 2.1 Schemas

Emotional Deprivation	The patient expects that others will never or not adequately meet his primary emotional needs (e.g., for support, nurturance, empathy, and protection). He feels isolated and lonely.
Abandonment/ Instability	The patient expects that significant others will eventually abandon him. Others are unreliable and unpredictable in their support and connection. When the patient feels abandoned he switches between feelings of anxiety, grief, and anger.
Mistrust and/or Abuse	The patient is convinced that others will intentionally abuse him in some way or that they will cheat or humiliate him. These feelings vary greatly and the patient is continuously on edge.
Social Isolation/ Alienation	The patient feels isolated from the world and believes that he is not part of any community.
Defectiveness/ Shame	The patient believes that he is internally flawed and bad. If others get close, they will realize this and withdraw from the relationship. The feeling of being worthless often leads to a strong sense of shame.
Social Undesirability	The patient believes that he is socially inept and physically unattractive. He sees himself as boring, dull, and ugly.
Failure	The patient believes that he is incapable of performing as well as his peer group. He feels stupid and untalented.
Dependence/ Incompetence	The patient feels extremely helpless and incapable of functioning independently. He is incapable of making day-to day decisions and is often tense and anxious.
Vulnerability to Harm and Illness	The patient believes that imminent catastrophe will strike him and significant others, and that he is unable to prevent this.
Enmeshment/ Undeveloped Self	The patient has an excessive emotional involvement and closeness with one or more significant others (often his parents), as a result of which he cannot develop his own identity.
Subjugation	The patient submits to the control of others in order to avoid negative consequences. The patient ignores his own needs because he fears conflict and punishment.
Self-Sacrifice	The patient focuses on voluntarily meeting the needs of others, whom he considers weaker than himself. If he pays attention to his own needs, he feels guilty, and he gives priority to the needs of others. Finally, he becomes annoyed with the people he is looking after.
Approval-Seeking*	The patient focuses excessively on gaining recognition, approval, and attention, at the expense of his own development and needs.
Emotional Inhibition	The patient inhibits emotions and impulses because he believes that any expression of feelings will harm others or lead to embarrassment, retaliation, or abandonment. He lacks spontaneity and stresses rationality.
Unrelenting Standards/ Hypocritical	The patient believes that whatever he does is not good enough and that he must always strive harder. He is hypercritical of himself and others, and he is a perfectionist, rigid, and extremely efficient. This is at the expense of pleasure, relaxation, and social contacts.
Negativity and Pessimism*	The patient is always focused on the negative aspects of life and ignores or plays down the positive aspects. He is frequently anxious and hyper-alert.

Table 2.1 (*Continued*)

Punitiveness*	The patient believes that people should be harshly punished for making mistakes. He is aggressive, intolerant, impatient, and unforgiving.
Entitlement/ Grandiosity	The patient believes that he is superior to others and entitled to special rights. He insists that he should be able to do or have what he wants, regardless of what others think. The core theme is power and being in control of situations or people.
Insufficient Self-Control/ Self-Discipline	The patient has no tolerance of frustration and is unable to control his feelings and impulses. He cannot bear dissatisfaction or discomfort (pain, conflicts, or overexertion).

* = Schemas that are not in the YSQ.

Over-Compensation. In the short term, these coping styles often provide some relief, but in the long run, they lead to difficulties in essential areas of life. Using a coping style is generally not a conscious choice, but an automatic reaction to a threatening or difficult situation. Coping styles may be particularly visible in the behavior of the patient, but they also contain cognitive transformations.

Surrender (to the schema). The patient gives in to his schema and adapts his feelings and thoughts to this end:

BEHAVIOR:	Repeating behavioral patterns from childhood by looking for people and situations that are similar to the circumstances that led to the forming of the schema.
THOUGHTS:	Selective processing of information, i.e., seeing only the information that corresponds with the schema and not the information that diminishes the schema.
FEELINGS:	The emotional pain of the schema is felt directly.

Avoidance (Schema-avoiding behavior). The patient avoids activities that trigger the schema and the emotions that accompany it. The result is that the schema is not open to discussion and it becomes impossible to have a corrective experience.

BEHAVIOR:	Active and passive avoidance of all kinds of situations that could trigger the schema.
THOUGHTS:	Denial of events or memories, depersonalization or dissociation.
FEELINGS:	Smoothing over feelings or feeling nothing at all.

Over-Compensation (Showing the opposite behavior in order to fight the schema)

The patient behaves, as much as possible, in the opposite direction from the core of his schema, in order not to be bothered by it. This leads to an underestimation of the influence that a schema can have, and also often to excessively assertive, aggressive, or independent behavior.

> ### Three kinds of coping styles
>
> Proceeding from the Abandonment/Instability schema, someone decides never to enter into a relationship again (avoidance). He thus gains temporary relief, because no one can hurt him by leaving him. However, in the long run, he becomes very lonely, because he avoids all intimacy.
>
> If he decides to compensate for his Over-Compensation schema, he starts looking for the "perfect relationship" with someone who will never abandon him. During the initial period of being in love, he might succeed, but after a while, when the partner wants to have more autonomy, he will claim the other person and demand constant availability. There is a good chance that the partner will not be able to tolerate this and will leave him. This way, the schema is confirmed.
>
> If he submits to the Surrender schema, he settles for a relationship that offers him insufficient support and security (e.g., with a partner who is often unfaithful or a on/off relationship). In a sense, this feels familiar, but in the long run, the patient remains lonely and unhappy.

BEHAVIOR: Showing behavior that is opposite (often exaggerated) to the schema.
THOUGHTS: Thoughts are opposite to the content of the schema as well. The patient denies that he has the schema.
FEELINGS: The patient masks uncomfortable feelings belonging to the schema with opposite feelings (e.g., power as a cover for powerlessness; pride as a cover for a sense of inferiority). However, the uncomfortable feelings may return if the over-compensation fails.

Normally, patients have only one coping style. Although a coping style such as Surrender can be dominant, in the course of time, you can see a patient adopting other coping styles as well. Surrendering to the Self-Sacrifice schema for a long period and in a very intense manner, in which thoughts about the wishes and interest of others are prominent, finally leads to exhaustion and a growing need to see their own needs fulfilled for once. Accordingly, this can lead to a (probably short) period of Over-Compensation. Sometimes the patient can strive for his own aims in an aggressive way, without having any consideration for others. Switching from Surrender to Over-Compensation is more abrupt and more strongly visible in severe forms of psychopathology (see Elliott and Kirby Lassen, 1999). If it all becomes too much, the patient may try to escape from the strong feelings that evoke Surrender or Over-Compensation by Avoidance. The patient may then, for instance, avoid situations in which something could be asked of him. He cannot keep this up for ever, so at some point this takes him back to Surrender or Over-Compensation. In this way, each of these coping styles leads to the maintenance of the schema.

Schema Modes

It appears that, particularly with the more complex personality problems, patients recognize themselves in many different schemas and in addition, deal with diverse coping styles in a flexible way. Therefore, mood and behavior changes can often occur within a very short period of time. This observation has resulted in the development of a so-called "schema mode model" for borderline personality disorder (and later also the narcissistic personality disorder by Young *et al.*, 2005). According to Young *et al.* (2005), schema modes are the instantaneous, continuously changing, but dominant states of mind a patient can find himself in. Whereas schemas are stable ("trait"), modes are short-term situations ("state"). And whereas a schema represents a one-dimensional theme (e.g., Defectiveness/Shame), a schema mode reflects a *constellation* of schemas and coping styles that are active at that moment (the Vulnerable Child, for example, consists of the Defectiveness/Shame schema and Emotional Deprivation; Lobbestael, van Vreeswijk and Arntz, 2007).

Schema modes, just like schemas, are not only present in people with a personality disorder, but play a role in everyone. The difference is the degree to which the modes operate independently from each other as well as their strength.

The healthier a person is, the more independent the modes are, and the less the maladaptive modes dominate. In an unpleasant situation, a healthy person can experience grief, anger, and the tendency not to think about it more or less simultaneously, and can control and integrate these emotions and this behavior. Someone with a personality disorder has much more difficulty. However, schema modes are never completely distinct from each other, so there is the idea of the patient having discrete parts. A schema mode is a state that is prominent at a certain moment. In the case of a patient with a few maladaptive modes, one mode is prominent, but the other modes remain in the background (see "simultaneous chess playing in a pinball machine," in Arntz and van Genderen, 2009).

After the development of a mode model for borderline and narcissistic personality disorder (Young *et al.*, 2003), a similar mode model for the other personality disorders was developed. However, these models are still in an experimental stage (Bernstein, Arntz and de Vos, 2007; Lobbestael *et al.*, 2007; Arntz, 2010; and see Part IV, Chapter 12 and Part VI, Chapter 2).

In Table 2.2, the modes that have been developed thus far are described. A number of modes have been investigated by Lobbestael *et al.* (2007), in terms of their psychometric qualities, and some are still in the experimental stage (Arntz *et al.*, 2009; Arntz, 2010). These last modes are, among other things, based on experiences with patients with both forensic problems and Cluster C personality disorders.

Because more research into the existence of modes in BPD has been conducted, and because the efficacy of ST with regard to these problems has been studied intensively (Young *et al.*, 2003; Giesen-Bloo *et al.*, 2006; Arntz, 2007; Arntz and van Genderen, 2009), the mode model for this disorder is described in detail.

Table 2.2 Schema modes

Child modes

Vulnerable Child	The patient believes that nobody will fulfill his needs and that everyone will eventually abandon him. He mistrusts others and believes that they will abuse him. He feels worthless and expects rejection. He is ashamed of himself and he often feels excluded. He behaves like a small, vulnerable child that clings to the therapist for help, because he feels lonely and believes there is danger everywhere.
Angry Child	The patient feels intensely angry, enraged, and impatient because his core needs are not being met. He can also feel abandoned, humiliated, or betrayed. He expresses his anger in extreme manifestations, both verbal and nonverbal, just like a small child who has an outburst of anger.
Enraged Child	The patient feels enraged for the same reason as the Angry Child, but loses control. This is expressed in offensive and injurious actions toward people and objects, in the same way as a small child hurts his parents.
Impulsive Child	The patient wants to satisfy his (non-core) desires in a selfish and uncontrolled manner. He cannot control his feelings and impulses and he becomes enraged and infuriated when his (non-core) desires or impulses are not met. He often behaves like a spoiled child.
Undisciplined Child	The patient has no tolerance of frustration and cannot force himself to finish routine or boring tasks. He cannot bear dissatisfaction or discomfort (pain, conflict, or overexertion) and he behaves like a spoiled child.
Happy Child	The patient feels loved, satisfied, protected, understood, and validated. He is self-confident and feels competent, appropriately autonomous, and in control. He can react spontaneously, is adventurous and optimistic, and plays like a happy, young child.

Maladaptive coping Modes

Compliant Surrender	The patient devotes himself to the desire of others in order to avoid negative consequences. He suppresses his own needs or emotions and bottles up his aggression. He behaves subserviently and passively, and hopes to gain approval by being obedient. He tolerates abuse from other people.
Detached Protector	The patient cuts off strong feelings because he believes that such feelings are dangerous and can get out of hand. He withdraws from social contacts and tries to cut off his feelings (sometimes this leads to dissociation). The patient feels empty, bored, and depersonalized. He may adopt a cynical or pessimistic attitude to keep others at arm's length.
Detached Self-Soother	The patient seeks distraction in order not to feel negative emotions. He achieves this by self-soothing behavior (e.g., sleeping or substance abuse) or by self-stimulating activities (being fanatical or occupied with work, the internet, sport, or sex).

Table 2.2 (*Continued*)

Child modes	
Over-Compensator Modes	
Self-Aggrandizer	The patient believes that he is superior to others and entitled to special rights. He insists that he should be able to do or have what he wants, regardless of what others think. He shows off and denigrates others to augment his self-esteem.
Bully and Attack	The patient wants to prevent being controlled or hurt by others, and therefore he tries to be in control of them. He uses threats, intimidation, aggression, and force to this end. He always wants to be in a dominant position, and takes sadistic pleasure in hurting others.
Maladaptive parent Modes	
Punitive Parent	The patient is aggressive, intolerant, impatient, and unforgiving toward himself. He is always self-critical and feels guilty. He is ashamed of his mistakes and believes he has to be punished severely for them. This mode is a reflection of what (one of) the parents or other educators used to say to the patient in order to belittle or punish him.
Demanding Parent	The patient feels that he must fulfill rigid rules, norms, and values. He must be extremely efficient in meeting these. He believes that whatever he does is never good enough and that he must strive harder. Therefore, he pursues his highest standard until it is perfect, at the expense of rest and pleasure. He is also never satisfied with the result. These rules and norms are also internalized by (one of) the parents.
Healthy mode	
Healthy Adult	The patient has positive and neutralized thoughts and feelings about himself. He does things that are good for him and this leads to healthy relationships and activities. The Healthy Adult mode isn't maladaptive.
Modes not yet investigated	
Angry Protector	The patient uses a wall of anger to protect himself against others, considered to be a threat. He keeps others at a safe distance with great displays of rage. However, his anger is more under control than that in the Angry or Enraged Child.
Obsessive Over-Controller	The patient tries to protect himself against supposed or actual threats by keeping everything under extreme control. He uses repetitions or rituals to achieve this.
Paranoid	The patient tries to protect himself against supposed or actual threats by containing others and exposing their real intentions.
Conning and Manipulative	The patient cheats, lies, or manipulates in order to achieve a specific aim, the purpose of which is to victimize others or to avoid punishment.
Predator	The patient eliminates threats, rivals, obstacles, or enemies in a cold, ruthless, calculating way.
Attention-Seeker	The patient tries to obtain the approval and attention of others by exaggerated behavior, erotomania, or grandiosity.

Mode Model in Borderline Personality Disorders

In order to meet the diagnosis borderline personality disorder, a patient must score on five out of nine criteria of the DSM-IV (American Psychiatric Association, 1994). Nevertheless, this descriptive diagnosis doesn't provide an explanatory model for the disorder. These patients have a number of characteristics in common, namely switching moods, problems with relationships, and uncertainty about their identity. Therefore, most patients aren't capable of completing their studies, finding suitable work, or entering into a stable relationship. The means of expression can be very different. One patient with a BPD may have many conflicts with the people around him, while another often withdraws and lives in a very isolated manner. By looking at the combination of schemas and coping styles, the therapist can get a better insight into this. Translating this information into a mode model makes the problems more understandable for the therapist and the patient.

The modes in a borderline personality disorder are:

> Linda is 21 years old when she is treated for her borderline personality disorder. She comes from a family of five children, in which, in particular, the two youngest children were neglected because the parents were alcoholics and couldn't handle the large family. Her parents were often verbally abusive and sometimes also physically abusive. Linda was more or less raised by her eldest sister, but when Linda was 10 years old, her sister left home. From that moment on, Linda's brother started to abuse her sexually. In order to keep this a secret, he threatened her and said that their parents wouldn't believe her anyway and that they would call her a whore. Linda has lived away from home for a year, and she dropped out of school after six months. At the moment, she lives on social security. To earn some money, she occasionally works in a coffee shop. She smokes a lot of cannabis. When she is desperate, she cuts her arms and legs. Recently, she made a suicide attempt.
>
> The therapist tries to find out who it was who said all those negative things about her, and so who modelled the Punitive Parent. In Linda's case, this was, in particular, her mother and her brother. Linda calls this "my punitive side" and she draws a very big ball, because it exerts the most control over her life. She calls the Detached Protector "ways to feel nothing" and this mainly consists of smoking cannabis and sleeping. At a very young age, Linda learned that she could protect herself best by going to her bedroom and locking the door. The thick lines between the Protector and the three other modes indicate that she feels a wall around her when she smokes cannabis or hides in her bed, through which she feels little, but is also not bothered by the Punitive Parent. Little Linda is bigger than angry Linda, because she isn't angry very often.

Healthy Adult

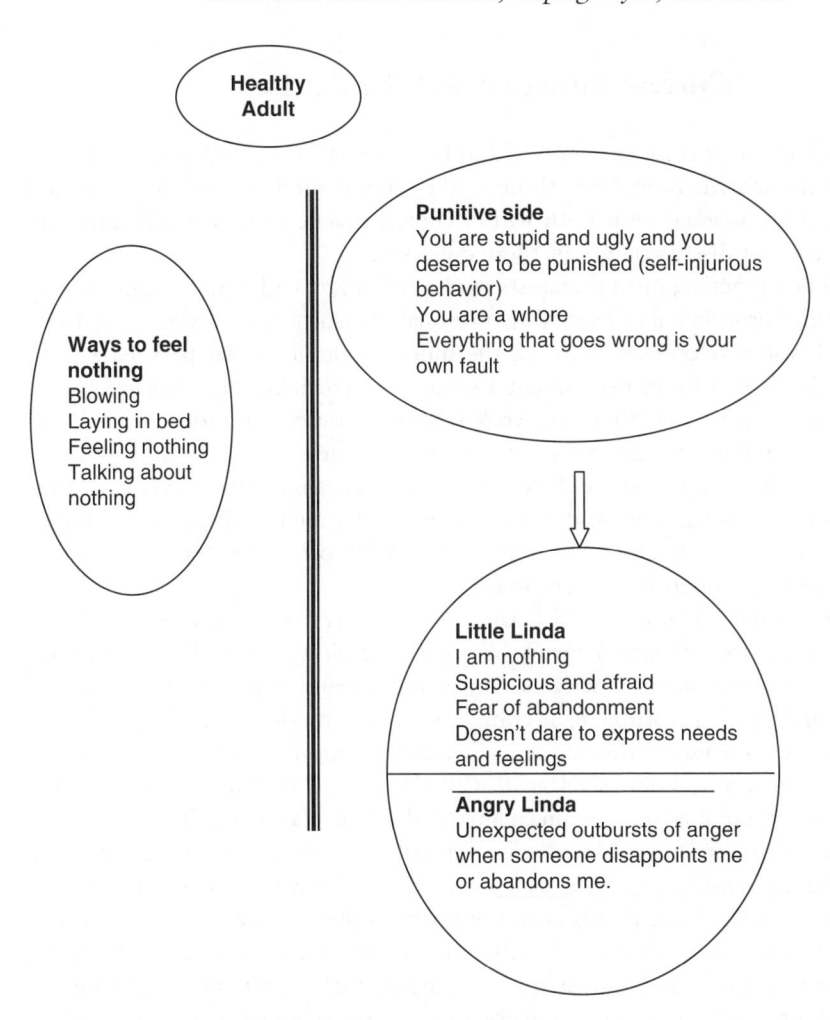

Ways to feel nothing
Blowing
Laying in bed
Feeling nothing
Talking about nothing

Punitive side
You are stupid and ugly and you deserve to be punished (self-injurious behavior)
You are a whore
Everything that goes wrong is your own fault

Little Linda
I am nothing
Suspicious and afraid
Fear of abandonment
Doesn't dare to express needs and feelings

Angry Linda
Unexpected outbursts of anger when someone disappoints me or abandons me.

Figure 2.2 Linda's schema mode model

- Vulnerable Child
- Angry Child
- Punitive Parent
- Detached Protector
- Healthy Adult

On the basis of the information obtained, the therapist and the patient make a mode model together in which the different modes are described as much as possible in the patient's own words. The patient can reflect on the degree to which the mode influences his life by drawing a bigger or smaller ball. He can also draw lines or arrows, which may clarify the model for him. In Figure 2.2, a mode model is shown which was made with the patient Linda.

The information about the schemas isn't put into the model, but it is important for the therapist to know which schemas play a role in each mode, so he knows which emotions and thoughts play a role if the patient is in a certain mode. The same goes for the information about the life history and therefore the origin of the modes (see also Part II, Chapter 6).

Current Situation and the Future

In the meantime, there is a distinction within the schema-focused approach between adherents of the schema model and those of the schema mode model. Schemas and schema modes are worked with both within clinical practice and scientific practice, and there is a lot of discussion about these concepts.

Within clinical practice, most therapists work particularly with schemas and coping styles, but with borderline and narcissistic personality disorders they also use a mode model. The latest development is to use the mode model for other personality disorders, but this is still in an experimental stage. The participants in the treatment studies of Arntz report that they can work well with these new mode models and that the patients recognize themselves well in these models.

Within scientific practice, research is carried out regarding newly developed concepts within each model. The study of and the developments within both models seem to be carried out relatively separately. But is it correct to design these two movements so independently of each other?

The mode model was established because patients with more severe (and in an emotional perspective, stronger) forms of psychopathology normally present with a complexity of simultaneously active schemas and varying coping styles, so that a transparent analysis of the problems is complicated. The mode model simplifies this, since the unit of analysis – the mode – is a combination of active schemas and coping styles. However, Lobbestael et al. (2007) showed that in the case of borderline patients, there are, once again, many modes that play a role. It appears that the mode model does not prevail in terms of frugality. Furthermore, more and more modes are being identified (at the time of writing 14 have been researched and seven proposed), something that is also found within the schema model. The question arises: is there really that much difference between the schemas and coping styles on the one hand, and modes on the other hand? Aren't most child modes similar to the surrender to, or over-compensation of, core schemas such as: Emotional Deprivation, Abandonment/Instability, Mistrust and/or Abuse, or Insufficient Self-Control/Self-Discipline? Aren't the maladaptive coping modes the surrender to schemas that originated as a reaction to the core schemas (e.g., isn't the Compliant Surrender the submission to the Subjugation schema)? Similarly, can the Bully and Attack mode not be seen as over-compensation of the Mistrust and/or Abuse schema?

Furthermore, it can be noted that a part of the modes includes externalizing problems. This is partly due to the fact that a number of modes were developed as an explanation for personality problems such as those described in the forensic field. In line with this, Rijkeboer (2005), in her analysis of the schema inventory, states that the existing set of schemas particularly represent internalizing problems. She therefore concludes that an extension of the set might be necessary, for instance with schemas that are more externalizing in nature.

These practically parallel developments illustrate that schemas and schema modes should cover a broad range of personality problems, and that both concepts are probably more related to each other than first assumed. At the moment, there are several initiatives underway, led by different researchers, to shed more light on this subject.

References

American Psychiatric Association (1994) *Diagnostic and Statistical Manual of Mental Disorders*, 4th edition (DSM-IV). Washington, DC: American Psychiatric Association.

Arntz, A. (2007) New insights from therapy. Borderline trial. Paper presented at the 2nd Congress of the International Society of Schema Therapy, Delft, September, 15–16.

Arntz, A. (2010) Schema Therapy for Cluster C personality disorders, in *Fortschritte der Schematherapie* (eds E. Roediger and G. Jacobs). Göttingen: Hogrefe-Verlag.

Arntz, A., Bernstein, D., Gielen, D. et al. (2009) Cluster C, paranoid, and borderline personality disorders are dimensional: evidence from taxometric tests. *Journal of Personality Disorders*, 23(6), 606–628.

Arntz, A. and van Genderen, H. (2009) *Schema Therapy for Borderline Personality Disorder*. Chichester: Wiley-Blackwell.

Arntz, A., van Genderen, H., and Wijts, P. (2006) Persoonlijkheidsstoornissen, in *Handboek Psychopathologie deel 2, Klinische praktijk* (eds W. Vandereycken, C.A.L. Hoogduin and P.M.G. Emmelkamp). Houten: Bohn Stafleu van Loghum, pp. 443–479.

Bernstein, D.P., Arntz, A. and de Vos, M.E. (2007) Schemagerichte therapie in de forensische setting, theoretisch model en voorstellen voor best clinical practice. *Tijdschrift voor Psychotherapie*, 33, 120–133.

Bowlby, J. (1988) *A Secure Base: Parent–Child Attachment and Healthy Human Development*. New York: Basic Books.

Cohen, P., Crawford, Th. N., Johnson, J.G. and Kasen, S. (2005) The children in the community study of developmental course of personality disorder. *Journal of Personality Disorders*, 19, 466–486.

Conway, M.A. and Pleydell-Pearce, C.W. (2000) The construction of the autobiographical memories in the self-memory system. *Psychological Review*, 107, 261–288.

Elliott, C. and Kirby Lassen, M. (1999) *Waarom Krijg Ik Niet Wat Ik Wil? Schemagerichte Therapie voor Meer Eigenwaarde, Daadkracht en Betere Relaties*. Utrecht and Antwerp: Kosmos-ZandK Uitgevers B.V.

Gallagher, K.C. (2002) Does child temperament moderate the influence of parenting on adjustment? *Developmental Review*, 22, 623–643.

Giesen-Bloo, J., Dyck, R., Spinhoven, P. et al. (2006) Outpatient psychotherapy for borderline personality disorder, randomized trial of schema-focused therapy vs. transference-focused psychotherapy. *Archives of General Psychiatry*, 63, 649–658.

Grover, K.E., Carpenter, L.L., Price, L.H. et al. (2007) The relationship between childhood abuse and adult personality disorder symptoms. *Journal of Personality Disorders*, 21, 442–447.

James, I.A., Southam, L. and Blackburn, I.M. (2004) Schemas revisited. *Clinical Psychology and Psychotherapy*, 11, 369–377.

Johnson, J.C., Cohen, P., Kasen, S., Smailes, E. and Brook, J.S. (2001) Association of maladaptive parental behavior with psychiatric disorder among parents and their offspring. *Archives of General Psychiatry*, 58, 453–460.

Lobbestael, J., van Vreeswijk, M.F. and Arntz, A. (2007) Shedding light on schema modes: a clarification of the mode concept and its current research status. *Netherlands Journal of Psychology*, 63, 76–85.

Maughan, A. and Cicchetti, D. (2002) Impact of child maltreatment and interadult violence on children's emotion regulation abilities and their socioemotional adjustment. *Child Development*, 73, 1525–1542.

Rijkeboer, M.M. (2005) *Assessment of Early Maladaptive Schemas. On the Validity of the Dutch Schema Questionnaire*. Academisch proefschrift, Universiteit Utrecht.

Rijkeboer, M.M., van Genderen, H., and Arntz. A. (2007). Schemagerichte therapie, in *Handboek persoonlijkheidspathologie* (eds E.H.M. Eurelings-Bontekoe, R. Verheul and W.M. Snellen). Houten: Bohn Stafleu van Loghum, pp. 285–302.

Sterk, F. and Rijkeboer, M.M. (1997) *Schema-Vragenlijst*. Utrecht: Ambulatorium Universiteit Utrecht.

Vonk, R. (1999) Schemas, in *Cognitieve Sociale Psychologie: Psychologie van het Dagelijks Denken en Doen* (ed. R. Vonk). Utrecht: Lemma, pp. 143–194.

Williams, J. M.G., Watts, F.N., MacLeod, C. and Mathews, A. (1997) *Cognitive Psychology and Emotional Disorders*, 2nd edition. Chichester: Wiley.

Young, J.E. and Brown, G. (1994) Young Schema Questionnaire, 2nd edition, in J.E. Young, *Cognitive Therapy for Personality Disorders: a Schema-Focused Approach*, rev. edition. Sarasota, FL: Professional Resource Press, pp. 63–76.

Young, J.E., Klosko, J.S. and Weishaar, M.E. (2005) *Schemagerichte Therapie. Handboek voor Therapeuten*. Houten: Bohn Stafleu Van Loghum.

Young, J.E., Klosko, J.S. and Weishaar, M.E. (2003) *Schema Therapy: a Practitioner's Guide*. New York: Guilford Press.

3
A New Look at Core Emotional Needs

George Lockwood and Poul Perris

Introduction

Over the past three decades Schema Therapy (ST) has evolved from an approach with a primary focus on core *beliefs* to one which now *places* core ***emotional needs*** at its center. The essence of ST involves helping patients meet their needs. From this vantage point, the better we can understand what they are and how to meet them, the more effective we will be.

Young developed ST by identifying internalized negative patterns or themes underlying the suffering that bring patients to therapy. He organized the themes into 19 distinct early maladaptive schemas (EMS), each implying a frustrated core emotional need. Substantial empirical data supporting EMS has been presented in numerous publications using the Young Schema Questionnaire (Young and Brown, 2003; Young, 2005). Furthermore, hypothesized need-thwarting experiences have been investigated using the Young Parenting Inventory (Young, 1999).

To advance our understanding of the process of meeting needs we believe it is important to explicitly define the need implied by each EMS as well as more fully delineate and operationalize the steps involved in needs being met. This would include identifying 1) the innate inclinations that humans are born with that provide the impetus and capacity to find and incorporate the relevant nutriments (e.g., neural networks and modes); 2) the need; 3) the nutriment that meets the need; and 4) the healthy patterns that result from needs being met, including the resulting internal representations (Early Adaptive Schemas) and the related behavioral inclinations (Adaptive Behavioral Dispositions). This would include an understanding of how needs interact and relate to one another. For example, their hierarchical nature, how they unfold over time and relate to critical periods, whether or not they cluster and form domains, and how they may be at odds or work synergistically. In

---

The Wiley Blackwell Handbook of Schema Therapy: Theory, Research, and Practice, First Edition.
Edited by Michiel van Vreeswijk, Jenny Broersen, and Marjon Nadort.
© 2012 John Wiley & Sons, Ltd. Published 2015 by John Wiley & Sons, Ltd.

this chapter we will take the initial steps toward building a model of core emotional needs within a framework defined by Early Maladaptive Schemas (EMS), Early Adaptive Schemas (EAS), and Adaptive Behavioral Dispositions (ABD). This will include a discussion of items 2–3 above, saving an exploration of related neural networks and innate modes for a later stage.

We will examine the trends emerging in regard to second-order factors occurring in factor analytic investigations of the YSQ, to identify what EMS and, by implication, what needs form natural groupings or domains. This will be used as a basis for comparison with other models of core emotional needs and to further our understanding of how EMS, EAS, and ABD relate to and interact with one another. We will begin with a discussion of the basic affirmative, trusting, and active stance ST takes toward core emotional needs (the foundation on which strategies aimed at specific needs are built). This orientation will be examined from the vantage point of evolution, physical anthropology, molecular biology, and ethology. Through these multiple lenses we will offer a perspective that suggests how and why ST's relatively unique approach to meeting needs can be transformative.

Needs, Temperament, and Parenting Styles

All of the EMS (except for Entitlement/Grandiosity and Self-Sacrifice) have shown significant correlations with the temperament dimension "negative affectivity" and the trait "neuroticism" in child, adolescent, and adult samples (Muris, 2006; Thimm, 2010; Rijkeboer and de Boo, 2010). Negative affectivity and neuroticism are, in turn, associated with greater parental needs of the child (Van den Boom and Hocksma, 1994). A prospective study that focused on the issue of how to best parent a needy child was conducted by Suomi (1997). The study investigated the developmental outcome of insufficient, normal, and exceptionally good parenting of infant rhesus macaque monkeys with both normal and "neurotic" temperaments. One of the findings was that infant monkeys with a normal temperament raised by inadequate parents (i.e., peers) developed behavioral and physiological characteristics of neurotic infants raised by normal parents. Infant monkeys with a neurotic temperament raised by normal mothers developed deficits in early exploration, exaggerated startle responses to minor stressors, a less secure attachment, and were more likely to remain at the bottom of the dominance hierarchy. Interestingly, infant monkeys with a neurotic temperament raised by parents with exceptionally good parenting skills (i.e., being notably loving, nurturing, and patient; qualities that are known to be essential for effective ST) expressed an even better developmental trajectory than infants with a normal temperament raised by normal parents. For example, they explored their environment more, displayed less behavioral disturbance during weaning, had an unusually secure attachment, rose to and maintained top positions in the dominance hierarchy, and became highly nurturing parents themselves. The developmental trajectory of normal infants raised by exceptionally good parents was the same as that when raised by normal parents. The extra nurturance seemed to make no difference.

Being a prospective study with primates, it allowed for control of all relevant variables throughout the period of investigation, making conclusions about causality more reliable than even the most tightly controlled prospective studies possible with humans. We view this study as a striking example of the potential advantages of a responsive and affirmative stance toward the needs of patients with a temperament characterized by neuroticism or negative affectivity. This study also introduces an alternative to the traditional diasthesis stress model that focuses solely on the negative impact stress can have when impinging on an area of vulnerability. Belsky and Pluess (2009) have introduced a new perspective called the "Differential Susceptibility Model," which suggests that some individual differences, as is the case for the neurotic rhesus macaques, can lead to bad outcomes in the face of adversity or very good outcomes in the context of enriched environments. Metaphorically, what was viewed as a source of fragility and as operating like glass, in the face of a stone, is now seen as something more like clay, that can form a deep impression for the better or worse.

Parallels can be seen between this investigation and an outcome study by Giesen-Bloo *et al.* (2006), in which ST was compared to Transference Focused Therapy (TFP) in the treatment of borderline personality disorder (BPD). ST was found to be twice as effective as TFP. The Schema Therapists in the study were selected and trained with a focus on being warm and highly nurturing in response to the BPD patient's intense affect and needs for soothing. This involved the therapists making direct contact with the client's Vulnerable Child (VC) mode, providing it with emotional nutriments such as soothing, reassurance, validation, understanding, and praise, along with empathic limits when needed. The experiences are seen as being internalized and thereby building the Healthy Adult part of the patient. TFP therapists, on the other hand, maintained a focus on the adult part of their patients, helping them gain a better insight into the nature of their needs and feelings and through this, learn how to better tolerate painful affect and self-sooth. A key difference between these two approaches, and between ST and almost all other therapies, is captured in this distinction between the internalization of "other-soothing" and training in "self-soothing." The former involves the assumption that the ability to self-sooth will grow spontaneously out of gratifying dependency needs. The latter involves a belief that directly gratifying patients' longings to be soothed and nurtured will do the opposite – impede and undermine the development of the capacity to self-sooth. Notably the nurturing monkey parents were operating on the basis of internalization of other-soothing. We do not necessarily see this as a difference between good and bad. For children with less sensitive temperaments, there appears to be little difference between normal and exceptionally loving parenting and many young children and patients with either temperament can be trained to self-sooth. Also, a large percentage of the patients treated with TFP derived significant benefit. We believe, however, that training an infant or child to self-sooth in response to these early core emotional needs can too easily become training in compulsive self-reliance and risks, with children with more sensitive or difficult temperaments, promoting the development of detachment from self and others as a means of coping with intense affect.

Needs, Temperament, Genes, and Molecular Biology

An intensive area of research for over a decade has involved an effort to identify genetic contributions to temperament, emotional functioning, and mental disorders.

Doing so will, among other things, allow us to develop a deeper understanding of the nature of needs and how they interact with the environment. Of particular significance to ST are two lines of investigation that have focused on the genetic correlates of neuroticism. Neuroticism is defined as a tendency to experience negative emotional states accompanied by anxiety or depression, anger, and guilt (Costa and McCrae, 1992) and to appraise events as stressful (Hurt *et al.*, 1984). There is a significant degree of overlap between this definition and features of EMS; thus, as mentioned earlier, it is no surprise that a correlation has been found between schemas and neuroticism. Many of the items that are used to assess the trait neuroticism as defined by the NEO PI-r (e.g., "I am easily disturbed," "I often feel blue") can be seen as signs of schema activation (Costra and McCrae, 1995). The serotonergic system is centrally involved in emotional functioning and has several commonly occurring genetic variations associated with it that influence affect. The short (s) allele of the 5-HTTLPR (serotonin transporter length polymorphic region) is associated with reduced serotonin transporter (5-HTT) protein availability and function (Canli and Lesch, 2007) compared with the long (L) form.

The first study to propose a correlation between the s allele and neuroticism was conducted by Lesch and colleagues (1996). This investigation inspired many subsequent attempts at replication. The results have been inconsistent with studies supporting (e.g., Gonda *et al.*, 2009) and not supporting (e.g., Willis-Owen *et al.*, 2005) this correlation. The majority of these studies were underpowered, with sample sizes being small relative to what is needed to draw conclusions based on the small effect size that can be attributed to a single gene. The studies that have been adequately powered (e.g., Willis-Owen *et al.*, 2005; Terracciano *et al.*, 2009) have not found a correlation, adding to the weight of current evidence in this direction.

Another line of investigation has looked at the possibility that the s allele is not itself correlated with negative affect but interacts with adversity, leading to neuroticism or such states as depression or anxiety in the face of negative life events. These studies have also led to inconsistent findings. A recent large-scale, highly powered study (Middeldorp *et al.*, 2010) and two meta-analyses (Munafo *et al.*, 2009; Risch *et al.*, 2009) support the notion that the s allele does not moderate the interaction between negative life events and neuroticism. The vast majority of this research has been conducted within the diathesis-stress framework and, as a result, has not considered the Differential Susceptibility or "Plasticity Hypothesis" by looking at the impact of both positive and negative life events on the link between the s allele and neuroticism. On the negative side, for example, the relative risk of developing a borderline or antisocial personality disorder has been shown to increase by a factor of 2 for each short allele (Gunderson and Lyons-Ruth, 2008). On the positive side, carriers of two short alleles have been found to have more pulvinar neurons (Young *et al.*, 2007). Pulvinar neurons are involved in the processing of visual signals sent to the limbic system via a subcortical route. More neurons mean a stronger connection and may be associated with a greater capacity to detect the emotional context of an environment. Short allele carriers express greater sympathetic reactivity when observing another person receiving a shock (Crişan *et al.*, 2009), suggesting a possible link to a greater capacity for empathy. In another study it was found that seeing a favorite person led to significantly higher amygdala activity in short allele carriers suggesting a higher reward value of positive interpersonal experience (Matsunagaa et al., 2010).

Homberg and Lesch (2011) have reviewed the many cognitive and emotional advantages that correspond to the greater sensitivity and emotional responsiveness that have been correlated with the s allele. They hypothesize that these advantages may counterbalance or completely offset the disadvantages and may explain the inconsistent findings referred to above. Working from the same premise Pluess, Belsky, Way, and Taylor (2010) studied the interaction between negative and positive life events in relation to neuroticism in individuals ($N = 118$) homozygous for s alleles and L alleles. Consistent with the plasticity hypothesis, they found that those with s alleles who experienced more negative life events had higher neuroticism scores and those experiencing more positive life events had lower neuroticism scores. Those with L alleles had consistent scores on neuroticism regardless of the number of positive or negative life events. Thus neuroticism may be a more stable trait for those with the L allele and less so for those with an s allele. It also may be that those with s alleles are more likely to be negatively impacted by a toxic childhood, develop schemas, look "neurotic" or borderline, and at the same time be exceptionally capable of benefiting from the enriched environment that ST offers. The plasticity hypothesis would also lead us to predict that the children who are likely to develop EMS when subjected to maltreatment are the most likely to develop strong EAS in the context of very loving and enriched environments. These early developing adaptive schemas may serve as strong buffers for later negative life events.

A study in line with this prediction was conducted by Antypa and van der Does (2010), who asked 250 university students about experiences of emotional abuse in childhood. Cognitive reactivity to sad mood was assessed using the Leiden Index of Depression Sensitivity scale. This measures habitual negative cognitive patterns and yields scores that remain high even when symptoms are low and thus overlaps significantly with our notion of an EMS. The results confirmed the plasticity hypothesis. Short allele carriers whose scores were very low on a measure of childhood emotional abuse had extremely low scores on the measure of cognitive vulnerability to depression and extremely high scores when they reported high scores on measures of abuse. Long allele carriers had moderate scores no matter what level of abuse they reported. Put another way, the short allele carriers were able to benefit far more from a good childhood than the long allele carriers. Again, this is very similar to what was found with the highly reactive rhesus macaques. It is important to note that while these recent findings are intriguing, replication with a well-powered study is needed to confirm or refute these observations. It is estimated that a sample size over 1,000 will be needed to have 80% power at a significance level of $p = 0.50$ (Munafo et al., 2008).

The L allele and the associated efficient serotonergic functioning may lead to greater self-reliance with more affective regulation occurring within one's own synapses. The s allele, associated with less efficient serotonergic functioning, may lead to an adaptive strategy that draws more on deep and enriched ongoing attachments to regulate affect. We could view this as emphasizing regulation across a "social synapse." This is a genetic variation that goes deep into our past as a species and, interestingly, humans and rhesus macaques are the only two species that have it. Humans and rhesus macaques are known as the "weed" species since both proliferate wherever they are placed in the world. It seems that both adaptive strategies (self-reliance and strong attachments) are important to the collective whole. ST, with its flexibility and responsiveness to the needs associated with both, seems well suited to capitalize on this important polymorphism.

The s allele also interacts with other genetic variations and, together, these may eventually be shown to contribute to a plasticity gradient. One example of relevance to ST is its interaction with the arginine vasopressin receptor 1a gene. Bachner-Melman *et al.* (2004) found that an aptitude and need for dancing was associated with the combined effect of the s allele and the vasopressin receptor. Dancing is a phenomenon that is believed to have begun close to our origin as a species and is related to a need for non-verbal emotional expression, attunement, and affiliation. These authors also found a correlation between the s allele and a propensity to react intensely and imaginatively to stimuli and for mystical and visionary experiences. This may be associated with a greater capacity for the creative use of imagery.

Another example of a finding in molecular biology applicable to ST, the plasticity hypothesis, and the process of meeting needs, pertains to the 7-Repeat allele of the DRD4 gene. This allele is associated with a less efficient dopaminergic system. Humans who carry this allele are more prone to impulsivity and to externalize their problems. Van Zeijl and colleagues (2007) conducted an outcome study with children who were judged to be at risk of externalizing disorders. The children in this group who carried the 7-Repeat allele and had parents trained in using positive-sensitive discipline (the experimental condition and a process that has much in common with empathic confrontation) were the only ones who showed a reduction in externalizing problems. These children also showed the least salivary cortisol in response to an experimental stressor and the most if the mother was assigned to the control group. Thus, we see a similar swing between a very good and a bad outcome.

We believe that the findings in molecular biology discussed above lend important interdisciplinary confirmation and support to ST's stance toward emotional needs, especially when treating client populations marked by impulsivity and/or negative affectivity. These findings can also provide an additional measure of reassurance and confidence to Schema Therapists while weathering the crises and emotional intensity of high-needs patients knowing that, over time, there is a kind of magic that unfolds through the process of remaining patient, affirming, sensitive, responsive, and, when necessary, firm in positive ways. This is also an important and hopeful message to the parents of children with challenging temperaments.

As helpful and encouraging as these initial findings are, it is important to know that we are at the early stages of developing a clear understanding of the way that genes influence needs and interact with life events. Any single genetic variation will account for a small part of the total variance in observable behavior. It is likely that a full explanation of a complex phenotype such as neuroticism will involve an interaction between several genes in interaction with the environment.

Core Emotional Needs and the Role of Mothers, Fathers, and Culture

We view the primary focus on the provision of training in self-soothing that characterizes most psychotherapies as an example of culture in conflict with core needs. We see this conflict as reflecting the way Western industrialized societies have fallen out of step with the wisdom of the nurturing monkey mothers and, as will be discussed below, out of step with the deeply etched impact of our hunter-gatherer past. This conflict can be organized around what we see as two primary modes through which core needs are met; a Maternal and a Paternal mode. Our conception of the Maternal mode involves experiencing the young child (or child within the patient) as an extension of one's self and feeling compelled to respond to cries with direct soothing and nurturing. The focus is on connecting, mutual empathy, and ongoing availability. The Paternal mode involves experiencing the child as separate, feeling less inclined to respond to her cry with direct soothing, and more likely to believe she will benefit by "crying it out" and thereby learn to deal with the distress on her own. The focus of the Paternal mode is on separateness and independence. It is important to note that we believe both sexes have the capacities inherent in both modes. In support of this is accumulating evidence that men can function well as objects of infant attachment and be competent care-givers (Pruett, 1998; Lamb and Lewis, 2004).

Both modes have an important place in development; however, in Western industrialized societies the Paternal mode often comes into play at the expense of the Maternal mode. A push for independence frequently starts in the first months or weeks of life, often with enthusiasm about how soon a child can learn to sleep through the night on her own. Another example is a belief that weaning or the transition to solid foods should occur in a certain number of months, the number determined more by the parents' or pediatrician's beliefs than the infant's inclinations. This has a parallel within psychotherapy of an early push toward self-soothing and independent functioning. The Paternal mode bias is reflected in the belief that a young child needs to be trained to self-sooth when it comes to a range of "demands" and that giving in to them will foster habits that will be difficult to break and a dependency that will impede the development of independence. This bias is also reflected in the belief that transitional objects are universal, normal, and healthy; a notion promoted by Winnicott (1953), but which Bowlby (1969) disagreed with. Bowlby viewed transitional objects as redirected attachment behavior due to the lack of availability of the primary caretaker, and thus symptomatic of a problem.

The existing research supports Bowlby's view. Transitional objects are most prevalent in Western cultures (Hobara, 2003) and correlate with the lack of continuous availability of a primary caretaker, especially at night. An example of the impact of this bias on brain development is seen in the results of the largest and most rigorous randomized control trial of human lactation to date (Kramer *et al.*, 2008). This study found that mothers who practiced prolonged and exclusive breastfeeding (the period under investigation was up to one year) had children with higher mean scores on all of the Wechsler Abbreviated Scales of Intelligence measures at 6.5 years of age than the children of mothers who did not. Randomization was based on the subset of mothers who were planning on nursing their children to begin with, so the reported results would be a significant underestimation of the effect on intelligence. It seems likely that nursing beyond one year, not necessarily exclusively, would contribute further to this impact on the brain since our phylogenic history has been based on weaning occurring somewhere between 2½ and 3½ years of age.

Studies investigating whether or not the effect is due to the properties of the long chain polyunsaturated fatty acids in human milk have led to inconsistent results

(Simmer, 2001; Simmer and Patole, 2004). This suggests that it is not human milk itself that produced the effect. The authors of the study hypothesize that the physical and/or emotional act of breastfeeding might lead to permanent physiological changes that enhance neurocognitive development and that the increased frequency and duration of maternal–infant contact associated with breastfeeding could increase verbal interaction between mother and infant, which might also accelerate this development. Nursing is a multidimensional relational experience that often involves prolonged eye contact, soothing, play, joy, and bliss, and a corresponding set of attitudes and inclinations on the mother's part toward her infant that seem likely to influence her response to other core needs. If indeed the quality of the relationship between mother and child is having this impact, this may be a demonstration of the profound contribution the Maternal mode can make to our brains when given freer rein than is typically the case. There is a growing body of empirical evidence that shows wide-ranging health benefits to both mother and infant from the practice of prolonged breastfeeding, including a stronger immune system and greater physical health later in life. Those familiar with the intricacies of prolonged breastfeeding know that life is far easier when this goes hand in hand with some form of infant–mother bed-sharing. Co-sleeping mothers are often able to sleep through nighttime nursing and quickly and easily respond to surfacing before it becomes crying. Parents who do not bed-share end up with more infant crying and frequent trips to and from a separate sleeping area. This quickly becomes exhausting.

From an evolutionary perspective, breastfeeding and bed-sharing are seen as an adaptive complex of behaviors that deepen synchrony and mutual regulation on multiple levels (McKenna and McDade, 2005). For example, bed-sharing leads to more frequent feeding which, in turn, leads to a greater intake of the immune properties of milk. Research (Keller and Goldberg, 2004) also suggests that responding to dependency needs at night through co-sleeping leads to the opposite of the heightened dependency many fear. This is reflected in greater levels of independence during the day as demonstrated, for example, by being more likely to dress oneself and to settle arguments with peers without needing to involve an adult. Despite the accumulating evidence, prolonged and exclusive breastfeeding and bed-sharing remain highly controversial. In fact, one of the most hotly debated topics in pediatric medicine over the past decade is co-sleeping. An entire issue of the journal *Infant and Child Development* was devoted to it (Goldberg and Keller, 2007). Research had yielded conflicting findings for and against it. More recently culturally influenced biases in how many of these investigations were conducted have come to light. For example, when investigators asked about frequency of night time surfacing it was scored as higher in the co-sleeping group and coded as a problem. When co-sleeping parents were finally asked how they felt about night time surfacing, few considered it to be a problem. Most saw it as a natural occurrence and were happy to be available to provide soothing and comfort if needed. It also became clear that children who were not co-sleeping were surfacing, but the parents were unaware of it (Ramos, Yougclarke and Anderson, 2007). This way of defining variables has a large impact on whether one concludes co-sleeping is beneficial or problematic and seems to be an instance of the Paternal mode emphasis on early independence biasing research. The confusion regarding the impact of the s allele may be due to a similar bias. Since the one study done by Suomi (1997) conducted over a decade ago, there has been little attention paid to the impact of the exceptionally loving and enriched environments associated with the Maternal mode and thus the latent strengths of the s allele that thrive with connection are often missed. If this kind of responsiveness is seen as indulgence or as giving in to unreasonable demands, it will be defined as problematic and not considered as a focus for investigation. Until the outcome study referred to above involving ST, this was the case in psychotherapy research. This more nurturing stance had either not been included (as has been the case for cognitive and behavioral approaches) or had been examined within the framework of being a limited and diluted variant of analytic treatment falling under the heading of supportive psychotherapy. In the latter case, the "pure gold" of interpretation was considered inferior to the "copper" of support and suggestion.

There are many valid reasons (economic, physical, and emotional) why caretakers may choose not to be highly responsive to core emotional needs. For example, it may involve more than can be given without feeling resentful or exhausted. In this case a different compromise between the infant's and caretaker's needs must be struck. This is not controversial. The essence of the controversy, as is the case with ST's stance toward core emotional needs, has to do with the idea that it is not good for a young child or patient to be responded to in this manner even if a parent or therapist is capable and able of doing so. Beyond it simply being something that is not wrong to do, we believe it is a stance toward core needs that can have a major impact on the trajectory of a child's and patient's emotional well-being over her lifetime when she has a more sensitive and challenging temperament. If we are correct, this is an important element to factor into the balancing of a parent's and child's needs. We believe early investments with these children will pay huge dividends; likewise with therapists and sensitive/challenging patients.

The Evolution of Hominid Parenting and Needs

The hunter-gatherer phase of human history represents the culmination of evolution's impact on our bodies, brains, and core emotional needs. The rapid changes since then have been primarily non-genetic and cultural. Thus hunter-gatherer childhood and hunter-gatherer parenting become key reference points for what can be considered "natural." Extensive anthropological investigations over the past decades (Konner, 2010) has shown that present-day hunter-gatherer parenting (and, by implication, those of our ancestors) is very much in line with ST's far more trusting and responsive stance toward core needs for connection. For example, there is immediate responsiveness to an infant's cries resulting in a substantially lower overall amount of crying than in industrial societies, less pain inflicted on infants, and less of an early focus on developing independence (the development of independence does not become a major focus until about the age of 6 years). This responsiveness includes frequent nursing, mother–infant co-sleeping, nursing and responsiveness through the night, ease and lateness of toilet training, and weaning no earlier than two years of age (most commonly between 2½ and 3½ years). It is a pattern consistent with the rest of the Old World monkeys and apes and thus appears to be deeply etched into the nature of our early development. Humans have diverged from monkeys and apes in the direction of greater infant vulnerability, suggesting an even greater need for trust and responsiveness to core needs for connection.

One of the key points of divergence from our ape cousins was our hominid ancestors beginning to walk upright. This led to a collision course between two anatomical trends that had a significant impact on our core emotional needs. First, bipedality led to the pelvis becoming narrower and more rigid and thus to a smaller birth canal. Second, it freed our hands for things like gesturing, carrying, and more advanced tool-making and use. This led to new habitats and larger, more complex group structures. This, in turn, created selection pressures for more intelligence and larger brains. Due to this conflict between larger-brained infants and narrower, less flexible birth canals, over the millennia infants needed to be born in a less and less mature state to be small enough for the narrowed passageway. This led to human infants becoming more vulnerable and needier for a longer period than any other species. This, in turn, would have created selection pressures for infants capable of expressing these intense and more far-ranging needs and for caretakers who had the capacity and sustained motivation to meet them. Beyond crying, two of the infant's capacities that are most significant in terms of the early expression of needs is the social smile and the capacity for sustained mutual gaze, both appearing between two and three months of age. In response to these emerging capacities, caretakers report that their feelings of love become much stronger. Out of this convergence between the infant's capacities for engagement and the mother's increased feelings of love the first form of social play, called "motherese" or baby talk, accelerates. This process becomes a second major dimension surrounding core needs that is added to the internalization of other-soothing in response to crying; the internalization of "other-joy" in response to gazing and smiling. Primates use facial expressions, gestures, and sounds to communicate and respond to needs. Within the human mother–infant bond these expressions have become more elaborate, intense, and exquisitely patterned and involve exaggerated and rhythmic facial expressions and sounds and movements that are captivating, joyous, and fun. In addition to soothing the infant, parents are now energetically entertaining it; building to climaxes that the infant breathlessly awaits the conclusion of, followed by peals of laughter and urges for more. This species-specific dance, with the accompanying experience of love and delight and frequent bursts of positive affect, may have been how natural selection transformed an infant with an increasingly burdensome set of needs into a highly sought-after bundle of joy (Dissanayake, 2000). In fact, caretaker responses share brain networks in common with those that become active in romantic love (Bartels and Zeki, 2004). The motherese phase, once considered trivial or even inane, is now considered to be pivotal in sculpting the social brain and leveraging plasticity (Carroll, 2005). Lockwood and Shaw (Part III, Chapter 5) discuss ways in which ST can be expanded to more fully incorporate this dimension of social play and internalization of other-joy.

A second key feature of human evolution was the expansion of what is called "middle childhood," which starts at about age six and continues to puberty. Other primates go straight from weaning to puberty so this is a massive and pivotal shift. Primary foci of early middle childhood involve developing independence and learning cultural knowledge. Late middle childhood, at about 10 or 11 years of age, marks the emergence of a capacity to more fully grasp the concepts of reciprocity and fairness and thus is a critical period for needs pertaining to adequate limits. One of the striking differences between the hunter-gatherer parenting baseline and current practices throughout the middle childhood phase is that most of this learning takes place through play (Konner, 2010). Our species-specific context led to the development of a relatively carefree and play-filled long middle childhood. Play was the primary mode within which the child's physical and social environment was explored and thus was a main early vehicle for developing autonomy and independence. This highlights both how far we continue to deviate from this pattern and the potential significance of play within the process of emotional growth and change (Lockwood and Shaw, Part III, Chapter 5).

Empirically-based Comprehensive Models of Core Emotional Needs

The discussion so far has applicability to the general stance and attitude we take toward our patients and their needs and to several dimensions that are key to the change process. As such, they form the foundation on which treatment rests and on which the technical details of therapy depend. If this foundation is not in place, one can have excellent technique and yet make no progress. If it is, then many of the technical details will fall into place naturally and there will a much larger margin for error. Patients knowing they are respected at their core, that their needs are trusted, understood, and readily responded to, that their latent strengths are seen and appreciated, and that the therapist enjoys and even takes delight in them as unique persons plays a significant role in the process of healing and growing. Beyond this foundation, more detailed guidelines are helpful in addressing specific needs. What follows is a discussion of comprehensive models designed to facilitate work at this level.

To scientifically substantiate a model of core emotional needs at least four criteria must be met. First, meeting or not meeting the need should lead to an increase or decrease in well-being and have effects that extend beyond psychological functioning to include other system levels, such as our brain, body, family, and community as demonstrated above. Second, each proposed need should make a contribution to well-being and not be derived from any other need. Third, the need should be evident universally (i.e., shown to appear and be operative in a broad range of cultures). Fourth, each should be consistent with and supported by what we know about evolution so that there is evidence that they have their origins in our early history as a species (Baumeister and Leary, 1995; Deci and Ryan, 2000; Flanagan, 2010).

There has been some work on core needs, most notably Baumeister and Leary's (1995) seminal paper on the need for belonging, which has a strong empirical foundation and meets the four criteria outlined above but is not an attempt at a comprehensive model. Other efforts (e.g., Reiss, 2008; Kenrick, Griskevicius, Neuberg and Schaller, 2010) are comprehensive and empirically based, but include a mixture of core emotional needs and what we see as non-core needs. Thus while interesting, important, and empirically based, they are less relevant to our model. This most likely derives from the fact that they were not developed within the context of understanding adults who were trapped in emotional pain and are not, therefore, intended as a framework for psychotherapy.

Flanagan (2010) proposes a comprehensive model of needs utilizing ethology to ground and augment direct observations in her clinical practice. Through this she has proposed six core needs organized in pairs: connection and autonomy, stability and change, and desirability and self-comprehension. Her model has some empirical support based on several of the criteria outlined above. What remains to be determined for the need for change, stability, desirability, and self-comprehension relates to the second criterion noted above since exploratory and confirmatory factor analyses will be required to substantiate that they do not derive from other needs or cannot be further subdivided. We consider the need for autonomy and connection to have some support based on the second criterion through the factor analytic studies that have been conducted with the YSQ, discussed below. Flanagan provides empirical support for her taxonomy based on the third (universality) and fourth (evolution) criteria mentioned above.

Working from the opposite end of the mental health continuum and starting at about the same time as ST, Deci and Ryan (2000) began developing Self Determination Theory (SDT), a comprehensive model of core psychological needs that has, over the past two decades, been developing some empirical support pertaining to three of the criteria outlined above (Deci and Ryan, 2000). SDT grew out of, among other things, Deci and Ryan's effort to integrate a range of empirical findings in studies of intrinsic motivation. Intrinsic motivation involves freely pursuing what one is naturally interested in for its own sake and is, in this respect, the opposite of being trapped in the pain of negative life patterns that has been the province of ST. This research looked at the types of social experiences that maintained or increased intrinsic motivation. Their efforts to identify the underlying themes of these experiences led to three main categories: autonomy, competence, and relatedness. They posited these as three core psychological needs since interactions that promote them are required for intrinsic motivation to be maintained or grow. At present their model has only limited support based on the second criterion listed above, since it lacks significant findings based on factor analytic investigations. Deci and Ryan (2000) provide evidence in support of their model based on the criteria of increases and decreases in well-being, universality, and evolution.

The Empirical Status of Schema Therapy's Current Model as it Relates to Needs

Schema Therapy provides indirect evidence in support of the first criterion mentioned above through a series of studies (Giessen-Bloo *et al.*, 2006; Farrell, Shaw and Weber, 2009; Nadort *et al.*, 2009) demonstrating dramatic and broad-based decreases in suffering and increases in positive functioning through a treatment that both patients and therapists understood as one that involved meeting core emotional needs as central to the process. Giessen-Bloo *et al.* (2006) also found that ST led to better and stronger treatment alliances and that the strength of this alliance was highly correlated with the outcome meaning, in essence, that patients liked getting their needs met, that the Schema Therapists were happy to meet them, and that this process had much to do with the gains in therapy. The patients in these studies all suffered from borderline personality disorder (BPD). BPD has been found to be characterized by high scores on almost all of the 18 EMS as assessed by the YSQ, indicating that the patients suffer from almost all of the negative patterns that have been identified and suggesting that they start treatment with an extreme degree and broad range of unmet needs.

The YSQ was developed to assess early maladaptive schemas as they are currently experienced and operating in a person's life and provides a basis for research on whether or not the originally proposed set of 16 patterns and the needs that they imply exist as distinct and separate entities. This gives us a way to test the implied needs against the second criterion (i.e., that each makes its own contribution to well-being and is not derived from any other). One of the most important tools for accomplishing this is factor analysis. Factor analytic studies have been conducted in the US, Australia, Spain, Korea, France, Turkey, and the Netherlands on both student and patient samples. (e.g., Schmidt, Joiner, Young and Telch, 1995; Lee, Taylor and Dunn, 1999; Welburn, Coristine, Dagg, Pontefract and Jordan, 2002; Cecero, Nelson and Gillie, 2004; Baranoff, Oei, Seong and Seok-man, 2006; Lachenal-Chavallet, Mauchand, Cottrauz, Bouvard and Martin, 2006; Soygut, Karaosmanoglu and Cakir, 2009). The initial studies were based on exploratory factor analyses and consistently found between 12 and 15 of the 16 schemas developed by Young with a higher degree of overlap with the proposed schemas tending to occur when patient samples were used and a lower degree with student samples. As supportive as these studies were of the schema model, exploratory methods can at most suggest the latent structure of variables. This structure must be later substantiated through confirmatory factor analysis. Two recent studies (Hoffart *et al.*, 2005; Rijkeboer and van den Bergh, 2006) have done this and found an even stronger convergence with the proposed set of 16 schemas than that arrived at in previous investigations. The later study is made stronger by the fact that it was the first to use a randomized item format. Another unique contribution was the use of a statistical technique that allowed the investigators to determine that the same patterns (factor structure) existed across normal and patient groups. This lends support to the universality of these patterns and the implied needs. In total, these studies substantiate the notion that at least 15 of the proposed 19 schemas are a fundamental and irreducible construct (a total of 19 have been proposed, including the Social Undesirability schema, but 18 are currently assessed by the YSQ). These studies also provide some evidence in support of the third criterion since the same patterns arose in many different parts of the world and within individualist and collectivist cultures. Three of the proposed 19 EMS are relatively new (Approval-Seeking/Recognition-Seeking, Negativity/Pessimism, and Punitiveness) and have not yet been examined through repeated factor analytic investigations. One EMS, Social Undesirability, was not found to be a separate factor in several factor analytic investigations and had been dropped from consideration in many subsequent studies, but was found as a separate factor by Rijkeboer and van den Bergh (2006).

The Core Emotional Needs Model

Our core emotional needs model (CNM) operationalizes hypothesized needs corresponding to each EMS as measured through the Emotional Core Needs Inventory (Perris, Young, Lockwood, Arntz and Farrell, 2008a), a measure of the degree to which people are currently perceiving their core needs are being met. Each need is proposed in association with a therapeutic nutriment as defined by the Reparenting Inventory (Perris, Young and Lockwood, 2010), developed to assess the degree to which patients see their therapist as meeting their needs and adequately responding to deficits identified in the Emotional Core Needs Inventory. The Adaptive Behavioral Dispositions Inventory (Perris, Young, Lockwood, Arntz and Farrell, 2008b) assesses the degree to which an individual is developing the Adaptive Behavioral Dispositions that are hypothesized to occur in response to the experiences assessed by the Limited Reparenting Inventory. These measures are currently being utilized in the context of several outcome studies. Information on how to obtain copies of these inventories can be found in the reference section in connection with each of the references listed above. The 15 EMS that have the most extensive empirical support and the corresponding needs, EAS and ABD, are presented in Table 3.1. Since we do not yet have an adequate empirical basis for the three most recently proposed EMS (Approval-Seeking/Recognition-seeking, Negativity/Pessimism, and Punitiveness) these have not been included.

Our definition of an EAS closely parallels that for Early Maladaptive Schemas. An EAS is a broad, pervasive theme or pattern, comprised of memories, emotions, cognitions, and neurobiological reactions regarding oneself and one's relationship with others, developed during childhood or adolescence, elaborated throughout one's lifetime, and leading to healthy functioning and adaptive behavioral dispositions. EAS are formed when a child/adolescent grows up in a family and sociocultural context that responds adequately to core emotional needs. They are internal representations of these positive patterns that take the form of flexible rather than rigid templates. These templates lead to traits and states that promote successful interpersonal and independent functioning and ongoing fulfillment of core emotional needs without harm to others. The early versions of these templates are positive yet relatively crude and simple. For example, a child with a Trust EAS will be generally trusting. As a child's cognitive capacities develop and needs continue to be adequately responded to, EAS are continually elaborated and refined, leading to later adaptive schemas characterized by integrated and fluid states and flexible, balanced, nuanced, and choiceful behavior. The child with a trust EAS becomes an adult able to make nuanced decisions about how much to trust a given individual in a given situation and thus is able to balance a tendency to be trusting with a reasonable degree of caution. While these later refinements and extensions are important, we hypothesize that the affective core is rooted in the early templates. This adaptive behavior is seen as the result of the Healthy Adult mode integrating and modulating the information and energy flowing from a comprehensive range of adaptive schemas and states. We see these executive functions of the Healthy Adult mode developing throughout the lifespan beginning in childhood.

CNM and Other Models of Core Emotional Needs

To make comparisons between CNM and the work of Flanagan, and of Deci and Ryan, it is necessary to draw on findings regarding higher-order factors since the published versions of both of these bodies of work are conceptualized on the domain level.

Table 3.1 Early maladaptive schemas, core needs, early adaptive schemas, and adaptive behavioral dispositions

Early Maladaptive Schema	Core Need in Relationships	Early Adaptive Schema	Adaptive Behavioral Disposition (Adult Form) The ability to
Abandonment/ Instability	A stable and predictable emotional attachment figure.	Stable Attachment	Find and maintain relationships with others who will be there when you need them in a predictable way and will not leave.
Mistrust/Abuse	Honesty, trustworthiness, loyalty, and the absence of abuse.	Basic Trust	Trust others' intentions and give them the benefit of the doubt and balance this with a reasonable degree of caution.
Emotional Deprivation	Warmth and affection, empathy, protection, guidance, and mutual sharing of personal experience.	Emotional Fulfillment	Form intimate relationships with significant others that include disclosing private needs, feelings, and thoughts and sharing love and affection.
Emotional Inhibition	A significant other who can be playful and spontaneous and who invites the same in you and others and encourages you to express emotions and talk about feelings.	Emotional Openness / Spontaneity	Express and discuss emotions freely; behave and respond spontaneously and without inhibition when appropriate.
Defectiveness / Shame	Unconditional acceptance of, and love for, one's private and public self along with regular praise and the absence of ongoing criticism or rejection. Encouragement to share areas of self-doubt and not keep them secret from others.	Self-Acceptance / Lovability	Be self-accepting and compassionate toward oneself and genuine and transparent to others.
Social Isolation/ Alienation	Inclusion in and acceptance by a community with shared interests, and values.	Social Belonging	Seek out and connect with social groups that share the same interests and values and the ability to find similarities and common ground with others.

(*Continued*)

Table 3.1 (*Continued*)

Early Maladaptive Schema	Core Need in Relationships	Early Adaptive Schema	Adaptive Behavioral Disposition (Adult Form) The ability to
Failure	Support and guidance in developing mastery and competence in chosen areas of achievement (educational, vocational, and recreational).	Success	Accomplish meaningful educational, work, and recreational goals.
Vulnerability To Harm Or Illness	A reassuring significant other who balances reasonable concern for harm and illness with a sense of manageability of these risks and models taking appropriate action without undue worry or overprotection.	Basic Health & Safety	Have a realistic sense of safety and physical resilience and enter into situations freely if they do not involve physical danger and respond calmly to minor physical symptoms. Be both confident and proactive regarding risks involving harm and illness.
Dependence/ Incompetence	Challenge, support, and guidance in learning to handle day-to-day decisions, tasks, and problems on one's own, without excessive help from others.	Healthy Self-Reliance / Competence	Handle everyday tasks and decisions without over-reliance on others, along with the ability to seek help when needed (being "independent but well connected").
Enmeshment/ Undeveloped Self	A significant other who promotes and accepts one having a separate identity and direction in life, and who respects one's personal boundaries.	Healthy Boundaries/ Developed Self	Have one's own life direction, convictions, beliefs, interests, and feelings and have appropriate boundaries between oneself and others.
Subjugation	Freedom to express needs, feelings, and opinions in the context of significant relationships without fear of punishment or rejection.	Assertiveness/ Self-Expression	Assert and express needs, feelings, and desires in relationships even when these differ from, or are in conflict with, significant others and, at the same time, remain open to compromise.

Table 3.1 (*Continued*)

Early Maladaptive Schema	Core Need in Relationships	Early Adaptive Schema	Adaptive Behavioral Disposition (Adult Form) The ability to
Self-Sacrifice	Balance in the importance of each person's needs. Guilt is not used to control expression and consideration of one's needs.	Healthy Self-Interest / Self-Care	Treat one's needs as no less important than anyone else's and find a healthy balance between getting one's needs met and helping others.
Unrelenting Standards/ Hypercriticalness	Guidance in developing appropriate (not too low, rigid, or extreme) standards and ideals and in balancing performance goals with getting other needs met (health, intimacy, relaxation) along with a forgiving attitude toward mistakes or imperfections.	Realistic Standards & Expectations	Flexibly adapt standards to one's abilities and circumstances and be forgiving of one's failures and imperfections.
Entitlement/ Grandiosity	Guidance and empathic limit-setting to learn the consequences for others of your actions and to empathize with others' perspectives, rights, and needs. Not made to feel superior to others and limits placed on unrealistic demands.	Empathic Consideration / Respect for others	Take the perspective of others, show consideration and respect for their needs and feelings, and experience oneself and others as having equal value.
Insufficient Self-Control/ Self-Discipline	Guidance and empathic firmness in forgoing short-term pleasure and comfort in order to complete day-to-day routines, responsibilities, and meet longer-term goals. Limits placed on expressing emotions that are out of control, inappropriate, or impulsive.	Healthy Self-Control / Self-Discipline	Forgo short-term gratification and immediate impulses for the sake of one's responsibilities to oneself and others and one's long-term goals.

© 2011, George Lockwood, Poul Perris, and Jeffrey Young. Unauthorized reproduction without written consent of the authors is prohibited. For more information, contact: Schema Therapy Institute Midwest, 471 West South Street, Suite 41 C, Kalamazoo, MI 49007 www.schematherapymidwest.com.

This will also be helpful as a way to understand how EMS and needs relate to and interact with one another and in determining whether there is an underlying structure to the proposed 15 core emotional needs. The findings at this level are less consistent than on the primary (schema) level. The two confirmatory factor analyses (Hoffart *et al.*, 2005; Rijkeboer and van den Bergh, 2006), again our strongest test of the model, produced inconsistent results; the former supported the existence of second-order factors and the latter did not. (This negative result was not stated explicitly in the published results and is based on personal communication with the principal investigator, Rijkeboer, 2010). Since the data from the two CFA studies of the YSQ are inconsistent, we cannot yet determine whether second-order factors provide a good-enough fit to the data. Therefore, we will discuss *trends* in the data that point to certain schemas that seem to cluster together. We caution readers against concluding, from the available data, that these clusters represent statistically meaningful factors, domains, or dimensions. We encourage further research to investigate these important questions so that we can reach more definitive conclusions in the future.

Looking at studies published in English, there are a few noteworthy trends that have emerged across all the major exploratory and confirmatory factor analyses conducted to date. Two higher-order factors appeared in five out of six studies, Disconnection/Rejection and Impaired Autonomy and Performance, and accounted for a significant percent of the variance in the YSQ (Schmidt *et al.*, 1995; Lee *et al.*, 1999; Cecero *et al.*, 2005; Hoffart *et al.*, 2006; Soygut *et al.*, 2007) (see Table 3.2). The EMS that have shown up in the Disconnection/Rejection cluster in three or more of these studies are: Mistrust/Abuse, Emotional Deprivation, Emotional Inhibition, Defectiveness, and Social Isolation. The EMS that have shown up in the Impaired Autonomy and Performance cluster in three or more of the above studies are: Failure, Vulnerability to Harm and Illness, Dependence, Enmeshment, Abandonment, and Subjugation.

Two other second-order factors also appeared in four of the five studies. Unrelenting Standards paired with Self-Sacrifice in four out of the five studies forming the Extreme Efforts factor, and Entitlement appeared on its own in one study and with schemas involving issues with self-control in three of the five studies forming the Impaired Limits factor. These trends suggest that these four groupings may eventually define an underlying structure for the 15 schemas and related needs (see Figure 3.1).

It is important to note that the Abandonment/Instability schema loaded on the Disconnection/Rejection factor in two studies and on the Impaired Autonomy and Performance factor in three others. Based on our clinical experience, we hypothesize that fear of abandonment has two origins. In association with the Impaired Autonomy domain it may develop out of a feeling of dependency and one's perceived lack of competence, and, in association with the Connection domain, may originate from a perception of others as unreliable. These two types of fear would involve addressing two discrete needs: for independence via the development of competence and confidence; and for a stable connection.

We again want to emphasize the speculative nature of the groupings we are proposing. The studies we base this on have various methodological limitations, a main one being the use of a non-randomized item format. In addition, coping styles and response biases can influence how a subject responds to the YSQ and certain patient

Table 3.2 Comparison of secondary factors (not in order of strength of factor loadings)

Schema Domains	Schmidt et al. (1995) P = 187, S = 1129	Lee et al. (1999) P = 433	Ceccro et al. (2005) S = 292 (44.41% of variance accounted for by 4 higher order factors)	Hoffart et al. (2005) Confirmatory Factor Analysis P = 888	Soygut et al. (2007) S = 150-1071
Secondary Factor 1 Disconnection/ Rejection	Mistrust/Abuse Emotional Deprivation Emotional Inhibition Defectiveness Abandonment Fear of Losing Control Insufficient Control	Mistrust/Abuse Emotional Deprivation Emotional Inhibition Defectiveness Social Isolation Abandonment	Mistrust/Abuse Emotional Deprivation *Emotional Inhibition Social Isolation	Mistrust/Abuse Emotional Deprivation Emotional Inhibition Defectiveness Social Isolation	Mistrust/Abuse Emotional Deprivation Emotional Inhibition Defectiveness Social Isolation
Secondary Factor 2 Impaired Autonomy and Performance	Failure Vulnerability to Harm and Illness Dependence Enmeshment Insufficient Self-Control	Failure Vulnerability to Harm and Illness Dependence Subjugation	Failure Vulnerability to Harm and Illness Enmeshment Abandonment Subjugation	Failure Vulnerability to Harm and Illness Dependence Enmeshment Abandonment Subjugation Insufficient Self-control	Failure Vulnerability to Harm and Illness Dependence Enmeshment Abandonment Pessimism
Secondary Factor 3 Extreme Efforts	Unrelenting Standards Self-Sacrifice, Insufficient Self-Control	Unrelenting Standards Self-Sacrifice	Unrelenting Standards Self-Sacrifice *Dependence/Incompetence *Insufficient Self-Control	Unrelenting Standards Self-Sacrifice	Unrelenting Standards Approval-Seeking
Secondary Factor 4 Impaired Limits	Entitlement	Entitlement Fear of Losing Control	Entitlement	Entitlement Insufficient Self-Control	Entitlement Insufficient Self-Control

P = patient sample; S = student sample;
* = a negative loading.

DISCONNECTION AND REJECTION	IMPAIRED AUTONOMY AND PERFORMANCE	Extreme Efforts	IMPAIRED LIMITS
Connection and Acceptance	Unimpaired Autonomy and Performance	Balanced Efforts	Adequate Limits
⬇	⬇	⬇	⬇
MISTRUST/ABUSE Basic Trust	**VULNERABILLITY TO HARM AND ILLNESS** Basic Safety and Health	**SELF-SACRIFICE** Healthy Self-Interest/ Self-Care	**ENTITLEMENT** Empathic Consideration/ Respect for Others
DEFECTIVENESS/ SHAME Self Acceptance/ Lovability	**DEPENDENCE/ INCOMPETENCE** Healthy Self-Reliance/ Competence	**UNRELENTING STANDARDS** Realistic Standards and Expectations	**INSUFFICIENT SELF-CONTROL** Healthy Self-Control/ Self-Discipline
EMOTIONAL DEPRIVATION Emotional Fulfillment	**ENMESHMENT/ UNDEVELOPED SELF** Health Boundaries/ Developed Self		
SOCIAL ISOLATION/ ALIENATION Social Belonging	**ABANDONMENT/ INSTABILITY** Stable Attachment		
EMOTIONAL INHIBITION Emotional Openness/ Spontaneity	**SUBJUGATION** Assertiveness/ Self-Expression **FAILURE** Success		

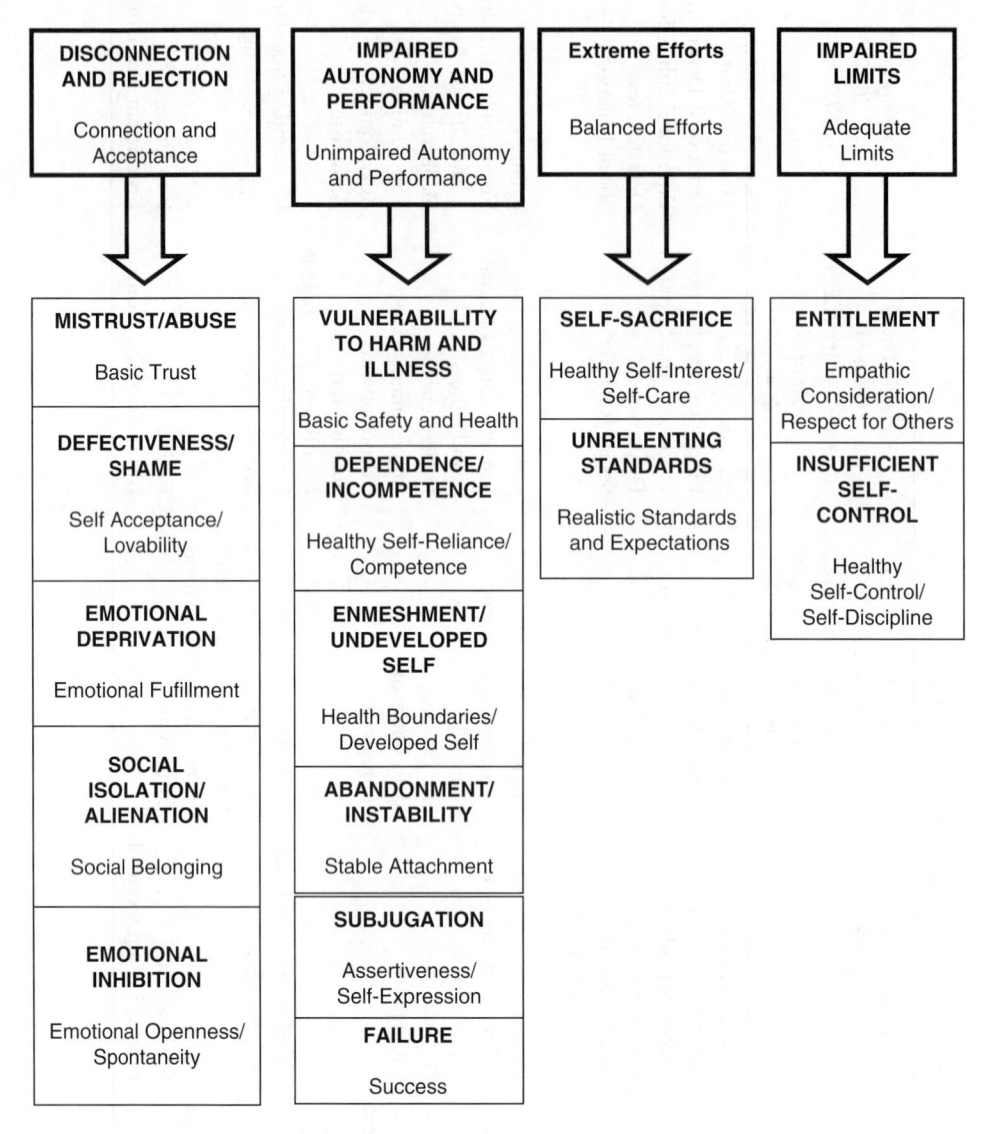

Figure 3.1 The four cluster EMS–EAS model

© 2011, George Lockwood, Poul Perris, and Jeffrey Young. Unauthorized reproduction without written consent of the authors is prohibited. For more information, write: Schema Therapy Institute Midwest, 471 West South Street, Suite 41 C, Kalamazoo, MI 49007 www.schematherapymidwest.com.

groups (e.g., those who internalize) may have biases that differ from others (e.g., those who externalize). Furthermore, it is sometimes difficult to determine whether or not there have been differences in the way the YSQ is scored. Addressing these limitations and challenges in future research will allow us to cast further light on these questions.

Using this tentative set of clusters as a basis for comparisons with the other comprehensive models, we find that the Connection/Acceptance cluster (the need and EAS counterpart to the Disconnection/Rejection cluster) overlaps with Deci and Ryan's and Flanagan's relatedness and connection need and further elaborates Deci and Ryan's (2000) concept of relatedness by way of the five schemas. The Autonomy and Performance cluster (the counterpart to the Impaired Autonomy and Performance cluster) overlaps with Flanagan's autonomy need and, while bearing a similar name, is not clearly aligned with Deci and Ryan's autonomy need in the way they define it. The Mastery and Success EAS (Failure EMS) seems closer to their need for competence. Schema Therapy views impairments in competence as an aspect of Impaired Autonomy. Thus some variant of a Connection and Autonomy/Independence need are found in all of these models and are the clearest points of convergence. These two domains also fit within the context of the key features of the evolution of hominid childhood: greater vulnerability (needs related to connection) along with a long middle childhood focused on the development of autonomy and independence. It seems likely, however, that these broad categories, as elaborated by CNM, are made up of a number of specific and irreducible needs that are central to the development of a full sense of connection and autonomy and that there are many other needs of no less importance and, perhaps, two key need pairings (adequate limits and reasonable expectations) that are not encompassed by these categories. While potentially helpful on a theoretical level, we would like to caution against the use of more abstract concepts, such as a need for connection or autonomy, with regard to clinical work since the empirical evidence indicates that these labels are very rough approximations of a range of schemas and implied needs that are most meaningfully and clearly captured at the schema level. Consequently, we see the CNM model, with its focus on the more complete range of EMS, hypothesized EAS, needs, and adaptive behavioral dispositions as a more useful guide for clarifying the process of meeting core emotional needs.

Summary

Recent empirical evidence emerging from a variety of scientific disciplines provides strong support for ST's trusting and responsive stance toward core needs for connection in work with patients suffering from attachment-based disorders such as BPD. The data suggest that this leads to an initial growth of independence that develops, to a considerable extent, spontaneously rather than primarily through early training in self-sufficiency. This route to independence is based on a fuller internalization of other-soothing and other-joy and, when begun early in life, appears to lead to stronger and healthier brains, bodies, and immune systems. An early phase of responsiveness in combination with positive and sensitive limit-setting and structure for the development of adequate impulse control is followed by a gradual shift toward a focus on the further development of independence. This approach is seen as overcoming cultural biases in relation to core needs for connection characteristic of parenting and psychotherapy in Western industrialized societies. Recent research also suggests that, through this process, our neediest patients, including those with BPD, have the potential to develop exceptionally deep, secure, and transformative attachments and that this can lead to the development of remarkable strengths and abilities. The research also points to the importance of play and joyful interactions in enriching and deepening the impact of attachment bonds. Taken together these elements are seen as forming the foundation on which ST strategies and techniques for meeting needs are built.

The Core Needs Model (CNM) expands on ST's current framework of EMS by developing the concept of EAS and related core emotional needs and adaptive behavioral dispositions. In this way we follow the implications of what we have learned over the past couple of decades about what can go wrong in childhood and adolescence to further elucidate the basic needs and patterns involved when things go well. Providing therapists and patients with a more comprehensive, nuanced, and clearer picture of what this looks like may facilitate the process of meeting needs and the development of positive life patterns over and above healing from negative ones. The EMS–Needs–EAS–ABD links offer us a window on the origins of negativity and positivity and allow us to add depth-oriented positive psychology to our current theoretical model.

Further research will be needed to confirm that needs, EAS, and ABD, like the EMS, are made up of unique and irreducible elements and that they are linked or correlated with EMS in the way we have proposed. Further research will also be required to determine whether EMS and core emotional needs will be best understood as independent constructs or as independent constructs that also form meaningful clusters or domains.

Acknowledgment

We would like to thank Jeffery Young for his invaluable guidance and input in the development of this chapter.

References

Antypa, N. and van der Does, W. (2010) Serotonin transporter gene, childhood emotional abuse and cognitive vulnerability to depression. *Genes, Brain and Behavior*, *9*(6), 615–620.

Bachner-Melman, R., Dina, C., Zohar, A. *et al.* (2004) AVPR1a and SLC6A4 gene polymorphisms are associated with creative dance performance. *PLoS Genetics*, *1*(3), 394–403.

Baranoff, J., Oei, T., Seong, H.C. and Seok-Man, K. (2006) Factor structure and internal consistency of the Young schema questionnaire (short form) in a Korean and Australian sample. *Journal of Affective Disorders*, *93*, 133–140.

Bartels, A. and Zeki, S. (2004) The neural correlates of maternal and romantic love. *Neuroimage*, *21*(3), 1155–1166.

Baumeister, R.F. and Leary, M.R. (1995) The need to belong: desire for interpersonal attachments as a fundamental human motivation. *Psychological Bulletin*, *117*, 497–529.

Belsky, J. and Pluess, M. (2009) Beyond diathesis stress: differential susceptibility to environmental influences. *Psychological Bulletin*, *135*(6), 885–908.

Bowlby, J. (1969) *Attachment and Loss*. New York: Basic Books.

Canli, T. and Lesch, K.P. (2007) Long story short: the serotonin transporter in emotion regulation and social cognition. *Nature Neuroscience 10*, 1103–1109.

Carroll, R. (2005) An interview with Allan Schore: the American Bowlby. www.thinkbody.co.uk/papers/interview-with-allan-s.htm.

Cecero, J.J., Nelson, J.D. and Gillie, J.M. (2004) Tools and tenets of schema therapy: toward the construct validity of the early maladaptive schema questionnaire–research version (EMSQ-R). *Clinical Psychology and Psychotherapy*, *11*, 344–357.

Costa, P.T, and McCrae, R.R. (1992) *Revised NEO Personality Factor Inventory (NEO PI-R) and NEOFFfive Factor Inventory*. Professional manual. Odessa, FL: Psychological Assessment Resources.

Crişan, L., Pană, S., Vulturar, R., *et al.* (2009) Genetic contributions of the serotonin transporter to social learning of fear and economic decision making. *Social Cognitive and Affective Neuroscience*, *4*(4), 399–408.

Deci, E.L. and Ryan, R.M. (2000) The "what" and "why" of goal pursuits: human needs and the self-determination of behavior. *Psychological Inquiry*, *11*, 227–268.

Dissanayake, E. (2000) *Art and Intimacy*. Seattle, WA: University of Washington Press.

Farrell, J., Shaw, I. and Webber, M. (2009) A schema-focused approach to group psychotherapy for outpatients with borderline personality disorder: a randomized controlled trial. *Journal of Behavior Therapy and Experimental Psychiatry*, *40*(2), 317–328.

Flanagan, C. (2010) The case for needs in psychotherapy. *Journal of Psychotherapy Integration*, *20*(1), 1–36.

Giesen-Bloo, J., van Dyck, R., Spinhoven, P., *et al.* (2006) Outpatient psychotherapy for borderline personality disorder: a randomized trial of schema focused therapy versus transference focused therapy. *Archives of General Psychiatry*, *63*(6), 649–658.

Goldberg, W.A. and Keller, M.A. (2007) Parent–infant co-sleeping: why the interest and concern? *Infant and Child Development*, *16*(4), 331–339.

Gonda, X., Fountoulakis, K., Juhasz, G. *et al.* (2009) Association of the s allele of the 5-HTTLPR with neuroticism-related traits and temperaments in a psychiatrically healthy population. *European Archives of Psychiatry and Clinical Neuroscience*, *259*, 106–113.

Gunderson, J. and Lyons-Ruth, K. (2008) BPD's interpersonal hypersensitivity phenotype: a gene–environment–developmental model. *Journal of Personality Disorders*, *22*(1), 22–41.

Hobara, M. (2003) Prevalence of transitional objects in Tokyo and New York. *Infant Mental Health Journal*, *24*(2), 174–191.

Hoffart, A., Sexton, H., Hedley, L.M. *et al.* (2006) The structure of maladaptive schemas: a confirmatory factor analysis and psychometric evaluation of derived scales. *Cognitive Therapy and Research*, *29*(6), 627–644.

Homberg, J.R. and Lesch, K.P. (2011) Looking on the bright side of serotonin transporter gene variation. *Biological Psychiatry*, *69*(6), 513–519.

Hurt, S.W., Widiger, T.A., Frances, A., Gilmore M. and Clarkin J.F. (1984) Diagnostic efficiency and DSM-III. *Archives of General Psychiatry*, *41*(10), 1005–1012.

Keller, M. and Goldberg, W. (2004) Co-sleeping: help or hindrance for young children's independence? *Infant and Child Development*, 13, 369–388.

Kenrick, D., Griskevicius, V., Neuberg, S. and Schaller, M. (2010) Renovating the pyramid of needs: contemporary extensions built upon ancient foundations. *Perspectives on Psychological Science*, 5, 292–314.

Konner, M. (2010) *The Evolution of Childhood*. Cambridge, MA: Harvard University Press.

Kramer, M.S., Aboud, F., Mironova, E. *et al*. (2008) Promotion of Breastfeeding Intervention Trial (PROBIT) Study Group. Breastfeeding and child cognitive development: new evidence from a large randomized trial. *Archives of General Psychiatry*, 65(5), 578–584.

Lachenal-Chevallet, K., Mauchand P., Cottraux J., Bouvard, M. and Martin, R. (2006) Factor analysis of the schema questionnaire-short form in a non-clinical sample. *Journal of Cognitive Psychotherapy: An International Quarterly*, 20(3), 311–318.

Lamb, M.E. and Lewis, C. (2004) The development and significance of father–child relationships in two-parent families, in *The Role of the Father in Child Development*, 4th edition (ed. M.E. Lamb). Hoboken, NJ: Wiley, pp. 272–306.

Lee, C.W., Taylor, G. and Dunn, J. (1999) Factor structure of the schema questionnaire in a large clinical sample. *Cognitive Therapy and Research*, 23, 441–451.

Lesch, K.P., Bengel, D., Heils, A. *et al*. (1996) Association of anxiety related traits with a polymorphism in the serotonin transporter gene regulatory region. *Science*, 274, 1527–1531.

Matsunagaa, M., Murakami, H., Yamakawac, K., *et al*. (2010) Genetic variations in the serotonin transporter gene-linked polymorphic region influence attraction for a favorite person and the associated interactions between the central nervous and immune systems. *Neuroscience Letters*, 468, 211–215.

McKenna, J. and McDade, T. (2005) Why babies should never sleep alone: a review of the co-sleeping controversy in relation to SIDS, bedsharing and breast feeding. *Paediatric Respiratory Reviews*, 6, 134–152.

Middeldorp, C.M., de Geus, E., Willemsen, G. *et al*. (2010) The serotonin transporter gene length polymorphism (5-HTTLPR) and life events: no evidence for an interaction effect on neuroticism and anxious depressive symptoms. *Twin Research and Human Genetics*, 13(6), 544–549.

Munafo, M.R., Freimer, N.B., Ng, W. *et al*. (2009) 5-HTTLPR genotype and anxiety-related personality traits: a meta-analysis and new data. *American Journal of Medical Genetics Part B*, 150B, 271–281.

Muris, P. (2006) Maladaptive schemas in non-clinical adolescents: relations to perceived parental rearing behaviours, big five personality factors, and psychopathological symptoms. *Clinical Psychology and Psychotherapy*, 13, 405–413.

Nadort, M., Arntz, A., Smit, J. *et al*. (2009) Implementation of outpatient schema therapy for borderline personality disorder with versus without crisis support by the therapist outside office hours: a randomized trial. *Behaviour Research and Therapy*, 47(11), 961–973.

Perris, P., Young, J. and Lockwood, G. (2010) Reparenting Inventory. www.cbti.se.

Perris, P., Young J., Lockwood, G., Arntz, A. and Farrell, J. (2008a) *Emotional Core Needs Inventory*. www.cbti.se.

Perris, P., Young, J., Lockwood, G., Arntz, A. and Farrell, J. (2008b) *Adaptive Behavioral Dispositions Inventory*. www.cbti.se.

Pluess, M., Belsky, J., Way, B., Baldwin, M. and Taylor, S. (2010) 5-HTTLPR moderates effects of current life events on neuroticism: differential susceptibility to environmental influences. *Progress in Neuro-Psychopharmacology and Biological Psychiatry*, 34, 1070–1074.

Pruett, K.D. (1998) The role of the father. *Pediatrics*, *102*(5 Suppl. E), 1253–1261.
Ramos, D.K., Youngclarke, D. and Anderson, J.E. (2007) Parental perceptions of sleep problems among co-sleeping and solitary sleeping children. *Infant and Child Development*, *16*(4), 417–431.
Reiss, S., (2008) *The Normal Personality*. Cambridge: Cambridge University Press.
Rijkeboer, M. (2010) Personal communication. October 31.
Rijkeboer, M.M. and van den Bergh, H. (2006) Multiple group confirmatory factor of the Young schema questionnaire in a Dutch clinical versus non-clinical sample. *Cognitive Therapy and Research*, *30*, 263–278.
Rijkeboer, M.M., van den Bergh, H. and Arntz, A. (2005) Relationships between early maladaptive schemas and the five-factor model of personality, in *Assessment of Early Maladaptive Schemas. On the Validity of the Dutch Young Schema Questionnaire* (ed. M.M. Rijkeboer). Amsterdam: Printpartners Ipskamp, pp. 93–114.
Rijkeboer, M.M. and de Boo, G.M. (2010) Early maladaptive schemas in children: development and validation of the schema inventory for children. *Journal of Behavior Therapy and Experimental Psychiatry*, *41*, 102–109.
Risch, N., Herrell, R., Lehner, T. *et al.* (2009) Interaction between the serotonin transporter gene (5-HTTLPR), stressful life events, and risk of depression: a meta-analysis. *Journal of the American Medical Association*, *301*(23), 2462–2471.
Schmidt, N.B., Joiner, T.E., Joung, J.E. and Telch, M.J. (1995) The schema questionnaire: investigation of psychometric properties and the hierarchical structure of a measure of maladaptive schemas. *Cognitive Therapy and Research*, *19*, 295– 321.
Simmer, K. and Patole, S. (2004) Long chain polyunsaturated fatty acid supplementation in preterm infants [update of Cochrane Database Syst Rev. 2000; (2):CD000375]. *Cochrane Database System* Rev. (1):CD000375. doi:10.1002/14651858. CD000375. pub2.
Soygut, G., Karaosmanoglu, A. and Cakir, Z. (2009) Assessment of early maladaptive schemas: a psychometric study of the Turkish Young Schema Questionnaire–Short Form-3. *Turkish Journal of Psychiatry*, *20*(1), 75–84.
Suomi, S. (1997) Early determinants of behaviour: evidence from primate studies. *British Medical Bulletin*, *53*, 170–184.
Terracciano, A., Balaci, L., Thayer, J. *et al.* (2009) Variants of the serotonin transporter gene and NEO-PI-R neuroticism: no association in the BLSA and SardiNIA samples. *American Journal of Medical Genetics Part B*, *150B*, 1070–1077.
Thimm, J.C. (2010) Personality and early maladaptive schemas: a five-factor model perspective. *Journal of Behavior Therapy and Experimental Psychiatry*, *41*, 373–380.
van den Boom, D.C. and Hocksma, J.B. (1994) The effect of infant irritability on mother–infant interaction: a growth curve analysis. *Developmental Psychology*, *30*, 581–590.
van Zeijl, J., Mesman, J., Stolk, M. *et al.* (2007) Differential susceptibility to discipline: the moderating effect of child temperament on the association between maternal discipline and early childhood externalizing problems. *Journal of Family Psychology*, *21*(4), 626–636.
Welburn, K., Corstine, M., Dagg, P., Pontefract, A. and Jordan, S. (2002). The schema questionnaire–short form: Factor analysis and relationships between schemas and symptoms. *Cognitive Therapy and Research*, *26*, 519–530.
Willis-Owen, A.G., Turri, M.G., Munafò, M.R. *et al.* (2005) The serotonin transporter length polymorphism, neuroticism, and depression: A comprehensive assessment of association. *Biological Psychiatry*, *58*, 451–456.
Winnicott, D.W. (1953) Transitional objects and transitional phenomena. *International Journal of Psycho-Analysis*, *34*, 89–97.

Young, J.E. (1999) *Young Parenting Inventory* (YPI) (on-line). New York: Cognitive Therapy Centre. www.schematherapy.com.
Young, J.E. (2005) *Young Schema Questionnaire: Long Form, Version 3.* New York: Schema Therapy Institute. www.schematherapy.com.
Young, J.E. and Brown, G. (2003) *Young Schema Questionnaire; Short Form, Version 3.* New York: Schema Therapy Institute. www.schematherapy.com.
Young, K., Holcomb, L., Bonkale, W. *et al.* (2007) 5-HTTLPR polymorphism and enlargement of the pulvinar: unlocking the backdoor to the limbic system. *Biological Psychiatry*, *61*(6), 813–818.

Part II
The Indication Process in Schema Therapy

Part II

1

The Case Formulation Process in Schema Therapy of Chronic Axis I Disorder (Affective/Anxiety Disorder)

Asle Hoffart

Introduction

For most affective and anxiety disorders, standard cognitive therapy models have been developed and empirically tested (Hawton, Salkovskis, Kirk and Clark, 1989). Although these disorders may develop on the basis of certain pervasive early maladaptive schemas (EMSs) as defined in Young, Klosko, and Weishaar (2003), the standard models almost exclusively address the present internal dynamics of the disorder. Thus, panic disorder may partly result from a Vulnerability to Harm schema originating in childhood, but the cognitive model of panic focuses the current interplay of specific catastrophic interpretations of bodily sensations, safety behaviors, and an internal focus of attention during panic attacks (Salkovskis and Clark, 1991).

Overall, these standard cognitive therapy models have proven to be effective and sufficient for many patients. However, a considerable subgroup may suffer from chronic anxiety and/or depression, despite having received presumably adequate psychological and/or pharmacological treatment. These patients may fail to progress during cognitive therapy due to schema-related issues. For instance, a patient may resist doing homework because she needs to compensate for a Subjugation schema. Another patient may collect abundant evidence that others do not react negatively to him, but a strong Defectiveness schema may still make him feel stupid and inferior in social situations. Others may improve, but relapse after treatment because of their schemas. For instance, a patient with panic disorder may experience reduced fear of bodily sensations and avoidance during therapy, but later a Vulnerability to Harm schema may make her see new dangers that fuel increased anxiety. Some may develop multiple Axis I anxiety and depressive disorders on the basis of certain

The Wiley Blackwell Handbook of Schema Therapy: Theory, Research, and Practice, First Edition.
Edited by Michiel van Vreeswijk, Jenny Broersen, and Marjon Nadort.
© 2012 John Wiley & Sons, Ltd. Published 2015 by John Wiley & Sons, Ltd.

schemas. In these patients, progress in one disorder as a result of treatment may not lead to the remediation of the others because the underlying schemas remain unchanged. Thus, maladaptive schemas may in various ways be involved in the maintenance of chronic anxiety and depression. Often, these schemas lead to comorbid Axis II personality disorders. In such cases Schema Therapy (ST) may be indicated.

The purpose of this chapter is to present the case formulation procedures and process within ST in cases of chronic anxiety and/or depression and illustrate this with a case example. The patient participated in an 11-week inpatient program that consisted of first an agoraphobia-focused phase and a second, schema-focused phase (Hoffart, Versland and Sexton, 2002). A cohort of patients with agoraphobia and Cluster C personality disorders treated in this program showed greater long-term improvement in interpersonal problems than a cohort of similar patients receiving psychodynamic treatment as usual (TAU) (Gude and Hoffart, 2008).

The Patient and the Treatment Context

The patient, Jane, was a 29-year-old married woman with no children who had suffered from panic attacks and social anxiety since she was 17. She had been given various psychological treatments and had been treated with antidepressants for several years. However, her problems persisted and she was ultimately admitted to the specialized inpatient program introduced above. In this program, patients are admitted in closed treatment groups with eight members in each. The first five-week agoraphobia-focused phase is based on the cognitive model of panic and agoraphobia (Salkovskis and Clark, 1991) and consists mainly of group sessions and behavioral experiments. The second six-week, schema-focused phase consists mainly of 9–10 individual sessions of 45-minutes duration, eight 90-minute group sessions, and between-session assignments. The case formulation process involving Jane as patient and the present author as therapist in the first three individual sessions of the second phase will be presented below.

The Case Formulation Process

Goals

A case formulation is developed during the initial phase of therapy. The case formulation process involves several goals, which are explained below. During this process, the Schema Therapist needs to attend to all these goals and specifically promote each of them at relevant points.

Treatment plan. A case formulation consists of an account of how the patient's EMS and maladaptive coping strategies used to handle these EMS maintain the patient's current problems. The overall strategy is first to list the patient's problems and identify their central features and then to identify the EMS and coping strategies that may maintain these problems. On the basis of the formulation, a *treatment plan* is made for how and when to address the identified maintaining factors.

Joint understanding of the formulation. As in standard cognitive therapy, one wants to empower the patient by making the therapy as transparent and understandable to him/her as possible. A joint understanding of the formulation contributes to such transparency. Furthermore, a joint understanding of what the patient's problems are and how they are maintained prepares the ground for a good alliance. In particular, the therapist and the patient are more likely to agree on the goals and tasks of therapy.

Reflective distance. When coming to therapy, patients usually lack understanding of their problems. The Schema Therapist helps patients identify their EMS and become aware of the childhood memories, emotions, bodily sensations, cognitions, and coping strategies associated with them. Once patients understand their EMS and coping strategies, they may adopt a reflective distance and thus begin to exert some control over their responses.

Self-compassion. Patients are often self-critical with regard to their problems. Schema-related responses, such as anxiousness, may evoke anger at self, self-blame, self-contempt, and even self-hate. During the case formulation process, such patients may see that their schema-related responses are understandable and reasonable in their childhood environment and become more sympathetic toward self. Most importantly, re-experiencing the painful emotions of the past may naturally elicit compassion for self.

Socialization to ST and mapping of resources. The case formulation work should demonstrate the schema approach in general, so that socialization to ST can begin. At the same time, the therapist notes the patient's resources in their reactions to this approach, resources that can be deliberately activated when needed in further therapy.

Hope. Patients with chronic anxiety and/or depressive disorders, strong EMS, and rigid coping styles are often profoundly demoralized. Hope may be instigated by a rationale that is understandable, easy to recognize oneself in, and brings order to the patient's problems. Clinical experience indicates that the schema model has these features.

Bonding. Schema Therapy involves the courageous endeavor to re-experience and communicate the most vulnerable states of childhood, those where the child desperately needed the care of adults but was not getting it (Young *et al.*, 2003). An initial step is therefore for the therapist and patient to form a secure emotional attachment so that the patient together with the therapist dares to approach these states. This bond is a crucial part of the alliance in ST and should be given particular attention and strengthened during the case formulation process.

Developing a problem list

The principles I use for developing a problem list follows those of Parsons (1995). The goal is to attain an overall survey of the patient's problems. The standard instruction is something like: "We need to get a survey of your problems. What do want help with? What is difficult in your life? We first enlist all kinds of problems – work difficulties, financial difficulties, health problems, housing problems, recreational difficulties – not only those that seem directly psychological. These other problems often influence the psychological, and also the other way around: the psychological ones may influence those other problems."

The therapist writes down the problems in a readable way, summarizes them frequently, and asks: "Is this the right way to put them? Have we left anything out?" Particularly important problems may get their own place in the list, although they are part of another problem also mentioned. For instance, "suicidal impulses" might appear under a problem labeled "depression" but might also appear as a separate problem. It is also useful to list separately problems that cut across other problems, for instance "unassertive." Problems are stated in concrete terms, and emotional, bodily, behavioral, and cognitive components of the problem are described. If possible, the problems are quantified (e.g., "Panic attacks, occurring daily"). The problems are preferably described in the patient's own words, and a mutually agreed problem list is strived for.

For Jane, the approach described above resulted in the following problem list:

1. *Social anxiety*. Anxiety-eliciting situations include having people behind, for instance in cinemas or churches, eating with half-acquaintances and seeing them in their eyes, and walking across open spaces while being observed by others. Catastrophic thoughts in these situations include that my head will shake visibly, that my voice will quaver, that I will walk unsteadily, and that I will not be able to resist my impulse to flee the situation.
2. *Sleeping difficulties*. Falling asleep may take up to three hours. Disturbed by worrying about future social interactions.
3. *Depression*. "I have been more depressed during the last week." Ruminates about two themes: "1) whether I will ever recover from my anxiety problems, elicited by the increase of 'bodily anxiety' last week; and 2) whether I have to move with my husband to a city because he has difficulties getting a job where we currently live. I strongly want not to move because I here live close to my family of origin and because our social circle in the city would involve academics who trigger my feelings of inferiority. I have diminished pleasure talking with other people, find it hard to get out of bed in the morning, and sometimes withdraw to my bed to avoid social situations."
4. *Low self-esteem*. "All my life I have had low self-esteem. I easily feel inferior to well-educated people with important work, also to my husband who is highly confident about his work skills. Very afraid of being judged as "unintelligent" by well-educated people and authorities. My self-esteem has increased a little after I took a lower-level university grade. I also feel very inferior and stupid when I have done something embarrassing when other people are present."

During the work with the problem list, I noted that Jane sometimes "softened" the description of her problems, for instance "I am not that depressed, I am still able to enjoy some activities." Perhaps she wanted to avoid giving the impression of being severely disturbed. This could be explored later.

Problem integration

After the list is completed, a *problem integration* phase follows, where the connections between the problems are explored. Thus, the therapist and the patient together assess whether some problems are primary and others more secondary and whether maintaining relationships exist between the problems.

The standard instruction is something like: "Before we decide what to address in the treatment, we need to look for possible relationships between your problems. Are they linked together in some way? Is it something that occurs to everyone? A certain thought? A feeling? A way of coping? Are some problems part of other problems? How do the problems influence each other? If you overcame this problem, would you still have this? If you got rid of this problem, what would remain?"

For Jane, it seems that the sleeping difficulties are part of the social anxiety. Furthermore, her depression seems partly reactive to her social anxiety and partly relates to her negative self-schemas and low self-esteem. On the basis of this integration, it seems pertinent to focus on her social anxiety and her low self-esteem in the further development of the formulation.

Diagnostics

Diagnostic precision is decisive, as the diagnostic categories provide connections to the cognitive models that are developed for each disorder (Hawton *et al.*, 1989). The listed problems indicate which diagnoses should be examined in more detail.

As indicated above, Jane participated in a research project where the diagnoses were determined in independent interviews. Before joining the cognitive program for agoraphobia, she reached the criteria for the following DSM-IV diagnoses: panic disorder with agoraphobia, social phobia, past major depression, and avoidant personality disorder. After the agoraphobia phase, she no longer met criteria for panic disorder with agoraphobia. Her fears during panic attacks of choking to death or having a heart attack had disappeared and panic attacks now appeared to be exclusively related to social anxiety. The social anxieties, on the other hand, were largely unchanged. The depressive symptoms had not yet lasted long enough to be diagnosed as current major depression.

Identification of schemas and coping strategies through situational analysis

Schemas involve patterns of reactions that are pervasive in a number of situations. Problematic beliefs, feelings, and behaviors that cut across situations, such as "unassertiveness" or "low self-esteem," are therefore a useful vantage point for identifying schemas and maladaptive coping strategies. Such general problems are focused in *situational analysis*. The standard instruction is: "You said that low self-esteem is a problem for you. We need to map this more accurately. When does this low self-esteem show itself? Do you have examples?" The therapist chooses two or three situations from those the patient mentions, finds a recent episode, which the patient remembers well from each of the situations, and analyzes these episodes using Figure 1.1 (Beck, 1995). If the problem is also a part of the symptom disorders, it is mandatory to include a symptom episode in the analysis.

```
┌─────────────────────────────────────────────────────────────────┐
│                    Early Maladaptive Schemas                    │
│   "I am worthless, inferior, unintelligent, stupid, like a leper" │
└─────────────────────────────────────────────────────────────────┘
                                │
┌─────────────────────────────────────────────────────────────────┐
│                          Assumptions                            │
│          "I must hide shaking/that I am unintelligent"          │
└─────────────────────────────────────────────────────────────────┘
                                │
┌─────────────────────────────────────────────────────────────────┐
│                      Maladaptive coping                         │
│     Avoid social situations, especially those involving authorities │
└─────────────────────────────────────────────────────────────────┘
```

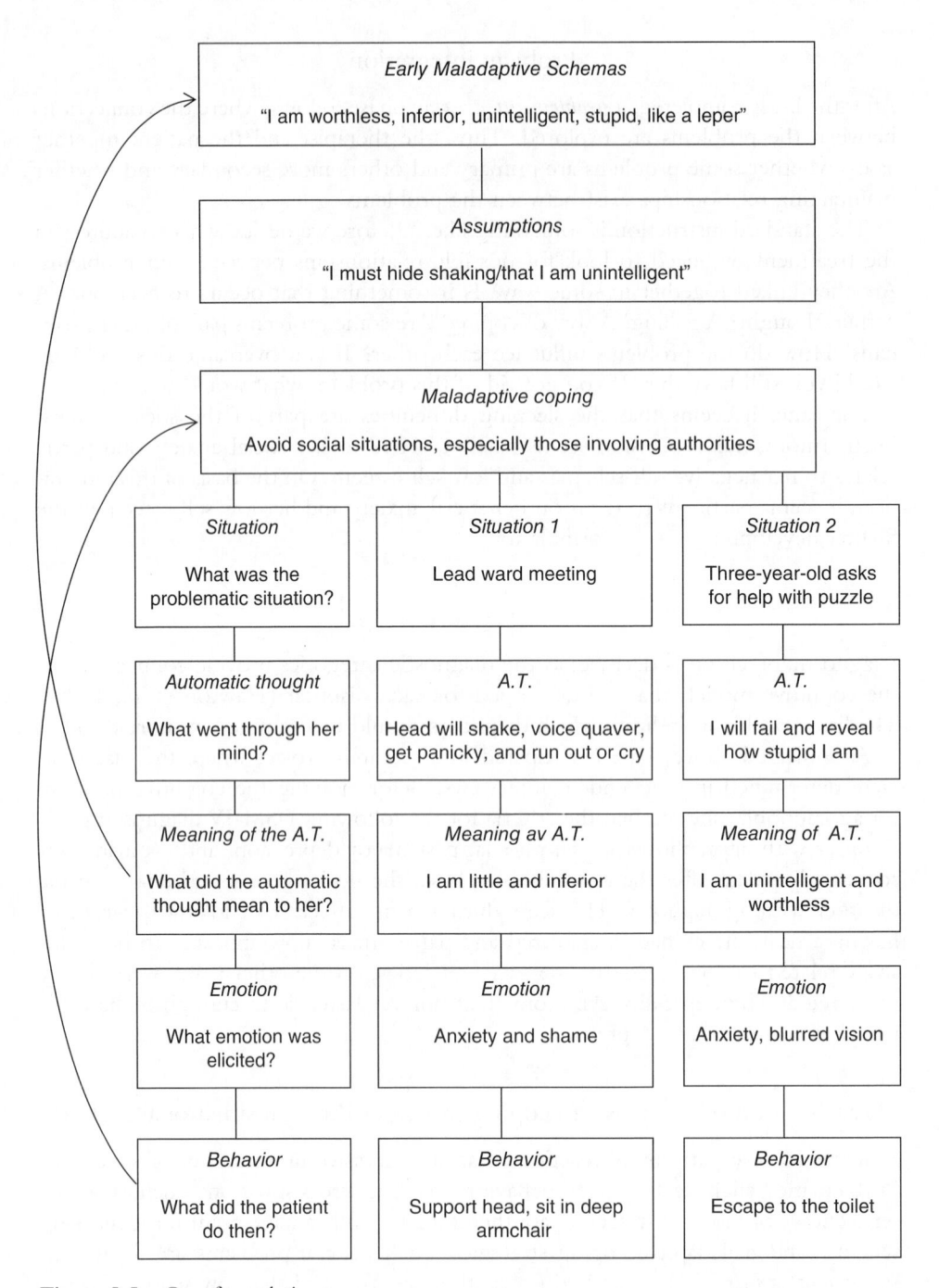

Situation	Situation 1	Situation 2
What was the problematic situation?	Lead ward meeting	Three-year-old asks for help with puzzle
Automatic thought — What went through her mind?	**A.T.** — Head will shake, voice quaver, get panicky, and run out or cry	**A.T.** — I will fail and reveal how stupid I am
Meaning of the A.T. — What did the automatic thought mean to her?	**Meaning av A.T.** — I am little and inferior	**Meaning of A.T.** — I am unintelligent and worthless
Emotion — What emotion was elicited?	**Emotion** — Anxiety and shame	**Emotion** — Anxiety, blurred vision
Behavior — What did the patient do then?	**Behavior** — Support head, sit in deep armchair	**Behavior** — Escape to the toilet

Figure 1.1 Case formulation

From consistency of meanings of the automatic thoughts and images across situations, a possible negative EMS and assumptions may be extracted. The behavior, on the other hand, indicates how the patient is trying to avoid, compensate for, or attenuate the activation of the EMS.

In Jane's case, we analyzed a forthcoming social situation – to lead the ward meeting taking place the next day. She was asked what she thought would happen according to the diagram in Figure 1.1. Questions such as the following were used: "When you lead the meeting, what do you think will happen to you? In your body? In your mind? What do you think others will notice? If they notice this, what do you think they will think? Will you do something to prevent these things from happening?" The analysis ended in thoughts about self being little and worthless. These thoughts reminded her of a fear of appearing unintelligent. This fear was in particular elicited in the presence of authorities and well-educated people, and we analyzed a salient episode where she was visiting a family where the husband was a professor and the three-year-old child asked her to put together a simple jigsaw puzzle. She reacted with high anxiety and blurred vision and could not see the puzzle pieces clearly. The results of the analysis of this episode are reported in the last column of Figure 1.1. She also disclosed that she generally put great effort into trying to prove to others that she is not stupid. For instance, she had taken a university degree partly for that reason. The general meanings and strategies were extracted and filled in the upper part of the figure.

After revealing her reactions in the "puzzle" episode, she asked me whether I thought she was an "odd creature." I told her that I could have similar experiences, feeling blocked when involuntarily being put to test. However, although I found this distressing, I did not feel odd for having such reactions.

Resources were exhibited during the situational analysis. First, she revealed a progressive attitude and socialization to the schema model in choosing to lead the ward meeting and thus confront her anxiety. Second, when investigating the meanings of her automatic thoughts in this situation, she spontaneously gained access to alternative thoughts such as "My fellow patients will not judge me for running out or crying" and her anticipatory anxiety subsided. This indicated a flexibility of thinking simply by reflecting on her automatic thoughts and meanings.

Focused life history

The situational analysis represents a temporally "horizontal" approach for assessing schemas and coping styles. In the development of a focused life history, the therapist complements the situational analysis with a temporally "vertical" approach through the patient's history. Whether the current schemas and coping styles identified through the situational analysis recur during the patient's life is explored. In particular, originating or prototypical experiences are sought. In this process, the interaction serves several purposes: it should strengthen bonding with the therapist; lead to identification of central childhood experiences; and lead to full exposure of the emotions connected to these experiences. Bonding is not only a part of this process, but to some extent a prerequisite for it.

To strengthen bonding, the therapist listens attentively to the patient's stories and also attends closely to the patient's reactions. This tends to elicit feelings of sympathy and warmth toward the patient, which in turn are expressed in the therapist's tone of voice and comments. To signal interest in the patient's experience and to facilitate the telling of the story, the therapist asks open-ended questions that encourage patients to express their needs and emotions. For example, the therapist may ask, "What are you feeling as you talk about that?" The patient's feelings are validated by the therapist's empathic reactions. These include sounds and exclamations ("How awful!") by which the patient's feeling state is acknowledged and shared, and statements that confirm the naturalness of feelings ("No wonder you were frightened") (Havens, 1979). When clearly abusive and bad behaviors are reported, supportive statements such as "I think this was a very nasty thing to say to you" are indicated.

In the second session, Jane was given as a homework assignment to think of and write down the answer to the question: "During your life, when have you had these feelings that you are inferior and worthless?" We focused on the episodes that she reacted to most intensely.

Comment about pimples. When participating at a handball tournament when she was 16, Jane experienced a very nasty comment from another girl. When Jane was sitting eating together with her team fellows, this girl exclaimed that she could not stand sitting there because Jane was so pimply. Jane left the table and withdrew to the toilets, crying. She felt "like a leper and inferior."

Comment about dirtiness. In her early teens, Jane was ashamed of her body, which she felt was big and ugly. For this reason, she avoided taking showers after gym sessions. When planning a trip with her class, a boy said that he would not sleep in the same tent as Jane because she never washed and was dirty. At this remark, she felt "like a leper and inferior." She remembered having avoided giving others a hug because of this.

Stepfather's punitive behaviors. During meals, she had been severely corrected by her stepfather for not behaving properly. He had approached in fury and violently pulled her hair. Strong anger at the stepfather was activated when telling about this. She connected her preoccupation of others' critical looks at meals with these incidents.

Left by her biological father. In this phase of therapy, she happened to bump into her aunt, her biological father's sister. Her mother and biological father had never lived together. She had grown up with her mother and, from the age of four, with her stepfather as well. The meeting with the aunt was very satisfying for her, and many thoughts and feelings in her relation to her father were evoked. She realized that she had usually coped with these feelings by denying her connection to this side of her family. She now admitted grief over her loss of contact and that she longed for more contact. She felt "forgotten, left behind, and worthless" by her biological father's absence and showed emotions of sadness and anger. She felt determined to approach her biological father in the future, and there had been some indications lately that he also wanted more contact with her.

She said that she had cried a lot when writing down the episodes. She felt as if she was back in time, back at the age of seven or eight years. This indicates that the purpose of accessing unintegrated memories was fulfilled (Conway and Pleydell-Pearce, 2000).

She broke her limits by telling the episode about pimples. She had not told anyone about this before and she felt ashamed to tell me. Afterward, she told me that she felt sad about having lived 27 years without being fond of herself. This could indicate that some self-compassion was about to emerge.

Schema inventory

The long-form version of the Young Schema Questionnaire (YSQ-L2; Young and Brown, 2001) contains 205 items and assesses 16 schemas. In clinical use, the therapist looks at the items for each schema separately, circling high scores (5s and 6s), and reviews the completed questionnaire with the patient (Young et al., 2003). The therapist uses the high-scoring items to prompt the patient to talk about each relevant schema by asking, "Can you tell me more about how this statement relates to your life?" Exploring two items for each high-scored schema in this way usually suffices to convey the essence of the schema. Young et al. (2003) have developed cognitive, experiential, behavioral, and therapy relationship strategies for each of the YSQ schemas, and identification of the patient's schemas thus provides a connection to these strategies.

Jane completed the YSQ-L2, but we did not discuss the ratings. She scored at least 1 standard deviation above the mean for Norwegian psychiatric patients (Hoffart et al., 2005) on the following five EMSs: Emotional Deprivation, Subjugation, Enmeshment, Defectiveness/Shame, and Failure to Achieve. Her endorsement of the schemas Subjugation, Defectiveness/Shame, and Failure was consistent with the hypotheses formed so far. However, her high scores on the schemas Emotional Deprivation and Enmeshment were surprising.

Imagery assessment

Through the assessment process so far, the therapist and the patient have built hypotheses about the patient's schemas and coping styles. Originating childhood experiences have been identified and the emotions connected to these events have been experienced to a greater or lesser degree. Emotional events such as the schema-related childhood experiences are mainly stored in the form of images (Conway and Pleydell-Pearce, 2000). Controlled imagery is therefore an efficient way to access these experiences. Therefore, provided sufficient safety and trust in the therapist has been established, the next step is to trigger the patient's schemas in the session through imagery.

Goals and rationale.   The goals of the imagery assessment are:

1. To more accurately identify those schemas that are central for the patient by eliciting core images – those connected with such primary emotions as fear, rage, shame, and grief – that are linked to the patient's EMS.
2. To help the patient feel and tolerate the emotions associated with the images/schemas more fully.
3. To better understand the childhood origin of the patient's schemas.

4. To link the origins of their schemas in childhood and adolescence with their current problems.
5. To provide a basis for self-compassion by experiencing the emotional pain of the image.
6. For the therapist, to experience the origins with the patient in order to understand them emotionally, thus creating a basis for empathic responding.

Patients are first provided a rationale for imagery work along the lines of these goals.

Imagery procedure. The vantage point for the imagery may be a problematic feeling, somatic sensation, or visual image of self (Hackmann, Clark and McManus, 2000). Patients are asked to close their eyes, relax, and let the emotion, sensation, or image come to mind. Then they are asked to go back in time and picture a situation in childhood where they had the same emotion/sensation/image. To make the imagery as vivid and emotional as possible, patients are instructed and helped to let the images appear spontaneously, to focus on the sensory features of the images, to report them in the present tense as if the imagined events are happening now, and to use the first-person pronoun to strengthen the experience that the events are happening to *them*. They are asked to provide as much detail as possible, including sights, sounds, smells, behaviors, bodily sensations, feelings, and thoughts. To ensure that all the frightening or otherwise distressing features of the situation are confronted, unreported details are elicited by asking questions such as "What can you see/hear/smell?" "What does his face look like?" "How are you feeling?" "What is going through your mind right now?" During imagery, the therapist's role is facilitative rather than directive. He/she should be careful not to suggest what to experience in the imagery. The imagery reliving continues until the visualized event appears to have come to an end.

Post-imagery discussion. Following the imagery, patients are asked how vivid it was, what they noticed about the experience, and what was surprising about it. In particular, they are asked to verbalize their sense of self and others during the worst moments of the imagined situation. This provides the most individualized formulation of the activated schema.

During the focused life-history discussions with Jane, it became clear that the episodes with her stepfather evoked the most intense emotions. However, talking about the episodes for the most part elicited anger. I thought she needed to get in touch also with her more vulnerable and directly schema-related emotions back then in order to work on them. These episodes were therefore selected as a target for imagery assessment.

She was asked to close her eyes, to place herself in a comfortable position in her chair, and was given grounding instructions including "feel that the chair is carrying you" and "feel that your body is becoming heavy." Then she was asked to let images of episodes in her childhood with her stepfather emerge. She immediately saw images of stepfather pulling her hair; he looked angry. When seeing this image, she became nauseous and asked me anxiously whether that was "normal." I reminded her that she had said that she was afraid of her stepfather in these episodes and that the nausea might be a natural part of this.

She reported that she saw both persons from outside and that she was so small compared to him. The nausea became worse and she felt that she had to vomit. I found a bucket that she could vomit into. She also felt a shivering sensation in her neck and was afraid that she would lose control of her head and shake visibly.

When I invited her to take a field perspective in the imagery and see the stepfather through her eyes during the event she was able to do that. I thought full reliving could also involve the pain sensations when he was pulling her hair; I therefore asked her whether she could feel pain but she reported that she did not. The fear of losing control over her head increased, and I asked her whether she did anything to keep control. She replied that she tensed her muscles and I asked her whether she would try something different now and let that tension go. I also asked her how bad it would be if she let me see her shaking.

In the post-imagery discussion, she expresses surprise that she becomes concerned about shaking her head when she imagines the episodes with her father pulling her hair, even though there is no one actually there behind her. She seems relieved to make these connections between her present fear of shaking, especially when there is someone behind her, and the past episodes with the stepfather. Her sense of self during these episodes was that she felt worthless.

Treatment Plan

The problem integration phase indicated that the social anxiety and her low self-esteem were the two central targets for change. In the further assessment, social anxiety was connected to physically abusive childhood episodes with her stepfather. Low self-esteem was determined as EMSs such as being worthless, inferior, unintelligent, and "like a leper." The treatment plan consequently involved imagery rescripting of fearful episodes with stepfather, so that she could be empowered in this relation. This empowerment and the performance of self-assertion assignments could help her be more self-assertive in current relationships and also become less anxious about her head shaking in social situations. In parallel, she should be encouraged to seek out social situations and learn that the feared outcome of being judged to be worthless does not occur. Her approaches toward her biological father should be monitored and supported.

Pitfalls and Tips

As elaborated above, schema work is a multilevel activity. It consists of verbal understanding, emotional experiences, and relational experiences. Any emphasis on one of these elements at the expense of the others may stall the therapeutic process. For instance, full emotional activation of schema-related experiences is a prerequisite for an adequate verbal understanding of schemas and coping strategies. A safe therapeutic relationship, in which the patient is ready to reveal shameful issues and trust the therapist's ability to tolerate and handle strong emotions, is a prerequisite for engaging in imagery work. Empathic listening and giving time to let emotional experiences evolve is important when making a focused life history. However, verbal summaries and selection of the most central childhood episodes based on a verbal analysis are necessary to prevent the life history slipping into an unending endeavor. I find that the simpler schema approach rather than mode work is appropriate and sufficient for most chronic affective/anxiety disorder patients. However, when the patient is highly self-critical, suggesting the internalization of a Critical/Punitive Parent mode, an analysis including this mode may be indicated.

References

Beck, J.S. (1995) *Cognitive Therapy: Basics and Beyond*. New York: Guilford Press.
Conway, M.A. and Pleydell-Pearce, C.W. (2000) The construction of autobiographical memories in the self-memory system. *Psychological Review*, 107, 261–288.
Gude, T. and Hoffart, A. (2008) Change in interpersonal problems after cognitive agoraphobia and schema-focused therapy versus psychodynamic treatment as usual of inpatients with agoraphobia and Cluster C personality disorders. *Scandinavian Journal of Psychology*, 49, 195–199.
Hackmann, A., Clark, D.M. and McManus, F. (2000) Recurrent images and early memories in social phobia. *Behaviour Research and Therapy*, 38, 601–610.
Havens, L. (1979) Explorations in the uses of language in psychotherapy: complex empathic statements. *Psychiatry*, 42, 40–48.
Hawton, K., Salkovskis, P., Kirk, J. and Clark, D.M. (1989) *Cognitive Behaviour Therapy for Psychiatric Problems: a Practical Guide*. Oxford: Oxford University Press.
Hoffart, A., Sexton, H., Hedley, L.M. *et al.* (2005) The structure of maladaptive schemas: a confirmatory factor analysis and a psychometric evaluation of factor-derived scales. *Cognitive Therapy and Research*, 29, 627–644.
Hoffart, A., Versland, S. and Sexton, H. (2002) Self-understanding, empathy, guided discovery, and schema belief in schema-focused cognitive therapy of personality problems: a process–outcome study. *Cognitive Therapy and Research*, 26, 199–219.
Salkovskis, P. and Clark, D.M. (1991) Cognitive therapy for panic attacks. *Journal of Cognitive Psychotherapy*, 5, 215–226.
Young, J.E., Klosko, J.S. and Weishaar, M. (2003) *Schema Therapy: a Practitioner's Guide*. New York: Guilford Press.

2
Schema Therapy for Narcissism – A Case Study

Wendy Behary

Developed for treating patients with borderline personality disorder (BPD), in response to the high number of schemas reported on inventories, consistently observable self-defeating coping styles, rapidly changing states of mind ("mode flipping"), and the predictable activation of schema clusters (bundling of schemas that erupt under specific exogenous or endogenous conditions, creating intense affect and debilitating behavior patterns), Young, Klosko, and Weishaar (2003) describe a specific Schema Mode Therapy to treat patients with narcissistic personality disorder (NPD). Working in the mid-1990s, Young and colleagues found that this patient population also appeared to demonstrate uniquely predictable schema profiles, coping styles, and emotional states, along with predictable external and internal conditions for schema-triggering (Ronningstam, 1998; Young et al., 2003; Behary, 2008a, 2008b).

While their affect appeared to be less intense and the schema count was not nearly as high as those of patients with BPD, patients with NPD seemed to consistently present with remarkably specific personality traits (early maladaptive schemas) and emotional/behavioral states (schema modes).

Typical schemas of a patient with NPD would include Emotional Deprivation, Defectiveness/Shame, and Entitlement as the most prominent and profound schemas within the profile, directly linked to the patient's core unmet needs.

We also frequently observe some combination of the following schemas (Young et al., 2003):

- Mistrust/Abuse
- Unrelenting Standards/Hypercriticalness
- Insufficient Self-Control/Self-Discipline
- Social Isolation/Alienation
- Failure

- Subjugation
- Approval-Seeking/Recognition-Seeking
- Punitiveness.

The Four Schema Modes of Patients with NPD

The Self-Aggrandizer mode

This is the default mode of the narcissist. In this mode the patient may act as if entitled, demanding, controlling, attention-seeking, approval-seeking, critical, or even abusive at times. This is the over-compensating ("fight") mode of the narcissist. The patient actively fights to avoid core feelings of shame and mistrust that are linked to the Lonely Child mode and the early unmet needs for unconditional love and acceptance. He distracts the therapist by showing off and challenging the proposed treatment.

The Detached Self-Soother/Self-Stimulator mode

In treatment, the narcissist automatically cuts off access to painful emotions linked to unmet needs and emotional longings. He will deny having any vulnerable feelings associated with potential loss, unwanted consequences, and difficult or traumatic past experiences. The hallmark schema – Shame – prohibits the narcissist from exposing these "weak" and humiliating human emotions. He may become cynical or accuse the therapist of underestimating his superior qualities, as compared to others, when it comes to dealing with difficult issues, thus flipping him back into his Self-Aggrandizing mode when challenged to experience the (Vulnerable) Lonely Child mode.

In the absence of an audience, the narcissist's detached mode will include excessive behaviors such as substance abuse, gambling, pornography and sexual preoccupation, working, eating, internet surfing, and other methods of escape and stimulation.

This mode is the equivalent of the "flight" response of the human survival system. When a human encounters a threat to his safety and stability – in the case of the narcissist, his humility and independence – one way of coping is to flee, avoid, shut down, or distract himself.

The Lonely Child mode

Beneath their "hiding places" and "fierce posturing" lies the Lonely Child mode. This is a subset of the Vulnerable Child mode. We call it the "Lonely" Child mode because we believe that the narcissist's vulnerability is founded in the feeling of being emotionally alone and prohibited from expressing the natural longings and needs to be held, loved, and nurtured (as every child does) unconditionally – without having to prove themselves. In the typical origins of narcissism they are made to feel ashamed of vulnerable emotions, while praised for extraordinary performance and achievement that is expected of them. They may also be taught that they are "special" and need not adhere to the rules of ordinary, conventional people. This sets them apart, adding to their sense of loneliness. The lack of attunement, empathy, and real nurturing in their early lives leaves them without the capacity and fluidity to effectively connect with others, furthering the loneliness.

When in this mode, the narcissist will strive to find stimulating or soothing activities as the feelings become intolerable to them. This state of loneliness and shame is unbearable for them; and at the more severe end of the spectrum, this concealed, forbidden side of their personality makes it difficult, if not impossible, for them to cultivate healthy and satisfying intimate relationships.

We postulate that the bedrock of effective schema mode treatment with NPD is founded in the therapy relationship. Here are the major strategies embodied in that work:

- The presence and maintenance of leverage – consistently confronting undesirable behaviors, reminding the patient of the consequences that he does not wish to face if his hurtful interpersonal style and behavioral transgressions with loved ones, the law, work-related situations, in therapy, and with others, do not cease (e.g., a partner leaving, losing a job).
- Limited (adaptive) reparenting approach – harnessing the moment-to-moment, interpersonal (transference and countertransference) experiences relevant to the patient's treatment goals, and bringing them into awareness through the use of empathic confrontation and limit-setting – the treatment room becomes a microcosm for the macro-reality of the narcissist (Behary, 2008b). Relevant self-disclosure is used to enhance empathy and attunement.
- Emotion-focused and cognitive-behavioral strategies (CBT) – persistent efforts are aimed at accessing and reparenting the Lonely Child mode of the narcissist through the use of imagery and transformational chair work (Young, 2003; Kellogg, 2009). CBT strategies include audio flashcards (Behary, 2008a), schema diaries, and behavioral role-plays aimed at the practice of reciprocity in conversations, expressing emotions and needs, and empathy for others. Ultimately, the narcissist is encouraged to employ his Healthy Adult mode in meeting the needs of the Lonely Child. In so doing, he becomes more able to let others see his vulnerability along with his (loveable) ordinariness. He learns that he does not have to be in performance mode, constantly proving his greatness, to be accepted.

Case study: Stephen

- The therapy relationship (self-disclosure, empathic confrontation, use of leverage)
- Identifying modes
- Using chair work in the early phase of treatment
- Audio flashcard

Stephen is a 52-year-old married man with an adult son. He is a successful broker working for a large Wall Street firm. He has been married to Linda for 25 years. She spends her time volunteering at the community shelter, and writing short stories.

History: Stephen grew up in an affluent home, his father was a very accomplished businessman, and his mother was a well-regarded figure in the community. Stephen was the eldest of three boys. He was always told that he was "meant for great things," "brilliant," and "very special." These accolades were not offered to Stephen for being a precious little boy who was curious, playful, sweet, and vulnerable like most children. They were offered for Stephen's athletic prowess, intelligence, "toughness" ("I never cried"), and his drive to achieve, beginning as early as his toddler years.

Stephen recalls having to comfort his distressed and sobbing mother when he was five years old after she had had a fight with his father – a common occurrence. He describes his father as intelligent, frightening, and very demanding of Stephen. But his brothers were always let "off the hook" when it came to his demands and expectations because they "were not as smart or coordinated." Stephen resented them but felt "better than them" at the same time.

Entering treatment: Stephen agreed to therapy after Linda finished reading my book on narcissism (Behary, 2008a) and said the book was written about him (and them). After several years of her own therapy and countless complaints about his mistreatment and neglect of her, their children, extended family, and friends, she issued an ultimatum: if he didn't make a commitment to work on his issues, she would end the marriage. He believed her and this mattered to him (leverage).

Like many narcissists, Stephen begrudgingly made the initial appointment and agreed to a "few visits" with me. Please note in the case below in parentheses the use of the terms *empathic confrontation, leverage, limit setting* (mostly in keeping Stephen accountable and in touch with his emotional state), and *self-disclosure*.

The use of limited reparenting occurred throughout the session: in tone, pace, persistence, eye contact, gesture, "realness vs. robotic" style, helping him to tolerate the frustration and discomfort he was experiencing without pushing me away or running away, which is so typical of narcissists.

This is the fourth session:

> W. Hello Stephen. How are you today?
> S. (*hurried*) I am fine, but frankly, I agreed to a few sessions, and now we are on what, our fourth visit?
> W. Yes, it is our fourth session, and if you recall, we agreed that we would talk about a forward plan after this session. You look annoyed or something. What's going on Stephen?
> S. (*sigh, eye roll*) Yes . . . Whatever. (*Looks at his watch*) Fine.
> W. You say "fine" but it doesn't look or sound like it's fine with you. What is it? You seem upset or triggered.
> S. We're wasting time. Let's get on with your prognosis. I have to cut this short as I have a phone conference with Tokyo in an hour.
> W. I can appreciate that you are a very busy man and that you deal with a lot of pressure from your firm and your clients. As you said, it makes you irritable with people when they push you and don't appreciate you. But why do you think you would take that frustration out on me right now... right after "hello"? (*persistence/limit-setting*)
> S. This is ridiculous. I am sorry that I brought it up. I am *paying* for this, you know.
> W. Actually it is neither ridiculous nor a waste of money. And this is not meant to be critical of you, but I sense that this might be an example of what Linda describes as part of the ongoing hurt she feels whenever she tries to discuss something

personal with you. You brush her off, dismiss her, and become insulting about the subject matter. Years of this have led her to this decision where you could lose her. (*leverage*)

S. Oh God. (*sighs*)

W. Now I can feel it happening with me. Here's the difference, Stephen: I am trained to understand your makeup, so I don't take it personally. Fortunately, however, I am human and that that allows me the capacity to appreciate what it might be like to be in Linda's shoes. I know that in the world of your family, it was very important for you to meet the very high standards that your parents expected, even demanded, from you. They had little tolerance for your emotional experiences. I understand how this idea about how to live in the world may have worked for little Stephen – to survive in that family and to feel some sense of value – but in this chapter of your life it only serves to increase the erosion in your connection to Linda, your son, and other loved ones and to perpetuate the loneliness that little Stephen has always felt. You could ignore this. But you would be ignoring a profoundly important problem. Does this feel right to you? (*self-disclosure and empathic confrontation*)

S. (*quietly glowering*) Okay, I get it. I just don't see what the big deal is anyway. I think women are all just so sensitive. I mean, yes, you have a point. But I am who I am. She has known this from the beginning.

W. Stephen, let me ask you again: Why do you think you are using that harsh and demeaning tone with me right now? (*persistence/limit-setting*)

S. (*angry/loudly*) Because maybe I just don't want to talk about . . . you know . . . that emotional crap. It's not me! I am not Mr. Sensitive Renaissance Man.

W. I know you don't want to talk about it, but why do you think you are so angry? I may be sensitive, but I know you get this complaint from men too. It can't be that *everyone* is just too sensitive, right? And even if that were true, wouldn't you be even more careful with the sensitive people who care about you? (*persistence/leverage*)

S. I don't know. You tell me. You're the expert.

W. Maybe Stephen, it's exactly what you said: that you don't want to talk about the emotional "crap" . . . because you were never allowed to be that kind of boy or man. I think actually you just don't want to feel your emotions, the ones that you have just like everyone else. And you don't want me to see that vulnerable side of you because I might judge "that guy" or not be impressed with "him," or disappoint "him." You said yourself that you had to grow up fast . . . you didn't really get to be a child. And now you get upset when anyone tries to get to know that side of you. The side that you were taught was weak. How does that seem to you? (*empathic confrontation*)

S. (*hanging on every word, less angry*) What do you want me to say? That my parents were bad parents and I turned into an asshole? That my wife is going to just suddenly end a 25-year marriage, and my son will take her side? That my partners appreciate nothing I do, even though I work harder than everyone and have no time for myself? I just don't know what you want me to say.

W. I only want you to say what feels right to you . . . and what makes you so angry with me right this moment. There is no right or wrong answer. (*persistence*)

S. (*somber*) I just don't know what to do. I mean, I'm not intentionally taking it out on you. I tell Linda and Mark [his son] the same thing. Can't a guy get a little mad sometimes?

W. Of course you can get "mad" sometimes. Feeling and expressing your emotions – even anger – is fine. It's the way you do that and the impact on other people, people you care about, that allows you to be heard and accepted or dismissed and rejected. When you are critical, cynical, blaming, or aggressive, Linda gets so distracted by her hurt and the need to protect her feelings, that she cannot even hear your needs.

By the way, when you just said it was "not intentional," I don't think it was intentional either. I think it's your way of protecting yourself too, but the problem is that it pushes people away. By the way . . . was that an apology, Stephen? (*empathic confrontation*)

S. I guess. But it's certainly never good enough for Linda.

W. Perhaps because this is *not* a "sometimes" event. And because your apology lacks a spoken understanding of the impact you have on the other person when you act this way. You don't just express anger or the feelings you are having, Stephen. You become critical, disparaging, and dismissive, as if you are trying to push the other person away. Linda grew up with a very explosive father. She, like most people, but especially given her childhood, has a very hard time when someone she loves is yelling at her or putting her down. You would never let anyone else treat her that way and yet you don't seem to be willing to protect her from that bullying part of you. (*other disclosure/limit-setting*)

S. (*agreeable*) Well maybe that's just who I am.

W. Actually I don't believe it is *who* you are. I think its *how* you become when you get triggered – you know, when someone tries to get near that "emotional crap" (*smiling*). You have this side of you that emerges, acting as a guard, not allowing anyone to enter that part of your world. You either try to distract them with entertaining news stories, or you get angry and cut them off, or you disappear to some other stimulating activity like your word puzzles or your investments. But the goal is to cut off contact with that side of you – the feeling side, the vulnerable side, that precious, child like side. Hell, you told me you weren't allowed to play or be silly, giggle or cry as a little boy. It was a serious house with lots of toys but no one to play with. Your dad, who was barely around, had you immersed in competitive sports, music, and academic tutoring sessions from the age of five. Your mom was either involved in community affairs, depressed, overprotective, or smothering you but unaffectionate, and needed a lot of attention from you. Your brothers were shipped off to your granddad's farm each summer to play, to fish, and go boating with your granddad. But, Little Stephen, despite all of his "gifts," did not get the nurturing, unconditional love, and affection he needed. And so you learned to tuck him in where no one could see him, not even you. You experienced him as too lonely, and you became ashamed of his neediness and imperfectness. Does that feel right to you? (*empathic confrontation*)

S. (*cynically*) So you're saying that I developed a multiple personality?

W. No Stephen, I am saying that we all have modes or ways of being. I am describing the modes that helped you as a child – helped you to perform all that was expected of you. But today, those same modes, while helpful with your work and your high degree of determination to succeed, hurt you in other ways – as in relationships where people just want to *be with you and feel cared for by you*, not simply watch you perform or disappear. (*leverage*)

S. (*surprised, softer*) Oh.

W. We have to access little Stephen and then help him to get his needs met. There are ways to do this, but we have to get those guards out of the way. (*limit-setting*)

S. Even if I agree with you, what can you possibly do – magically rewrite my history? I am not a child anymore. This seems silly.

W. You're right. We cannot change your history, but we can change the way you hold the story in your mind. By taking better care of little Stephen – who is, by the way, still a part of you – we heal him, and this has a profound effect on your relationships with others, with Linda. You won't have to be burdened by old demands to keep hiding your emotions. Once you can feel him, you will learn how to appreciate how others feel too.

S. Linda says that narcissists have no empathy.

W. You have a hard time understanding and allowing yourself to experience your emotions. You become so ashamed of what you feel that you bury your vulnerability by blaming others and shutting down. (*empathic confrontation*) You first have to learn to understand your own emotional side and then it will be easier to understand others. In fact, right now it feels a little better between us, easier to talk. Can you sense it too?

S. (*looking uncomfortable*) Oh . . . I don't know . . . maybe, but I am not really sure what you mean.

W. Can you feel the fear or the loneliness? Linda says, as sad as it makes her feel, she could truly end this relationship. What is that like for Little Stephen? (*leverage*)

S. It sucks for him and for me.

W. Yes, I imagine it does. From that chair over there [therapist motions to another chair in the room where Stephen should sit] would you be willing to be "Little Stephen" and have him tell the Angry/Detached Stephen (*points to another chair opposite the "child" chair*) what he is feeling, in the first person?

S. (*moves into the chair, stammers a little*) Okay . . . Um . . . I guess I feel scared and I don't like being alone.

W. And what does he need?

S. (*as Lonely Child*) I don't know (*pause*) maybe some time to just be, uh, you know, some rest, somebody caring about me.

W. Yes, of course. Okay, now from that chair [directs Stephen to change seats] be the detached/guarded side of you – let's call him "Tough, Guarded Stephen" – who says feelings are silly and it isn't worth feeling them even if you were aware of them. And make the best case to "Little Stephen" that you can for why not.

S. (*moving to another chair*) Well . . . feeling bad makes you unproductive, and makes me drink a lot, and makes me uncomfortable. What's the point? And besides, I am not a little boy anymore.

W. Okay. Now I am going to play the part of the wiser and healthier side of Stephen and we'll call this side "Healthy Adult Stephen," and I will say to the Guard: "Yes, it's true that I have grown up, but it seems that when you are running the show I do self-defeating things like not focusing well at work, being hurtful and avoidant, and that's without any up-front awareness of my emotions. Seems that your job to cut off feelings is pretty tough, and I end up feeling worse and making poor choices anyway. But you keep trying to cover up all of my pain by bullying and blaming others and saying that I don't really care, and people are stupid and silly."

S. Yeah, but it could be even worse if I let myself be upset all the time.

W. (*in Healthy Stephen role*) True, but if I let myself really get to know the hurt I feel inside and I gain some true comfort and understanding, I will find relief and will not need to live in this seemingly transparent hiding place you created for me. It only leads me to the very outcome I dread – Linda leaving me.

S. I am not willing to sit around and cry all day and feel sorry for myself!

W. (*in Healthy Adult role*) I would not need to do that because Wendy, and Linda, and (me) "Healthy Stephen" will provide the comfort and caring to "Little Stephen," who needs support and acceptance of his feelings. We can help him to feel more secure and less lonely, help him to develop more confidence in being acceptable and lovable just for being him.

S. (*sounding more vulnerable*) Oh.

W. (*moves back to her original chair*) What are you feeling, Stephen?

S. A little weird.

W. (*smiles*) Actually, you sound a little more real, honest . . . like you belong in that chair (*points to the Child chair*). Okay – let's debrief for a moment. Stephen, would you please stand up for a second and take a look at these sides of you [points to the chairs] and tell me what you notice about them. What is it that we are up against here in our work?

S. (*clears his throat and straightens his tie*) Well, other than the foolishness of this imaginary game, I can see that the "Guard" is very tough and in charge of the decisions; and sometimes he is a quiet type and sometimes he is a big shot or a bully; and this is probably what you are trying to defeat, right?

W. And what do you think?

S. I guess so. Otherwise, I will keep doing the same thing, and that kid over there (*points to "Little Stephen" chair*) . . . he gets nothing.

W. Yes, that feels right to me too. We must help "Little Stephen" to feel lovable and connected to the people that want to love him, not for all the things *he does* but for who *he is*. . . . Good. Nice work, Stephen. I know this is hard for you. I am proud of you. How does that feel so far? Anything feel different already? (*limited reparenting*)

S. I think it feels right. And, you know, no one really ever stood up to me like you just did. I know I am not easy. But, this work won't be easy either! I can promise you that! (*Cheshire cat grin*)

W. No, it won't. But I am up for it if you are. We must agree to respect each other's rights and feelings even when it feels frustrating and scary. I can get frustrated at times too, Stephen. So this is also my responsibility and commitment to you, too. Is that a deal? (*limit-setting*)

S. (*reluctantly*) Yeah, yeah . . . Deal. But you probably have no idea what it's like in my world.

W. Are you asking me Stephen . . . if I get it?

S. No, I know you don't really.

W. Well, not exactly as you experience it. But I trust you will help me with that. I do know, however, something about the struggle to show others my needy and fragile side. I also had to learn how to tolerate and express my vulnerable side. (*self-disclosure*)

S. (*interested, nods*) Hmmm . . . Okay.

W. Okay – a little take-home practice. (*Stephen grimaces*) I am going to make an audio flash card and send it to your e-mail tonight. I would like you to listen to it daily, especially when you feel triggered to become bullying or you find yourself locked away in distractions.

(*Therapist takes out MP3 recorder and speaks into it. This can also be a written flash card.*)

Here's what I want to say:

"Hi Stephen, perhaps you are just checking in, or maybe you are feeling triggered and have found yourself under the influence of the 'Tough Guard' or the 'Big Shot.' Take a moment, and with eyes closed, see if you can feel your vulnerable feelings. See if you can see – and feel – 'Little Stephen'? Notice him. What does he need? Does he need some attention, some affection, understanding, holding? Imagine giving 'Little Stephen' what he needs – even if only for a few minutes. Notice what got you upset. What was the triggering event? How did you handle it? What needs to be repaired and with whom? Be sure to include some sense of how it feels for Linda or whoever might be on the receiving end of your anger, your bullying, or your detachment. Express remorse with an appreciation for the impact your behavior has on them . . . their experience . . . not to just get yourself off the hook. It is not your *fault* that you have these modes, but it is your *responsibility* to change them and to be accountable to the people who get hurt by them even though this is not your intention. Remember, it is the *how* you are that gets in your way and becomes unacceptable, not *who* you are."

Okay, Stephen?

S. Okay . . . Got it . . . Thanks . . . See you next week.

References

Behary, W.T. (2006) The art of empathic confrontation: working with the narcissistic client. *Psychotherapy Networker*, 75–81.

Behary, W.T. (2008a) *Disarming the Narcissist: Surviving and Thriving with the Self-absorbed*. Oakland, CA: New Harbinger.

Behary, W.T. (2008b) *Disarming the Narcissist*. www.disarmingthenarcissist.com.

Behary, W.T. and Dieckmann, E. (2011) Schema therapy for narcissism: the art of empathic confrontation, limit-setting, and leverage, in *The Handbook of Narcissism and Narcissistic Personality Disorder: Theoretical Approaches, Empirical Findings, and Treatments* (ed. W.K. Campbell and J.D. Miller). Hoboken, NJ: John Wiley & Sons, pp. 445–454.

Behary, W.T. and Dieckmann, E. (2011) Schema therapy for pathological narcissism: the art of adaptive re-parenting, in *Treating Pathological Narcissism* (ed. J.S. Ogrodniczuk). Washington, DC: American Psychological Association.

Kellogg, S.H. (2009) Schema therapy: a gestalt-oriented overview. *Gestalt, 10*. www.g-gej.org/10-1/schematherapy.html.

Ronningstam, E. (1998) *Identifying and Understanding the Narcissistic Personality*. New York: Oxford University Press.

Young, J.E. (1999) *Cognitive Therapy for Personality Disorders: a Schema-Focused Approach*, 3rd edition. Sarasota, FL: Professional Resource Exchange.

Young, J.E. and Behary, W.T. (1998) Schema-focused therapy for personality disorder, in *Treating Complex Cases* (eds N. Tarrier, A. Wells and G. Haddock). Chichester: John Wiley & Sons.

Young, J.E. and Brown, G. (2001) *Young Schema Questionnaire: Special Edition*. New York: Schema Therapy Institute.

Young, J.E. and First, M. (2004) *Schema Therapy: an Integrative Therapy for Personality Change*. www.schematherapy.com.

Young, J.E. and Flanagan, C. (1998) Schema-focused therapy for narcissistic patients, in *Disorders of Narcissism* (ed. E.F. Ronningstam). Washington, DC: American Psychiatric Press.

Young, J.E. and Klosko, J.S. (1993) *Reinventing Your Life*. New York: Plume.

Young, J.E., Klosko, J.S. and Weishaar, M. (2003) *Schema Therapy: a Practitioner's Guide*. New York: Guilford Press.

3
Assessment for Schema Therapy

Anoek Weertman and Hilde de Saeger

Assessment for psychotherapy, and in particular Schema Therapy (ST), is a process that usually follows implicit rules and knowledge. Empirical data supporting differential selection and treatment planning on the basis of personality factors are scarce (Verheul, 2007). In general, one usually first determines whether someone is eligible for psychotherapy, and if so, which form of psychotherapy may be most applicable to this individual. This chapter mainly focuses on the indicators that may determine whether ST is chosen. Indicators useful in determining setting (outpatient, day treatment, or inpatient) and format (individual or group therapy) will also be discussed. The indicators discussed in this chapter are drawn both from current research literature and clinical experience. Although there is no straightforward scientific proof for the use of these indicators (see Critchfield and Benjamin, 2006), there is indirect scientific support in the sense that the majority of these indicators are used in studies that investigate and show the effectiveness of ST (Svartberg, Stiles and Sletzer, 2004; Giesen-Bloo et al., 2006; Weertman and Arntz, 2007). These research results indicate that patients with DSM-IV (APA, 1994) diagnosed borderline and Cluster C personality disorder may be applicable for ST. No systematic research has been conducted with regard to the other personality disorders. There are, however, case studies of other Cluster B and Cluster A personality disorders, and there is no reason why ST should not be used for other Cluster B disorders when the indicators discussed later in this chapter are met. It is, however, not possible to make a good assessment on the basis of DSM-IV classifications only. Several authors agree that besides DSM-IV classifications, factors such as motivation, mental capacity, and ego-strength play an important part in the decision to include a patient for a particular psychotherapy (Vermote, 2006). In order to take these factors into account, complementary diagnostics, including structural diagnostics, are often necessary.

The Wiley Blackwell Handbook of Schema Therapy: Theory, Research, and Practice, First Edition.
Edited by Michiel van Vreeswijk, Jenny Broersen, and Marjon Nadort.
© 2012 John Wiley & Sons, Ltd. Published 2015 by John Wiley & Sons, Ltd.

Indicators for Schema Therapy

1. Possible existing Axis I disorders do not interfere with treatment focusing on personality problems, or have already been treated.
2. Patient and therapist agree that the core of the patient's problems have to do with long-standing, repeated patterns of thinking, feeling, and behaving, traceable to the patient's youth. The therapy will therefore mainly focus on changing these well-established patterns.
3. The patient is motivated to commit to long-term treatment.
4. Due to the active role of the Schema Therapist, Schema Therapy is, in terms of the Big Five, suited both to patients who are very open and patients who are very introverted. The structure that the therapist brings provides containment to patients who are very open, while offering a safe environment in which the therapist's active approach enables more introverted individuals to slowly open up.

> Maisy is a 45-year-old woman who self-refers with recurrent complaints of depression, a strong sense of defectiveness, problems with decision-making, and dependency on others. She finds it difficult to stand up for herself, puts herself last, and is very afraid of losing others. In the past, she has had several forms of therapy for depression. Cognitive behavioral therapy has proven most helpful, but her sense of defectiveness and dependency has remained unchanged. She has had these feelings for as long as she can remember.
>
> Maisy is the youngest of three children. As a child she was, on the one hand, unwanted (she was born out of wedlock), and on the other, overprotected. She was always told that she was good for nothing and has always worked beneath her capacity. She has always relied heavily on her mother, who tried to protect her. In friendships, and also in relationships with men, she is very easily influenced. She lived in a cult for years and could only get out when a new leader figure came into her life. During the periods she was alone, when there was no one to lean on, she became depressed. Based on the DSM-IV, a relapsed depressive disorder was diagnosed plus a dependent personality disorder. Through therapy she wants to learn how to prevent a new depressive episode and become more self-confident and independent, less doubtful, and regain the feeling that she can cope with life on her own.

Contraindications

It is generally advised that if a patient is diagnosed with Axis I conditions that have not yet been treated, they should be addressed with evidence-based techniques before continuing with ST. Contra-assessments include:

1. Severe Axis I complaints that make a treatment focused on a personality disorder impossible (e.g., severe mood disorders, severe addiction that requires detoxification,

psychological disorders, or severe eating disorders). In any of these cases it is preferable to treat the Axis I disorder first, before considering ST.
2. Disorders that make it difficult to diagnose a personality disorder (e.g., developmental disorders such as ADHD, autism, or a form of autism). According to van Genderen and Arntz (2005), developmental disorders complicate treatment with ST because ST is based on the belief that the development of the patient may be disrupted or stagnated, otherwise normal development would have been possible.
3. When patients cannot bear any deregulations and when severe destructive behavior is present, such as self-injurious behavior or suicidal tendencies.

> Diana is a 20-year-old woman, who is referred following several suicide attempts. She has severe mood swings and feelings of gloominess and emptiness. She is very impulsive, often quarrels with others, and changes jobs frequently. She uses alcohol to temper her mood. Furthermore, she reports sleeping problems: difficulty falling asleep and staying asleep, and nightmares. She has self-injured since she was 11 years old. She reports that there is very little that she likes, she has a great need for stimulation, and is bored all the time. She says that alcohol and drugs make her feel alive and fill the emptiness, besides dealing with her low moods. She also states that she has no control over herself whatsoever. She doesn't always feel so bad, and that is why she has never had structured help. She has always walked out of therapy prematurely.
>
> The patient grew up in a very unsafe, criminal environment, where she was emotionally neglected by her mother and emotionally abused by her father. She often witnessed emotional and physical abuse of her mother by her father. Both parents were often under the influence of alcohol or drugs. Diana decided early on that she couldn't trust others and she avoids intimacy. On the other hand, she has a tendency to feel strongly dependent and make herself dependent. In terms of DSM-IV, she presents with a dependency on several substances, a depressive disorder, recrudescence, and a borderline disorder with dependency tendencies. For Diana, a treatment primarily focused on emotion regulation and the prevention of giving in to impulse (e.g. a Linehan treatment) seems appropriate in the short term. Her motivation in terms of committing to a long-term treatment program fluctuates strongly. She has no idea that her problems have to do with her personality development.

Setting indicators

With regard to the setting and frequency of ST, the same factors are taken into consideration as for psychotherapy in general. Until now, only individual ST has been scientifically researched and shown to be effective. Although its use is widespread in the Netherlands, there has thus far been no research on the relative efficacy of day treatment and inpatient settings. The assessment for day treatment and inpatient settings is therefore based on clinical knowledge and experience, but is not yet scientifically supported. Currently, there is most evidence for the effectiveness of individual ST. Sessions are required more than weekly for severe personality problems such as borderline personality disorder (Dutch Work Council personality disorders, concept version, 2008).

The severity of the problems, the length and severity of the symptoms, lack of effect of previous treatment, the number of areas of functioning that are affected, social roles (still working, caring for children, partner, parents), and the quality of the social network strongly influence the choice for outpatient, day treatment, or inpatient setting. Severe problems and a lack of social roles or social network point toward treatment in a (day) inpatient setting, whereas less severe symptoms and the existence of social roles and a social network, point to outpatient ST. As far as the choice of format (individual or group) is concerned, there is a difference between ST in an outpatient group and ST in a (day) inpatient group setting, whether or not combined with individual ST. The choice of setting often corresponds with the choice of format in the sense that most (day) inpatient ST treatments are carried out in groups. Where an outpatient ST is concerned, it is important to estimate to which degree the patient is capable of learning from others and can feel safe enough to benefit from group treatments. In cases of severe trauma that must be worked through individually, and where there is also extreme distrust, group ST is not recommended.

When forming groups, the schedules of individual patients have to be taken into account. For instance, including several patients who score high in the domain of Impaired Limits can cause a great feeling of insecurity in a group. ST is mainly an individually focused treatment, even when given in a group. Therefore, fewer demands are made on the patients with regard to the issues concerning the division of attention, the ability to learn from others and increase of contact, than within most other group psychotherapeutic settings such as psychodynamic group psychotherapy.

Alternatives to Schema Therapy

If a therapist thinks that therapy focused on personality disorder is indicated, but the patient has no insight into his problems and the effect of a treatment focused on personality, it is advisable to consider an initial evaluation. This may consist of motivational talks or an initial evaluation where the patient and the therapist map out the problem, for instance by forming a holistic theory to give the patient more insight into what he needs in treatment. When a patient still tends to externalize his behavior, an initial evaluation group can be very helpful, because a patient is confronted with his problems and his role in them to a greater degree in a group as opposed to in individual contact. In an initial evaluation group, shame can be conquered and recognition and acknowledgment can lead to motivation for further ST.

When the emphasis is on problems with impulse control and destructiveness, and patients cannot bear deregulation (i.e., are very sensitive to crises), both dialectic behavior therapy (DBT) and mentalization-based treatment (MBT) are good options. Furthermore, STEPP (Systems Training for Emotional Predictability and Problem-Solving) may be considered. This treatment is especially indicated when there is a severe emotion regulation problem and the patient has no opportunity whatsoever to enter a therapeutic alliance or is incapable of self-reflection. This can be the case when dealing with severe Axis I disorders, such as drug abuse or psychotic disorders, or in those with limited cognitive ability.

This is not to suggest that ST is applicable for everyone diagnosed with a personality disorder. It is an intensive treatment that should be considered only when less drastic and less costly treatment methods do not meet the needs of the patient.

Approach

A thorough intake assessment is needed for diagnosis and treatment planning. The most important terms and measurements associated with the decision process are discussed below. Before examining the current approach further, the use of categorical diagnoses according to the DSM-IV (American Psychiatric Association, 1994) combined with structural diagnoses deserves further explanation. The DSM-IV is the most widely used classification system for personality disorders in current inpatient practice. The advantage of using DSM-IV is therefore that it simplifies communication and it is widely accepted that there are sufficiently reliable and valid instruments available to diagnose personality disorders using DSM-IV. However, there are also disadvantages, two of which will be discussed here:

1. DSM-IV only includes a limited "coverage" of patients with personality disorders. Many people who experience problems with their personality do not qualify for a formal Axis II classification;
2. There are often big and meaningful differences between patients with the same classifications (Verheul, 2007).

The classification itself is seldom sufficient for treatment planning. In addition to the classification, information about (among other factors) the severity of the disorder, psychiatric comorbidity, the presence of psychological skills, and contextual factors (e.g., the social support system) can be helpful when selecting the most effective and efficient treatment program (Dutch Work Council personality disorders, concept version, 2008). Information about these factors is required in order to make an assessment regarding the format and setting of the ST.

The most commonly used model for intake and assessment combines an unstructured clinical interview, a semi-structured interview, and questionnaires.

Unstructured clinical interview

The unstructured clinical interview serves several purposes:

1. to clarify complaint(s), estimate the severity of the complaint;
2. to clarify the request for help;
3. to collect information about relevant biographical data, such as family background, current social situation, working situation, traumas;
4. to gain insight into the quality of personal relationships;
5. to estimate frustration tolerance, impulse control, and level of anxiety;

6. to gain insight into the individual's ability in terms of self-awareness and motivation;
7. to examine the possibilities for increased contact.

Besides collecting data from questionnaires, the interviewer also has the important task of connecting with the patient during the intake assessment, as well as conducting test interventions. Connecting is conducted from a non-directive standpoint, with acceptance, empathy, and authenticity. This serves to establish a secure relationship and examine the possibility for a stronger therapeutic alliance. Test interventions can consist of confrontation (indicating inconsistencies), interpretation (demonstrating connections), or clarification. The whole array of mainly directive interventions has the purpose of examining whether the patient can make a disturbance in the pathological balance, productive in relation to the problems, and that within the given cooperation (Cornelissen, 1993). In short, the goal is to establish to what extent a patient can benefit from psychotherapy, whether more supportive and structural interventions are necessary, or if a more open approach can be used. For example, does someone have a stable self-image, and can drug abuse be stopped?

The manner in which somebody makes initial contact is also an important factor. Which position does the individual take? Is the patient comfortable with closeness? Is there reciprocity and a growing therapeutic alliance? These are all important questions that cannot be answered from questionnaires or semi-structured interviews, but the answers may become clear in a less structured intake assessment.

Semi-structured interviews

Semi-structured interviews are preferable when assessing the reliability and efficiency of DSM-IV disorders. The use of semi-structured interviews raises the possibility of questioning DSM-IV disorders efficiently, by which information about the severity, duration, and frequency of the symptoms can be ascertained. This prevents overdiagnosis. In the Netherlands, as well as in the international literature, the structured interview for the assessment of DSM-IV Axis I disorders (SCID-I: First, Spitzer, Gibbon and Williams, 1996; Dutch translation: van Groenestijn, Akkerhuis, Kupka, Schneider and Nolen, 1999) and the structured clinical interview for the assessment of DSM-IV Axis II disorders (SCID-II: First, Spitzer, Gibbon, Williams and Benjamin, 1997; Dutch translation: Weertman, Arntz and Kerkhofs, 2000) are frequently used. SCID-I systematically asks about the following Axis I disorders: mood episodes, psychotic and related symptoms, psychotic differentiation, mood differentiation, drug abuse, anxiety disorders, somatoform disorders, eating disorders, adjustment disorder, and several other disorders. SCID-II consists of modules for all 11 personality disorders, where the questions are classified according to disorder. Furthermore, an appendix for depressive personality disorder and passive aggressive personality disorder is added.

Questionnaires

In addition to unstructured and semi-structured interviews, questionnaire research can be done. For example, the NEO-PI-R (Dutch adaption: Hoekstra, Ornel and de

Fruyt, 1996) is often used to measure the five personality dimensions according to the Big Five. Within these five dimensions, six important aspects that define the dimension in question are measured. It has a total of 30 scales. The value of using the NEO-PI-R is that this tool is not specifically developed to measure the pathological aspects of personality. It also highlights the healthy facets of the personality that are relevant for the assessment. For instance, conscientiousness is admitted in the NEO-PI-R. This factor provides a good assessment of someone's level of persistence, which is essential in psychotherapy.

A still relatively unknown inventory is the Severity Index for Personality Pathology (SIPP; Andrea *et al.*, 2007). This is a self-report index used to measure the generic and variable components of personality disorders. It consists of 118 questions, grouped into 16 facets: frustration tolerance, emotional regulation, self-control, aggression regulation, stable self-image, capacity for self-reflection, self-respect, feeling appreciated, respect for others, giving meaning, joy, cooperation, intimacy, long-term relationships, responsibility, and reliability. With this tool an individual's adaptive and less adaptive personality features may be mapped out.

The Minnesota Multiphasic Personality Inventory (MMPI; Dutch adaption: Derksen, Sloor, Mey and Hellenbosch, 1993) is also frequently used to measure personality characteristics. Current inventories used to assess conditions are the Symptom Checklist (SCL-90; Dutch adaption: Arrindell and Ettema, 2003) and the abridged version of the SCL-90, the Brief Symptom Inventory (BSI; Dutch adaption: de Beurs, 2004).

The choice of inventories is large and depends on the availability and knowledge of the researcher.

Complementary diagnostics

When the use of ST is indicated and the patient has accepted this decision, specific diagnostics can be made. In the case of ST, at the very least the schema and mode inventories (as described in Part II, Chapter 5) are used following the assessment. When the assessment shows that clinical schema treatment is required, it is preferable to map out the personality structure in more detail. To do this, projective material can be used. In an inpatient setting, the personality structure is always examined in great detail, because the inpatient environment has such a regressive character that it is not applicable for ego-weak patients. An obsessive-compulsive personality disorder, according to DSM-IV, can serve to hold together the ego-functions of a weakly structured patient. If this patient is challenged to let go of disruptive schemas too soon, he could become psychotic. The structural diagnostic serves to expose the strength and weakness of the individual's personality structure to the therapist at an early stage.

If necessary, IQ can also be assessed. To benefit from intensive psychotherapy, an individual must have sufficient intellectual capacities. An IQ of less than 80 is regarded as problematic. Psychotherapy is about letting go of old patterns and acquiring new ones. Furthermore, it is important that a patient can make his own connections and has sufficient integrative capacities. In someone with an IQ below 80 these skills are often poorly developed.

Pitfalls and Tips

As argued earlier in this chapter, classification alone says little about assessment because other factors, such as impulse control, anxiety level, motivation, and treatment preferences, all play an important role. Assessment in person rather than by written questionnaire is essential. It is important to pay attention to improve congruence between what a patient asks for and what kind of treatment is offered. Furthermore, it is essential to explain both the treatment and how the treatment choice was made. Bearing in mind that motivation for treatment is a predictor of success, the importance of this should not be underestimated. (Dutch Work Council personality disorders, concept version, 2008). Both a lack of good diagnostics and unnecessary burdening of the patient with diagnostics should be avoided. A multi-step model is preferable.

The Future

As far as the authors are aware, to date there have been no evidence-based models for assessment regarding personality disorders. There is a literature in which general guidelines for assessment are discussed but this is not focused on specific disorders. For example, in the Systematic Treatment Selection (STS) model of Beutler, Moleiro, and Talebi (2002) general principles of change are described and this model serves as a guideline for clinicians to develop extended treatment methods. Cape and Parry (2000) have developed a set of guidelines used to allocate adult patients to the most appropriate psychological treatment. It is not known if these models can be applied to personality disorders. Currently, van Manen and colleagues (submitted for publication) are researching a clinical decision model that can help select the most (cost-) effective psychotherapeutic treatment for patients with personality disorders. Similar research into choice of therapeutic context, setting, frequency, and duration is still in an early stage merits priority.

References

American Psychiatric Association (1994) *Diagnostic and Statistical Manual of Mental Disorders*, 4th edition. Washington DC: American Psychiatric Association.

Andrea, H., Verheul, R., Berghout, C. *et al.* (2007) Measuring the core components of maladaptive personality: Severity Indices of Personality Problems (SIPP-118). *Report of the Viersprong Institute for Studies on Personality Disorders (VISPD), in Cooperation with the Department of Medical Psychology and Psychotherapy*, Erasmus University Rotterdam, the Netherlands.

Arrindell, W.A. and Ettema, J.H.M. (2003) *Symptom Checklist, SCL-90*. Lisse: Swets & Zeitlinger.

Beutler, L.E., Moleiro, C. and Talebi, H. (2002) How practitioners can systematically use empirical evidence in treatment selection. *Journal of Clinical Psychology*, 58, 119–212.

Cape, J. and Parry, G. (2000) Clinical practice guidelines development in evidence based psychotherapy in *Evidence-based Counselling and Psychological Therapies* (eds N. Rowland and S. Goss). London: Routledge, pp. 171–190.

Cornelissen, C.L.M. (1993) Het eerste gesprek: indicatiestelling en selectie, in *Handboek Groepspsychotherapie* (eds T.J.C. Berk, M.P. Bolten, E. Gans and H.G.Y. Koksma). Houten: Bohn Stafleu Van Loghum.

Critchfield, K.L. and Benjamin, L.S. (2006) Integration of therapeutic factors in treating personality disorders, in *Principles of Therapeutic Change that Work* (eds L.G. Castonguay and L.E. Beutler). London: Oxford University Press.

De Beurs, E. (2004) *Brief Symptom Inventory, Handleiding.* Leiden, Nederland.

Derksen, J.J.L., Sloor, H., de Mey, H.R.A. and Hellenbosch, G. (1993) *MMPI-2 Handleiding bij Afname, Scoring en Interpretatie.* Nijmegen: PEN.

Dutch Work Council personality disorder (Werkgroep richtlijn persoonlijkheidsstoornissen) (2008, January) *Multidisciplinaire Richtlijn Persoonlijkheidsstoornissen: Richtlijn voor de Diagnostiek en Behandeling van Volwassen Patiënten met een Persoonlijkheidsstoornis.* Uitgever: Trimbos-Instituut, Utrecht.

First, M.B., Spitzer, R.L., Gibbon, M. and Williams, J.B.W. (1996) *Structured Clinical Interview for DSM-IV Axis I Disorders (SCID-I).* Patient edition (SCID-I/P, Version 2.0). New York: Biometric Research Department.

First, M.B., Spitzer, R.L., Gibbon, M., Williams, J.B.W. and Benjamin, L. (1997) *Structured Clinical Interview for DSM-IV Personality Disorders (SCID-II).* Washington, DC: American Psychiatric Press.

Genderen, H. van and Arntz, A. (2005) *Schemagerichte Cognitieve Therapie bij Borderline Persoonlijkheidsstoornis.* Amsterdam: Uitgeverij Nieuwezijds.

Giesen-Bloo, J., Van Dyck, R., Spinhoven, P. *et al.* (2006) Outpatient psychotherapy for borderline personality disorder: randomized trial of schema-focused therapy vs. transference focused psychotherapy. *Archives of General Psychiatry,* 63, 649–658.

Groenestijn, M.A.C., Akkerhuis, G.W., Kupka, R.W. *et al.* (1999) *Gestructureerd Klinisch Interview voor de vaststelling van DSM-IV Axis I stoornissen.* Lisse: Swets Test.

Hoekstra, H.A., Ornel, J. and de Fruyt, F. (1996) *NEO Persoonlijkheidsvragenlijst.* Lisse: Swets & Zeitlinger.

Manen, J.G. van, Kamphuis, J.H., Visbach, G.T. *et al.* (in press) In search of patient characteristics that may guide empirically based treatment selection for personality disorder patients – A concept map approach. *Journal of Personality Disorders.*

Svartberg, M., Stiles, T.C. and Sletzer, M.H. (2004) Randomized, controlled trial of the effectiveness of short-term dynamic psychotherapy and cognitive therapy for Cluster C personality disorders. *American Journal of Psychiatry,* 161, 810–817.

Verheul, R. (2007) Klinische bruikbaarheid van dimensies versus categorieën in de diagnostiek van persoonlijkheidsstoornissen, in *De Toekomst van Persoonlijkheidsstoornissen: Diagnostiek, Behandeling en Beleid* (eds R. Verheul and J.H. Kamphuis). Houten; Bohn Stafleu van Loghum.

Vermote, R. (2006) Indicatiestelling bij borderline persoonlijkheidsstoornis: bevindingen vanuit de psychodynamisch psychotherapeutische kliniek en onderzoek, in *Tot de Puzzel Past, Psychodiagnostiek in Methodiek en Praktijk* (eds P. Claes, P. Bijttebier, T. Vercruysse, L. Hamelinck and E. De Bruyn). Leuven: Acco.

Weertman, A. and Artnz, A. (2007) Effectiveness of treatment of childhood memories in cognitive therapy for personality disorders: a controlled study contrasting methods focusing on the present and methods focusing on childhood memories. *Behaviour Research and Therapy,* 45, 2133–2143.

Weertman, A., Arntz, A. and Kerkhofs, M. (2000) *Gestructureerd Klinisch Interview voor DSM-IV Persoonlijkheidsstoornissen.* Lisse: Swets Test.

4
The Use of Experiential Techniques for Diagnostics

Anoek Weertman

The use of experiential techniques is a key feature of Schema Therapy (ST) and a way in which this therapy clearly distinguishes itself from traditional cognitive behavioral therapy. The rational vision that lies behind the use of experiential techniques is the hypothesis that schemas are formed in early youth, often in the period in which the child is not yet capable of fully verbalizing experiences (see Beck *et al.*, 2004, p. 89; see also Arntz and Weertman, 1999). This lack of verbalization becomes apparent in the diagnostic stage of ST; patients are often not capable of expressing their schemas in words. If the verbalization of schemas is difficult, a diagnosis based solely on self-report is not sufficient. Furthermore, patients often have little perception of their own functioning, because of the ego-syntonic character of schemas. It is therefore difficult for them to clearly express their problems. Experiential techniques are tools that make the schemas and schema modes immediately visible in the therapy room. In addition, experiential techniques are also helpful when there is a reasonable recognition of schemas, but when the schemas are not felt intensely. Experiential techniques can be useful, for example, in determining to what extent a patient is capable of experiencing emotions.

In Practice

In this chapter, experiential techniques described in literature, and, as far as is known, most commonly used in practice, will be discussed. Given that the use of experiential techniques is still under development, the overview is not complete. When using experiential techniques, it is essential to follow the process of the patient and help him come closer to often difficult emotions rather than to rigidly follow concrete guidelines for the application of these techniques. Therefore, working with experiential techniques requires a high degree of flexibility and insight in the therapist's approach. Furthermore, it is important that the therapist is capable of dealing with extreme emotions and is aware of not avoiding these emotions as expressed by the patient. Several techniques are discussed further by means of concrete steps and case histories.

Approach

The therapeutic alliance

The therapeutic alliance may be the most experiential element of therapy because the patient has all kinds of experiences directly in the presence of the therapist. At the same time the therapist directly experiences the schemas of the patient while being in contact with him.

During the diagnostic stage, the therapeutic alliance requires more attention for a number of reasons:

1. During the first sessions, an important start is made in building the therapeutic alliance.
2. When the therapist starts to work with the therapeutic alliance from the beginning of the diagnostic stage, the patient will become familiar with this and it will be a rational part of further treatment.
3. What happens within the therapeutic alliance and how patients react to interventions focused on the therapeutic alliance provides a lot of information that is important for diagnostics.

(For the meaning of the therapeutic alliance and its structure in ST, see Young, Klosko and Weishaar, 2005, pp. 187–217; van Genderen and Arntz, 2005, pp. 45–62).

In ST, empathic confrontation and limited reparenting are the two main characteristics of the therapeutic alliance. In ST, it is assumed that the old maladaptive schemas will be activated within the therapeutic alliance. In this sense, ST is no different from psychodynamic-oriented therapies.

An important difference that sets ST apart from psychodynamic psychotherapy is that the therapist openly and immediately discusses what is happening within the therapeutic alliance and refers to this in terms of schemas, modes, and coping styles (see Young *et al.*, 2005). Although there is much more to add regarding the therapeutic alliance in ST, this chapter is primarily about how to use the therapeutic alliance as a diagnostic tool. The primary focus is *to give meaning to what happens within the therapeutic alliance in terms of Schema Therapy*.

The therapist can put the therapeutic alliance into action as a diagnostic tool by:

1. *Observation of the behavior of the patient within the therapeutic alliance.* Through observation, the therapist acquires data about the patient's schema.
2. *Checking what the therapist himself experiences while in contact with the patient.* It is relevant that the therapist internalizes the emotions, thoughts, and behaviors

the patient evokes, and checks which possible schemas are triggered by the therapist.
3. *Discussion with the patient about what will happen in the therapeutic relationship.* If a patient's schema is activated in the therapeutic alliance, the therapist can help the patient diagnose which schema this is. Through questioning, the therapist can then examine what has happened. Possible questions are:
   – *What exactly happened? (e.g., what did the therapist do?)*
   – *What did the patient think about that, what did he feel, and what was his reaction in terms of his behavior?*
   – *To check the patient's coping style, did he surrender to his schema, avoid it, or over compensate?*
4. *By starting limited reparenting, and by observing how the patient reacts to this, the therapist can estimate what the needs of the patient are.* From the first meeting onward, the therapist will structure the contact through limited reparenting in the form of emphatic reacting, validating, structuring, and restricting, through which the therapist can measure the patient's reactions to the different interventions.

Below is a case study of a discussion with the patient about what happens in the therapeutic alliance. The patient is a 39-year-old woman who has recently formed a

---

T: I notice that you say very little about your contact with Jonathan, although this relationship is still very important to you.
P: Yes, that's right. I would rather not discuss it with you at all.
T: Can you tell me a bit more about why you don't want to talk to me about it?
P: Well, I just don't want to. I don't think it's necessary. I would rather talk about the problems that I have at work.
T: And what do you notice about me?
P: You are asking more and more questions. The less I say, the more you ask.
T: What do you think when I keep asking you about your relationship?
P: That I want to keep it to myself. That it is none of your business.
T: Mmm. Anything else on your mind?
P: It feels like you are my mother. She also always wanted to know everything. I was not allowed to keep anything to myself, and definitely not when it was about boyfriends. And if I did say something, and took them home with me, she acted so horribly that she always ruined it for me, and those boyfriends would never come to my place again. It was as if she begrudged me having a boyfriend.
T: And when we talk about Jonathan, does it feel the same as it used to with your mother?
P: Yes, then I get the feeling that you want to take it away from me, even though I somehow know that it is not true.
T: But apparently it feels that way. How exactly do you feel?
P: I cut myself off, but I'm also angry, angry that you keep nagging.
T: You feel angry, and you notice that you are cutting yourself off. Do you feel anything else, or is this the most important feeling?
P: I am also afraid – afraid that this relationship will fail too.

relationship with a new boyfriend (Jonathan). She is very nervous about this relationship, and is often preoccupied with it. When the therapist asks her how things are going, her answers are very brief.

If what happened becomes clear within the therapeutic alliance, the therapist can choose to explore with the patient the situation that was triggered from the past. In the example above, the therapist can ask how the mother reacted, what she did, and how the patient experienced that. Next, the therapist and the patient can check in which situations this continues and see if it can be expressed in schema terms. In the example above, this could work by continuing to ask questions about the mother who deliberately made the patient look like a fool when she took not only boyfriends but any friends home. This resulted in social isolation, but also nourished her Mistrust schema.

Guided imagery

The goal of guided imagery is similar to that of other experiential techniques in the assessment phase, namely the easier assessment and instinctive experiencing of core schemas and modes. In addition, guided imagery is specifically useful in terms of gaining a perception and understanding of the origin of schemas and modes. By going back from the present to situations from childhood that have contributed to the entrenchment of the schemas, a link between the recent problems and the source in childhood can be made (see also Young *et al.*, 2005, p. 129). Different versions of guided imagery are described. However, the basic steps are discussed below. Variations are possible, depending on the experience of the therapist and the effect on the individual patient.

1. Explain what you are going to do.
2. Ask the patient to relax, sit straight up, feet on the floor, shoulders relaxed.
3. Ask the patient to imagine a safe place from the present or the past, real or imagined.
4. Ask the patient to recall a strong emotion in his current life.
5. From that feeling, ask for a situation in their childhood (as young as possible) in which the patient had similar feelings.
6. Ask the patient to return to the safe place.
7. Evaluate.

For more details of step 1–6, see Arntz and Weertman (1999), Young *et al.* (2005), and van Genderen and Arntz (2005). Below is a fragment of an evaluation of guided imagery (step 7).

> The patient is a 45-year-old man who says he has had sleeping problems for his whole life. He does everything he can to delay going to sleep, and if he sleeps, he often wakes very early. He regularly suffers from nightmares. During an imagery session, a memory comes up that his father, after too much drinking, regularly got into his bed, and then pushed him out. His father was also often aggressive during the day.

T:	Well, what did you think about it?
P:	Pff, I suddenly felt that fear and alertness again.
T:	Can you still feel that here and now, that you have to be alert, because otherwise you can be caught unexpectedly?
P:	Yes, actually I'm always on my guard. I am now. I know exactly how I could get away from here. Whenever I enter a place, I always look for the escape route first. Not so much at home, but I think I sleep badly because my father often comes back in my nightmares and beats me up.
T:	I think that the feeling of alertness that you have described and that bothers you so much if you can't sleep, goes very well with your Mistrust and/or Abuse schema. And I think the situation with your father that has just come to light is a very clear example of a situation that underlies that schema. A child's bed should be a truly safe place, and that basic form of safety was not there for you.

Role-play

Role-play often assists both the patient and the therapist to gain more insight into the patient's (coping) behavior, and what this behavior evokes in the other. It is perhaps an open door, but role-play is not applicable for situations in which physical contact or threat took place. In these instances, the same steps are followed as for the treatment with role-play, but the phases of role-reversal and practice of the new behavior are omitted. The goal is not to change, but to acquire insight into the behavior, thoughts, and emotions of the patient. To be quite clear, the steps of role-play during the assessment are summarized here:

1. Pre-discussion of the situation: the therapist briefly explains the purpose of the role-play and the patient gives instructions to the therapist for his role.
2. The original situation is repeated whereby the patient plays himself and the therapist plays the other.
3. Evaluation about what the patient has experienced during the role-play. What did he feel, think, and do? Do these situations occur more often? What did the other do?
4. The therapist tells the patient what he noticed about the behavior of the patient and checks if the patient recognizes this. If he does, a check is made to see whether this behavior can be placed within ST terms.

Role-reversal is not normally used during the assessment phase, because patients can find it very confrontational to see themselves played by someone else. Therefore, it is very important that the therapeutic alliance is safe enough. However, if the patient has no insight into his own behavior, it may sometimes be necessary to switch roles, whereby the patient plays the other person and the therapist plays the patient. Afterward, it is again important to evaluate what the patient experienced in the role of the other.

> David is a 29-year-old man and during his first sessions he is mainly very socially adapted in his contact with the therapist. He scores very highly on the Subjugation schema, often choosing relationships in which he submits himself and crosses his own boundaries strongly. Even so, he still gets into conflicts on a regular basis. To get a clearer view on this, the therapist suggests a role-play with reference to a recent incident at work. The patient briefly describes the situation, and instructs the therapist on the role as a colleague. During the role-reversal, it is noticeable that the patient leans forward, coming across as very forceful, and not allowing the therapist to have his say. This provokes irritation in the therapist in his role as a colleague. In the evaluation, the patient recognizes that he doesn't allow the other to speak and that he keeps a tight control over the conversation. When the therapist confronts him with his feelings and thoughts, he realizes that he was mainly very afraid, afraid to have to adapt to the other (Subjugation schema). In order to prevent that, he starts to dominate and control (Over-Compensation schema). In this way, the role-play offers a good overview of the fact that, besides the Subjugation schema, he also uses the Over-Compensation schema as a coping style for his Subjugation schema. This had not become clear within the therapeutic alliance.

Chair work

Chair work is used within the treatment of a borderline personality disorder in order to break loose from the punishing or protecting mode (van Genderen and Arntz, 2005, p. 95). This technique is less often used for assessment purposes (although it can be). The technique is especially applicable if the patient has conflicting feelings. This can be seen in his behavior (e.g., having no trust in therapy, but still attending the session), as an incongruence in feeling and thinking. Often these patients report that they know something rationally (e.g., that they are worthwhile), but that it doesn't feel that way. Chair work is often used to show these different aspects and gain more insight into the different modes. This is achieved by asking the patient to repeatedly switch chairs when he expresses another aspect, most of the time another mode, of himself. By literally changing seats, it is easier for the patient to let go of certain aspects of himself and in that way to make a better separation between different modes or schemas.

An example of the use of chair work as an assessment tool:

> The patient is a 38-year-old woman, who said in her third session that she wanted to stop her therapy. Accordingly, the therapist explores the feelings and thoughts of this mode and checks with the patient whether there are more sides to name.
>
> P: Therapy is not helping me. I am restricted; my father cannot handle emotions. It is all useless.

> T: It seems that you have made up your mind beforehand that the therapy will not work.
> P: Yes, that's right. Why would it work, lead to something? I'm already a failure. (*Said angrily*)
> T: You look angry when you say this.
> P: Yes, that's how I feel. It is all useless anyway.
> T: I suggest that we try to map out your feelings about this therapy a bit more. We can do that by putting different feelings in different chairs. Is that OK for you?
> P: As long as I don't have to talk to a chair. I won't do a stupid thing like that.
> T: You don't have to do that yet. I only want to ask you to switch chairs to make it clearer for you what you feel and think, and to separate this from other feelings and thoughts that play a role at the moment.
> P: Well, OK, I guess I have to. I will sit here first. (*She doesn't look at the therapist and sits in the chair next to her*)
> T: What's the name of that chair?
> P: Do I have to give a name to the chair as well? (*Still angry*)
> T: Yes, try to express what this chair stands for, for what feeling.
> P: I don't feel like it.
> T: OK, so we'll call this chair the "I don't feel like it" chair. What do you feel when you sit in this chair?

Creative experiential techniques

As far as the author knows, there is no literature that describes how creative experiential techniques can be used within the frame of assessment in ST. However, in 2006 an article was published by Haeyen in which she describes how imagery can be used in expressive therapy. Because creative experiential therapy is a subject in itself, this paragraph will only briefly report what kind of material creative experiential therapy can provide for diagnostics. Creative experiential therapy has an experiential character in the sense that a lot of it is focused on perception and less on verbalization. As with other experiential techniques, it also applies to creative experiential therapy that creative experiential techniques are mainly indicated for patients who have difficulty in verbalizing their schemas and modes, and for patients who cannot easily get in touch with their feelings. When difficulty in making contact with the body is the main issue, techniques from psychomotor therapy (PMT) can be useful. For example, the Angry Child mode can become very clear in a game where a patient starts throwing a ball too hard, or breaking material and crossing other people's boundaries. The Detached Protector, among others, will become visible when a patient literally does not attend the game, is too hard on himself, does not feel any injuries, or does not perceive that someone has crossed his own boundaries. PMT can also visualize to what degree the Happy Child mode applies, and PMT offers insight into how the patient can get into contact with that mode.

In art, it can become very clear how someone experiences himself by making self-presentations in images. Especially the child modes (e.g., the Vulnerable Child) often become very visible in drawings and images. On the other hand, it can also visualize what the Healthy Adult mode looks like in drawings and other images. In art therapy, the Detached Protector is also clearly visible when patients make fragmented work they can't reflect on (because they are out of contact with themselves) or they cannot be creative, just stick strictly to the assignment, and are unable to talk about it.

Pitfalls and Tips

In general, the use of experiential techniques should never be a goal in itself, but a way to obtain information about schemas, schema modes, schema processes, and coping styles via a different channel. Whether these techniques can be applied is strongly dependent on the patient's ability to integrate feelings. If someone is susceptible to psychotic decompensation or dissociation, it is advisable to postpone experiential techniques until the treatment phase when there is more trust in the therapeutic alliance and when the alliance is more developed. Therefore, it is important to make an early estimation of the possibility for disintegration.

In the therapeutic alliance, it is essential that the therapist is attentive and has a good insight into his own schemas, so that he does not become emotionally entangled.

As described above, chair work is especially useful in gaining insight into the different modes of the patient. Guided imagery is mainly suitable for obtaining more insight into the origin of schemas and finding out which schemas and modes are linked to current problems. Imagery is suitable in situations where there is a suspicion of abuse or maltreatment. In such situations, it is safer to address such issues in imagery rather than using more directive approaches, such as role-play or chair work. When using guided imagery, it is very important not to proceed too fast. It is often hard for the therapist to make patients relive painful feelings from the past without using an intervention (as done later in the treatment by rescripting during imagery). Role-play is very suitable in situations where more insight into coping styles is required. Creative experiential techniques are very useful for patients that have difficulties in making direct contact with their own body or with the therapist. Patients can then still verbalize their problems indirectly through material or play. However, potential pitfalls include using experiential techniques either too soon or too often, as well as waiting too long and using too little of these interventions. Diagnostics regarding ego-strength and the danger of decompensation prior to treatment (see also Part II, Chapter 3) can be useful for estimating when and how often the use of experiential techniques is required.

The Future

The techniques described in this chapter are mainly used during the early sessions of the treatment. Although the different experiential techniques have been described in the literature, there is a need to emphasize the use of these techniques as therapeutic tools with different groups of patients and in different settings (outpatient, day treatment, inpatient, individual, and in a group). Currently there is hardly any scientific data for the use of these techniques for assessment. Research into the efficacy of these techniques for assessment is very welcome. Furthermore, the description of diagnostic creative experiential techniques within ST and the integration of these techniques with more verbal techniques are still in their infancy. Therefore, there is a need for concrete guidelines for the use of creative experiential techniques for assessment in ST.

References

Arntz, A. and Weertman, A. (1999) Treatment of childhood memories: theory and practice. *Behaviour Research and Therapy, 37*, 715–740.

Beck, A.T., Freeman, A. and Davis, D.D. (2004) *Cognitive Therapy of Personality Disorders*, 2nd edition. New York: Guilford Press.

Genderen, H. van and Arntz, A. (2005) *Schemagerichte Cognitieve Therapie bij Borderline Persoonlijkheidsstoornis*. Amsterdam: Uitgeverij Nieuwezijds.

Haeyen, S. (2006) Imaginatie in beeldende therapie: een schema-gerichte benadering. *Tijdschrift voor Vaktherapie, 1*, 3–9.

Young, J.E., Klosko, J.S. and Weishaar, M.E. (2005) *Schemagerichte therapie: Handboek voor Therapeuten*. Houten; Bohn Stafleu van Loghum. Translation of Young, J.E., Klosko, J.S. and Weishaar, M.E. (2003) *Schema Therapy: a Practitioner's Guide*. New York: Guilford Press.

5
Clinical Use of Schema Inventories

Alexandra Sheffield and Glenn Waller

Introduction

In the past decade schema-based models of psychopathology have received increasing attention from researchers and clinicians (Riso, du Toit, Stein and Young, 2007). In response to this interest, a number of measures of schema content and process have been developed. Some are explicitly presented as measures of schemas (e.g., the different incarnations of the YSQ), some are presented as measures of the beliefs that are commonly associated with schemas, for example Cooper *et al.*'s (1997) EDBQ-NSB scale, and others are presented as measures of the schema-level core beliefs associated with the personality disorders (e.g., Beck and Beck's PBQ, 1991). However, it is important to begin by stressing that no individual inventory actually measures schemas, with their cognitive, emotional, behavioral, motivational, and physiological elements. Most measure cognitive content (i.e., core beliefs) and some address cognitive processes (i.e., the maladaptive coping strategies that reinforce schemas). Therefore, it is important to bear in mind that most of what is discussed here are measures of the different cognitive elements of schemas. However, this limitation does not reduce the clinical utility of the measures. The schema inventories reviewed in this chapter are all questionnaire-based and so rely on subjective self-reports. This chapter will focus on the clinical utility of the measures rather than their psychometric utility (see Part VI, Chapters 4 and 5), considering those that we have found helpful and those that we have not found useful in our clinical practice.

Clinical Practice

Schema inventories are useful clinical tools if they help develop accurate individual case formulations and hypotheses regarding clinical targets. If used properly (i.e., discussed with the patient rather than used only by the clinician), they can aid engagement and socialization to schema-based models. They also have the wider potential utility of explaining the development and maintenance of different psychological disorders. Finally, they can be used to measure the effectiveness of treatment, both for the individual and for broader clinical groups (see Part III, Chapter 11). We tend to use schema inventories at the beginning and end of treatment, although they can be used at any stage in therapy (e.g., to review progress when working on a particular core belief). However, while schema inventories can provide important information in helping to understand individual psychopathology, they should be interpreted carefully and with their limitations (e.g., psychometric properties) in mind.

While the majority of schema inventories to date have developed from Young's (1994) work, there are others that merit consideration. This review will consider measures of schema content, schema processes, the origins of schemas, and schema modes. It will also consider alternative ways of achieving the same clinical goal and of elaborating on those measures in clinical practice. We should stress that it is critical not to rely on any such inventory for purposes of evaluation or diagnosis. The schema inventories are more useful in identifying and addressing targets in individualized treatment for psychological disorders. As part of this pattern of assessment, formulation, and treatment planning, it can be particularly valuable to consider both schema content and process, using different measures.

Approach: Clinical Utility and Functions

Schema inventories have a number of clinical uses, including assisting in assessment, formulation, planning treatment, and assessing outcomes. However, there are also limitations to such measures that have to be borne in mind when employing them. These advantages and drawbacks will be detailed in this section.

Hypothesizing about the presence, role, and function of schemas

Schema inventories can provide rich clinical information on conditions where schemas are thought to play a role in the continuation of the problem (e.g., Riso *et al.*, 2007). Different schema inventories can help to develop hypotheses about the following:

- Cognitions that might be driving personality-level pathological responses. These include:
    - the Young Schema Questionnaire [YSQ[1]]; the Young-Atkinson Mode Inventory (YAMI) (Young, Atkinson, Arntz and Weishaar, 2005) and its revision, the Schema Mode Inventory (SMI) (Young *et al.*, 2007; see also Part VI, Chapter 5);

---

[1] The YSQ comes in a number of editions, some of which have been shown to be comparable (e.g., Stopa, Thorne, Waters and Preston, 2001; Waller, Meyer and Ohanian, 2001). Therefore, when talking about this measure we will use the generic term YSQ, specifying the version only when that is relevant.

- the Personality Beliefs Questionnaire (PBQ) (Beck and Beck, 1991) and its recently developed short version, PBQ-SF (Butler, Beck and Cohen, 2007);
- the Personality Disorders Beliefs Questionnaire (PDBQ) (Arntz, Dreessen, Schouten and Weertman, 2004);
- the Negative Self-Beliefs scale of the Eating Disorder Beliefs Questionnaire (EDBQ-NSB) (Cooper, Cohen-Tovée, Todd, Wells and Tovée, 1997).
- What maladaptive processes might be maintaining the problem (e.g., Young-Rygh Avoidance Inventory, YRAI; Young and Rygh, 1994; Young Compensation Inventory, YCI; Young, 1995).
- What early experiences might be relevant to schema development (e.g., Young Parenting Inventory, YPI; Young, 1999).

As stated above, none of the schema inventories measures the full range of elements that are conceptualized to make up schemas as they are defined in different models (e.g., Young, 1994; Beck, 1996). Most address cognitive process and/or content, rather than factors such as emotions, physiology, behavior, and motivation. Therefore, they cannot truly measure schemas, though they retain clinical utility. It is also important to consider that some of the original measures (YPI, YCI, YRAI) have been shown to be inadequate in their original conception, and that they make more sense if scored into different scales from those originally proposed. For example, Luck, Waller, Meyer, and Lacey (2005) have developed revised versions of the YRAI (YRAI-R) and YCI (YCI-R), and Sheffield and colleagues (2005) have developed a revised version of the YPI (YPI-R). Similarly, some of the measures have been shown to be longer than is necessary and have been issued in short forms that have equal clinical utility (e.g., the versions of the YSQ-S; the PBQ-SF – Butler *et al.*, 2007; the SMI – Young *et al.*, 2007). We find that these revised, abbreviated forms have clinical utility that is equal to or better than the originals.

The information gathered from schema inventories can complement, but not substitute for, comprehensive clinical assessment. The hypotheses developed from responses on different inventories can play a part in engaging the patient and developing a shared formulation of the patients' difficulties. Such a formulation can then indicate targets for intervention strategies by demonstrating the need to challenge specific core beliefs, schema modes, or the compensatory processes that maintain the patient's difficulties.

Measuring Outcome

We find that some schema inventories are useful for the measurement of the effectiveness of psychological therapies (e.g., YSQ, PBQ, PDBQ, YAMI/SMI). However, one cannot assume that a decrease in scores on these measures over the course of therapy is necessarily indicative of a good outcome. The following considerations are important:

- It is important to have a good working knowledge of scoring procedures, normative data, and the meaning of subscale scores on each inventory. Some indices represent relatively positive, functional characteristics in some circumstances; for example, the cognitive-emotional avoidance scale of the YCI-R appears to reflect a healthy, non-pathological way of coping with emotions (Luck et al., 2005). Similarly, some items may reflect an accurate perception of past experiences (e.g., the YSQ subscale emotional deprivation item: *"Most of the time, I haven't had someone to nurture me, share him/herself with me, or care deeply about everything that happens to me"*). Therapy may be dependent on the individual's capacity to learn that while this is true of the past, it does not have to be true in the future. Thus, clinical change does not require that this perception of the past should change.

- If an individual uses avoidance or idealization as a way of coping with underlying schemas, they may score low on schema inventories such as the YSQ. If therapy is then effective in helping the individual rely less on avoidance and idealization, they may become more aware of their schemas and score higher on these measures later in therapy.
- Schema inventories are designed to measure broad, personality-level constructs rather than Axis I symptomatology. Therefore, given that it is possible for patients to improve at the symptom level and not at a schema level (and vice versa), schema inventories should always be used alongside measures of Axis I symptomatology to provide a more detailed analysis of outcome.

General Limitations on Clinical Use

Each inventory has its limitations. However, they all share the general limitation that responses are affected by recall bias and that the inventories reflect individuals' perceptions of reality rather than reality itself. However, it can be argued that recall bias is crucial to the accurate measurement of schemas because they are maintained partly by selective attention to, or distortion of, information, which then reinforces them. Similarly, it can be argued that it is perceptions that should be the focus of investigation, because it is perceptions that impact on and reflect psychopathology (e.g., Parker, 1983). Therefore, as long as clinicians are clear that schema inventories measure recall biases and perceptions, and not reality *per se*, their construct validity is upheld. Finally, as mentioned above, it is likely that schemas will influence one's reporting on each of the inventories, which could lead to important information being missed (e.g., not wanting to report one's abandonment cognitions for fear of being rejected from therapy due to being a "nuisance").

Choosing a Schema Inventory to Use

The choice of inventories depends very much on what the clinician wants to determine. Of course, the choice will be guided primarily by hypotheses regarding case presentation and clinical need. As has already been noted, schema inventories are often measures of core beliefs and the underlying cognitive processes, rather than the full range of cognitions, behaviors, physiology, motivation, and emotion that is encompassed by the term "schema" (e.g., Beck, 1996). For example, the abandonment subscale of the YSQ measures the cognitive content of an abandonment schema (i.e., the core belief *"Others will inevitably abandon me"*). It does not measure the other aspects of the schema, such as the anxiety associated with the belief, the physiological response to its activation, the memories it evokes, or the behavior that one might use to avoid or cope with it. In addition, the measures do not always reflect the proposal that schemas are invariant, since they are mood-dependent (e.g., Stopa and Waters, 2005). This finding leads to three alternative conclusions: schema activation is variable (e.g., schemas are accessed differently if one's mood is different); schemas are not invariant (e.g., they are influenced by current mood); schema inventories do not measure schemas as they are usually defined. There are also issues of psychometric validity of the different measures (see Part VI, Chapters 4 and 5).

In our experience, there are several measures of schema elements that are useful, but several that are not.

Optimum measures of core beliefs

In general, we find the YSQ useful for addressing core beliefs in clinical settings. This measure has been translated into a number of languages, sometimes more than once. It is not possible to recommend particular translations, since there have been no published comparisons of the relevant versions. The YSQ (both the short and long versions) has been shown to have robust psychometric properties across a number of studies, with comparable factor structures and internal consistencies (e.g., Stopa, Thorne, Waters and Preston, 2001; Waller, Meyer and Ohanian, 2001; Welburn, Coristine, Dagg, Ponetgract and Jordan, 2002; Hoffart, Sexton, Hedley, Wang, Holthe, Haugum, Nordahl, Hovland and Holte, 2005; Baranoff, Oei, Cho and Kwon, 2006), and association with more fundamental personality factors (Thimm, 2010). There is less agreement about the factor structure of this measure with younger groups (e.g., Rijkeboer and de Boo, 2010; Vlierberghe, Braet, Bosmans, Rosseel and Bögels, 2010).

In case formulations, we conceptualize the core beliefs by dividing them into two types: central beliefs and compensatory beliefs. This division has recently been outlined in detail (Waller, Kennerley and Ohanian, 2007). Central core beliefs are those that represent the damage done to the individual's self-concept during development, while compensatory core beliefs are those beliefs that are developed in order to cope with or avoid these central negative self-beliefs. A case example is given below that illustrates the importance of distinguishing these two types of belief:

Anna: central vs. compensatory beliefs

Anna was a 44-year-old woman with bulimia nervosa, depression, and obsessive-compulsive disorder. She completed the YSQ-S early in treatment to facilitate the development of a formulation of her interpersonal difficulties as well her bingeing. She scored well above norms on the following core beliefs: Abandonment, Subjugation, Emotional Inhibition, Mistrust/Abuse, and Social Isolation. Clinical questioning supported their presence, but through discussion with Anna about the origins and functions of these beliefs, it became clear

> that not all the schemas were central beliefs; in fact, many were compensatory beliefs. Anna developed Abandonment and Mistrust/Abuse beliefs in response to perceived experiences of abandonment and punishment by her family. To try to avoid further abandonment and punishment, she developed the compensatory beliefs (Subjugation, Social Isolation, Emotional Inhibition). They manifested themselves in the following behaviors:
>
> - She would generally avoid relationships, or in any social situation would be constantly anxious and hypervigilant for signs that someone disliked her. If she perceived any such sign (often mistakenly), she would quickly withdraw (Social Isolation).
> - She would always let others make decisions and would go along with them even if she disliked and felt angry about what they decided (Subjugation).
> - She would hide her genuine feelings from others and would try to be exactly like whoever she was with (Emotional Inhibition).
>
> Continued use of these behaviors in all her interactions led to a failure to develop genuine mutual, trusting relationships. This pattern led to widespread rejection, isolation, and mistrust by others and hence reinforced the central schemas of Abandonment and Mistrust/Abuse.

The YSQ has been through many incarnations, so it is important to be clear about the version that is being used. The current long version of the YSQ has 205 items and addresses 16 core beliefs rather than schemas. In contrast, the most widely used short version addresses 15 core beliefs, while the most recent iteration (long and short versions) adds a further three (Young, 2005). There are also variants of the short form in terms of item order (random vs. clustered) and target age groups (while the original was devised around adults, there is a version that has been slightly reworded for adolescents; Simmons, 2000). Our experience is that the short version encourages full completion of the scale and that the versions that have the items clustered (e.g., YSQ-S1) are much easier to interpret by eye. We do not find that there is any loss of clinical richness, and patients do not report any impact of item clustering (frequently scoring adjacent items from the same scale as 1 and 6). The additional three scales in the most recent version of the YSQ (Young, 2005) do not seem to add greatly to our clinical formulations, but that conclusion might be a consequence of which specific clinical population is being considered. Therefore, our current recommendation is to employ the YSQ-S with 75 items, with the items clustered in groups of five for each of the 15 scales. However, YSQ scores show systematic drops over time and it might be more valid to use alternate subsets of the YSQ items when measuring change across therapy (Rijkeboer, van den Bergh and van den Bout, 2005). It is also possible to use the short inventories that are given in the Young and Klosko (1993) self-help book to help patients to identify many (but not all) of the schemas in the YSQ.

Other measures merit consideration. The EDBQ-NSB scale consists of 10 items, within a measure whose other items are specific to the eating disorders. However, this scale appears to reflect the construct represented by the YSQ Defectiveness/Shame scale, and we find that it lacks clinical richness for a range of disorders. In particular, it lacks the interpersonal element that is key to many of the YSQ scales.

The other measure that we would recommend is the PBQ, a 126-item scale. This measure has many similarities to the YSQ at the level of individual items. However, the scoring of the PBQ is based on clustering the core beliefs that are specific to individual personality disorder pathologies. Thus, while the YSQ can be used to identify the common core beliefs that underpin a range of disorders, the PBQ is used for identifying the cognitive elements of individual personality disorders. The PDBQ (Arntz *et al.*, 2004) was derived from the same conceptual base as the PBQ, and has similar properties and utility. However, the PBQ has been more widely validated (Beck *et al.*, 2001; Butler, Brown, Beck and Grisham, 2002; Jones, Burrell-Hodgson and Tate, 2007; Bhar, Brown and Beck, 2008), and the short version, PBQ-SF (Butler *et al.*, 2007) has excellent clinical potential. Thus, either measure – PBQ or PDBQ – can be used clinically, but the PBQ has greater support at present.

To summarize, the selection of a measure of core beliefs depends on the clinical hypotheses that underpin that measurement. We find the PBQ and PDBQ useful in identifying personality pathology at an early stage in assessment and formulation, when behavioral manifestations of specific personality disorders have not yet emerged. In contrast, we find the YSQ more useful for formulation and treatment planning, particularly because it allows us to consider both the role of the central beliefs and the ways in which compensatory beliefs can result in behaviors that are not otherwise explicable (e.g., the use of impulsive behaviors to block emotional arousal; the avoidance of social interaction to reduce fears of being abandoned; perfectionist behavior to manage fear of failure).

Measures of schema processes

Young (1994) describes a number of core schema-level cognitive-behavioral processes/coping styles that ensure the survival of a schema, even when the conditions under which it developed no longer apply (e.g., the maintenance of an abandonment core belief that developed following multiple loss experiences in childhood, even in the absence of any such experiences since then). The YCI was developed to address schema compensation, and the YRAI assesses schema avoidance. We find the YCI and YRAI to be less useful than the YSQ. The YCI can be interpreted (Luck *et al.*, 2005) as a measure of the primary avoidance of emotional arousal (using behaviors and cognitions to avoid the triggering of emotional states). This manifests as longer-term patterns of behavior (e.g., restrictive eating, social isolation), cognitions (e.g., perfectionism, obsessionality), and emotions (e.g., emotional instability). However, this is not apparent in the existing measure or in its conception. It is easier to use the YSQ to demonstrate these links in case formulation (e.g., the presence of an unrelenting standards belief paired with a failure belief). The YRAI addresses the secondary avoidance of affect (Luck *et al.*, 2005), where emotions are blocked once they have been triggered (e.g., through aggression, alcohol use, self-harm). Again, we find this measure to be less clinically relevant than simply identifying impulsive behaviors.

Measures of schema development

There are many measures of developmental factors that might have an impact on psychopathology, including measures of perceived abuse and parenting style. The YPI is the only such measure developed to explain the development of specific schemas. It is a long measure, which asks the individual to report on the behaviors of each parent separately. As with many other indices of parental behavior (Leung, Thomas and Waller, 2000), this measure shows some association with core beliefs. However, the specificity of the YPI scales is poor (Sheffield et al., 2005). Therefore, we find that there is no advantage to using this measure compared with other measures of parental behaviors (e.g., Parker, Tupling and Brown, 1979; Mountford, Corstorphine, Tomlinson and Waller, 2007), which have the benefit of being substantially shorter. Our clinical practice is to use our clinical interview and formulation to develop a picture of the developmental factors that have resulted in the development of both central and compensatory core beliefs, rather than the YPI.

Measures of schema modes

The first measure of such modes was the YAMI, which has been developed into the SMI (Young et al., 2007) (see Part VI, Chapter 5). These measures address styles of interacting with the world that are dependent on a number of linked schemas being activated. The scales often have similarities to those reflecting other construct measures (e.g., measures of core beliefs, coping styles, mood, and dissociation). Those similarities mean that the schema mode measures can be redundant when carried out within a comprehensive clinical assessment. The alternative perspective, of course, is that it is the other measures that are redundant. However, these are hypotheses that remain to be tested. Currently, there are no clinical norms for the SMI that allow the clinician to consider the normative or pathological nature of the individual's scores.

A key difficulty of the schema mode measures (YAMI and SMI) is that the model underlying such measures is state-dependent, where "schema flipping" means that only one mode is likely to be activated at a time, so that the score on the YAMI is likely to be a measure of immediate state, changing over time and circumstance. If this is the case, then it can be hypothesized that external manipulation should influence scores (cf. Stopa and Waters, 2005). Therefore, it is dangerous to assume that a score on the YAMI reflects how the person will be under different circumstances. For example, the state dissociation reflected by the YAMI Detached Protector scale is likely to appear much lower when the individual is focused in the immediate emotional state (e.g., when the Punitive Parent mode is active). Therefore, if the mode theory is accurate, the measure can be seen only as a measure of immediate state, rather than longer-term traits. In a clinical setting, the Detached Protector mode is more likely to be seen than other modes, but the most informative clinical experience is likely to be when the modes change in response to what goes on in the clinical setting. Formal measures of modes are unlikely to reflect the dynamism underlying such constructs.

Scoring systems

While some schema inventories have formal scoring criteria (e.g., PBQ, PDBQ, EDBQ-NSB), the measures developed by Young (YSQ, YCI, YRAI, YPI, YAMI) have been distributed with "informal" scoring criteria, where the focus is on the number of items where the individual scores 5 or 6. While that is a good "eyeball" method of identifying pathological core beliefs, we find it more useful to take item mean scores for each scale in order to show the broader changes over time that we aim to achieve through treatment. This approach helps to deal with the fact that some scales seem to return relatively high scores even among non-pathological cases. In particular, the YSQ unrelenting standards scale can yield a lot of high scores among non-clinical individuals, reflecting the fact that perfectionism is a trait that can be functional as well as dysfunctional, according to the circumstances. The more formal scoring systems for these measures (Beck and Beck, 1991; Cooper et al., 1997; Waller et al., 2001) have led to the development of normative scores.

Interpreting Schema Inventories

Interpreting schema inventories requires good, informed clinical judgment. As outlined above, one needs to understand their scoring procedures, normative data, and the meanings of different subscales. Measures such as the PBQ, PDBQ, and EDBQ-NSB are relatively easy to interpret since they are measures of negative central core beliefs. The PBQ and PDBQ are particularly easy to link to specific personality disorders, since that is the function of the measures, and the items have clear face validity.

With the YSQ, it has also been stressed that it is necessary to distinguish two types of core belief: central and compensatory (Waller et al., 2007). In particular, it is important to understand that compensatory beliefs have developed as functional responses to the central beliefs, but that they have failed to adapt to changing circumstances. Thus, over time, compensatory beliefs become maladaptive and reinforce the central beliefs. For example, a subjugation schema might develop to protect an individual from the negative impact of mistrust/abuse core beliefs that resulted from an abusive early environment. However, a style of letting others be in control leaves the individual vulnerable to further abuse later in life, thus reinforcing the mistrust/abuse belief.

Interpretation of other measures is dependent on their clinical psychometric properties (i.e., do they measure what they say they measure?). For example, we have already described how the YSQ can provide a better measure of compensatory mechanisms than the YCI. Similarly, indices of impulsive and compulsive behaviors (e.g., the Multi-Impulsivity Scale; Evans, Searle and Dolan, 1998; or the Vancouver Obsessional Compulsive Inventory; Thordarson et al., 2004) can be more effective than the YRAI and YCI in this respect. Thus, it can be argued that the YCI and YRAI are redundant. The YPI is particularly hard to interpret as Young (1999) has suggested, since the evidence suggests that the parental elements do not neatly relate to the core beliefs that they were designed to address (Sheffield *et al.*, 2005). Other measures of parental behaviors (e.g., the Invalidating Childhood Experiences Scale; Mountford *et al.*, 2007; and the Parental Bonding Inventory; Parker *et al.*, 1979) can be as effective as using the YPI in addressing potentially pathological environments in early years.

When interpreting schema inventories, it is also important to administer state measures of general psychopathology (e.g., the Brief Symptom Inventory; Derogatis, 1993) and consider the consequences of behaviors such as substance misuse. Comorbid Axis I disorders (e.g., anxiety, depression) can temporarily bias the results of schema inventories (e.g., Stopa and Waters, 2005), and substance misuse can induce states that could otherwise be interpreted as reflecting schema-level problems (e.g., substance-related dissociation can appear to be a manifestation of the Detached Protector mode on the SMI, rather than being a consequence of that mode). Such biases can lead to incorrect hypotheses about the presence and role of schemas, and can result in unnecessary or inappropriate treatment interventions. A case example drawn from our practice in the eating disorders illustrates the importance of under-

> ### Lizzie: a case of mistaken core beliefs
>
> Lizzie was a 23-year-old woman with both borderline and bulimic features. She attended for treatment following the birth of her first child since she did not want to continue her impulsive behaviors as a model for her daughter. Her YSQ-L score indicated relatively few pathological core beliefs. The principal pair of core beliefs was shown by very high scores on the Defectiveness/Shame and Emotional Inhibition scales. However, it was hard to arrive at a meaningful formulation that linked these beliefs when we discussed her history. Eventually, we concluded that her Emotional Inhibition beliefs were so strong that they meant that she was unable to think about her childhood as being emotionally unsupported. Thus, when asked to respond to items such as: "I haven't had someone to nurture me, share him/herself with me, or care deeply about everything that happens to me," she judged her entitlement to such support as being so low that she had no way of judging others as having let her down emotionally. Hence, her scores on this scale were all so low that the inventory failed to pick up on this core belief. Thus, it became necessary to amend her formulation to include this belief system. However, as she began to eat more regularly, her mood improved dramatically, as is often the case when carbohydrate levels are increased in the diet of eating-disordered patients. Many of the cognitions that had been labeled as reflecting a defectiveness core belief (e.g., "I'm unworthy of the love, attention, and respect of others") began to reduce substantially, suggesting that the inventory scores had been influenced adversely by Lizzie's physiologically influenced mood state.

standing the case from a clinical perspective, as well as having the results of such inventories.

The case examples described in this chapter reflect the strengths of the schema inventories, showing how they can contribute to the development of clinical targets and treatment approaches. However, they show that clinical interviews, case formulations, and awareness of treatment efficacy in the individual case are needed to understand and verify (or refute) those conclusions.

Pitfalls and Tips

Table 5.1 gives a set of rules to remember when using schema inventories. It summarizes the most common set of errors that we find clinicians make when using such measures and gives tips that we find useful in reminding clinicians how to use these tools:

Table 5.1 Rules to remember when using schema inventories

- No inventory measures the full range of cognitions, emotions, behaviors, and physiological factors that reflect schemas, and it is important to recognize that these inventories tell us only part of the story. For example, the YSQ is widely used, but many clinicians treat it as a measure of schemas rather than the measure of core beliefs that it actually is.
- It is important to distinguish central core beliefs from the compensatory beliefs when using such inventories to understand cases (see first case example above).
- There is currently no clear evidence that these inventories allow us to map early experiences neatly onto schema development. It is important to remember the mediating and moderating influence of other factors (e.g., temperament, experiences in later life) that can influence schema development. Some of those experiences are relatively subtle (e.g., invalidating environments), compared to the overt experiences that are described in the trauma literature.
- It is important to formulate the origins of the compensatory beliefs, as well as the central beliefs. This allows us to understand why different individuals respond to the same central belief in different ways.
- By definition, the inventories reflect subjective impressions. It is therefore important to remember that they measure constructs that are based on perceptions of one's experiences. These perceptions are affected by recall bias and current experiences or mood states. The inventories do not measure real experiences, facts, or memories, though this fact does not necessarily impair their utility, as individuals respond to those subjective experiences.
- Patients and clinicians disagree at times when rating schema constructs (e.g., Lobbestael, Arntz, Löbbes and Cima, 2009).
- Patients and clinicians tend to describe schemas as being external entities ("Your schema made you . . ."). It is important to remember that this is not the case and that each individual has the capacity to work with those schemas.

The Future

While the schema inventories have many clinical uses, it is important to be aware of their limitations, as outlined in this chapter. While many of these limitations can be addressed within good clinical practice, there remains the overarching fact that the schema inventories that have been developed to date do not reflect the broad concept of a schema and the relation of such schemas to personality (e.g., Beck, 1996). Therefore, to avoid constructing inaccurate hypotheses about pathology, it is critical for users to be clear about what the schema inventories actually measure. Meaningful interpretations can be obtained only when analyzed alongside information gathered from clinical interviews, and such interpretations should always be informed by the inventory's limitations and by comparison with the normative data available.

References

Arntz, A., Dreessen, L., Schouten, E., and Weertman, A. (2004) Beliefs in personality disorders: a test with the personality disorders belief questionnaire. *Behaviour Research and Therapy*, 42, 1215–1225.

Baranoff, J., Oei, T.P., Cho, S.H., and Kwon, S.M. (2006) Factor structure and internal consistency of the Young Schema Questionnaire (short form) in Korean and Australian samples. *Journal of Affective Disorders*, 93, 133–140.

Beck, A.T. (1996) Beyond belief: a theory of modes, personality and psychopathology, in *Frontiers of Cognitive Therapy* (ed P.M. Salkovskis), Guildford Press, New York.

Beck, A.T., and Beck, J.S. (1991) *The Personality Belief Questionnaire*. Bala Cynwyd, PA: Beck Institute for Cognitive Therapy and Research.

Beck, A.T., Butler, A.C. et al. (2001) Dysfunctional beliefs discriminate personality disorders. *Behaviour Research and Therapy*, 39, 1213–1225.

Bhar, S.S., Brown, G.K., and Beck, A.T. (2008) Dysfunctional beliefs and psychopathology in borderline personality disorder. *Journal of Personality Disorders*, 22, 165–177.

Butler, A.C., Beck, A.T., and Cohen, L.C. (2007) The Personality Belief Questionnaire – short form: development and preliminary findings. *Cognitive Therapy and Research*, 31, 357–370.

Butler, A.C., Brown, G.K., Beck, A.T., and Grisham, J.R. (2002) Assessment of dysfunctional beliefs in borderline personality disorder. *Behaviour Research and Therapy*, 40, 1231–1240.

Cooper, M., Cohen-Tovée, E., Todd, G. et al. (1997) The eating disorder belief questionnaire: preliminary development. *Behaviour Research and Therapy*, 35, 381–388.

Derogatis, L. (1993) *The brief symptom inventory: administration, scoring, and procedures manual* (3rd edition). Minneapolis, MN: National Computer Systems.

Evans, C., Searle, Y., and Dolan, B. (1998) Two new tools for the assessment of multi-impulsivity: The "MIS" and the "CAM." *European Eating Disorders Review*, 6, 48–57.

Hoffart, A., Sexton, H. et al. (2005). The structure of maladaptive schemas: a confirmatory factor analysis and a psychometric evaluation of factor-derived scales. *Cognitive Therapy and Research*, 29, 627–644.

Jones, S.H., Burrell-Hodgson, G., and Tate, G. (2007) Relationships between the personality beliefs questionnaire and self-rated personality disorders. *British Journal of Clinical Psychology*, 46, 247–251.

Leung, N., Thomas, G.V., and Waller, G. (2000) The relationship between parental bonding and core beliefs in anorexic and bulimic women. *British Journal of Clinical Psychology*, 39, 203–213.

Lobbestael, J., Arntz, A., Löbbes, A., and Cima, M. (2009) A comparative study of patients and therapists' reports of schema modes. *Journal of Behavior Therapy and Experimental Psychiatry*, 40, 571–579.

Luck, A., Waller, G., Meyer, C., and Lacey, H. (2005) The role of schema processes in the eating disorders. *Cognitive Therapy and Research*, 29, 717–732.

Mountford, V., Corstorphine, E., Tomlinson, S., and Waller, G. (2007) Development of a measure to assess invalidating childhood environments in the eating disorders. *Eating Behaviors*, 8, 48–58.

Parker, G. (1983) *Parental overprotection: a risk factor in psychosocial development*. New York: Grune and Stratton.

Parker, G., Tupling, H., and Brown, L.B. (1979) A parental bonding instrument. *British Journal of Medical Psychology*, 52, 1–10.

Rijkeboer, M.M., and de Boo, G.M. (2010) Early maladaptive schemas in children: development and validation of the schema inventory for children. *Journal of Behavior Therapy and Experimental Psychiatry*, 41, 102–109.

Rijkeboer, M.M., van den Bergh, H., and van den Bout, J. (2005) Stability and discriminative power of the Young schema questionnaire in a Dutch clinical versus non-clinical population. *Journal of Behavior Therapy and Experimental Psychiatry*, 36, 129–144.

Riso, L.P., du Toit, P.L., Stein, D.J., and Young, J.E. (2007) *Cognitive schemas and core beliefs in psychiatric disorders: a scientist-practitioner guide*. New York: American Psychological Association.

Sheffield, A., Waller, G., Emanuelli, F., Murray, J. and Meyer, C. (2005) Links between parenting and core beliefs: preliminary psychometric validation of the Young parenting inventory. *Cognitive Therapy and Research*, 29, 787–802.

Simmons, J. (2000) Depressed adolescent girls and their mothers. Unpublished doctoral dissertation, University of Oxford.

Stopa, L., Thorne, P., Waters, A., and Preston, J. (2001) Are the short and long forms of the Young schema questionnaire comparable and how well does each version predict psychopathology scores? *Journal of Cognitive Psychotherapy*, 15, 253–272.

Stopa, L., and Waters, A. (2005) The effect of mood on responses to the Young schema questionnaire: short form. *Psychology and Psychotherapy: Theory, Research and Practice*, 78, 45–57.

Thimm, J.C. (2010) Personality and early maladaptive schemas: a five-factor model perspective. *Journal of Behavior Therapy and Experimental Psychiatry*, 41, 373–380.

Thordarson, D.S., Radomsky, A.S., Rachman, S. et al. (2004) The Vancouver Obsessional Compulsive Inventory (VOCI). *Behaviour Research and Therapy*, 42, 1289–1314.

van Vlierberghe, L., Braet, C., Bosmans, G. et al. (2010) Maladaptive schemas and psychopathology in adolescence: On the utility of Young's schema theory in youth. *Cognitive Therapy and Research*, 34, 316–332.

Waller, G., Kennerley, H., and Ohanian, V. (2007) Schema-focused cognitive behavioral therapy with eating disorders, in *Cognitive schemas and core beliefs in psychiatric disorders: a scientist-practitioner guide* (eds L.P.. Riso, P.L. du Toit, D.J. Stein, and J.E. Young), New York: American Psychological Association, pp. 139–175.

Waller, G., Meyer, C., and Ohanian, V. (2001) Psychometric properties of the long and short versions of the young schema questionnaire: core beliefs among bulimic and comparison women. *Cognitive Therapy and Research*, 25, 137–147.

Welburn, K., Coristine, M., Dagg, P. et al. (2002) The schema questionnaire – short form: factor analysis and relationship between schemas and symptoms. *Cognitive Therapy and Research*, 26, 519–530.

Young, J.E. (1994) *Cognitive therapy for personality disorders: a schema focused approach* (2nd edition). Sarasota, FL: Professional Resource Exchange.

Young, J.E. (1995) *Young Compensatory Inventory*. New York: Cognitive Therapy Centre. www.schematherapy.com.

Young, J.E. (1999) *Young Parenting Inventory*. New York: Cognitive Therapy Centre. www.schematherapy.com.

Young, J.E. (2005) *Young Schema Questionnaire (YSQ-L3)*. New York: Cognitive Therapy Centre. www.schematherapy.com/id55.htm.

Young, J.E., Arntz, A. *et al.* (2007) *Schema Mode Inventory (SMI version 1)*. New York: Schema Therapy Institute.

Young, J.E., Atkinson, T., Arntz, A., and Weishaar, M. (2005) *The Young–Atkinson mode inventory (YAMI-PM, 1B)*. New York: Schema Therapy Institute.

Young, J.E., and Klosko, J.S. (1993) *Reinventing your life*. New York: Plume.

Young, J.E., and Rygh, J. (1994) *Young–Rygh Avoidance Inventory*. New York: Cognitive Therapy Centre. www.schematherapy.com.

6
Case Conceptualization in Schema Therapy

Hannie van Genderen

It is essential that problems are mapped out as completely as possible before starting treatment (e.g., Young, Klosko and Weishaar, 2003; Beck, Freeman, Davis and Associates, 2004; Arntz and van Genderen, 2009). This gives insight to both therapist and patient regarding which schemas are playing a role, how they originated, and what their influence is on current problems. The aim is not only to map out the problems as completely as possible, but also for the therapist to understand the patient's problems as fully as possible, and for the patient and the therapist to formulate a shared explanation of the problems in the patient's own terms. A good case conceptualization makes it a lot easier to design a treatment plan and it offers valuable indications to handle the therapeutic alliance.

The verbal data are collected, written on a case conceptualization form and inserted into a two-dimensional model, in order to show the links between the different elements. Two different kinds of model are used: the case conceptualization model for schemas and the mode model for schema modes.

In Practice

Since developing an effective case conceptualization with the help of the form and a model is in every Schema Therapy (ST) training program it is likely that in practice most therapists will develop one. Developing a good case conceptualization takes more than two sessions. In certain settings, this isn't possible because the number of psychotherapy sessions has been cut. Therefore, the question is whether conceptualizations are developed in all cases. Aside from this, whether there is a link between a good case conceptualization and an adequate treatment is questionable (see discussions about scientific foundations in Henry and Williams, 1997; Perris, 1999; Bieling and Kuyken, 2003; Kuyken, Fothergill, Musa and Chadwick, 2005). Patients often mention that they understand their problems better after developing their case conceptualization and that consequently they are more motivated to start therapy.

Approach

Case conceptualization form

The case conceptualization form includes information about the patient's current problems, schemas, schema modes, and coping styles, as well as a description of temperament, education, and other relevant events in the patient's life. The therapist tries to describe the problems as far as possible in the patient's own words. Therefore, depression may be described as "often feeling down" and social phobia as "afraid of others in company and being silent most of the time." Subsequently, the therapist describes how he thinks that his schemas will interact with the patient's schemas. He doesn't share this part with the patient, but with the peer supervision group. Finally, the outlines of the treatment are described.

The therapist tries to map out the information as fully as possible, while summarizing the information. If he includes too much detail, the case conceptualization phase will be long, and this will be rather discouraging, especially for the patient. Besides, more information doesn't always offer more insight into the problems. The therapist can discuss the form with the patient; however this is not necessary. What the form actually provides is a stepping-stone, in order to structure the information and to check whether it is complete. On the basis of the information from the case conceptualization form, the therapist develops a case conceptualization model in order to show how the problems are connected. This model is always developed together with the patient.

In some cases the therapist will not have enough information to develop a good case conceptualization and may be under the impression that certain schemas and coping styles are relevant, but the patient disagrees. The therapist can try to get more information by using the downward arrow technique or imagery in order to give the patient more insight into the nature and severity of his problems. However, this shouldn't become a conflict. The therapist must sometimes build up a trusted relationship with the patient in order to ensure he receives sufficient relevant information.

The case conceptualization is a working model that can be modified during therapy whenever new insights arise. It isn't immutable. For example, it is common for the patient to speak in positive terms about his parents at the beginning of the therapy, but revise this image later. Interim evaluations are recommended in the case of long-term therapy, to review the case conceptualization and the treatment plan, and, if necessary, adjust it.

Administering the case conceptualization form

The therapist and the patient complete the case conceptualization form together. The form has a certain order that can be followed with most patients. However, a therapist should not stick rigidly to this if doing so prevents a smooth-running inventory of

> Sarah is a shy 28-year-old woman, who cries a lot and finds it difficult to talk about her problems. She has just finished her social skills training program, but with little results. She is still afraid to express her feelings or to stand up for her interests in relation to others. Her therapist refers her to personality disorder treatment, because Sarah's problems are more the result of her personality problems, and the symptoms haven't improved.
>
> Sarah is living with her boyfriend, whom she wants to leave, but she doesn't make this clear to him and she doesn't take the necessary steps to do so. She has a university degree and works as an architectural draughtswoman. Her manager thinks that she does a very good job "technically speaking," but that she doesn't communicate well with her colleagues.
>
> Sarah was raised in a socially isolated family. They were the only family from Friesland, in the north of the Netherlands, living in a village in Limburg, in the south of the Netherlands. Her parents always kept themselves at a distance from the community. Her father was hard-working, but he was often overworked. During this period, the family had to be considerate to him and her mother devoted all her attention to him. Sarah has a sister, who is one year older, and a brother who is seven years younger. Her brother had asthma and also needed a lot of attention from their mother. At first, Sarah describes her childhood as normal, but further questioning shows that her mother really paid no attention to her at all. Her father was only interested in how well the children did at school; otherwise, he was only concerned with himself. Sarah's sister avoided the family by spending a lot of time with friends. Sarah didn't have many friends and she spent most of her time alone in her room.

the problems. What must be administered for each part is described next, and Sarah's form is used as an example.

Short description of the patient. In this short description, a number of facts about the patient are given (e.g., age, current relationship with partner, children, and/or relevant others). In addition, there is a short description of daily activities (e.g., job, education, or the lack of this, and the problems that the patient has with that).

Current symptoms and problems. Current symptoms and problems have a large effect on the life of the patient or her surroundings. The symptoms and problems can be derived from the symptom inventory. In Sarah's case, these are depression and social phobia. In addition, problems with relationships are described. Sarah mentions her anxiety about conflicts and expressing her opinion and feelings at work, to her boyfriend, and to friends. The therapist summarizes the problems in a few general categories (e.g., problems with relationships). In many cases the therapist will also indicate a few problems that the patient doesn't initially recognize to be issues. However, he must not impose his perception on the patient. The schemas and coping styles are a normal way of thinking and experiencing in the eyes of the patient, and if the therapist

> ### Sarah's case conceptualization form
>
> *Short description of the patient*
>
> *Sarah is a 28-year-old woman, who has lived with Peter for approximately five years. Sarah would like to end the relationship, but Peter doesn't. She has a university degree and has worked as an architectural draughtswoman at a firm of architects for a year. In addition to this, she attends courses in the evening. She likes her work, but she has little contact with her colleagues. She also has little social contact. Peter is unemployed and does little to find work.*
>
> *Sarah is the middle child of a family of three children (sister > 1 year and brother <7 years). She often goes to her parents' because she feels obliged to, not because she likes to go home. Her brother still lives with her parents and she meets him there. She has less contact with her sister; however, their relationship is quite good.*

> Sarah's therapist notices that she is always busy with her work and further studies. She works many more hours than she is paid for and she sets herself high standards in her work. Sarah thinks that's normal and initially she doesn't want to interpret this in the problem description. Only after she took on more assignments and, as a result, couldn't sleep well, was she willing to add this problem, albeit reluctantly.

refers to certain things as a problem, which the patient doesn't experience as such, there is a risk of misunderstanding and alienation between therapist and patient.

The therapist can also obtain information from a third party. This happens, for example, with criminal behavior or difficulties with relationships with somebody who has an Entitlement/Grandiosity or Insufficient Self-Control schema. Relevant information about the therapeutic alliance can be described under current problems if the patient experiences it this way. For example, "mistrust with regard to the therapist and the therapy." However, if there is no consensus about this behavior, the therapist may decide to place this under the heading "Therapeutic alliance."

Relevant schemas (pitfalls). Information about the schemas, derived from the Young Schema Questionnaire (YSQ) (Young and Brown, 1994; Dutch translation and adjustment: Sterk and Rijkeboer, 1997) and other questionnaires, information that the therapist collects during the first sessions but also from the reports of others, is used.

Sarah's case conceptualization form

Current symptoms and problems

1. She is feeling down, and has little pleasure in life, and she has nothing besides her work.
2. She remains distant in social contacts.
3. She doesn't risk conflicts.
4. She has problems with relationships.
5. She works too hard.
6. At work her colleagues complain because she has little contact with them.

Sarah's case conceptualization form

Relevant schemas (pitfalls)	*Average score*
1. Emotional Deprivation (I am not important)	3.5
2. Social Isolation/Alienation (I am substantially different from others)	4.2
3. Self-Sacrifice (You must always think about others first)	4.7
4. Unrelenting Standards /Hypercriticalness I want to get everything right)	5.2

Sarah tended to avoid her Emotional Deprivation and Social Isolation/Alienation schemas. Therefore, she doesn't have examples for these, and the therapist must be more active in looking for such examples. Sarah does recognize the other two schemas.

The therapist doesn't only use cognitive techniques, but also experiential techniques, in order to map out all schemas (see also Part I, Chapter 2).

Which situations or events can evoke which schemas (pitfalls)? The therapist and the patient try to describe links between current problems and the schemas. Sometimes it is very difficult to get information about a schema, especially in the presence of a strong avoiding or over-compensating coping style. In this case, continuing to ask questions, using the downward arrow technique or imagery, is necessary to get enough information. However, there are also patients who, after having discussed the schemas and reading about them, begin to discover the influence of their schemas on their problems themselves.

Sarah's case conceptualization form

Which situations or events can evoke which schemas (pitfalls)? (mention the most important)

Situation		Schemas/pitfalls
1.	Performance interview at work. My manager tells me that I must cooperate more with my colleagues and that I should ask for things.	Social Isolation/ Alienation Unrelenting Standards/ Hypercritical
2.	My boyfriend doesn't do much housekeeping, so I do it.	Self-Sacrifice Emotional Deprivation
3.	My friend always decides what we are going to do and this is often something with his friends. I never say anything about it.	Self-Sacrifice Social Isolation/ Alienation
4.	My boyfriend took the car, therefore I had to go by bicycle in the rain.	Self-Sacrifice
5.	I always keep working until everything is done.	Unrelenting Standards/ Hypercritical

Coping styles: How do I handle my schemas (pitfalls)? It is not only during the first sessions, but also later in therapy, as mentioned above, that a better understanding the patient's coping styles is gained. It isn't always easy to discover whether a certain behavior is surrender to a schema or the avoiding/over-compensating of a schema (see Part I, Chapter 2). The YSQ, supplemented by the Young–Rygh Avoidance Inventory (Young and Rygh, 1994), the Young Compensation Inventory (Young, 1995), and the Young Parenting Inventory (Young, 1994), can offer some decisive answers, in combination with information provided by the patient himself. Since the YSQ was investigated in detail and the other questionnaires were not, using the scores on the YSQ as a guiding principle is recommended.

The case conceptualization is a joint project of the therapist and the patient. Therefore, especially at the beginning of the therapy, the therapist will attempt to focus, as much as possible, on the patient's point of view. If a patient doesn't recognize

Sarah's case conceptualization form

Coping styles: How do I handle my schemas/pitfalls?
  Give for each schema (Surrender, Avoidance, or Over-compensation)

Schema Pitfall	Surrender (behavior that leads to surrender to the schema)	Avoidance (behavior that leads to avoiding the schema)	Over-compensation (reversed behavior, which leads to "overstraining" the schema)
1. Emotional Deprivation	She has a boyfriend who neglects her	She has no real friendships	She sometimes demands her friend's attention very ineptly
2. Social Isolation/ Alienation	She always notices the differences between herself and her colleagues	She has no contact with colleagues	She changes to fit in study groups
3. Self-Sacrifice	She puts her boyfriend's and family's needs before her own	She avoids starting new relationships	She sometimes loses her temper with her boyfriend
4. Unrelenting Standards/ Hypercriticalness	She is always working or studying	She puts off discussing her work with colleagues	

a specific coping style, the therapist tentatively concludes that this isn't present. The case conceptualization model is a working model and doesn't have to be perfect from the start. However, it is worth investigating whether the patient handles, or has handled, other coping styles. It is very rare that a patient keeps to one coping style for very long, without switching to another coping style (see Part I, Chapter 2). In order to discover this, it is often necessary take a wider perspective and involve another period or other circumstances in the patient's life. If the patient has the Emotional Deprivation schema and is not currently in a relationship, you might see the Avoidance coping style. But when he was in a relationship with a neglectful partner (Surrender), there could have been times when he forcefully demanded her attention (Over-Compensation). In the outline of the coping styles, the therapist always provides an example of the behavior that is characteristic for the specific coping style in that schema.

Schema modes. Because it appeared that patients with a borderline personality disorder had a large number of schemas and coping styles, Young (2003) developed the so-called schema mode model. The schema mode model for narcissistic personality disorder was added later. Recently, more schema modes have been developed, and for most of the other personality disorders a mode model was developed in accordance with the DSM-IV (see Part I, Chapter 2). Questionnaires that attempt to measure modes are the YAMI and the SMI-r (Lobbestael, van Vreeswijk, Spinhoven, *et al.*, 2010). In particular, when there are many schemas with switching coping styles it is more efficient to develop a schema mode model, and therefore also to describe the schema modes. However, when patients have few schemas, indicating the modes is not compulsory, but could add some extra information. When a schema mode model is used, a case conceptualization model for the schemas isn't necessary since a schema mode model will suffice. Nevertheless, it is strongly recommended that the therapist maps out all schemas, so that it becomes clear which schemas are linked to which modes. In Sarah's case, the therapist started with a case conceptualization model for schemas, but mentioned the different schema modes that in his opinion were also playing a role.

Temperamental and biological factors of the patient. Here, the patient's original temperament is described, as well as important biological facts. Besides the child's temperament, other factors in the child's nature can also play a role in the development of

---

Sarah's case conceptualization form

Child mode

Vulnerable Child

Coping modes

Compliant Surrender
Over-Controller

Parent mode

Demanding Parent

> ### Sarah's case conceptualization form
>
> *Temperamental and biological factors*
>
> *Sarah was a quiet, sensitive, and anxious child who could often be found alone reading in her room. She had a lot of perseverance and often tried to fit in with others. She found school work easy, and she was sometimes bullied because of this. She completed her university studies successfully.*

> ### Sarah's case conceptualization form
>
> *Character and parenting style of the father*
>
> *Father was always working and made great demands on himself and others. He was frequently overworked and then became even more critical and verbally aggressive. He didn't have much time for his children; he was only interested in their school results. Her father came from Friesland, in the north of the Netherlands, and had difficulties adjusting in Limburg, in the south, in particular, because he wanted everything to be done his way.*
>
> *Character and parenting style of the mother*
>
> *Mother was quiet, withdrawn, and cold. Her focus was the father when he was overworked, and her son, because he was often ill. Mother was also from Friesland and had few social contacts.*

the personality pathology – for example, intelligence and physical health. Information from a third party (e.g., the school) can be used to complete this profile.

Upbringing. All relevant aspects of development by the most important parent(s)/caregiver(s) can be described here. If there are other caregivers (stepparents or grandparents, older siblings), the therapist will include these under "other caregivers." Traumatic events (e.g., physical or sexual abuse) are also noted here.

Other relevant memories of influences during the patient's childhood. Other relevant influences on the development of the patient's schemas are the school (e.g., being bullied) and environment (e.g., being raised in a dangerous area) or other circumstances (e.g., fled from a war zone).

> ### Sarah's case conceptualization form
>
> *Other relevant memories of influences during the patient's childhood (influences of the peer group, traumatic events)*
>
> *Sarah's sister fled from the house and her brother was often ill. At school, she was shy and had little contact with other children. She was never allowed to bring friends home, because it was too much for her father. The only way to get any attention was by getting good school results.*

> ### Sarah's case conceptualization form
>
> *Underlying assumptions that the patient extracted from the childhood experiences mentioned above*
>
> *If I don't try very hard, I will fail.*
> *It's better to stay away from others, because I don't belong.*
> *My opinions don't matter.*
> *I can't leave my boyfriend, because he will go to pieces.*
> *If I end this relationship, I will never find someone else.*
> *If I express my opinion, my friends will let me down.*
> *I can't ask for help at work, because they will think I'm stupid.*
> *I must be there for everyone all of the time.*
> *Not finishing something or putting it off is a sign of weakness.*

Underlying assumptions that the patient extracted from her childhood experiences. In order to clarify how all the information gathered so far affects the daily life of the patient, we describe a few underlying assumptions. These are general rules of life explaining how the patient thinks and assumes he should act.

Schemas of the therapist and their interaction with schemas of the patient. Considering the importance of the therapeutic alliance, it is also of major concern to describe the interaction between therapist's schemas and those of the patient in the case conceptualization form. The therapist knows his own schemas and investigates how these can influence the therapeutic alliance positively or negatively. The therapist describes the interaction in such a way that it becomes clear how his and the patient's schemas can be mutually enhancing. He formulates several hypotheses and shares

> ### Sarah's case conceptualization form
>
> *Therapeutic alliance*
>
> *As a result of the therapist's Unrelenting Standards/Hypercriticalness schema, he wants to develop a perfect case conceptualization. Sarah doesn't recognize the Emotional Deprivation schema and doesn't want to include this in the case conceptualization. The therapist keeps insisting, and Sarah feels misunderstood. She doesn't attend the next session. The therapist is irritated because his case conceptualization is delayed (Unrelenting Standards/Hypercriticalness schemas become stronger). He doesn't call Sarah to make a new appointment, but writes her a brief note giving her a new appointment. In doing so, he enhances Sarah's Emotional Deprivation schema. She avoids contact with the therapist by secluding herself or by being late for appointments. It will require more effort from the therapist to finish the case conceptualization. And so on.*

them with his peer supervision group or supervisor. Returning to this part of the case conceptualization is recommended, particularly when the therapy seems to be stagnating.

Treatment plan. If things go well, the case conceptualization can show where to place emphasis in the treatment plan. Both the attitude of the therapist in the alliance and the planning of the techniques, which should be used with this specific patient, are described here. In particular, the emphasis and the order of the techniques used in the course of therapy are described here. The outlines are discussed with the patient, if this hasn't been done during the case conceptualization.

Case Conceptualization Model for Schemas

In order to report the links between current problems, schemas, coping styles, and information about caregivers, and any other relevant information about the past of the patient diagrammatically, the therapist summarizes the case conceptualization form and links them in a model. It is possible to choose a case conceptualization model for schemas or a schema mode model for schema modes. The case conceptualization model for schemas is similar to the holistic theory of cognitive behavioral therapy. The difference is that in addition to the current problems and relevant information, the schemas and coping styles are also reported (see Figure 6.1).

If a patient has many schemas, it is probably better to move directly to the mode model. In all other cases, a combination (of several schemas within a ball) is possible. In the case conceptualization model for schemas, links with past and current problems

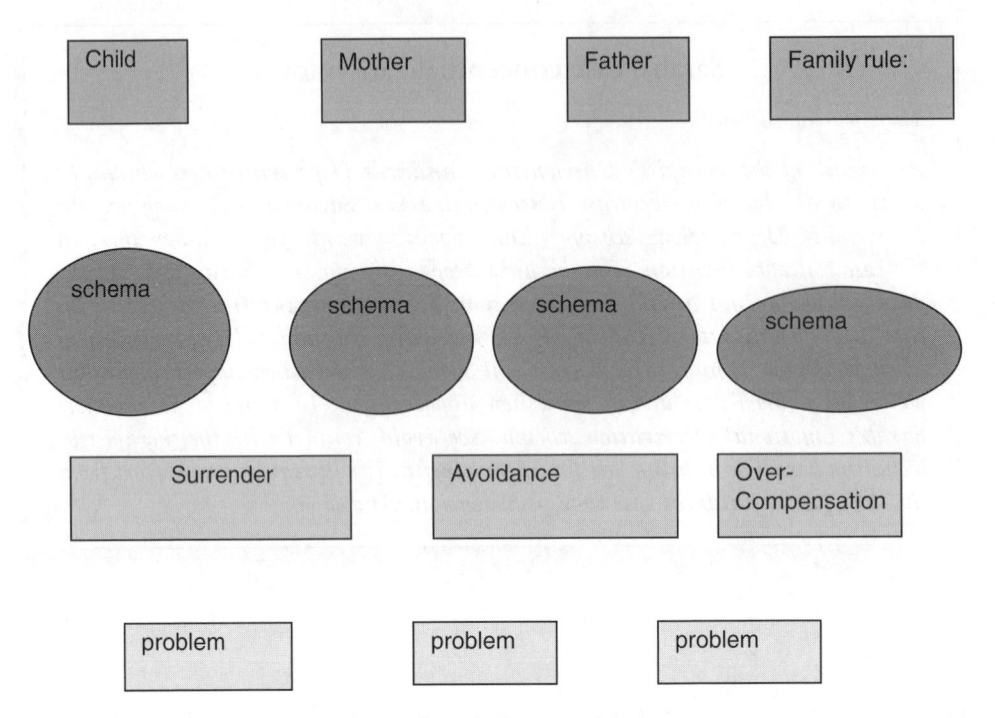

Figure 6.1 Example of the case conceptualization model

are mapped. This is not the case in the schema mode model, but because it is more concise and simpler, patients find it easier to understand. In both cases, the aim is to develop the model together. While discussing the information that has already been recorded on the form, the therapist has, if possible, already made links between current problems, the schemas, and the patient's life history. When developing a model, it is much easier for many patients to start with current problems and, in addition, search for links with the schemas and coping styles. After this, links with childhood are described. For patients who are reticent or denying of their past, it is difficult to make a link between their background and the schemas. That does not necessarily imply that you have to make a perfect model immediately. The model can be adapted with the passage of time when new information arises. Figure 6.1 shows a basic model without any arrows.

The number of squares and balls aren't prescriptive. The therapist draws as many squares as needed to describe all relevant issues. In general, the "child" square summarizes what is described in the form under temperamental and biological factors. The "father" and "mother" squares give information about the parents' character and parenting style. Family rules consist of set phrases from the family of origin, such as "we will never air your dirty washing in public." If there are many schemas, some therapists choose to put the four or five schemas with the highest scores or the schemas from the same domain together. As long as this doesn't oversimplify the problems, this can be a useful solution. The same goes for current problems: there is no harm in briefly summarizing these. Sarah's case conceptualization model is described in Figure 6.2.

Case Conceptualization in Schema Therapy 137

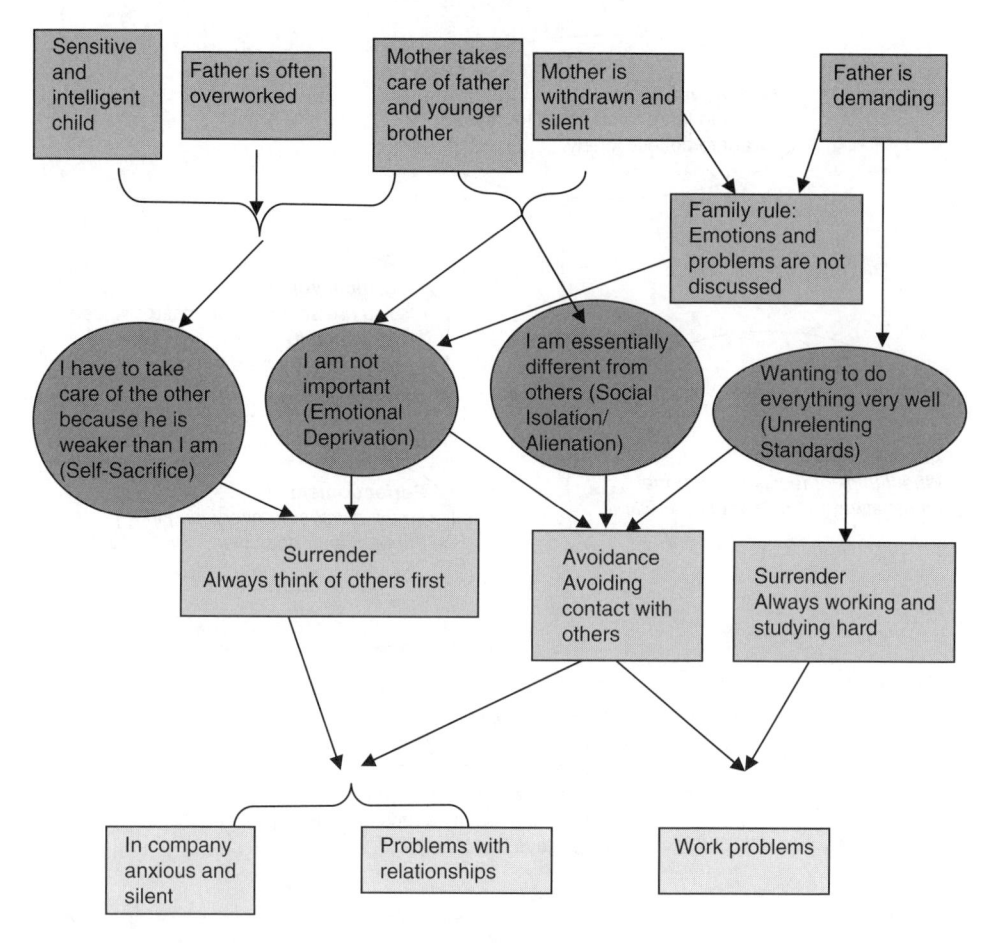

Figure 6.2 Sarah's case conceptualization model

The Schema Mode Model

Developing a schema mode model for borderline personality disorders has been described in Part I, Chapter 2. In Sarah's case the modes are:

- Vulnerable Child
- Compliant Surrender
- Over-Controller
- Demanding Parent

The mode model describes what the modes are called in the patient's own terms and the size of the balls give an impression of the importance of the mode (see Figure 6.3).

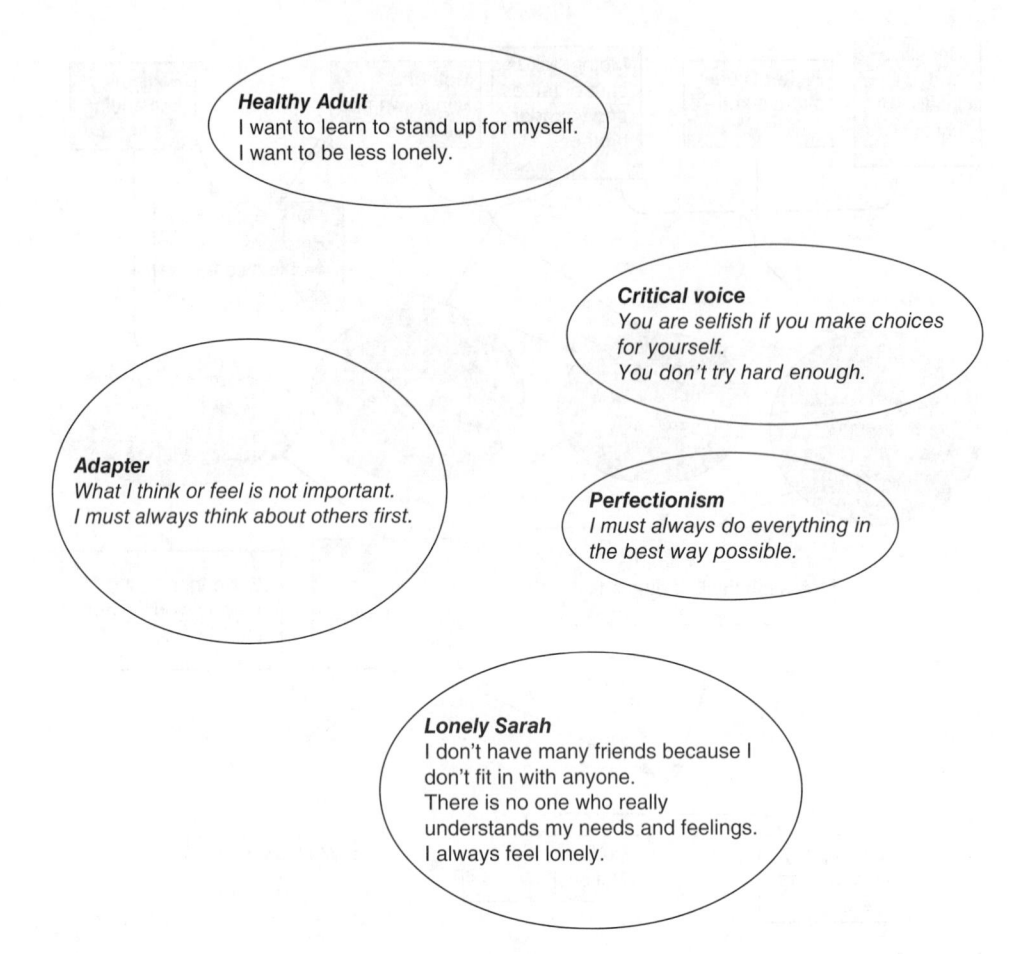

Healthy Adult
I want to learn to stand up for myself.
I want to be less lonely.

Critical voice
You are selfish if you make choices for yourself.
You don't try hard enough.

Adapter
What I think or feel is not important.
I must always think about others first.

Perfectionism
I must always do everything in the best way possible.

Lonely Sarah
I don't have many friends because I don't fit in with anyone.
There is no one who really understands my needs and feelings.
I always feel lonely.

Figure 6.3 Mode model: Sarah

Sarah's mode model

Sarah calls the Compliant Surrender "the adjuster" and the Obsessive Over-Controller "perfectionism." These two modes are very large. She can indicate what she would like to be (Healthy Adult), but she doesn't know how she can achieve this. When she does something in her own interest, the first thing that comes to her mind is that she is selfish and she doesn't try hard enough; she calls this "the critical voice." Initially, she doesn't recognize the Vulnerable Child mode, because the adjuster and her perfectionism control most of her life. But after several imageries in order to search for the origin of her schemas, she realizes that she has always been very lonely. Therefore, this mode is called "lonely Sarah."

Pitfalls and Tips

Confusion about schemas and coping styles

When investigating schemas and coping styles, sometimes the question arises whether something belongs to a schema or to a coping style. In other words, in Sarah's case is over-adjusting a coping style (Avoidance) of Emotional Deprivation? Or does the patient have the Self-Sacrifice schema? In most cases, both schemas are present, but one may be a reaction to the other. In the example above, the adjustment to others means surrender to self-sacrifice and at the same time the avoidance of emotional deprivation. The only way to find out which is a schema and which a coping style is to ask the patient and to bring in the YSQ scores. When someone has high scores on both schemas, then both schemas are most likely present. A lower score doesn't indicate that the schema isn't present; there can be a case of Avoidance or Over-Compensation while administering the YSQ.

The patient doesn't see the links between schemas and the past or present

When making links in the case conceptualization model, some patients experience difficulty making links between their past and the schemas. This mostly has to do with the fact that the patient doesn't want to speak ill of his family and has little sense of what a normal upbringing is like. If the usual techniques to make these links don't help, the best thing for the therapist to do is to agree with the perceptions that the patient already has and complete and adjust the model during the therapy. It might also help to search for other terms. *"My father was very preoccupied with himself"* sounds much better than *"My father was selfish."*

It is also possible for the therapist to see links that don't in fact exist. Since this therapy takes longer than symptom-focused therapy, the simple but effective advice is to wait until gray areas become clearer.

The link between the therapist's own schemas and the patient's is neglected

The therapist may have difficulties here, because he doesn't know his own schemas that well. To complete the schema questionnaire himself might help, as well as discussing this in the peer supervision group or in supervision. In general, it can be supposed that a therapist should start with schema therapy only if he has sufficient personal insight and if he has good supervision, in which this subject can be discussed as necessary.

Too many schemas and arrows, which make the model unclear

In practice, developing a case conceptualization model can be more complicated than the description of it shows. In particular, when there is a case with many schemas and links between all elements, the arrows may criss-cross, which won't make the

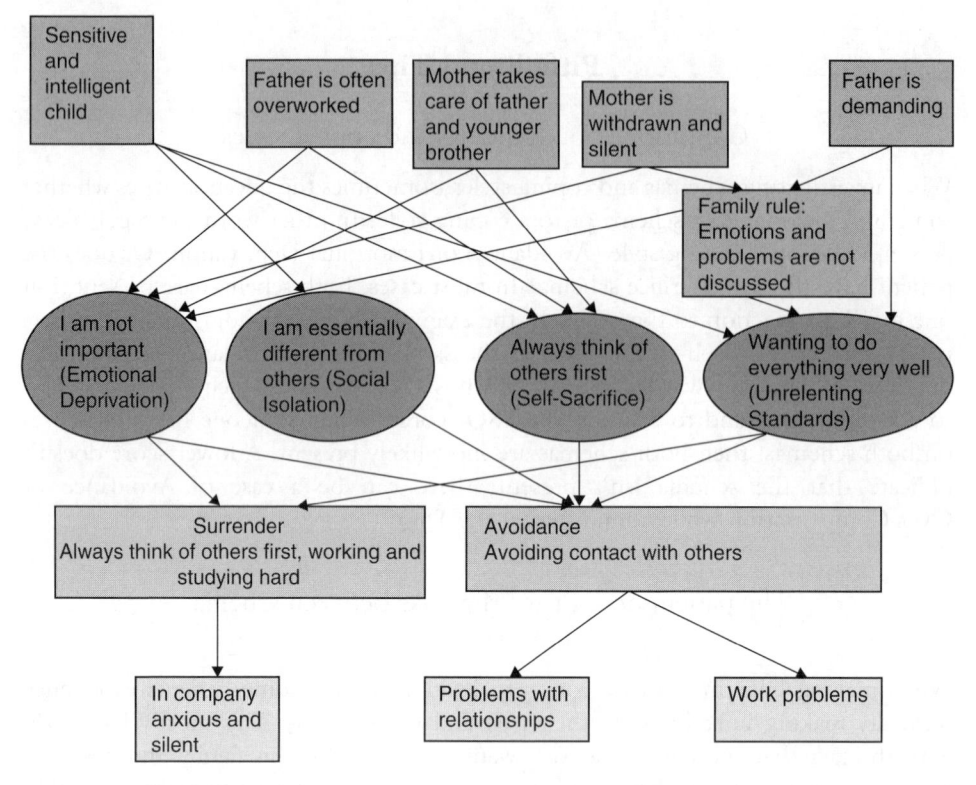

Figure 6.4 Model for Sarah

model easier to understand. Where there are too many schemas, the therapist can choose to put some of them in one domain. However, the disadvantage is that the model will become too general and won't explain enough. An alternative is to summarize the mass of information in a mode model.

A more technical solution is to move the schemas and use more terms. Furthermore, it is sometimes useful to mention a coping style twice. Figure 6.2 would be similar to Figure 6.4 if these steps weren't taken.

Developing just a model and no form

Due to time and outcome pressure in Dutch mental healthcare institutes, some therapists develop only the case conceptualization model and skip administering the form. In these cases, there is a high risk that the information will be incomplete. This provides a short-term gain of time, but in the long term, can lead to mistakes, stagnation in therapy, or under treatment. Another risk is that the problems that are an obstacle for Schema Therapy aren't discovered. When Schema Therapy is indicated, it may be assumed that short-term, symptom-focused therapy has already been attempted, and the outcomes were insufficient. It is worthwhile spending more time on the link between these problems and in greater depth before starting the treatment.

The Future

The question of whether the conceptualization model for schemas or the mode model will dominate, or whether both models will be used in tandem, is an interesting one. It may be possible for the two models to be integrated into one. However, developing an assessed case conceptualization before the beginning of Schema Therapy is required. It is essential for the patient to understand what his problems are and on what the treatment will be focused. For the therapist, it is important to reveal which schemas and modes are relevant in order to select the treatment techniques and to adjust the therapeutic alliance to the core schemas. Which concept of the case conceptualization would add most to this should be investigated in the future.

References

Artnz, A. and Genderen, H. van (2009) *Schema Therapy for Borderline Personality Disorder*. Chichester: Wiley-Blackwell.

Beck, A.T., Freeman, A., Davis, D. *et al.* (2004). *Cognitive Therapy of Personality Disorders*, New York: Guilford Press.

Bieling, P.J. and Kuyken, W. (2003) Is cognitive case formulation science or science fiction? *Clinical Psychology: Science and Practice*, 10(1), 52–69.

Henry, L.A. and Wiliams, R.M. (1997) Problems in conceptualization within cognitive therapy: an illustrative case study. *Clinical Psychology and Psychotherapy*, 4, 201–213.

Kuyken, W., Fothergill, C.D., Musa, M. and Chadwick, P. (2005) The reliability and quality of cognitive case formulation. *Behaviour Research and Therapy*, 43, 1187–1201.

Lobbestael, J., Vreeswijk, M.F., van Spinhoven, P., Schouten, E., and Arntz, A. (2010) The reliability and validity of the Schema Mode Inventory-revised (SMI-r). *Behavioural and Cognitive Psychotherapy*, 238, 437–458.

Perris, C. (1999) A conceptualization of personality-related disorders of interpersonal behaviour with implications for treatment. *Clinical Psychology and Psychotherapy*, 6, 239–260.

Sterk, F. and Rijkeboer, M.M. (1997) *Schema-Vragenlijst [Schema Questionnaire]*. Utrecht: Ambulatorium, Utrecht University.

Young, J.E. (1994) *Young Parenting Inventory*. New York: Cognitive Therapy Center of New York.

Young, J.E. (1995) *Young Compensation Inventory*. New York: Cognitive Therapy Center of New York.

Young, J.E. and Brown, G. (1994) *Young Schema Questionnaire*, 2nd edition. In J.E. Young, *Cognitive Therapy for Personality Disorders: a Schema-focused Approach*, rev. edition. Sarasota, FL: Professional Resource Press, pp. 63–76.

Young, J.E., Klosko, J.S. and Weishaar, M.E. (2003) *Schema Therapy: A Practitioner's Guide*. New York: Guilford Press.

Young, J.E. and Rygh, J.L. (1994) *Young–Rygh Avoidance Inventory*. New York: Cognitive Therapy Center of New York.

Part III
Schema Therapy Techniques

1

Schema Therapy for Eating Disorders
A Case Study Illustration of the Mode Approach

Susan Simpson

Introduction

Eating disorders are notoriously difficult to treat, with only a relatively limited proportion responding to standard cognitive behavioral therapy (CBT). A significant number of sufferers develop chronic symptoms and less than half of those with bulimia nervosa (BN) are symptom-free at follow-up (Fairburn *et al.*, 1991) with a typical drop-out rate of about 25% (Shapiro *et al.*, 2007). Anorexia nervosa (AN) has the highest mortality rate of any psychiatric disorder (Vitiello and Lederhendler, 2000). Of those who are weight-restored, 35–50% relapse after "full" recovery (Herzog *et al.*, 1999; Carter, Blackmore, Sutander-Pinnock and Woodside, 2004). There is scant evidence for the efficacy of CBT with AN (Bulik, Berkman, Brownley, Sedway and Lohr, 2007) with poor acceptance for treatment and high drop-out (Halmi *et al.*, 2005).

Several factors may interfere with engagement in and effectiveness of therapy for this client group, in particular ambivalence around change and the ego-syntonic nature of the symptoms, especially in AN (Vitousek, Watson and Wilson, 1998). There is a high level of comorbidity in the eating disordered population (Blinder, Cumella and Sunathara, 2006). Nature of this comorbidity is complex, with factors such as malnourishment and unreliability of self-report in this population confounding the accuracy of measurement of eating and personality pathology (Vitousek and Stumpf, 2005). The prevalence of personality disorder (PD) is high – up to 69% of sufferers may meet diagnostic criteria for at least one personality disorder, and of these, 93% may have concurrent Axis I comorbidity (especially affective disorders, anxiety disorders, and substance misuse) (Braun, Sunday and Halmi, 1994; Sansone,

Levitt and Sansone, 2006). Borderline PD is most prevalent in those with BN and binge-eating/purging-type AN; and obsessive-compulsive and avoidant PD most common in restricting-type AN and binge-eating disorder (Sansone, Levitt and Sansone, 2004; Cassin and von Ranson, 2005; Levitt and Sansone, 2006). Those patients who fit into the EDNOS (Eating Disorders not Otherwise Specified) category may have even more severe and widespread personality pathology than the "pure" disorders (Herzog, et al., 1992). Evidence from studies on eating disorders indicate that the presence of rigid personality pathology (e.g., perfectionism, narcissistic defenses) and PDs (particularly avoidant and obsessive-compulsive) adversely effects outcomes (Gillberg, Råstam and Gillberg, 1995; Santonastaso, Friederici and Favaro, 1999; Diaz-Marsa, Carrasco and Saiz, 2000; Bizeul, Sadowsky and Rigaud, 2001; Milos, Spindler, Ruggiero, Klaghofer and Schnyder, 2002; Sutandar-Pinnock, Blake, Carter, Olmsted and Kaplan, 2003; Grilo et al., 2007; Waller, Sines, Meyer, Foster and Skelton, 2007). Avoidant PD has a prevalence of approximately 25% in AN (Skodol et al., 1993; Diaz-Marsa et al., 2000), but is common across all eating disorders (Grilo et al., 2003). The pattern of pervasive behavioral, emotional, and cognitive avoidance that is characteristic of avoidant PD is evident from early adulthood. Interpersonal avoidance is particularly prominent, such as keeping others at a distance and avoiding intimate relationships. These avoidant traits precede the onset of eating disorders, which may indicate that they function as both risk and maintaining factors in this population (Troop and Treasure, 1997; Troop, Holbrey and Treasure, 1998; Schmidt and Treasure, 2006). Evidence indicates that even after recovery these traits remain intact (Casper, 1990).

There is some consensus that in order to maximize effectiveness and minimize risk of relapse, eating-disordered sufferers with schema-level beliefs (i.e., unconditional beliefs about oneself in relation to others and the world) require a sophisticated treatment model that specifically addresses both eating and personality pathology in a focused and intensive way (Leung, Waller and Thomas, 2000; Bruce and Steiger, 2006; Hinrichsen and Waller, 2006; Simpson, Morrow, van Vreeswijk and Reid, 2010; Simpson and Slowey, 2011). The transdiagnostic "enhanced CBT" (CBT-E) model (Fairburn, Cooper and Shafran, 2003) attempts to address some of these factors by offering additional "modules" on top of the standard CBT approach. However, this is essentially a maintenance model, with an almost exclusive here-and-now focus and minimal attention paid to the early origins of underlying schema-level representations.

The schema mode model (Young, Klosko and Weishaar, 2003) is distinctly suited to the eating disorder population, particularly those with personality disorders, complex problems, and interpersonal dysfunction. This model explicitly addresses schemas (and associated core beliefs), emotions, behaviors, and interpersonal difficulties, with the therapeutic relationship as the primary vehicle for change. ST techniques specifically target the entrenched belief systems and high levels of avoidance characteristic of both personality disorders and complex eating disorders that frequently interfere with progress in a conventional CBT setting (Taylor, Parker, Bagby and Bourker, 1996; Dennis and Sansone, 1997; Leung et al., 2000; Waller, Ohanian, Meyer, Osman, 2000; Waller, Dickson and Ohanian, 2002; Mountford and Waller, 2006; Waller, Kennerley and Ohanian, 2007). One of the focal guiding strategies in ST is the development of a formulation and treatment plan that addresses the underlying functions of eating disorders. This has been highlighted in previous literature as critical to effective treatment with this population (Vitousek *et al.*, 1998; Wildes, Ringham and Marcus, 2010).

Eating disorder modes are parts of the self that can be conceptualized as states that are to some degree dissociated from each other. In spite of their lack of integration, they are mostly experienced as ego-syntonic, especially the dysfunctional parent and coping modes. Although some modes are more "split-off" than others, to some extent they are all maladaptive, rigid, and sometimes unacknowledged. I propose 11 schema modes linked to eating disorders, adapted from the 10 schema modes identified by Young, Klosko and Weishaar (2003). As shown in Table 1.1, the Critical and Demanding modes (which frequently operate in alliance) set unrealistically high standards and deprive, attack, and punish the Child modes, typically using the body as a target for shame and humiliation. The Critical/Demanding modes treat emotional neediness with disdain, thereby triggering high levels of shame in the Shamed/Deprived Child mode. When the distress experienced in Deprived/Shamed Child mode is too great, they flip into the Detached Self-Soother mode to block out emotional pain and to soothe themselves in a detached way (e.g., by bingeing, vomiting, alcohol, sleep). The "Needy" Child feels deprived and seeks nurturance in an impulsive and entitled manner, thereby incurring further messages of disgust from Dysfunctional Adult modes. The Perfectionistic Controller mode is used as a primary avoidance mode, whereby the eating disorder sufferer compulsively uses restrictive and ritualistic eating, body checking, and exercise in an attempt to control and "improve" their body shape and/or weight, with the aim of reducing the perceived risk for schema-triggering and further humiliation and shame. This mode functions as a pervasive mechanism that blocks emotion. Perfectionism is linked to the Unrelenting Standards schema and covers a range of other domains, including general appearance, work, studies, and cleaning. This mode compensates for at least one of the following underlying schemas: Failure, Defectiveness/Shame, Emotional Deprivation, and Subjugation. It is strongly reinforced by short-term feelings of achievement and pride when self-imposed rules and ideals (e.g., for thinness) are fulfilled. In this mode, the client can appear "healthy" and in control of their life and is therefore more likely to minimize the existence or severity of the eating disorder. The Compliant Surrender mode also typically compensates for an underlying Defectiveness/Shame schema, allowing the client to avoid rejection (and schema-triggering) by pleasing others, allowing them to take control, and meeting their needs. However, this mode gives control to others, thereby reinforcing perceptions and fears associated with loss of control. Bingeing can therefore occur in the context of the Critical mode (as self-punishment or deprivation); Detached Self-Soother (as avoidance/escape from emotional pain or emptiness); and the "Needy" Child mode (as a backlash in response to feeling controlled or deprived by other people (as well as one's own modes); i.e., "I'll take what I want!").

Case Study – Nicki

Presenting problems

Nicki was referred to the service by her General Practitioner. She was a 41-year-old woman with longstanding BN. She recalled a 21-year history of eating large

Table 1.1 Eleven hypothesized schema modes linked to complex eating disorders (adapted from the modes described in Young, Klosko and Weishaar, 2003)

Child Modes

- **Shamed / Deprived Child**: feels rejected, hurt, unwanted, ashamed, anxious, panicky, lost, unattractive, and inferior. Feels like a lonely child that is valued only by "proving" herself to others (e.g., achievement, physical appearance) and/or meeting others' needs. Because the most important emotional needs of the child have generally not been met, the child usually feels empty, anxious, alone, and undeserving of love. Feels ashamed of normal emotions and needs due to explicit or implicit message from parents that these are unacceptable or unmanageable. Feels different and inferior due to perceived physical flaws. Feels disempowered due to prolonged bullying, exclusion and/or over-control by caregivers. Criticism, abuse, and bullying may lead to a sense of being socially unacceptable, unattractive, and ashamed at an emotional and a bodily "felt-sense" level. Craves a sense of safety and control due to feeling overwhelmed by feelings of powerlessness (i.e., powerless to change the experience of being unacceptable/ shameful).
- **"Needy" Child**: Feels desperate for nurturance, protection, and attention. Takes what she can get. Impulsive bingeing, overdoses, and self-harm function as ways of seeking nurturance. Acts on impulses, in a self-focused or uncontrolled manner to get one's own way without regard to possible consequences to self or others. Rebels against demands to be "good." This mode is often suppressed since emotional needs are viewed as shameful.
- **Angry Child**: Feels intensely angry because emotional needs not being met. Expresses anger through passive-aggressive means (e.g., withdrawal, irritability, lashing out). Anger is usually suppressed, as it is experienced as being "out-of-control," which is viewed as unacceptable and shameful.
- **Happy Child**: As described in original model. Views body as an integrated part of the "self" and uses it appropriately for play and pleasurable activities.

Maladaptive Coping Modes

- **Compliant Surrender**: As described in original model. Passively allows others to take control or even openly gives control to others in an attempt to increase the likelihood of gaining emotional nurturance and social acceptance and reduce the chance of criticism and humiliation.
- **Detached Protector**: As described in original model. The effort required to block emotion may result in physical pain such as constriction in the throat/chest. Keeps relationships at superficial level. Restriction (starving oneself) and over-exercise (as well as other compulsive behaviors such as workaholism, drug, and alcohol use) can function by preventing schemas being triggered in the first place, by allowing person to shut off from relationships and the demands of life. Compulsive bingeing can also work this way by pervading all of a person's thinking space while they plan what they will eat and then allowing them to completely switch off from everything else while bingeing. May become angry and defensive (Angry Protector) if feeling threatened by potential loss of control (e.g., when prompted to explore possible disadvantages associated with eating disorder).
- **Detached Self-Soother**: Shuts off emotion by engaging in solitary activities that will soothe, stimulate, or distract them from uncomfortable feelings. These behaviors mostly function in an impulsive manner to avoid acute distress after schemas have been triggered. Bingeing, exercise, drugs, and alcohol (and vomiting) can be used as a way of trying to block strong emotions and to self-soothe (whilst bypassing the Critical mode and/or Shamed Child mode). Subsequently, vomiting may follow as a way of "cancelling out" the feelings of shame and guilt triggered by bingeing. These behaviors are also self-soothing during episodes of generalized anxiety, linked to schemas that may be "primed" but not fully triggered (e.g., "free-floating" feelings of emptiness and vulnerability linked to the emotional deprivation schema).

Table 1.1 (*Continued*)

Perfectionistic Controller Mode
- This mode develops as a result of lack of attention/nurturance during childhood, or attention that was largely dependent on performing at a very high level. The child learns that they will only be seen to be worthwhile if they are "special" (e.g., regarding work/study/dieting achievements, weight, shape, appearance). This mode thereby compensates for underlying feelings of defectiveness or inferiority by actively seeking accolades or trying to appear "perfect" or superior to others.
- Compensates for strong emotions associated with fear of being ignored, hurt, or rejected and losing control (e.g., of emotions, eating, body shape/weight).
- May be self-absorbed, competitive, over controlling, attention seeking, wanting to be seen as special. Compares self constantly with others and is hyper-vigilant to signs that one may be inferior in some respect (e.g., body shape, skin, clothing, outward expression of happiness).
- Uses "thinness" and/or physical "perfection" to inflate sense of self and may take pride in "flaunting" this as a sign of their superior self-control and discipline. This may involve using diet and hours of daily exercise to hone body shape and weight; placing excessive emphasis on clothes, hairstyles, and makeup; spending hours on appearance before leaving home.
- Imposes a simplifying and tangible set of [dietary and weight-related] rules. Often the child has experienced a combination of inadequate emotional nurturance alongside excessive overprotection and is frightened by the unpredictability and complexities of growing up. Dietary rules and regulations provide a sense of direction and purpose in an otherwise confusing and frightening world and a substitute for true emotional nurturance and connection. When these rules are met, they also compensate for the hitherto absence of a sense of achievement and pride in other life domains, especially for those with Failure and Unrelenting Standards schemas.
- *Invests significant energy in planning ahead to ensure that life is predictable and controllable. Exerts control through:*
    - Prioritizing safety and certainty at all costs. Excessive adherence to routine.
    - Focusing control on a particular aspect of one's life or self (e.g., body) or may strive for a state of complete self-control, whilst denying one's own needs completely, thereby defying basic human instincts and desires.
    - Hyper-vigilance to signs that events are not unfolding as planned or that one cannot completely retain control (e.g., over eating/weight/shape).
    - Engaging in compulsive checking behaviors to provide reassurance that body weight/shape is not spiraling out of control, and that one is completely "safe" from the risk of criticism.
    - Constant rumination and compulsive thinking focused on determining the "correct" way of behaving, which is intended to relieve feelings of anxiety and guilt triggered by dysfunctional parent modes.
    - Use of restriction (of eating) as a way of controlling others and/ or keeping others close (geographically, rather than emotionally) and to compensate for unmet needs for connection and nurturance.
    - Use of eating disorder as a compensatory "relationship" that is safer and more reliable than acknowledging emotional needs, connecting with other people, and risking rejection/ humiliation.

(*Continued*)

Table 1.1 (*Continued*)

Adult modes
Demanding Mode:
- Functions as the internalized voice of a parent or a combination of sources. In many cases this mode develops from the implicit meaning they deduced from the lack of emotional nurturance or attunement during childhood, alongside the perception that their needs were seen as unacceptable or unmanageable to the parent. This voice then evolves into an internalized self-dictator that demands that one behaves the "right" way, and criticizes and humiliates the child for having normal needs and/or for being unacceptable or undesirable in some way.
- May use body as a tangible target on which rules and standards can be imposed, especially if a parent was openly body and/or weight-conscious. Believes that there is one "right" healthy diet that she should adhere to at all times without fail. Believes that she should strive to achieve a self-determined ideal weight through some combination of excessive dieting and exercise, diet pills, diuretics, and laxatives. Believes that breaking one's dietary rules will lead to loss of self-control, excessive weight gain and ultimately, undesirability.

Critical Mode:
- Internalized voice of parent or significant others (e.g., school bullies). The tone of this mode is harsh, critical, and unforgiving. Signs and symptoms include self-loathing, self-criticism, self-denial, self-mutilation, body dysmorphia, suicidal fantasies, and self-destructive behavior.
- Punishment may be directed toward the body and take the form of cutting or depriving oneself (e.g., of food) and talking about one's body or appearance in mean, harsh tones.
- Functions as a punitive screen or filter through which one views oneself. Expresses harsh messages of disgust, criticism, and labeling toward body. Distorts perception of body-image through internalized (felt-sense) shame/disgust and associated images of body as unattractive/ugly. Can be triggered by behaviors that may lead to weight gain (e.g., not sticking to strict diet, eating food from their 'bad' food list), perceived signs of possible weight gain (e.g., bloating; compliments such as "you look healthy"; tightness of clothes) which are then used as evidence for 'fatness' and 'unattractiveness') and experiencing and/or expressing 'unacceptable' emotions. Expresses disgust regarding eating disorder symptoms and inability to exercise strict dietary control.

The Healthy Adult:
- As described in original model. The body is valued as an important aspect of the 'self' that needs to be cared for. Able to view oneself in a balanced way and to recognize inherent worth and attractiveness.

---

quantities of food over a period of two to three hours in an uncontrolled way at least seven to eight times per week. During binges she described feeling "spacey." Food consumed during binges was mostly that which came under her "forbidden" category, including chocolate bars, sweets, biscuits, as well as breakfast cereals, bread, and takeaway pizza. Binges were followed by feelings of extreme guilt and vomiting. She exercised vigorously every morning at her local gym for at least an hour. If she missed a session, she was overcome with feelings of guilt throughout the day and found it difficult to concentrate on her work as a project manager. On weekends she

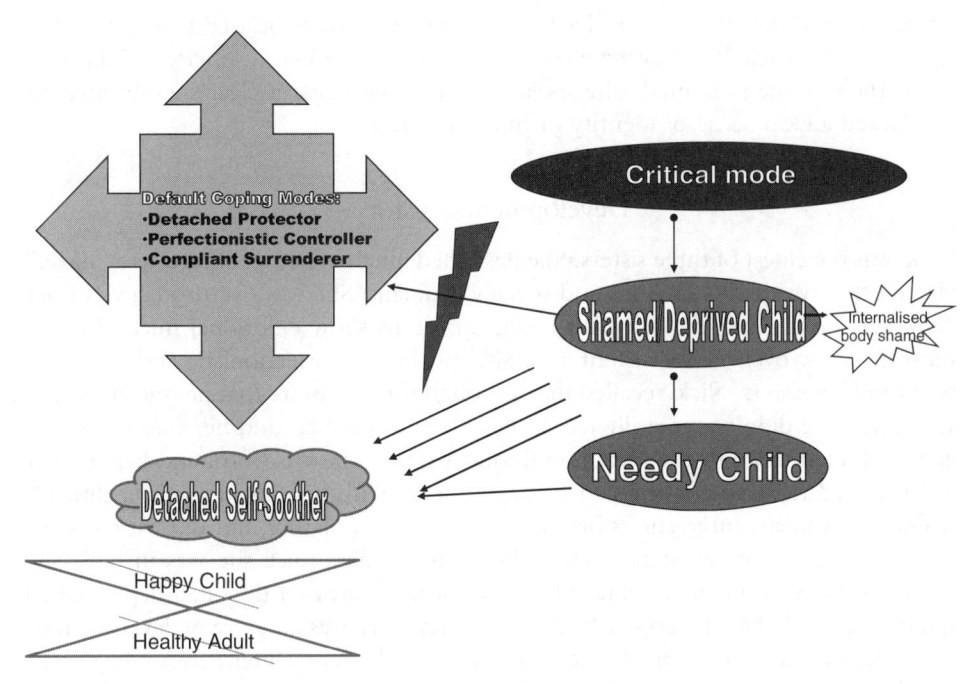

Figure 1.1 Eating disorder modes

mostly stayed at home and avoided social events. Her partner (with whom she was living) frequently expressed frustration about her lack of sociability and preoccupation with her weight. Nicki described feeling self-conscious and was preoccupied with thoughts that others saw her as "fat" and "unattractive." She avoided wearing tight-fitting or summery clothes and holidays at beach resorts (which would have involved wearing swimwear). She felt that her body was the "wrong shape" and that her thighs and hips were lumpy and out of proportion with the rest of her body. She compared herself with other women in a hyper-vigilant way, noticing whether others were thinner or "better proportioned" than her. This interfered with her ability to carry out and remain focused on conversations with others. She had been told by others that she came across as aloof and sometimes arrogant. She described experiencing high levels of distress and shame whenever she ate more than she had planned, weighed herself, or was invited out for a social event. On numerous occasions she had been invited to go out and then found that she couldn't decide what to wear. Whatever outfit she chose triggered thoughts that it might make her look fat, followed by high levels of shame, anxiety, and low mood that could continue for several days. She was often irritable and did not want to get out of bed in the mornings. Her partner and children learned to avoid her during those times. She described feeling disgust when she looked at her body in a mirror and therefore minimized this when possible. However, she frequently checked her body with her hands throughout the day, especially her hips and bottom.

Nicki was very smartly dressed at her initial sessions. She had clearly spent a great deal of time preparing herself, with immaculate makeup, hair, and clothing (triggering the therapist's own "Demanding mode" with associated thoughts about appearing disheveled!). Nevertheless, there was something distinctly "child-like" about the way she presented. She spoke in a way that made it clear she was anxious and lacked a clear sense of identity or inner direction.

Developmental history

Nicki was the eldest of three sisters. She described much of her childhood as a "haze." Her mother was highly anxious and socially avoidant. She was overprotective of her daughters on the one hand, whilst being unable to show emotional nurturance or warmth in any overt or consistent way. She was highly perfectionistic and critical of Nicki and her sisters. Nicki recalled that although she was aware that her mother cared about her, she didn't ever really feel loved. Her mother had told her that her father had continued to go to the local pub frequently after she was born, and her mother had resented the fact that she had to stay at home with her. Nicki found it difficult at first to recall any interactions between herself and her father, but did witness conflicts between her parents, and heard their raised voices once she was in bed. She described these events in a detached, matter-of-fact way, as if they had happened to someone else. As her therapist I had a sense that there was an extreme level of emotional deprivation that "whitewashed" her childhood. Her feelings had not been validated at any level and she was left feeling that her existence was an inconvenience.

Nicki had a shy, introverted disposition and she recalled feeling self-conscious in social situations from a young age. Her family lived outside a village, restricting her access to social events after school hours. At school she had one or two close friends, but she was bullied at secondary school. This took the form of subtle sniggering and pointing during class times, being called "ugly" and "spot face," being excluded and laughed at during physical exercise classes, and being actively ostracized by peers during school-breaks. Her mother was overweight and frequently went on fad diets in an attempt to lose weight. Her father was contemptuous of her mother and made it clear that he found her unattractive due to her weight. Nicki was of normal weight during childhood. She attended a gymnastic class throughout her early teens but this was stopped at the age of 15 as her mother felt she should be concentrating on school exams. This was followed by a rapid change in her body shape, as she began to gain weight.

At the age of 16 she went on her first diet under the guidance of her mother. Although she initially lost a small amount of weight, she regarded the diet as ineffective and was left feeling that she had failed. By 18 she had tried several fad diets and was restricting her diet severely, whilst exercising for several hours each day. She described a period of AN at the age of 19, characterized by restrictive eating and purging. At that time her body mass index (BMI) dropped to 14 (normal range 18.5–24.9) for approximately one year. Following this, she described a gradual onset of binge eating and purging and at the time of referral her BMI was stable at 18.

Treatment history

Nicki had attended a CBT group for eating disorders in the past with some individual support. She had found this helpful in terms of making insights and links between her eating behaviors, thoughts, and feelings in the here-and-now. She had also seen a dietician for nutritional advice. Her eating behaviors had not improved, but she had found the support helpful. She said that she had resigned herself to the "fact" that the eating disorder was "who I am" and that she could not imagine herself existing without it. She had also had a trial of Fluoxetine 60 mg for a period of four months approximately two years previously, but had not found this helpful.

DSM-IV diagnosis (American Psychiatric Association, 2004)

Axis I: Bulimia Nervosa (307.51); Dysthymic Disorder (300.4); Generalized Anxiety Disorder (300.02)
 Axis II: Avoidant Personality Disorder (301.82)

Formulation

Nicki's hypothesized formulation is shown in Figure 1.2. *Emotional Temperament* sensitive, eager to please, passive, shy. Her *Core Unmet Needs* were a lack of emotional nurturance and (unconditional) acceptance from both parents during childhood, alongside a lack of safety due to the ongoing threat of being bullied for a prolonged period during her school years. Nicki experienced minimal opportunities for developing autonomy and she was expected to follow quite rigid family rules with little scope to make her own choices. She experienced few opportunities to develop her identity, due to a lack of opportunity to make choices and minimal individual attention or praise. On the basis of information provided by more distant family members, it was hypothesized that the ingredients for a healthy attachment relationship with her parents (e.g., "tuning in" to her needs and "mirroring" or reflecting emotions) were absent from very early in her life. Both parents were emotionally detached and focused on their own problems. Shape and weight were linked to self-worth through observing her mother struggling with her weight and her father criticizing her and treating her with disdain for being overweight. Nicki's needs and feelings were invalidated, and play and spontaneity were discouraged. Nicki was sensitized to her mother's avoidance of her own emotional distress and thereby learned to protect her mother from her "bad" feelings through detachment. Nicki learned that closeness to others would lead to humiliation and rejection. She developed self-protective strategies to keep relationships as superficial as possible and to finish relationships that became too close. Checking behaviors (e.g., flatness of stomach) increased preoccupation with appearance. Physical side-effects (dental decay, acne) reinforced her belief that she was unattractive and associated feelings of shame.

Her BN served the function of providing a "safe" relationship that would occupy her mind and give her a daily challenge and *raison d'être*, which also provided a sense of hope that she could feel good about herself if only she reached her target "ideal" weight. The vicious diet–binge–vomit cycle that developed provided a way of occupying her mind in order to avoid the emptiness and meaningless of a life devoid of close relationships. In the short term, the daily challenge was reinforced by the sense of pride that resulted from successful dieting and weight loss. In the longer term, her sense of failure was reinforced by loss of control over her eating, reinforcing feelings of shame around the perception that this was a self-imposed cycle that was entirely her own fault.

Childhood

- Shy disposition.

- Parental conflict: Mum controlling, overprotective, critical. Dad absent, rejecting.

- High expectations to live up to mother's perfectionistic standards.

- Lack of emotional nurturance, encouragement, support.

- Compared negatively with siblings.

- Made to feel an "imposition"; that my needs were unimportant.

- Lived out of town; minimal contact with peers; socially isolated.

- Bullied at high school.

- Stopped gymnastics at 15; followed by weight gain.

- Began dieting at 16 years old.

- Weight loss through restrictive eating and excessive exercise.

↓

Schemas

- I am worthless; I am inferior; I am fat and ugly. *(Defectiveness)*

- I am too needy; no one can ever give me what I need. *(Emotional Deprivation)*

- I am different; I don't belong here. *(Social Isolation)*

- If others get to know the real me, they will reject me or leave me. *(Abandonment)*

- I'm a failure, not good enough. *(Failure)*

- I must strive to be the best in everything I do – mistakes are intolerable. To be loved and accepted I have to be perfect/special/the best. (*Unrelenting Standards*)

- Others will hurt me, put me down. *(Mistrust)*

- I must give in and do what others want or I will be rejected. *(Subjugation)*

- I must sacrifice myself and put others' needs first. *(Self-Sacrifice)*

Figure 1.2

Shamed/Deprived Child	Critical Mode (the "Bully")	Detached Protector ("Blocker")
• Feels anxious and empty, alone, unwanted, unloved. • Afraid of being humiliated, rejected, or laughed at. • Feels ashamed and "disgusting" (bodily felt-sense). • Wants to hide from others.	• Toby (partner) doesn't really like you – you'll just end up looking stupid when he sees what you're really like and rejects you. No one will ever love you; you are too ugly. • You are completely out of proportion; your stomach is huge! • Look at her; she's much prettier than you! • You have ruined everything by eating that cake – it has already turned to fat!	• Dieting, exercise, and preoccupation with weight/shape helps to block out painful feelings of depression and chronic emptiness and gives life a safe "focus" and purpose • Pushes others away – friendships are superficial
Perfectionistic Controller	**Angry Child**	**Detached Self-Soother**
• Sticking to my diet and keeping to my exercise regime makes me feel confident and in control. I need to know exactly what I have to do to make sure nothing bad happens. • The most important thing in life is to look good and to have a perfect body. • The thinner I am, the better person I will be and the more others will like me; If I let go of the control, my weight will spiral and I'll be rejected again. • Compulsive checking – "I need to lose fat off my stomach. Must exercise more!"	• Irritable and sullen if partner perceived as inattentive. • Protests by angrily withdrawing from others when feeling hurt, left out, or not understood. **"Needy" Child** • Bingeing on food as desperate attempt to satiate dietary and emotional needs. • Impulsive clothes shopping.	• When feeling low (e.g., after eating unplanned foods) uses bingeing, vomiting, and alcohol to block shame and anger. • Uses work and exercise to occupy mind, avoid difficult feelings **Compliant Surrender** • Spends most of her time cooking and cleaning for others. • Goes along with partner's plans and ideas, and children's demands. Rarely tells them what she needs. • Hands over control to therapist: "What should I do? Can you fix me?"

Figure 1.2 (*Continued*)

Phase 1: (Sessions 1–6) Comprehensive assessment

- Nicki's therapy began with a full developmental assessment of her eating disorder and exploration of her background. Throughout this period, the therapist was gently probing to identify links between childhood issues, relationships, and current patterns and difficulties. Nicki commented that even attending therapy was experienced as extremely shameful and she was aware that what she was looking for was a "quick-fix" solution to her difficulties. She talked about her eating problems in a detached way. She became tearful when questioned about the connections between eating disorder symptoms and difficult feelings or events in her life. She then lowered her head and said in a quiet voice that she "hated" it when she was emotional and reassured the therapist that it wouldn't happen again. This led to some discussion about where and how she had learned to see her feelings as shameful, how other family members dealt with distress, and the explicit and implicit messages her parents had conveyed to her as a child about her emotions as undesirable and a burden on others.

- The assessment explored the onset of her eating disorder and the links between fluctuations in eating disorder symptoms and events within significant relationships. The function of her eating disorder as a psychological survival mechanism was explored in the context of her childhood environment and clear absence of emotional connection, nurturance, and empathy.

Phase 2: (Sessions 7–18) Cognitive Behavioral Therapy (CBT-BN) and Schema-focused Cognitive Therapy (SFCT)

- CBT-BN: Nicki was asked to fill out food diaries to be used as the basis for exploring relevant triggers for binge-eating and self-critical thinking. The following session she returned with diaries uncompleted. She explained that she had started to fill them out, but when her eating behaviors deteriorated and bingeing increased she tore up the sheets. We explored her feelings of shame in relation to the prospect of sharing her diaries, linked with expectations of being humiliated or "told off." In order to prioritize therapeutic bonding and to avoid any disruption to the development of trust at this early stage of therapy, I made a note of this as a probable indication of a Mistrust/Abuse schema and/or Defectiveness schema, and suggested that this might be something she could try once she felt ready to take a step toward increasing her self-awareness and testing out my response to her completed diaries. I reassured her that I would check with her regularly about when she might feel ready to take this step.
- We examined the advantages and disadvantages of the eating disorder in her life, including dental decay, acne, feelings of loss of control, heightened feelings of guilt and shame, difficulties attending social events due to fear of eating in public, and preoccupation with her body that disrupted concentration at work. Although she initially felt that there were no fears associated with giving up her eating disorder, she then surprised herself by identifying that the absence of her eating disorder was linked to the presence of (unacceptable) low mood, that the eating disorder was something she could rely on (unlike "relationships" with people), and without it she would feel lost and alone.
- Together we agreed on the terms of a contract, stating the consequences of weight loss during treatment ("non-negotiables"), the points at which other professionals would become involved in her care, and it was agreed that we would be working toward a normal BMI weight range.
- Standard CBT-BN techniques (Wilson and Fairburn, 1998) were used to identify cognitive distortions and core beliefs linked to eating behaviors. Nicki was given educational material on nutrition and the dangers of dieting and advice on gradually introducing regular meals and snacks. A number of behavioral strategies were suggested in order to help her minimize binges and normalize her eating patterns. Together, we began to develop a list of Nicki's "good" and "bad" foods for gradual desensitization. After six CBT sessions there had been no improvement in the frequency of binges and the ST model was adopted.
- After filling out the Young Schema Questionnaire (YSQ-L2; Young and Brown, 1990), the origins and maintenance strategies for her main schemas were explored in detail.

- ST cognitive strategies were used to challenge her primary schemas, including Reviewing the Evidence (where evidence from the past and present is identified to support and refute schemas), and Healthy vs. Schema voice dialogue (where this evidence is used to conduct a dialogue between the healthy voice and the schema voice). These exercises gave Nicki preliminary experience whereby she was able to see her schemas as only part of her rather than all-consuming, and enabled her to begin to consider the possibility that she may also have a healthy part. Although this exercise led to cognitive rather than emotional change, it increased her awareness of the role of her schemas in driving and maintaining her eating disorder and low self-esteem.
- Schema diaries were used to identify how schemas were triggered by relevant events such as sensations of bloatedness, eating "bad" foods, breaking dietary rules, perceived criticism or disapproval from others when others didn't recognize her emotional needs, others trying to get closer to her, comparisons of self with others who were thinner or considered more attractive, and the presence of "negative" emotions.
- Imagery assessment revealed core themes in her relationships. These included memories of being humiliated and teased as a child by peers at school, her mother telling her when she was a child that "making a fuss" (i.e., expressing distress) was "naughty," expressions of contempt and disgust by her father, especially during mealtimes, overt rejection of mother by her father for being "disgustingly overweight," and feeling alone and isolated in her bedroom.

Phase 3: (Sessions 19–29) Getting to know the eating disorder modes

- Introducing the modes: Nicki was introduced to the concept of modes as facets of the personality that are currently active for an individual, often triggered by particular situations. A mode formulation diagram was configured on the basis of data from her Schema Mode Inventory (SMI; Young et al., 2007) and self-report (see Figure 1.2). Modes were labeled and identified as they arose in sessions.
- Linking modes with childhood and current relationships: Nicki recognized that the Detached Protector was a mode that had existed for as long as she could remember. Through the Imagery Assessment exercise, we learned that this coping mode developed as a way of protecting herself from being hurt and humiliated by others and connecting with "unacceptable" emotions and needs. It was evident that this was one of her main "default" modes (i.e., she spent most of her life in this detached, disconnected state). We explored how the Detached Protector blocked distress linked to her Shamed/Deprived Child mode and kept relationships at a very superficial level. As we began to look back through her childhood, it became clear that there was a dearth of emotional connection or attunement to her needs. She was unable to recall a time that she had ever been able to talk to anyone about her feelings or distress, and she had adopted an "independent" stance from an early age. Her Detached Protector mode had been there from as early as she could remember, blocking her relationships with others and preventing her from further hurt. She recalled feeling close to one girl at secondary school, but she decided to end this relationship without any sense of the reason

why. In retrospect, she saw that it had been safer to restrict interactions with others to a superficial level. She recalled her Detached Protector mode helping her to cope when bullied at school by allowing her to block all feelings of shame and humiliation. Her Critical/Demanding mode was identified with her parents' strict rules, her father's derogatory comments, the way he looked at her, and the cruel and punitive tone of the school bullies. Nicki was able to link this mode to her unrealistically high dietary standards and the disgust she felt for her body. She labeled it the "Bully."

- Identifying the function of coping modes: The function of coping modes was explored in depth, especially that of the Compliant Surrender in maintaining relationships, albeit at a superficial level; the Detached Self-Soother by impulsively blocking negative feelings and distracting her after schema triggering (e.g., by bingeing, vomiting, self-harm, alcohol abuse); and the Perfectionistic Controller in providing a short-term source of self-esteem and pride. We explored the origins of the Perfectionistic Controller as a coping mode that over-compensated for her underlying sense of herself as defective and unlovable. The Imagery Assessment exercise identified the Perfectionistic Controller mode as a way of allowing her to feel "better" than the people who were bullying her by being thinner and thereby "achieving the unachievable." Although the effects were short-lived, the Perfectionistic Controller could take her to another "world" where she could set herself new ideal weight targets, and then re-set them once they were reached or after they were sabotaged through binges. She described this as a "seductive" mode that gave her a "buzz," making her feel more confident, "special," and sometimes even superior to others. After exploring the function of this mode, she flipped into the Shamed/Deprived Child mode, and suddenly became quiet and tearful. She described being horrified at how shallow and superficial she was in this mode, and how shameful it was to be living in such a self-focused way. I reiterated the role of the Perfectionistic Controller as a survivor part, and we explored the good intention behind this mode by enabling her to feel good about herself and to retain a sense of control (and pseudo-self) in an environment that had undermined her self-worth and identity.
- Nicki was shown how to fill out the schema mode diaries, which had been adapted to include eating behaviors. This was to increase her awareness of "flipping" between modes on a moment-to-moment basis between sessions and to give her a model to begin to make sense of events and her subsequent reactions and impulses.
- Nicki was also asked to draw pictures of both an imagined 'safe place' and her modes with colored pens, one-by-one for homework. This facilitated the exploration of the feelings and physical felt-sense of each mode in preparation for imagery and mode dialogue work. Nicki drew her own bedroom for her safe place. She drew a huge black domineering "monster-looking" creature as her Critical mode. Her Shamed/Deprived Child was depicted as a small figure crouched on the floor, hunched forward as if protecting herself, with tears visibly falling. Her Perfectionistic Controller was glamorous and flawless, with a thin figure and stylish outfit and hair. She had an air of aloofness and arrogance, and Nicki portrayed her as inward-looking with an excessive emphasis on appearance. The Detached Protector was drawn as a happy smiling mask, but with eyes fixed in a

detached gaze. The Detached Self-Soother was drawn as a frenzied whirlwind creating space between her and the outside world. As her early sessions had indicated, her Healthy Adult was still at a very early stage of development. Nicki felt unable to draw this mode, and so she was asked to be aware of how this mode might begin to take shape as her therapy progressed, with a view to attempting this later in therapy.

Phase 4: (Sessions 30–60) Schema mode therapy for eating disorders bypassing the Detached Protector and Perfectionistic Controller

- It was often difficult to reach or make a connection with Nicki's Shamed/Deprived Child side during sessions due to blocking by the Perfectionistic Controller and Detached Protector. When in the Perfectionistic Controller mode she did not want to talk about her eating disorder, preferring to justify these behaviors in the light of being a "fit and healthy person." When gently pressed to look at underlying feelings she would flip into the Detached (Angry) Protector mode, where she would remain for a week or two after sessions.
- Reconnecting with feelings: In imagery sessions it was discovered that she blocked feelings due to her longstanding expectation of being shamed for experiencing and expressing distress. She would "talk the talk" during these sessions, but it was clear that there was a lack of expressed emotion even when describing traumatic memories. We talked about ways of learning to reconnect with feelings and to stay with them through using relaxation imagery and then gradual desensitization to memories that evoked difficult feelings (e.g., an argument with her partner, eating a "bad" food). When talking about difficult issues in therapy she was asked to be mindful of the emotions being triggered and to recognize the mechanisms by which the Detached Protector tried to block these (e.g., breathing became more shallow and constricted, leading to lightheadedness and "fuzziness").
- Nicki's difficulty tolerating distress made it hard for her to do the emotional work required for healing schemas. She was open about wanting a "quick fix" that would be simple and tangible, and if possible avoid "messy" and shameful emotions. She missed sessions on three occasions due to spending excessive time in bed, increased bingeing, and alcohol use to block out feelings following difficult sessions.
- Mindfulness was introduced as a way of helping her to increase her awareness and emotional acceptance of modes as they "flipped" and the feelings and thoughts associated with each of these. A short mindfulness exercise was used at the start and end of each therapy session as a way of desensitizing her to this practice, which was initially seen as anxiety-provoking. Over time she learned to use mindfulness, and especially yoga, to help her develop tolerance of her emotions and to learn to stay with them rather than immediately dismissing them. Through mindfulness she became acutely aware of a high level of chronic anxiety and agitation linked to her Shamed/Deprived Child mode – something she had previously worked hard to block out with her coping modes.
- Regular mode dialogues were carried out with the Detached Protector ("Blocker") mode.

> | THERAPIST (T): | Little Nicki is so upset and she needs my help. She is hurting. Why won't you let her show how hurt she is? Be that part of you- the "Blocker" mode- that is trying to stop her from showing how hurt she is . . . |
> | --- | --- |
> | NICKI (N) (as the "Blocker"): | You might hurt her. That's what always happens. Other people always make fun of you when you get upset. It's not good to show your feelings. It's a burden on other people. |
> | T: | Have you seen me making fun of little Nicki at all? Is there anything that I might have said in therapy that might make it difficult for you to trust me? |
> | N: | No, but that's what has always happened before. It's just not right to show your feelings, that's all I know. She'll just end up feeling hurt and stupid all over again. |
> | T: | I can understand that little Nicki has been hurt before and no one has been there for her to help her through it. You have protected her from all that hurt, so it must be hard for you to risk trusting me or anyone else to talk to little Nicki. The trouble is that I can only help little Nicki to feel better and to get what she needs if I can talk to her and ask her what she is feeling. Do you think that it might be possible to experiment with giving her a chance to talk to me and see if it helps her? Is there anything that we can do that might help you to feel safer and to let me talk to her for two or three minutes to start with? |
> | N: | I could try, but it would be better if you turned your chair around so I don't feel you are staring at me. |
> | T: | Thank you . . . let's try that . . . |
>
> Over several sessions the Blocker allowed the therapist to begin to connect with the Deprived/Shamed Child.
>
> After 10 months of therapy, the therapist gradually began to emphasize the importance of the Blocker allowing the Shamed Child to connect intimately with others, so that she could engage in real relationships with trusted others who could then begin to meet her needs.

Building the Healthy Adult and healing the Shamed/Deprived Child

- Limited reparenting within the therapeutic relationship was the main mechanism for the gradual development of Nicki's Healthy Adult mode. In therapy I focused on providing an antidote for some of her unmet needs, such as through being empathic, nurturing, and as open as I could about my own therapeutic decisions and boundaries. My main task at first was to validate her feelings as they arose and to work with her to try to identify modes linked to her emotional states whilst building a formulation. I tried to maintain the perspective that she was highly ashamed at the core. This helped me to manage my own frustration when she missed sessions and avoided set homework tasks. I offered her my e-mail address to contact me if she needed more help managing her modes between sessions. This was provided as an encouragement to recognize and ask for her needs to be met – something that had been actively discouraged by her family. Nicki was often apologetic and required a great deal of encouragement to learn to ask me for support between sessions. E-mails were found to be a manageable way of responding to difficulties when I was able to find the time through the course of a day. This was clearly set up as a form of regular support during working hours only.

- Audio flash cards (recorded directly onto Nicki's MP3 player) were used to provide reassurance and encouragement for the Shamed/Deprived Child and validation of her needs.
- Mode dialogues with the Detached Protector usually took place before attempting reparenting imagery, whereby the Shamed/Deprived Child was accessed through an image and asked what she was feeling and what she needed. This allowed Nicki the opportunity to experience being in the Child mode while learning to ask the therapist to provide the nurturance and protection that she missed out on during childhood.
- Imagery rescripting: On one occasion early in therapy, Nicki came to the session feeling distressed after attending a 3D body image session (described later). She had clearly flipped into Shamed Child mode and described feeling ashamed and disgusted with her body, especially her stomach and hips. In imagery she was asked to see herself as Little Nicki and to describe where she was and what she was seeing/hearing/thinking/feeling. She saw herself in the classroom as a six-year-old being laughed at and called "porky" by a group of boys sitting next to her. She described suddenly having the physical sensation of feeling "big," of her thighs and stomach expanding (perceiving herself as she experienced others' perceptions of her). She felt sick, alone, unprotected, and humiliated. I asked her if she would allow me to enter the image. She agreed and imagined me coming into the classroom. I then explained that I was there to help little Nicki. I asked little Nicki what she needed from me. She replied that she needed to feel safe, to not be so ugly and picked on by the boys. I told her: "Now I want you to see that I am taking your hand. I am saying to the boys 'Stop being so mean. It's horrible to treat other children like that. Think about how you would feel if someone said that to you. Nicki is a great little girl and she's always been nice to you. You are just picking on her because you think you can get away with it. Well, that's enough. It has to stop, and if not I will have to tell your headmaster about your behavior. From now on, I want you to start thinking about how you can be kind to other children. No more teasing'. I am leading you out of the classroom to a nice comfortable room nearby where you are safe. How are you feeling now?" Little Nicki replied that she was feeling better, but still felt it must be her fault, that there was something wrong with her. As the therapist in the image I reassured her "The boys were being mean and showing off to each other. That's

bad behavior and not your fault. But they can't tease you now because I am here to protect you from them. You are a lovely little girl and you always do your best. You are beautiful already, just as you are. You are just right. Can you look down and see yourself as you really are now? Your arms and legs and tummy are all just the way they are supposed to be. I am going to remind you lots and lots that you are beautiful, just in case you forget. How are you feeling now? Is there anything you need from me just now?" Little Nicki replied that she needed a hug. I told her: "Can you see me hugging you in the image? Can you feel it? You can have a hug whenever you need one. You deserve lots of hugs to remind you of how lovable you are." Little Nicki said afterward that she enjoyed being hugged, but it felt strange, and part of her (the Blocker) wanted to detach. As we repeated the imagery rescripting with several similar images (i.e., focused on the school bullying and being humiliated by her father), Nicki began to internalize a sense of being lovable and acceptable in both an emotional and bodily sense. Her Healthy Adult mode was introduced into imagery sessions and after over a year of therapy was gradually able to take on the role of protecting and nurturing little Nicki. There seemed to be something about the physical contact (being hugged, having her hair stroked) with the therapist within the images that enabled her to develop more positive and healthy physical associations with her bodily felt-sense.

- This was reinforced through a range of other "self-nurturing" homework exercises that were planned in a gradually desensitizing manner, including manicures, pedicures, baths, swimming, yoga, play (e.g., spontaneous games and positive touch with her children) and eventually back massages by her partner. She was very reluctant to try many of these activities, and strong encouragement and praise were required to enable her to take these steps toward allowing her Healthy Adult to nurture her Shamed/Deprived Child mode.
- This self-nurturing work gradually facilitated the reduction of her "Needy" Child and Detached Self-Soother modes. Instead of resorting to impulsive bingeing and self-harm when distressed, she was encouraged to recall the image of her Healthy Adult comforting little Nicki. She also learned to use a range of other activities to help her through the emotional pain linked to being in little Nicki mode, including coloring in, kneading play dough, listening to classical music, listening to mindfulness sessions that I had recorded for her, and hugging a large soft bear.
- Through mindfulness she became gradually aware of the comings and goings of her modes. Self-compassion exercises were used to begin the process of develop a Healthy Adult mode. This included asking her to write about parts of herself she felt ashamed of or hid from others and then writing compassionate letters to her Shamed/Deprived Child mode. This was a slow and uncomfortable process for Nicki.
- Flash cards were used to prepare for difficult situations, to rehearse self-compassion, and a schema decision-making chart was used to help her to make compassionate (rather than automatic) choices.

Additional work with "Needy" Child and Angry Child modes

As Nicki's mindfulness practice became more regular, she began to become aware of the short, "mini-moments" between experiencing an impulsive urge and acting it out. In sessions we used visualization to help her to practice responding differently to her urges and managing the anxiety through healthy self-soothing.

- "Urge surfing" (a mindfulness practice which enables you to acknowledge and experience strong urges whilst "surfing" on top of the urge, rather than being drawn "down" into the behavior linked to it (www.mindfulness.org.au/URGE%20SURFING.htm#TeachingUrgeSurfingToClients) was also practiced in and out of sessions as a way of increasing the sense of self-efficacy and control experienced by her Healthy Adult mode.
- As her Healthy Adult mode grew in strength she began to express her needs and opinions more openly in her relationships with others. As she started to feel more in control of her role within her relationships and to make decisions based on her own needs, her "Needy" Child mode became less prominent.
- On the rare occasions that her Angry Child mode appeared in sessions, imagery was used to encourage her to express anger openly, rather than "acting out" her anger. This was initially met with a great deal of resistance, since she had become used to suppressing feelings of anger due to fear of rejection. When she was a child, her father had become loud and domineering when she had expressed any form of anger or even minor discontentment. Her mother had withdrawn from her and become sullen. It became clear in imagery that she feared this response from me as the therapist. Over a period of many months, through limited reparenting imagery and imagery rescripting we were able to desensitize her to feelings of anger and to allow her to gradually express these in a safe way. As she became used to owning these feelings, she became less reliant on self-harm as a mechanism for expressing (suppressed) anger.

Combating the Critical "Bully" mode

- Imagery rescripting: Nicki's "Bully" mode was very critical of her Shamed/Deprived Child, especially around eating and appearance. It set high standards and if these were not met, she was criticized severely. The Bully mode was curtailed in therapy through imagery rescripting (largely focusing on challenging her father's critical attitude during childhood). Nicki began to make a caricature of her Bully mode out of clay. This was a way of exploring this mode in a safe and controllable way, and starting to distance her healthy part from it enough to start to see it in a less scary way. She also drew an image of her Bully mode on a white T-shirt. This was used in mode (chair) dialogues, whereby she put the T-shirt on when she was playing the part of the Bully mode, and took it off and draped it over the chair when she was in the Healthy Adult or Shamed/Deprived Child chairs. When her Healthy Adult mode began to strengthen toward the latter part of therapy, she began to take the Bully mode T-shirt out of the room and leave it outside the door to allow us to move on with other therapy exercises.
- Mode dialogues and imagery restructuring sessions focused on combating the Critical mode as described by Young, Klosko, and Weishaar (2003). Here is a short excerpt:

Chair work dialogue: combating the punitive parent

BULLY (B) (*played by Nicki*):	You're so ugly and disgusting. No matter how much you diet you'll never be remotely attractive. No one will ever like you while you look like that . . . what a state!
HEALTHY ADULT (HA) (*played by therapist*):	You can't talk to little Nicki like that. She's only a little girl. She's doing the best she can. She needs to be encouraged. When you're mean to her you make her feel worse and worse about herself. You're making her hide away because she's scared of you. It's not acceptable to treat her like that.
B:	I'll do what I like. It's true that she's disgusting and she's hardly got any friends. Those that she does have just feel sorry for her. She's a disgrace.
THERAPIST (T):	Stop being so mean to her. It's hard for her to make friends because you make her feel small when others get close. It's completely wrong to treat a child like that and superficial to make judgments about her appearance. She's actually very lovable but you don't bother to spend the time to get to know her.
B:	Back off – who are you to say that? You don't know what she's really like.
T:	I am getting to know her very well because I've taken the time to talk to her and to understand who she really is. You have to stop taking your problems out on her. It's not fair to do that. You're an adult and it's your responsibility to deal with your own past. You are the one that has to stop this pattern of abuse that has come down through the generations.
B:	I'll do what I want.
T:	I'm going to remove you until you can recognize that your behavior has to change [*takes T-shirt out of the room*].
T (*to Nicki*):	This isn't your fault. You're perfectly lovable as you are. The Bully has to learn to stop treating you like this and to stop this pattern of hurting others. You deserve to be loved and together with your Healthy Adult mode I'm going to help you.

- Nicki also found a "theme song" which she played when the Bully mode was particularly strong – "I am beautiful" (by Christina Aguilera)
- Flash cards were used to combat the Bully mode (see example below).

Empathic confrontation with the Perfectionistic Controller ("Glam Nicki")

- Nicki's approval-seeking, over-compensatory behavior was confronted gently, while being mindful not to devalue her and the function of this mode. The rationale for this was to help her to identify her true feelings of emptiness and

> ### Dealing with criticism flash card
>
> At this moment I am feeling depressed and angry because I was criticized. This has triggered my "Bully" mode. This mode developed in the past when I was bullied and criticized at school. They made me feel that I was a failure. The Bully mode represents what I learned from those school bullies and it still puts me down. Although the Bully mode makes me feel that I'm different, that I don't fit in and there is something wrong with me, the reality is that others do like me, they enjoy having me around and most people think I'm good fun. The evidence for this healthier point of view is my friends have told me that they enjoy my company and that I have brought a fun atmosphere to my workplace. I'm upfront and a good communicator. When others are critical, it's usually about their own schemas and problems. That is why, although I want to go to bed, restrict my eating, and vomit, it would be healthier for me to stand up to the Bully mode and protect little Nicki. I need to eat well and nurture little Nicki. I can remember that everyone is criticized from time to time and that is no excuse for the Bully mode to attack me. I can accept myself. I am lovable as I am.

loneliness (behind her Shamed/Deprived and "Needy" Child modes) as her reason for being in therapy, and to ask her to express her emotions and needs.
- I needed to be careful when doing this work not to react to her tendency to dismiss both what I was suggesting and the therapy in general. She clearly enjoyed the feelings of being in control associated with this mode, and easily flipped into Angry Protector mode if she perceived that I was threatening this "safe" state. This would result in her angrily claiming that there was nothing wrong with her dieting and exercise behaviors and implying that the therapy (i.e., the therapist) was failing by not giving her the help she needed to stop bingeing. (I recognized that this sometimes triggered self-doubt linked to my own schemas.)
- Acknowledging function of coping mode: It was important to acknowledge that change and overcoming the eating disorder equated to her giving up the Perfectionistic Controller mode – which had given her a source of pride, achievement, and being "special." Resisting the control of others and resisting her compulsion to eat was an important part of the identity of the Perfectionistic Controller. Therefore, it was important to acknowledge the positive and protective function of the disorder and the strength of will required to restrict eating or the excitement of a binge.
- Audio-taping sessions: To assist with "breaking through" Glam Nicki mode between sessions Nicki was asked to listen to a tape of the session at least once a week. She was also asked to write a short summary of what she had learned after each session to try to make connections between sessions, which was otherwise constantly undermined by Glam Nicki denying that anything had been learned in therapy.

- An example of an empathic confrontation with Nicki that occurred during session 18 is shown below, and an adjunctive dialogue with the Angry Protector.

Phase 5: (Sessions 40–60) Schema-based behavioral change. The final part of therapy overlapped significantly with the previous phase of therapy and focused largely on reinforcing behavioral changes that had been initiated throughout therapy.

- Standard CBT techniques were reintroduced to work with remaining eating behaviors (residual bingeing and vomiting).

Empathic confrontation – Perfectionistic controller

N (*as Glam Nicki*): I don't really see what the point is of all this mode work. To be honest it all feels a bit silly. I kind of feel quite happy with how things are going at the moment. But I've put on some weight with these changes to my diet and I didn't really anticipate that or agree to it. I'm just going to feel worse about myself if I don't try to lose it and get back to the weight I was. I'm not going to look good in my bikini and I've already booked my summer trip.

T: I can see that losing weight and being thin makes you feel good about yourself and in control. But I really wonder if what lies underneath is little Nicki who is feeling unattractive and unlovable. I understand that in Glam Nicki mode you try to feel good and confident through being thin and that part also thinks that you will be liked or admired more for being thin. This part of you learned to think this way because you were criticized and bullied for your appearance as a child and you learned to use your appearance to feel good about yourself.

N: Look, this is who I am. My diet and exercising is healthy. And it makes me feel good about myself. Why on earth would I want to stop that?

T: Nicki, I care about you, not how thin you are, not how pretty you are, not how expensive your clothes are. The problem is that I don't feel I get a true connection with you when you try to block your feelings by presenting yourself in a flawless way. I feel more connected with you when I see the real you and when you express your emotional needs directly.

N: Yes, but it makes me feels too vulnerable to do that, like I'll be at the bottom of the pile all over again. I can't believe that people will really like me when they see what I'm like.

T: Although I understand that you are afraid that others won't accept the real you (just like the bullies at school), I want you to start to practice showing others your real self more. This is because I think this is the only way you can learn to develop real

> relationships with people (who are emotionally available) and to experience real acceptance and love. This is a much more authentic way of living your life and although it feels risky, it is the only way that you will get what you need. And because I genuinely like and care for the real you, I believe that others will too. What you were taught when you were a child is superficial and wrong.
>
> N (*flips into Angry Protector mode*): I am feeling a bit annnoyed to be honest. I want this session to be over. I really don't see the point of all this.
>
> T: I wonder if the angry part of you is feeling frightened of connecting and of being nurtured, even though it is what little Nicki needs? I understand that its scary for Glam Nicki to let go of some of the control. When I try to nurture little Nicki it feels safer to block me out and to stick to what helps you feel in control. I know how important exercise and healthy eating are for you and I can see you have worked really hard to feel good about your body. I can see that some of the time that makes you feel good. But I'm concerned to see how stressed and unhappy you are about the eating problems and worried that you might be pushing yourself too hard. I'd like to see if you can think about how it might be to let me in to talk about these issues, even though they make you uncomfortable. Although it feels scary, it is the only way we can start to allow little Nicki to get what she really needs. Would that be OK with you?

- Mindfulness was introduced during eating in order to increase awareness of the role of modes in sabotaging normal eating patterns. In this final stage of therapy, Nicki was more skilled at recognizing and dealing appropriately with the modes as they arose.
- Couples therapy: Throughout therapy, work on the Compliant Surrender mode had focused on enabling Nicki to increasing her awareness of her needs and feelings, and teaching her to communicate clearly and assertively. She was able to practice this within the therapy relationship and encouraged to actively practice this in her relationships outside therapy. This led to some conflicts in her relationship with her partner, where she had previously been compliant and quiet. Both partners remained committed, and relationship counseling was embarked on as a way of renegotiating the dynamics of their relationship. Nicki commented that her relationship with her own children was significantly better than before therapy – she was more attuned to their needs and better able to play and meet their demands in a spontaneous way.
- Body-image work was the focus of several sessions. Nicki learned to use urge surfing to reduce her urges to compulsively check her body with her hands, and

noticed a substantial reduction in intrusive thoughts (driven by the Perfectionistic Controller) related to her appearance.
- Exposure work/behavioral experiments: She began to work actively on showing herself in public without excessive makeup and immaculate hair. This began with a visit to the corner shop, and eventually she was able to attend work and social events with minimal makeup. Using a flash card to challenge the Perfectionistic Controller helped her to stay focused on the rationale for this work. Nicki gradually worked toward wearing shorts in public and then her swimsuit at the public swimming pool. These tasks caused immense anxiety, but with the help of preparative imagery and flash cards, she was gradually able to overcome her self-consciousness and work toward self-acceptance.
- Mirror exposure and having a 3D scan of her body (produced both in picture and computer graphic format) was also used in the latter part of therapy as a way of triggering the Critical mode. This allowed us to practice dealing with the Critical mode in its full "glory" while practicing self-acceptance.

Outcome

Nicki made significant progress in therapy, both in terms of overcoming her detached *modus operandi* and the over-compensatory mechanisms she had been using to boost her self-worth and to "hold her identity together." Her dieting had stopped altogether by session 25. Bingeing and vomiting reduced significantly by session 30 and by the end of therapy she had been abstinent for over a month. Scores on the Eating Disorder Examination Questionnaire (EDE-Q; Fairburn and Beglin, 1994) showed that her global score had reduced from 4.59 at pre-therapy to 0.98 (well within normal range for non-clinical population) at post-therapy. Scores on her YSI-L2 also showed a reduction from a total mean score of 76 to 25. She was able to recognize and deal appropriately with her modes more of the time and actively practiced mindfulness to try to maintain this awareness. I noticed a significant growth in her Healthy Adult mode through the process of therapy. During the first 40 or so sessions, this was less evident, as much of the effort in therapy at that time was on bypassing the Detached Protector and perfectionistic controller modes. In imagery sessions she was gradually able to take a more active role in taking care of the Shamed/Deprived Child mode and to stand up to the Critical mode. The therapeutic relationship played an important role in helping her to make the shift from valuing herself on the basis of her body shape and weight to valuing herself as a whole person. The empathic confrontation exercise was an important part of this process, by strongly encouraging her to take the steps needed to let go of her eating disorder as her only source of self-esteem, while building real connections in her relationships with others. This was a frightening process for Nicki and at times she really struggled to let this part of herself go. Although it is not possible to include details of all techniques in this chapter, it is important to note the significance of experiential work with this client group, who tend to be more comfortable with the cognitive aspects of therapy. Validating and showing compassion toward the "Needy" and Shamed/Deprived Child modes are of paramount importance, through a combination of limited reparenting, restructuring imagery, and mode dialogues.

Given the motivational and engagement issues associated with treating this client group, the great strength of the schema mode model is how easily the concepts are understood and resonate emotionally with clients. It provides a meaningful framework for each person's eating behavior within the context of their childhood, adolescence, and adulthood. The model aims to enable clients to stay with the painful underlying feelings rather than avoid them through a process of working with the schema modes and gradual exposure. Incorporating mindfulness into the schema model also introduces the concept of "mental space" before acting on urges to binge, vomit, restrict, or exercise, which allows the patients the opportunity to make a conscious choice in what may otherwise be experienced as compulsive automatic behaviors. Increasing clients' capacity to conceptualize their difficulties within this model can significantly reduce the shame associated with having an eating disorder.

Acknowledgements

Special thanks to Calum Munro, Michiel van Vreeswijk, and Emma Morrow for their extremely helpful ideas and comments on the earlier versions of this chapter.

References

American Psychiatric Association (1994) *Diagnostic and Statistical Manual of Mental Disorders*, 4th edition (DSM-IV). Washington, DC: American Psychiatric Association.

Bizeul, C., Sadowsky, N. and Rigaud, D. (2001) The prognostic value of initial EDI scores in anorexia nervosa patients: a prospective follow-up study of 5–10 years. *European Psychiatry*, 16, 232–238.

Blinder, B.J., Cumella, V.A. and Sanathara, V.A. (2006) Psychiatric comorbidities of female inpatients with eating disorders. *Psychosomatic Medicine*, 6, 454–462.

Braun, D.L., Sunday, S.R. and Halmi, K.A. (1994) Psychiatric comorbidity in patients with eating disorders. *Psychological Medicine*, 24, 859–867.

Bruce, K.R. and Steiger, H. (2006) Prognostic implications of personality disorders in eating disorders, in *Personality Disorders and Eating Disorders: Exploring the Frontier* (eds R.A. Sansone and J.L. Levitt). New York: Routledge, pp. 247–262.

Bulik, C., Berkman, N., Brownley, K., Sedway, J. and Lohr, K. (2007) Anorexia nervosa treatment: a systematic review of randomized controlled trials. *International Journal of Eating Disorders*, 40, 310–320.

Carter, J.C., Blackmore, E., Sutander-Pinnock, K. and Woodside, D.B. (2004) Relapse in anorexia nervosa: a survival analysis. *Psychological Medicine*, 34(4), 671–679.

Casper, R.C. (1990). Personality features of women with good outcome from restricting anorexia nervosa. *Psychosomatic Medicine*, 52, 156–170.

Cassin, S. E. and von Ranson, K.M. (2005) Personality and eating disorders: a decade in review, *Clinical Psychology Review*, 25(7), 895–916.

Dennis, A.B. and Sansone, R.A. (1997) Eating disorder and personality disorders, in *Handbook of Treatment for Eating Disorders* (eds D.M. Garner and P.E. Garfinkel). New York: Guilford Press, pp. 437–449.

Diaz-Marsa, M., Carrasco, J.L. and Saiz, J. (2000) A study of temperament and personality in anorexia and bulimia nervosa. *Journal of Personality Disorders*, 14, 352–359.

Fairburn, C.G. and Beglin, S.J. (1994) Assessment of eating disorders: Interview or self-report questionnaire? *International Journal of Eating Disorders*, 16, 363–370.

Fairburn, C.G., Cooper, Z. and Shafran, R. (2003) Cognitive behavior therapy for eating disorders: a "transdiagnostic" theory and treatment. *Behavior Research and Therapy*, 41, 509–528.

Fairburn, C.G., Jones, R., Peveler, R.C. *et al.* (1991) Three psychological treatments for bulimia nervosa: a comparative trial. *Archives of General Psychiatry*, 48, 463–469.

Gillberg, I.C., Råstam, M. and Gillberg, C. (1995) Anorexia nervosa 6 years after onset: Part I. Personality disorders. *Comprehensive Psychiatry*, 36, 61–69.

Grilo, C.M., Pagano, M.E., Skodol, A.E. *et al.* (2007) Natural course of bulimia nervosa and of eating disorder not otherwise specified: 5-year prospective study of remissions, relapses, and the effects of personality disorder psychopathology. *Journal of Clinical Psychiatry*, 68, 738–746.

Grilo, C.M., Sanislow, C.A., Skodol, A.E. *et al.* (2003). Do eating disorders co-occur with personality disorders? Comparison groups matter. *International Journal of Eating Disorders*, 33, 155–164.

Halmi, K.A., Agras, S.W., Crow, S. *et al.* (2005) Predictors of treatment acceptance and completion in anorexia nervosa: implications for future study designs. *Archives of General Psychiatry*, 62(7), 776–781.

Herzog, D.B., Dorer, D.J., Keel, P.K. *et al.* (1999) Recovery and relapse in anorexia nervosa and bulimia nervosa: a 7.5 year follow-up study. *Journal of the American Academy of Child and Adolescent Psychiatry*, 38(7), 829–837.

Herzog, D., Keller, J., Sacks, N., Yeh, C. and Lavori, P. (1992) Psychiatric comorbidity in treatment seeking anorexics and bulimics. *Journal of the American Academy of Child and Adolescent Psychiatry*, 31, 810–818.

Hinrichsen, H. and Waller, G. (2006) The treatment of avoidant personality disorder, in *Personality Disorders and Eating Disorders: Exploring the Frontier* (eds R.A. Sansone and J.L. Levitt). New York: Routledge, pp. 213–230.

Leung, N., Waller, G. and Thomas, G. (2000) Outcome of group cognitive-behavior therapy for bulimia nervosa: the role of core beliefs. *Behavior Research and Therapy*, 38, 145–156.

Levitt, J.L. and Sansone, R.A. (2006) Avoidant personality disorder and eating disorders, in *Personality Disorders and Eating Disorders: Exploring the Frontier* (eds R.A. Sansone and J.L. Levitt). New York: Routledge, pp. 149–162.

Milos, G., Spindler, A., Ruggiero, G., Klaghofer, R. and Schnyder, U. (2002) Comorbidity of obsessive-compulsive disorders and duration of eating disorders. *International Journal of Eating Disorders*, 31, 284–289.

Mountford, V. and Waller, G. (2006) Using imagery in cognitive-behavioral treatment for eating disorders: tackling the restrictive mode. *International Journal of Eating Disorders*, 39, 533–543.

Sansone, R.A. Levitt, J.L. and Sansone, L.A. (2004) The prevalence of personality disorders among those with eating disorders. *Eating Disorders*, 13(1), 7–21.

Sansone, R.A., Levitt, J.L. and Sansone, L.A. (2006) The prevalence of personality disorders in those with eating disorders, in *Personality Disorders and Eating Disorders: Exploring the Frontier* (eds R.A. Sansone and J.L. Levitt). New York: Routledge, pp. 23–39.

Santonastaso, P., Friederici, S. and Favaro, A. (1999) Full and partial syndromes in eating disorders: a 1-year prospective study of risk factors among female students. *Psychopathology*, 32, 50–56.

Schmidt, U. and Treasure, J. (2006) Anorexia nervosa: valued and visible: a cognitive-interpersonal maintenance model and its implications for research and practice. *British Journal of Clinical Psychology*, 45, 343–366.

Shapiro, J.L., Berkman, N.D., Brownley, K.A. *et al.* (2007) Bulimia nervosa treatment: a systematic review of randomized controlled trials. *International Journal of Eating Disorders*, 40(4), 321–336.

Simpson, S., Morrow, E., van Vreeswijk, M. and Reid, C. (2010) Group schema therapy for eating disorders: a pilot study. *Frontiers in Psychology for Clinical Settings*, *1*(182): 1–10.

Simpson, S. and Slowey, L. (2011) Video therapy for atypical eating disorder and obesity: a case study. *Clinical Practice and Epidemiology in Mental Health 7*, 38–43.

Skodol, A.E., Oldham, J.M., Hyler, S.E. *et al.* (1993) Comorbidity of DSM-III-R eating disorders and personality disorders. *International Journal of Eating Disorders*, *14*, 403–416.

Sutandar-Pinnock, K., Blake, W.D., Carter, J.C., Olmsted, M.P. and Kaplan, A.S. (2003) Perfectionism in anorexia nervosa: a 6–24-month follow-up study. *International Journal of Eating Disorders*, *33*, 225–229.

Taylor, G.J., Parker, J.D.A., Bagby, M. and Bourker, M.P. (1996) Relationships between alexthymia and psychological characteristics associated with eating disorders. *Journal of Psychosomatic Research*, *41*(6), 561–568.

Troop, N.A., Holbrey, A. and Treasure, J.L. (1998) Stress, coping, and crisis support in eating disorders. *International Journal of Eating Disorders*, *24*, 157–166.

Troop, N.A. and Treasure, J.L. (1997) Psychosocial factors in the onset of eating disorders: responses to life-events and difficulties. *British Journal of Medical Psychology*, *70*, 373–385.

Vitiello, B. and Lederhendler, I. (2000) Research on eating disorders: current status and future prospects. *Biological Psychiatry*, *47*, 777–786.

Vitousek, K.M. and Stumpf, R.E. (2005). Difficulties in the assessment of personality traits and disorders in eating-disordered individuals. *Eating Disorders*, *13*, 37–60.

Vitousek, K.M., Watson, S. and Wilson, G.T. (1998) Enhancing motivation for change in treatment-resistant eating disorders. *Clinical Psychology Review*, *18*(4), 391–420.

Waller, G., Dickson, C. and Ohanian, V. (2002). Cognitive content in bulimic disorders: core beliefs and eating attitudes. *Eating Behaviors*, *3*, 171–178.

Waller, G., Kennerley, H. and Ohanian, V. (2007) Schema-focused cognitive behavior therapy with eating disorders, in *Cognitive Schemas and Core Beliefs in Psychiatric Disorders: a Scientist Practitioners' Guide* (eds L.P. Riso, P.T. du Toit and J.E. Young). New York: American Psychiatric Association, pp. 139–175.

Waller, G., Ohanian, V., Meyer, C. and Osman, S. (2000) Cognitive content among bulimic women: the role of core beliefs. *International Journal of Eating Disorders*, *28*, 235–241.

Waller, G., Sines, J., Meyer, C., Foster, E. and Skelton, A. (2007) Narcissism and narcissistic defences in the eating disorders. *International Journal of Eating Disorders*, *40*(2), 143–148.

Wildes, J.E., Ringham, R.M. and Marcus, M.D. (2010) Emotion avoidance in patients with anorexia nervosa: initial test of a functional model. *International Journal of Eating Disorders*, *43*(5), 398–404.

Wilson, G.T. and Fairburn, C.G. (1998) Treatments for eating disorders, in *A Guide to Treatments that Work* (eds P.E. Nathan and J.M. Gorman). New York: Oxford University Press, pp. 501–530.

Young, J.E., Arntz, A., Atkinson, T. *et al.* (2007) *The Schema Mode Inventory (SMI)*. New York: Schema Therapy Institute.

Young, J. and Brown, G. (1990) *The Young Schema Questionnaire – Long Version (YSI-L2)*. Cognitive Therapy Center of New York.

Young, J.E., Klosko, J. and Weishaar, M.E. (2003) *Schema Therapy: a Practitioner's Guide*. New York: Guilford Press.

2
Treating OCD with the Schema Mode Model

Ellen Gross, Nicola Stelzer and Gitta Jacob

Introduction

Obsessive-compulsive disorder (OCD) is highly heterogeneous and with a prevalence rate of 1–3% (Robins *et al.*, 1984) and a six-month prevalence rate of 1–2% (Myers *et al.*, 1984) is the fourth most common psychiatric disorder. It is associated with significant morbidity (Kaplan and Saddock, 1998), impaired quality of life, and poor social functioning (Eisen *et al.*, 2006). Men and women are affected equally. Only 1% of patients receive inpatient treatment (Goodwin, Guze and Robins, 1969). Studies show that up to 66% of patients with OCD display Axis II disorders (Rasmussen and Tsuang, 1986). Approximately 90% of patients complain about low self-esteem and up to 70% state that it impacts their career (Hollander *et al.*, 1996–97).

Cognitive behavioural therapy (CBT), with the essential procedures of Exposure and Response Prevention (ERP), is the empirically established psychotherapy of choice (Abramowitz, Taylor and McKay, 2009). Some 40–80% of patients respond to this therapy (Hand, 1995; Foa *et al.*, 2002; Abramowitz, 2006) by showing more than a 30% reduction of Y-BOCS scores after treatment. Cognitive therapy combined with exposure therapy shows high effect sizes of 0.3–1.6 (Vogel *et al.*, 2006) and has proven to be most effective in inpatient treatment (Voderholzer and Hohagen, 2009). If psychotherapy is combined with pharmacotherapy (e.g., serotonin reuptake inhibitors: SSRI), effect sizes show even better results for treatment outcome (Foa *et al.*, 2005; NICE, 2005; Koran *et al.*, 2007; Voderholzer and Hohagen, 2009).

However, research to date indicates that approximately 50% of patients do not respond satisfactorily (Stanley and Turner, 1995; Baer and Minichiello, 1998). In many OCD cases, symptoms persist as standard treatment does not lead to full remission (Pigott and Seay, 1997; Ackerman and Greenland, 2002; Steketee and Pigott, 2006).

Poor response is predicted by severe major depressive disorder (MDD), which is common in approximately 70–80% of OCD patients (Rasmussen and Eisen, 1988), predominance of obsessions and mental neutralizing (Rufer *et al.*, 2006), early onset (AuBuchon and Malatesta, 1994; Abramowitz, 2006), comorbid PTSD (Gershuny, Baer, Radomsky, Wilson and Jenike, 2003), greater initial severity of symptoms (Keijsers, Hoogduin and Schaap, 1994), longer illness duration and greater severity (Goodwin *et al.*, 1969), as well as tic disorders and comorbid personality disorder. Yet some studies on these predictors yielded less conclusive or even opposing results (e.g., Fricke *et al.*, 2006). Early childhood trauma seems to be associated with negative treatment outcome since it is associated with early onset, higher symptom severity, and personality disorder (PD) symptoms (Gershuny *et al.*, 2008; Maier, Kuelz and Voderholzer, 2009). Fricke and colleagues (2007) found 42% of OCD patients had suffered physical abuse, 20% sexual abuse, and 43% severe emotional deprivation. Sexually abused patients seem to have a seven-fold higher risk of developing OCD (Saunders *et al.*, 1992). Intrusive mental images are also very common in OCD (Hackmann and Holmes, 2004; Rachman, 2007) and correlate with severity of OCD and poor response to regular CBT (Speckens, Hackmann, Ehlers and Cuthbert, 2007).

Patients who respond positively to treatment say that "talking about emotions" was the most relevant aspect (Kuelz *et al.*, 2009). To have been "in touch with their emotions" seems to be the most crucial element in treatment progress and quality of life (effect size 5.12) and shows higher effect sizes than "executed exposures" (effect size 4.72). In addition, the therapeutic relationship correlates highly significantly with the treatment outcome (all examples from Kuelz *et al.*, 2009).

The problems to be faced in treatment of OCD include:

- High rate of non-responders (10–50%)
- Many patients show relapse after treatment
- Patients experience chronic feelings of shame and guilt
- Blocked emotions and needs; high rates of emotional detachment
- Feeling of lack of control
- Feeling of "incompleteness" (uncertainty, dissociative symptoms)
- High rates of trauma and emotional deprivation

(Hoffmann and Hofmann, 2004; Kuelz *et al.*, 2009)

Current Status

We consider Schema Therapy (ST) with the schema mode model described by Young, Klosko, and Weishaar (2003) and Arntz and van Genderen (2009) as a more promising approach for severe OCD cases with weak response to regular CBT, especially patients with chronic OCD, trauma history, and comorbid personality disorders. We presume that a schema therapeutic approach may help these patients toward a more positive treatment outcome and therefore stable long-term results by establishing a Healthy Adult, who is enabled to take control and nurture the traumatized and deprived Vulnerable Child. Schema Therapy also aims directly at obstacles such as detachment (as stated above) by working with compensatory modes, which often block emotions and reduce the effectiveness of exposure sessions. ST is also well known for its specialized therapeutic alliance of "limited reparenting" and "limit-setting." As stated by Young and colleagues (2003), the therapeutic relationship and the contact with emotions seem to be crucial for a positive treatment outcome. The relationship is often not clearly labeled in common CBT where schema therapy offers a specific, manualized approach.

Recent studies have shown that schemas such as Social Isolation, Vulnerability to harm or illness, and Pessimism/Negativity occur more often in OCD patients than in healthy controls (Atalay et al., 2008). Specific mode models have been suggested for BPD and narcissistic PD (Young et al., 2003), avoidant, dependent, obsessive-compulsive, paranoid, and histrionic PD (Lobbestael et al., 2008), as well as for forensic patients (Bernstein, Arntz and de Vos, 2007). To our knowledge a mode model for OCD has yet to be developed.

We assume that emotional problems due to traumatic memories, connected to negative treatment outcome, severely interfere with improvement in OCD. ST may therefore be the right approach to reduce the interference for these patients. Nevertheless, it is possible that cognitive processing and/or behavioral features or circumstances also interfere with therapy outcome. Further research is needed here.

Approach

We propose to work in OCD with a model that incorporates the individual personal pathology of the disorder as well as the functionality of the OCD behaviour and symptomatology. The specific OCD symptoms can be conceptualized differently in the mode model, depending on the personal pathology.

Ongoing studies confirm that certain modes and schemas in OCD patients are much more highly activated than in other psychiatric disorders or healthy controls (Stelzer et al., in progress). Most patients with whom the authors worked showed a mode model as presented in Figure 2.1. This model should be considered as an

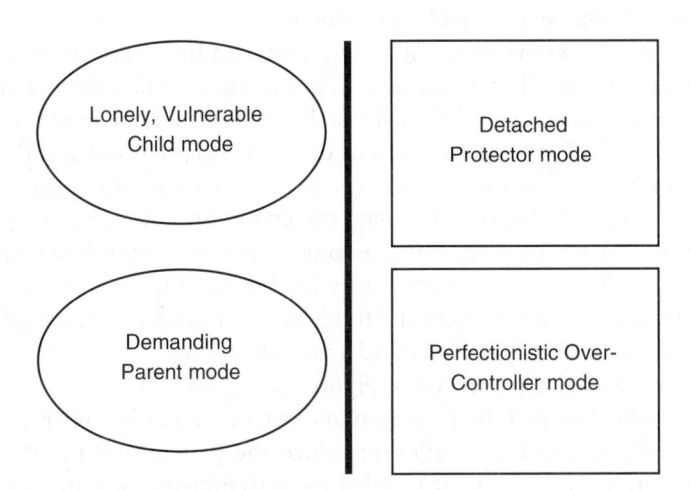

Figure 2.1 Example of a mode model of OCD

approximate concept that requires further research. Accordingly, OCD symptoms can in some cases be conceptualized as a compensatory mode such as a Perfectionistic Overcontroller mode or a Detached Protector mode. The Detached Protector mode interferes mostly within therapy, creating obstacles in the treatment room, whereas the Overcontroller mode can be addressed in exposure and response prevention (ERP) sessions.

In order to illustrate and conceptualize our model, we present case reports of two patients.

Case 1 Mary

Mary B. is a 31-year-old, currently unemployed bank assistant. She has suffered severe compulsions and coexisting obsessions for 20 years. She washes her hands up to 40 times a day, combining it with a counting ritual. Her washing and cleaning relates particularly to a fear of contamination with different pathogens or poisonous substances. She is also obsessed with checking and controlling. Her OCD leaves her socially isolated. She suffers from depressive symptoms (e.g., suicidal thoughts) as well as aggressive impulses, which lead to self-harming behavior (cutting or burning herself) to regulate emotional stress in harmful interpersonal relationships.

Her father died from cancer when Mary was 11 years old. She felt guilty and responsible for his death, because she remembered having touched his knee the day before he died. After his death, she developed the compulsions and began isolating herself.

At school, she merely had casual friends. She still has trouble establishing warm, healthy relationships with caring and supportive friends, believing that she has no right to these. Mary had previously been in many in- and outpatient treatments for her OCD, none of which had been successful.

In talking about functionality it was shown that Mary needs the OCD to calm her Demanding Parent mode that urges her to achieve certain unrelenting standards. This mode resembles her mother's voice from when Mary was young. Mary always had to fulfill her mother's wishes, not daring to stand up for herself. Her OCD "helps" her to reject requirements and to regulate distance to others, and therefore creates a sense of apparent control and autonomy.

Schemas like Defectiveness, Abandonment, Failure, Social Isolation, and Subjugation are present. The Vulnerable Child mode contains feelings of loss, fear, defectiveness, and shame. The dysfunctional Demanding Parent mode resembles the prohibition of needs. Her OCD symptoms can be conceptualized as a Detached and Angry Protector mode, reducing aversive, negative feelings and preventing others from getting too close to her or demanding something from her. Her compulsions also rebalance the striving for her needs and autonomy despite the presence and predominance of her Maladaptive Parent and Compensatory modes. Her OCD symptoms are also her only known strategies to ask for help and to regain social contacts. Through them Mary is able to make social contact in a seemingly controlled way.

Mary's mode model is presented in Figure 2.2.

This mode model helped the patient in understanding her behavior. It also helped to build a strong therapeutic relationship since the patient and the therapist were working with the same concept. It enabled them to prepare their strategies together in therapy. The patient felt validated in her experience.

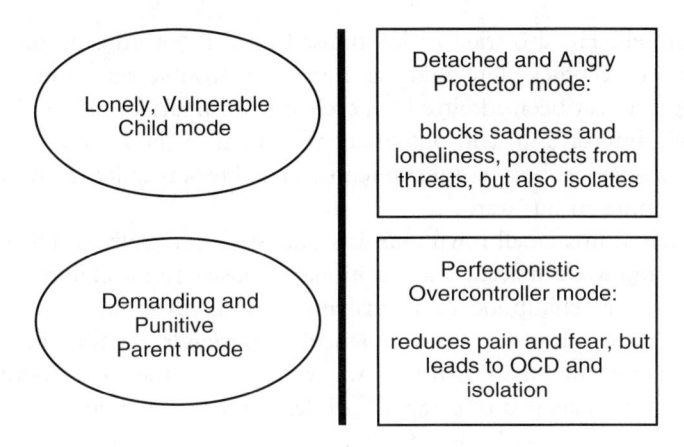

```
┌─────────────────┐     │  ┌──────────────────────┐
│                 │     │  │ Detached and Angry   │
│ Lonely, Vulnerable│   │  │ Protector mode:      │
│   Child mode    │     │  │                      │
│                 │     │  │ blocks sadness and   │
└─────────────────┘     │  │ loneliness, protects from│
                        │  │ threats, but also isolates│
                        │  └──────────────────────┘
                        │
┌─────────────────┐     │  ┌──────────────────────┐
│                 │     │  │ Perfectionistic      │
│ Demanding and   │     │  │ Overcontroller mode: │
│   Punitive      │     │  │                      │
│  Parent mode    │     │  │ reduces pain and fear, but│
│                 │     │  │ leads to OCD and     │
└─────────────────┘     │  │ isolation            │
                        │  └──────────────────────┘
```

Figure 2.2 Mode model of Case 1

Problems arose in therapy when Mary did not enter an emotional process but reported "emotional numbness" during exposure sessions. She occasionally fell into dissociative or angry states and fulfilled exercises "just for the sake of the therapist." In addition, she would sometimes protest firmly when ERP sessions were underway and refused to do planned exercises. This triggered self-devaluation, anger, and self-hatred as well as sadness and helplessness. Emotional numbness and anger were connected with the Detached/Angry Protector mode, self-devaluation with the Demanding and Punitive Parent mode, and intensive feelings of sadness and fear with the Vulnerable Child mode. These "dead-end" situations could be resolved by use of experiential techniques like chair work to explore and confront the dysfunctional modes as well as imagery to bypass them. Eventually, it became possible to reach the needs of the Lonely and Vulnerable Child mode, to support the child in venting its sorrow, and to calm and soothe it by means of imagery techniques and limited reparenting. Important work was also done by building a strong Healthy Adult mode to enable Mary to take control, regain self-esteem, and protect and support herself without having to resort to OCD behaviors. Through these interventions she developed the courage and motivation to continue CBT by allowing her emotions to be evoked and to adapt to them. She was capable of proceeding with ERP sessions, which helped her to regain resources.

Case 2 Carl

Carl is a 45-year-old retired, divorced gardener. He has suffered from heavy compulsions since the age of 15. He fears impulses that would harm him or others, such as turning the steering wheel the wrong way while driving a car or looking into the sun until his eyes hurt badly. This leads to high levels of uncertainty, exertion, and nervousness. Carl therefore intends to reduce his tension by intensive cognitive reconstructuring and compulsive behavior such as rechecking and reorganizing. High tension also intensifies his tic disorder. This disorder first developed at the age of 11, when he experienced great stress at school, and it emerges when he has to perform to certain standards. In his youth, he suffered from self-injuries by cutting his skin to punish himself. He also tried to kill himself once by overdosing on medication. Occasionally, he becomes quite angry and gets into trouble with others.

Carl had previously been admitted to psychiatric hospitals for his OCD and depression, receiving intensive in- and outpatient treatment in the form of standard CBT with exposure sessions, but without much success. He was quite frustrated and pessimistic on coming to our ward.

Carl was raised in a small town and was one of several siblings. His father was a heavy drinker and was physically and emotionally abusive to the children and his wife. Carl remembers his childhood as a terrifying period, resembling a "concentration camp," in which he was never allowed to meet with friends. He lived in constant fear of his father's punishments. When Carl was young, his father tried to kill him once with an ax, but he managed to escape. Carl describes the moment his father died in an accident when Carl was 14 as a "relief."

Carl also has problems in relationships. He fears most being abandoned and became severely depressed and suicidal after his divorce. His feeling of defectiveness creates intense shame and punitiveness against himself. He longs for companionship, understanding, and emotional nourishment but prevents himself from seeking and enjoying healthy social contacts due to the fear of being rejected.

His OCD fulfills functionality in terms of "overcontrolling" everything to feel safe and being perfectionistic so that "nothing cruel might happen." Since he sees himself as a potential aggressor, Carl does not allow himself to stand up for himself. Mental images concerning his aggressive obsessions are extremely distressing for him, because they are very vivid and emotionally exhausting. His tic disorder "helps" him to avoid stressful situations, eventually leading to frustration, unrelenting standards, and self-hatred.

In Carl's case, the Defectiveness, Punitiveness, Pessimism, Emotional Deprivation, and Abandonment schemas are present. In terms of the mode model, we conceptualize the need for safety and emotional warmth as the Vulnerable Child mode. Carl's angry behavior when core needs are not met is conceptualized as an Angry Child mode. His Punitive Parent mode contains his negativity, hatred, and self-injury. His tic disorder is conceptualized as a Detached Protector mode, providing a means to block aversive emotions. His OCD is a maladaptive compensatory way of controlling himself by overcontrolling everything to establish a slight sense of safety. It is therefore described as a Perfectionistic Overcontroller mode.

Carl's mode model is presented in Figure 2.3.

The model helped Carl to understand the rationale and functionality of his OCD behavior and to establish a new way of working with the therapist. After creating a therapeutic alliance by limited reparenting, most work was done by fighting the strong Punitive Parent mode to support the Vulnerable Child mode, as well as to calm and validate the Angry Child mode. Problems in therapy occurred mostly when the punitive mode interacted negatively, for example in exposure sessions, bullying the vulnerable side by devaluing its needs, and trying to terrify the developing Healthy Adult mode. The therapist worked as a Healthy Adult role model, using chair dialogues and imagery exercises to reduce and overcome the Punitive Parent mode. After several sessions, Carl was able to regain control by developing his Healthy Adult side, to reduce the avoiding detachment and perfectionism carefully, and to proceed in continuing his exposure therapy successfully.

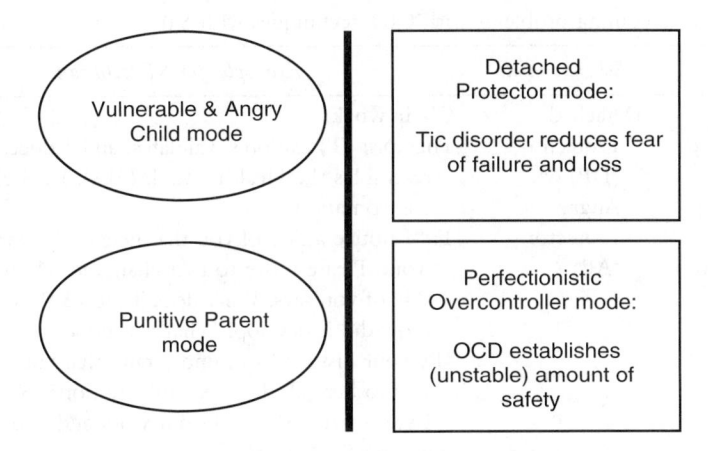

```
┌─────────────────┐         ┌─────────────────────┐
│                 │         │     Detached        │
│ Vulnerable & Angry │      │  Protector mode:    │
│   Child mode    │         │                     │
│                 │         │ Tic disorder reduces fear │
└─────────────────┘         │   of failure and loss │
                            └─────────────────────┘

┌─────────────────┐         ┌─────────────────────┐
│                 │         │   Perfectionistic   │
│ Punitive Parent │         │ Overcontroller mode:│
│     mode        │         │                     │
│                 │         │  OCD establishes    │
└─────────────────┘         │  (unstable) amount of │
                            │       safety        │
                            └─────────────────────┘
```

Figure 2.3 Mode model of Case 2

Pitfalls and Tips

To point out the proposed benefit of the mode concept for OCD patients we present in Table 2.1 the standard CBT techniques where you can get stuck and how ST can help bypassing them.

The Future

We reported the new concept of combining standard CBT for severe, chronic OCD with an OCD-related schema mode model for cases with a lack of response to prior treatment and severe negative outcome predictors, and we illustrated the concept with two case examples. Patients who had responded poorly to several OCD treatments finally benefited from this treatment, since it was possible to overcome treatment obstacles with ST interventions. Patients state that the mode model was crucial for their restrengthening and success in CBT therapy.

In our view, the mode model is well suited to conceptualize treatment problems in OCD therapy and to look for strategies to overcome them. The most important ST interventions reported by the patients were education about the mode model, therapeutic relationship, imagery, and chair work. These interventions helped the patients to make progress in exposure therapy (overcoming the compenstory modes) and enabled them to build a stronger Healthy Adult mode. Imagery exercises were mostly used to rescript the dysfunctional, painful intrusions and harmful inner pictures and memories.

The schema mode model is a developmental model, focusing on the unmet basic emotional needs of children. In our view, the need for stability, expression, and

Table 2.1 Overcoming problems with CBT techniques with ST

Situation	Schema mode	Examples for ST techniques
The patient refuses to do Exposure and Response Prevention (ERP).	Detached Protector (DP) or Angry Protector (AP)	**Chair work:** Therapist (T) explores, validates, and reduces DP/AP, resembles the Healthy Adult (HA). Uses empathic confrontation. T: "I notice a side of you that gets in the way of our work. Please move to that chair and tell me what this side of you says. What does it mean? Why is it there? How did it develop? What is it good for?" "By your history I can understand that you needed this side to bear all these painful emotions. Nonetheless, I see that it also blocks our work and disables your process in therapy."
Patient does not feel any emotions during ERP sessions.	DP	**Imagery or empathic confrontion** T uses imagery work to bypass DP and reach Vulnerable Child (VC) underneath. T: "Please close your eyes now and go back to a situation where you felt anxious as a child." T reassures the VC; fights the Punitive Parent (PP) if necessary.
Patient dissociates often during sessions.	DP Vulnerable child (VC)	**For empathic confrontation use chair work to confront DP** T confronts DP, uses chair work to explore it, and works with Healthy Adult (HA), to enable HA to stand up to DP. T: "I notice this side of you again. Please move to that chair." (T explores and validates DP, aims to understand its functionality.) "Please come to this chair and talk as your own HA with the DP. Tell him what you want, what your goals are." "I want to talk to your HA. What do you need to fight the DP? Which skills might help you?" **Imagery** T uses imagery to offer safety and limited reparenting to VC. "I understand now that your VC is too afraid to let the DP go. Let's do some imagery work. Please go to a situation in your childhood where you felt this unsafe and terrified as you do now." (T steps into imagery later on and fights the dysfuntional parent modes).
Patient claims he is too bad to deserve help.	Punitive parent (PP)	**Imagery** T steps into image, fights the PP. T (in image to PP): "You are not allowed to tell such nasty things to your son. He is a wonderful child. He deserves to be loved. I want you to stop yelling at him at once." **Chair work** T fights the PP by putting it in a chair (empty chair technique). T does NOT put patient into chair of PP. Patient stays in chair of HA (or VC).

Table 2.1 (*Continued*)

Situation	Schema mode	Examples for ST techniques
Patient feels he has to exercise more, that he is not doing it right.	Demanding Parent (DemP)	**Chair work** T fights the DemP by putting it in one chair, explores it, stands firmly up to it. Encourages HA part of patient to echo T. T (to DemP): "You say that Carl is lazy and does not work hard enough. You are not right. He does an excellent job. You'd better shut your mouth and listen to what he has to say. He is able to find out what he wants by himself. He does not need you putting pressure on him." T (to HA): "Please say to your DemP what you want it to do." If necessary, imagery is used to fight the DemP in a childhood situation.
Patient is burdened with painful images, cries, is tormented.	VC	**Imagery** T uses imagery to establish safety and reframe the image. T helps and reassures the VC. T: "Can you put me there into the picture? May I stand next to you and hold your hand?" "We can tell the aggressor to step back. Do you want him to be put in jail? We can ask for an army to take him away. Can you see him getting trapped? He will never come back to haunt you." "Do you want to go to a safe place like your grandma's garden? Let's go there and play some soccer, if you like."
Patient claims that the OCD has diminished by standard CBT whereas his emotions, such as anger and fear, are still there.	VC Angry Child (AC)	**Imagery** T uses imagery to get in touch with the patient's emotions. T reassures VC, helps AC to ventilate anger. T does limited reparenting in imagery to work on emotional needs. **Chair work** T tries to explore and validate AC. T (to AC): "Tell me what you are angry about. What went wrong? Is there more you are angry about?"
Patient clings to OCD behavior, continues to fulfill obsessions and compulsions.	Perfectionistic overcontroller (PO)	**Empathic confrontation and chair work** T confronts and explores PO, elaborates Pros and Cons, resembles HA of patient. T (acts as HA toward PO): "All these compulsions you want me to do – what are they good for? You are not helping me, your control is shallow and weak. You hurt and bother me. I don't want you to play such a major role in my life anymore!" T puts patient into chair of HA, supports patient in diminishing PO. Goal: to continue with ERP to reduce PO.

sharing of feeling, acceptance, and autonomy has often not been met in complex OCD cases. Many of the patients we worked with stressed suppressing spontaneous feelings or meeting rigid, internalized rules and expectations of performance and ethical behavior. This emphasis often comes at the expense of self-expression and close relationships. Lacking the possibility to function independently in childhood due to a dysfunctional family environment may lead to a schema of vulnerability, as studies have shown (Atalay et al., 2008). In work with these patients the use of ST elements may in our view be crucial for therapy outcome.

For now, our patients and staff accept the interventions gratefully and like the model. Further research must clarify whether the model applies to a larger group of OCD patients. We are preparing a randomized controlled trial to establish more well-measured methods and to retest the model with a larger sample to enable clearer conclusions.

References

Abramowitz, J.S. (2006) The psychological treatment of obsessive-compulsive disorder. *Canadian Journal of Psychiatry*, 51, 407–416.

Abramowitz, J.S., Taylor, S. and McKay, D. (2009) Obsessive-compulsive disorder. *Lancet*, 374, 491–499.

Ackerman, D.L. and Greenland, S. (2002) Multivariate meta-analysis of controlled drug studies for obsessive-compulsive disorder. *Journal of Clinical Psychopharmacology*, 22(3), 309–317.

Arntz, A. and Genderen, H. van (2009) *Schema Therapy for Borderline Personality Disorder*, 1st edition. Chichester: Wiley-Blackwell.

Atalay, H., Atalay, F., Karahan, D. and Caliskan, M. (2008) Early maladaptive schemas activated in patients with obsessive-compulsive disorder: a cross-sectional study. *International Journal of Psychiatry in Clinical Practise*, 12(4), 268–279.

AuBuchon, G. and Malatesta, V.J. (1994) Obsessive-compulsive patients with comorbid personality disorder: associated problems and response to a comprehensive behavior therapy. *Journal of Clinical Psychiatry*, 55(10), 448–453.

Baer, L. and Minichiello, W.E. (1998) Behavior therapy for obsessive-compulsive disorder, in *Obsessive-Compulsive Disorder: Practical Management* (eds M.A. Jenike, L. Baer and M.E. Minichiello). St. Louis, MO: Mosby, pp. 132–164.

Bernstein, D., Arntz, A. and de Vos, M. (2007) Schema-focused therapy in forensic settings: theoretical model and recommendations of best clinical practice. *International Journal of Forensic Mental Health*, 6(2), 169–183.

Eisen, J.L., Mancebo, M.A., Pinto, A. et al. (2006) Impact of obsessive-compulsive disorder on quality of life. *Comprehensive Psychiatry*, 47(4), 270–275.

Foa, E.B., Franklin, M.E. and Moser, J. (2002) Context in the clinic: how well do cognitive-behavioral therapies and medication work in combination? *Biological Psychiatry*, 52, 989–997.

Foa, E.B., Liebowitz, M.R., Kozak, M.J. et al. (2005) Randomized, placebo-controlled trial of exposure and ritual-prevention, clomipramine and their combination in the treatment of obsessive-compulsive disorders. *American Journal of Psychiatry*, 162(1), 151–161.

Fricke, S., Köhler, S., Moritz, S. and Schäfer, I. (2007) Frühe interpersonale Traumatisierungen bei Zwangserkrankungen: Eine Pilotstudie [Early interpersonal traumatization in obsessive-compulsive disorders: a pilot study]. *Verhaltenstherapie*, 17, 243–250.

Fricke, S., Moritz, S., Andresen, B. et al. (2006) Do personality disorders predict negative treatment outcome in obsessive-compulsive disorders? A prospective 6-month follow-up study. *European Psychiatry*, 21(5), 319–324.

Gershuny, B.S., Baer, L., Radomsky, A.S., Wilson, K.A. and Jenike, M.A. (2003) Connections among symptoms of obsessive-compulsive disorder and posttraumatic stress disorder: a case series. *Behaviour Research and Therapy*, 41, 1029–1041.

Gershuny, B.S., Baer, L., Parker, H. et al. (2008) Trauma and post-traumatic stress disorder in treatment-resistant obsessive-compulsive disorder. *Depression and Anxiety*, 25(1), 69–71.

Goodwin, D.W., Guze, S.B. and Robins, E. (1969) Follow-up studies in obsessional neurosis. *Archives of General Psychiatry*, 20(2), 182–187.

Hackmann, A. and Holmes, E.A. (2004). Reflecting on imagery: a clinical perspective and overview of the special issue of *Memory* on mental imagery and memory in psychopathology. *Memory*, 12(4), 389–402.

Hand, I. (1995) Outpatient behavior therapy in obsessive-compulsive disorders. *Fortschritte der Neurologie Psychiatrie*, 63(1), 12–18.

Hoffmann, N. and Hofmann, B. (2004) *Expositionen bei Ängsten und Zwängen [Exposure Therapy in Anxiety Disorders and Obsessive-Compulsive Disorders]*. Weinheim: Beltz.

Hollander, E., Greenwald, S., Neville, D. et al. (1996–97) Uncomplicated and comorbid obsevive-compulsive disorder in an epidemiologic sample. *Depression and Anxiety*, 4(3), 111–119.

Kaplan, H.I. and Sadock, B.J. (1998). *Synopsis of Psychiatry*, 8th edition. Baltimore, MD: Williams and Wilkins.

Keijsers, G.R., Hoogduin, C.A. and Schaap, C.P. (1994) Predictors of treatment outcome in the behavioural treatment of obsessive-compulsive disorder. *British Journal of Psychiatry*, 165(5), 781–786.

Koran, L.M., Hanna, G.L, Hollander, E., Nestadt, G. and Blair Simpson, H. (2007) Practice guideline for the treatment of patients with obsessive-compulsive disorder. *American Journal of Psychiatry*, 164, 1–56.

Kuelz, A.K., Hassenpflug, K., Riemann, D. et al. (2009) Psychotherapeutic care in outpatients – results from an anonymous therapist survey. *Psychother Psych Med*, 60, 194–201.

Lobbestael, J., Vreeswijk, M.F., van, Arntz, A. and Spinhoven, P. (2008) *The Reliability and Validity of the Schema Mode Inventory–revised (SMI-r)*.

Maier, S., Kuelz, A.K. and Voderholzer, U. (2009). Traumatisierung und Dissoziationsneigung bei Zwangserkrankten: Ein Überblick [Traumatization and the tendency to dissociate in obsessive-compulsive patients]. *Verhaltenstherapie*, 19, 219–227.

Myers, J.K., Weissmann, M.M., Tischler, G.L. et al. (1984) Six-month prevalence of psychiatric disorders in three communities 1980–1982. *Archives of General Psychiatry*, 41(10), 959–967.

NICE (National Institute for Health and Clinical Excellence) (2005) Obsessive-compulsive disorder: core interventions in the treatment of obsessive-compulsive disorder and body dysmorphic disorder. *Clinical Guideline, 31*. London: NICE.

Pigott, T. and Seay, S. (1997) Pharmacotherapy of OCD. *International Review of Psychiatry*, 9, 133–147.

Rachman, S. (2007) Unwanted intrusive images in obsessive-compulsive disorders. *Journal of Behavior Therapy and Experimental Psychiatry*, 38, 402–410.

Rasmussen, S.A. and Eisen, J.L. (1988) Clinical and epidemiologic findings of significance to neuropharmacologic trials in OCD. *Psychopharmacology Bulletin*, 24(3), 466–470.

Rasmussen, S.A. and Tsuang, M.T. (1986) Clinical characteristics and family history in DSM-III obsessive-compulsive disorder. *American Journal of Psychiatry*, 143(3), 317–322.

Robins, L.N., Helzer, J.E., Weissmann, M.N. et al. (1984) Lifetime prevalence of specific psychiatric disorders in three sites. *Archives of General Psychiatry*, *41*, 949–958.

Rufer, M., Fricke, S., Moritz, S., Kloss, M. and Hand, I. (2006) Symptom dimensions in obsessive-compulsive disorder: Prediction of cognitive-behavior therapy outcome. *Acta Psychiatrica Scandinavica*, *113*, 440–446.

Saunders, B.E., Villeponteaux, L.A., Lipovsky, J.A., Kilpatrick, D.G. and Veronen, L.J. (1992) Child sexual assault as a risk factor for mental disorders among women: a community survey. *Journal of Interpersonal Violence*, *7*, 189–204.

Speckens, A.E., Hackmann, A., Ehlers, A. and Cuthbert, B. (2007) Imagery special issue: intrusive images and memories of earlier adverse events in patients with obsessive-compulsive disorder. *Journal of Behavior Therapy and Experimental Psychiatry*, *38*, 411–422.

Stanley, M.A. and Turner, S.M. (1995) Current status of pharmalogical and behavioral treatment of obsessive-compulsive disorder. *Behavior Therapy*, *26*, 163–186.

Steketee, G. and Pigott, T. (2006). *Obsessive-Compulsive Disorder: The Latest Assignment and Treatment Strategies*, 3rd edition. Salt Lake City, UT: Compact Clinicals.

Voderholzer, U. and Hohagen, F. (2009) *Therapie psychischer Erkrankungen. State of the Art [Therapy of Psychiatric Disorders. State of the Art]*, 3rd edition. Munich: Elsevier/Urban and Fischer-Verlag.

Vogel, P.A., Hansen, B., Stiles, T.C. and Götestam, K.G. (2006) Treatment motivation, treatment expectancy, and helping alliance as predictors of outcome in cognitive behavioral treatment of OCD. *Journal of Behaviour Therapy and Experimental Psychiatry*, *37*(3), 247–255.

Young, J.E., Klosko, J.S. and Weishaar, M.E. (2003) *Schema Therapy: a Practitioner's Guide*, 1st edition. New York: Guilford Press.

3
Techniques within Schema Therapy

Michiel van Vreeswijk, Jenny Broersen, Josephine Bloo and Suzanne Haeyen

Treatments from different theoretical frameworks are offered to patients with personality problems. In part due to this development, Schema Therapy (ST) is growing, a growth that is driven further by the positive outcomes of efficacy studies into ST in patients with a borderline personality disorder (Giesen-Bloo *et al.*, 2006).

In this chapter, the authors restrict themselves to techniques used in ST. Longer descriptions of techniques, indications for ST, and pitfalls can be found, among others, in Young, Klosko, and Weishaar (2003), Beck, Freeman, and Davis (2004), van Vreeswijk and Broersen (2006), Haeyen (2007), Muste, Weertman and Claassen (2009), and van Genderen and Arntz (2010). These are sources used while writing this chapter; references are only cited below if they are different from these.

In Practice

Scientific interest in treatment strategies for patients with a borderline personality disorder (BPD) is enormous. A study in the US (Sharp *et al.*, 2005) investigated the use of therapy techniques for patients with BPD and showed that cognitive behavioral therapy (CBT) is the most frequently used treatment method for this group of patients, followed by psychodynamic therapy, or a combination of the two. The techniques most often used were the training in problem-solving behavior, here-and-now focus techniques (e.g., patient education, non-suicide contract, family/relatives counseling), cognitive restructuring, validating experiences, and anger management.

Less often reported techniques included interpretation of the unconsciousness, non-directivity, mindfulness training, Socratic dialogue, and ST techniques. The last finding is noteworthy because of the worldwide growth of ST and the increasing evidence of its efficacy. A possible explanation is that ST is new and still developing.

The Wiley Blackwell Handbook of Schema Therapy: Theory, Research, and Practice, First Edition.
Edited by Michiel van Vreeswijk, Jenny Broersen, and Marjon Nadort.
© 2012 John Wiley & Sons, Ltd. Published 2015 by John Wiley & Sons, Ltd.

Table 3.1 Therapeutic techniques within Schema Therapy (Arntz and Bögels, 2000; van Genderen and Arntz, 2010)

	CHANNEL		
FOCUS	Feeling	Thinking	Behavior
Outside therapy	• Role-playing present • Imaginary situations present • Exercise feeling emotions • Exposure to showing emotions	• Socratic dialogue • Formulating new schemas • Schema dialogue • Flash cards • Positive journal	• Behavioral experiments • Role-play skills • Trying out new behavior
Within therapy	• Limited reparenting • Empathic confrontation • Setting boundaries • Role-reversal: therapist–patient	• Identifying schemas of the patient in the therapeutic alliance • Challenging ideas about the therapist • Identifying schemas of the therapist • Disclosure	• Behavioral experiments • Confirming functional behavior • Training of skills with regard to therapeutic alliance • Modeling therapist
Past	• Imaginary rescripting • Role-playing past • Chair-work technique • Writing letters	• Reinterpreting events in the past and integrating into new schemas • Historical tests	• Trying out new behavior on old core figures

Approach

Schema Therapy is an integrative psychotherapy, partly based on CBT, Gestalt Therapy, attachment theory, object relations theory, and constructivist and psychoanalytic schools. However, in general, therapeutic techniques within ST can be divided into three groups: cognitive interventions, experiential interventions, and behavioral interventions. These techniques can also be described by indicating if these changes are realized through feeling, thinking, or behavior. These techniques are also focused on life outside therapy, the events that occur in therapy, or experiences from the past (Arntz and Bögels, 2000; van Genderen and Arntz, 2010). Table 3.1 shows these techniques.

In this chapter, the techniques are briefly explained. Over the years, additional techniques have been developed within ST. These are also discussed.

Therapeutic alliance

In ST, the therapeutic alliance is seen as an important tool. The therapeutic alliance offers the opportunity for so-called "limited reparenting". Unfulfilled needs can be met (within the limitations of therapy) in the present. A patient who, as a child, wasn't allowed to be angry can learn that the therapist won't abandon him when he is angry with the therapist. The therapist will also invite the patient to express his anger in full. If the therapist has made a mistake, the therapist can admit it and, together with the patient, check what this means to him. For example, which schemas and modes come to the fore in the therapeutic alliance? What (from the past) does it remind the patient of? What does the patient need?

> Andrew was raised with a father who abused and assaulted him. As a consequence, he often feels anxious and belittled when others interrupt him or when they continue to discuss something that isn't important to him. This issue, and how it affects the therapeutic alliance, is discussed regularly in therapy. Andrew finds it very difficult to tell the therapist what he doesn't like in the alliance. He is afraid that the therapist will explode just like his father used to do. Because of this, he puts his feelings aside and adapts again and again (Subjugation schema). After the therapist recognizes this anxiety and continues to ask about the contact that Andrew has with his father, they discuss the advantages and disadvantages of Andrew suppressing or hiding his emotions in the therapeutic alliance and also in other relationships. Gradually, Andrew comes to realize that concealing his emotions results in others not seeing him. His Emotional Deprivation schema is maintained because of this. Andrew agrees to start an experiment within the therapeutic alliance whereby he is to express what he doesn't like in the alliance. Although he is very afraid of this, he also wants to practice expressing his irritations within this alliance.

If necessary, the therapist will give advice and feedback to increase the healthy growth of the alliance. The therapist can, for instance, offer patient education about mental disorders and dealing with others, and, for example, suggest that the patient reads (schema-focused) self-help books (Young and Klosko, 1994). Where necessary, the therapist, as a good parent, can restrict the maladaptive behavior of the patient and confront him (emphatically) with any destructive behaviors that may be present. Video and audio recording of sessions can be used to let the patient hear again what was discussed in the session and to understand how the therapist and patient react to each other. It gives the patient an opportunity to learn to observe; to see whether he may have jumped to conclusions about what the therapist said, and to make it easier to return to what was discussed in previous sessions. Furthermore, the therapist can use cognitive, behavioral, and experiential techniques to assist the therapeutic alliance.

Cognitive interventions

The therapist can use the downward arrow technique to trace core beliefs/schemas. The therapist continues to ask what it means for a patient if a certain thought proves to be true – what it would mean for the patient, his self-image, other people, and the world around him. The schemas and modes of a patient can also be tracked and challenged by the use of a schema and/or modes diary.

When a patient gains more insight into which schemas and modes he has and when they occur, there is a moment in which it is wise to make an advantage and disadvantage analysis per schema and mode to assess what the advantages and disadvantages are of having certain schemas and modes. Following this, the therapist can discuss with the patient whether he is prepared to change anything about the severity of his schemas/modes.

A historical test is a technique that allows the patient to look for evidence that is in favor of or against schemas, both in the present and the past. The patient is invited to bring in as much (factual) evidence for a schema as possible and to search for (factual) counter arguments that illustrate why the schema has no right to bother the patient that much.

A visual analog scale (VAS) is used to challenge the black-and-white thinking of a patient. For this purpose, multidimensional evaluation can be used. A patient who thinks from his Defectiveness/Shame schema, and believes that everybody thinks he is stupid, can be challenged with these techniques. This may encourage him to appreciate others and himself on many levels, in order to come to a more nuanced outcome instead of an all-or-nothing outcome.

When a patient suggests a certain link between two variables, this can be challenged through two-dimensional reflection (Padesky, 1995). For example, a patient who thinks from his schemas that only beautiful people have a partner may be asked to place himself and others on the dimension "beauty" and on the dimension "having a partner." As in the multidimensional evaluation, this technique can lead to differentiated thoughts.

In the case of an excessive sense of guilt or a tendency to place responsibility outside oneself, the patient can be asked to complete a pie chart. For example, with regard to a "situation of guilt," all possible factors that may play a role in this situation are thought of. In addition, the patient first gives a slice of the pie to all named factors and after that to himself. In this way, the patient learns that there are more factors that play a part in this situation, and so the schema is challenged.

Patients tend, stemming from their schemas, to focus only on things that go wrong, which confirms the schema. A positive journal can help the patient to take the edge off his schemas. The patient is asked to examine events that are contrary to his schemas.

On flash cards, a patient writes in brief what is in favor of the schema and what is a healthy way to deal with it. Patients are advised to keep flash cards in their pocket or wallet. When the schema is triggered, they can look at the flash cards where alternative and more helping thoughts/behaviors are described.

Experiential interventions

Experiential techniques focus on experiencing and expressing emotions that are linked to (past) situations that, in turn, led to the development or maintenance of the schemas and modes. Writing a very angry, uncensored, not-to-be-sent letter is an example of a more experiential approach toward the schemas. However, the term experiential technique often reminds one more of imagery, (historical) role-play, and chair work.

Preceding the imagery, training is given regarding having an (imaginary) safe place in order to give the patient the option to go there during an imagery if necessary. Next, the therapist moves to the negative memory during the imagery, as if it were happening again in the here and now. In this way, the patient can be confronted with this negative experience in a safe way and can give a different meaning to this experience, both on a cognitive and an affective level. It is also possible for the therapist to use the imagery for so-called rescripts, as Andrew's case shows.

> As a result of an experience in which Andrew (A) felt very small when his boss was angry with him, he does an imagery exercise with rescripting, together with his therapist. From a very safe place, he goes back to a memory where he, as a seven-year-old, was shouted at by his father.
>
> T: What is happening? How old are you? Where are you now and who is with you?
> A: I'm in my room and my father enters roaring. I'm seven years old and I dropped a little plate by accident. My father is very angry. I'm afraid he is going to hit me.
> T: What else is happening?
> A: He starts to yell at me and he comes closer and closer. He looks very angry and he is raising his hand. I want to run away, but I can't.
> T: Andrew, is it OK if I come and stand next to you in this situation and help little Andrew to protect himself against his very angry father?
> A: (*nods anxiously*)

> The therapist "steps" into the image that Andrew has created and restricts the father. The therapist explains to the father that it isn't necessary to become that angry, that it makes Andrew very afraid, which means he can't even apologize to his father. When the father becomes calmer, the therapist asks little Andrew what he would like from his father. What would he like to say to his father, and what would he like to hear from him?

In rescripting, but also in (historical) role-play, it may be necessary for the therapist to perform as a continuation of the Healthy Adult mode of the patient. For example, the situation can evoke too many emotions in a patient for him to react in a healthy way, or the patient may not know how to react adequately.

Role-play can be used to represent (past) situations and to check with the patient what he experiences in the role-play, and what the other experiences in this situation (role-reversal). Furthermore, the patient can practice reacting in a more adequate way in the situation, whether or not with the introduction of the Healthy Adult, who supports the patient and helps him to express his desires/needs, and to restrict his impulsiveness.

Chair work makes it possible to give a chair to the different modes in the patient and to make contact with each of them separately. This makes it easier, for example, to dismiss the Punitive and Demanding Parent mode, to get through to the Detached Protector and/or the Detached Self-Soother, and to approach the Vulnerable Child mode. The patient learns how to deal with each of his modes from the Healthy Adult and/or Happy Child.

Behavioral interventions

Relaxation exercises can be introduced in therapy at different moments. For example, relaxation exercises can be used when a patient easily feels stressed or worries a lot, and is therefore less able to react to the Healthy Adult or Happy Child.

In the case of harmful behavior (self-injury, threatening others), the therapist, together with the patient, tries to explore, in a neutral, non-punitive way, what the harmful behavior consists of. The function of the behavior is also explored, and it is established whether specific moments can be identified in which harmful behavior occurs or intensifies. Although it isn't usually expected that the patient's harmful behavior will stop immediately, sometimes it is necessary to set firm boundaries with regard to the behavior. A clear explanation of the damaging consequences of this behavior and an exploration (together with the patient) of possible alternatives can help the patient to stop this behavior without feeling rejected or misunderstood.

The therapist continually stimulates the practicing of appropriate behavior. A patient who never goes to parties is stimulated to go and to try to get in touch with people instead of withdrawing into himself. Within therapy, it is also possible to work on developing (social) skills. How you make contact without withdrawing shortly afterward, or laying a claim to someone, are examples of skills that can be developed in training. The therapist compliments the patient on the steps that he takes in behavioral change. Even if the behavior experiment seems to fail, it is still successful because the patient broke through his avoidance and the experiment can offer valuable information about how a patient can handle the situation differently the next time.

Additional techniques within Schema Therapy

Cognitive behavioral therapeutic techniques, experiential techniques, and the therapeutic alliance were some of the first techniques in the development of ST. In the last few years, ST techniques has increased with the use of creative experiential and mindfulness-based techniques.

Creative experiential therapy. Because creative experiential therapy provides both expressive and structural possibilities, it fits closely to specific themes in personality problems (e.g., emotion regulation and impulse regulation). Creative (more commonly know as Art Therapy), experiential therapy is about acting and experiencing, becoming aware, expressing, becoming visible, but also remaining partly masked. This means that you can feel in control of expression and behavior. People with personality problems often have a vague or negative self-image and they get entangled in intense emotions that immediately elicit a certain reaction in them. Creating is experiencing and the action of creating contents of feelings and thoughts demands structure of perception of thoughts, and can therefore help the patient to organize feelings and thoughts.

Within creative experiential therapy, reflection takes place on different levels and refers to different processes; behavior, the content of the perception, the cognition which is created, and the level of social functioning. People with borderline problems mainly switch from feeling to impulsive behavior or are controlled by negative thinking about their behavior. Therefore, integrating feelings, behavior, and thoughts is an important goal. In order to frame experiences and improve integration, it is important to verbalize experiences that have been gained in the therapy. In this way, mentalization skills can be worked on (Bateman and Fonagy, 2005; Haeyen, 2005).

The use of experiential treatment techniques fits in well with the character of the different creative experiential techniques. In practice, you can see that a translation from ST to creative experiential therapy is made, and this occurs in such a manner in more and more places, as well as in inpatient, outpatient, and day treatments. According to the experts, creative experiential therapy can be integrated into therapy and used in addition to ST. This point of view is taken by the Dutch panel of creative therapists (Haeyen, 2005) and it is also supported by the literature (Thunnissen and Muste, 2002; de Jong, 2003; Haeyen, 2006). It is recommended that creative experiential therapy is investigated within ST.

Different modes are triggered within creative experiential therapy. Child modes are evoked by emotional reactions to materials and working methods involving playing. Parent modes emerge because, for example, a patient may look rigidly and punitively at his own work; the work is judged and considered to be not good enough. Fighting the Demanding and Punitive Parent can be practiced. Feelings and expressions linked to child modes can be validated, recognized, and made important. The therapist can work with limited reparenting by using soft materials, comforting music, and by occupying comforting roles within role-play. Because the therapist has material and working methods/experiential techniques at his disposal, the relationship between patient and therapist becomes less direct but the medium within this therapeutic alliance starts to play an important role. The medium evokes reactions and provides structure, feedback, and comfort, and in this way, it also functions in the field of reparenting without losing the patient's own responsibility.

Experiences within creative experiential therapy are mostly about discovering, improvising, experimenting, and instinctively acting in the present. It brings important core feelings to expression in the present (Smeijsters, 2007). In more structured working methods, the first matter of importance is emotional organizing.

In ST, experiential techniques such as imagery are used. ST provides a framework, for example, to work within art therapy with concrete personal experiences and to investigate underlying schemas. Following the imagery, an attempt is made to create an external shape from the inner images by creating these images in material.

Crystallizing that which came forward in the imagery creates the possibility of making choices, to be able to distance oneself, and evokes renewed reflection on the experiences. It is important to be able to distinguish/separate present and past, but also to mark an emotional experience, and to see the connections between present and past. Through artwork important experiences are intensely felt, confirmed, and embedded, both in holding on to positive feelings and in meaningful experiences of being able to take action as an adult about experiences of the past. That which was previously less clear becomes clear. It becomes apparent and visible which schemas play a role, what the change within the schema looks like, and with this, what this change can look like in the day-to-day life of the patient. The results of a group of 48 patients who completed a questionnaire after an imagery exercise within art therapy confirm this and show that the expressive aspect of therapy adds something essential (Haeyen, 2006). Results in research, using the Schema Mode Inventory-R (SMI-R, Young *et al.*, 2008), comparing between week 1 and week 13 of treatment including Visual Art Therapy were: - a strong significant decrease of the mode of the Demanding parent (0.00, p-value<0.01), a significant decrease of the mode of the Impulsive child (0.021, p-value<0.05) and the Enraged child (0.053, p-value<0.10). The conclusion was that there's a change in schema modes, especially in the decrease of demandingness, impulsivity and destructive anger. Also an increase of free and happy predominant emotional states was shown in the results (Haeyen, 2011).

Former patient Karen

I remember very well where it all started. In the individual therapy, I came to the point where I wanted to express the feelings that I have with experiences in my youngest years (until I was four years old). You can search for the words but I didn't connect, my vocabulary just didn't connect. The idea of a number of individual sessions of art therapy came up. In art group therapy I had noticed that art therapy worked well for me. I am rational and analytic by

> nature but that keeps me from my emotions. In art therapy, you do not use words, but you literally have to feel. The individual art therapy focused on the little child in me that was insecure, hurt, scared, alone, and neglected; a very emotionally charged child. As an adult, I had no idea how to deal with that. I felt that part of me but I was afraid of it because of all its impact. I ignored it. What art therapy achieved is that I started to look at that little child. That was very intense but it was also very nice to meet that little child. A pottery figure that I made of a little girl expressed very well how I felt then. I felt excluded from the family, not a part of it, different. The writing assignment in the art therapy sessions started as a fantasy story, told in the third person, but soon changed into a story about me. Still it felt good to start it as a fantasy. Otherwise it would be too confrontational; it would go too fast. Later on I was asked to bring the adult and the child together in one image, to bring them into contact with each other. I then made an image of a large hand that carried a small hand. This made me realize that as an adult I can care for the little child inside me. A merging of different positions in the image occurred. I used to place confirmation of myself very much in the hands of others. I can now offer myself that confirmation, even though it is only a thin layer. I can now tell that small vulnerable part of me: "It's hard, but that's OK." The core of the therapy process for me is that I learned to connect with the vulnerable part in me, with my feelings that go along with that, and that I learned to take care of that part of me.
>
> (Haeyen, 2007)

Mindfulness-based techniques. Although meditation or mindfulness (MBCT) is mentioned as an intervention within ST, there are few extended descriptions about how these techniques can be used (for exceptions, see Bennet-Goleman, 2001; van Vreeswijk, Broersen and Schurink, 2009; also see Part III, Chapters 6–10). Many patients with personality problems have comorbid Axis I disorders for which MBCT is proven to be the effective treatment method (for an overview article, see Schurink, 2006). Furthermore, patients with personality problems have a tendency to react in a sensitive way based on (old) learned experiences. In certain situations, a schema is triggered and then, in automatic pilot, a patient becomes defensive, offensive, or completely withdraws from the therapeutic alliance, or his own emotions and needs.

Implementing schema-focused MBCT teaches the patient to look at thoughts, behaviors, emotions, and physical experiences without automatically reacting from schemas or modes. A patient learns to look at something with renewed interest, as if seeing it for the first time and therefore without attaching a value judgment to it. When there are very intense worries, emotions, or physical experiences, the patient learns to be mindful about them, without the need to change them immediately. Allowing the presence of intense observations without behaving in an automatic fashion can lead to the realization that schemas and modes come and go, and that desperately trying to control or avoid this will only lead to tunnel vision, as opposed to having several options to hand.

> Monica does a lot for others. Even though she has many things to do herself, she will drop her own work to help someone else as soon as they ask her. Furthermore, she tends to feel the need to do everything extremely well, and she continues as long as is necessary to finish something. The following description is part of a discussion between Monica and her therapist, after they completed a mindfulness-based exercise.
>
> T: You have just told me that you realized something in the exercise. Can you tell me more about it?
>
> M: Yes. Yesterday I was busy working on a project that I have to finish for tomorrow, until a colleague came to ask me for help with another complicated project that she has to finish next week. I got up immediately and I went to give her a hand. The result was that a few hours later, I hadn't got any further with my own project and I was completely stressed until just now.
>
> T: Then what happened?
>
> M: I was worried that I'm not going to manage it. I was angry with myself that I didn't start work on the project before. I was angry that I went to help others. During the exercise, I also felt anger coming over me toward my colleague, because she came to ask me for help when she knew I was too busy and because she wouldn't have helped me straight away herself. When I allowed myself this feeling, allowed the thoughts and physical experiences with a neutral, curious perception, without letting myself be dragged away in my anger, I became calmer. I felt I was becoming less strict with myself, and less abused/cheated by others.

Pitfalls and Tips

In their enthusiasm, many therapists want to set to work (too quickly) when they hear and read about ST. The techniques employed can come across as very easily applied. Experience shows that it is important that therapists take both a ST course and a cognitive behavioral therapy course. Furthermore, not every patient is suited to ST. It is also the case that, for example, it is easier to work with schema-focused experiential techniques with patient A, and with cognitive techniques with patient B, whereas for patient C a constructive therapeutic alliance may make a big improvement. It is necessary that a therapeutic experience in the choice and implementation of schema techniques is built up under supervision and with a peer supervision group.

The Future

In daily practice, additional schema techniques (e.g., techniques of creative experiential therapy – art, expressive, music and psychomotor therapy – and mindfulness-based techniques) have been developed. Further investigation is necessary to understand which techniques work best for which patient. The best moment for implementing a certain technique also needs further scientific investigation and an understanding of which ST will be the most important for an optimal therapeutic result is required.

References

Arntz, A. and Bögels, S. (2000) *Praktijkreeks Gedragstherapie: Schemagerichte Cognitieve Therapie voor Persoonlijkheidstoornissen.* Houten: Bohn Stafleu and van Loghum.

Bateman, A.W. and Fonagy, P. (2005) *Psychotherapy for Borderline Personality Disorder. Mentalization-based Treatment.* New York: Oxford University Press.

Beck, A.T., Freeman, A. and Davis, D.D. (2004) *Cognitive Therapy of Personality Disorders*, 2nd edition. New York: Guilford Press.

Bennet-Goleman, T. (2001) *Emotional Alchemy: How the Mind Can Heal the Heart.* New York: Harmony.

Genderen, H. van and Arntz, A. (2010) *Schematherapie bij Bordeline Persoonlijkheidsstoornis.* Amsterdam: Uitgeverij Nieuwezijds.

Giesen-Bloo, J., van Dyck, R., Spinhoven, P. et al. (2006) Outpatient psychotherapy for borderline personality disorder. Randomized trial of schema-focused therapy vs. transference-focused psychotherapy. *Archives General Psychiatry*, 63, 649–658.

Haeyen, S. (2005) *Verslag paneldiscussie creatief therapeuten richtlijn persoonlijkheidstoornissen.*

Haeyen, S. (2006) Imaginatie in schemagerichte beeldende therapie. *Tijdschrift voor creatieve therapie*, 1, 3–10.

Haeyen, S. (2007) *Niet uitleven maar beleven, beeldende therapie bij persoonlijkheidsproblematiek*, Houten: Bohn Stafleu and van Loghum.

Haeyen, S. (2011) The connecting quality of Art therapy. Effects of Art therapy in the treatment of personality disorders. *Introduction of an Art therapy Questionnaire.* Apeldoorn/Antwerpen: Garant Uitgevers n.v.

Jong, N. de (2003) *Ben ik in beeld? De Muziektherapeutische Behandeling van de Narcistische Persoonlijkheidsstoornis, Volgens de Schemagerichte Therapie.* Afstudeerscriptie Muziektherapie, Conservatorium, Saxion Hogeschool Enschede.

Muste, E., Weertman, A. and Claassen, A. (2009) *Handboek Klinische Schematherapie.* Houten: Bohn Stafleu van Loghum.

Padesky, C.A. (1995) Schemaveranderingsprocessen in cognitieve therapie. *Psychotherapie*, 4, 395–423.

Schurink, G. (2006) Mindfulness: integratie in de cognitieve gedragstherapie. *Gedragstherapie*, 39, 281–292.

Sharp, I.R., Gregg, R., Henriqies, G.R. et al. (2005) Strategies used in the treatment of borderline personality disorder: a survey of practicing psychologists. *Journal of Contemporary Psychotherapy*, 35(4), 359–368.

Smeijsters, H. (2007) *Lezing "Emotion focused Vaktherapieën."* bij Studiedag GNOON vaktherapie te GGNet Apeldoorn, Nederland.

Thunnissen, M.M. and Muste, E.H. (2002) Schematherapie in de klinisch-psychotherapeutische behandeling van persoonlijkheidsstoornissen. *Tijdschrift voor Psychotherapie*, 28, 385–401.

Vreeswijk, M.F. van and Broersen, J. (2006) *Schemagerichte therapie in groepen. Handleiding voor therapeuten.* Houten: Bohn Stafleu van Loghum.

Vreeswijk, M.F. van, Broersen, J. and Schurink, G. (2009) *Mindfulness en Schematherapie; Praktische Training bij Persoonlijkheidsproblematiek.* Houten: Bohn Stafleu van Loghum.

Young, J.E. and Klosko, J.S. (1994) *Reinventing Your Life.* New York: Plume.

Young, J.E., Klosko, J.S. and Weishaar, M.E. (2003) *Schema Therapy: a Practitioner's Guide.* New York: Guilford Press.

4
On Speaking One's Mind: Using Chairwork Dialogues in Schema Therapy

Scott Kellogg

Introduction

Schema Therapy (Young, Klosko and Weishaar, 2003) is an integrative psychotherapy that utilizes cognitive, behavioral, psychodynamic, and gestalt concepts and techniques in the treatment of severe Axis I and Axis II pathology. One of the distinguishing features of ST is the central importance of experiential techniques – specifically imagery and chairwork dialogues. These gestalt techniques have played an important role in the development of both the schema-focused and the schema mode models. In fact, Jeffrey Young has discussed the central role that his own experiences with a gestalt therapist had on his life and his work (Collard, 2004).

The aim of this chapter is to provide a brief introduction to the use of chairwork in psychotherapeutic practice. Through the use of clinical vignettes and case examples, some of the many ways of using chairwork will be demonstrated and their relevance to schema therapists will be clarified.

History and Background

What is chairwork? At its most essential, there are two basic forms of psychotherapeutic dialogue. In the first, known as the "empty chair" dialogue, the patient is invited to sit in one chair and to imagine a person in the opposite chair. Typically, this is a person with whom they have some kind of "unfinished business" or unresolved emotional connection. In the second form, the patient is often working with inner conflicts. In the case of a decision, they can express a viewpoint in one chair and then switch to the one opposite to express the alternative view. This is known as the two-chair dialogue.

Chairwork is most often associated with the Gestalt Therapy of Frederick ("Fritz") Perls, the charismatic and controversial psychiatrist who popularized this way of working during the 1960s (see Shepard, 1975; Gaines, 1979; or Clarkson and Mackewn, 1993 for a full biographical portrait). While he played a significant innovative role, he was not the originator of the technique. In the 1950s, Jacob Moreno, the creator of psychodrama, held a weekly group in New York City and Perls appears to have been a fairly regular attendee (Leveton, 2001). It was Moreno who invented chairwork – something Perls publicly acknowledged in *The Gestalt Approach* (1973).

Invited to California in the early 1960s, Perls discovered the Esalen Institute in Big Sur and decided to make it his home. In an effort to draw attention to his therapy, he first did large-scale demonstrations in which he used the chair technique on stage (Clarkson and Mackewn, 1993). He then moved to the workshop format that would eventually lead to his becoming world-famous. His model was to work with people one-on-one; that is, to do individual therapy in a group setting (Perls, 1969). People who participated in these groups frequently spoke of having life-changing experiences (Gaines, 1979).

The work that he did at Esalen would eventually become known as California gestalt or West Coast gestalt (Naranjo, 1993). In my opinion, he actually created a second version of Gestalt Therapy that really had little to do with the one that had been first outlined in the foundational 1951 volume *Gestalt Therapy: Excitement and Growth in the Human Personality* (Perls, Hefferline and Goodman, 1965). The creative developments of this period are captured in *Gestalt Therapy Verbatim* (Perls, 1969), which contains transcripts of lectures and chairwork sessions that he gave and held at the Esalen Institute. It was here that the basic chairwork structures that are used today were crystallized (Kellogg, 2009b).

Like many of the great figures in the field of psychotherapy, Perls was a very complex man. Seen as a therapeutic genius by some (E. Polster, in Wysong, 1978), he was filled with darkness and light, and engendered strong feelings in most who engaged with him.

After his death, the Gestalt Therapy world was polarized, with many therapists in New York and Cleveland favoring the model outline in the 1951 book. Over time, this faction gained ascendance and there was an increasing rejection of the work that Perls had done in California and of chairwork itself (Naranjo, 1993). As Isidore From, one of the earliest gestalt therapists, put it, "psychodrama . . . is not consistent with the method of Gestalt Therapy" (1984, p. 9).

The paradoxical result was that chairwork, the technique that had come to epitomize Gestalt Therapy, was generally disowned by the Gestalt Therapy establishment (Kellogg, 2009a, 2009b). This "orphaning" process continues today; Woldt and Toman (2005), for example, in a leading textbook, barely mention this way of working.

While gestalt therapists were jettisoning chairwork from their armamentarium, many other therapists were trying to incorporate it into theirs. These would include Robert and Mary Goulding in their Redecision Therapy (Goulding and Goulding, 1997), Arnold Lazarus in his Multimodal Therapy (Lazarus and Messer, 1991), and

Leslie Greenberg (Greenberg, Rice and Elliott, 1993) in his Process-Experiential/Emotion-Focused Therapy. Marvin Goldfried (1988; Samoilove and Goldfried, 2000) and Dave Edwards (1989) both explored ways of integrating it with cognitive behavioral therapy, and Jeffrey Young would, of course, make it a central component of Schema Therapy (Young *et al.*, 2003).

External Dialogues

In much of the clinical and research literature, psychotherapeutic dialogues are referred to in terms of furniture arrangements, i.e., "two-chair" and "empty" chair. It is, perhaps, time to let go of this convention and organize our use of these therapeutic encounters in terms of whether they are "external" or "internal"; that is, did the therapist ask the patient to dialogue with a person or object outside of him- or herself or with an internal force or experience? (Kellogg, 2004). As psychotherapists gain confidence with this way of working they will want to flow back and forth between the internal and external realms; in addition, they may find it helpful to use more than two chairs at any given instance.

For Perls (1969; Perls *et al.*, 1965) the phrase "unfinished business" covered much of the interpersonal work that he did with patients. This would include ongoing difficulties with significant others, imagined conflicts in the future, and losses and traumatic experiences from the past. Engaging with these situations psychodramatically allowed the patient to move from "talking about" to "talking to" (Perls, 1969). In terms of past events, future anxieties, or situations that occurred outside of the therapy session, it allowed for a process of "presentification" in which everything could be worked through in the here and now (Naranjo, 1993).

Clinically, three of the more common external dialogues involve grief, trauma, and assertiveness. In terms of grief and loss, patients may be blocked or stuck in the past in a variety of ways. To encounter patients in practice who are having difficulty overcoming a romantic loss or who seem to be trapped in a state of mourning after a death is, perhaps, not that uncommon. Patients, however, may be struggling with other, less obvious losses as well. A man or woman may lose a job or position that they had for a long time or one that they had worked hard to achieve. Other people may have had ambitions that they were never able to fulfill, and some may need to say goodbye to geographical locations that were important to them (Goulding and Goulding, 1997). Each of these may benefit from a process of working through and letting go, and chairwork can play a vital role in this process.

Tobin (1976) has laid out a classic gestalt structure for "saying goodbye." When a patient wants to do this, he or she is invited to put the grieved other in the "empty chair," which is placed opposite to where they are seated. The therapist encourages the patient to try to "see" the lost or missing person in the other chair. "What does he look like? How is he dressed? What are you feeling as you look at him?" These questions help to deepen the experience and engage the patient in the dialogue.

Gestalt therapists have consistently emphasized the importance of balance and patients are encouraged to express the emotion that first emerges as they view the imagined other in the opposite chair. Ultimately, they should be invited to express the love, anger, fear, and grief that they feel for the person (Perls, 1973).

This process may take a single session or it may take several. At some point, however, the patient will be invited to formally say goodbye. In some cases they will agree to do this, in others they will not. The latter are now seen as having made an existential decision to remain actively connected to a person who is no longer in their life, which means that they are no longer a "victim" of a grief process (Tobin, 1976).

A woman and her husband were told that their 13-month-old baby had a heart defect and, in consultation with their physician, chose surgery as a remedy. Unfortunately, the baby died and the mother had been blaming herself for 16 years. The therapist first asked her to imagine the baby sitting in the chair opposite and to speak with her about what happened and how she was feeling. After conveying her guilt and grief, the therapist then invited her to switch seats and now speak from the perspective of the baby. What emerged was that the "baby" said that she, too, had wanted a full life and that if she had been able to, she would have chosen the operation as well. In essence, the "baby" told the mother that she did the right thing. With this, an enormous load was lifted from the mother and there was some resolution of her grief and loss (Stevens, 1970).

Experiences with trauma and abuse are tragically common in psychotherapy practice and ST is particularly focused on the processing and working through of experiences of mistreatment and abuse. Chairwork can be used to create a kind of "psychotherapeutic theater" (Gaines 1979) in which many important conversations and dialogues can take place. For example, patients and therapists can speak with and nurture the abused child while also confronting the abuser and those who knew about the mistreatment yet did not protect the child.

Looking at the work of Goulding and Goulding (1997), a helpful dialogue structure emerges from their practice. They "put" the visualized perpetrator in the opposite chair and then asked the patient to verbalize the following aspects of his or her experience: 1) "This is what you did to me," followed by the details of the abuse; 2) "This is how it affected me at the time" – i.e., "I felt damaged, ashamed, dirty, and humiliated"; and 3) "This is how I have lived my life since then" – i.e., "I have not trusted others," "I have used drugs and alcohol destructively," or "I have allowed others to misuse me."

The goal of this work is for the patient to make a decision to no longer live in the shadow of the mistreatment, to make a decision that they will live in *defiance* of what has been done to them. This is called a *redecision*. The next step would be for them to say: 4) "I am no longer going to live my life this way. I will act and relate to myself and others in ways that reflect my taking control of my life and treating myself with love and respect." Examples of these kinds of redecisions include: "From now on, I am going to find trustworthy people, and I will trust them. Everyone is not like you." "I enjoy sex today in spite of what you did to me. You are no longer in my bed." "I can laugh and jump and dance without guilt, because my fun didn't cause you to rape me! It was your perversity!" (Goulding and Goulding, 1997, p. 248). This work has clear parallels to the process of fighting the maladaptive schema and its origins.

In an example concerning emotional abuse, a woman put her grandmother in the opposite chair and said to her: "I hate being here with you. You constantly talk about dying and death, death, that's it, every day, every day. . . . I resent the times you called me a tramp. . . . I was never a tramp! You always said, 'You'll become pregnant.' I never did things like that. But you always said I was no good, a slut. . . . I resent you for not trusting me, for not letting me be a young person. I resent you for dragging me to cemeteries to see dead graves. . . . I *resent* that . . . " (Engle, Beutler and Dalrup, 1991, pp. 180–182).

In this scenario, the patient is given an opportunity to say the things that she probably could not have said as a child or teenager. She is also being given an opportunity to claim authority and speak with anger and forcefulness. At the end of the encounter, the patient told her grandmother, "I feel stronger. I'm in control, not you" (Engle *et al.*, 1991, p. 182).

Assertiveness training and behavioral rehearsal come from the behavioral tradition. In fact, Wolpe (1982) originally called this way of working "Behavioristic Psychodrama." In a way, assertiveness training can be seen as helping people to find their voice, to claim their voice, to access power, and to defend themselves. It gives them both the right and the ability to say "yes" or "no" and to engage with the world in a stance of respectful desire. In this regard, chairwork can help all kinds of patients become more positively forceful in their lives; it may be particularly helpful to those who have traditionally had more limited access to power, such as women and disenfranchised or marginalized groups.

In my practice, a patient complained that her boyfriend was critical of her beliefs and esthetic choices, and she was particularly upset that he criticized her taste in music. I asked her to imagine him sitting in the opposite chair and to tell him that she did not like this behavior, that she had the right to listen to the music that she liked, and that she wanted him to stop. We worked on this repeatedly so that she would feel more comfortable using stronger language and claiming ownership of her feelings and desires. We also worked on the tone and volume of her voice. She went home and confronted him and he apologized and agreed to stop the behavior. This was a powerful moment in the therapy and it led to a general shift in their relationship because she now felt that she could ask for what she wanted.

Internal Dialogues I

In a ST framework, chairwork dialogues can function as either a cognitive technique or an experiential technique (Young *et al.*, 2003; Kellogg and Young, 2006; Kellogg, 2009a). In the external dialogues, chairwork served as an experiential technique in the grief and abuse scenarios and a mixed experiential/cognitive function in the assertiveness work.

With the internal dialogues, these two approaches are more clearly delineated. Both Cognitive and Schema Therapists have used chairwork dialogues as a way of challenging problematic beliefs and schemas. The belief can be stated in one chair and the evidence to the contrary can be presented in the other. For example, the patient can express their belief and fear that they will fail a test in one chair and then switch to the other chair and make the case that, with proper preparation, he or she has always passed (Leahy and Holland, 2000). These *corrective* dialogues can involve the development of a counter-script as a way to prepare a comprehensive argument (Kellogg, 2004).

In *Schema Therapy*, there is a case in which Young works with a woman named Ivy, whose problem is her relationship with a friend named Adam (Young et al., 2003). The fundamental issue is one of inhibition – she listens to his problems but feels blocked when it comes to sharing the details of her life. While a part of her would like to redress this situation, she has a Self-Sacrifice schema that tells her that she does not have the right to speak up and express her needs and desires because that would be selfish.

Working with Young, she is able to have a dialogue with the schema where she gets angry about the damage it has caused her while also affirming the new healthy schema that prizes reciprocity. After successfully challenging the schema, she does imagery work and is able to confront her mother, who was the source of the schema. All of this gets crystallized when she says to the mother, "It cost me too much to take care of you. It cost me my sense of self" (p. 148). She eventually has a meeting with Adam and is successfully able to speak about personal matters.

On a technical level, gestalt therapists encourage patients to give voice to both sides in a strong and vigorous manner. When they say the new perspective, they are making it more vital and meaningful. When they argue for the old schema, they are taking possession of it. In this way it becomes less automatic and more under their control (Perls et al., 1965).

Furthering the link between chairwork and cognitive therapy, Bishop (2001) has affirmed that the thoughts of cognitive therapy can be re-envisioned as voices. Edwards (1989) felt that the processes involved in both chairwork and imagery were forms of cognitive restructuring, and Goldfried (1988) spoke about the importance of "hot cognitions" and how chairwork could help create them. The psychodramatic quality of this way of working would be beneficial as it would more likely lead to neurobiological activation and, therefore, more lasting change.

The mode model anchors ST within a broader effort to integrate concepts of multiplicity of self into psychotherapeutic practice. As Stiles has written, "An emerging understanding considers people not as separate, unitary individuals, but rather as mosaics or communities of different voices" (1999, p. 3).

In schema mode work, one of the central goals is the creation and/or strengthening of the Healthy Adult mode. This mode, which may develop in part from the internalization of the assertive qualities of the therapist, also develops from ongoing dialogues with other modes such as the Punitive Parent, the Demanding Parent, the Impulsive Child, the Vulnerable Child, and the Detached Protector. This kind of engagement is a process that takes time and it involves work outside the session.

However, using the idea of modes more generally, it is fine to say that at the heart of many patients' problems is a conflict between a part that wants to do something (Desire) and a part that is afraid (Fear). Another version of this includes a third voice that judges (Critic) and often inhibits the desire part through challenging his or her right to act. The Critic and Fear voices are, in fact, often connected in some way.

The Decision paradigm is perhaps the most basic of the internal dialogues. When a patient is faced with a choice – "Should I stay in my marriage or leave?" "Should I pursue the job opportunity or continue with my company?" – it is helpful to start by doing a Decisional Balance (Marlatt and Gordon, 1985). With this technique the patient clarifies the positives and negatives of one course of action and the positives and negatives of the other. Using this as orienting information, one voice can be created that embodies both the positives of that perspective and the negatives of the opposite, and vice versa. The therapist can then integrate this as he coaches the patient through the dialogue. (It should be noted that more than two voices may emerge in this process, which would then require the use of more than two chairs.)

One of my patients had been wrestling with job unhappiness. He had previously run his own company for a number of years, but due to economic shifts, he had to close it and was now working for a large firm. He was very unhappy with the commute and did not like reporting to others and meeting their needs and requirements. This part of him wanted to leave and re-engage in some kind of entrepreneurial activity. Another part, however, was very worried about money. He felt that as he was getting older he needed financial security. The result of this conflict was frequent states of anger, anxiety, and depression.

We did a two-chair dialogue in which he strongly, clearly, and emotionally made the case for each perspective. He went back and forth a number of times until he felt that he had fully expressed the energy that was contained in each voice. The outcome was that he was able to more fully commit to staying in his current job since he was now much less conflicted and more at peace. A year after the therapy ended he was still working in that position.

It is important for the therapist to be as thorough as possible when working with a decision. This means that the therapist may want to question and challenge the perspectives that are being embodied in each of the chairs. One additional technique is to go to the future and have the patient imagine how their life is at that time and how they feel about the decision they made (Fabry, 1988). For example, starting in one chair, the patient can be asked: "Ten years ago today, you made the decision to leave your wife and end your marriage. How are you doing today? What is your life like? What was it like in the first few years after you left her? How do you feel about having made the decision to leave?" The patient then switches to the other chair, and the therapist continues: "Ten years ago today, you were in a state of crisis. Despite the difficulties you were going through, you decided to stay with your wife and reaffirm your marriage. How are things today? What is your life like? How did things go after you made that decision? How do you feel about having decided to stay?" In this way, the many facets involved in the choice are considered.

Internal Dialogues II

There is another way to approach internal phenomena that is not currently a part of ST, but is, nonetheless, quite powerful. Perls (1969), in a synthesis of psychodynamic, humanistic, and Jungian thinking, emphasized the importance of inner polarities and their integration (Polster, 1987). He believed that either through direct injunctions, cultural norms, or unfortunate circumstances people learn that some aspects of themselves are acceptable while others are not. The parts that are not acceptable are then disavowed, repressed, and, frequently, projected onto the world (Baumgardner, 1975).

For example, patients may have gotten the message that it is acceptable to be intellectual but not aggressive, financially oriented but not artistic, nurturing but not sexual, social but not ambitious, or aggressive but not tender. The result is that people suffer from a form of emotional crippling in which they do not have access to all of their inner resources. From this perspective, the conflict between the acceptable and unacceptable parts of the self is seen to be at the root of many patients' problems with depression and anxiety.

For Perls (1969), the answer lay in reclaiming the disowned polarity, giving voice to it, and integrating it in a creative and useful way. His way of discovering and re-owning these projections involved the enactment and embodiment of difficult life situations and the creation of polarity dialogues based on dream imagery.

Erving Polster worked with a minister in the 1960s. The minister wanted to give a sermon on the conflict in Selma, Alabama – a place where the police had used dogs to attack Civil Rights marchers. While this was an issue that he felt quite disturbed by, he was afraid that his sermon would not be effective. Polster invited him to practice this in the session and found that it was, in fact, lacking in passion and interest.

Going to the opposite polarity, he asked the minister to stand up and tell the story of Selma as if he were one of the policemen. As he did this, he spoke with much more emotion and energy. His voice was louder, he clenched his fists, he told stories, and was generally more confident. Polster then asked him to give the sermon again, but this time he should say it in the manner of the policeman. This time the sermon was quite compelling and it resonated with Polster and, ultimately, with his congregation.

As they explored the issue of forcefulness and aggression, it turned out that the minister had always looked up to the bullies in his school. He had admired their energy and confidence, even though they had attacked him and called him a sissy. The polarity that he had developed was that bullies were vital, but bad, while victims were moral and good, but lacked aggression. Through this work, he was able to claim his own vitality and strength while holding on to his moral center. The result was that he could become both forceful *and* righteous (Polster and Polster, 1973).

An Integrated Example

A striking example of chairwork that utilizes both external and internal techniques comes from the work of Xu Yi Ming. In 1999 there was a catastrophic earthquake in Taiwan that led to many deaths and much upheaval. Ming led a grief and bereavement team to various schools and villages where they used psychodrama to help the survivors process their grief and trauma.

A boy at the Pu Li Elementary School, who had lost his father in the quake, was being criticized by others because he was not demonstrating the kind of grief that was expected in Taiwanese culture. When the team spoke with the boy, they came to realize that the father had been a violent and abusive alcoholic who had mistreated both the boy and his mother. The boy was in a state of conflict because while he was relieved that his father was gone, he now feared that his mother could be taken as well. He was also feeling stressed because his mother had become much more possessive.

Ming first invited the boy to sit in one chair and play his father. As he got more comfortable in the role he began to imitate his father's drunken speech. He started to curse and he acted out the beating of a child. This imagined beating was quite intense and he laughed, cried, and seemed hysterical at times. The therapist then had him go to another chair and speak to his father in the first chair. With encouragement, he was able to express the deep unhappiness and hatred he felt for the father. At the end, he kicked the "father" chair over repeatedly as he expressed his rage.

When this was finished, Ming put two new chairs in front of the boy. One chair was for his anger and hatred and the other chair was for the part of him that wanted to be hugged and taken care of, the part of him that was capable of love and forgiveness. Using the shuttling technique (Perls, 1973; Daniels, 2005), Ming repeatedly asked him to go back and forth between the two chairs – first expressing hatred and then expressing love. At the end, he said to the boy:

> I can see now you feel much better and released. Now you sit on this chair, you are the boy of love and forgiveness. You said to that empty chair that represents your hatred and anger, "Get away. I place all my hatred and anger on you. Now I want to bury you together with my dead father". The boy did so according to the director's advice. He looked tired but peaceful. (Chang, 2005, p. 291)

In this case, Ming utilized several powerful interventions. When the boy played the father, he was able to re-enact the trauma while also sharing it with others. When he switched chairs, Ming gave the boy the freedom to express his anger and hatred in a safe space that was temporarily removed from the disapproving greater culture while also validating the boy's right to have those feelings. In the final two-chair dialogue, he had the boy give voice to his loving and angry parts or modes, and, using the shuttle technique, he worked on affirming the boy's complexity of self. At the end, he encouraged him to bury the angry part with his father. In this way, he created a greater distance between the boy and his angry/hateful mode – perhaps even going so far as to externalize it.

Pitfalls and Tips

Chairwork is a deceptively simple, yet extremely powerful technique. Schema Therapy is, fundamentally, an active therapy and it calls practitioners to a stance of measured therapeutic boldness. This means that therapists, when creating chair dialogues, must work to create appropriately high levels of emotional intensity since this is necessary for the deep and profound healing that they are trying to foster. Since this will lead to some necessary patient discomfort, clinicians must also be careful that they do not push patients too fast or too hard. This balance is, perhaps, something that can only be learned through practice.

The Future

The creative, yet scientifically based use of experiential techniques is one of the great strengths of ST. For many clinicians, imagery and chairwork are the skills with which they have had the least experience; this means that the growth and development of these techniques within in a ST context will depend on the quality and quantity of training available. In a way, chairwork is a "low-threshold" intervention in that through reading articles and watching DVDs, many clinicians can learn enough to use the technique in a rudimentary, yet effective form. Further expertise can be developed through attending workshops, receiving supervision from Schema Therapists versed in the technique, and using it in a personal therapy context.

As was discussed earlier, the second form of internal chairwork dialogues involves the use of projections and polarities. This is a very profound way to work; however, it is not a method that is currently used under a ST rubric. I believe that the challenge of finding ways to add these kinds of dialogues to the clinical armamentarium is one that is worth taking up because it will add a valuable dimension to the healing work.

Conclusion

Chairwork is a powerful, creative, and effective therapeutic technique that can be used with a wide array of clinical problems. Schema Therapists can specifically use it to rework painful and traumatic experiences, to challenge maladaptive schemas, and to engage in mode dialogues and mode restructuring. It is my hope that the cases presented here have provided therapists with some useful and inspiring examples.

References

Baumgardner, P. (1975) *Gifts from Lake Cowichan*. Palo Alto, CA: Science and Behavior Books.
Bishop, F.M. (2001) *Managing Addictions: Cognitive, Emotive, and Behavioral Techniques*. Northvale, NJ: Jason Aronson.
Chang, I.I. (2005) Theatre as therapy, therapy as theatre transforming the memories and trauma of the 21 September 1999 earthquake in Taiwan. *Research in Drama Education*, 10, 285–301.
Clarkson, P. and Mackewn, J. (1993) *Fritz Perls*. Thousand Oaks, CA: Sage.
Collard, P. (2004) Interview with Jeffrey Young: reinventing your life through schema therapy. *Counselling Psychology Quarterly*, 17, 1–11.
Daniels, V. (2005) The method of "shuttling" in the gestalt working process. *Gestalt!* 9, n.p. www.g-gej.org-91/corner.html (accessed September 30, 2007).
Edwards, D.J.A. (1989) Cognitive restructuring through guided imagery, in *Comprehensive Handbook of Cognitive Therapy* (eds A. Freeman, K.M. Simon, L.E. Beutler and H. Arkowitz). New York: Plenum Press, pp. 283–297.
Engle, D., Beutler, L.E. and Dalrup, R.J. (1991) Focused expressive therapy: treating blocked emotions, in *Emotion, Psychotherapy, and Change* (eds J.S. Safran and L.S. Greenberg). New York: Guilford Press, pp. 169–196.
Fabry, J. (1988) *Guideposts to Meaning: Discovering What Really Matters*. Oakland, CA: New Harbinger.
From, I. (1984) Reflections on Gestalt Therapy after thirty-two years of practice: a requiem for gestalt. *Gestalt Journal*, 7, 4–12.
Gaines, J. (1979) *Fritz Perls: Here and Now*. Millbrae, CA: Celestial Arts.

Goldfried, M.R. (1988) Application of rational restructuring to anxiety disorders. *The Counseling Psychologist*, *16*, 50–68.

Goulding, M.M. and Goulding, R. (1997) *Changing Lives through Redecision Therapy*. New York: Grove Press.

Greenberg, L.S., Rice, L.N. and Elliott, R. (1993) *Facilitating Emotional Change: The Moment-By-Moment Process*. New York: Guilford Press.

Kellogg, S.H. (2004) Dialogical encounters: contemporary perspectives on "chairwork" in psychotherapy. *Psychotherapy: Research, Theory, Practice, Training*, *41*, 310–320.

Kellogg, S.H. (2009a) Schema Therapy: A gestalt-oriented overview. *Gestalt! 10*(1): www.g-gej.org/10-1/schematherapy.html (accessed October 26, 2011).

Kellogg, S.H. (2009b) Response to Bloom, Fodor, and Brownell. *Gestalt! 10*(1): www.g-gej.org/10-1/Kelloggresponse.html (accessed October 26, 2011).

Kellogg, S.H. and Young, J.E. (2006) Schema Therapy for borderline personality disorder. *Journal of Clinical Psychology*, *62*, 445–458.

Lazarus, A.A. and Messer, S.B. (1991) Does chaos prevail? An exchange on technical eclecticism and assimilative integration. *Journal of Psychotherapy Integration*, *1*, 143–158.

Leahy, R.L. and Holland, S.J. (2000) *Treatment Plans and Interventions for Depression and Anxiety Disorders*. New York: Guilford Press.

Leveton, E. (2001) *A Clinician's Guide To Psychodrama*, 3rd edition. New York: Springer.

Marlatt, G.A. and Gordon, J.R. (1985) *Relapse Prevention*. New York: Guilford Press.

Naranjo, C. (1993) *Gestalt Therapy: The Attitude and Practice of an Atheoretical Experientialism*. Nevada City, DA: Gateways/IDHHB Publishing.

Perls, F.S. (1969) *Gestalt Therapy Verbatim*. Lafayette, CA: Real People Press.

Perls, F.S. (1973) *The Gestalt Approach and Eye Witness to Therapy*. Palo Alto, CA: Science and Behavior Books.

Perls, F., Hefferline, R.F. and Goodman, P. (1965) *Gestalt Therapy: Excitement and Growth in The Human Personality*. New York: Dell.

Polster, E., and Polster, M. (1973) *Gestalt Therapy Integrated: Contours of Theory and Practice*. New York: Brunner/Mazel.

Polster, M. (1987) Gestalt Therapy: evolution and application, in *The Evolution of Psychotherapy* (ed. J. Zeig). New York: Bruner/Mazel, pp. 312–322.

Samoilove, A. and Goldfried, M.R. (2000) Role of emotion in cognitive behavior therapy. *Clinical Psychology: Science and Practice*, *7*, 373–385.

Shepard, M. (1975) *Fritz*. New York: E.P. Dutton.

Stevens, B. (1970) *Don't Push the River*. Lafayette, CA: Real People Press.

Stiles, W.B. (1999) Signs and voices in psychotherapy. *Psychotherapy Research*, *9*, 1–21.

Tobin, S.A. (1976) Saying goodbye in Gestalt Therapy, in *The Handbook of Gestalt Therapy* (eds C. Hatcher and P. Himelstein). New York: Jason Aronson, pp. 371–383.

Woldt, A.L. and Toman, S.M. (2005) *Gestalt Therapy: History, Theory, and Practice*. Thousand Oaks, CA: Sage.

Wolpe, J. (1982) *The Practice of Behavior Therapy*, 3rd edition. New York: Pergamon Press.

Wysong, J. (1978) An oral history of Gestalt Therapy, part three: a conversation with Erving and Miriam Polster. www.gestalt.org/postview.htm (accessed September 11, 2010).

Young, J.E., Klosko, J.S. and Weishaar, M.E. (2003) *Schema Therapy: A Practitioner's Guide*. New York: Guilford Press.

5
Schema Therapy and the Role of Joy and Play

George Lockwood and Ida Shaw

Introduction

Three overriding dimensions of parenting and limited reparenting are the minimization of negative affect (e.g., soothing and comforting), the amplification of positive affect (e.g., sharing wonder, playfulness, and joy), and managing impulsiveness through adequate structure and limit setting. We see each of these as having important roles in meeting core emotional needs but that, for a variety of reasons, the amplification of positive affect as relatively underutilized in psychotherapy. Most psychotherapy is still focused on the serious business of relief from pain and suffering and maintaining adequate boundaries, and much less on fostering play, happiness, and joy. In Grawe's (2007) extensive studies of therapeutic process he found that therapists often miss opportunities to convey positive, need-satisfying experiences because they are too busy focusing on other things. From another vantage point, Schore (2003) has pointed out that research on the mother's role as amplifier and regulator of infant joy and the central role this has in the "wiring" of the social brain has yet to be digested fully into the psychotherapy world (Carroll, 2005). Our goal in this chapter is to further this integration. While psychotherapists are beginning to incorporate techniques emerging from the positive psychology movement (Seligman, 2002; Frisch, 2006), much of this work focuses on helping the adult side of the patient through the use of cognitive and behavioral techniques and less of it involves direct engagement with the child side of the patient and a focus on the early roots of positivity. Here we discuss what we consider to be "depth-oriented" positive psychology, an approach that is especially applicable for patients who have missed out on the early building blocks of positivity and who do not yet have the capacity to benefit from the use of strategies such as gratitude journals or the identification and use of strengths (Seligman, Steen, Park and Peterson, 2005). We will first provide a general overview of the theory and technique we have developed around joy and play and then discuss specific applications within individual and group modalities.

Theory

Joy, play, and early maladaptive schemas

A focus on the amplification of positive affect and play as central features of core emotional needs can expand our view of a number of schemas. For example, the notion of Emotional Deprivation moves beyond the calming, comforting, and reassuring aspects of warmth, affection, empathy, protection, and guidance that have been its focus to an inclusion of joy and playfulness. The capacity for joy, like the capacity for empathy and attunement, is, to a significant extent, learned. It is dependent on a parent who is able to experience joy and who can share it with an infant or child without over stimulating her (Schore, 2003). While the instinct to play is universal, play itself is a language that is dependent on others for its development and elaboration (Sutton-Smith, 1974). A parent's participation in, and expansion of, a child's play has a critical role in this elaboration and in the enrichment of the bond between parent and child.

A second schema that is expanded by this focus on positivity is Shame/Defectiveness. It involves a sense of being unlovable, badness, or inferiority, for example, and implies a need to feel loved and accepted. Beyond this, we see as equally important the need to feel that ones we love take a delight in who we are at our core and cherish us. A parent who has the capacity to experience this with her child and a therapist who is able to take a delight in his patients and the process of working with them adds an important dimension to the process of growth and change that goes beyond the traditional warmth, genuineness, and positive regard. This is something that is often picked up on, not necessarily consciously, by the patient in the early sessions and makes a significant difference in their sense of safety and engagement in the treatment. A patient began to experience this dimension of attachment and articulated to me (George) what many patients need but are unaware of or are too fearful of hoping for this way:

> "One of the things I have needed and have never gotten is to be cherished. My parents never did that. I didn't get that in my first marriage at all. I feel loved by my current husband [but] at the same time it is not quite the same as the little girl place of feeling cherished. I don't want to put that on him. I feel it here with you and at the same time it is so unfamiliar and I fear I will lose it."

Joy, play, and modes

From the vantage point of the amplification of positive affect, we propose the addition of what we call the Playful/Exuberant Child mode to the list of core Child modes. We view it as conceptually and phenomenologically distinct from the Vulnerable, Angry, Impulsive, and Contented Child modes. Panksepp (1998) has identified the play system as one of the seven emotional building blocks of the mammalian brain and thus lends support to conceptualizing it as a distinct mode. Its fundamental and central role is reflected in the fact that the play system involves an instinct shared by all mammals. It is likely to have a subcortical basis.

The zenith of the play instinct occurs between the ages of three and six years. Within this age range children are at the peak of their capacity to enter into imaginary worlds and of their urge to invite us to join them. We have found that especially imaginative children who have been deprived of parental involvement in their imagination during this phase and who have been otherwise deprived of emotional nurturance develop a Detached Imaginative World mode. This is a variant of the Detached Self-Soother mode. However, rather than the minimization of pain as in the case of detached self-soothing it involves imaginative attempts to meet needs, solve problems, and amplify positive affect that become detached from intimacy. A creative and enriching force within the child ends up isolating them.

Practice

Assessing joy and play deprivation

Patients are often unaware that they have experienced emotional deprivation because this is a result of sins of omission rather than commission and they are not as apparent as experiences such as abuse, criticism, punishment, or subjugation. A patient is even more likely to be unaware of being deprived of shared play and joy. Much of the early play and joy that is critical to the developing self and brain occurs before the patient can consciously remember it. The first from of social play, "motherese" or baby talk, reaches a zenith beginning at about three months of age. In addition, in many family cultures parents don't see it as their role to play with their children. Play is seen as trivial, non-essential, or a realm that is the province of peers or siblings. Some patients may be aware of being play-deprived but don't see it as significant. For patients who are less sensitive or imaginative by nature it may not be but for others, once they experience what they have missed, they often have strong feelings of loss.

I (George) have found that play and joy deprivation usually becomes apparent after the initial standard assessment phase, including inventories and imagery assessment. None of the inventories currently directly assesses these experiences. One way it surfaces is in the course of checking in with the Vulnerable Child mode after an initial connection has been established around addressing higher-profile sources of pain. If, for example, connecting with the "little self" (as will be demonstrated in a case example later) the patient has a neutral or good image that comes to mind, I will find out if the parents are involved and if so, in what way. For example, one patient was picturing herself in her backyard near a sandbox. She wanted to play in it and it became clear that her parents were never a part of this. When I asked her if she would like me to join her, she was open to it. She liked the idea but it felt odd to her. As we began to play in the sand together within the image, the play became quite involved and animated. She really enjoyed it and it became clear over several sessions with her desire to return to the play that this experience was enriching and deepening our connection with one another. In later images involving quiet moments of sitting on a dock together and dangling our feet in the water she felt deep sadness at the realization that neither her mother nor father ever took time to quietly enjoy being with her.

Interventions

Inspired phone calls

Early in the treatment of BPD spectrum patients some Schema Therapists will call to check in on a patient if they have been going through an especially difficult time and are concerned about them. This can help the patient know the therapist genuinely cares about how she is doing and in building trust and closeness. This also applies to the other end of the spectrum of patient experiences; when a therapist is feeling happy for a patient because things are exceptionally good. When I (George) find myself thinking about a patient in between sessions after they have made a significant breakthrough or step forward in therapy or in their life, I will sometimes call to share my happiness for him. This inevitably means a great deal.

Seeing the "playful little self"

A common technique in ST of BPD spectrum patients is to superimpose an image of the patient as a four-year-old during challenging junctures to help the therapist maintain empathy. This can help the therapist respond to the patient as they would to a young child rather than an adult since this more accurately captures where the patient is coming from. Seeing the four-year-old in the adult during the non-challenging times and, as a loving parent would, finding what is endearing about him utilizes this strategy on the opposite end of the spectrum. We find that this can help the therapist pick up on or create opportunities for playful connection, find greater enjoyment in working with a patient, and fuel the development of a warm and secure attachment. While this may seem like a lot to ask of a therapist and there may be some patients that a therapist is not able to resonate with in this way, doing so will yield distinct advantages. Just as a patient can sense if a therapist respects her, a patient knows if a therapist genuinely enjoys and likes working with her. This dimension, along with caring and respect, establishes a key foundation on which all the other techniques involving the amplification of positive affect and play are built. If a therapist cannot reach this place instinctively, using the strategies discussed in this chapter will come across as rote and be counteracted by the many channels of non-verbal communication. Research has demonstrated that subtle facial expressions (most significant being those formed by the muscles around the eyes and the corners of the mouth), tone of voice, gestures, gaze, body posture, and rhythmic crescendos and decrescendos of interaction are transmitted rapidly and registered within 40 milliseconds and appraised within 100 milliseconds (Carroll, 2005). Thus a great deal of what is being exchanged on an emotional level occurs more rapidly than the therapist or patient can be consciously aware of and is most likely the primary driving force behind the developing attachment. While a therapist cannot consciously control these exchanges, if his heart and gut are in the right place, the automatic levels of exchange are much more likely to flow in the desired direction.

Play within the Therapeutic Relationship

Play is a varied and fascinating phenomenon and can be about many things (e.g., mastery, living more fully, attachment, power, release, compensation, happiness) and take on many forms (e.g., open-ended imaginative play, sports, humor, games, festivals, daydreams). Since ST is a flexible, integrative approach that addresses a broad range of needs it lends itself to drawing freely from the many forms and functions of play. The focus for patients with problems rooted in early attachment will initially be on meeting needs for connection. Play and positive affect within this context is at its most meaningful when it clarifies, organizes, and builds on what is emerging within the child or patient in terms of her needs and core self. In this respect, the use of play for these patients at this phase of therapy parallels the early forms and functions of play between parent and infant or young child. This involves a playful mode on the part of the therapist in which he can flow with the spontaneous impulses and twists and turns coming from the patient and is free to introduce twists and turns in response or to introduce novel ways to elucidate and meet needs. It becomes a co-created dance oriented around the patient's core self and drawing on the therapist's Playful Child mode. For example, I (George) had a BPD spectrum patient who was in the process of experiencing a more sustained connection with her Vulnerable Child mode. This was putting her in touch with painful feelings, especially sadness and fear. She had maintained a numb state in which she was able to be productive and effective in a very demanding career but had no intimacy in her life. Due to the pain she was now experiencing and the difficulty in maintaining her previous level of effectiveness, she was beginning to question if it was worth remaining connected to her "little self." As she struggled with the trade-off between the increase in pain and her awareness that numbing again meant closing the door to intimacy she said, "You know, I could use a good laugh." I had been thinking about helping her to feel more comfort and safety and having her close her eyes and picture a soothing, safe place but realized that she was asking for fun not comfort. I thought for a moment about doing this kind of imagery anyway since being funny on demand is not one of my strengths and I was hoping it would be close enough to what she needed. Then it occurred to me that I knew some amusing magic tricks and asked her if she would like to see one (I had some on hand for children I was working with). This, needless to say, caught her by surprise. She said she definitely would like to. The trick involved my having rabbit-shaped sponges disappear from my hands and appear in her hands and then two rabbits turning into many rabbits and her unsuccessfully guessing at various junctures what was going to happen next. It ended up with us both laughing a lot. I also offered to meet with her sooner than our next scheduled time, which she appreciated and agreed to. She ended the hour saying she was feeling much better. I suspected it was in response to both the joyful moments at the end, along with the caring expressed through the extra hour. When she returned the following session she said she had thought back to the magic trick repeatedly through the week laughing to herself about it and that she had continued to feel better. A couple of months later she had referred back to this juncture as a turning point. She felt like she had been "saved by a magic trick." We both understood that there were many additional things that were involved in her progress. She expressed this most recently in saying that this was the first time she felt that she was in a healthy relationship that was really focused on her in a genuine and caring way. There are many other elements that were meaningful to her that are part of "standard Schema Therapy," such as my self-disclosure and a note/flash card I wrote for her. Nevertheless, the joyful and playful moments have been very meaningful additions over and above this. While much of this was lower profile than the magic trick it still has a special place in her memory of our work together.

Play can also be introduced not just in response to the patient but by the therapist in an effort to co-construct a new dimension of positive connection. One of my first experiences with this and one that impressed on me the power of this kind of intervention was with a patient who had experienced extreme emotional deprivation from both parents. She also wondered if she had been sexually abused by her father because of her fear of and longing for touch. She might initially feel comforted by it and then shift to feeling like the touch was bad and wrong and lose control physically and emotionally, having seizure-like reactions. At the same time she felt she needed to experience touch to feel connected and cared for. She knitted and had a ball of yarn with her one session. I suggested that we hold a piece of it between our hands and explore ways to play with it around touch and connection as a way to create a new positive and safe experience. We came up with lots of interesting and fun ways, including variations on "cat's cradle," rolling the ball of yarn around and between our hands and jointly tossing it into the air and one or the other of us trying to catch it and laughing a lot when we missed or ended up in awkward positions. This led to some other connection-oriented kinds of play; playing jacks, my doing a cups and balls trick, and our exploring a toy together that I had. At our next session she said that over the long period of time that I had talked to her about warmth and closeness she had never known what they meant until the experience of our last session. She has two grown children, is a loving mother, and had played with them when they were young, but experiencing this from the other side (being nurtured by play rather than nurturing) and directed toward her "little self" was a completely new experience for her. She had often expressed to me that I did not feel "real" to her. As a result of the spontaneous and self-revealing nature of the play, I now felt more real. Over repeated periods of yarn play across a number of sessions we created a new experience of touch which, for the first time, felt deeply comforting to her.

We know intuitively that the play impulse comes from deep within ourselves and when expressed freely and spontaneously is a core form of non-verbal self-disclosure. I have found that this is one of the reasons some therapists can initially find it difficult to become more playful with their patients. It is, on the other hand, the reason the interactions can feel more real, grounded, and connecting. I am referring here to higher-profile forms of play. Play, on the other hand, is so imbedded in what we do that it can be difficult to tease it out as a separate phenomenon. It can be expressed in the form of humor, verbal repartee, facial expressions, gestures, or eye contact that lighten the mood and foster trust and closeness, or it can be taking place within us as we "play with" different ways of understanding or experiencing a patient.

Play can also be used to "go through the back door" when a patient and therapist are in a repetitive cycle. For example, a patient had been in an Angry Detached Protector mode for several sessions with my gently and steadily working to bypass it with some limited success. I asked her as she angrily settled in at the start of a session if she would like a jelly bean. She asked somewhat animatedly, "Do you have some?" I said I did (again drawing on supplies I had for my work with children) and brought out a bag of gourmet beans as she began to soften. We spent some time trying out and commenting on the different flavors and colors and then (I can't recall if she or I came up with the idea first) started making each other concoctions like an ice-cream sundae with combinations of flavors. She felt that this experience helped her to connect with me and she was grateful for my having gotten her out of her being stuck in anger. I subsequently have incorporated other kinds of connection-oriented play experiences to help further trust and attachment and as an alternative to draw on when she gets stuck in an angry mode. She has referred to the spontaneous and surprising new positive experiences that I have introduced and we have developed together as "jelly-bean moments."

Imagery as Play, Play in Imagery, and Playing as Dreaming

Imagery work in Schema Therapy is itself a form of play. The therapists asks the patient to, for example, imagine a safe place and pretend that they are there, are their child self, are their parent or are expressing anger toward their parent. As with play and a child who is pretending to be a pirate or princess, the patient knows that this is both not real in terms of the external world (they are not a child and their parent isn't in the room) but at the same time is real in terms of feelings, thoughts, inner voices, and memories. Not being tied to and fully committed to the real world allows children at play and patients doing imagery work to be freer to feel, think, and do things than they would otherwise. As a result, they often do so with more emotional intensity and conviction than they would in real life. The imagery becomes a staging area for the discovery and creation of new aspects of the self that can eventually "go live." Perhaps the "as if" element of play and imagery work is an alternative to the physical paralysis that occurs when we dream. They may serve to keep us safe to freely experience thoughts and feelings and trial actions as we integrate and consolidate past experience or prepare for the future. That fact that both also become rigid and repetitive when overwhelmed by trauma and are both established therapeutic avenues for undoing this rigidity also point out their pivotal role in our emotional well-being. Perhaps playing is the waking version of dreaming.

Greater degrees of dissociation lead to the parts of the self being experienced as more real and less "as if." When this happens, imagery work can feel less safe. For example, the Vulnerable Abandoned Child cannot be tried on for size if, once connected with, the patient becomes totally subsumed by it. The central organizing capacity (i.e., Healthy Adult mode) from which this experience can be reflected on and integrated is weak. When imagery with the wounded parts of the self loses its "as if" quality, explicitly bringing play into imagery can be an effective way of creating safety and building trust. One way of accomplishing this is by finding and connecting with the Playful Child mode through imagery. It can be viewed as a way of introducing an element of "as if" when the "as if" quality of the imagery is at risk of being lost. Patients who have had an extensive history of childhood sexual abuse and have difficulty accepting comfort and experiencing trust within an image involving their "little self" are often able to trust and enjoy the therapist entering the image to play. For example, one patient was able to feel some initial tentative safety and comfort as her four-year-old self when I (George) offered her some pillows and a blanket in the image. I then asked her if there was anything she would like to do that would be fun for her. She was open to this but didn't know what she wanted. I asked if she would like to draw and she liked that idea. I said I had a box of 50 crayons with all kinds of colors and new sharp points, that I was opening the lid of box for her, that they smelled really good, and asked if she would like to smell them. She said she really liked the smell and that she wanted to draw a tree with grass, sky, and sun. I drew in a big swing and asked her if she would like to step into the picture and try out the swing. She liked this and I pushed her up to big long gliding arcs and while doing that shared with her a real memory I had from my childhood of a big swing like this that I loved. This was followed by our stepping out of the image and her drawing some new things on the page (the next was a sandy area on a hill top) and our re-entering the image to play in the sand with trucks and cars that she had with her. When I needed to bring the image to an end it was difficult for her to leave it since she was feeling so good being with me. Her initial tentativeness had shifted to a very engaged, trusting, and vividly experienced playful and spontaneous interaction. The vividness and flow that develop in this kind of experience occur through drawing on one's own sense of joy and play from childhood and on experiences of play with one's own and others' children as a source for direction and knowing how to make it fit and feel right for the patient's little self. A therapist does not have to be a parent to do this effectively, but it will undoubtedly help. What is essential is that the therapist has good access to her Playful Child mode and has a reasonable degree of happiness and joy in her life.

Play, Imagery, and Modes

Integrating play into Schema Therapy involves creating new positive experiences through the capacity to be joyful, spontaneous, and playful while keeping track of and responding to the schemas and modes that are triggered. To accomplish this both the therapist's Playful Child mode and Healthy Adult mode need to be engaged. The central aim of play and the amplification of positive affect in ST is meeting the patient's needs. Thus the direction and form the play takes and its content, rather than necessarily being free-form and open-ended, are determined by the patient's needs. The play could end up being free-form and open-ended if the need is for freedom and spontaneity. Alternatively, it may be about protection, warmth, love, mutuality, authenticity, optimism, or competence, among other things. A secondary goal is bypassing maladaptive coping modes (e.g., the Detached Protector mode). Even though play can often accomplish this more quickly than working directly with these modes, it will almost always lead to a Maladaptive Coping or Maladaptive Parent mode being triggered. Consequently, it is important to be alert for this and directly check in to see how these modes are reacting.

The following case example illustrates this process. It is also an example of the early assessment of play/joy deprivation and demonstrates the extra degree of freedom that develops when introducing "as if" play into the "as if" of the imagery. This enhanced plasticity can allow more to be experienced and expressed with greater intensity and clarity on the part of both patient and therapist.

Mary had been deprived of love and understanding from her mother and was controlled, subjugated, harshly criticized, and pressured to be perfect by both parents. She said she never felt good enough and that she didn't talk much with either parent; things remained on a superficial level. Mary was regularly told by both parents that she was too dramatic, cried too much, and asked too many questions. She said she was trained to be stoic and repressed and wanted to break free of that. Just before our current session a friend had asked her, "If you could be in touch with your wild self, your true nature, what would that woman do?" As she reflected on the question she decided that she would like to "burn the Tupperware" and not settle for leftovers and scraps at the table of life anymore. She wanted the full meal but found it hard to stay with this desire because she would start to feel scared. I (George) asked her if she would like to use the imagery we had been doing in earlier sessions to connect with this deeper self. She liked this idea. As Mary closed her eyes she recalled an experience when she was six years of age of being on a beautiful mountain top with her family. It smelled good and she could see "forever." She was looking at the beautiful flowers and grass, feeling perfectly content and sensing that there was magic in this place. It became clear that this good feeling went with her being in her own world apart from her parents. They would be thinking about joy concrete things, unaware that she was finding the flowers beautiful and that she was wondering if there were fairies nearby and if other girls had been in this place before and what they might have been doing. I asked if she would like me to stand with her atop the mountain. She liked the idea. I let her know that I really liked being with her and getting to know the things that made her happy and that she wondered about. I asked what she would like to do and she said she wanted to make a shelter together. Within our shared imaginary space, we built one with stones and grass for the floor. This led to her wanting to pretend that we were characters from the book *Little House on the Prairie*. She didn't want to be the mother because she said she ends up being mean and controlling when she plays mothers so she decided I would be the dad (called Paw in the book) and she would be his beloved daughter. My role as the dad was informed by what I knew of what she needed. I let her know how much I loved her, liked spending time with her, and told her some of the things that were special about her. What follows is the interaction and dialogue from this point in the session:

> MARY: Are you proud of me, do you think I am good enough the way that I am?
> GEORGE: Yes, I am really proud of you. I am proud of your heart and sensitivity, your imaginativeness and enjoyment of the world around you and your creativity. I am very proud of you.
> MARY: (*began to feel sad and to experience a longing in anticipation of what she was getting from me going away*)
> GEORGE: I know this is hard and also part of your sensitivity and something that is good. I know that this sense of closeness and love and being appreciated for who you are is so important and that means more to a girl than anything else in the world. I know that because it is so important that you really want to hang on to it and that you need lots of it, to be able to

hear these things a lot. I also know that you are feeling the difference between this and what you experienced . . . what you have missed and that that also makes you feel sad in not having this with your real dad. (*She is nodding her head in agreement through this*). It is a natural thing to be feeling now and I want you to know it is OK to feel sad, that we can be open to all the feelings that come up and I am going to be here for you.

MARY: I don't want to feel strange for feeling sad, I want to feel normal. I don't want to feel like there is something wrong with me all the time.

GEORGE: I really like this part of you, that you feel things and feel things deeply. I think that is something that is special about you and not something that is bad. I know that you can also feel love just as strongly as you feel sadness and that you can get very excited about things and really love nature . . . it is part of what I really enjoy about you.

MARY: I get scared that I will never stop feeling this way. Then I don't know what to do because I am small and I don't have anyone to talk to.

GEORGE: I know that we can trust you and that we can trust these feelings and that you are good and that what you need and want is good. I trust you completely. I know that you are feeling sad because you are getting something now that is important to you and that the feelings of sadness are something that we will move through and that they will be feeling less as you get enough of what you need (*She is nodding her head in agreement.*) and we know what is right in terms of what you need by staying connected with you and how you are feeling. It is not something that we decide from the outside . . . something that is just told . . . it is something that we discover from staying in touch with how you are feeling. The feelings of sadness are from missing what you need, not having the full meal, it is when you are getting crumbs and you are dealing with Tupperware. We need to stay with the full meal long enough. You are good and I really care about you and I really enjoy the real you and I really like knowing how you are feeling deep down and when I know that I can be closer to you and help you be happy.

MARY: My heart is hurting. It is a very old feeling. (*Shaking her head, putting her hand to her heart, and looking pained.*)

GEORGE: Do you want me to be sitting next to you or for me to put my arm around you? Would that help with that feeling? What would help you . . . your heart?

MARY: I don't even know.

GEORGE: If I am Paw, and you are my girl that would be my instinct, to sit beside you and to put my arm around you and hold you and let you know that it is OK. (*she is nodding her head, yes*) and to let you know that I understand. Would you want me to do that?

MARY: (*Nods her head, yes*).

GEORGE: Do you want me to do it in the image or in real life? (*I am being careful here about the boundary between "as if" and real so that I am sure she feels safe.*)

MARY: I am imagining that Paw is holding me and that he is like a big bear of a man and he feels soft and big. (*She makes clear that she prefers to keep it "as if" and imagines something that feels just right for her.*)

GEORGE: (*I bring this "as if" further to life and flow with it in the direction of giving her more of what I sense she is needing.*) Yes, I am holding you now and I

> understand and I know what that feeling in your heart is about. It is about needing love and that the love you have can be felt. I am right here and you are good and you are beautiful to me through and through. I want you to be able to feel all the feelings that you have and be who you are and to know that I am right here and that the love I have for you is not going away, that there is nothing that can shake it.
>
> MARY: It's funny, it feels better just because I said that.
> GEORGE: That's good. I am glad.

I checked in with her Detached Protector mode at the end of the hour (this mode had been identified in earlier sessions and was called the "Eagle"). She said it came up a little bit when I asked her if she wanted me to hold her. She realized at that moment that she was not comforted when she felt that way when she was small. She recalled being told, "Don't act like that." She said she is used to trying to make herself feel comforted but that it is like a little girl who doesn't really know what to do versus a grown-up woman who has a lot more power and a lot more knowledge and understanding. The big part of her would try to comfort the little part of her that couldn't have that. She talked about a strong clash between the part of her that wanted to be comforted by physical contact from me when I offered it and the part of her that fights it and does exactly the opposite of what would help her to feel better and how this perpetuates her feelings of estrangement and loneliness. At the end of the session I asked her about coming back in her mind to the shelter we created and to me being there and available to help her. She liked the idea and said that she needs things like that that she can come back to and hold on to. She talked about her mind being drawn to create narrative and stories and that this would provide a place to come back to so that it doesn't feel like she is always starting from scratch, trying to pull herself back together on her own.

This was a start for a safe, warm, and loving space that we were playfully and vividly creating together as represented by the shelter. In the session that follows it becomes clear that the fluidity of the imaginative play largely bypassed the Eagle that had strong reactions to it after the session. We pick up at the start of the next session.

> MARY: One of the things I was realizing about being in the little shelter with "Paw" was that I'm not really used to that. It was sort of like, "Wait a minute, get over there. What are you doing here?" I don't even know how to integrate the idea that I would not be by myself. So when I was feeling stressed this week I would think, "Well, you could go to the shelter and you could just take a breath and use it like a visualization, as a place to go to and be present in and then it would be like, What are you doing here?"
> GEORGE: I will be Paw.
> MARY: What are you doing here?
> GEORGE: I am here because we made this together and I know it's something that you wanted and also a little bit ago you wanted a hug from me and that

	felt good to you. I am happy to leave you to have space if you want or to be a few feet away or wherever feels right for you and also to come back if you want me to be here. So what at the moment would you like? Would you like me to move back a little bit and still be sitting here, would you like me to walk away for a little while and be in calling range?
MARY:	Well, I think that the shelter is too small. You are all bent over so I am worried about you . . . that you are not really comfortable. It is too short and too narrow so in my mind I want us to push it out and make it taller so that it feels more spacious and less confining so that you might bump into me or touch me when I didn't want you to. I am realizing that I did not even think that I could ask you to leave.
GEORGE:	Yes, you can do that. I can see that you are wanting room for you and that you are also wanting room for me and don't want me to bump my head. I know that you are thoughtful and caring and that you also need your space. All of that is important so I am going to get some more stones and make a bigger room here so that it will go over my head so I can stand and we can move about more easily.
MARY:	So say again so I can hear again, why you are here?
GEORGE:	I am here because no one was with you to notice what you were thinking or how you were feeling. Your brother was off throwing rocks and your mother and father were off doing some other things and I noticed that you were looking at the ocean and the forest and I like you and I was curious to know what you were thinking and how you were doing and also what you wanted. I like you being happy and I know that one of things you wanted to do was to make something together. Remember that?
MARY:	Um hum.
GEORGE:	. . . and so we made this place and then we got some grass to make it soft. That is how I got here.
MARY:	I am feeling like some part of me is worried that you are going to take over their job.
GEORGE:	Take over your parents' job?
MARY:	No, it's more like the Protector part is worried that somehow you are infringing on their turf. And that's not what you are trying to do at all. You are not trying to be a protector part . . .
GEORGE:	Is this the Eagle?
MARY:	Yes. I hadn't realized it until I was sitting in here and I could feel that this part is wanting a wall . . . and I don't feel like I really want that.
GEORGE:	As the Eagle you are concerned that I am going to try to push you out? Is that right?
MARY:	Yes. That you are trying to "MUSCLE IN ON MY TERRITORY" yah know. "I'VE GOT THIS COVERED" yah know. "WE DON'T NEED THE STONE THING."
GEORGE:	Well . . . I respect you and I know you've been around for a long time and you have done a *good* job of protecting little Mary and I am glad of that. I think that little Mary likes the "stone thing." It made her feel good and helped her relax. I am not here with the idea of just pushing you away and I also know that with all the good that you do for her that you can stand in the way of little Mary having closeness and having more caring and love. I know that you feel that you need to do that to make

	sure she is all right, that it is kind of a survival thing but what I also know is that I am safe and that you don't need to worry and that I can be with little Mary and that I can be good to her and I also want you to feel comfortable. Tell me, would you like me to go away? . . . I can tell you that if I were to go away that I would be concerned that little Mary would miss out on things because I know that she likes this place and I know she likes closeness and can like me to be around. Tell me what your thoughts and feelings are.
MARY:	As you were talking it is like the little Mary part could get bigger and stronger like a deflated blow-up sort of feeling that then pushes the wings [of the Eagle] open. Inside the wings it's very dark. It's like being inside a box some of the time and I don't even know that it's happening, so when you were talking the Mary part was getting stronger and there was a feeling of the wings going down [*not folded over forming a wall in front*].
GEORGE:	So you are feeling as little Mary that you have more room and are not being boxed in.
MARY:	Yes, it's like the automatic first thing is, "Be afraid and close in."

As little Mary is feeling safe and connected I ask her what she would like. She decides she would like to ride bikes together.

MARY:	. . . let's ride our bikes. Let's ride and go really fast and feel the air blow our hair back and go up and down the hills on top of the mountain and stop and look. Let's like be just in motion, moving, feeling like we are part of the whole fabric of the sky and the mountain and just be . . . let's just be.
GEORGE:	That sounds good. I would love to do that.
[*little later in the session once we are on our way*]	
GEORGE:	. . . Can you tell me what's happening now as were riding?
MARY:	. . . just feeling very peaceful inside and free. I'm feeling very free of not being closed in. It's not dark. You can see the sky's a big bowl and I'm not worrying about anything and I'm not afraid. I feel your companionship.
GEORGE:	That's really good. I'm happy about that. I like this. I like riding. I like the freedom and I like going up hills and down hills and going up to the top of the mountain and being able to see everything and to just be together, and to see the things that you are discovering and to be able to show you interesting things I see. It feels really good to me. It really feels good knowing you are feeling that sense of peacefulness. That's wonderful . . . and I know that being able to feel that and feel the freedom and have a sense of me being with you . . . that that's really good.
MARY:	That's funny. Then there was this moment when there was like . . . "Are you a part of me?" So now the Eagle's back . . . right, "Are you a part of me?" The Eagle has to know, "WHO ARE YOU? WHAT ARE YOU TRYING TO DO?"
GEORGE:	I'm not a part of Mary. I'm a friend of Mary's and I care about her, and I'm here to help her to be able to feel good and be happy and to help her to

be able to have closeness, and closeness, that means that she can be who she is, completely free and not have to work at it and just to know that I'm here and that I like her for who she is. . . . What do you think about that?

MARY: Does everyone have someone else? People aren't alone inside themselves?

GEORGE: I think that everyone who feels happy and feels secure inside has that.

MARY: We didn't know that . . . (*tears are welling up and her hands begin to cover her face*)

GEORGE: I know. . . . I know.

MARY: (*sobbing*)

GEORGE: Yes, I know.

MARY: (*sobbing*)

GEORGE: It's OK.

MARY: (*starts gasping and grabs a paper tissue*).

GEORGE: (*I move my chair over to her*) I know it's hard. This is something that is really basic. Mary: (*sobbing*)

GEORGE: It's basic and something that you've needed all along and couldn't find and didn't really understand.

MARY: (*sobbing*) I didn't.

GEORGE: I know that hurts because it's something that is a really big thing to realize that wasn't there and hasn't been there.

MARY: (*beginning to compose herself*) OK. Now I am in my real self, so is this like I was not *attached* to my parents . . . my mother, is that what were really looking at here? I mean that you know that I know about infant development. Is that what the real issue is here do you think?

GEORGE: There was an attachment but it wasn't a healthy attachment, it wasn't an attachment that included fully who you are and your heart and your soul, and it didn't have the closeness that you've needed.

MARY: So this feeling of always, always being alone . . . other people don't feel that like I do, do they?

GEORGE: Right. . . . I guess we could say that there was a part of you that wasn't attached. The part of you that would feel things strongly, that had questions about things, that would get upset about things. This part of you had no place to go. The imaginative part of you that wanted to play . . . a really big basic part of you that was just on her own. It's sad (*I feel tearful*) because it is so . . . central to being able to be happy and being OK. There was so much that you had going on inside that you wanted to share that is wonderful and that I really enjoy . . . your perspectives and your curiosity, and the interesting thoughts you have, and your imaginativeness . . . and that was lost on them and that was a shame.

I have found that the establishment of this rich and strong foundation also fuels later phases of treatment and can make processes such as battling the Punitive Parent mode an easier and more effective process. For example, incorporating the stone shelter in imagery work with Mary expressing anger toward her mother enabled her to express this more fully and powerfully than she was able to do without it. The stone shelter remains a reference point for us in terms of little Mary and a warm and full sense of closeness. It is now quite large and spacious with blue curtains in the window.

In the following section we turn from individual work to a focus on the application of play in group therapy with patients with BPD. This has been an important dimension (the two authors of this chapter might say the "secret ingredient") of a protocol that has demonstrated extremely effective outcomes in a recent randomized control trial (Farrell *et al.*, 2009) and in this respect adds empirical validation to the power of play with adults. The use of play in this context, as discussed above in individual work, is not a process that is brought in toward the end of a course of group therapy or at lighter moments, but is something that is used from early on and woven into work with difficult and serious problems. Play within group Schema Therapy generally requires more planning and structure than play in individual Schema Therapy. While more structured to start with, there is a great deal of flexibility and spontaneity that develops around this and where it ends up is anyone's guess.

Working with Play in a Group

Play should be fun, but for many adult patients with BPD working in a group setting, even the idea of play can be very stressful and far from enjoyable. Different schemas, core beliefs, and coping styles get triggered by the presence of others when you ask some patients to participate in play. Take for example the Punitive Parent mode; it can be heard in statements like "This is stupid. It's a waste of time. I don't deserve to have fun and besides play is for babies." They roll their eyes at others, shake their head with a look of disgust, or make disapproving comments like "You are acting very immature." "If you guys could see how silly you look you wouldn't be doing that." Some patients state that initially they were afraid of engaging in playful activities because they feared others would see that they didn't know how to play and then would judge them, in the end, only adding to their feelings of defectiveness. It is imperative to address the importance of play with the group members and to discuss, confront, and work through the maladaptive schemas. Usually, talking about the reasons for and benefits of play can quiet and diminish the Punitive Parent interference. As the process begins to unfold, it is important to encourage and celebrate their growth as they discover play's healing benefit's. When there are group members that continue to be hesitant and to refuse to join in the group play activity it is important to be patient and accept where they are, suggesting that they try to imagine (from their safe place) participating without their Punitive Parent yelling at them.

Group Play Activities

The following are examples of playful activities that we have found to be effective over the course of our many years of group work with BPD patients.

The face game

Each group member is given a balloon to blow up and soft felt pens. They are instructed to draw a face on the balloon showing how they feel. Before they name how they feel the other group members try to guess. This is a fun and safe way to begin talking about feelings, why we have them, and how we can meet the needs underneath them.

Building a safe house

After a group discussion on ways to take care of the Vulnerable Child, one group member shared that she had an image of a safe house filled with love that she takes her inner child to. Several members really liked the idea of a safe house and said how nice it would be to have such a place. We could all build one in our imagination then share how we decorate it, chimed one. Hey, why don't we build a dolls' house together and call it our safe house, said another. So from the idea the actual building of a house began. This was a wonderful learning experience for everyone. The women learned how to work together, use tools, follow a blueprint, deal with design issues, likes and dislikes, delegate jobs such as sanding and painting, and worked out which room they would decorate. They learned how to work within a budget, but best of all they shared laughter, joy, and a sense of pride and mastery at their contribution to the building of the safe house.

The Olympics

One evening on an inpatient unit, the patients were complaining about being bored because nothing was on television but the Olympics. I said, "Let's have our own Olympics." Soon the excitement spread, ideas were born, and plans were made to put on our own games for the viewing audience (the staff). After working together for two evenings constructing banners, flags, and costumes we were ready to start with our opening ceremony. One therapist acted as the master of ceremonies announcing each country (patient) as they entered the hall. Here comes Canada, wearing a beautiful moose hat, waving her maple leaf flag. Next is Italy sporting a lovely jacket in white, orange and green, wait a minute, what is that on her head, yes it's a plate of spaghetti. Each country was introduced in this manner and was met with loud applause and cheers. The anthem Children of the World was sung and the games were declared opened. The countries competed in *Downhill Skiing*: wearing shoe boxes on their feet and carrying an egg on a spoon the participants had to maneuver around various obstacles to the finish line. The same course was used for the *Luge*, lying on the floor on a torn cardboard box with the use of their hands and feet; it was quite a sight to see. Many games were played over the course of the evening and each was met with shared laughter, joy, and a sense of belonging. The closing ceremonies ended with hot chocolate and donuts. The patients talked about this shared experience many times and always with large grins, smiles, and twinkling eyes.

Keepsakes, memories, and connection boxes

We came up with the idea of a making a Vulnerable Child box that the patients could use at home especially during times when the Vulnerable Child was triggered. We used shoe boxes and decorated them with colorful and decorative papers. Stickers, cut outs, button, ribbons, and other materials were used as well to adorn these boxes. The patients were encouraged to collect things that would remind them that their Vulnerable Child was safe and cared for and that they mattered: things like a small smooth stone from the beach, or crayons, bubble gum, and pictures. The therapist wrote positive affirmations on cards. Patients made things for each other, tapes of relaxing music, book marks, all of which worked like transitional objects. Patients reported that they never knew how to comfort their Vulnerable Child before, but now they open their box and read to the child, tell them where the objects came from, read the messages, listen to the tapes, blow bubbles with their gum, etc. They discovered that by doing these things they were becoming a healthy adult taking care of their Vulnerable Child.

Playing with anger

Anger is very frightening for many patients. They associate trauma, abuse, pain, and fear at the mere mention of it. Asking them to engage in play to deal with anger is met with great hesitancy, fear, and skepticism. However games like tug-of-war or stomping and popping balloons are a safe and effective way to release anger. The patients begin to realize that movement and play are good tools for releasing anger and much better than shoving it down and numbing out. Making sounds, like who can make the best cow sound or the loudest pig grunts, is a game that is safe and fun. It can be the first step for the patients to claim their voice. Being able to say "STOP" and "NO" when they are feeling anger can be taught through the use of play. The patient also discovers that nothing bad happens when they get angry and that they can control it.

Play is a powerful tool that helps troubled patients work through their experiences of abuse and trauma. Play breaks through the blocks of mistrust and fear. It provides experiences where they can feel and learn to trust. It can shatter the beliefs that they are unworthy. Play is an enjoyable experience for both the therapist and the client because it is a safe way to attend the needs of the Vulnerable Child, the Angry Child, the Happy and Joyful Child as well as other schema modes. It can be an effective way to begin working on banishing the Punitive Parent and play becomes a part of the Healthy Adult regime.

Pitfalls and Tips

There are many times when a playful impulse would be intrusive. For example, if a patient is feeling more intense feelings of anger, sadness, or fear, a playful intervention would be likely to backfire. A patient's Vulnerable Child mode must be feeling safe and settled enough to be open to play. Play will then engage the core self and be part of healing and growth rather than become an expression of the Detached Protector or Detached Self-Soother mode. Similarly, it makes a big difference if the therapist's little self is feeling safe and settled enough for play. If not, attempts to introduce play may become rote or repetitive. While the therapist's child self is important for inspiration and energy, as mentioned earlier, it is important that this be overseen by the Healthy Adult mode so that the inspiration and energy is in service of the patient's needs. Play can become a distraction when it is used to avoid painful feelings or difficult issues and it can become forced when it is used to compensate for feelings of pain or vulnerability. An important example of play and joy losing touch with the Healthy Adult mode and being co-opted by avoidant or compensatory modes of the therapist is when it becomes sexualized. A focus on the delightful/ precious little self of the patient is very different from a focus on the patient as a sexual object.

Perhaps the main ingredient that fosters the productive use of play and joy in the therapy process is the capacity to have fun with and enjoy our patients and our work. This involves taking care of our little self through an emphasis on intrinsic goals, such as exploring, discovering, learning, connecting, caring, and growing over and above extrinsic goals like how we look, how well we are doing, how we rank, or doing things the right way.

Creating an office space that invites play can also help. I (George) have a doll'-house-size tree house with winches, pulleys, and figures that sits on a table behind me. It is the product of a collaboration between little George and adult George. I initially designed it as something to inspire both an adult's and child's imagination and used it for play with my own children. It and other designs that were created to foster adult involvement in children's open-ended imaginative play were later produced by several toy companies. Photos of these can be found at www.schematherapymidwest/schematherapy/treatment. I will on occasion have a patient who comes in for a first consultation who says something like, "Oh, cool. Why don't we just play!" This kind of comment would probably not be elicited as often if I had a bust of Freud sitting behind me. The objects occasionally show up in dreams and the figures in the tree house have recently became part of sessions with a patient as she talks about what she imagines their life is like and what they are up to. I respond based on what I "know" about them; a knowing informed by what I believe she needs to hear.

Having objects on hand that will be helpful as links between your own and your patient's child self is helpful. Jelly beans, balls, magic tricks, musical instruments, balloons, pillows, towels, bubble wrap, crayons, and magic markers are examples. Choosing things with which you and your patient can resonate (as a parent introduces new and delightful aspects of their world to a child when she is ready) can help to make this playful link fluid, real, and fun. New patients will often lead to entirely new inspirations.

Summary

The authors of this chapter naturally gravitate toward play. A couple of years ago when I (George) was making a case for the addition of the Playful Child mode within Schema Therapy theory during a phone conference call I later found out that Ida Shaw (who was in the background of the call) was feeling gleeful about this proposal (and perhaps dancing a jig). Play is in our genes. As we have given all this fun deeper thought, we realize that play is a fundamental part of all of our genes, our mental health, and what makes us human. This has provided us with just the excuse we needed to bring even more play into our work and to spend more time talking and writing about it. What a delight! We hope in the process of doing so that we can pass on what we are discovering about the important place of joy and play within our lives and our therapies and further the process of the psychotherapy world digesting more fully the mother's (and father's) role as amplifier and regulator of infant joy and play and the central role this has in the wiring of the social brain.

References

Carroll, R. (2005) An interview with Allan Schore; the American Bowlby. www.thinkbody.co.uk/papers/interview-with-allan-s.htm.

Farrell, J., Shaw, I. and Webber, M. (2009) A schema-focused approach to group psychotherapy for outpatients with borderline personality disorder: a randomized controlled trial. *Journal of Behavior Therapy and Experimental Psychiatry*, 40(2), 317–328.

Frisch, M. (2006) *Quality of Life Therapy*. Hoboken, NJ: John Wiley & Sons.

Grawe, K. (2007) *Neuropsychotherapy*. Mahwah, NJ: Lawrence Erlbaum.

Panksepp, J. (1998) *Affective Neuroscience: The Foundations of Human and Animal Emotions*. New York: Oxford University Press.

Schore, A. (2003) *Affect Dysregulation and Disorders of the Self*. New York: W.W. Norton.

Seligman, M. (2002) *Authentic Happiness*. New York: The Free Press.

Seligman, M., Steen, T., Park, N. and Peterson, C. (2005) Positive psychology progress. *American Psychologist*, 60(5), 410–421.

Sutton-Smith, B. (1974) *How to Play with Your Children*. New York: Hawthorn Books.

6
Schema Therapy, Mindfulness, and ACT – Differences and Points of Contact

Erwin Parfy

Introduction

Recent years have seen a remarkable split in the further development of the cognitive-behavioral approach. On the one hand, there is Jeffery Young's Schema Therapy (Young, 1994; Young, Klosko and Weishaar, 2003), rooted in detailed analysis of problematic life-patterns, identifying moments of vulnerability, grief, and unmet needs in the individual's past. Change processes here are driven by a deeper understanding of the inner conditions and their history, focusing all efforts on imagining alternative and much healthier ways of experiencing important relationships. On the other hand, inspired by Jonathan Kabat-Zinn (1990, 1994) and his therapeutic adaptation of the Buddhist meditation practice as mindfulness-based stress reduction (MBSR), there is Marsha Linehan (1993) with dialectical behavior therapy (DBT) and later Steven Hayes (Hayes, Strohsal and Wilson, 1999) with acceptance and commitment therapy (ACT). For work with depression, Segal, Williams, and Teasdale (2002) called this therapeutic style mindfulness-based cognitive therapy (MBCT). All these approaches have one thing in common: they outline a more pragmatic way of coping with the moment now, searching for change potential in an accurate observation of experiences without any rush to interpretation or assessment. This should promote an accepting attitude toward life as it is, building up a sound basis for a more value-oriented commitment to the future. Analyzing past experiences in relationships to arrive at a more differentiated picture of one's self can lead to verbal illusions, which could imprison us.

In order to start thinking about differences and possible points of contact between these two mainstreams in the cognitive-behavioral tradition we will first summarize their central characteristics.

Current Status

Schema Therapy (ST) is close to the human sciences, concerned with general valid statements about neurobiological preconditions, developmental, and basic needs, as in Bowlby's Attachment Theory (Bowlby, 1969, 1973, 1980). It is a conceptualization of humans whereby emotional forces are functional signals in the body. These signals are expressed in relationships, calling for helpful responses from significant others. Their support is necessary for rebalancing the organism – and not just in early childhood. In general, this is a causal-analytic view, where the body is regulated on many levels by circuits of feedback loops to meet basic needs. An observed emotional boosted process reflects recurrent interactional themes, while the emerging experience is organized against a background of past experiences from a neurobiological entity, conceptualized as a schema. If these ultimately (re)constructed and verbal categorized entities are identified as maladaptive, they become targets for therapeutic change strategies.

Questionnaires were developed to appraise the intensity of each schema (see Part VI, Chapter 4) or schema mode (see Part VI, Chapter 5). The outcome helps us to formulate individual case conceptualizations. So as a consequence of being asked, for example, about childhood circumstances, the personal rating of verbal statements in the questionnaire leads primarily to hypothetical stories about what might be causing current problems. Subsequently, therapeutic dialogues and imagery work allow much closer access to the subjective reality of the patient. But of course, this reality is always shaped by verbalization. Nevertheless, it is handled as concrete – the named schema is accepted as a fact. Very straightforward procedures are proposed to weaken the influence of every schema or schema mode, being designed logically to link inherent interactional themes and open up possible corrective experiences. Therefore, the therapeutic approach, with its clearly connected target–method relations, promises powerful control over unhappy involvement in one's own past.

Hayes' ACT looks for the opposite. Attempts to get a grip on our emotional pitfalls are here identified as a main part of the problem. The more we want to avoid moments of sorrow and grief, the more we experience them. But our language suggests that the principles of creative power, successfully approved in the outside world, could be applied to our inner world too. Following this idea, fighting endless battles against undesirable aspects of our own experience are part of the daily program. Rooted in the philosophy of language, ACT tries to undermine verbal conceptualizations like that and enable direct access to experience, willing to accept it as it is, even if it is painful. Allowing experiences to come and go without opposing them is the proposed way to a more open attitude toward what will come next. Searching for reasons that look in the other direction – toward the past – merely puts obstacles in the way of our attempt to rid ourselves of sorrow.

Table 6.1 The main differences between ST and ACT (MBCT)

Schema Therapy	ACT (MBCT)
Analyzing causality	Control as the problem
Individual case conceptualization	Defusion of language
Needs in relationships	Observing pure experience

At this point a warning might be appropriate: to polarize ST and ACT in this way ultimately is an artifact of our language and its tacit logic too. It suggests a neither/nor constellation, but if we look more closely at the concrete therapeutic interventions beyond both general and even verbal conceptualizations, similarities can be observed. For example, one of the main interventions in ST is imagery of past situations with painfully frustrated needs. Although it is doubtless intended to overwrite the experiences of helplessness with a glimmer of hope and possible personal strength, the therapeutic attitude is far from trying to achieve this by getting it under direct control (which would not work in any case). Time and room are made to unfold all the emotion-tinged, largely distressing memories, and an accepting atmosphere is created. And to be honest, no one who works with this method can predict what will happen exactly. Both the therapist and the patient are well advised to be willing at this moment of interpersonal closeness to deal with anything that comes up. Finding words for it without valuing the experience as good or bad is an attitude that seems to be very similar to practiced mindfulness. Limited reparenting has much to do with acceptance with regard to the exploratory child behavior as a central quality for a nurturing environment.

On the other hand, ACT tries to weaken the influence of our rational senses and reason with exercises, which enables the patient to take his cognitive products less seriously. Critical and wounding words in our mind are kept at a distance by metaphorical reframing and so-called "cognitive defusion." The words and their intention are visualized, for example, as unwanted passengers in a bus driven by the person who is suffering. Or the therapist plays the "critical sense," while the patient listens to the therapist's comments. Both exercises give the opportunity to realize that self-injurious thinking is unhelpful. They empower a self-conscious attitude independent of our thinking. The idea behind this seems to be very similar to the strategies of ST, where unrelenting standards or Punitive/Demanding Parent modes are worked out to externalize them. This helps to free the patient of perplexity and enable more self-caring in opposition to them (even if the task in ST terms is formulated in military terms, and therefore control-seeking, as "combating" these modes).

These points of contact encourage us to transform the neither/nor constellation from the initial overview into an either/or statement belonging to the details of therapeutic interventions (listening to Marsha Linehan's vote for dialectical solutions here). But before we can take the next steps in this direction, it would be helpful to specify the therapeutic attitudes, the emotion-supported convictions "between the lines." These attitudes are generating possible therapeutic interventions with an important spin on what is said. So maybe the different interactional styles of the ST and ACT approaches could alternate or complete in its own time.

Table 6.2 Possible points of contact

Schema Therapy	ACT (MBCT)
Imagery	Mindfulness
Limited reparenting	Acceptance
Combating parent modes	Distance from critical sense/reason

Table 6.3 Therapeutic attitudes – each in its due time!

Schema Therapy	ACT (MBCT)
Yes to neediness	Autonomy of the observing consciousness
Therapeutic loyalty and knowledge	Paradoxical therapeutic style
Emotional validation	Distancing from emotion/cognition

Believing in the central importance of human attachments, ST is always on the side of neediness, addressed to the main attachment figures. The therapeutic attitude is characterized by intense loyalty if someone is missing longed-for responses from significant others. It validates expressions of grief with far-reaching willingness. Working with schema modes (e.g., using different chairs for different parts of the person), therapists also insist on opening the way for recognizing the needs of the Vulnerable Child. The therapeutic style structures the process in the direction of the case conceptualization, leading the patient to those points of his inner world that are generally specified from the model as crucial. We can say that the therapist claims a position of knowledge about the path to follow.

Contrary to that, ACT is convinced of the strength of the observing consciousness, allowing autonomy and independence from fresh cognitions, emotions, or impulses, even if they are driven by basic needs. So the therapeutic style impresses with partly paradoxical effects. Statements are formulated in such a way that the listener is referred back to his own conscious experience, coming from the therapist, who is equally trapped as every human being is in his own cognitive world. The implicit message is that we should not cling to the past. Being able to let go is modeled by the therapist, who does not insist on his own ideas at all times. The ACT approach allows transparency about the struggle with language, thoughts, and emotions, which the therapist experiences too. Even if it becomes evident that therapist and patient are "in the same boat," the therapist tries to demonstrate how to avoid further entanglement.

If we ask now for more concrete bridging from the viewpoint of ST, the question necessarily arises of how to integrate mindfulness-based strategies into the structure of our therapeutic procedures. But if ST is really what it claims to be – an integrative approach – this should be its touchstone.

Approach

When therapists are open to different concepts, convinced that one perspective alone cannot do justice to our complex lives, they have a problem. In daily practice quite often there are moments when ideas from somewhere else come into our mind. For me, coming from the field of Attachment Theory and having identified a lot with ST, they all come from the corner where ACT/MBCT is located. But for our current task these moments are exactly what we need in order to examine the closer circumstances of integration. Are insights into the tacit limitations of the original model possible? Is it a chance to switch therapeutic attitude in order to go further in the therapeutic process? Can other strategies and exercises be helpful, and if so, how should we validate them?

Let us start with the examination. There is, for example, a point after repeated imagery work where the deep emotional contact with past traumatizing situations and their restructuring with visualized helping figures allows new experiences of holding and nurturing relationships. But the deeper the original trauma, the harder it is to stabilize an optimistic and future-oriented perspective. Too many situations are triggering schemas and coping modes, and even if they are much weaker or adapted than at the beginning of therapy, they are not completely absent. So quite often it is not possible to fulfill the target method promises of the ST model as well as suggested, despite our willingness to commit to endless corrective imagery work. In that case patients are in danger of assessing their continuing vulnerability as failure. The inherent logic of the model comes up against its limits and there are no other strategies available within the need-supporting therapeutic attitude. Of course, there is a need for a peaceful inner world, but this may not attainable by intensifying more of the same therapeutic efforts. Inner peace in the long term could be nearer if we accept the presence of need-frustrating circumstances and our emotional pain in reaction to them in the short term. At this point in the therapeutic process the gate is opened for ACT-correlated ideas.

In ST there are very helpful strategies to identify interpersonal themes. But even if you can gain access to the Vulnerable Child at the core of all grief, quite often it is not easy to keep in touch with this mode, because the wished-for emotional openness directly clashes with the compulsive search for control. Of course, there are many points within ST where the theme of control is problematized, for example, in schemas such as Mistrust/Abuse, Vulnerability, Emotional Inhibition, or Unrelenting Standards, and also in the Angry Child, Over-Compensator, Detached Protector, or Demanding Parent schema modes. But although the suggested therapeutic strategies get close to the problematic manner of control in many ways, something more explicit is missing. If you cannot access the controlling behavior by addressing your efforts directly to the emotional needs, rational insights into the inner dynamic and likely consequences must be given a second chance. Therefore, basic education about this with the help of appropriate ACT strategies could strengthen the Healthy Adult. Even the therapeutic attitude itself should model the willingness to tolerate tensions and "unfinished business" within the process. If therapists resist moments of their own vulnerability, there is hope for the patient that control is not so important in any case.

Last but not least there is the opportunity to introduce mindfulness as a competency and a skill to deal with insecurity, ambivalence, and pain. This capability is understandable as one of the main wanted parts of the established Healthy Adult. It aids stability against psychic distortions in general. Focusing on one's own breathing, labeling all upcoming cognitive, emotional, or physical irritations, and then gently bringing the observing consciousness back to the breathing is a starting point. This could be learned in sessions or at the same time in some meditation courses. Practicing mindfulness in everyday life on a regular basis, even if it is individually adapted to one's talents and current capabilities, develops patience in dealing with one's own, mostly very vivid, experienced mind.

More concrete docking points are in ST work with Unrelenting Standards and all the problematic Parent modes. ACT exercises and metaphors are very easily

Table 6.4 Possibilities of integration

Possible ST Docking Points	Additional ACT/MBCT Facets
Persisting vulnerability to triggers	Modeling an attitude of acceptance
Treatment of compulsiveness/rumination	Education about "control as the problem"
Confrontation with insecurity and pain	Practicing mindfulness as a skill
Concrete schema and mode work	ACT exercises and metaphors

integrated and enrich the original approach. For example, viewing cognitions and emotions from a bridge as endlessly passing trains and trying to stay on the bridge instead of jumping on the train could be a very powerful picture. Or visualizing an unwanted emotion with its color, texture, and form, then visualizing the next emotion in reaction to the unwanted first one, could show the enduring character of our feelings. Instead of fighting it, it could be healthier to carry our pain like an unwanted child with us. Many of these compact and convincing ACT ideas can be integrated without any contradiction to ST procedures. Their effectiveness is validated with help of the patient's assessment: if they experience these interventions as crucial, we should not withhold them.

To summarize: we can say first that it would be helpful to model an accepting and non-controlling therapeutic attitude in a more conscious applied manner than outlined before, especially in cases where target-method efforts have reached their limits. Second, general education about the pro and cons of striving for control could help in the treatment of many disorders. Learning to trust even if life seems to be very insecure is necessary. Third, many meditation techniques depend on personal preferences and resources are suitable for enhancing mindfulness as a self-stabilizing mode. Finally, ACT exercises and metaphors are easily introduced into our well-established treatment of maladaptive schemas and modes. Two case vignettes illustrate these suggestions.

Pitfalls and Tips

When we talk about mindfulness and meditation we touch on Eastern philosophy and Buddhism, which could be problematic. The therapist's religious convictions could be declared, but should never be discussed intellectually. Mindfulness is a quality of experience and therefore arguing about it is clearly a road down a cul-de-sac. Mindfulness has nothing to do with a faith in "something great or miraculous," even if some people – inspired by a meditation-friendly atmosphere – start searching for "enlightenment" in order to become superior to everyone else. If we do this, we are in danger of enhancing the Self-Aggrandizer mode by talking about meditation in a way that treats it as a "special experience."

On the other hand, mindfulness is not a skill that is automatically built up purely as a consequence of disciplined training. It needs a high level of compliance and mental motivation, which is more a question of individual identification with the path to it than forcing oneself in this direction with therapeutic authority. The Eastern

Mary, a 39-year-old mother of two daughters, aged 13 and 15 years, is married to the boss of a small plumbing company, where she works part-time as secretary. She came to therapy with generalized anxieties about her health. She suffered from headaches and her heartbeat was irregular and rapid. She also ruminated about the health of her daughters. The older one has mild epilepsy and the younger shows asymmetrically developing breasts. Mary consulted many specialists to clear possible serious dangers behind the symptoms, but in the end no one could reassure her. Additionally, she ruminated about her performance as a mother who is so emotionally fragile that her daughters too are at risk of becoming anxious and shy. In her worst-case fantasies they could end up unable to be integrated in society as she felt herself to be. Mary hated herself for this, and her anger was directed at her husband too, who was not sympathetic to her situation.

In the Schema Questionnaire she rated very high in Vulnerability to harm or illness and Failure to Achieve, but less high in Self-Punitiveness. Searching for the triggers was easy – physical signs and sensations were stimulating catastrophic thinking. But Mary could not habituate because in the end all medical prognoses about her daughters and herself were uncertain (a year later she had surgery to control her irregular heartbeat, something her father had undergone, but in his case with little success – hereditary influences were diagnosed as relevant). So every therapeutic strategy that was striving to counterbalance her fears was on shifting ground. We used flash cards with helpful thoughts, validated her needs for more emotional support from her husband, and searched for a more self-conscious and self-nurturing attitude in her social life. Nevertheless, the intensity of her reaction to uncontrolled and even uncontrollable body circumstances was overwhelming as before.

When I started to focus on this strong and aggressive attitude toward insecurity, paired with uncompromising thinking about final solutions, we turned things around. Mary realized how unacceptable it was for her to take these borders of knowledge and influence as a natural part of human existence. It was very hard for her to try doing less rather than more of the same – instead of surfing the internet for new medical websites, it could be better to sit in the garden and listen to the birds, for example. Mindfulness came into our therapy. More and more she got a glimpse of tranquility within her daily battles against incomprehensible body sensations. Finally, Mary developed a good feeling for the moment when her emotional waves got higher. She entered her bedroom as an oasis of peace, observed her breathing, and held a beautiful stone in her hands, which reminded her of the last seaside holiday. Even if it was not easy at times to focus on herself in that way, she was convinced about the fact that every other direction in these moments could only make it worse.

> John, a 46-year-old husband and father, worked in a university library. His son was mentally disabled and at 18 years old behaved like a very demanding child and burdened the whole family with his aggressive enforced obsessive-compulsive rules. There was no possibility of getting day care for his son. Many institutions had offered this in the past, but after a short time they withdrew their offer because the son disrupted any form of group setting. John himself suffered from obsessive-compulsive thoughts and habits that had to be acted out to mitigate his own inner tensions. This could be identified as over-compensation for his more anxiety-driven tendency to subjugate himself under the pressure of his private life. His wife and their parents were very demanding too, demonstrating that even handling the son is not the real problem. John escaped from all this by involving himself in many idealized pursuits (extreme sports, special intellectual interests, sexual role plays) which allowed him a parallel life of Self-Aggrandizement. But because he acts impulsively first and then with perfectionistic obsession, these experiences tighten the screw of pressure.
>
> Early in therapy we gained access to his Vulnerable Child, Impulsive Child, and over-compensating tendency, answering pressure of the outer world with intensifying inner pressure to reach for "higher goals." We did a lot of chair work, trying to enforce the Healthy Adult to support the overcharged boy, stop the impulsiveness, and relativize the search for self-aggrandizement. But although his sense of inferiority and restriction could be expressed and validated comprehensively, he could not stop "high-speed involvement" in his vivid and obsessive-compulsive fantasies. He doubted our therapy's ability to break through these patterns by demanding more effort, because this only would increase his tension. So I took him to where he was and tried to build a bridge to ACT-correlated ideas. We agreed to experiment with acting against his inner impulses: breaking off where he is on the edge of starting something new, observing the waxing and waning of his impulsivity and letting the fantasies pass without becoming involved in them. The advice was generally "doing less than more". After short time John realized that he could achieve silence and freedom, qualities missing in his life before. This experience changed how he dealt with his interests and with his family too. He reduced the number of interactions and claimed more protected time for himself, where he enjoyed the possibility for "self-reflection" without pressure (what was in the end very similar to mindfulness practice).

tradition offers many variants to approximate this mental quality and in the Western tradition too there are possibilities in sports, arts, and handicrafts to cultivate an attitude of mindfulness. With therapeutic creativity a personal gate to it can be opened for everyone. But it needs much more time than, for example, training in progressive muscle relaxation to gain entrance to this quality of inner distance. In my view it is not only a skill (to reach something desirable), it is more an attitude to deal with the experienced transformations in life and the principal fact that there is no final ground to root our existence in. We as therapists, like our patients, have to stabilize by being willing to be in perpetual motion, which could be a good model for our daily therapeutic challenges.

The Future

Maybe ACT exercises and metaphors, and regular mindfulness practice, are not the most complicated for integration. It is an open attitude in general, which is hard to realize if you think of schema terms as concrete and even neurobiological given entities. Talking about that is scientifically correct, but to ease changing processes in dialogue with patients it might be better in advanced stages of the therapeutic process to rid ourselves of verbal fixation in schema terms. Openness to all experiences should not be diminished by the need to categorize them. I hope that in the future two things will be possible for Schema Therapists: 1) to support with clear and precise structuring the problematized field of experience in order to get in touch with the vulnerability that has its origins in the past, encouraging the expression of grief and pain, and making alternative forms of experience accessible; 2) to model openness to live life without preconceptions, even if this means that the biographically rooted schema case conceptualization loses in importance as the patient becomes willing to stay on his own. After "climbing the ladder to free oneself" there is no need to hold on to the ladder – for the schema therapeutic footprints have been blown away by "the winds of change."

References

Bowlby, J. (1969) *Attachment and Loss. Vol. 1: Attachment.* London: Hogarth Press.
Bowlby, J. (1973) *Attachment and Loss. Vol. 2: Separation: Anxiety and Anger.* New York: Basic Books.
Bowlby, J. (1980) *Attachment and Loss. Vol. 3: Loss: Sadness, and Depression.* New York: Basic Books.
Hayes, S.C., Strohsal, K.D. and Wilson, K.G. (1999) *Acceptance and Commitment Therapy – an Experiential Approach to Behavior Change.* New York: Guilford Press.
Kabat-Zinn, J. (1990) *Full Catastrophe Living: Using the Wisdom of Your Body and Mind to Face Stress, Pain and Illness.* New York: Delta.
Kabat-Zinn, J. (1994) *Wherever You Go, There You Are: Mindfulness Meditation in Everyday Life.* New York: Hyperion.
Linehan, M.M. (1993) *Cognitive-Behavioral Treatment of Borderline Personality Disorder.* New York: Guilford Press.
Segal, Z., Williams, M. and Teasdale, J. (2002) *Mindfulness-based Cognitive Therapy for Depression.* New York: Guilford Press.
Young, J.E. (1994) *Cognitive Therapy for Personality Disorders: a Schema-focused Approach.* Sarasota, FL: Professional Resource Press.
Young, J., Klosko, J. and Weishaar, M. (2003) *Schema Therapy: a Practitioner's Guide.* New York: Guilford Press.

7
Why Are Mindfulness and Acceptance Central Elements for Therapeutic Change in Schema Therapy Too?
An Integrative Perspective

Eckhard Roediger

Introduction

The attitude of mindfulness is at the heart of Buddhist meditation (Thera, 1962). Following an innovative article published by Walsh (1980) and the conceptual work of Varela, Thompson, and Roach (1991), Kabat-Zinn (1982) introduced mindfulness into Western psychology in the early 1980s and started research on it. Since than it has influenced some major approaches, including Marlatt's relapse prevention and urge surfing concept (1994) and Linehan's dialectical behavior therapy (1993).

There is some evidence for the measurable beneficial effects of meditation: an increase in high-amplitude gamma oscillation and a pattern of highly synchronized activity in the left frontal–parietal lobes are regarded as an expression of an alert, integrative, self-reflective state (Lutz, Greischar, Rawlings, Ricard and Davidson, 2004). Increased prefrontal activity has been consistently found (Cahn and Polich, 2006) and comparable changes have been seen in PET and *f*MRT studies too (Pizzagalli and Shackman, 2003). Meditators also show increased levels of antibodies after receiving an influenza vaccination compared to a control group (Davidson *et al.*, 2003). They are less susceptible to optical illusions and show lower trait markers for anxiety and depression (Tlocynski, Santucci and Astor-Stetson, 2000), to name a few findings.

However, in this chapter we are not talking about meditation, but its "heart," the mindfulness attitude. Mindfulness means in essence moment-to-moment attention and awareness of its spontaneously arising content without trying to change it: "Thoughts are just suggestions and feelings, just feelings! You don't have to follow them – watch them come and go!" Or, in the words of an old Chinese saying: "You cannot stop a bird flying over your head, but you can keep it from building a nest in your hair." This is the basic attitude of meditation and allows us to distance ourselves from our spontaneous tendency to identify ourselves with what we feel or do – what Segal, Williams and Teasdale (2001) call the "doing-mode." By contrast, in a mindful state we experience ourselves as a constantly present internal observer, who is independent of the changing content of our consciousness. Segal and colleagues call this the "being-mode."

Current Status: The So-Called Third Wave In Behavior Therapy

This process is a core element of all so-called third-wave therapies (Hayes, 2004), beginning with mindfulness-based stress reduction (MBSR), Kabat-Zinn (1990), Linehan's (1993) dialectical behavior therapy (DBT), Acceptance and Commitment Therapy (ACT) (Hayes, 1999), cognitive-behavioral analysis system of psychotherapy (CBASP) (McCullough, 2000), mindfulness-based cognitive therapy (MBCT) (Segal, Williams and Teasdale, 2001), and meta-cognitive therapy (MCT) (Wells, 2008). Although heterogeneous in their approach, they all include a disidentification movement as a core element. Some practice mindfulness (or meditation) explicitly (DBT, MBCT, and MBSR), some make implicit use of a mindful altitude (ACT, CBASP, and MCT). However, all these therapies claim to contribute fundamentally to the further development of behavior therapy, as the cognitive therapy of the second wave did. What is common to these metacognitive approaches? While cognitive therapy tries to reappraise the *content* of an irrational thought, all the third-wave therapies take a more distant look at the thinking *procedure* itself (disregarding its content) by judging it as generally dysfunctional and refraining from arguing with it. In an approximate but impressive manner, Salkovskis labeled the thought rumination of an OCD patient in a workshop "brain trash" (personal communication, 1993). If patients are able to keep a necessary distance from their thinking process and take a fresh look at their emotional core needs, this is more effective than disarming every single distorted thought, one by one. Herbert and Forman (2011) regard a metacognitive approach in general as more promising than a cognitive one. Incidentally, trying to fulfill emotional core needs actively goes beyond Buddhism. However, here we are talking about psychotherapy, not religion.

Schema Therapy (ST) finds itself at the cutting edge, because on the one hand it uses cognitive strategies to "fight the early maladaptive schemas" (Young *et al.*, 2003). But on the other, when it comes to label the intrusive thoughts of a Demanding or Punitive Parent as a whole, places them on a special chair in a chair work session (Kellogg, 2004) and finally ejects them from the room, it is more like a metacognitive approach. This kind of work doesn't waste much time battling dysfunctional thoughts, but gets rid of them, focuses attention on the Vulnerable Child and its needs, and tries to fulfill them with the resources of the Healthy Adult. The distancing and detaching movement of this procedure is in its essence similar to the Buddhist way of distancing oneself from one's thoughts and letting them pass (although the atmosphere in a chair work session and the change part is much more active, goal-directed, powerful, and combative). If we compare schema and mode work, working with the schema model is closer to cognitive therapy, whereas the mode model invites us to work in a more metacognitive way. To go deeper into this metacognitive style of ST, let's take a closer look at the schema mode model and how the Healthy Adult works.

Looking Deeper into the Schema Mode Model

The model distinguishes between schemas and modes. Schemas are the "footprints" of former, emotionally relevant experiences in the neural structure of the brain. In a behavior analysis system (Kanfer and Scheffl, 1988) these traits are part of the O-Variable (see Figure 7.1). Schemas serve as attractors that lead the flow of neural activation into preformed pathways: I see what I know and I do what I (already) can. So we find ourselves caught in our "life traps" (Young and Klosko, 1993).

New internal or external stimuli (S) activate the existing schemas and elicit modes as complex current mood states, including emotions, thoughts, and physiological activations. Thus, we never perceive a schema itself, only as it is expressed in modes as their transient expression (*states*). The schema model strictly separates schema activation from coping behavior. "Behavior is schema driven, but it is not part of the schema" (Young *et al.*, 2003). By this means, we can separate the modes into Internal Child and Parent modes (Ri) and external coping modes (Re) (see Figure 7.1).

Unconditional schemas lead to primary emotional responses (Child modes), conditional schemas mirror core beliefs, which lead to automatic thoughts in the form of "voices of the internalized significant others" inducing behavior tendencies (Parent modes). Both internal modes are activated simultaneously and merge into coping modes as the currently best solution; for example, if the anger of an Angry Child cannot be expressed because a Punitive Parent prohibits it, a self-mutilating behavior (Detached Self-Soother) might be the solution. It is a core therapeutic goal to bypass the coping modes and access the Internal Child and Parent modes in order to disempower or "impeach" the Parent modes and fulfill the needs of the Child modes. In the case above, we can overcome self-mutilating behavior if we disarm the Punitive Parent and allow the Angry Child to vent his anger. Initially the anger has to be acknowledged and accepted, as well as the existence of the words of the Punitive Parent. This requires a mindful, nonjudgmental look at the thoughts and feelings hidden behind the Detached Self-Soother. Therefore, the therapist acknowledges, labels, and validates the anger of the Child mode and the accusations of the Parent mode as given and thus supports the patient to accept them himself. Then the patient can switch to a Healthy Adult perspective and look for an adequate way to express the anger of the Angry Child and take a fresh look at the Punitive Parent's position.

How Does the Healthy Adult Really Work?

The function of the Healthy Adult mode in the process of behavior change can be compared to shifting gear (Schore, 1994). This takes place in three steps:

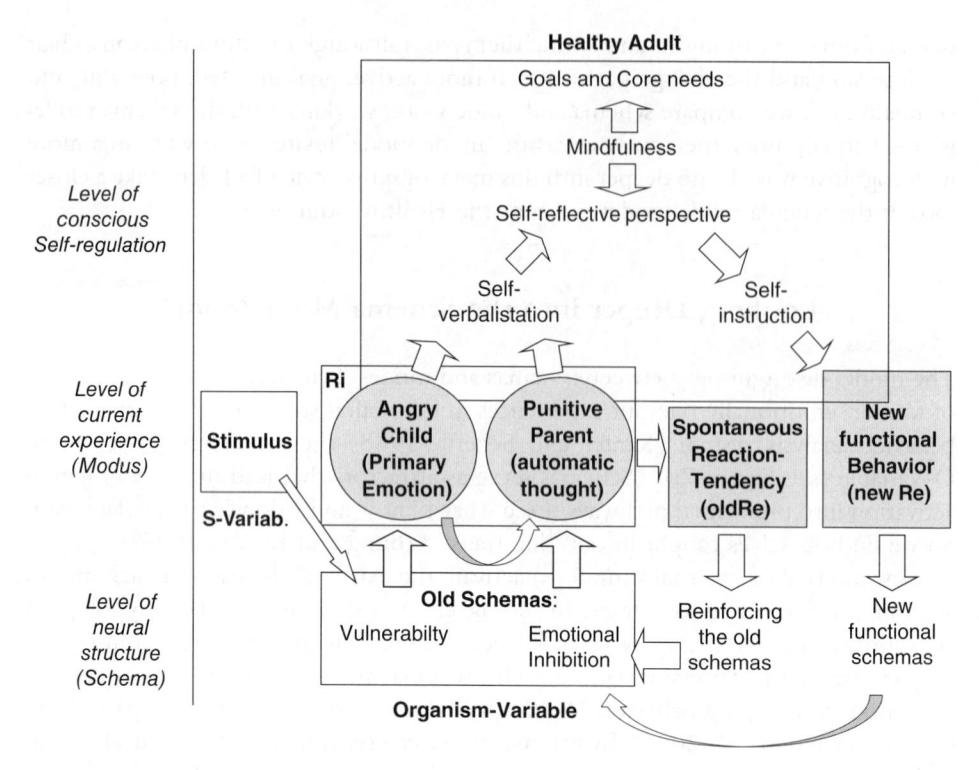

Figure 7.1

1. Become aware that the current gear isn't working well and shift out (Disidentification).
2. Reappraise the situation from a distance and select a better gear (Perspective change).
3. Shift to the new gear forcefully (Behavior pattern-breaking).

The following vignette gives an example of how these three steps work in Schema Therapy:

1. Peter arrives at the session full of suppressed anger complaining about a work colleague. The therapist induces a change into a self-reflective state by asking: "Hey, Peter, can you see what you are doing?" And after a pause: "Look at your feelings. What mode are you currently in?" The therapist doesn't react to the content of Peter's complaints, but helps him to label them and then focus on the underlying emotions from an observer's perspective. Peter needs the therapist's support to get out of his emotional quagmire. Mindfulness is essential as a first step to change any behavior: if we aren't aware of our schema activations, putting them into a labeling self-verbalization, and abstaining from reacting with our existing coping modes, there is no chance of changing anything and we will remain feeling trapped. There is no way to shift gear!
2. Switching into a self-reflecting perspective allows us to look into the "schema drawers" and recognize the modes as a result of personal schema activation and

not only as externally triggered. This helps Peter get in touch with the Angry Child behind his over-compensating insults. Imagery work is very helpful to detect and accept current mode activations that result from prior childhood wounds. In the imagery Peter could see that he has always been irritated by his younger brother, but his parents obliged him to be tolerant because "you are the older brother." In a chair work session Peter's Healthy Adult got in touch with his anger and, supported by the therapist's validations, he was able to accept it as a result of childhood schema activation. Looking through his "best friend's" eyes, he could see that any child in his place would have felt the same. This perspective change allowed him to reappraise the voices of his Punitive Parent mode and he decided he would no longer obey them. He selected a new gear.

3. At the end of the chair work session the therapist supported Peter to confront the Punitive Parent by speaking up to them in a powerful manner. Finally, he was coached in how to express anger toward his colleague appropriately in a role-play. "Shifting to this new gear" induces behavior pattern-breaking, constructs new schemas, and inhibits the activation of old ones. Finally, the core sentences of such an exercise serve as implicit self-instructions (Meichenbaum and Goodman, 1971) in similar situations outside therapy and help to induce new reactions (see Figure 7.1), for example, "I can actively express my needs now and fight for my rights!" By repetition and exercise they build up new neural footprints and modify the old schemas, or at least the activation of them. This is what "schema healing" is about. The effects (consequences) can be recorded in a schema diary and the new rules support the Healthy Adult to reappraise schema activation situations and "shift gear." So step-by-step self-efficacy grows and proves that the Healthy Adult is right and not the voices of the Punitive or Demanding Parent (Bandura, 1977).

While the first two steps are quite similar to Buddhism, the third step goes beyond the mindfulness and acceptance attitude, because the aim of Buddhism is not to bring about change. Schema Therapy, like DBT, tries to combine Eastern acceptance and Western change strategies in a balanced way. Bennet-Goleman (2001) describes what a synthesis of ST and Buddhism could look like.

Pitfalls and Tips

If we accept mindfulness as essential for change, we have to look for ways to train our patients in taking this perspective. Mindfulness can be trained formally or informally. The formal way is by meditation. The first pitfall is that patients usually don't think they can spare the time needed. A way out is to start informal mindfulness training, for this is what the peasants in ancient China did, since they didn't have free time either. Implicit mindfulness training means focusing attention fully on what we are doing right now. If I am clearing the table, I watch my hands and covertly comment: "My right hand takes the plate and the left one the cup, I am careful not to drop them. I walk to the kitchen, I place them close to the sink . . ." The ongoing mental description of what we are doing helps us keep the focus on the here and now. Focusing attention here and now initially can be trained in the session by letting the patient describe out loud and in detail what he or she sees in the room they are sitting in. This immediately calms any overwhelming emotion.

The next pitfall is that patients recognize the immediate effects, but argue that they can't do this all day long. Why not? As soon as we perceive intrusive thoughts or unpleasant feelings, we shift gear into the mindfulness exercise described above. We label the dysfunctional thought or feeling, accept its appearance without getting emotionally involved, let it go, and refocus on the here-and-now activity: "I am walking along the street, there is a blonde girl in front of me, a red car passes, to my left there is a florist . . ." We are the master of our mind! In a metaphor: there is only one seat in our mind for conscious thinking. If we sit there in a mindful state, there is no room for automatic thoughts!

Some patients find it difficult to switch into the hidden observer perspective. Depending on the patient's setup, we can suggest they are watching themselves through a camera, from a bird's eye view, through the eyes of their best friend or a wise man – or even a guardian angel if they have a religious background.

Another pitfall is simply that patients forget to practice mindfulness during the day. Therefore, it is helpful to link regular daily activities with moments of mindfulness, for example, taking the stairs at the office, going to the restroom, entering the train station, standing in a queue, waiting for a green traffic light. In those moments we actively switch into the observer perspective, watch the current thought content, perceive the sensations of our body, and focus on our breath for a few moments. One or two minutes, five or six times a day, are sufficient.

A further problem is that changing the focus of attention requires willpower. Some patients claim they aren't strong enough to do it. We can train our willpower (or self-control) by means of a simple exercise: every time you feel the urge to do something in a specific way, do the opposite. If you want to get out of bed with the right leg first, stop and start with the left leg. When you want to put on your shirt first, start with your trousers. Instead of having bacon, choose cheese for breakfast. When you want to cross the street in front of a car, let it pass and go behind it. (Note: Do not do this exercise the other way round!) You can proceed to not letting a word slip from your tongue or acknowledge a welling anger, and just let it go . . .

Last but not least, patients complain that they cannot practice mindfulness at night when intrusive thoughts keep them from sleep. Because we cannot stop thinking, it helps to divert attention away from the head to somewhere else in the body! Changing the attention focus must be accompanied by accepting that we cannot induce sleep actively, distancing ourselves from our Demanding Parent and telling them that somehow we will be there the next day, even if we won't be perfect. If we ignore him, the body will take the sleep it needs.

Conclusions and the Future

Implicitly, the attention part of mindfulness and creating a distance from thoughts or emotions is part of almost all psychotherapy and is not essentially new. Even exposure includes this mental movement when someone has to rate his or her level of fear. The feeling says: "It is overwhelming, I am going to die!" Rating requires comparing the current level of fear with a possible minimum and maximum. This means mentally moving from one pole to the other. A purist might say: This is hidden cognitive avoidance, but it is essential for the reappraisal of the intensity of the fear, which is probably more important for the effects of exposure and an antecedent of the habituation itself (Salkovskis, Clark, Hackmann, Wells and Gelder, 1999).

The term "mindfulness" affords us a new look at this first step. According to Shapiro, Carlson, Astin, and Freedman (2006), it enables "reperceiving" by changing perspective as a first step to bring about better self-regulation by "value clarification" and new goal-setting. In addition, the non-judgmental and acceptance part is important to create a distance from the emotional drag, permits "exposure" to negative emotions, and allows more flexible behavior responses. This is a specific "Eastern" contribution to psychotherapy, which helps to balance a change-directed "Western" therapy style. Thus, goal-attaining provides satisfaction on a high level of activity, but only for a short time unless the next challenge comes. However, "suffering derives from desire" and reducing estimations and readjusting goals also lead to reduced stress activation and consistency, at least at a lower level of activity (see Figure 7.2).

Some disorders are so severe, that, due to external and internal limitations, persisting and greater changes are hard to achieve. Therefore, we might start therapy with a focus on change and, over the course of therapy, we end up accepting certain limitations and revise our primary goals. Moreover, the older we get the more limitations we have to accept cannot be removed. So training in acceptance opens up an important resource in coping with circumstances we cannot change (see Part III, Chapter 6). At the least, an "autoplastic" change in our expectations (Piaget, 1962) under a consistency perspective (Grawe, 2004) might be as effective as an "alloplastic" change in the environment (see Figure 7.2). Of course, acceptance is not new, but part of strategies to overcome grief (Kübler-Ross, 1973).

Mindfulness is the counterbalance to the powerful impact of our schema activations (see Figure 7.1) and allows us to switch to a more distanced, self-reflective level of functioning. In brief: It helps us to keep our heads above the waves of emotion and saves us from drowning. This "mind-over-mood" attitude (Greenberger and Padesky, 1995) is a core element of our work and can be taught to patients as described. As a second element of Buddhist origin, acceptance allows peace of mind

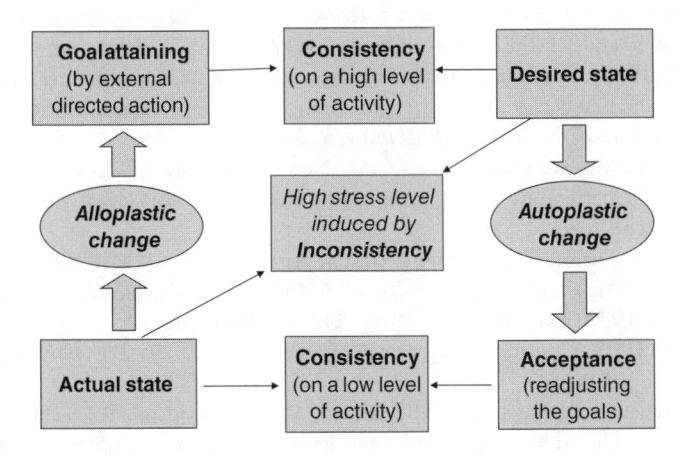

Figure 7.2

even under limited conditions. As pointed out above concerning mindfulness, a new term allows us a fresh look at this important therapeutic attitude. I am avoiding the term "strategy" at this point, because, from a purist Buddhist point of view, it might be illegitimate to use this religious-based non-desiring attitude in a goal-directed manner (Herbert, Forman and England, 2009). By contrast, Hayes (2002) suggested investigating mindfulness and acceptance scientifically despite their religious roots to introduce them into Western psychology. Perhaps there is a certain kind of "protection" against abusing mindfulness and acceptance in a "cold" or strategic manner: we won't be able to convince patients to practice mindfulness and acceptance if we don't do it ourselves! Besides enriching our personal life, this broadens our therapeutic repertoire to help people gain more confidence and peace of mind (see also Part III, Chapter 9).

References

Bandura, A. (1977) Self-efficacy: towards a unifying theory of behavioural change. *Psychological Review; 84*(2), 191–215.

Bennet-Goleman, T. (2001) *Emotional Alchemy: How the Mind Can Heal the Heart*. New York: Harmony.

Cahn, B.R. and Polich, J. (2006) Meditation states and traits: EEG, ERP and neuroimaging studies. *Psychological Bulletin, 132,* 180–211.

Davidson, R.J., Kabat-Zinn, J., Schumacher, J. *et al.* (2003) Alteration in brain and immune function produced by mindfulness meditation. *Psychosomatic Medicine, 65,* 564–570.

Grawe, K. (2004) *Psychological Therapy*. Goettingen: Hogrefe & Huber.

Greenberger, D. and Padesky, C.A. (1995) *Mind over Mood: a Cognitive Therapy Treatment for Clients*. New York: Guilford Press.

Hayes, S.C. (2002) Acceptance, mindfulness, and science. *Clinical Psychology: Science and Practice, 9,* 101–106.

Hayes, S.C. (2004) Acceptance and commitment therapy, relational frame theory, and the third wave of behavioral and cognitive therapies. *Behavior Therapy, 35,* 639–665.

Herbert, J.D. and Forman, J.M. (2011) *Acceptance and Mindfulness in Cognitive Behavior Therapy: Understanding and Applying the New Therapies*. Hoboken, NJ: Wiley.

Herbert, J.D., Forman, J.M. and England, E.L. (2009) Psychological acceptance, in *General Principles and Empirically Supported Techniques of Cognitive Behavior Therapy* (eds W. O'Donohue and J.E. Fisher). Hoboken, NJ: Wiley, pp. 77–101.

Kabat-Zinn, J. (1982) An out-patient program in behavioral medicine for chronic pain patients based on the practice of mindfulness meditation: theoretical considerations and preliminary results. *General Hospital Psychiatry, 4,* 33–47.

Kabat-Zinn, J. (1990) *Full Catastrophe Living*. New York: Delta.

Kanfer, F.H. and Schefft, B.K. (1988) *Guiding the Process of Therapeutic Change*. Champaign, IL: Research Press.

Kellogg, S. (2004) Dialogical encounters: contemporary perspectives on "chair work" in psychotherapy. *Psychotherapy: Theory, Research, Practice, Training, 41,* 310–320.

Kübler-Ross, E. (1973) *On Death and Dying*. Oxford: Routledge.

Linehan, M.M. (1993) *Cognitive-Behavioral Treatment of Borderline Personality Disorder*. New York: Guilford Press.

Lutz, A., Greischar, L.L., Rawlings, N.B., Ricard, M. and Davidson, R.J. (2004). Long-term meditators self-induce high-amplitude gamma synchrony during mental practice. *Proceedings of the National Academy of Sciences of the US, 101*(46), 16369–16373.

Marlatt, A. (1994) Addiction, mindfulness, and acceptance, in *Acceptance and Change: Content and Context in Psychotherapy* (eds S.C. Hayes, N.S. Jacobson, V.M. Folette and M.J. Dougher). Reno, NV: Context Press, pp. 175–197.

McCullough, J. (2000) *Treatment for Chronic Depression: Cognitive Behavioral Analysis System of Psychotherapy*. New York: Guilford Press.

Meichenbaum, D.H. and Goodman, J. (1971) Training impulsive children to talk to themselves: a means of developing self-control. *Journal of Abnormal Psychology*, 77, 115–126.

Piaget, J. (1962) *Play, Dreams, and Imitation in Childhood*. New York: W.W. Norton.

Pizzagalli, D. and Shackman, A.J. (2003) Affective neuroscience, in *Handbook of Affective Neuroscience* (eds R.J. Davidson, K.R. Scherer and H.H. Goldsmith). New York: Oxford University Press.

Salkovskis, P.M. (1993) Personal communication.

Salkovskis, P.M., Clark, D.M., Hackmann, A., Wells, A. and Gelder, M.G. (1999) An experimental investigation of the role of safety-seeking behaviours in the maintenance of panic disorder with agoraphobia. *Behaviour Research and Therapy*, 37, 559–574.

Schore, A.N. (1994) *Affect Regulation and the Origin of the Self: The Neurobiology of Emotional Development*. Hillsdale NJ: Erlbaum.

Segal, Z.V., Williams, J.M.G. and Teasdale, J.D. (2001) *Mindfulness-based Cognitive Therapy for Depression: a New Approach to Preventing Relapses*. New York: Guilford Press.

Shapiro, S.L., Carlson, L.E., Astin, J.A. and Freedman, B. (2006) Mechanisms of mindfulness. *Journal of Clinical Psychology*, 62, 373–386.

Thera, N. (1962) *The Heart of Buddhist Meditation*. New York: Weiser.

Tlocynski, J., Santucci, A. and Astor-Stetson, E. (2000) Perceptions of visual illusions by novice and longer-term meditators. *Perception and Motor Skills*, 91, 1021–1026.

Varela, F.J., Thompson, E. and Roach, E. (1991) *The Embodied Mind: Cognitive Science and Human Experience*. Cambridge, MA: MIT Press.

Walsh, R. (1980) The conscious disciplines and the behavioral sciences: questions of comparison and assessment. *American Journal of Psychiatry*, 137, 663–673.

Wells, A. (2008) *Metacognitive Therapy: a Practical Guide*. New York: Guilford Press.

Young, J.E. and Klosko, J.S. (1993) *Reinventing Your Life*. New York: Penguin.

Young, J.E., Klosko, J.S. and Weishaar, M.E. (2003) *Schema Therapy: a Practitioner's Guide*. New York: Guilford Press.

8

Mindfulness and ACT as Strategies to Enhance the Healthy Adult Mode

The Use of the Mindfulness Flash Card as an Example

Pierre Cousineau

Introduction

Schema Therapy interventions aim at reducing the influence of maladaptive schemas and coping modes on behavior while enhancing the adaptive Healthy Adult mode. This is accomplished through cognitive, behavioral, experiential, and relational strategies (Young, Klosko and Weishaar, 2003).

In the last decade, some clinicians and researchers have argued there was a "third wave" in cognitive behavioral therapy (Hayes, 2004a, 2004b). Acceptance and Commitment Therapy (ACT) is an important actor in this third wave (Hayes, Strosahl and Wilson, 1999; Luoma, Hayes and Walser, 2007), and mindfulness is also associated with the third wave although as a technique it existed long before that. In fact, mindfulness has been in existence for well over 2,000 years. However, its influence on many types of psychological interventions in the Western world has been more recent (Kabat-Zinn, 1990; Segal, Williams and Teasdale, 2001; Hayes, Follette and Linehan, 2004; Germer, Siegel and Fulton, 2005; Siegel, 2010).

The goal of this chapter is to provide some examples and avenues of reflection on the integration of mindfulness and ACT's strategies into Schema Therapy. Although there is a sound body of empirical evidence supporting the fields of ST, ACT, and mindfulness, there has not yet been any research to support the integration of these therapeutic strategies.

Schemas and Memory

In *The Developing Mind*, Siegel (1999, p. 24) defines memory as follows:

> Memory is more than what we can consciously recall about events from the past. A broader definition is that *memory is the way past events affect future function*. Memory is thus the way the brain is affected by experience and then subsequently alters its future responses.

Memory is often divided into two broad categories: implicit and explicit (Siegel, 1999; Grawe, 2004). Implicit memory is mostly connected to bodily sensations, emotions, perceptual categorization, mental models, behavior tendencies, and behavior responses. For example, we may experience an attraction or an aversion toward somebody we meet for the first time without knowing why. The other kind of memory, explicit memory, is best understood by its strong link to language. It is conceptual and narrative. Conceptual memory has to do with categorization according to perceptual features and other dimensions. For example, the differences between humans, animals, and plants are associated with conceptual memory. In everyday language, memory is often confused with narrative memory. That is, language allows the organization of implicit memory into a narrative sequence, the story we tell ourselves and others. Constructivists consider narration more as an act (creation of coherence, of meaning) than as a faithful reproduction of reality (Neimeyer and Raskin, 2000).

These definitions suggest that maladaptive schemas and dysfunctional strategies rely heavily on implicit memory. It is not surprising then that experiential and relationship strategies have come to play such an important role in schema modification and that an important criterion for progress is behavior pattern-breaking (Young *et al.*, 2003; Arntz and van Genderen, 2009).

However – and this comes as no surprise either – patients will most often present their problems on an explicit level. For example, a patient with a Defectiveness schema will say, "I am unlovable," one with a Failure schema, "I am stupid." Most of the time verbal interventions won't significantly change their belief. A typical response to cognitive schema confrontation would be, "Even if I know a lot of people appreciate me or like what I do, this doesn't change the way I feel deep inside, which is that something is wrong with me."

So there is that simple utterance "I am unlovable" and there is "a feeling deep inside." Where do we intervene?

Levels of Intervention

ACT proposes a theory of language referred to as Relational Frame Theory (RFT; see Hayes, Barnes-Holmes and Roche, 2001; Törneke, 2010). While it is beyond the scope of the present chapter to present the theory in detail, suffice it to say that in RFT, language is seen as contextual and should never be taken at face value. So when someone says, "I am unlovable," there is a whole context surrounding this simple sentence. What may it look like? That is, suppose for a moment that George is attending a social gathering and he notices Jane (antecedent and consequent stimulus control; see Wilson, 2008). At this point in his life he is single and longing for a partner (need for connection; see Flanagan, 2010). Seeing Jane as a potential partner triggers implicit memories of past rejections (Vulnerable Child mode: physiological reactions like "voice quavering," somatic sensations such as a "knotted stomach") and he feels the urge to flee the situation (behavioral tendency). George concludes that Jane could never be attracted to him since he is unlovable (self-narrative statement, Attributive function, Defectiveness schema), that the situation would bring him suffering (expectation), so he finally chooses to avoid Jane (behavioral response). So this short utterance, "I am unlovable" is the end product of very complex memories and processes:

> [Such] beliefs are multilayered organizations of networks that intermingle physiological, emotional, and cognitive schemes and processes in a complex pattern that creates an experience of the self as unlovable." (Whelton and Greenberg, 2001, p. 90)

Once explicitly conceptualized, this cognition will become another stimulus in a chain of behaviors. Wilson (2008) underlines that stimuli and responses make up functional units and that the distinction between them is useful only for practical reasons. The complexity of these processes makes us understand why the sole cognitive disputation of such dysfunctional beliefs is often like a drop in the ocean.

As Schema Therapists, we are regularly confronted with patients experiencing acute distress (Vulnerable or Angry Child), which in turn triggers dysfunctional coping responses. This will be addressed through the ST process. But is there a way to intervene rapidly and directly on the patient's "multilayered organizations of networks"? In our experience mindfulness and ACT techniques can prove to be significant aids in this regard. Mindfulness and ACT techniques are not symptoms, cognitions, behaviors, or schema-specific. They constitute meta-level interventions. Siegel (2007, 2010) writes that mindfulness has an impact on the mind, which he defines as the process that regulates the flow of energy and information within ourselves. In schema mode language, we would say that mindfulness and ACT techniques might constitute a way to enhance the Healthy Adult mode by proposing tools to cope with schemas when these are triggered. In order to do so, we adapted Young's flash card to integrate some of those techniques into the therapeutic process (Cousineau, 2010; Dionne *et al.*, 2010).

Approach

Mindfulness flash card

The mindfulness flash card is a four-step intervention. The main goals are to enhance the patient's tolerance to subjective discomfort, to promote an observer position within their mind's eye, and to replace automatic dysfunctional responses by chosen actions, in other words to replace automatic reactions by deliberate responses. In our experience, patients rapidly learn these tools that permit a fast, multilayered intervention (implicit and explicit levels). The mindfulness flash card also promotes a sense of control over emotionally loaded complex reactions that were driving patients' lives into directions they did not want.

Let's now go through the four steps of the mindfulness flash card.

> 1. *Right now, in the present moment, I feel.* *Instructions:* I simply stay with what I feel (affects and bodily sensations) for a few minutes. I observe what I feel without trying to change anything. If what I feel changes, I simply stay with the new feeling. I don't judge what is happening and I don't follow my thoughts; when a thought pops up, I notice the presence of that thought (I may say "a thought") and I return to what I am feeling. The philosophy behind this exercise = what is, is ("I fully realize that my schema has been triggered").

The patient has first been introduced (ideally, the session before the presentation of the mindfulness flash card) to experiential acceptance. We often use[1] what Harris (2007) refers to as an expansion (or acceptation) technique (Observe – Breathe – Create space – Allow). The main idea is to provide tools that facilitate exposure to emotional intensity. Staying with the bodily sensations of an emotional state without struggling with thoughts or urges to act is most often an astonishing experience for patients. Even if it is not the goal of the exercise (that point has to be stated clearly), patients regularly report that their bodily sensations change (in intensity, or even in nature).

Greater tolerance to intense emotions mitigates the strength of the automatic association between subjective states and the urge to act (dysfunctional coping responses to schema-triggering). During a therapy session, this exercise could be performed with mental imagery techniques in order to trigger the subjective experience of the schema in the present moment.

George in our example would be asked to stay with his bodily sensations of a "knotted stomach" and an "urge to flee." Feeling without responding will constitute a new experience and will eventually add to the repertoire of options.

This first section is essential for the next steps of the mindfulness flash card. We will see later that Sound Judgment (step 3) requires a pause in the habitual automatic responding sequence in order to allow a new way of processing information. Referring to Siegel (2007), we could hypothesize that this process relies on the strengthening of prefrontal activity.

> 2. *Why do I have this reaction?* *Instructions:* Why do I have that reaction? Which schema has been triggered? Where does it come from? (hypotheses about the schema's origin).
>
> Schema identification sets a target for change. The schema has been learned in a period of life where options were quite limited. It is very important that

---

[1] We recommend two books to the patient: for Schema Therapy, *Reinventing Your Life* (Young and Klosko, 1993) and for Acceptance and Commitment Therapy, *The Happiness Trap* (Harris, 2007).

> the patient realizes that the schema has been learned, so he doesn't identify with it ("I have a schema. I am not my schema"). In this perspective, ACT has an interesting concept called self-as-context (Luoma *et al.*, 2007); translated in the present theory, it means that the schema is a testimony of our learning history, *not* of how we are.

The very act of naming a schema also has the advantage of favoring a form of mentalization, for example, creating a healthy distance from the affective experience (which the patient learned to tolerate better in step 1). Mentalization has been shown to be helpful in affect regulation (Fonagy, Gergely, Jurist and Target, 2002).

Schema identification has an additional "collateral" positive effect. Human beings are story tellers (Siegel and Hartzell, 2003). Schema Theory offers a language that permits a more hopeful "rescripting" of the patient's life story. In our example, it would be quite different for George to say to himself that, in response to his father's harsh criticisms, he has learned to perceive himself through the Defectiveness schema, rather than firmly believing that he is an uninteresting and unlovable person. We can see in the following excerpt a parallel between a Schema Therapist and a good parent:

> Children try to understand and make sense out of their experiences. Telling your children the story of an experience can help them integrate both the events and the emotional content of that experience. Such an interaction with you can greatly help them make sense out of what happened to them and gives them the experiential tools to become reflective, insightful people. Without emotional understanding from a caring adult, a child can feel distress or even a sense of shame." (Siegel and Hartzell, 2003, Location 668 in Kindle book)

That dimension of ST is not often underscored. As when a parent is with a child, the Schema Therapist is helping the patient to integrate events and their emotional content and interpret their meaning in his life. This can be assimilated to the reparenting role of the Schema Therapist, which is helping the patient to make sense of his life.

> 3. *Sound judgment. Instructions*: Take the time to carefully reflect on this situation. What do you feel is really true? Is there any doubt, even the shadow of one, about the truthfulness of your schema? Is your actual interpretation of this situation in conflict with your needs and values?
>
> *Questions that may help*: Have there been occasions in the past in which what you felt was true was in fact false? In this unique situation, what are facts, what are interpretations? What would be the opinion of people close to you? Describe carefully the context of that situation. If it weren't for your fears, your guilt, or your anger, what would you choose to do?
>
> See thoughts, words, and images for what they are, that is plain thoughts, words, and images. Defuse yourself from their content – how useful are they to your needs or values?

The main goal of the present section is to create a distance from the false "emotional truth" of the schema by getting in touch with some other subjective experience (bodily felt sense; Gendlin, 1982); that is to instill doubt about the schema's gross, unrefined vision. The person doesn't have to be totally convinced of the schema's distortion, but there has to be *some kind of rift in the belief.* Once this rift is reasonably established, this opens up space for the Happy Child or Healthy Adult modes to emerge, giving the therapist the opportunity to support and reinforce them. At that point, there are bases to work on the patient's healthy goals.

What is the difference between a "pure" cognitive confrontation and what is proposed in this section? We want the patient to *experience* his "doubt" to a certain degree. Any means (as long as it is ethical) that will create a felt fissure in the belief is good. Let's look at an example of an obsessive-compulsive patient with a Negativity/Pessimism schema.

When Nadia leaves home, she always fears that her front door isn't properly closed or locked, so she compulsively returns and checks it. She has a dog that she holds dear to her heart and she couldn't bear the thought of losing him. The therapist used the following scenario to create another context: if she was offered a million dollars to make the right choice – the door is either closed and locked, or it isn't – what would she choose? The patient smiled broadly (bodily felt sense); she suddenly realized that she would have been the most stunned person in the world had she found her door opened or unlocked! This small destabilization was enough to convince her that it was worthwhile to try a new behavioral pattern when leaving home (Just Action – step 4).

Many ST techniques could be used to create a felt fissure in the schema's belief. Historical role-play is one. It offers an opportunity for the person to experience how she was drawn to distorted conclusions about herself by self-attribution of parents' difficulties (Defectiveness schema). Many techniques found in the present volume offer opportunities to create some level of doubt about the validity of the schema.

We have also found much utility with ACT's Defusion and Self-in-context strategies while working with this section of the mindfulness flash card. We saw earlier that George believes that he is an "unlovable" person, and that his Defectiveness schema triggered an avoidance response although he was attracted to Jane. A Defusion technique in this case could look like this: we would teach George how to become more aware of the present context and how it prompts the "I am unlovable" utterance. George would then be invited to reflect: "I am presently saying to myself that I am unlovable," and later, "I am conscious that I am presently saying to myself that I am unlovable." This will very often impoverish the schema's compelling persuasiveness.

Self-in-context goes a step further. George has learned to define himself most of the time as "unlovable," this is a conceptualized self. But he may become aware of an observer self, a part of him from which events are known, including the event of calling himself "unlovable." Most probably he will have had at times (even if rarely in case of a strong schema) other experiences of himself. What is the common denominator between these different, even opposite experiences? It is the fact that George is the one who experiences all of them (the "I" or first-person position). This part is more fundamental than any conceptualized self he may adopt. Becoming aware of such a perspective (process over content) lessens the potency of the schema.

What do such different therapeutic strategies such as historical role-play, scenario rescripting with mental imagery, defusing, and self-in-context have in common? If they work, the patient will experience himself differently and will then need a new cognitive coherence to fit that experience. Most often the new felt sense is closer to the Happy Child or Healthy Adult modes. If it is, it is an opportunity for the therapist to support and validate this new experience. If it isn't, then the situation needs further processing. Again, the idea is to get some rift in the schema's experience and belief. A felt sense that is closer to healthy modes will provide the basis on which to build a new behavioral pattern. The identification of significant values in ACT has similar functions. In order to choose the direction in which to go (the next step, Just Action), we have to get the feeling we do it for meaningful reasons. This is the goal of the Sound Judgment's section, to build up personal conditions that will favor a wiser choice.

> *4. Just action. Instructions:* In the current situation, considering what is conceivable, what I know, what is possible, and which means I can rely on, what is the optimal action?
> Once this optimal action is identified, I choose to do it – and I do it whatever I feel.

While I can't select which thoughts, images, feelings, or urges will show up, I can voluntarily choose a behavior. Then, the Just Action is simply to do it.

George has learned to tolerate the unpleasant feelings (shame and fear), and his urge to avoid associated with his being attracted to a woman. He recognizes the "I am unlovable" self-evaluation linked to his Defectiveness schema. He has developed a new perspective on these issues: the way he feels about himself has been learned, it isn't a factual description of who he really is. His avoidance strategy doesn't serve his need for a close relationship and his values about wanting a family. So, he consciously chooses to counteract his avoidance tendency by taking steps to introduce himself to women he is attracted to. He no longer surrenders to his learned automatic patterns (the schema). Similarly, Nadia will voluntarily stop her compulsive tendency to check the door again and again. To make this more likely, Nadia has learned to stay with her anxiety for longer periods of time, to identify the triggering of her Negativity/Pessimism schema, and to develop a different frame of mind about the checking context. Even if her compulsion to verify is still compelling, she now has a clear feeling that this isn't good for her since it increases her dysphoria and prevents her participation in more rewarding activities.

It is important to verify if the person already has the behavioral responses in her repertoire. If not, the therapist has to find ways to teach them. George may need some social skills training; Nadia some attentional skills training (being mentally present when checking).

Not acting according to a schema has a very important impact. It gives the opportunity to experience something different, a new response and its consequences (positive reinforcement, we hope). If schemas are memories, new experiences create new memories. In time, those new memories will compete with the schemas.

It is very important to expect relapses since the old memory configurations are very well established. We reframe it in terms of normal learning experiences. The new memory configurations need to "fire" together for a while before they can constitute significant alternatives to schemas.

Conclusion

Schema Therapy, mindfulness, and ACT are three fascinating and well-established models of therapy. As Schema Therapists, we found it very useful to integrate mindfulness and ACT techniques into our working models. The goal of ST is to modify schemas so that a person's behavior becomes more congruent with his needs (ACT would say with his values). In that sense any ethical strategy is good if it meets that goal. That is exactly our clinical experience with the mindfulness flash card. It is a powerful tool that allows us to intervene rapidly on "multilayered organizations of networks" and promote the Healthy Adult mode (adaptive strategies). Research in this area is most welcome.

References

Arntz, A. and van Genderen, H. (2009) *Schema Therapy for Borderline Personality Disorder*. Chichester: Wiley-Blackwell.

Cousineau, P. (2010) Un thérapeute des schémas qui a croisé l'ACT [A schema therapist who met ACT]. *Le Magazine ACT, Hors-série*, 3, 5–7 (www.lemagazineact.fr) (accessed October 26, 2011).

Dionne, F., Blais, M.C., Boisvert, J-M., Beaudry, M. and Cousineau, P. (2010) Optimiser les interventions comportementales et cognitives avec les innovations de la troisième vague [Optimizing behavioral and cognitive interventions with third wave innovations]. *Revue Francophone de Clinique Comportementale et Cognitive*, XV, 1–15.

Flanagan, C.M. (2010) The case for needs in psychotherapy. *Journal of Psychotherapy Integration*, 20, 1–36.

Fonagy, P., Gergely, G., Jurist, E. and Target, M. (2002) *Affect Regulation, Mentalization, and the Development of the Self*. New York: Other Press.

Gendlin, E.T. (1982) *Focusing*. New York: Bantam Books.

Germer, C.K., Siegel, R.D. and Fulton, P.R. (2005) *Mindfulness and Psychotherapy*. New York: Guilford Press.

Grawe, K. (2004). *Psychological Therapy*. Göttingen: Hogrefe & Huber.

Harris, R. (2007) *The Happiness Trap*. Boston, MA: Trumpeter Books.

Hayes, S.C. (2004a) Acceptance and commitment therapy, relational frame theory, and the third wave of behavioral and cognitive therapies. *Behavior Therapy*, 35, 639–665.

Hayes, S.C. (2004b) Acceptance and commitment therapy and the new behavior therapies, in *Mindfulness and Acceptance: Expanding the Cognitive-Behavioral Tradition* (eds S.C. Hayes, V.M. Follette and M.M. Linehan). New York: Guilford Press pp. 1–29.

Hayes, S.C., Barnes-Holmes, D. and Roche, B. (2001) *Relational Frame Theory: A Post-Skinnerian Account of Human Language and Cognition*. New York: Plenum Press.

Hayes, S.C., Follette, V.M. and Linehan M.M. (eds) (2004) *Mindfulness and Acceptance: Expanding the Cognitive-Behavioral Tradition*. New York: Guilford Press.

Hayes, S.C., Strosahl, K.D. and Wilson, K.G. (1999) *Acceptance and Commitment Therapy: an Experiential Approach to Behavior Change*. New York: Guilford Press.

Kabat-Zinn, J. (1990) *Full Catastrophe Living: Using the Wisdom of Your Body and Mind to Face Stress, Pain and Illness*. New York: Delta.

Luoma, J.B., Hayes, S.C. and Walser, R.D. (2007) *Learning ACT: an Acceptance and Commitment Skills-Training Manual For Therapists*. Oakland, CA: New Harbinger.

Neimeyer, R.A. and Raskin, J.D. (2000) *Constructions of Disorder: Meaning-Making Frameworks for Psychotherapy*. Washington, DC: American Psychological Association.

Segal, Z.V., Williams, J.M. and Teasdale, J.D. (2002) *Mindfulness-based Cognitive therapy for Depression: a New Approach to Preventing Relapse*. New York: Guilford Press.

Siegel, D.J. (1999) *The Developing Mind: Towards a Neurobiology of Interpersonal Experience*. New York: Guilford Press.

Siegel, D.J. (2007) *The Mindful Brain: Reflection and Attunement in the Cultivating of Well-Being*. New York: W.W. Norton.

Siegel, D.J. (2010) *The Mindful Therapist: A Clinician's Guide to Mindsight and Neural Integration*. New York: W.W. Norton.

Siegel, D.J. and Hartzell, M. (2003) *Parenting from the Inside Out*. New York: Tarcher (Kindle Books).

Törneke, N. (2010) *Learning RFT: An Introduction to Relational Frame Theory and its Clinical Application*. Oakland, CA: Context Press.

Whelton, W.J. and Greenberg, L.S. (2001) The self as a singular multiplicity: a process-experiential perspective, in *Self-Relations in the Psychotherapy Process* (ed. J.C. Muran). Washington, DC: American Psychological Association.

Wilson, K.G. (2008) *Mindfulness for Two: an Acceptance and Commitment Therapy Approach to Mindfulness in Psychotherapy*. Oakland CA: New Harbinger.

Young, J.E., Klosko, J.S. (1993) *Reinventing Your Life*. New York: Plume Book.

Young, J.E., Klosko, J.S. and Weishaar, M.E. (2003) *Schema Therapy: a Practitioner's Guide*. New York: Guilford Press.

9
Teaching Mindfulness Meditation within a Schema Therapy Framework

David Bricker and Miriam Labin

Introduction

Meditation has a rich history that goes back thousands of years, far beyond the development of scientific psychology and Schema Therapy. While the exact origins of meditation cannot be known, there is agreement that some form of it existed in Asia thousands of years ago. This history is not only long but also has considerable breadth; all major religious traditions have included some form of meditation as part of their rituals.

The twentieth century led to exciting new advances in these centuries-old traditions. As the world grew smaller with unprecedented developments in communication, knowledge of meditation spread from Asia to the West. In the 1960s this process accelerated as the Beatles studied with Guru Maharishi Mahesh Yogi in India and popularized his work in Transcendental Meditation. As the popularity of meditation spread, a multitude of empirical studies were conducted that showed its benefits on health and psychological well-being (Wallace, 1970; Benson, Malvea and Graham, 1973; Goleman and Schwartz, 1976; Shapiro, 1980).

It was not long before psychologists began to integrate meditation into other treatments. Marsha Linehan (1993) included meditation as part of dialectical behavior therapy. Concurrently, Jonathan Kabat-Zinn (1990) began writing about meditation and stress reduction. As part of this trend many ST practitioners included meditation as part of their treatment protocols. An informal survey of Schema Therapists attending the ISST conference in Coimbra, Portugal in 2008 showed that about half were already teaching meditation to their clients.

The Wiley Blackwell Handbook of Schema Therapy: Theory, Research, and Practice, First Edition.
Edited by Michiel van Vreeswijk, Jenny Broersen, and Marjon Nadort.
© 2012 John Wiley & Sons, Ltd. Published 2015 by John Wiley & Sons, Ltd.

While for the most part meditation provided benefits to our patients, problems were encountered along the way. Segal, Williams, and Teasdale (2002) cite several in teaching meditation to psychotherapy clients, among them resistance to homework, attitudes toward practice, coping with painful emotions, boredom, difficulties in staying focused, avoidance of negative emotions, preconceptions about what meditation is, and dealing with the dialectic between acceptance and action.

Taking into account some of these pitfalls as well as the nature of Schema Therapy, the intention of this chapter is to present a method for teaching meditation that makes it easy for the patients to learn meditation as part of ST. ST is a unique form of therapy and the manner in which meditation is taught can be adapted to it so that it is integrated into the therapy process. We advocate that meditation should not be taught as a stand-alone technique, but rather as something that is integrated into the entire therapeutic process.

We suggest a method in which clients learn a variety of brief mindfulness exercises and are also trained on when and how to apply each of them. Clients develop the ability to choose a meditation that supports their ability to cope better with the current situation in the context of the schema mode that they are experiencing.

In order to best integrate meditation into ST we divide it into seven components:

1. Awareness
2. Choice and Intention
3. Relaxation
4. Letting Go
5. Here and Now Focus
6. Nonjudgmental Acceptance
7. Values

For each of the components we will discuss the nature of the component and how it is a part of meditation. We will then discuss how to teach patients to use this technique. Finally, we will give examples of how each particular component is related to the process of ST.

Awareness

One of the most important themes in meditation is moment-to-moment awareness, which means directing attention and fully engaging your experience in the current moment. Being "in the moment" is seen as a positive value. Thus, if you are eating an apple, this kind of meditation would direct you to focus on the sensations that arise while you are eating, such as the taste and texture of the apple on your tongue. Likewise, when one is at a movie or engaged in a social event, the ideal is to be aware of what is going on at the moment it occurs.

There are many variations on this theme in meditation. One can meditate by focusing on different parts of the body, for instance by noticing how our weight shifts from one foot to the other as we walk. The following body-scan meditation increases awareness to bodily sensations.

Exercise: guided body scan meditation

Take a moment to get comfortable. Become aware of your breathing. Notice how air effortlessly and rhythmically enters your nose or mouth and how your lungs expand on the in-breath. Now notice how your lungs contract on the outbreath and the air leaves your body. Focus on different parts of your body as you breathe.

Now focus on your hands and fingers. Notice how both hands and all of your fingers feel.

Now shift your focus to your forearms . . . and then to your upper arms. Notice all of the feelings and sensations. See if you can detect different feelings in different parts of your arms.

Now pay attention to your shoulders and neck. Just notice what you are feeling in these areas. Notice any sensations that you feel.

Now notice your feet and your toes. Try to feel as much of your feet and toes as possible. See what they feel like.

Now notice your ankles and your calves. Notice the sensations, notice how they feel.

Now be aware of your thighs. Notice how they feel. Notice any sensations in your thighs.

Now shift your attention to your groin and your lower abdomen.

Now focus on your chest and back. Notice any sensations, mentally taking stock of any sensations you find.

Now direct your attention to your face. Notice your forehead, your eyes, your cheeks, your jaws, your lips. Just notice what these areas feel like. Become aware of any sensations you can connect with.

Awareness and Schema Therapy

Awareness of internal processes is central to any system of psychotherapy. Patients come to us with complaints about failed relationships and negative emotions. But they are not aware of the schemas and modes that they will soon be confronting. It is our job to help them to become aware of their inner thoughts and feelings so that we can engage them in ST. By teaching them awareness exercises we make it easier for them to pay attention to what is happening inside them so they can deal with it in therapy. The following example of a patient who presents with emotional detachment illustrates how awareness can be used as part of ST.

Choice and Intention

Box 1:

When Debora first presented in therapy she showed minimal affect. She said that her husband wanted her to start therapy. According to him, it was impossible to engage her in any emotional talk since she always turned to something she had to do for work and had a difficult time just sitting in one place and discussing emotional issues. Debora's husband was describing her Detached

> Protector mode. However, her facial expressions and demeanor suggested that underneath her strict appearance there was an Angry mode that she was struggling with. She would often drink alcohol in order to avoid her angry feelings. Her husband felt that he couldn't talk to her anymore and threatened to divorce her unless she came to therapy. Debora said that she felt very uncomfortable having "emotional talks." She realized that she had trouble recognizing her emotions even when she was alone. She told the therapist that as a child, her mother responded negatively by mocking her when she expressed her feelings and her father was very cold, aloof, and uninvolved with his family.
>
> Debora's first assignment was to simply ask herself: What am I thinking about right now? What am I feeling right now? Later, Debora learned the body-scan meditation. Gradually, she became more aware of her emotions and felt less uncomfortable staying with her emotions instead of deflecting from them. She noticed that she often felt angry about different needs that were not being met. This opened the possibility for her to listen to her anger and express her needs to her husband and other people who were close to her. By becoming aware of her Detached Protector mode she was able to notice more about the negative patterns in her life so she could confront them with her therapist.

In mindfulness meditation "choice and intention" have always formed a core component. It simply means that you can shift your attention to what you want to focus on and avoid distractions. It does not mean forcing yourself not to think about any certain thoughts; it is about what you want to focus on, not what you want to avoid. When your mind is wandering, you gently shift your thinking back to where you want it to be. The exercise below includes instructions on how to meditate by simply paying attention to your breathing.

Exercise: counting breaths

Begin by sitting comfortably in a chair, in a way that makes it easy for you to breathe slowly and relax. Simply pay attention to your breathing. Feel the air coming in through your nose, going in to your abdomen and going out again. Let your mind follow your breath a couple of times.

First, focus on the in-breath and say the number "one" as you breathe in. Then think the word "out" as you breathe out. Then say the number "two" on the next in breath. And think the word "out" as you breathe out.

Continue to follow every breath, counting as you breathe in and saying the word "out" in your mind very softly. When your mind wanders and you find yourself thinking about something else, gently bring it back to the breathing, counting as you breathe in and saying the word "out" to yourself. Practice doing that for a couple of minutes.

Continue to follow every in-breath saying a number to yourself very softly. You can combine focusing on the air going out while saying the word "out" and focusing on the air coming in while saying a number: "one–out", "two–out," and so on. When your mind is wandering bring it back to the breath with the minimum amount of effort, simply continuing to count and focusing on the air coming in and out.

Choice and intention and Schema Therapy

Clients learn that when feeling depressed or anxious they can shift attention to something else rather than continue to focus on the negative thoughts. They apply this mindfulness training to other life situations by simply asking a few questions such as: What would I like to think about right now? What is in my best interest right now? At work, for example, they can choose to shift their focus away from their depressed thoughts and focus on current tasks.

Relaxation

> **Box 2:**
>
> Ella is a 23-year-old graphic designer with a core schema of Defectiveness and Shame. She always felt defective in some major way. Her mother was very critical of her and her father was remote. One of her core childhood memories is of her mother smacking her for not tidying her room as her father watches from another room, not saying anything. Ella frequently thought: "I'm strange and boring" and "nobody loves me." Such thoughts were bothering her daily and causing her a lot of distress. She had limited social interactions because she was afraid that people would not like her when they got to know her. She kept a few friends from high school, but did not acquire new friends in college and never had a boyfriend.
>
> Despite her difficulties, Ella recognized a healthier part of her that helped her resist these negative thoughts. When she was in a healthy mode she thought: "This is stupid. I'm exaggerating. I know that people who are close to me love and appreciate me." During the course of Schema Therapy, Ella learned to shift her attention to her breath whenever she felt overwhelmed by negative thoughts. After she was able to shift her focus to her breathing, it also became easier for her to shift her focus to her Healthy Adult mode. Her experience of her healthy side increased together with her positive view of herself. She felt less defective and more in control. As a result, she began to expand her social interactions and even started dating.

Although some psychologists disagree, we believe that relaxation is an essential component of meditation. When we experience excessive anxiety it is hard for us to concentrate. Although we can go through the steps of various meditation exercises while feeling high arousal, it would be hard to benefit from the exercises without feeling a modicum of calmness in order to concentrate.

There are two simple relaxation techniques we show clients: slow deep breathing and progressive muscle relaxation (PMR). Reduction of stress in PMR is done by releasing tense muscles. While releasing tension, clients learn the difference between stress and relaxation.

Exercise: slow, deep breathing relaxation

Begin by sitting comfortably and paying attention to your breathing. Try to breathe slower and slower. Let the air go all the way in through your nose to your abdomen. Stop for a second. And now let all the air out through your mouth. Notice your breathing becoming deeper and slower as you continue to breathe in and breathe out. As your breathing is going in and out you are becoming more and more relaxed.

Exercise: progressive muscle relaxation

Begin with slow, deep breathing. Let your breathing becoming deeper and slower as you inhale the air through your nose and exhale through your mouth. Let's start by making a fist in your right hand. Hold it and notice how it feels like. Hold it some more and then let go. Notice how it feels when you let go.

Now, try doing the same with your left hand. Make a fist and notice how it feels. Hold it some more and then let go. Notice how it feels when you let go. Study the differences between tension and relaxation.

Now let's continue with your right arm. Pull it up toward your shoulder and tense the muscles of your right arm. Hold it and notice how it feels. Hold it some more and then let go. Notice how it feels when you let go.

Now, try doing the same with your left arm. Pull it up toward your shoulder and notice how it feels. Hold it some more and then let go. Notice how it feels when you let go. Study the differences between tension and relaxation.

Continue with your shoulders. Pull up both of your shoulders toward your ears. Hold them and notice how they feel. Hold them some more and then let go. Notice how it feels when you let go. Study the differences between tension and relaxation.

Let's move on by tensing the muscles of your face. This is done by closing your mouth and your eyes tightly. Hold this position and notice how it feels. Hold it some more and then let go. Notice how it feels when you let go. Study the differences between tension and relaxation.

Let's continue with the abdominal muscles. Tense the abdominal muscles, holding them tightly. Study the tension in your abdominal muscles. Now, let go and notice the sensations that come with the relaxation. Notice the difference between tension and relaxation.

Continue with your right leg. Pull it straight up in the air while tensing your muscles. Hold it and notice how the tense feels. Hold it some more and then let go. Notice how it feels when it is relaxed.

Let's move on to your left leg, tensing the muscles of your left leg by pulling it straight up in the air. Hold it and notice what it feels like. Hold it some more and then let go. Notice how it feels when you let go. Study the differences between tension and relaxation.

Let's move to your right foot. Point your right foot. Feel the tension in your foot while you are pointing it and study the sensations that come along with this tension. Hold it some more and then let go. Notice what it feels like when it is relaxed.

Now point your left foot. Feel the tension in your foot while you are pointing it and study the sensations that come along with this tension. Hold it some more and then let go. Notice how it feels when you release the tension. Study the differences between tension and relaxation.

Relaxation and Schema Therapy

Relaxation practice is relatively easy to learn by following the therapist's directions. Relaxation by itself rarely solves complex issues, such as the client's Vulnerability schema in the example above, but it offers an immediate relief and a sense of control and efficacy.

> **Box 3:**
>
> Yvonne felt anxious almost all the time. She was always worried about her health and well-being and about the well-being of her family. Yvonne was suffering from a Vulnerability schema, perceiving herself as weak and unable to cope. She often checked her body, looking for lumps that might indicate she had cancer and checked for palpitations fearing that something was wrong with her heart. She asked her husband many times during the day for reassurance that she is healthy. She also called her children many times during the day to check that they were well.
>
> Yvonne was diagnosed with hypochondria and general anxiety disorder. One of her major complaints was of severe muscle tension that tended to increase when she was overwhelmed with health concerns and other worries. We offered her PMR, which reduced some tension and was very relaxing for her. In the context of ST, PMR was framed as a coping tool that increased her ability to cope with anxiety.

Letting Go

In CBT and ST we teach clients to gain perspective over their thoughts and re-examine whether these thoughts correspond with reality. The "letting go" meditation also teaches clients to gain perspective over their thoughts, but in a different way. The idea is to let the thoughts just pass through your mind, acknowledge them, but not engage in them or analyze them. This meditation is specifically useful when the client experiences obsessive thoughts, concerns, or any kind of ruminative thinking.

Exercise: floating leaves on a stream

Close your eyes. Imagine that you are in the woods on a warm, sunny day sitting by a beautiful stream. The water flows over the rocks and descends downhill. You hear the calming sounds of the water and the trees above you. As you gaze down at the stream you notice that there are leaves floating down the stream.

Now become conscious of your thoughts. Each time a thought pops into your head imagine that you write it on a leaf and let the leaf float away down the stream with your thought on it. If you think in words, put them on the leaf as words. If you think in images, put them on the leaf as an image. Watch as the leaves disappear and the thought disappears with it.

The goal is to stay beside the stream and allow the leaves to keep flowing by. Don't try to make the stream go faster or slower; don't try to change what shows up on the leaves in any way. If the leaves disappear, or if you mentally go somewhere else, just notice that this has happened and gently direct your attention back to watching the leaves on the stream. Watch your thoughts as they are being written on each leaf and let them flow down the stream.

> **Box 4:** Letting go and Schema Therapy
>
> Jeff could not get his ex-girlfriend, Stacy, out of his mind. Jeff had an Abandonment schema and always had a hard time when ending a relationship. His parents divorced when he was five years old and he remembers their divorce as being very traumatic for him. One of his core memories is of his parents yelling at each other and totally ignoring him. Since the divorce they were not available to him or, as in his words: "It's like they were there but not really there." His father was often out of the state on business trips and his mother was very preoccupied with herself and always looking for new partners, so she was emotionally unavailable to him. As a result, Jeff developed an Abandonment schema.
>
> Although Jeff and Stacy separated a year ago, his thoughts about her interfered with his daily routine. He had difficulties concentrating at work, became forgetful and uninterested in seeing his friends or meeting other women. Jeff was taught the letting go meditation. Whenever Stacy's face came to mind he would visualize putting it on a leaf. He did the same with thoughts such as: "How could she leave me?" which were bothering him. Soon, his ability to concentrate improved. He learned that when he is in his Surrender schema mode his tendency to think about Stacy increases. The letting go meditation helped him realize that thinking about Stacy would not help him get her back or feel better. Actually, he felt much better when he was able to focus on his job and enjoy the company of his friends.

Here and Now Orientation

One of the most important themes in mindfulness meditation is being in the here and now, or being in the present, rather than the past or future. Clients who apply this meditation learn that negative thoughts and feelings often arise in relation to past and to future events, but much less in relation to the present moment.

Exercise: tracking your thoughts in time

Keep your eyes open and take a few slow deep breaths. Now, just let your mind wander and start noticing your thoughts and feelings and where your awareness goes.

As long as you are focused on the present continue to look straight ahead. When you begin to think of something from the past, turn your head to the left. Then when your thoughts return to the present, look straight ahead once again. And when you find yourself thinking about the future, look to the right.

> **Box 5:** Here and now orientation and Schema Therapy
>
> Sam, aged 42, married, is very successful at his work as a computer programmer. His boss likes him and always says he can trust him. However, Sam became frustrated because other people got raises and promotions before him, even when he was sure that they did not produce as much as he did. He had difficulty expressing his frustration and felt that he was being used by his boss. Sam has a Self-Sacrifice schema, the tendency to always put others ahead of himself while neglecting his own needs. At home, he also felt unappreciated and whenever he complained to his wife she became defensive and angry. Lately, he began feeling more depressed and angry and decided to seek treatment.
>
> As Sam practiced the "tracking your thoughts in time" meditation, he noticed that he mostly had thoughts about the past: "I got what I deserve," "I'm angry that others got promoted and I didn't"; and thoughts about the future "I'll never get what I deserve," "My boss will never appreciate my skills." However, Sam also noticed that for the brief moments that he focused on the "here and now" he felt more focused and somewhat calmer.
>
> This exercise was helpful as part of an overall plan to help Sam to deal with his Self-Sacrifice schema. By doing the exercise he was able to put his problems in perspective. He was able to become less angry and could focus on expressing his needs in an assertive way in the present. He tried to approach difficult issues with his wife by focusing on the present and putting aside thoughts about the past and the future. This approach proved to be very rewarding. Eventually, Sam approached his boss and began to get some of the benefits he deserved.

Non-Judgmental Acceptance

In mindfulness meditation, acceptance has always been a core component aiming to help clients recognize thoughts and feelings without involving judgment. The goal is to view all experiences, all thoughts and feelings, within a framework of acceptance rather than evaluation and criticism. As a part of meditation, when a thought comes into your head the goal is to let yourself have the thought and just observe it.

We can say that the opposite of having a schema is accepting who you are as a person. So, for example, if you have thoughts such as "I think I'm a bad person" and "How could I get into this stupid fight and say all these negative things." Instead of judging yourself you start thinking: "I accept who I am and that I make mistakes, but I choose not to judge myself. I just accept that I made this mistake." The goal is to be accepting of whatever your experience is.

Exercise: accepting your thoughts

Close your eyes and gently focus your attention on whatever you are thinking about. Every time you notice that you are aware of something take a moment to notice what it is that you are thinking about. Then identify what it is and think: "I accept that I am thinking about this now." For example, if you find that you are worrying about an upcoming event, think to yourself: "I'm having worried thoughts about the event" and then "I accept that I'm having worried thoughts." If you notice feeling sad, think to yourself: "I'm having feelings of sadness" and add: "I accept that I'm having feelings of sadness," and so on.

Do the same thing no matter where your awareness goes. With any thoughts, feelings, observations, memories, sensations just notice where your awareness is going, identify it, and think about accepting the experience.

Box 6: Acceptance and Schema Therapy

Tina, aged 22, always felt anxious about public speaking and other social situations. She started psychotherapy after her first year of college, during which she had a hard time presenting in class, going to parties, and participating in other social events. Tina often experienced a Critical Parent mode in which she was criticizing herself for the way she appeared and behaved.

Tina's core childhood memory was of her mother yelling at her in front of guests about not doing well in school. Her parents were very demanding and she grew up feeling that nothing she did was good enough for them. Even when she excelled in a test they would compare her to others in the class and assume that the test was not hard for her. So, she usually was not praised for her successes, but severely criticized when she did not meet her parents' standards.

She was bothered by her blushing during presentations, which was accompanied by thoughts such as "Everyone can see that I'm anxious" and "They probably think I'm a bad presenter and a bad student." Tina was diagnosed with social anxiety. As part of ST, Tina was taught acceptance meditation.

In generalizing from meditation to real life Tina's first goal was to accept her blushing and her anxiety while presenting in class. She practiced accepting her anxious thoughts, feelings, and sensations. She noticed that when she accepted her anxiety she felt less anxious over time. She was still anxious at the beginning of the presentation, but with acceptance her anxiety subsided and as she continued talking, she felt much less anxious. She also became an active participant in college parties and other social events.

Tina's tendency to criticize her performance demonstrates her Critical Parent mode since she grew up with parents who showed merely conditional love in response to achievements, giving her the message that she was never good enough. When she caught herself going into a Critical Parent mode she would practice gently shifting to thoughts such as "I accept myself the way I am."

Values

Working on values is different from practicing any other kind of mindfulness meditation. Values are not feelings or thoughts, but are a representation of one's sense of self and choices of life directions. Kabat-Zinn (1994) recommends that we ask ourselves: "What is my job on the planet?" or "What do I care about so much that I would pay to do it?" This can be done in conjunction with any mindfulness exercise or simply by thinking about the questions.

The following is an example of an exercise that can help clients connect with their life values.

Exercise: trusted adviser imagery

Close your eyes. Imagine that you are walking along a path in a very beautiful forest. Enjoy the peace and quiet of the forest around you. Now, imagine that you are about to meet a person whom you can trust to always be there for you, someone who is wise and always has your best interests at heart, who always cares about you. This wise man or woman has wisdom and insight to give you. As you approach you clarify the question that you want to ask.

You reach this person and you ask your question.

Listen to the response that this trusted adviser gives to you.

This exercise can easily be simplified. Clients may just think about a decision to be made and then simply close their eyes and be aware of their breathing for a few minutes. Often they will have much greater clarity about the issue afterward.

Box 7: Values and Schema Therapy

Tom, aged 40, recently divorced, was going through a mid-life crisis. He had been working as an investment banker since graduating from college and was doing very well. However, he did not feel satisfied. He always loved visual art and specifically painting. He kept it as a hobby for many years, but felt that he was missing his true life passion. He wanted to focus exclusively on learning and teaching art. Tom experienced a real dilemma: Should I quit my job and focus on my passion? Is this really what I want to do or just part of this crisis that I am going through? Tom was afraid that when painting became his "day job" he might feel bored with it too at some point.

We guided Tom through the wise man imagery. Tom imagined his grandfather, who always deeply cared about him, as the wise man. Eventually, Tom decided to take a leave of absence for six months from his job as a trial period before he made a decision about quitting his job. He thought that this would give him a chance to evaluate what his life as an artist would look like and to still return to his job if things didn't work out. He told the therapist that the imagery with his grandfather gave him a lot of insight and a sense that he had someone that he could lean on.

Conclusion

In conclusion, the outline presented here is not intended to be seen as a final statement about the one correct way to teach meditation, but rather as a framework that skilled therapists can use to make their work in ST more effective for more clients. Therapists can experiment with the different components and see which ones work best with their individual styles. Likewise, various clients will find that they prefer different types of meditation. There are countless examples of meditation exercises available and new ones are created every day. These methods can easily be integrated into our framework to make it fuller and more helpful.

Finally, there is no need to limit ourselves to these seven components. Psychologists may prefer to look at other attributes, or skills, such as connectedness, aliveness, appreciation, love, or contentment as core components. Some researchers (Gilbert and Tirch, 2008; Tirch, 2010) have begun to look at compassion as a core component in meditation. As ST evolves, the integration of meditation will continue in creative ways that will add to greater knowledge and efficiency in both fields.

References

Benson, H., Malvea, B. and Graham, J. (1973) Physiologic correlates of meditation and their clinical effects in headache: an ongoing investigation. *Headache*, 13(1), 23–24.

Gilbert, P. and Tirch, D. (2009) Emotional memory, mindfulness, and compassion, in *Clinical Handbook of Mindfulness* (ed. F. Di Donna). New York: Springer Science, pp. 99–110.

Goleman, D.J. and Schwartz, G.E. (1976) Meditation as an intervention in stress free activity. *Journal of Consulting and Clinical Psychology*, 44, 456–466.

Kabat-Zinn, J. (1990) *Full Catastrophe Living: Using the Wisdom of Your Body and Mind to Face Stress, Pain and Illness*. New York: Dell.

Kabat-Zinn, J. (1994) *Wherever You Go, There You Are: Mindfulness Meditation in Everyday Life*. New York: Hyperion.

Linehan, M. (1993) *Cognitive-Behavioral Treatment of Borderline Personality Disorder*. New York: Guilford Press.

Segal, Z., Williams, J. and Teasdale, J. (2002) *Mindfulness-based Cognitive Therapy of Depression: a New Approach to Preventing Relapse*. New York: Guilford Press.

Shapiro, D.H. (1980) *Meditation: Self-Regulation Strategy and Altered State of Consciousness*. New York: Aldine.

Tirch, D. (2010) Mindfulness as a context for the cultivation of compassion. *International Journal of Cognitive Therapy*, 3(2), 113–123.

Wallace, R.K. (1970) Physiological effects of transcendental meditation. *Science*, 167, 1751–1754.

10
Schema-Focused Mindfulness: an Eight-Session Protocol

Michiel van Vreeswijk and Jenny Broersen

In 2006, the idea to offer mindfulness techniques in Schema Therapy in a structured program was developed and this protocol was published in the Netherlands in 2009 (van Vreeswijk, Broersen and Schurink, 2009). In that period, mindfulness techniques were increasingly being implemented in ST and this continued in the years thereafter (see Part III, Chapters 6–9). However, for patients with personality problems, there was no structured training program for the implementation of these techniques in ST. It is a development that has hardly been investigated.

Mindfulness techniques were investigated in two randomized studies into relapsing depression (Taesdale *et al.*, 2000; Ma and Taesdale, 2004) and for some other symptoms reports of implementation, uncontrolled studies, and some case descriptions are known (see Baer, 2003, 2006; Bohlmeijer, Prenger, Taal and Cuijpers, 2010; Hofmann, Sawyer, Witt and Oh, 2010 for meta-analyses and reviews).

This chapter describes in brief an eight-session protocol for schema-focused mindfulness (for a more extended protocol see van Vreeswijk, Broersen and Schurink, 2009) and is developed in particular for patients with personality disorders who find schemas and modes difficult to grasp.

In Practice

Schema Therapy is an integrative psychotherapy, based on cognitive behavioral therapy, Gestalt Therapy, bonding therapy, object relations, and the constructivist and psychodynamic schools. The therapeutic techniques used in ST can roughly be divided into three interventions: cognitive, experiential, and behavioral (see Part III, Chapter 3). The therapeutic alliance is also essential part of ST. Imagery exercises, chair work techniques, and role-play are examples of the techniques. Sometimes relaxation exercises and mindfulness techniques are added. The implementation of

The Wiley Blackwell Handbook of Schema Therapy: Theory, Research, and Practice, First Edition.
Edited by Michiel van Vreeswijk, Jenny Broersen, and Marjon Nadort.
© 2012 John Wiley & Sons, Ltd. Published 2015 by John Wiley & Sons, Ltd.

mindfulness techniques in patients with personality disorders isn't a new development: Linehan used it in dialectical behavior therapy. This is about learning mindfulness techniques without using meditation. In mindfulness training such as described in this protocol, (shortened) meditation exercises are used.

Learning mindfulness techniques can give the patient a new perspective. By becoming aware of the schemas and modes that are triggered in a situation. Through a mindfulness based and a non-judgmental attitude, room is created to make well-considered choices concerning the way in which the patient wants to react to the triggering of his schema and modes, instead of reacting on automatic pilot. The following case illustrates a patient who follows the schema mindfulness protocol (see Box 1).

In practice, this experience shows that patients find imagery exercises less difficult when they practice mindfulness exercises more often. In the mindfulness exercises, patients are asked to close their eyes and focus completely on themselves. The same is asked of them in the imagery exercises.

In practice, it seems that the implementation of mindfulness techniques is complex for both the therapist and the patient, as the case illustrates (see Box 2). The patient is confronted with a new therapy method and it takes a long time to feel comfortable and safe with this. The occasional use of mindfulness techniques in patients with severe personality problems sometimes meets a lot of resistance. Awareness of emotions, modes, and schemas can be painful and confrontational. For impulsive patients slowing down in a therapy session by means of a mindfulness exercise is often impossible without extensive practice. A clear framework with a full explanation of the method and purpose of this technique is required to safeguard security. For this reason, the choice was made to group the mindfulness techniques in a module, especially focused

Box 1:

Davy talks about how he is very angry with his wife. Yesterday evening, a friend was visiting and she sided with this friend. Davy became angry, but tried to control himself. Over the past year he has abused his wife regularly. Eventually, he could no longer control himself and exploded, even though the children were at home.

The therapist starts the session with a schema mindfulness exercise; this time he makes Davy aware of the triggering mode that occurred in the situation last night.

During the evaluation of the exercise, Davy is surprised – his Angry Child mode is now less present. More room has been created. He is aware that the Vulnerable Child mode is also present, but is overshadowed by the Angry Child mode. He remarks that he actually feels very afraid – afraid that his wife will let him down and will eventually leave him. Actually, he has been fearful in relationships with others his whole life. He realizes that he never lets this show. Through this exercise, he sees his modes as "the children in a family." They all are entitled to attention and sometimes the silent child, in this case the Vulnerable Child mode, should be given more attention. An Angry Child must be held in check sometimes. Because of this awareness, he manages to step out of the Angry Child mode and intends sharing this awareness with his wife when he returns home.

> **Box 2:**
>
> In the schema day-treatment group, Susan usually started a discussion of the events of the previous week at the beginning of the session. This time, she is full of a conflict she has had with her boyfriend after she drank too much wine and injured herself. With increasing stress, her suspicion rises and she becomes more impulsive. She can hardly control herself whilst telling her story and this makes the group members uneasy. The group therapists had planned to try a mindfulness technique in this schema day-treatment group. They have never tried this technique before with this group. After a short explanation of the purpose of the technique, they ask the group members to close their eyes and focus on themselves. During the exercise, which both therapists participate in, the group becomes very uneasy. Some do not participate and Susan is obviously very upset by the fact that she cannot finish her story. The feeling of insecurity within the group increases. The group therapists also feel very uncomfortable and curtail the exercise. After the session, they decide not to use this technique for the time being.

on patients with personality problems. In eight sessions, the patients are taught the (basic) mindfulness techniques, in which the schemas and modes are also a focal point. This protocol is a training, which means that acquiring skills is the main purpose.

Approach

Mindfulness and Schema Therapy: Practical Training for Personality Problems (van Vreeswijk, Broersen and Schurink, 2009) describes a protocol that can be offered as a separate training or as part of individual or group ST in outpatient or inpatient settings. The book consists of a manual for trainers and a workbook for patients, and includes two CDs with schema mindfulness exercises.

Prior to commencing, schema questionnaires are completed and the results are discussed with the patient. Attention is paid to potential pitfalls arising from schema and mode triggering. This makes it difficult to regularly complete the exercises in the workbook for a patient with the Insufficient Self-Control/Self-Discipline schema. By discussing this with the patient prior to the training and by presenting it as a challenge, he is more motivated to finish the training. Based on the results of the questionnaires, the three highest scoring schemas and modes are identified. Establishing this helps the patient and the trainer to focus during the early stage of the training. Explanation about the training protocol is also important in the discussions preceding this training protocol. Usually, one or two assessment sessions are sufficient to determine whether a patient is suitable. If necessary, the trainer can suggest more sessions, for example when he questions the patient's motivation.

Session 1

Explanations about the concepts and working methods of mindfulness and Schema Therapy are the focus point of this session.

The regular basic mindfulness exercises ("raison" exercise and body scan) are completed and the patient is asked to choose a small daily activity that he is going to pay close attention to. The patient is also asked to complete a mindfulness questionnaire at set times. This is a tool to help the patient become more aware of the extent to which his mindfulness fluctuates and to stimulate him to think about the possible cause of this, without the implication that an immediate change has to be made. The session concludes with a short mindfulness exercise.

Session 2

This session begins and ends with a short mindfulness exercise. The patient is told that from now on every session will begin and end like this. The theme of this session is to observe the surroundings with more awareness. Situations from the past week are evaluated through an mindfulness based and stimulating attitude of the trainer. Homework is discussed. Situations in which the patient was not satisfied or in which things didn't go as he expected are reviewed with awareness. Possible schema triggering is tentatively tested. During the session, a mindfulness exercise focused on becoming aware of the surroundings is practiced.

Session 3

This session focuses on breathing. Breathing can be used as a neutral anchor in moments of upheaval or painful emotions. During this session, there is also an exercise focused on painful events and the possible origin of schemas and modes. This is not always easy for the patient, but everyday practice proves that this exercise is often used when a patient is aware of his difficulties. The patient with the Insufficient Self-Control/Self-Discipline schema often comments that he is becoming bored with the training at this point. He tends not to listen to the CDs and no longer reads the workbook. The novelty of the training has gone and he has switched his attention to other stimuli. A patient with the Unrelenting Standards/Hypercriticalness schema often comments that he should be feeling better by now and the therapy should have yielded results. The trainer reminds the patient of the assessment in which potential pitfalls originating from the schemas and modes were discussed, when necessary. This helps the patient to look at the training from a different perspective.

Session 4

Broadening awareness of schemas and modes starts in this session. The exercise with attention for difficulties has often triggered a lot of issues and offers enough material for a follow-up with other exercises. One of the exercises is "Getting to know your schemas even better" (van Vreeswijk, Broersen and Schurink, 2009).

In this session, there is also an exercise in juggling with a mindfulness based attitude. After this exercise, which often brings about many changes in modes, the coping schema that the patient uses is discussed.

"Getting to know your schemas even better"
Practice in experience
Start by focusing your attention on your breathing. Where do you feel it? . . . Focus your attention on the part of your body where you feel your breath. It could be that you feel your breathing by focusing on your abdomen as it moves up and down with every breath you take. It could be that you feel your breathing in your nose when the air enters and exits with every breath you take. Focus on where you are most aware of your breathing . . . What makes you aware that you are inhaling and exhaling?

When you're ready, focus your attention on the memory that evokes this much emotion for you . . . Bring your attention to what you now experience physically, emotionally, and mentally . . .

Now be aware of your breathing . . . Focus your attention on that part of your body where you are most aware of your breathing. . . .

Practice part
After you have completed the experience exercise, you can ask yourself what you have experienced, what you have been made aware of. It can help to close your eyes or to keep them closed when you try to answer the questions or you can stare at an imaginary point.

Ask yourself whether you have reacted to the situation in an unusual way. Would others have reacted the same way in this situation? . . . What was the effect of your behavior on others? . . . Did your behavior lead to an increasing intensity of emotions? . . . Did it lead to more overreacting or to avoidance? . . . If your reaction, your thoughts, or your emotions were different or more intense than at the moment where you reacted from your Healthy Adult mode, you are dealing with a schema that is activated at that moment. What triggered your schema? . . . Did you feel excluded from the group (Social Isolation/Alienation schema)? . . . Did you have the idea that others can do everything better than you and that things always goes badly for you (Failure schema)? . . . Or did you forget your appointment, forget to bring your things, fail to finish your work, buy things you didn't need (Insufficient Self-Control/Self-Discipline schema)? . . . Each schema has its own unique triggers. If you are aware of what is happening, what you feel, think, do in a certain situation, this offers a new opportunity to become aware and search for what triggered your schema.

What were your feelings? . . . Where in your body did you feel your emotions most? . . . Each schema has its own color of emotions and its own place in your body. You can learn to recognize your schemas by the composition and intensity of the emotions that arise in certain situations . . . What were your thoughts? . . . Did you, for example, start to worry whether you had hurt the other by demanding attention, whether you had short-changed the other (Subjugation schema)? . . . Where do these thoughts, feelings, behaviors come from? . . . If you dare not to tell a friend that you feel vulnerable and damaged (Defectiveness/Shame schema), then it could be that you were bullied because

> you were different from the others in the past, for example, softer/not as tough . . .
>
> I will now to count slowly to three and at three you can open your eyes again. Before moving straight into the action mode, take some time to focus your attention on yourself and on the surroundings you are now in . . . 1 . . . 2 . . . 3 . . .

Session 5

What is probably the most difficult subject will be discussed in session 5: accepting. For many patients, it is important that something will be done with feelings such as pain, distress, anger, and anxiety. Avoiding, fighting against it (overstraining), or resigning to it are strategies that occur often. Accepting what it is without feeling the need to always do something about it is often new to them. Next to the psycho-education, mindfulness based exercises, focused on accepting everything that is present at that moment (schema/mode triggering) will be done.

Session 6

The patient is invited to investigate schemas. Are schemas based on facts? As well as the minfulness based exercises, there is homework that is focused on the cognitions that belong to a specific schema. Patients are stimulated to let go of schemas and modes and to accept them less as the absolute truth.

Session 7

In the mindfulness exercise, the Healthy Adult and Happy Child are explicitly approached, but the present schema-confirming and schema-negating thoughts and behaviors are also elicited. Attention is paid to what is needed to help the Healthy Adult and Happy Child to grow.

Session 8

The Healthy Adult and Happy Child are the focus, but also what someone needs in contact with the other. This will be done by the exercise "Mindfulness to yourself as a child and as an adult" (van Vreeswijk, Broersen and Schurink, 2009).

In the last session, the patient starts to juggle again. During this exercise, which is focused on juggling with awareness and throwing in cooperation with the other, the patient becomes aware in a playful manner of what he now needs in his contact with the other.

"With attention to yourself as a child and as an adult"
Practice in experience part 1
Sit up straight with your back against the back of your chair. Place both your feet on the ground. Close your eyes and focus on your breathing. Focus on the part of your body where you are most aware of your inhaling and exhaling . . . If you notice that your attention wanders to thoughts or images, congratulate yourself that you have become aware of this. Then focus once again on your breathing . . .

Practice part 1
After you have completed the experience exercise above, we ask you to keep your eyes closed or to focus on an imaginary point, while you move into an attentive do-position with attention on your breathing. Imagine a place where you feel safe . . .

Maybe there is someone there whom you trust and love . . .

Maybe you are in a place where it's nice and warm and where the mood is relaxed, a place where you feel safe, protected and supported, a place where you can be yourself, a place where you don't have to pretend to be better or stronger than you feel at this moment . . .

Evoke feelings thoughts and images with MINDFULL and accepting wisdom. Do not judge what comes into your mind. Know that you can always return your attention to your breathing in the safe place you're in. . . . Maybe something is triggered from the time your schemas and mood states originated. Maybe you experience a link between the pattern of your emotional reactions and how they originated. Select something you know you can study with awareness. If something comes up that evokes too much, save that for a moment when you can handle it. If this is the case, search for something you can look at with awareness. If someone comes to mind with whom you experienced that you did not get what you needed, bring this person into your consciousness with awareness. Imagine that this person looks at you with an open mind and approaches you with awareness, that he wants to listen to you and be there for you and your needs. . . . Allow yourself to tell this person what you want to say openly and honestly. Don't hold anything back. Take your time to reflect on what you want to say, and then say it. Tell this person what you need from him openly and with awareness for your needs. For example, that he is more present, more sensitive, more attentive, or caring. Use those words that fit you best. If necessary, use your breathing as an anchor. This can help you to talk calmly and to say what you want to say to this person. . . . See how the other listens to you and hears you. See how the other appreciates that you are openly discussing your feelings, thoughts, and your needs. . . . Let the other say what you need to hear him say in your consciousness, whatever that may be. Let him say what feels good for you. . . .

Experience part 2
After the other has spoken in a supportive way to you, return to your breathing once again with awareness. Notice how your breath enters and leaves your body.

> Be aware of your physical experiences. . . . Be aware of the presence or absence of emotions and thoughts. . . . Allow emotions, physical experiences, and thoughts with awareness without censoring or criticizing them. Study them as if you are seeing them for the first time. . . . If you notice that your attention wanders, that you are going into automatic pilot, acknowledge this. Be aware of it for a moment and then return to the last thing you looked at with awareness. . . . Now focus your attention on your breathing, on your stomach, chest, throat, mouth, or nose, on the part of your body where you are aware of your breathing without having to change anything about it. . . .
>
> *Practice part 2*
> After you have completed the experience exercise above, you can ask yourself what you have experienced, what you have looked at with awareness. It can help to close your eyes and keep them closed when you try to answer the questions for yourself, or you can focus on an imaginary point. Where do you feel your breathing? . . . . What do you feel in your body? . . . . Which emotions are there? . . . . What does it feel like to evoke thoughts and images without censoring them? . . .
>
> What does it feel like to make the other listen to you and to let the other say what you would like to hear? What do you observe? . . . Which emotions do you feel? . . . Where do you feel it in your body? . . .
>
> I will now count slowly to three and at three you can open your eyes again. Before moving straight into the action mode, take some time to focus your attention on yourself and on the surroundings you are now in . . . 1 . . . 2 . . . 3 . . .

Follow-up or further treatment

For some patients, termination of the treatment is indicated because it fits in with the help they require or because they have had a long history of treatment before this. In these cases the mindfulness schema protocol is given as a separate module without the intention of offering follow-up therapy. After this protocol ends, there are two follow-up sessions during which how the patient managed to deal with the techniques that were taught in the training is discussed. If the protocol is part of continuing Schema Therapy, beginning and ending each session with a short schema mindfulness exercise is advised. Experience teaches that this benefits the affect regulation and the patient will keep doing the schema mindfulness exercises on his own. Patients who have had schema mindfulness training appear to be more open to other experiential techniques within Schema Therapy.

Pitfalls and Tips

This example (see Box 3) describes a patient who apparently seems to be making progress through schema mindfulness. However, in a case such as this, a therapist needs to be aware of the Detached Protector mode that seems to be increased

> **Box 3:**
>
> Marc tells his mindfulness trainer that he has been doing well over the last few weeks. He has had three sessions of the schema-focused mindfulness protocol thus far. The therapist asks Marc how he notices that things are going well with him. He is no longer preoccupied with what people think of him. It doesn't bother him as much. Marc is pleased with this. He is also considering quitting his job, because money is not important after all. The schema mindfulness exercises help him to relax, help him not to feel anything anymore. "It doesn't get any better," Marc says.

> **Box 4:**
>
> Frank, a 40-year-old Schema Therapist, has had flu for a few days, but he still feels he has to go to work. He has many patients and has just started the therapy phase with several of them. He is afraid that cancelling a few sessions will cause a delay in the therapeutic process. Today, he has a number of sessions with patients with whom he has started a schema-focused mindfulness protocol, but the day starts badly when he arrives at work late and he has to rush to his first patient. During the session Frank remarks that he is a little absentminded. He thinks about how to make up for the lost time that was caused by the delay. His patient who experiences many emotions with the mindfulness exercises asks for advice. She wants solutions for the painful emotions she experiences. For Frank, this feels like she is not cooperating. Doesn't she understand that mindfulness is all about not being action-oriented?

through the schema mindfulness exercises. An exploration of which state of mind a patient is in, and what brought about this state of mind, is the first step a schema therapist can take here. Furthermore, it is important to explain to the patient that the purpose of schema mindfulness isn't for people to detach themselves. Although practicing schema mindfulness can give more inner peace, the goal is that a patient learns to experience his emotions, schema-triggering, and modes with an open attitude. How to choose the manner in which he wants to react can be a follow-up step.

For therapists who apply mindfulness techniques in ST it is important to regularly do a mindfulness exercise themselves. A therapist with a heavy case load that moves from one appointment to the next will easily form a rushed impression of the patient and is less capable of listening with an open and inquiring attitude to what the patient is saying. Pressure is placed on limited reparenting in this way and there is a chance that the therapist will make hasty assumptions about what is going on. For example, he may rush to diagnose which schemas or modes are triggered in this patient and offer instant solutions.

In this case (see Box 4) described, the therapist himself isn't mindful and he appears to be in the Demanding Parent mode. During the session he is not capable of listening to the patient with an open and interested attitude and so cannot be a

> **Box 5:**
>
> Julia is touchy and easily becomes jealous when her boyfriend talks to other women. Yesterday, she was very annoyed that he didn't do the housework. During the evaluation of the mindfulness exercise, she is particularly aware of the Angry Child mode. In the exercise she is also asked to be aware of other mood states that might be present. It appears that Julia is afraid, but because of the Angry Child mode, she is not conscious of this. It is significant that she takes little notice of what is happening to her boyfriend.

> **Box 6:**
>
> After five sessions, two group trainers, who provide the schema-focused mindfulness protocol to a group of 10 participants with personality disorders, notice that they are beginning to doubt themselves. In each session, there is a lot of criticism of the mindfulness exercises. Allen, one of the participants, is a little detached, somewhere else with his thoughts. He looks angry. Jacky is annoyed by the slowness and voice of the group trainer. She thinks that there should be more room for the evaluation of the events of the previous week. She also thinks that there isn't enough attention given to evaluating the exercises. The other participants are quiet; it seems as if they don't dare say anything. The group trainers feel that they can't get it right with this training group.

role model for her. Even stronger, the message he puts across is that the patient should be able to do this. Her action orientation and Demanding Parent mode can become further encouraged by this. With an impulsive patient who doesn't practice, this therapist would not have been sufficiently capable of investigating why. A patient who falls asleep during the exercises would probably be neglected by the therapist in this session, yet it could be investigated with the patient whether falling asleep is a form of schema avoidance.

In all cases it is important that the therapist regularly observes himself, the patient, and the therapeutic alliance with an attentive attitude. This doesn't always occur. It is a challenge to be aware of switching to automatic pilot and moving back to the attentive Healthy Adult every single time.

The Angry Child mode can sometimes create such an intense feeling that there is little room to observe what is happening to the other person. In this case (see Box 5), the potential pitfall can be that the therapist focuses the mindfulness exercise only on Julia's schema and mode-triggering. She can have a new perspective if the focus is broadened by focusing on the emotional experience of her boyfriend and to give attention to his possible schema and mode triggering. This can improve her empathy and understanding for her boyfriend. The new perspective can help her to turn off the automatic pilot, after which she can make a conscious choice about how to deal with her triggered schemas and modes at that moment.

This case (see Box 6) illustrates that group processes also take place in training groups and that there can be a lot of anxiety and insecurity within a group. A potential pitfall is that trainers focus too much on the group therapeutic process. It is, after all, a training in which learning skills is the goal, and not group therapeutic working. However, it is important to build sufficient cohesion in training, in order to make it safe enough for the participants to learn these skills. Implementing this protocol, there surely are many more potential pitfalls, see van Vreeswijk, Broersen, and Schurink (2009).

References

Baer, R.A. (2003) Mindfulness training as a clinical intervention: a conceptual and empirical review. *Clinical Psychology: Science and Practice 10*, 125–143.

Baer, R. (ed.) (2006) *Mindfulness-based Treatment Approaches. Clinician's Guide to Evidence Base and Applications.* Burlington, VA: Elsevier.

Bohlmeijer, E., Prenger, R., Taal, E. and Cuijpers, P. (2010) Meta-analysis of the effectiveness of mindfulness-based stress reduction therapy on mental health of adults with a chronic disease: what should the reader not make of it? *Journal Psychosomatic Research, 69*(6), 614–615.

Hofmann, S.G., Sawyer, A.T., Witt, A.A. and Oh, D. (2010) The effect of mindfulness-based therapy on anxiety and depression: a meta-analytic review. *Journal of Consulting and Clinical Psychology, 78*(2), 169–183.

Ma, S.H. and Taesdale, J.D. (2004) Mindfulness-based cognitive therapy for depression: replication and exploration of differential relapse prevention effects. *Journal of Consulting and Clinical Psychology 72*, 31–40.

Taesdale, J.D., Segal, Z.V., Williams, J.M. *et al.* (2000) Prevention of relapse/recurrence in major depression by mindfulness based cognitive therapy. *Journal of Consulting and Clinical Psychology 68*, 615–623.

Vreeswijk, M.F. van, Broersen, J. and Schurink, G. (2009) *Mindfulness en Schematherapie: Praktische Training bij Persoonlijkheidsproblematiek.* Houten: Bohn Stafleu van Loghum.

11

The Impact of Measuring
Therapy Results and Therapeutic Alliance

Michiel van Vreeswijk, Jenny Broersen and Philip Spinhoven

"Information is knowledge" and "knowledge is power" are well-known expressions. Within psychotherapy, these statements are mainly reserved for researchers who write about therapy efficiency or for diagnosticians who want to map out a patient's problems. But what is the impact of measuring on the patients themselves? Does therapy have a greater effect if the patient receives feedback about his therapy, as measured by some predetermined tool? Is it useful to give feedback to therapists about the progress of therapy?

This chapter describes the method by which measurement tools can be used within Schema Therapy. Specifically, it examines how feedback on test results can be given to patients, how to deal with feedback regarding therapy results, and what the effect on patients and therapists will be examined. In addition, the clinical experience of the authors and the work of Lambert and colleagues, who have conducted much research in this area, will be used (see Lambert, 2005; Lambert et al., 2008).

In Practice

Systematically measuring a patient's progress in therapy is increasingly used in Dutch institutes. An example is the Routine Outcome Monitoring (ROM) procedure, as used by the Rijngeest group in Leiden and other Dutch institutes (de Beurs, 2005).

For this procedure, the patient completes, using a computer, a number of general and disorder-specific questions. In addition, the patient undertakes structured interviews with a research assistant. These measurements are carried out throughout the treatment and the results are taken into consideration regarding (changes in) the treatment plan.

Thus far, this method of monitoring progress in therapy is restricted to Axis I disorders and ROM isn't yet available for patients being treated for personality disorders. However, "The [Dutch] Work Council recommends the monitoring of treatment progress, especially in cases of long-term treatment, in order that any possible therapeutic stagnation will be detected in time, enabling a revision of the assessment to be carried out where necessary" (Werkgroep richtlijn persoonlijkheidsstoornissen [Concept Dutch Multidisciplinary Guideline Personality Disorders], 2008, p. 47). How the monitoring in Schema Therapy takes place isn't developed in great detail.

What are the advantages of routine outcome monitoring during Schema Therapy?

1. *Improvement as positive confirmation:* Measured positive therapy results, no matter how small, can be a positive confirmation for both patient and therapist of the work that has been done so far. This evidence of progress can also provide support in times of difficulty by acting as a reminder that progress has been made.
2. *Early detection of deterioration in symptoms/schemas and modes:* Deterioration in symptoms during therapy is found in 5–10% of patients (Lambert and Ogles, 2004). Approximately 40% don't experience any effect from the treatment (Hansen, Lambert and Forman, 2002), and a small proportion experience a negative result (Lambert, 2005). Taking the optimistic view that patients will experience improvement, therapists appear to be poor at predicting which patients will relapse and eventually experience a negative result (Norcross, 2003; Hannan *et al.*, 2005). They tend to dismiss psychometric data. Therapists are unable to identify which relapses are acceptable and when they should take action (Lambert, personal correspondence, 2007). It remains to be seen if relapses in patients with personality disorders are a necessary step, in order to increase insight into illness without therapeutic interference (increasing frequency of sessions, adapting treatment interventions, reconsidering medication policy, reconsideration diagnosis).
3. *Observing negative progress in therapy is a benefit:* Evidence from controlled studies, where a group of patients receiving systematic feedback (F group) on the progress of their therapy is compared with a group not receiving feedback (NF group), reveals that almost twice as many patients from the feedback group recover. In addition, this group experiences fewer relapses (Lambert *et al.*, 2001, 2002). Feedback appears to be especially important for patients who relapse during therapy, regardless of when they experience this relapse. Furthermore, it emerges that the advantage of feedback is greater when provided by more experienced therapists than by inexperienced therapists (Lambert *et al.*, 2002). These therapists may require more peer supervision and supervision tools.
4. *Evaluating treatment policy is useful throughout therapy:* Although previous research shows that therapy results can be predicted based on the extent of progress at the beginning of therapy and that these results continue to apply following therapy (Haas *et al.*, 2002), a study in progress shows that the result of therapy can best be predicted by the most recent measurement (Percevic *et al.*, 2006). Early progress in therapy is only predictive of outcome for therapies in which the duration of therapy is predetermined. In all other cases, the results of the most recent measurement are used as a reference point either to extend the duration of therapy or to adapt treatment strategies.

Approach

The use of measurement results within Schema Therapy

Within GGZ Delfland and G-kracht psycho-medical center in Delft (The Netherlands), patients receive a questionnaire package at the beginning of Schema Therapy, the contents of which include a schema questionnaire (SQ, Dutch version; Sterk and Rijkeboer, 1997; YSQ L2, English version Young and Brown, 2003), the schema modes questionnaire (SMI-1 Dutch version; Lobbestael, van Vreeswijk, Arntz and Spinhoven, 2010; SMI 1.1 English version Young et al., 2008), one or two personality questionnaires, and a symptom questionnaire. The results are discussed with the patient in the assessment session, during which the patient will be asked if he recognizes the results and whether there are any examples in his life in which certain schemas or modes were active. Any possible differences between the results of the questionnaires and the patient report, or what emerged from previous treatments, are examined with the patient. In this way, a start is made on increasing the patient's awareness and insight into his illness, giving psycho-education and working toward a case conceptualization. The patient receives a copy of the test report, as well as an explanation of how, throughout the treatment, from time to time, the same set of questionnaires will be given as a means to measure the progress of the therapy (see Figure 11.1, see page 286).

During predetermined evaluation sessions, the patient is asked to complete the SQ (English version: YSQ L2), SMI-1 (English version: SMI 1.1), a symptom list, and the client appreciation thermometer (Trimbos, 2003). The results are compared with the benchmark. Differences (both negative and positive changes) are added to a test report, which can be discussed with colleagues, Schema Therapists, and the patient. Before the results are discussed with the patient, he is asked if he has noticed progress, if he has any ideas about the factors that influence the progress or relapses, and what he expects from the results of the questionnaires. This increases the possibility that the patient will formulate his own opinion instead of basing his opinion on the results of the questionnaires. Following this, the results are submitted as feedback, and the similarities and differences between the ideas of the patient and the results of the questionnaires are discussed. The therapist then gives his opinion about any progress or relapses. Finally, both patient and therapist discuss their further expectations from the therapy and any possible adaptations where necessary. If progress is sufficient and the aims of the therapy have been satisfied, follow-up sessions will be scheduled, as well as a date set on which the therapy can be brought to a conclusion.

The Meaning and Interpretation of Outcome in Schema Therapy

Although completing the questionnaires demands considerable time from the patient and writing a test report also asks for a time commitment from the therapist, on the whole, the effort is deemed worthwhile. Many patients recognize themselves in the test results, and they feel they are being taken seriously. The results from evaluations

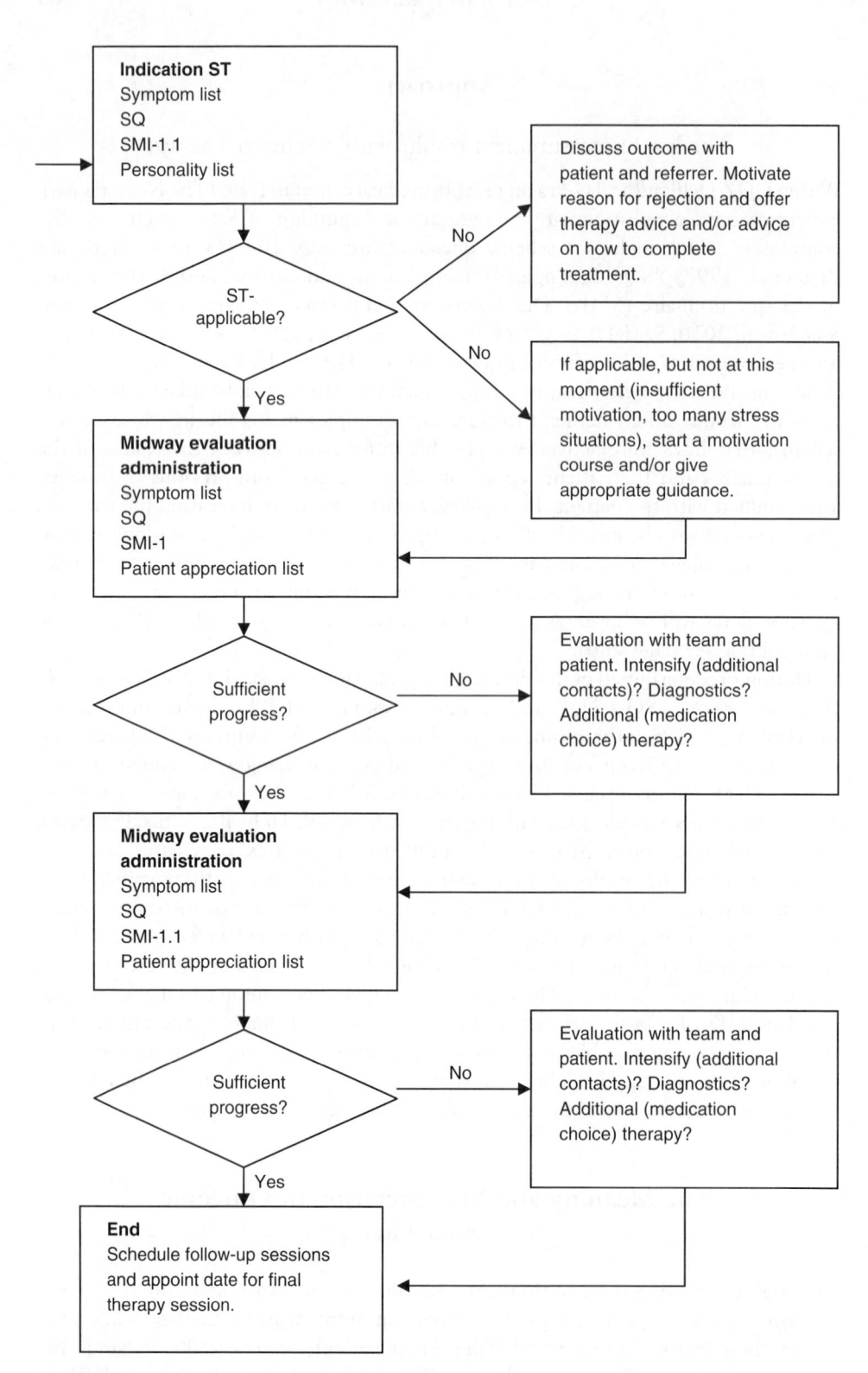

Figure 11.1 Flowchart evaluation process for Schema Therapy, as implemented in, for example, ST treatment in Delfland and G-kracht, Psycho-Medical Center, Delft (The Netherlands)

> John has a strong Failure schema. Every session, he begins by examining all the things that have gone wrong. He has formed an image of himself as someone who does little and someone who when he does do something, always fails. He concentrates solely on where he has failed. The midway evaluation reveals that the patient shows a lot of progress on both symptoms level and schemas and modes. His therapist discusses the results with John in relation to his self-image as someone who always fails. It emerges that the patient is afraid to be in the Healthy Adult mode, afraid to take responsibility and enjoy life. John and the therapist look for alternative ways of dealing with this anxiety, rather than continuing schema-confirming and schema-avoiding behavior.

during the therapeutic process and from final evaluations can act as a confirmation of the patient's feelings. In this way, the tests can provide further confirmation of positive therapy results. Likewise, when a patient shows improvement in the questionnaires, but doesn't experience any improvement himself, the results can be used for therapy intervention.

During the midway evaluation (see Box above), some patients show a (further) relapse or stagnation at the symptom level and/or in the severity of schemas and modes. These results can come as a surprise to some patients, who believe that everything is going well. In these cases, the therapist and the patient look for possible explanations for the difference between the test results and the patient's ideas about this. Causes for discrepancy can be:

1. The result of a temporary situation (e.g., the death of a loved one), but in general the patient is performing better, as the concrete changes in his daily life and in therapy show.
2. A certain aspect in their life is going so well (e.g., a patient in love) that the patient experiences every part of his life as going well.
3. The patient suppresses his feelings in contact with others and the therapist, but (somehow) realizes that things are getting worse.

In these cases, interventions, including reality testing, an advantage and disadvantage analysis regarding change, determining the patient's motivation to change, as well as psycho-education about Schema Therapy and mental symptoms should be started. Furthermore, it is important that the test results are taken seriously, and that the patient and therapist together examine what the patient needs – either a continuation of the therapy policy or adaption of the therapy interventions.

A similar open attitude is adopted toward test results that confirm the suspicions of the patient (and of the therapist) in cases of stagnation or deterioration. This open and neutral attitude often makes it easier for patients to express criticism regarding the therapy. In doing so, a situation where patients feel their problems aren't being recognized, as may have been the case in the past (schema triggering Emotional Deprivation), is prevented.

For "not on track" patients, Harmon *et al.* (2005) suggest additional interventions in the field of working alliance, patient motivation, and social networking. The interventions suggested are illustrated with examples from the authors of this chapter. They concentrate on Schema Therapy, but do not claim to be exhaustive on the subject. For specific ST interventions, see Part III, Chapter 3.

Working alliance: interventions

Narrative reviews and a meta-analysis of the role of therapeutic alliance indicate that there is a consistent connection between the quality of the therapeutic alliance at the beginning of the treatment and the final treatment result, regardless of the therapeutic orientation (Martin, Garske and Davis, 2000; Orlinsky, Ronnestad and Willutzki, 2004). In this, the quality of the working alliance as judged by the patient seems to have more predictive value than the quality as judged by the therapist. This positive connection can be attributed, only in part, to symptom reduction at the beginning of the treatment. The quality of the working alliance, therefore, is more than just an expression of the patient's appreciation of the course of the treatment. However, the therapeutic alliance is most often studied in the context of psychodynamic and experiential treatments. It also appears to be important within the framework of cognitive and cognitive behavioral treatments (Waddington, 2002). It is likely, especially in the treatment of personality disorders, that the therapeutic alliance plays a crucial role (Young, Klosko and Weishaar, 2003; Beck, Freeman and Davis, 2004). This can be because personality disorders are characterized by chronic and invalidating interpersonal problems, which interfere with starting and maintaining a therapeutic alliance.

The importance of the working alliance for treatment of personality disorders can be divided into different aspects. First, based on the available research, it seems that the quality of the working alliance, as judged by the patient at the beginning of the treatment, predicts a more positive treatment result for cognitive therapy for patients with an avoiding or obsessive-compulsive personality disorder (Strauss *et al.*, 2006), and a better treatment result of Schema Therapy for patients with borderline personality disorder (Spinhoven, Giesen-Bloo, van Dyck, Kooiman and Arntz, 2007). Furthermore, for ST patients with an anxiety disorder and Cluster C personality features, the mutual commitment of therapist and patient, as judged by independent assessors, predicts a decrease in the credibility of the schemas treated in therapy but not the extent of symptom reduction throughout the course of the treatment (Hoffart, Sexton, Nordahl and Stiles, 2005). Finally, it has been shown that the quality of the early working alliance, as judged by both therapist and patient, predicts a premature termination of treatment. This is important, because the dropout rate in personality disorders can be as high as 67% (Perry, Banon and Ianni, 1999; Leichsenring and Liebing, 2003). These results indicate that a good therapeutic alliance from the beginning of treatment can help keep patients in treatment and contributes to a more positive overall result. This is in particular a challenge for the therapists of patients with particularly dysfunctional interpersonal skills for whom it seems that the therapeutic alliance is less well established at the beginning of the treatment (Strauss *et al.*, 2006).

Furthermore, outcomes from the few studies that have been done show that the development of the working alliance throughout the course of treatment is very important. This concerns both the more global development of the working alliance, as measured in several treatment sessions, as well as changes in the therapeutic alliance, measured in fewer sessions. In ST treatment of patients with a borderline personality disorder, it has been concluded that when the patient judges that the therapeutic alliance developed well in the first year of the treatment, the treatment result is more positive in the following phase (Spinhoven *et al.*, 2007). This result accords with clinical experience that building and developing a good therapeutic alliance in the first phase of the treatment is required in order to successfully treat more damaging themes in later phases of the treatment.

When the development of the therapeutic alliance is examined in detail, it seems that the development varies per session, and that these minor changes in the quality of the therapeutic alliance are also of therapeutic importance. A certain type of change is the so-called "working alliance rupture." This is related to difficulties in maintaining the working alliance or dealing with a sudden deterioration in it. These ruptures occur mainly when the patient's core schemas are activated during treatment, when activated core schemas start to play a role in the treatment sessions, or when the therapist fails to take enough time for problems that arise within the therapeutic alliances. Focusing on identifying and working on these working alliance ruptures can help to mitigate the effect of maladaptive schemas and offer corrective experiences to counter this change (Beck *et al.*, 2004). Research into cognitive therapy in patients with an avoiding or obsessive-compulsive personality disorder shows that a sharp decrease in the quality of the therapeutic alliance followed by an equal increase in the quality of the working alliance is associated with a better therapy result.

In summary, the above findings suggest that it is important for the therapist to closely monitor the quality of the therapeutic alliance and to discuss this with the patient throughout the course of treatment. A good working alliance is a reasonable predictor of therapy dedication and better treatment results. Positive development of the working alliance seems to create a solid base from which to work constructively on more damaging problems for patients in later phases of the treatment. In particular,

> After having some initial problems at the beginning of his Schema Therapy, Peter, who has few social contacts and easily feels rejected (Abandonment/Instability and Mistrust and/or Abuse schema), begins to show some progress. He learns to show and discuss more of his vulnerable side. The therapist then falls ill and the treatment is discontinued for several weeks. On resuming the therapy, it is difficult to reconnect with Peter. The therapist explores, in an open and non-defensive manner, how Peter experienced the interruption of therapy and encourages him to express his negative feelings about this. Peter discovers that expressing his anger and mistrust doesn't destroy the therapeutic alliance and begins to see that the interruption caused a triggering of the old schemas of Abandonment/Instability and Mistrust and/or Abuse. After the differences between the current therapy situation and previous situations have been explored, the therapeutic alliance is restored. They can then continue the treatment with, for example, historic role-playing around themes such as abandonment and rejection by his parents.

the therapist should not ignore sudden fluctuations in the quality of the therapeutic alliance. It is precisely these working alliance ruptures that offer possibilities for identification and treatment of the activation of maladaptive schemas within the therapeutic alliance. They contribute to a more positive development of the therapeutic alliance over time and to achieving schema change and a better treatment outcome.

Considering the significance of the therapeutic alliance, an important question is which interventions a therapist has at his disposal to optimize the quality of the therapeutic alliance. As traditionally emphasized in client-centered therapy, this is specifically a matter of therapeutic attitude. Both cognitive therapy and Schema Therapy rightly emphasize the importance of an open and empathic relationship, which enables the therapist to give psycho-education and to function as a role model for the patient (Beck et al., 2004). Schema Therapy uses "limited reparenting" when the therapist partly fulfills the unrequited needs of the patient in an attempt to develop healthier schemas (Young et al., 2003). This is in sharp contrast to the more psychodynamic-focused treatment, such as transference-focused psychotherapy or mentalization-based psychotherapy, in which an active and supporting relationship with the patient is considered counterproductive and even anti-therapeutic (Bateman and Fonagy, 2004).

Apart from these general attitudes and interventions, the therapist also has more concrete interventions at his disposal, for productive treatment of working alliance ruptures. Table 11.1 gives an overview with examples.

Table 11.1 Working alliance interventions

Working alliance interventions (Harmon et al., 2005)	Working alliance interventions ST
Discuss the working alliance.	How does the patient view the therapist and which schemas and modes play a role in this? A patient with the schema Mistrust/Abuse won't take the therapist easily into his confidence.
Offer and ask for feedback regarding the working alliance.	To give and ask for feedback can lead to triggering the Abandonment/Instability schema. Mention this explicitly when you give and ask for feedback.
Spend more time on the experiences of your patient.	To what extent does the patient feel emotionally deprived by the therapist?
Spend time on agreeing goals and steps, in order to achieve them, and adapt if necessary.	A patient with the Insufficient Self-Control/Self-Discipline schema can have goals that vary continuously and he can feel the long-term goals take too long. In this case, look for short-term goals.
Take responsibility for the possible contribution of the therapist to the disruption of the working alliance.	A therapist can overcharge a patient due to their Unrelenting Standards/Hypercritical schema. Recognize if the working alliance is disturbed in part as a result of this.

Table 11.1 (*Continued*)

Working alliance interventions (Harmon et al., 2005)	Working alliance interventions ST
React to resistance from the patient by allowing more space/autonomy and discuss the resistance in an acceptable tone of voice.	What is the reason for the patient feeling cornered? Which situations in the past is the patient reminded of? What does the patient expect from the therapist regarding his attitude toward him?
Give (regularly) a rationale for therapy interventions.	Explain how the therapeutic alliance or relationships with group members can lead to the triggering of schemas and how therapy relationships can be used to treat experiences from the past.
Focus on subtle signals that indicate something may not be right with the therapeutic alliance.	Coming late, remaining silent, or not doing homework can fit into the Insufficient Self-Control/Self-Discipline schema, but can also be a way of schema avoidance in the Subjugation schema. Explore this with the patient.
Allow the patient to discuss negative feelings regarding the therapeutic alliance.	Show that expressing anger doesn't directly destroy the working alliance and connect this with the possible Abandonment/Instability schema. If necessary, limitations can be offered in a clearly and regularly manner, as a model for the patient.
Explore with the patient his anxiety about expressing negative feelings about the therapeutic alliance.	Patients with the Subjugation, Self-Sacrifice, Approval and Recognition Seeking, Abandonment/Instability schemas prefer to avoid confrontations. Explain that expressing irritations toward the therapist is healthy and necessary for an equal working alliance.
Give more positive feedback.	Patients with the Failure schema continuously believe that therapy won't succeed. Discuss progress, admit failures, and invite the patient to keep a record of all his positive changes.
Deal with questions such as: What happens on the process level? Is this a case of emotional entanglement?	Which schemas and modes of the therapist are triggered by the patient?
Discuss therapist–patient and therapy–patient matching.	Do the patient and therapist have a good working alliance or are they each other's schema allergies? Does the patient approve of the schema-focused treatment model?
Discuss mutual therapy relationship experiences.	Which schemas and modes (Emotional Deprivation, Abandonment/Instability, Failure, Demanding or Punitive Parent) were triggered when the therapist was late calling the patient in from the waiting room several times? What did the patient experience when the therapist asked emphatically about a certain situation? Discuss also what the therapist feels in such situations. What are the similarities and differences between the experiences of patient and therapist in these situations?

(*Continued*)

Table 11.1 (*Continued*)

Working alliance interventions (Harmon et al., 2005)	Working alliance interventions ST
ST therapeutic alliances in group therapy 1. Where there is an increasing presence of Detached Protectors in the group, the therapist, as a role model, can try to get the patient who is most in the Detached Protector mode, out of this mode by inviting him emphatically to make contact, to validate and to accept his vulnerable side. Explain that the patient is a member of a group, and that he can receive help from the group if he lets them. 2. When there are no irritations, the group therapists can offer psycho-education on the expression of anger in a relationship and the importance of this. They can invite group members to criticize each other and the therapist. 3. With an increase in unacceptable behavior (threatening self-injurious behavior/suicide, running away, or staying away from group therapy) the therapists can set boundaries in an emphatic manner, offering feedback on the behavior they experience from the patient and researching ways to deal with this within the patient group.	

Patient motivation: interventions

Not every patient with personality problems is consistently motivated to carry out therapy homework, attend appointments, or recognize existing problems (Werkgroep richtlijn persoonlijkheidsstoornissen, 2008, p. 67).

Many patients, like Frances, look for rapid results from the therapy. They want to get rid of their negative feelings and thoughts quickly. They believe that working on their problems for a long period of time is too complicated, if they cannot have an absolute guarantee of success. Other patients, who don't directly get what they ask for from the therapist, can feel emotional shortcomings, or abandoned. Some patients

> Frances has problems with her studies. She uses drugs intermittently and regularly drinks large amounts of alcohol. She has a difficult relationship with her parents, who believe she is capable of achieving more in life than she has done thus far. These disagreements escalated to the point where they kicked her out of the house. Frances often doesn't show up for her Schema Therapy or arrives late for sessions. When the therapist tries to raise this issue, she answers with "How interesting . . . How important . . . " When Frances is confronted with her Detached Protector attitude, she becomes emotional. She insists that she would like to change, but that it all takes so long and she has to work so hard at it (Insufficient Self-Control/Self-Discipline). She feels very lonely (Social Isolation/Alienation) and misunderstood (Emotional Deprivation).

feel extremely healthy when the critical stress goes and/or when they are in love. These factors can lead to a decrease in motivation for therapy and in some extreme cases a (premature) ending of the therapy. Interventions focused on increasing the motivation of patients are described in Table 11.2.

Table 11.2 Patient motivation interventions

Patient motivation interventions (Harmon et al., 2005)	Patient motivation interventions ST
Ask open questions about problem behavior. Invite more discussion about this behavior. Attention in itself can lead to awareness and change.	Formulate a case conceptualization with the patient in which possibly guided by his autobiography, he can describe his problems and the relationship with his schemas and modes.
Discuss the negative and positive effects of the behavior.	Discuss the toughness of schemas and modes. Produce an advantage and disadvantage analysis regarding schema change.
Give advice and psycho-education on the negative consequences at a time when patients are able listen to it.	Discuss with the patient the negative consequences of schema avoidance, schema confirmation or schema compensating behavior. Use concrete examples from the life of the patient. Describe the changes that would be possible if the patient confronted the schemas and modes.
Show confidence in the power of the patient in his capacity to change.	Point out aspects of the Healthy Adult and the Happy Child mode that arise from the concrete situations the patient describes.
Avoid giving solutions. Focus on exploring and allowing ambivalent feelings in a patient.	Why does the patient find it difficult to change his schemas/modes? Fear of the loss of loved ones? Fear of accepting responsibility? Search for a new identity? Explore this in a neutral and interested manner.
Avoid focusing on obvious problems when it is clear that patient and therapist aren't focusing on the same problem behavior. Probably, there is problem behavior that the patient doesn't yet dare to acknowledge.	In patients with the Defectiveness/Shame schema it is wise to first extend an open and friendly invitation to discuss anything that bothers him. The therapist can point out that he also experiences shame. This can assist the patient.

ST patient motivation-interventions within group therapy
1. Invite other group members to talk about their experiences regarding change. Which schemas/modes are resistant to change? How much effort does it cost them? What improvement has it offered them? Did they achieve a quick result or has it taken a while?
2. Stimulate the group to ask each other questions and recognize each other's situations, without coming up with solutions right away. Fellow patients tend to feel the need to help the other, sometimes in order to remove an ambivalence that has emerged within the group. Offering solutions will only lead to more feelings of alienation between an unmotivated patient and his more motivated co-patients.
3. Make themes such as anxiety and Defectiveness/Shame into group subjects. Sharing these feelings leads to more understanding and can stimulate an unmotivated patient to show more of his vulnerability.

Social support: interventions

> Barry has had few friends in his life. He has always felt like an outsider. When he is invited to parties, he often doesn't go (avoidance of Social Isolation/Alienation). He wants to be free of the idea that he doesn't fit in. After a successful start to therapy (he tries to go to parties more often), he relapses when his girlfriend breaks off the relationship because she finds him too boring. His Defectiveness/Shame schema is triggered as a result of this. He withdraws into his house and rarely goes out. Besides having some contacts through the computer or on MSN, he gives up hope of ever fitting in.

"The progress of therapeutic improvement is greater when the patient has more social support to fall back on (Werkgroep richtlijn persoonlijkheidsstoornissen, 2008, p. 47). A loss of social support can have a large influence, particularly on a patient who already has a limited social network and who simultaneously feels the need to expand this, but doesn't really dare to and/or isn't able to. The loss of loved ones can lead to a patient clinging desperately to those who are still around, which runs the risk that these people will then distance themselves. In some cases a patient withdraws himself from nearly all social contact, as was the case with Barry.

It is very important for therapists to carry out good diagnostic work in situations such as this. Is this a case of (social) anxiety? To what extent is it a matter of social ineptitude or of structural social disability? When it isn't a matter of social disability it may be worth considering referring a patient to group Schema Therapy. Social anxiety as well as other anxieties (e.g., abandonment anxiety) can be treated in this way. Patients often experience recognition and understanding within the group, and they learn (social) skills from one another. Other social support interventions are also effective, as described in Table 11.3.

Table 11.3 Interventions to benefit social support

Social support interventions (Harmon et al., 2005)	Social support interventions ST
Refer to group therapy (as a supplement to individual therapy).	Patients in which the Social Isolation/Alienation and Defectiveness/Shame schemas play an important role can benefit from group Schema Therapy. It feels less shameful to hear that others struggle with similar thoughts and feelings.
Encourage the patient to participate in a self-help group.	Ask a patient to do his homework or read and discuss a schema-focused therapy book with a safe support figure.
Role-play to facilitate social skills.	Role-play in which the Healthy Adult supports the vulnerable side of the patient when he struggles with his Social Isolation/Alienation or Defectiveness/Shame schema. The Healthy Adult can motivate the patient to try more helpful thoughts and behavior.

Table 11.3 (*Continued*)

Social support interventions (Harmon et al., 2005)	Social support interventions ST
Invite significant others of the patient for a session.	Offer psycho-education about the effect of schemas and modes on relationships/friendships, to support figures. Invite a support figure. Ask the patient in a neutral, non-punishing manner, what aspects of the relationship he would like to improve and how the other can help to achieve this.
Refer the patient to biofeedback when social anxiety has an effect on quality and quantity of relationships.	Apply schema mindfulness techniques by which the patient learns to reveal anxiety (think of Social Isolation/Alienation, Emotional Deprivation, Defectiveness/Shame).
Use desensitization techniques.	Behavioral experiments in which the patient practices social situations: break out of social isolation, inquire about the way others perceive him. Imagery exercises in which the patient comes into contact with others and faces schemas and modes.
Encourage social activities, team sports, and voluntary work.	Discuss how schemas and modes can be triggered in social activities. Study the manner in which maladaptive schema coping can be changed.
Discuss the patient's social network.	Make a sociogram about the past, present, and future with a patient. Discuss how the relationships with people in the sociogram are influenced by schemas and modes.
Discuss subjects that are about confidence in others.	Discuss whether the patient suffers from the Mistrust and/or Abuse schema and explore how this influence can be reduced when entering into social situations.
Encourage the patient to become friends with others who might need a friend.	Explain that more people suffer from schemas, because of which they enter into little contact with others. A patient will not only help himself but will also help others by entering into friendships with this knowledge.

ST social support interventions in group therapy
1. Invite the group to ask the patient actively what he needs to make more contact with the group members.
2. Stimulate group members to talk about situations in which they felt social anxiety, and how they dealt with it (regardless of what the result was) and if desired, what they gained in breaking the pattern.
3. Stimulate the group to understand/accept that everyone has his own way of making social contact; that there is no right or wrong. Discuss, if necessary, the Demanding Parent mode or the feeling of deprivation that occurs when someone else reacts differently in a social situation than how the patients would prefer.

Pitfalls and Tips

Implementing a schema-focused ROM procedure can be a good tool in treatment. However, it is no sinecure. Implementation of this system without the support of management, administration, and ICT isn't advisable. It is necessary for both patients and therapists to invest time and effort when following a ROM procedure. If this procedure doesn't work well, it leads to feelings of failure and emotional withdrawal from the patient. This can put added pressure on the therapeutic alliance.

Furthermore, the implementation of a Schema Therapy ROM procedure demands motivation and training from the therapists. It should not be assumed that every therapist has sufficient understanding of the tools and the feedback necessary. In addition, the benefit of using a feedback system is not likely to be understood by all therapists. Some therapists view it as a means for management to control their way of working. Others believe that a clinical impression encompasses more than what can be measured. It is advisable to investigate how therapists feel about the implementation of a schema-focused ROM procedure, and to check what they need by way of education and training before beginning.

Midway evaluations aren't always positive. This can have repercussions on both patient and therapist. It is important that when the therapist is advised to discuss the test results in peer supervision, he realizes explicitly the impact of the feedback on the patient. Questioning which schemas could be triggered and discussing possible risky behavior is advisable, particularly with patients who appear to react in a healthy way, but who are actually over-compensating or switching into the Detached Protector. Outstanding good results also deserve extra attention and discussion with the patient. Does the patient seek respite from mental health interventions? Is there a chance of relapse, and if so, what situations could lead to renewed schema-triggering? It is important that the therapist doesn't rely solely on test results, but keeps an open and critical attitude, and that he uses the test results as a therapy method instead of an aim in itself.

The Future

No study has been conducted into the effect of routine outcome measuring within Schema Therapy for people with personality problems. The scientific research into routine outcome monitoring is mainly restricted to the treatment of (very) short-term Axis I disorders particularly with the Outcome Questionaire-45 (OQ-45, Lambert *et al.*, 1996). That the bulk of research is limited to Axis I disorders is partly due to the fact that most measurement tools are developed for these disorders, and therefore they are the best regulated. Meanwhile, validation studies into Dutch schema and modes questionnaires have taken place (see also Part VI, Chapters 4 and 5). As a result of these studies it will be possible to determine when patients achieve significant clinical recovery, and if they then fall into the range of Healthy Adults regarding schemas and modes. (For the theoretical thesis concerning the calculation of patients who achieve significant clinical recovery or otherwise, see Lambert, Hansen and Bauer, 2008.) Systematically collecting the data of patients who undergo Schema Therapy makes it possible to predict therapy results, taking into consideration the severity of the pathology of a patient. Patients and health insurers increasingly demand a reliable calculation of the results of such treatment.

To facilitate the implementation of routine outcome monitoring within Schema Therapy, it is important that ST questionnaires, such as the SQ (English version YSQ L2) and the SMI-1 (English version SMI 1.1), are built into computer software.

When therapists give feedback to patients, it is advisable to provide them with the information verbally and with the help of diagrams. There is some evidence that offering written feedback, including diagrams, increases its positive effect (Harmon et al., 2005).

Systematically monitoring the progress of therapy offers increased possibilities of developing a study to determine which patients benefit most from this therapy method, which patients are at risk of ending the treatment prematurely, and when predictions of successful Schema Therapy can be made.

References

Bateman, A. and Fonagy, P. (2004) *Psychotherapy for Borderline Personality Disorder. Mentalization-Based Treatment.* New York: Oxford University Press.

Beck, A.T., Freeman, A. and Davis, D.D. (2004) *Cognitive Therapy of Personality Disorders*, 2nd edition. New York: Guilford Press.

Beurs, E. de (2005) *Routine Outcome Monitoring in het LUMC en Rivierduinen.* www.lumc.nl/3010/algemeen/Routine%20Monitoring.pdf.

Haas, E., Hill, R.D., Lambert, M.J. and Morrell, B. (2002) Do early responders to psychotherapy maintain treatment gains? *Journal of Clinical Psychology*, 58(9), 1157–1172.

Hannan, C., Lambert, M. J., Harmon, C. et al. (2005) A lab test and algorithms for identifying clients at risk for treatment failure. *Journal of Clinical Psychology*, 61(2), 155–163.

Hansen, N.B., Lambert, M.J. and Forman, E.V. (2002) The psychotherapy dose-effect and its implications for treatment delivery services. *Clinical Psychology: Science and Practice*, 9, 329–343.

Harmon, C., Hawkins, E.J., Lambert, M.J., Slade, K. and Whipple, J.L. (2005) Improving outcomes for poorly responding clients: the use of clinical support tools and feedback to clients. *Journal of Clinical Psychology*, 61(2), 175–185.

Hoffart, A., Sexton, H., Nordahl, H.M. and Stiles, T.C. (2005) Connection between patient and therapist and therapist's competence in schema-focused therapy of personality problems. *Clinical Psychology and Psychotherapy*, 3, 249–258.

Lambert, M.J. (2005) Emerging methods for providing clinicians with timely feedback on treatment effectiveness: an introduction. *Journal of Clinical Psychology*, 61(2), 141–144.

Lambert, M.J. (2007) Personal communication.

Lambert, M.J., Burlingame, G.M., Umphress, V. et al. (1996) The reliability and validity of the outcome questionnaire. *Clinical Psychology and Psychotherapy*, 3, 249–258.

Lambert, M.J., Hansen, N.B. and Bauer, S. (2008) Assessing the clinical significance of outcome results, in *Evidence-based Outcome Research* (eds A. Nezu and C. Nezu). Oxford: Oxford University Press.

Lambert, M.J. and Ogles, B.M. (2004) The efficacy and effectiveness of psychotherapy. *Bergin and Garfield's Handbook of Psychotherapy and Behavior Change*, 5th edition (ed. M.J. Lambert). New York: Wiley, pp. 139–193.

Lambert, M.J., Whipple, J.L., Smart, D.W. et al. (2001) The effects of providing therapist with feedback on client progress during psychotherapy: Are outcomes enhanced? *Psychotherapy Research*, 11, 49–68.

Lambert, M.J., Whipple, J.L., Vermeersch, D.A. et al. (2002) Enhancing psychotherapy outcomes via providing feedback on client progress: a replication. *Clinical Psychology and Psychotherapy*, 9, 1–103.

Leichsenring, F. and Leibing, E. (2003) The effectiveness of psychodynamic therapy and cognitive behavior therapy in the treatment of personality disorders: a meta-analysis. *American Journal of Psychiatry*, 160, 1223–1232.

Lobbestael, J., van Vreeswijk, M., Spinhoven, P., Schouten, E. and Arntz, A. (2010) Reliability and validity of the short Schema Mode Inventory (SMI). *Behavioural and Cognitive Psychotherapy*, 38, 437–458.

Martin, D.J., Garske, J.P. and Davis, M.K. (2000) Relation of the therapeutic alliance with outcome and other variables: a meta-analytical review. *Journal of Consulting and Clinical Psychology*, 68, 438–450.

Norcross, J.C. (2003) Empirically supported therapy relationships, in *Psychotherapy Relationships That Work* (ed. J.C. Norcross). New York: Oxford University Press, pp. 3–16.

Orlinsky, D.E., Ronnestad, M.H. and Willutzki, U. (2004) Fifty years of psychotherapy process-outcome research: continuity and change. *Bergin and Garfield's Handbook of Psychotherapy and Behavioral Change*, 5th edition (ed. M.J. Lambert). New York: Wiley, pp. 307–390.

Percevic, R., Lambert, M.J. and Kordy, H. (2006) What is the predictive value of responses to psychotherapy for its future course? Empirical explorations and consequences for outcome monitoring. *Psychotherapy Research*, 16(3), 364–373.

Perry, J.C., Banon, E. and Ianni, F. (1999) Effectiveness of psychotherapy for personality disorders. *American Journal of Psychiatry*, 156, 1312–1321.

Spinhoven, P., Giesen-Bloo, J., van Dyck, R., Kooiman, K. and Arntz, A. (2007) The therapeutic alliance in schema-focused therapy and transference-focused psychotherapy for borderline personality disorder. *Journal of Consulting and Clinical Psychology*, 75, 104–115.

Sterk, F. and Rijkeboer, M.M. (1997) *Schema-Vragenlijst*. Utrecht: Ambulatorium Universiteit Utrecht.

Strauss, J.L., Hayes, A.M., Johnson, S.L. et al. (2006) Early alliance, alliance ruptures, and symptom change in a nonrandomized trial of cognitive therapy for avoidant and obsessive-compulsive personality disorders. *Journal of Consulting and Clinical Psychology*, 74, 337–345.

Trimbos (2003). *Nieuwe "Thermometers" voor cliëntwaardering GGZ*. www.trimbos.nl/default4103.html.

Waddington, L. (2002) The therapy relationship in cognitive therapy: a review. *Behavioural and Cognitive Psychotherapy*, 30, 179–191.

Werkgroep richtlijn persoonlijkheidsstoornissen (conceptversie January 2008) *Multidisciplinaire richtlijn Persoonlijkheidsstoornissen: Richtlijn voor de diagnostiek en behandeling van volwassen patiënten met een persoonlijkheidsstoornis*. Uitgever: Trimbos-Instituut, Utrecht.

Young, J., Arntz, A., Atkinson, T. et al. (2008) *Schema Mode Inventory Version 1.1*. Cognitive Therapy Center of New York.

Young, J. and Brown, G. (2003) *Young Schema Questionnaire: Long Form*. Cognitive Therapy Center of New York.

Young, J.E., Klosko, J. and Weishaar, M.E. (2003). *Schema Therapy: a Practitioner's Guide*. New York: Guilford Press.

Part IV
Schema Therapy Settings and Patient Populations

Part IV

1
Inpatient Schema Therapy for Patients with Borderline Personality Disorder – a Case Study

Neele Reiss, Gitta Jacob and Joan Farrell

Background

Schema Therapy (ST) is a promising comprehensive treatment for borderline personality disorder (BPD) with a growing body of research evidence, both in the outpatient individual and group setting. Individual ST has demonstrated efficacy for a broad range of BPD psychopathology and critical psychosocial outcome measures, such as quality of life and cost-effectiveness (Giesen-Bloo *et al.*, 2006; Asselt *et al.*, 2008). The group ST (GST) model developed by Farrell and Shaw (1990, 1994) has been tested in one RCT (Farrell, Shaw and Webber, 2009). Effect sizes in this study were large, suggesting that ST may be even more powerful when delivered in a group format. In inpatient settings a combination of group and individual ST has been successfully implemented (Reiss, Lieb, Arntz, Shaw and Farrell, in preparation). In this chapter we describe the case of Lara, who took part in a ST inpatient program for patients with BPD.

Case Description: Patient Background and Presenting Problems

Lara was a 26-year-old woman with a primary diagnosis of BPD, who had repeatedly been in inpatient psychiatric treatment from the age of 22. Although most of her hospitalizations had been brief, they had been very frequent due to acute crises. At

---

The Wiley Blackwell Handbook of Schema Therapy: Theory, Research, and Practice, First Edition.
Edited by Michiel van Vreeswijk, Jenny Broersen, and Marjon Nadort.
© 2012 John Wiley & Sons, Ltd. Published 2015 by John Wiley & Sons, Ltd.

the time of admission, Lara had not worked for more than two years, although she had finished school to become an Emergency Room nurse and had worked in this profession for a short amount of time.

Lara was raised by her mother, who had divorced her father when Lara was two years old. Her mother told her that her father had walked out on the family and did not want contact with Lara. When she was six years old, Lara was told that her father had fought in court for the right to see his daughter ever since the divorce. Meanwhile, Lara's father had moved to a distant city, so she could only see him during vacations. While life with her mother was very difficult, Lara had a stable relationship with her father and looked forward to every vacation that she could spend with him, but her mother repeatedly put obstacles in the way to prevent these visits. Lara's mother continued to tell her that her father did not want her, which hurt Lara. Her mother had abused alcohol ever since Lara was born and frequently physically abused her daughter when intoxicated. Lara remembered that her mother often told her that she looked like her father. When drunk, Lara's mother would insult her repeatedly and tell her that she was the cause for her mother's misery. When her mother was unable to perform normal adult functions because she had a hangover, Lara tried to step into her role. At an extremely young age, Lara did the housework and even called in sick for her mother when intoxication prevented her from going to work.

In school, Lara was always an outsider; she had no friends. She wasn't allowed to bring friends home and had difficulties mixing. Her grades were good, but Lara didn't enjoy school because she was frequently bullied. Her mother told her that this was her own fault and that Lara had to learn to defend herself. Lara remembers that she always wished her mother would help her, but she never did.

In her romantic relationships, Lara often found herself attracted to partners who would not fulfill her need for stability and mutual respect. Lara felt that it was her responsibility alone to make the relationship work. At the start of a new relationship she over-engaged, trying to be the "perfect" girlfriend. Lara felt constant pressure to perform to her own "perfect" standard. After a short time, when the relationship settled in to everyday life, Lara felt burdened by the amount of work she had taken on and angry when her partner left her at home to go out with his friends. She became jealous of any female friends her partner had and started checking his text messages, e-mails, and Facebook profile. In arguments with her partners, she would verbally and even physically attack them and threaten to commit suicide. In therapy Lara often spoke about the contrast between her boyfriends' mothers, who adored her for her responsibility and working so hard for the relationship, and her boyfriends, who had to deal with her aggressive and suicidal behaviors, which no one else knew about.

Psychological treatment had been offered to Lara from the age of 15, when one of her teachers noticed her emotional difficulties. Lara always stopped going to outpatient sessions after a few hours. She said that she couldn't trust therapists or anyone outside of her closest relations, so it didn't make any sense for her to spend time in therapy. During her last month in nursing school, Lara took an overdose of alcohol and prescription medication when her relationship with her boyfriend ended so as "not to feel the pain" anymore. She reported that she longed to die every day. When she was taken to hospital after a drinking binge, Lara learned that she had been pregnant and had miscarried. She went into an inpatient crisis intervention program at that time. She finished nursing school shortly afterward, but was only able to work for a few weeks before another crisis intervention hospitalization was required. Lara was hospitalized for most of the year during the two years before she started the Schema Therapy program. These hospitalizations included an inpatient dialectical behavior therapy (DBT) program, which she described as helpful in improving her emotion regulation. However, she reported that she had felt so abandoned at discharge that she immediately started having suicidal thoughts again and was rehospitalized.

When Lara came to ST inpatient treatment, she reported that she would frequently injure herself with razorblades when she was angry with her boyfriend or hated herself. She described chronic thoughts of suicide, which she attributed to feeling useless and unable to live up to her own standards. Her current relationship was at stake, because she threatened suicide after an argument with her boyfriend by climbing on the roof of a nearby building. Her boyfriend followed her and "rescued" her. Lara spoke of this suicide attempt without showing any emotion, although she repeatedly stated her hopelessness.

Schema Therapy Case Conceptualization and Course of Psychotherapeutic Treatment

Inpatient ST for patients with BPD is a 12-week structured program with a combination of individual and group ST sessions. Patients attend approximately two hours of group therapy daily following the goals for BPD treatment described by Young, Klosko, and Weishaar (2003). Ultimately, by changing schemas and modes, the primary goals of treatment are to help patients change dysfunctional life patterns and get their core needs met in an adaptive manner outside of therapy. Lara's treatment described here illustrates the progression of this work through the course of inpatient treatment.

At the beginning of treatment patients complete several questionnaires, including the Schema Mode Inventory (SMI; Lobbestael, van Vreeswijck, Spinhoven, Schouten and Arntz, 2010; Reiss *et al.*, in press). Within the first four weeks of treatment a ST case concept is made in individual therapy and presented to the treatment team (Figure 1.1). This conceptualization is used to guide the patient's psychotherapeutic work on reducing their dysfunctional modes and strengthening their functional modes.

A complex disorder such as BPD cannot be "cured" in 12 weeks. One primary focus of inpatient ST is to help patients get into and stay in outpatient treatment. In Lara's case, she described difficulties trusting other people – even therapists – which prevented her from establishing a working therapeutic relationship.

At the beginning of treatment, Lara attended a ST psycho-education group in which she learned about schemas, modes, and the goals of ST regarding mode change. In early individual ST sessions it became clear that Lara had a strong Detached Protector mode that prevented her from getting the help she needed in an inpatient setting or everyday life.

Working on the Detached Protector mode

In ST group sessions Lara learned about the function of the Detached Protector mode in her childhood. Lara understood that she had learned to detach from her

Case concept of Lara

Little vulnerable and abused Lara
- Fearful and sad
- Hopeless

Little angry Lara
- Anger and jealousy in close relationships
- Physical and verbal attacks of partners

Punitive Mother mode
- history of invalidation and abuse
- self hatred, self injury, suicide attempts

Demanding Parent mode
- "you are responsible"
- Perfectionism

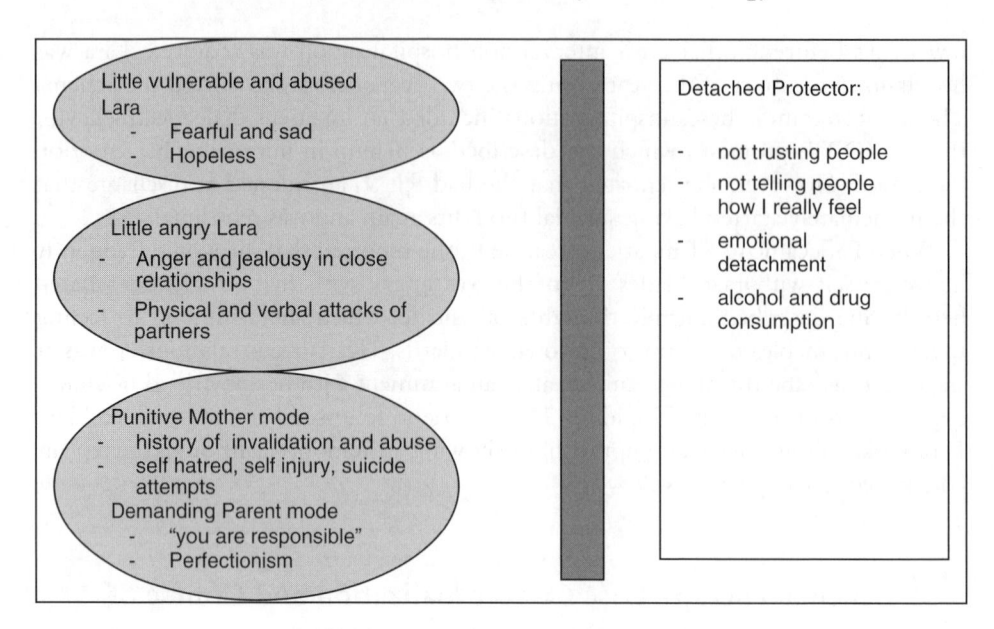

Detached Protector:
- not trusting people
- not telling people how I really feel
- emotional detachment
- alcohol and drug consumption

Figure 1.1 Case concept of Lara

feelings when her mother drank and physically and emotionally abused her. She discussed the pros and cons of her present use of the Detached Protector mode with fellow group members. In an experiential exercise Lara learned that due to her strong Detached Protector mode, she was unable to get physically close to other patients, whom she actually liked. In individual ST chair work was used to empathically confront the Detached Protector mode. Lara found out that she had people in her life (e.g., one close friend) whom she wanted to be close to and whom she felt she could trust. Her individual therapist worked on establishing a therapeutic relationship with her, in which she could feel safe and experience that her needs were important. For example, the therapist visited Lara's room to check on her or say goodbye before she left work. In mode awareness work Lara was able to use daily monitoring to become more aware of the triggers for her Detached Protector mode and in the schema skills group she learned specific skills that helped her get out of this maladaptive coping mode (e.g., focusing on her need and trying to fulfill it).

Within a few weeks Lara was able to notice when she switched into Detached Protector mode and sometimes could apply skills to get out of it and use a more adaptive behavior. In individual and group therapy Lara was able to open up more and express her feelings and needs. As Lara was in Detached Protector mode less often, her Dysfunctional Parent and Maladaptive Child modes occurred more frequently.

Dysfunctional Parent modes

Demanding Parent mode. Lara's Demanding Parent mode was triggered in many different situations and was often seen by others as the Healthy Adult mode. When in Demanding Parent mode, Lara would try to accomplish many tasks at the same time and could succeed for a while. However, as a consequence she felt exhausted and overwhelmed by the demands, a state that led to self-injurious behavior. With her fellow patients Lara discussed the differences between being in Demanding Parent and Healthy Adult mode. On a cognitive level Lara said that her thoughts were dominated by "You have to . . . ," "You must not . . . ," and "It is your responsibility to . . . ". Another patient said that she felt constantly under pressure. Lara was able to empathize with that. In ST group, patients identified the typical behaviors they would engage in when in Demanding Parent mode. They also found out that, when the norms of the Demanding Parent mode were not fulfilled, Punitive Parent mode followed and very quickly suicidal thoughts came into their minds. In mode awareness group Lara learned to distinguish between how she felt in Demanding Parent mode and how she felt in Healthy Adult mode. She also learned that listing the factual demands of a situation helped her switch into Healthy Adult mode. Then she could try to meet those demands at her own pace. In schema skills group patients could develop skills to get out of the Demanding Parent mode, such as asking their peers if a certain goal is achievable. In individual ST the therapist helped Lara to develop weekly plans, which took both her personal needs and her responsibilities into account. After a while Lara decided that getting feedback and support from others was helpful in dealing with her Demanding Parent mode. In modes-in-interaction group Lara worked conscientiously on her interpersonal skills. During group sessions she was able to talk about some of her needs in the relationships with her peers at the unit. At times Lara caught herself switching into Demanding Parent mode and being confronted with her own unrelenting standards when she was asked to do chores at the unit. Sometimes she managed to ask for help from the nurses, but when in Demanding Parent mode she heard cognitively distorted messages such as "You have to do it by yourself", or "You are too stupid to do even the easiest things by yourself." In individual ST Lara learned that when she felt the need for support but couldn't voice it appropriately, she switched from Demanding Parent mode into Angry Child mode. In Angry Child mode she reacted aggressively toward others, and that drove people away.

Demanding Parent and the Angry Child modes were among the most difficult for Lara to work on during inpatient schema therapy. In outpatient therapy Lara continued her work on Demanding Parent mode, since it was repeatedly triggered in her work.

Punitive Parent mode. After Lara overcame Detached Protector mode in a few situations, her chronic suicidal thoughts became more apparent. She talked about feeling worthless and a burden on others. Although Lara could identify the thoughts as her own, she often identified her mother's voice when she was in her Punitive Parent mode. In ST group an effigy of the patient's Punitive Parent mode was developed. Lara wrote sentences such as "Nobody wants you," "No one would miss you if you were dead," "You don't deserve any better!" on the cloth, which she had heard echoing in her head for years. Lara was astonished to find out that other patients heard similar statements. Although Lara had no difficulty telling her peers that she felt their Punitive Parent messages were absurd, she had a difficult time believing that the same applied to her Punitive Parent messages. Imagery exercises in individual ST helped Lara to identify root experiences with her mother, which were linked to her Punitive Parent mode. In imagery change work Lara's therapist stepped into the images and saved young Lara from her drunken mother's abuse and took her to her father's house, where Lara felt safe. In individual ST, mode awareness group and schema skills group Lara worked on recognizing early signs of Punitive Parent mode and how to fight it. With her therapist she made mode memory cards and a tape, in which she could hear good parent messages in her therapist's voice. In chair techniques and mode role-plays in groups Lara started to fight her Punitive Parent herself with the help of her peers.

Punitive Parent mode was a challenge during inpatient treatment. Lara had multiple episodes in which her Punitive Parent mode became so strong that she injured herself while on the unit. Fighting her Punitive Parent mode, especially in situations where Lara felt she could turn to no one for help, was difficult for her. At the end of inpatient treatment Lara told her therapist that her Punitive Parent mode was still there, but that there were moments in which it was quiet. Her hope was that these moments would become longer and more frequent in the future.

Maladaptive Child modes

Vulnerable Child mode. At the same time that the Punitive Parent mode became obvious through suicidal thoughts, Lara's Vulnerable Child mode appeared. Lara realized that because she had been living in Detached Protector mode for so long, her life had become lonely and it was difficult for her to share her feelings with others or connect with them. When Lara was in Vulnerable Child mode she withdrew to her room, hid under her blankets, and cried. At the beginning of treatment, Lara stated in individual ST that she "hated" her Vulnerable Child mode. She said, "I think it is useless. It is useless to cry and to think somebody will be there for you, because nobody will. And it is a burden to others to be such a wimp." These messages were identified as Punitive Parent messages. In ST group Lara learned about the healthy needs of children and how they remain present in Vulnerable Child mode if they were not met. With other ST patients she discussed in schema skills group who her Vulnerable Child felt secure with, which objects helped to soothe her, and how she could fulfil the needs of her Vulnerable Child when in this mode. In individual ST, Lara learned how to take good care of her Vulnerable Child mode. These imagery exercises were a first step toward self-compassion and better self-care. In mode awareness group Lara found that it helped her to be aware of the needs of her Vulnerable Child mode, even if she could not fulfill them right away. This awareness kept them from amassing and making her feel miserable. Over the course of treatment Lara made efforts to fulfill her Vulnerable Child needs. Unfortunately, at the end of inpatient treatment, Lara's Punitive Parent mode often prevented her from getting her needs met and made her feel bad about having them. What did change as a result of treatment was that Lara knew that it was her Punitive Parent mode that made her feel she did not deserve to have her needs met and, even if it was difficult for her, she no longer wanted to listen to this mode. At the end of inpatient treatment she allowed herself to engage in activities and do things that made her feel good. In her daily plan she gave herself one hour of free time, in which she would only do things that addressed her current needs. She also found out that her Vulnerable Child liked to be hugged by friends and other patients when she felt alone. Towards the end of treatment, when she was afraid to be left alone, being hugged by a friend was a very powerful soothing skill for her Vulnerable Child mode.

Angry Child mode. Because the Angry Child mode was not seen very often in our inpatient setting in Lara's case, little work was done on it during Lara's inpatient treatment. Lara had reported that her suicide attempts occured while in the Angry Child mode, at times when she wanted close others to see how much she was suffering. In individual ST, mode analyses of these situations were done so that Lara could understand the chain of events that led to those suicide attempts. In ST, group exercises were conducted to help patients learn about boundaries and how to defend these boundaries in a socially acceptable way. In modes-in-interaction group Lara learned to verbalize that she felt upset about something without threatening others. In body therapy and in fun exercises such as tug-of-war, Lara worked on the physical experience of anger and found out that anger could be experienced safely, without having to harm herself or others. Lara reported at the end of inpatient treatment that her Angry Child mode was still difficult for her to deal with, especially with her boyfriend. When she succeeded in accessing the underlying need of her Angry Child mode she was able to verbalize the need and manage the situation in a socially acceptable way.

Adaptive modes

During inpatient treatment therapy work is done to make patients aware of and strengthen the two adaptive modes: Happy Child and Healthy Adult.

Happy Child mode. Most BPD patients did not experience a happy childhood in which they could engage in spontaneous playful activities such as games with their friends. Therefore, it seems to be a crucial experience for them in treatment to learn how to enjoy playful activities, both alone and with their peers. The inpatient ward can be a good place to learn how to play. In art classes, Lara discovered her talent for drawing cartoons. She and the other patients enjoyed the cartoons she created, which were based on things that happened during her day. Lara and her peers discovered that watching "girlie" movies and eating pizza in bed at night were ways to nurture their Happy Child. Experiencing the Happy Child mode and being allowed to experience a child's joy and happiness allowed Lara to learn about a different aspect of herself and to explore her likes and dislikes. Including playful activities and times with friends in her daily life, allowing room for the Happy Child mode, was an important step for Lara to establish a more balanced life.

Healthy Adult mode. When Punitive Parent mode was discussed in ST group and many patients decided that they wanted to fight it, Lara went into Detached Protector mode. It was difficult for her to speak in group and only toward the end of group could she say that she was scared, but that she couldn't talk about it yet. In individual ST Lara managed to overcome Detached Protector mode completely by saying, "I don't know what will be left of me, if my Punitive Parent mode is gone. Maybe there is nothing else, maybe I will just be hollow. It scares me." That was when Lara and her therapist started talking in more detail about Healthy Adult mode. Lara felt that she did not have a Healthy Adult mode. So Lara and her therapist recorded parts of Healthy Adult mode on a flip chart. Lara found that she already had some of the parts that form a Healthy Adult identity and she also identified the aspects that she did not yet have. She could also identify the modes, such as Punitive Parent mode or Detached Protector mode, that interfered with the parts of a Healthy Adult identity. One part of Healthy Adult mode that she found especially difficult was having a stable sense of self-esteem. Since Lara's Punitive Parent mode destroyed any positive feedback by making her feel that she did not deserve it, Lara had to work on not listening to the Punitive Parent mode interference. She often said that this was really difficult for her, because Punitive Parent mode got louder and louder at the beginning of ST, then finally, very slowly, became quieter. As a first step, Lara worked on accepting positive feedback regarding her work in art therapy (i.e., her cartoons). She started working on things that were harder for her and that had mistakes in them. At those times both Demanding Parent mode and Punitive Parent mode would assert their voices. Accepting mistakes and still getting positive feedback was very hard for Lara. At the end of treatment Lara felt that her Healthy Adult was strong enough in the area of work that she asked her legal guardian to help her arrange for an internship in the protected job market. She did not want to go back to being a nurse because she thought the constant demands in this job would trigger her Demanding Parent mode and that she would not be able to stay in the job for long. To the inpatient treatment team, this seemed like a healthy decision and they supported it.

To work on establishing personal qualities as a Healthy Adult in ST group, patients wrote positive feedback for each other on little cards. Lara picked out the feedback cards that she could accept. The group discussed the different characteristics that people have (e.g., tolerant, loud, funny, chaotic) and every group member marked what they thought their level of each characteristic was on a scale. Lara found this exploration of her Healthy Adult qualities interesting and that it was helpful to get to know herself better.

After Inpatient Treatment

After Lara left inpatient treatment, she did not find an outpatient therapist immediately. She called nurses at the unit or her inpatient therapist when she felt she needed help or was in crisis, at the rate of about once a month, until she found an outpatient therapist about a year later. Lara had one crisis hospitalization for a few days during this period, but she did not injure herself or make a suicide attempt.

Regarding work, she had to go through a phase of testing and a phase of waiting, but about six months later she did get an internship in the protected job market. A year later she called the unit to talk about a new part-time job that she was very happy with. She said that all was not well and she still needed her outpatient treatment, but that she had the impression that life was improving. Her relationship had not worked out, she had just moved to the city where her new job was and she had to find a new therapist there, but she felt she had enough support to manage.

Summary

During her inpatient ST treatment Lara worked on reducing her Detached Protector mode and fighting her Punitive Parent mode. Through experiencing safety and stability in the therapeutic relationships with her individual and group therapists and the nursing staff, and finding an environment in which she could experience supportive peer relationships with other BPD patients, Lara developed and strengthened her Healthy Adult and her Happy Child modes and her Vulnerable Child mode could be present and comforted. The combination of individual and group ST offers both the intimate relationship to one's individual schema therapist, in which the full capacity of limited reparenting can unfold, and the healthy "family" environment, including siblings in groups, where conflicts among patients can occur and be solved in a way in which nobody is hurt or excluded from the group. From a clinical point of view, the combination of individual and group format in intensive ST settings seems to be beneficial for severe BPD patients like Lara, but more extensive research on the topic is needed.

References

Asselt, A.D. van, Dirksen, C.D., Arntz, A. *et al.* (2008) Outpatient psychotherapy for borderline personality disorder: cost-effectiveness of schema-focused therapy vs. transference-focused psychotherapy. *British Journal of Psychiatry*, 192(6), 450–457.

Farrell, J.M. and Shaw, I.A. (1990) Emotional awareness training for borderline personality disorder patients: a treatment manual. Unpublished manuscript for NIH RO3, Indiana University School of Medicine, Indianapolis.

Farrell, J.M. and Shaw, I.A. (1994) Emotional awareness training: a prerequisite to effective cognitive-behavioral treatment of borderline personality disorder. *Cognitive and Behavioral Practice*, 1, 71–91.

Farrell, J.M., Shaw, I.A. and Webber, M.A. (2009) A schema-focused approach to group psychotherapy for outpatients with borderline personality disorder: a randomized controlled trial. *Journal of Behavior Therapy and Exerimental Psychiatry*, 40, 317–328.

Giesen-Bloo, J., van Dyck, R., Spinhoven, P. *et al.* (2006) Outpatient psychotherapy for borderline personality disorder: randomized trial of schema-focused therapy vs. transference-focused psychotherapy. *Archives of General Psychiatry*, 63, 649–659.

Lobbestael, J., van Vreeswijck, M., Spinhoven, P., Schouten, E., & Arntz, A. (2010). Reliability and validity of the short schema mode inventory (SMI). *Behavioral and Cognitive Psychotherapy*, 38, 437–458.

Reiss, N., Dominiak, P., Harris, D., Knörnschild, C., Schouten, E. & Jacob, G.A. (in press). Reliability and validity of the German version of the schema mode inventory. *European Journal of Psychological Assessment.* doi:10.1027/1015-5759/a000110

Reiss, N., Lieb, K., Arntz, A., Shaw, I.A. and Farrell, J.M. (submitted) Responding to the treatment challenge of patients with severe BPD: results of three pilot studies of inpatient schema therapy.

Young, J.E., Klosko, J.S. and Weishaar, M.E. (2003) *Schema Therapy: a Practitioner's Guide*. New York: Guilford Press.

2
Individual Schema Therapy
Practical Experience with Adults

Pien van den Kieboom and Daan Jonker

Individual Schema Therapy is the most common treatment approach in Schema Therapy (ST). This approach has developed gradually. Treatment of patients with (severe) personality problems is hard to describe in phases. During their lifetime, these patients are confronted with stressful situations more often than average, and this often requires attention in individual treatment. Patients may struggle with problems in relationships, education, or work, and in managing personal finance. Sometimes the threat is so overwhelming that a crisis follows. The individual therapist is confronted with the patient's problems and is challenged to focus on them, without losing sight of ST techniques.

Individual Schema Therapy is discussed in the literature (e.g., Young and Pijnaker, 1999; Arntz and Bögels, 2000; Schacht and Peeters, 2000; van Genderen and Arntz, 2005). Young, Klosko, and Weishaar (2003, 2005). For borderline and narcissistic personality disorders, they developed a "schema modes concept." With these patients several schemas may be active at the same time and coping styles switch abruptly. Connecting the different modes seems to work better with this group. For other personality disorders, a similar schema modes concept has been investigated (Bernstein, Arntz, and de Vos, 2007; Lobbestael, Vreeswijk, and Arntz, 2008).

The effectiviness of individual ST for patients with borderline personality disorders was first examined in a randomized control trial (Giesen-Bloo et al., 2006). Following this study, several experiments investigating the implementation of individual ST for patients with borderline problems took place in eight Dutch mental healthcare institutes (Nadort et al., in progress). There are also studies being run for individual ST with regard to other personality disorders (Bamelis et al., 2006–10).

Thanks to these studies, it is to be expected that individual ST will be further adapted and improved in the near future. This chapter describes individual outpatient therapy. Although it is not always possible to describe the entire therapy, it can be divided into phases (Arntz and Bögels, 2000; van Genderen and Arntz, 2005, Nissen and Poppinger, 2008). These phases are summarized and attention is also given to potential difficulties that may stand in the way of treatment.

The Wiley Blackwell Handbook of Schema Therapy: Theory, Research, and Practice, First Edition.
Edited by Michiel van Vreeswijk, Jenny Broersen, and Marjon Nadort.
© 2012 John Wiley & Sons, Ltd. Published 2015 by John Wiley & Sons, Ltd.

In Practice

> Jane was a 35-year-old woman, diagnosed with borderline personality disorder. She had had inpatient and outpatient therapy since childhood. She was now in therapy following a suicide attempt, in which it seems that severe relationship problems played a role. Her childhood was characterized by emotional deprivation, abandonment by her mother at the age of 12, and abuse during her stay in foster homes. She accepts treatment cynically: "Doing this again probably won't help."

> Maisy, aged 27 years, often lies in bed for days at a time, and comes for outpatient treatment because of depression, problems studying, and outbursts of anger, especially in her relationship. She still has a lot of contact with her parents, whom she sometimes phones in the middle of the night, because she doesn't know what to do. Sometimes they go over to her place to calm her down, but they don't know what to do with her either. At the assessment, a borderline personality disorder is diagnosed, and she accepts the proposed ST.

The process of ST is in line with what is advised by the Dutch Work Council personality disorders, concept version (Werkgroep richtlijn persoonlijkheidsstoornissen, 2008):

> Outpatient individual psychotherapies are evidence-based treatments for personality disorders, but are used mainly for borderline personality disorders, the dependence and avoidance personality disorders and the personality disorder Not Otherwise Specified. Depending on the stage of the treatment and the capacities of the patient, there is usually more emphasis on the supportive elements in the beginning and more emphasis on the insight-oriented elements later on. Motivational techniques and diagnostic interventions are of great value in this phase (prior to the treatment), especially because patients with personality disorders are not self-motivated from the beginning.

Approach

Individual ST can be divided into six phases:

1. Diagnostics.
2. Growing a therapeutic alliance.
3. Symptom management.
4. Challenging dysfunctional assumptions/thoughts.

5. Trauma process/schema change.
6. End of Treatment.

In practice, these phases are seldom well defined and strictly separated.

Establishing a therapeutic alliance starts in the diagnostics phase. Symptom management plays an important role throughout all phases. In the end phase, difficulties in the earlier phases may be briefly evoked due to anxiety of abandonment. However, the therapy can roughly be divided into points of particular interest, following a logical order.

Diagnostics

During the intake and assessment for ST, motivational techniques and schema inventories are used. At the beginning of the treatment, it should be realized that:

- Schema Therapy is a long-term treatment; this has to be allowed for within the mental healthcare institute.
- It is important to have one therapist for ST.
- In case of a crisis or severe self-injurious behavior, it is possible to have an assessment for additional treatment, such as Linehan training, STEPP training, or a module CGT (Slee, 2008).

As recommended by the Dutch Work Council personality disorders (concept version, 2008), patients and the people close to them are informed that it is essential that right from the beginning of a diagnosis/assessment, which often starts with a crisis, they take the matter seriously, and that the patient is treated with respect.

> Jane was very reserved in the first months of therapy, and she was always angry with the therapist about something (e.g., if he was a few minutes late, didn't listen attentively, or didn't explain something clearly). She remained angry until the therapist talked to her about her anger, and named it as the Detached (angry) Protector (Young et al., 2005, p. 44; 2003), who protected her from entering into a relationship where she might get hurt. Little by little, she dared to let go of the Detached Protector. An important contribution to this was that she agreed to have a session with her sons. The fact that her sons liked the therapist, and, as it were, gave permission for the treatment, helped.

> Maisy said she would love to start therapy, but repeatedly cancelled her appointments. She often called in tears just before the scheduled time, to say that she wouldn't be able to come because she was in such bad shape. The therapist continued to make appointments for her and encouraged her to come. The therapist didn't get angry with her, but confronted her in an empathic way: he said that he couldn't be a good therapist for her if he let her miss her therapy, when he knew that she needed it so badly. Maisy's confidence grew, and after six months, she consistently attended each appointment.

Growing a therapeutic alliance

It is clear that growing a therapeutic alliance starts in the first evaluation phase. To set the tone, it is important to be reliable and available to the patient and important others, to take time to motivate them, and set limits on self-injurious behavior.

Growing a therapeutic alliance isn't a technique in itself; the therapeutic alliance grows throughout all phases. This is in part due to good implementation of strategies and techniques that belong to a specific phase, and especially because of the two main therapeutic strategies in Schema Therapy: limited reparenting and empathic confrontation (Young *et al.*, 2003, 2005).

The most important work that has to be done in this phase is patient education of the disorder, to explain the rationale behind the therapy, and creating a case conceptualization (see Part II, Chapter 6). This is to give patients insight into the connection between their complaints, schemas, and modes that bother them, and the important relationships and events from their childhood. It is important to establish the connection between complaints, schemas, and case history together with the patient (Arntz and Kuipers, 1998).

The involvement of other important persons can be significant too.

> Maisy got little understanding from her parents about the strong emotions that she sometimes felt, and they had even less sympathy for her lack of energy, which meant that she could not continue with her studies or hold down a job.
>
> When she told her parents about her therapy her mother was very disparaging about it. In a session with her parents, who were invited by letter, the diagnosis of borderline personality disorder and the complaints Maisy suffered from were explained. The content of therapy was discussed in general. This resulted in more understanding and support from her parents. After this session, the mother called the therapist to ask for advice. The therapist explained that conversations would take place only in the presence of her daughter. Therefore, Maisy got more confidence in the therapist, and her parents encouraged their daughter to discuss her problems in therapy.

Symptom management

It is wise to start by treating symptoms that can lead to quick results. Often, excellent results can be achieved with the treatment of, for example, sleeping problems, difficulty in maintaining normal levels of activity, or problems with a physical condition.

A big problem for many patients, especially those with borderline disorders, is fluctuating emotional states. Emotions can build up tension and can lead to anxiety and sometimes to self-injurious behavior. It is important to analyze why certain emotional states are aroused and which schemas or modes are triggered. Following this, an approach and an emergency plan (treatment plan) outlining alternative behaviors

> A weekly activity schedule was constructed with Maisy. Sleeping during the day was limited to a minimum. Furthermore, the therapist made an MP3 file with relaxation exercises and a "safe place." Maisy could use these exercises to fall asleep, at first with and later without MP3 files. Later in the treatment, she could use them to temper any tension that was building up.
>
> In the case of the urge to self-injurious or suicidal acts, Maisy agreed to call the therapist, even outside business hours. She called the therapist at 2 a.m. to say she had taken an overdose, but wanted to say goodbye to him.

for each emotional state can be made. Offering the mindfulness mode can be helpful. With mindfulness techniques, the patient can learn to see strong emotions as transitory and learn to create distance from them and cope with them (Linehan, 1993a, 1993b; Kabat-Zinn, 2000).

Where there is suicidal behavior or self-injurious behavior, the frequency of contact must be increased.

It is important to ask about suicidal tendencies and the intentions toward that behavior. Which schemas are activated and in which modes do these occur? How does this behavior fit within the concept of therapy? Together with the patient, alternatives to self-injurious tendencies can be examined (e.g., movement, or the experience of non-injurious pain such as putting one's hands in icy water). The patient or therapist could also help to prevent this behavior by informing important others, and this is an option to be discussed. The possibility of having contact with a co-therapist, or contact by telephone with extra phone support outside office hours when the therapist is not available, can prevent self-injurious behavior. The use of medication, participation in DBT, mindfulness, and cognitive behavioral therapy focused on self-injurious behavior (Slee, 2008; Slee, Garnefski and Spinhoven, 2008) are also options. A voluntarily admission is a good option that allows patients to have a safe place in the short term.

Challenging dysfunctional assumptions/thoughts

The tracking and correction of problems that underlie faulty interpretations is a recurring activity. For that purpose, there are several useful techniques, for example, schema dialogues, imagery dialogues, chair work, the advantages and disadvantages of this way of thinking, rating on a visual analog scale, pie chart technique, flash cards, the evidence in the present and in the past, and positive journals (Beck *et al.*, 2004; see also Part III, Chapter 3).

In general, the problem in this phase is not one of making errors, but rather the characteristic persistence of all-or-nothing thinking (the extremes). Furthermore, there is the impossibility of putting oneself in someone else's shoes. This leads to precision work, and often many sessions have to be undertaken, working with several perspectives and techniques, to teach the patient how to think differently.

> At first, Jane saw every second that her therapist was late as total abandonment. Unexpected absence was also unbearable. It seemed that there was an important turn in the treatment after two weeks of the therapist's unexpected absence. The therapist came with the personal disclosure that his father had died and he thought it was relevant to inform the patient personally. In this way, it was possible for the therapist to check whether the patient held the idea that he had lost interest in her and that this had been the reason for his absence. His disclosure made the patient realize, for the first time, that she was dealing with a man of flesh and blood, someone who had also had a father. The following sessions were, among other things, about the loss of her own father. She also started to become better able to deal with the fact that the therapist wasn't always on time; she could even make jokes about it and arrive late herself.

Schema change and possible trauma processing

In this phase, a common method is imagery with rescripting, role-playing of past situations, and role-playing in the present (see Part III, Chapter 3). The most common therapeutic approach remains reparenting. Sometimes EMDR is of value, if the therapist is trained for this, but the usual method of rescripting is especially applicable to more complicated experiences. A simple trauma is rare (de Jongh and ten Broeke, 1998).

In an imagery exercise with rescripting, the patient could recall this memory. First with the help of the therapist, and later with her Healthy Adult mode, she could let her father know that she did have the right to her own place in her life. With EMDR, her strong feelings of anxiety that belong to the image of that memory could be desensitized and the negative cognition "I have no rights at all" could change to "I have the same rights as anyone else." For this patient, the complication in treatment was that she spent almost every weekend at her parents' home, where she was again exposed to disparaging treatment by her father. Everything that was built up in therapy came under attack at home. Therefore, they agreed that she would greatly decrease the amount of contact with her father, as long as she wasn't capable of setting limits to his behavior. Later, she could tell him what his treatment meant to her, and she made it clear to him that she would no longer put up with it. Unfortunately, her father was completely unsympathetic, and though it caused her a lot of pain, she voluntarily ended contact with him.

> Jane now lived a more balanced life with a new boyfriend. That gave her room to explore painful memories. With imagery (in which the trained safe place technique used regularly) a situation was created in which an indecent assault occurred when Jane was 11. On the day of the assault, Jane's parents apparently had a huge fight when Jane came home. From that moment on, Jane was the one who had to comfort her mother and there was no room for her own story. In the imagery, she finally told her story to her mother, who was listening this

time, and offered words of consolation. Encouraged for that purpose by "adult Jane," she evoked "little Jane" in the image to help her. This experience of assault possibly contributed to the occurrence and maintenance of some important schemas. At that time, she concluded that she was worthless. Partly for this reason, she developed avoiding styles, such as staying in bed all day.

The message Maisy received from her very strict, domineering father was that there was absolutely no safe place for her anywhere. This belief continued to inform her adult life. There was nowhere that she felt really at ease, and she always had a bag with her, even as a child, filled with important survival gear (emergency rations, clothes, important addresses, precious pictures, her teddy bear). She had a very clear memory of an event, that was typical for her, which helped her to develop the idea that "there is no room for me," coming from the Emotional Deprivation schema.

End of treatment

In the last phase, attention is given to any remaining symptoms. Announcing the end of therapy, and discussing the results, allows the opportunity to use relapse as an exercise to cope with this new stage of life in a competent way. The patient can make a plan for the last phase and for the period after therapy. New behavior has to be practiced in role-play.

Maisy, who is now married and pregnant with her first child, had been allowed to consult the therapist on demand over the last two years. The run-down went very gradually, and although she still finds it a little scary, she agrees the treatment really will end. She and the therapist agree that the session where she will bring her baby will be the last one.

Jane's completion of the treatment is different.

With full agreement, the end of her treatment is worked up to. The date is more or less settled. However, the general practitioner throws a spanner in the works. He is the one who has to prescribe her medication, because the contact with the psychiatrist will also stop. Initially, the GP refuses, because he had been satisfied with the care Jane received during difficult moments in the past years. Therefore, they agree that the GP can refer to the psychiatrist in the event of a relapse.

Pitfalls and Tips

In each phase, the therapist can encounter pitfalls; some are specific to a certain phase; others are more general. Several are discussed below, as well as tips on how to deal with them.

Start of treatment

> Jane was given an assignment to read the first chapters of the book *Reinventing Your Life* (Young and Klosko, 1994). However, she not only read the first chapters but also completed the rest, and got to work on the chapter about separation anxiety. She noticed that she was very clingy with her partner. Naturally, her partner agreed with her and told her that he didn't get enough time to spend on his own hobbies and work, because of her (suicidal) crisis. He was motivated to create more distance right away. Of course, there had to be negotiation about this all-or-nothing reaction, but the couple found a good solution for this.

The expectation that one can start immediately by running through the different phases in Schema Therapy can lead to disillusionment. Often, preliminary work has to be carried out, probably called counseling, taking into account the current restrictions regarding the number of psychotherapy sessions that are permitted. This depends on the institution where the treatment takes place. Well-meaning relatives can interfere at the start of the treatment by being too critical or refusing to let the patient go. Therefore, the advice is to involve supportive relatives in the treatment. In cases of self-injurious and risky behavior it is important that the therapist recognizes the Protector mode and negotiates about abandoning this mode in stages. Furthermore, the therapist can consider risky behavior as a primary focus and treat this behavior with CBT in cases of self-injurious behavior.

It is also important to provide good information about both the problems and treatment, and to act with patience and determination when confronted with the ambivalence of the patient to commit himself to the therapist's care. The therapist can use self-analysis to this end (Young *et al.*, 2003, 2005).

Crisis and extra phone support[1]

The pitfall in a crisis is that the therapist can end up in the role of the Punitive Parent, because he confronts the patient about the unacceptable behavior without being empathic.

In a crisis, it is important to get into contact with the Vulnerable Child. First, the therapist has to advise on how safety can be created or increased, and involve others if necessary. Furthermore, the next appointment, in which an evaluation can be made as to how the patient ended up in this situation, and how the crisis can be explained according to the schema model, is brought forward. Which mode was the patient in and why was it activated? A step-by-step plan or crisis plan can be made with the patient, to recognize mounting tension and to plan what to do in order to break through, and in this way, reduce self-injury behavior. The use of "Bed on indication"

---

[1] Many institutes within current Dutch mental healthcare have a facility at their clinical wards, which temporary or long-term outpatients can use 24 hours a day for extra phone support; they can also ask for a bed at difficult moments.

> ### Telephone support
> Because the therapist wanted to be certain that Maisy would phone in a crisis, they came to the agreement that she would first practice making a phone call at an appointed time. Such an agreement is judicious: the patient can practice, and the therapist can be certain that telephone access is used correctly.

and offering extra phone support would be applicable in this situation. A possible time-out with safe family and friends could also be beneficial, with the condition that it is clearly agreed with the people involved what to do and what not to do. It is advisable to actively involve confidential advisors in developing a crisis plan, if they are available.

Dealing with authorities

Throughout treatment, problems with social security administration and other authorities can influence the life, complaints, and treatment of the patient. A potential pitfall is that the therapist underestimates these problems and doesn't give enough attention to them during treatment. Helping to write letters, call social services, and practice conversations in role-play is considered to be part of limited reparenting.

> Jane had come a long way in her treatment. In agreement with her partner, they decided to split up. She didn't have anywhere to live at first and it took another six months before she could move to a new apartment. During this time, the focus was on the present and sorting out all kind of things.
>
> After she moved, it appeared that her social security benefit was not paid, the tax authorities were behind with her file, and the landlord wouldn't wait any longer for the rent. In an empty home, with only a charity food supply and no social support, she made a serious suicide attempt when she was threatened with eviction, which resulted in hospitalization.
>
> Even her therapist was not able to cope with the extent of her social and emotional grief. With the support of social workers from the institute and a lawyer, they managed to keep the apartment during her hospitalization.
>
> Her social security benefit was paid, and even the tax authority paid. She made a new start. Impulsively, she bought a far too expensive aquarium, but this kind of "self-harmful behavior" is currently under control.

Comorbidity

During treatment, the matter of comorbidity often arises. Anxiety and mood are often easily treated with medication.

The use and abuse of drugs and medication should remain a matter of discussion. Whenever there is a high level of anxiety, medication can be a good remedy, but a disadvantage can be that it keeps the patient in the Protector mode and hampers the treatment.

> ### Cormorbidity
>
> Maisy seemed to misinterpret the glass of wine that she drank before going to sleep. It mostly turned into drinking the whole bottle. As she restricted this, her sleeping pattern and nightmares decreased remarkably.

Therapeutic alliance

The urge to "score" too quickly as a therapist is a potential pitfall and is counterproductive, especially in the treatment of long-existing schemas. The therapist needs to realize that if the schemas and modes of the patient are shaken up, an existential anxiety will be aroused. Although schemas cause many problems these problems are often very familiar and reliable, the only certainty in life. It is important that the therapist is aware of his own schemas, which can play a role. Supervision and peer supervision are essential for this.

The anxiety and anger that can be evoked in the therapist can lead to rejection and punitive behavior toward the patient, a repetition of his past experiences. Obviously, limits for destructive and verbally aggressive behavior have to be set at the outset. Furthermore, the patient should have the opportunity to express anger fully, even though it seems unrealistic. It is important to have empathy with underlying schemas, to name them, and to make connections with previous experiences. Following this, a reality check can start: Was it realistic to become that angry? It is also important to search for alternative explanations together with the patient, point out misinterpretations and exaggerations, but also recognize the realistic components.

Another potential pitfall within the therapeutic alliance is that the therapist gets stuck in reparenting. In this case, the therapist doesn't help the patient gain independence. The focus on the patient clashes with the patient's need for confrontation and verification of reality. It is very important that the therapist gains insight into his own schemas and works with it. In this way, the therapist and patient can move into the completion phase together. In supervision or peer supervision, or by making a case conceptualization, difficulties within the alliance can be analyzed (Sprey, 2000).

Relational aspects

Problems within partner relationships and with intimacy often occur in the completion phase of schema change. At this time, the patient may be ready to take a different and more equal role with their partner, which might lead to conflicts. The partner will see the therapist as not objective (which is mostly the case). Therefore, it is advisable to refer them for this problem to relationship counseling service or to a sexologist.

The Future

The demand for ST treatment is increasing since it appears to be both effective and safe. The mental healthcare services will have to guarantee the minimal conditions necessary for therapists to implement this treatment well. This requires training, ongoing gains in expertise, peer supervision, supervision, and the support of management and colleagues.

A peer supervision group is also necessary in order to stay alert to the schemas of the therapist himself, and how these can conflict with those of the patient, or how they can influence therapy in a negative way. Because of the current climate within Dutch mental healthcare institutes, where the pressure on production is high and there remains little space for supervision and peer supervision, it is not easy to organize this. A solution might be to get into contact with one or more colleagues in a less formal way. It is also possible to search through the Schema Therapy register for like-minded people who are willing to form a peer supervision group.

Currently, the implementation of individual ST for borderline personality disorders in Dutch mental healthcare institutes is being researched in an implementation study (Nadort *et al.*, in progress). This study is an investigation of the conditions that are necessary to implement this treatment successfully, for example, providing compensation for the patient's contribution to psychotherapy, embedding within the ward, peer supervision, and supervision. Furthermore, this study examines the effect of telephone availability out of office hours.

References

Arntz, A. and Bögels, S. (2000) *Schemagerichte Cognitieve Therapie voor Persoonlijkheidsstoornissen*. Houten: Bohn Stafleu van Loghum.

Arntz, A. and Kuipers, H. (1998) Cognitieve gedragstherapie bij borderline persoonlijkheidstoornis, in *Behandelingsstrategieën bij Borderline Persoonlijkheidsstoornis* (eds W. van Tilburg, W. van den Brink and A. Arntz). Houten: Bohn Stafleu van Loghum, pp. 42–64.

Bamelis, L., Arntz, A., Bernstein, D. *et al.* (2006–10) *Psychological Treatment of Personality Disorders: a Multicentered Randomized Controlled Trial on the (Cost-)Effectiveness of Schema-Focused Therapy*. Promotietraject, University of Maastricht.

Beck, A.T., Freeman, A., Davis, D.D. *et al.* (2004) *Cognitive Therapy of Personality Disorders*. New York: Guilford Press.

Bernstein, D., Arntz, A. and Vos, M.E. de (2007) Schemagerichte therapie in forensische settings: theoretisch model en richtlijnen voor best clinical practice. *Tijdschrift voor Psychotherapie*, 33, 120–139.

Genderen, H. van and Arntz, A. (2005) *Schemagerichte Cognitieve Therapie bij Borderline Persoonlijkheidsstoornis*. Amsterdam: Uitgeverij Nieuwezijds.

Giesen-Bloo, J., Dyck, R., Spinhoven, P. *et al.* (2006) Outpatient psychotherapy for borderline personality disorder: a randomized clinical trial of schema focused therapy versus transference focused psychotherapy. *Archives of General Psychiatry*, 63, 649–658.

Jongh, A. de and Broeke, E. ten (2003) *Handboek EMDR, een Geprotocolleerde Behandelmethode voor de Gevolgen van Psychotrauma*. Lisse: Swets & Zeitlinger.

Kabat-Zinn, J. (2000) *Handboek Meditatief Ontspannen, Effectief Programma voor het Bestrijden van Pijn en Stress.* Haarlem: Becht.

Linehan, M.M. (1993a) *Cognitive-Behavioral Treatment of Borderline Personality Disorder.* New York: Guilford Press.

Linehan, M.M. (1993b) *Skills Training Manual for Treating Borderline Personality Disorder.* New York: Guilford Press.

Lobbestael, J., Vreeswijk, M.F. van and Arntz, A. (2008) An empirical test of schema mode conceptualizations in personality disorders. *Behaviour Research and Therapy,* 46(7), 854–860.

Nadort, M., Dyck, R., Smit, J.H. et al. (in progress) *Implementation of Out-patient Schema-focused Therapy for Borderline Personality Disorder in General Psychiatry.*

Nissen, L. and Poppinger, M. (2008) Eine Fallkonzeption zur Schematherapie nach Jeffrey Young. *Verhaltenstherapie and psychosoziale Praxis,* 40(2), 269–280.

Schacht, R. and Peeters, R. (2000) *Schemagerichte Therapie voor Moeilijke Mensen: een Nieuwe Uitdaging voor de Cognitieve Gedragstherapie.* Leuven: Garant.

Slee, N. (2008) *Cognitive-Behavioral Therapy for Deliberate Self-harm.* Academisch proefschrift. Universiteit Leiden.

Slee, N., Garnefski, N. and Spinhoven, P. (2008) Protocollaire behandeling voor jongeren met zelfbeschadigend gedrag, in *Protocollaire behandelingen voor kinderen en adolescenten* (eds C. Braet and S. Bögels). Amsterdam: Boom.

Sprey, A. (2000) *Praktijkboek Persoonlijkheidsstoornissen: Diagnostiek, Cognitieve Gedragstherapie en Therapeutische Relatie.* Houten: Bohn Stafleu van Loghum.

Werkgroep richtlijn persoonlijkheidsstoornissen (2008) *Multidisciplinaire Richtlijn Persoonlijkheidsstoornissen. Richtlijn voor de Diagnostiek en Behandeling van Volwassen Patiënten met een Persoonlijkheidsstoornis (Conceptversie).* Utrecht: Trimbos-instituut.

Young, J.E., Klosko, J. and Weishaar, M.E. (2003) *Schema Therapy: a Practitioner's Guide.* New York: Guilford Press.

Young, J.E., Klosko, J.S. and Weishaar, M.E. (2005) *Schemagerichte Therapie: Handboek voor Therapeuten.* Houten: Bohn Stafleu van Loghum.

Young, J.E. and Pijnaker, H. (1999) *Cognitieve Theapie voor Persoonlijkheidsstoornissen. Een Schemagerichte Banadering.* Houten: Bohn Stafleu van Loghum.

3
Schema Therapy for Couples: Healing Partners in a Relationship

Travis Atkinson

Introduction

Intimate relationships can play a key role in helping heal a client's early maladaptive schemas, enabling core needs to be met. As an integrative model, Schema Therapy (ST) incorporates the latest evidence defining the nature of couples' distress, utilizes highly accurate predictors for relationship separation and longevity, and applies interventions to help couples make lasting changes. The ST model offers an expansive compass to help the couples therapist assess and differentiate core maladaptive themes underlying relationship distress, and provides a detailed strategy for the therapist to guide couples toward meeting both personal and relationship needs.

ST for couples can help partners access and reprocess key emotions connected with schemas to help create healthy, adaptive coping strategies and modes in a relationship. Early maladaptive schemas can be reinvented, establishing healthy schemas of the self and secure connections in the couple's relationship. ST for couples can be used specifically with couples in distress, or as a supplement to individual therapy, with the partner teaming up with the therapist to help heal early maladaptive schemas. Core maladaptive schemas, coping strategies, and modes can threaten the creation and establishment of a "secure base" for each partner in a relationship to explore the world, and can destroy a "safe haven" in the relationship where each partner can count on the other for attention, love, and support (Bowlby, 1988). In individual therapy, the therapist practices limited reparenting to become the "secure base" for the client, and the therapy session becomes the "safe haven." In couples therapy, the therapist works with the couple to help each partner become the primary "secure base" for the other, and for the relationship to become the "safe haven" (Johnson, 2003a).

In many situations, several individual sessions may be needed for schemas to erupt during the one-on-one session. In couples therapy, the presence of the partner can instantly ignite raw core emotions of the early maladaptive schemas, providing a rapid and intense emotional experience. The therapist helps each partner quickly identify schemas, coping strategies, and modes in-session with the partner, and choreographs "corrective emotional experiences" for each partner to reprocess and heal schema wounds (Alexander and French, 1946). Models of self and others can be tested with a partner in the session, and corrective experiences can contradict early maladaptive schemas. The couple experiments with healthy "theories," maladaptive schemas become dormant or are healed, and healthy schemas become realities.

Clashes and Healing: Mode Cycles in Couples

Maladaptive schemas and coping strategies play out in the couple's interaction process and can create intense schema clashes and mode cycles, primarily triggered by schemas in the first domain: disconnection and rejection. Unmet needs for security and satisfying attachment result in a mode cycle. Each partner's need for stability, safety, nurturance, love, and belonging is thwarted. The schemas of Abandonment, Mistrust and Abuse, Emotional Deprivation, and Defectiveness filter couple interactions and cause acute emotional states, followed by physiological arousal and an urge to act. Distressed couples can respond to a perceived threat to themselves or the relationship using three basic maladaptive responses to danger: *fight* (child modes of Angry, Enraged, or Impulsive Child; compensation modes of Self-Aggrandizer or Bully and Attack; and the Demanding or Punitive Parent modes), *flight* (avoidance modes of the Detached Protector or Detached Self-Soother), or *freeze* (the Compliant Surrender mode). The result in the couple's dynamic is a mode cycle that limits options and creates patterns that perpetuate schemas (Young, Klosko and Weishaar, 2003).

When a partner experienced a depriving or threatening situation in the past (childhood, a relationship, or a trauma or betrayal in the present relationship), he or she may have used his or her coping strategies to survive. In an adult intimate relationship, when key emotions associated with core schemas erupt, the same adaptive strategies used in the past constrict and narrow present options. Needs go unmet. The most intense fears of the partner are more likely to occur, but as a result of the coping strategies and modes reinforcing the schemas (Young *et al.*, 2003). Mode cycles can ignite more intensely and rapidly in specific couples' dynamics, especially when one or both partners has a strong Mistrust and Abuse schema, or have features of borderline or narcissistic personality disorder. More rigid, intense mode cycles can also form when a partner experiences a significant betrayal or abandonment in the relationship that erupts and supports a schema (Johnson, 2004).

Maladaptive mode cycles create clashes that may correlate highly with separation or divorce, and a flexible, adaptive mode cycle can promote healing and relationship longevity (Gottman, 1994). Rather than responding equally in an interaction, maladaptive mode cycles escalate negativity and reject a partner's influence (Gottman, 1999). Awareness between partners diminishes, effective support-seeking is inhibited, and emotional responsiveness is sidetracked (Mikulincer and Shaver, 2007). Common maladaptive mode cycles follow patterns of rigidity and create relationship clashes. An anxious partner turns to his or her significant other for soothing, but while emotionally overwhelmed through an ambiguous strategy that can push the partner away, and simultaneously unable to comfort or assist the other partner (Begley, 2007). A

> Maladaptive mode cycles include: 1) a fight/flight loop. The most common in distressed couples, an example includes Mary pursuing John to connect by criticizing him for being late (Punitive Parent), but John walks into another room to watch football on television, tuning Mary and the relationship out (Detached Protector); 2) a fight/fight loop. For instance, both Tim and Liz shift into their Punitive Parent mode when Tim becomes contemptuous toward Liz, rolling his eyes after she makes a mistake with their finances, and Liz criticizes Tim, calling him a "control freak"; 3) a fight/freeze loop, such as when Kim criticizes Peter for talking to a female co-worker at an office party, and Peter shifts into his Compliant Surrender mode, passively submitting to Kim's attacks; 4) a freeze/freeze loop, when Chris and Pat both shift into the Compliant Surrender mode, perpetuating their schemas by not asking for their needs to be met; and 5) a flight/flight loop. Both Gail and Art live parallel lives, scheduling their own activities away from each other without any emotional engagement, stuck in a Detached Protector mode (Young et al., 2003).

detached partner manages upsets independently, disconnecting from his or her significant other (Goleman, 2006).

The healthy mode cycle in a couple occurs when both partners flexibly shift between the Healthy Adult, Vulnerable Child, and Contented Child modes. Partners communicate coherently with each other and experience collaborative discourses. Whether favorable or not, the couple's description and evaluation of relationship experiences are consistent (Siegel, 1999). A healthy mode utilizes the Healthy Adult to take risks, learn new ideas, and update models of the self and world, strengthening an ability to reflect on schemas (Fonagy and Target, 1997). The ability of each partner to successfully repair maladaptive mode cycles and heal schemas is a goal of ST, resulting in the couple building and sustaining a secure bond.

In a couple's dynamic, several schemas can clash simultaneously. Using a mode cycle framework, the therapist identifies the couple's main maladaptive interaction style, their prototypical cycle that reinforces each partner's schemas. A key goal for the therapist is to help the couple shift into adaptive interactions with each other that invite responses that can heal schemas, creating a sense of hope and safety in the relationship that can secure the relationship bond.

Application

Assessment and education phase

Preparation and beginning the couple's therapy process. Creating a strong therapeutic relationship with the couple starts at the initial contact with the therapist. With a warm, inviting voice, the therapist builds a connection with the partner in the relationship who is scheduling the initial appointment. The therapist conveys confidence in working with couples experiencing similar themes, or refers to appropriate alternatives.

During the first contact, ideally the therapist assesses several criteria before meeting the couple for the first appointment. Questions may include the following: is one or both of the partners in crisis? Is violence part of the dynamic? If so, the therapist assesses whether the level of violence requires a referral to an appropriate agency specializing in battering programs. Are any present or past psychiatric diagnoses applicable for either partner? Is one or both partners abusing substances or chemicals, or experiencing other addictions? If yes, further assessment may be needed to determine if couples therapy is appropriate. Do other potential contraindications apply? Although brief, the first contact assesses a couple's needs and matches them with the most appropriate resources.

If the couple is suitable for relationship therapy, the therapist outlines the process the couple can expect. Generally, the assessment phase includes initial conjoint sessions, an individual session with each partner, and an additional conjoint "feedback and goals" session. Intervention sessions follow the assessment process, usually conjointly, though occasional individual sessions may be needed. Depending on the severity of the couple's prototypical mode cycle and the specific Domain 1 schemas, many couples can expect 15 to 20 highly focused intervention sessions to meet their goals of relationship satisfaction. However, if one or both partners experience an acute schema, such as Mistrust and Abuse, or a particularly rigid mode cycle, such as a disengaged flight/flight loop, the number of intervention sessions needed may double or triple (Johnson, 2003b).

Questionnaires can help the therapist assess both individual and relationship issues. The questionnaires include: the Young Schema Questionnaire (YSQ-3), the Young Parenting Inventory (YPI), the Schema Mode Inventory (SMI), the Beck Depression Inventory (BDI-II), and the Beck Anxiety Inventory (BAI). The YSQ-3 and YPI help the therapist conceptualize the schemas of each partner. The SMI can help the therapist identify the prototypical mode cycle.[1] Higher scores on the Beck inventories for depression and anxiety may help signify the need for one or both partners to address symptoms that may be negatively impacting on the relationship (Young et al., 2003).

Goals of the assessment conjoint sessions. The therapist works to frame the treatment for the couple. As the couple first sits in the therapist's office, they ideally face each other to increase awareness of nonverbal cues and to develop "mindsight," a capacity for insight and empathy (Siegel, 2007). The therapist asks the couple to summarize what is motivating them to seek therapy at this time. The therapist monitors nonverbal communications between the couple, assessing the quality of the connection and each partner's emotional sentiment toward the other as they discuss key moments of the relationship.

---

[1] Three relationship questionnaires may help further assess couples. As of writing, the Dyadic Adjustment Scale (DAS) and the Revised Conflict Tactics Scale (RCTS), and the Weiss-Cerreto Marital Status Inventory (MSI) are not available in Dutch. The DAS is a highly reliable measure of relationship satisfaction assessing dyadic satisfaction, consensus, cohesion, and affectional expression. For DAS scoring, the mean is 100, with a standard deviation of 15. Relationships in the first four years generally score 15–20 points above the mean. A distressed couple usually has at least one partner scoring below 85. Couples who separate or divorce typically score 70 or below. On the Weiss-Cerreto, separation potential is predicted when a partner's score exceeds 4. The therapist also assesses the couple for violence, and the RCTS is widely used to detect physical aggression in a relationship. Higher scores may signify referring a couple to a violence program instead of couples therapy (Gottman, 1999).

Attaining a detailed history of the relationship may include asking questions, including: What do you remember about the first time you met? What were your first impressions of each other? What attracted you to each other? What stands out about your first six months together? What led to your making a serious commitment together? When did you notice tension in your relationship, and how did that get played out? What do you remember about your wedding or ceremony, and honeymoon? What adjustments did you experience the first year you lived together? With the arrival of your first baby, how did your relationship evolve? What experiences stand out as really good times and as distressing times in your relationship? How is your relationship different now compared with during your first 8–10 months together? Do you know examples of happy and distressed relationships? What is different between these couples? How does your relationship compare to these couples right now? What are your goals in our work together? What questions do you have about relationship therapy? (Gottman, 1999).

The therapist asks the couple to complete the questionnaires and bring them in for the following conjoint session. Additional homework may be assigned, based on the couple's needs. The therapist works to create and build a strong therapeutic relationship with both partners, carefully reflecting and validating each one's perspectives and experiences. By the end of the first session the couple feels the therapist understands them and the specific culture of the relationship. The therapist assesses for any personal schemas activated with each partner and the relationship dynamic, and continues working with that understanding, or seeks additional supervision to limit any potential negative effects. For instance, a therapist with an intense Detached Protector may feel overwhelmed with a fight/fight mode loop and conclude that the couple is hopeless, rather than stuck in a cycle that can be broken.

The second conjoint session seeks to illuminate the interaction process of the couple and identify their prototypical mode cycle from among the five most common loops (fight/flight, fight/fight, flight/flight, fight/freeze, or freeze/freeze), connecting schemas that trigger mode cycles. The therapist compares higher scores on each partner's SMI with actual patterns between the couple in the session. After checking with the couple, the therapist asks each partner what key moments stand out since the first session. The therapist notes interaction patterns of the relationship. The couple has the opportunity to discuss themes and content issues that repeatedly get them stuck in a negative mode cycle, usually the chronic issues of the relationship. The therapist asks the couple to model what it would look if he or she were a fly on the wall watching a conflict between them. For instance, the therapist instructs:

> "Jill and Chris, I want to understand how you are in a conflict together. I'd like to see what happens for both of you when you talk about the issue of whether you both want children." The therapist tracks each moment of what they are describing, asking repeatedly, "And then what happens?" The therapist notes the mode cycle emerging from the couple's interaction, including schemas and coping styles, and compares this to the SMI results. After play-by-play descriptions, the therapist asks the couple to engage in a conflict on a subject that has not been resolved in their relationship. The therapist may ask permission to record the couple engaging in the conflict. The therapist might say, "I'd

> like you both to turn to the other and start discussing an upsetting, unresolved topic, and do the best that you can within a 10-minute period to resolve this topic. I'll observe without interjecting. When you finish, we'll talk about how it was for both of you."

The therapist analyzes the interaction, labeling the prototypical mode cycle, noting key schema eruptions, and linking mode cycles to the main complaints each partner has about the relationship and his or her unmet needs. The therapist conceptualizes key themes to present during the feedback session, along with specific strategies to address in the intervention sessions. After taping, the therapist asks both partners how they experienced the most difficult parts of the interaction. The couple begins to identify specific cues that trigger key emotions, how they cope when they are upset, and their mode cycle. The therapist notes areas of strength in their dynamic, and continues to reflect and validate both of their perspectives, working to secure a strong therapeutic relationship. The couple leaves the session with a sense of hope and inspiration that they've started to become aware of their negative interaction patterns stemming from their schemas, a necessary step on the road to positive change. The therapist assigns tasks to complete before the next session, including relevant chapters in *Reinventing Your Life*, and appropriate relationship exercises.

Individual sessions. Referencing the questionnaires, the therapist asks each partner for information about significant events in the relationship, and personal history. The therapist starts the session by discussing rules of confidentiality and secrets.

> "A key element in the couples therapy process is for both partners not to have major secrets from each other, related to the relationship. This means that if you disclose something to me that John doesn't know about, such as an affair or an addiction problem, you agree to disclose it to John within one month. I will not personally disclose it to him. If you find it difficult to reveal, I will work with you to help make it easier for you. After a month, if you have not told him, our work together in relationship therapy will have to stop. We make this commitment because if there is a major secret, our work together may be limited in its effectiveness, and I want to do all that I can to help both of you improve your relationship. I've also found it much easier for couples to repair damage in a relationship when secrets are disclosed, rather than discovered."

During the individual session, a primary objective is to reinforce the therapeutic alliance. The therapist reflects each partner's experiences, as described in individual schema treatment, in a manner that helps reveal key schemas, coping strategies, and modes. Using the self-assessment questionnaires, the therapist labels and discusses the origins and functions of each schema, coping style, and mode in each partner's developmental history. The therapist asks for a detailed relationship history, identifying life patterns in partner selection and past relationship problems, and links key schemas and modes to the current relationship problems and life situations. The therapist conducts an assessment imagery exercise that includes childhood images of mother, father, and other significant parent figures, and links the partner's needs and emotions from childhood images with his or her current relationship (Young *et al.*, 2003). Who did the partner confide in and turn to for comfort as a child? How did that figure respond? How did the partner cope with his or her environment as a child? (Johnson *et al.*, 2005). The therapist discusses the cues of schemas and modes from the past and compares these triggers to relevant conflicts with the partner in the relationship. During this discussion, the therapist carefully reflects and validates the partner's coping strategies and modes originating from his or her core schemas, helping him or her feel validated rather than shamed.

Next, the therapist discusses each partner's relationship satisfaction and level of commitment to his or her present relationship. Who does each partner confide in now and get emotional support from? The therapist accesses each partner's level of engagement in the therapy process. In addition, knowing that a partner cares can help sustain even a severely distressed relationship and may predict a more promising outcome in couple's therapy (Johnson, 2004).

> Sex and passion are also discussed during the individual session.
> "On a scale of 1 to 10, how would you rate your companionate love and chemistry with Pat? How much passion and romance do you feel right now? What was it like in the beginning of your relationship? Has that changed, and if so, when?"

The therapist assesses for initial and present attraction levels and how the couple's mode cycle influences sex and intimacy in the relationship.

An ongoing affair is a contraindication for success in couples therapy, and the therapist asks both partners during the individual sessions to disclose any emotional or romantic affairs. Additional contraindications may include violence, substance abuse, and differing agendas. While therapeutic discretion must be used, one or two situations that become physically violent do not necessarily equate with a pattern of abuse. Additionally, emotional violence can also derail couples therapy. Both partners must feel safe enough to experience raw emotions together in the therapy session without the threat of a violent response. If safety cannot be established with the therapist, a referral to a domestic violence program may be appropriate. After a program is successfully completed, if safety can be established, couples therapy may continue (Johnson, 2004).

Couples therapy may not be effective if a partner is actively abusing a substance or experiencing other addictions, using an entrenched Detached Protector mode to block or numb emotions. Healing emotional experiences can only occur when access to emotions is possible. If a partner is using an addiction as part of his or her Detached Protector mode and refuses to address his or her behaviors, couples therapy may be discontinued. The therapist works with the partner of the addict to make decisions, and suitable referrals may be provided for individual therapy or support groups (Gottman, 1999).

In some cases, one partner may have an agenda that the therapist cannot ethically support. For instance, if the main goal of one partner is to have the therapist convince the other partner to do something the other partner does not want to do, couples therapy may not be appropriate (Johnson, 2004). The therapist directs each partner to appropriate treatment if the issues can better be addressed elsewhere, including crisis situations of depression, anxiety, bipolar disorder, or anger management. The therapist also diagnoses applicable personality disorders, including BPD, narcissism, or obsessive compulsive disorder features, and makes appropriate individual referrals as needed.

Feedback session. The final stage of assessment occurs when the therapist meets with both partners and summarizes their strengths, difficulties, and themes in the relationship. The therapist educates them about their prototypical mode cycle, and the schemas and coping strategies in common clashes. The questionnaires and information attained during the assessment process are summarized. The therapist discusses a time frame for the couple's therapy sessions, taking into account both partners' histories, the severity of their schemas, and the intensity of the mode cycle. A couple rapidly flipping into an intense, rigid mode cycle usually requires more sessions. The therapist carefully instills hope in both partners, and answers any questions they have. Homework is assigned to help the couple identify what happens for both of them outside of the session when their mode cycle erupts. The therapist also assigns continued reading relevant to their schemas in *Reinventing Your Life* (Young and Klosko, 1993).

Change

Intervention sessions focus on helping each partner identify maladaptive mode cycles, and assist each partner to "reparent" the core needs of the other. The couple works to create a flexible and fluid interaction style together, sustaining the Healthy Adult/Vulnerable Child/Contented Child mode cycle.

Cognitive techniques. Throughout the intervention process, the therapist addresses cognitions each partner experiences originating from schemas, helping each partner restructure his or her beliefs of self and about his or her partner in the relationship. A goal for the couple is to develop a healthy working model of intimacy. When partners describe a mode cycle they are experiencing, the therapist intervenes using *cognitive work* to communicate an understanding of the origins of schemas for both partners, and to validate the partner's experience. The therapist then empathically tests the validity of each schema in the present relationship and helps the partner put the situation into a healthier, more realistic perspective. Evidence from all periods of both partners' lives is gathered to fight the schemas and discredit reinforcements, especially core schemas in the disconnection and rejection domain. Since both partners are involved in the process, they may assist each other in relating to their core themes. The therapist focuses on the couple's mode cycle or the interaction process between them, not the content of the fights. If the therapist examines only the content of a conflict, the couple may not address the modes that cause the interaction styles that perpetuate schemas.

The therapist practices mode dialogues between the voices of core modes and schemas and the Healthy Adult. For instance, to help a partner connect with the Vulnerable Child mode, the therapist says:

> "Pat, right now I noticed that your voice began to tremble and your body started to shake. If we gave a voice to that part of you, what would she say?" The therapist helps Pat to experience the Vulnerable Child, and for her partner to identify when Pat is in that mode. The therapist models for the partner how the Healthy Adult can respond to the Vulnerable Child mode. "A part of you right now is so afraid of losing John, so afraid that the pattern might repeat, that once again you'll be all alone, just like little Pat. Is that right? It's scary to be in this place, where you love John so much and don't want to lose him. I want you to know that you're not alone in this. I'm here with you, and I'll help you through this place." The therapist models a Healthy Adult providing an antidotal experience through calming, comforting, and soothing a Vulnerable Child, validating the emotions being triggered, and testing the reality of the situation. A Healthy Adult can then give the Vulnerable Child appropriate guidance and advice, if applicable. Both partners are able to identify their mode cycle, core unmet needs, and antidotes to get those needs met.

The therapist helps the couple write a flash card for recurring mode cycles in the relationship, linking core schemas to the cycle. The couple reviews the flash card regularly and uses it when an unhealthy mode cycle erupts to build a case against their schemas. Rationally, the couple disproves the validity of schemas and recognizes how schemas are perpetuated through the mode cycle (Young *et al.*, 2003). Additional homework may be assigned, including books related to relationships such as *The Seven Principles for Making Marriage Work* by J.M. Gottman. The therapist helps link predictors for separation in relationships, including criticism, defensiveness, contempt, and stonewalling with the couple's mode cycles and offers alternatives for adaptive cycles (Gottman and Silver, 1999).

Experiential techniques. With a cognitive understanding of their mode cycle solidified, the therapist begins to include more experiential work with the couple in the intervention process. Couples therapy allows the therapist to access, expand, and process intense emotional experiences with both partners present in the session, often activating more intense emotions than individual therapy. For instance, provoked by a partner, the therapist will more likely observe one partner flipping into a Punitive Parent mode towards the other partner, which may be difficult for the therapist to produce in individual therapy. In the couple's therapy context, the therapist can use the heightened affect resulting from the mode cycle as an entry into the couple's schemas. Rather than a report of outside events in a distanced way, the therapist witnesses the couple's mode cycle in session. The therapist can assist a partner to provide an antidote through the Healthy Adult to the other partner's schemas, providing a "corrective emotional experience" (Alexander and French, 1946).

A key part of experiential work is the therapeutic relationship. If both partners feel validated and understood by the therapist, they may feel safer to connect with their more vulnerable emotions. The therapist can then link erupting schemas and modes connected with the emotions. Several techniques can be employed by the therapist

> The therapist actively works to stop a partner's Detached Protector mode from dampening or exciting emotions. For instance, a therapist would say, "Pat, let me slow you down. What just happened inside for you, right before the wall came up? What were you experiencing inside, right at that moment when Jill said she wanted to run?" The therapist redirects the partner to focus on a key moment of emotion, feeding back the key moment when the Detached Protector arose, helping the partner capture his or her Vulnerable Child.

to help intensify and expand the more vulnerable emotions. For instance, the therapist can reflect key elements of the mode cycle with each partner, validating, legitimizing, and understanding emotional reactions. Key phrases verbalized by each partner are linked to schemas and repeated to heighten the partner's emotions. The therapist can also heighten vulnerable emotions by leaning forward and lowering and slowing his or her voice when speaking to a partner's Vulnerable Child mode. Working with an Angry Child mode, the therapist expresses empathy by raising his or her voice to match the emotional state of a partner in an assertive mode. When the partner feels understood, he or she may feel safer to enter Vulnerable Child mode. In addition, images and metaphors can be directly applied to relationship situations to heighten vulnerable emotions and connect to schemas (Johnson, 2004).

During experiential work, the couple is able to connect and label emotions that relate to each mode, and core schemas driving the mode. Additionally, the therapist works experientially with the couple to help them move beyond labeling their emotions from a distance: they engage their emotions in-session, describing rather than explaining their emotional experience without becoming overwhelmed by them (Ekman, 2003).

The therapist uses imagery, dialogues, and role-plays to link each partner's childhood and past experiences with his or her current relationship. Each partner empowers his or her Healthy Adult: asserting rights and needs appropriately, grieving for losses, and facing and healing traumas. The therapist also helps each partner write letters (rarely sent) to parents and significant relationship figures influencing the development of the schemas, helping the partner feel the pain of the Vulnerable Child and accessing a Healthy Adult to confront and set the record straight (Young and Klosko, 1993).

In imagery, both partners confront a parent or caregiver and protect and comfort their Vulnerable Child. They are able to discuss what they needed from their significant figure but did not get. The image can shift to scenes where each partner has felt let down, betrayed, or abandoned by his or her partner, discussing unmet needs, the emotions connected with the scene, the schemas erupting, and the urges to act. Each partner is able to confront his or her schemas directly, in the presence of the partner. Imagery allows the couple to access and express his or her Vulnerable Child, helping the other partner safely hear the message without feeling attacked. Often the partner experiences a desire to soothe the other's Vulnerable Child. Eventually, the partner uses a Healthy Adult voice in the imagery scene to provide the antidotal experience the other partner longs for.

Another experiential tool in the couple's therapy process occurs when the therapist conducts mode dialogues, instructing each partner to enact key emotions with each

> The therapist helps Jane identify that she flips into her Angry Child mode to cope with the terror her Vulnerable Child experiences related to the possibility of Bill leaving her (Abandonment). Once she makes this connection, the therapist asks her to tell Bill what she feels when she's terrified of losing him. The therapist asks Jane how she experienced telling Bill about her fear in the Vulnerable Child voice. She describes her fear to expose "little Jane" to Bill. The therapist supports Jane's strength, and turns to Bill and asks how he experienced Jane telling him how afraid she is of losing him. Bill expresses compassion toward Jane, and how much safer he feels with her compared to her angry voice. He is able to identify his own sadness, uncovering his Vulnerable Child and his longing for Jane's approval. The therapist asks Bill to talk to Jane through his Vulnerable Child's voice, and the mode dialogue continues. The couple has flipped from a fight/flight loop into a healthy loop of a Vulnerable Child and Healthy Adult. Both partners can be heard and understood, and are more likely to get their needs met.

other, including any significant schema injuries and wounds of the relationship with his or her partner. A mode dialogue helps each partner access emotions linked to their mode cycle, and shift to an adaptive cycle.

Initially in treatment, the therapist focuses on both partners. However, as therapy continues, the therapist may focus on a partner in a Detached Protector mode to help him or her become more engaged in the process. Until emotions are accessed, the other partner will most likely feel anxious and progress may feel limited (Young et al., 2003). Once the therapist empathically confronts the Detached Protector, and the partner flips into a Vulnerable Child mode, the therapist can focus on an Angry Child, or Punitive or Demanding Parent mode. The therapist protects the transition from Detached Protector to Vulnerable Child, blocking any attacking modes of a partner. They express vulnerabilities and longings for connection with each other during the session, modeling antidotes to schemas.

The therapeutic alliance. The therapeutic relationship helps identify and heal each partner's schemas and modes erupting during sessions. As in individual therapy, the therapist works to establish a strong therapeutic alliance. However, a break in an alliance is highly likely when working with two individuals over time in couples therapy. The therapist must be sensitive and vigilant to address any misunderstanding or hurt a partner may feel from the therapist. Progress may stop until the alliance is repaired. The therapist links relevant personal information of the partner to in-session triggers, labeling cues of a schema, and associated emotions and coping strategies. Through reparenting, the therapist helps the partner rebuild safety and trust in the therapeutic alliance (Young et al., 2003).

Behavioral pattern-breaking. Behavioral pattern-breaking helps each partner rehearse behavioral changes together to break mode cycles and dysfunctional life patterns. During behavioral pattern-breaking, the therapist clarifies self-defeating mode cycles, and models and practices healthy behaviors. Additionally, the therapist uses imagery, mode dialogues, and flash cards to help the couple confront blocks to behavioral change. The therapist also combines cognitive and experiential work to empathically confront each partner, helping the couple shift from an unhealthy mode cycle to a Vulnerable Child/Happy Child/Healthy Adult mode cycle. Rituals of connection in the relationship are created that become repeated and predictable, such as affectionate greetings and partings (Gottman and DeClaire, 2001).

Resolution sessions. As couples navigate their mode cycle and healthier experiences emerge, the therapist solidifies gains in the therapy process and begins to prepare for termination of the therapy process. The therapist underlines differences between the prototypical mode cycle and the healthier dynamic in the couple. The couple's improved connection helps them have the confidence to better handle conflicts and meet each other's core needs, providing "soothing responses" in the relationship (Gottman, 1999). The couple's growth and strengths are validated, and the couple commits to continued work in a more secure relationship. The therapist analyzes self-assessment questionnaires, such as the SMI, to confirm the strength of healthier mode cycles in the relationship. The therapist makes a plan with the couple for occasional tune-up or follow-up sessions, with defined intervals.

Tips and Pitfalls

Several possibilities can limit or halt progress in couples therapy. First, the therapist must thoroughly evaluate each partner for contraindications. If the therapist assesses that a partner is in crisis and in need of an intervention, such as treatment for major depression, anxiety, or bipolar disorder, the therapist works to get appropriate individual treatment, either separately or combined with couples therapy. As with individual therapy, the therapist confers with other professionals involved in treatment, such as a provider managing psychotropic medications.

Confidentiality can also be a pitfall in the couple's therapy process. The therapist reminds both partners that any individual contact is conducted as if the partner is included in the conversation, and the therapist does not deviate from this.

Addictions can also lead to pitfalls in couples therapy. If the therapist observes that, despite several interventions, one partner is stagnating, substance abuse or other addictions should be ruled out.

In the therapeutic relationship, the therapist must carefully maintain the connection with both partners simultaneously. This can often be a difficult balancing act, especially when a partner triggers the therapist's own schemas. If the therapist does not quickly repair a break in the relationship, the couple may discontinue therapy. Both partners may experience schema eruptions at the same time. When the therapist makes a mistake or upsets one partner, he or she quickly works to repair the injury and return the couple to safety in the therapy session. The therapist may lose focus at times, and the couple may drift. Before every session, the therapist identifies where the couple is in the process of therapy, and designs relevant tasks for the couple to address where they may be stuck or need more attention. Are they working primarily with cognitive, experiential, behavioral, or combined themes? What schemas are being activated, and is the partner providing antidotes to each schema? What is the couple's prototypical mode cycle and is it shifting to a healthier cycle? The therapist assigns homework at the end of each session based on the couple's needs.

The Future

ST for couples offers a structured framework integrating several effective therapeutic techniques into one model. While ST has not yet been extensively researched specifically for couples, its integrative approach is ripe for research to build and expand on the successful outcomes of emotionally focused couple therapy and behavioral couple therapy (Johnson, 2004). With ST, not only can a couple feel relieved from relationship distress, but also each partner may recover from chronic, lifelong wounds originating from schemas. The goal of building hope and safety into the relationship allows each partner to become accessible and responsive to the other's needs, facilitating forgiveness, reconciliation, and healing of core schemas.

References

Alexander, F. and French, T. (1946) *Psychoanalytic Therapy: Principles and Application.* New York: Ronald Press.
Begley, S. (2007) *Train Your Mind, Change Your Brain.* New York: Ballantine Books.
Bowlby, J. (1988) *A Secure Base.* New York: Basic Books.
Ekman, P. (2003) *Emotions Revealed.* New York: Owl Books.
Fonagy, P. and Target, M. (1997) Attachment and reflective function: their role in self-organization. *Development and Psychopathology, 9,* 679–700.
Goleman, D. (2006) *Social Intelligence.* New York: Bantam Book.
Gottman, J.M. (1994) *What Predicts Divorce?* Hillsdale, NJ: Erlbaum.
Gottman, J.M. (1999) *The Marriage Clinic.* New York: Norton.
Gottman, J.M. and DeClaire, J. (2001) *The Relationship Cure.* New York: Three Rivers Press.
Gottman, J.M. and Silver, N. (1999) *The Seven Principles for Making Marriage Work.* New York: Three Rivers Press.
Johnson, S.M. (2003a) *Emotionally Focused Couple Therapy with Trauma Survivors: Strengthening Attachment Bonds.* New York: Guilford Press.
Johnson, S.M. (2003b) A guide for couple therapy, in *Attachment Process in Couple and Family Therapy* (eds S.M. Johnson and V.E. Whiffen). New York: Guilford Press, pp. 103–123.
Johnson, S.M. (2004) *The Practice of Emotionally Focused Couple Therapy.* New York: Brunner-Routledge.
Johnson, S.M., Bradley, B., Furrow, J. *et al.* (2005) *Becoming an Emotionally Focused Couple Therapist.* New York: Routledge.
Mikulincer, M. and Shaver, P.R. (2007) *Attachment in Adulthood.* New York: Guilford Press.
Siegel, D.J. (1999) *The Developing Mind.* New York: Guilford Press.
Siegel, D.J. (2007) *The Mindful Brain.* New York: Norton.
Young, J.E. and Klosko, J.S. (1993) *Reinventing Your Life.* New York: Plume.
Young, J.E., Klosko, J.S. and Weishaar, M.E. (2003) *Schema Therapy: a Practitioner's Guide.* New York: Guilford Press.

4

Introduction to Group Schema Therapy

Joan Farrell

In Part IV some of the Chapters describe a number of different approaches to using Schema Therapy (ST) in a group, with different patient populations, in a range of settings (outpatient, inpatient, day treatment) in the US, the Netherlands, and Germany. ST in groups is described by Young (2010) as the "third phase in the development of ST" and as having great promise. Using ST in a group format is not a particularly new development (Farrell and Shaw, 1994; Young and Pijnakker, 1999; van Vreeswijk and Broersen, 2006; Muste, Weertman and Claassen, 2009), however the publication of studies to evaluate the group models described here is more recent. Open-trial pilots have demonstrated effectiveness (Andrea, 2008; Reiss, Lieb, Arntz, Shaw and Farrell, submitted; van Vreeswijk, Spinhoven, Broersen and Eurelings-Bontekoe, unpublished), however, some of the results have limited availability. One randomized controlled trial (RCT) ($N = 32$) of group ST (GST) (summarized in Farrell and Shaw, 1994) for patients with borderline personality disorder (BPD) demonstrated the group model's effectiveness in reducing BPD symptoms, global psychiatric symptoms, and improved function with very large effect sizes (mean = 2.4) (Farrell, Shaw and Webber, 2009). GST is currently being evaluated in a large multi-site RCT ($N = 448$) in four countries (Arntz and Farrell, 2010) in which two years of a primarily GST condition are compared to a balanced GST and individual ST (IST) condition, with a treatment as usual (TAU) control.

Farrell, Shaw, and Reiss describe GST, which was developed as a comprehensive treatment for patients with BPD. This model has been tested as described above and demonstrated effectiveness in both outpatient and inpatient settings. GST was developed and refined by Farrell and Shaw over the last 25 years and parallels the development of ST by Young (1990; Young et al., 2003) and Arntz (2004; Arntz and van Genderen, 2009). The GST model is theoretically and conceptually consistent with ST. The major differences between the two lie in the strategic adaptation of standard ST interventions such as imagery change work and mode role-plays to actively include the entire group. In this model two equal co-therapists are seen as necessary in order to maintain the attachment with patients that is a core component of ST. Unlike interpersonal or process-oriented groups, the therapist role is an active and directive one, based on the developmental level and needs of the group. Patients with BPD are primarily in child modes in the early stages of treatment, so active "parents" are needed. A major difference between the GST model here and cognitive therapy and skills groups (e.g., dialectical behavior therapy) is that the therapeutic factors of groups (summarized in Yalom, 1995) are harnessed strategically to catalyze and augment the active ingredients of ST (i.e., limited reparenting, experiential and cognitive change work, and behavioral pattern-breaking). The full integration of experiential and cognitive work in the same GST session differentiates it from the models presented in the other chapters. GST is the group ST model being tested in the international RCT led by Arntz and Farrell (2010).

Muste describes the use of a group format in a day hospital and inpatient setting. He emphasizes the need for safety and transparency, with attention paid to the therapeutic climate of the group. This group program divides sessions into a cognitive component and a less structured component. Muste's group is described as a "work group" in which schemas and modes that impair the group process are identified and worked with. In this model group, individual and even family sessions are combined according to a patient's needs and what he describes as their "ego strength." Muste thinks that aspects of DBT, Acceptance and Commitment Therapy and mindfulness can be used in group ST. This is a controversial opinion in the ST community because of the possible conflict of these models with the limited reparenting therapist style crucial to ST.

Van Vreeswijk and Broersen present a short-term group program SCBT-g, which was developed for a mixed patient group with Cluster B and C personality disorders. SCBT-g has a published workbook and protocol (in Dutch). This model focuses primarily on the cognitive and behavioral techniques of ST and is described as sharing aspects of both the "classic behavioral" group therapy and interpersonal group therapy. SCBT-g, like GST, considers the different phases that a group passes through and their impact on which ST interventions are chosen in a session. The authors stress the importance of not sticking so rigidly to the protocol that the group therapeutic process and the emotional process of the patients are not attended to. Preliminary (unpublished) outcome data support the efficacy of this model (van Vreeswijk et al., unpublished).

Aalders and van Dijk describe integrating ST with a psychodynamic group model. This model is described as contraindicated for patients who are currently suicidal or self-injuring, aggressive or abusing drugs, and they limit the number of narcissistic, BPD, and Cluster C patients. Consequently, this model is more restrictive of patient population treated than the others in these chapters. They divide their sessions into an hour of ST techniques followed by an unstructured hour, which they describe as focusing on "psychodynamics." The first hour includes standard ST interventions such as imagery rescripting in which the focus is on an individual with the group observing or involved, role-play, and diary cards. The second hour has no agenda and patients may introduce any topic. As with traditional interpersonal process groups, members are encouraged to react to each other freely. In contrast, the Farrell-Shaw GST prohibits using this group model for BPD patients since it is an approach designed to engender conflict and high emotions.

As these chapters demonstrate, the therapy group is an effective modality for ST, which can be particularly effective for remediating the interpersonal effects of schema driven and mode behavior of a variety of patients. The ST group provides practitioners with a closer analog to the family of origin, which appears to add power to the experiential and cognitive interventions of ST and offers a microcosm of the "outside-of-therapy" world in which to practice behavioral pattern-breaking. There are some disagreements among the models of ST groups represented here (e.g., whether psychodynamic and ST therapist approaches can be reconciled, how outside group contact should be dealt with, how the group itself is employed as an agent of change). These and other issues raised still need to be investigated empirically. The various group models have varying levels of support by outcome studies. The large effect sizes reported (Farrell *et al.*, 2009) and observed clinically (Reiss *et al.*, submitted; van Vreeswijk, *et al.*, unpublished) strongly suggest further exploration of the promise of ST in groups for difficult-to-treat patient populations.

References

Andrea, H. (2008) Cohort klinische schematherapie; data uit Sceptre onderzoek [Cohort clinical schema therapy: data from Sceptre research]. Personal communication.

Arntz, A. (2004) Cognitive therapy for borderline personality disorder, in *Cognitive Therapy of Personality Disorders* (eds A. Beck *et al.*). New York: Guilford Press.

Arntz, A. and Farrell, J.M. (2010) New international developments in schema therapy for borderline personality disorder. Symposium at the World Congress of Associations for Behavioral and Cognitive Therapy, Boston, MA. June 6.

Arntz, A. and Genderen, H. van (2009) *Schema Therapy for Borderline Personality Disorder*. New York: Wiley.

Farrell, J.M. and Shaw, I.A. (1994) Emotional awareness training: a prerequisite to effective cognitive-behavioral treatment of borderline personality disorder. *Cognitive and Behavioral Practice*, 1, 71–91.

Farrell, J., Shaw, I. and Webber, M. (2009) A schema-focused approach to group psychotherapy for outpatients with borderline personality disorder: a randomized controlled trial. *Journal of Behavior Therapy and Experimental Psychiatry*, 40, 317–328.

Muste, E., Weertman, A. and Claassen, A. (2009) *Handboek Klinische Schematherapie*. Houten: Bohn Stafleu van Loghum.

Reiss, N., Lieb, K., Arntz, A., Shaw, I.A. and Farrell, J.M. (submitted) Responding to the treatment challenge of patients with severe BPD: results of three pilot studies of inpatient schema therapy.

Vreeswijk, M.F. van and Broersen, J. (2006) *Schemagerichte Therapie in Groepen (Handleiding)*. Houten: Bohn Stafleu van Loghum.

Yalom, I.D. (1995) *The Theory and Practice of Group Psychotherapy*, 5th edition. New York: Basic Books.

Young, J.E. (1990) *Cognitive Therapy for Personality Disorders: a Schema-Focused Approach*. Sarasota, FL: Practitioner's Resource Series.

Young, J.E. (2010) Schema therapy, past, present and future. Keynote address to the Conference of the International Society for Schema Therapy, Berlin, Germany, July.

Young, J.E., Klosko, J.S. and Weishaar, M.E. (2003) *Schema Therapy: a Practitioner's Guide*. New York: Guilford Press.

Young, J.E. and Pijnaker, H. (1999) *Cognitieve Therapie voor Persoonlijkheidsstoornissen, een Schemagerichte Benadering*. Houten: Bohn Staffleu van Loghum.

5

Group Schema Therapy for Borderline Personality Disorder Patients
Catalyzing Schema and Mode Change

Joan Farrell, Ida Shaw and Neele Reiss

Introduction

The adaptation of Schema Therapy (ST) techniques for use in the group modality is an important theoretical and practical development. In a time of shrinking healthcare resources, group ST (GST) is a cost-effective alternative that could increase treatment availability. The GST model described here can be used with a range of personality disorders and Axis I symptoms (e.g., depression and anxiety), just as individual ST can. Those applications are in development and have not yet been tested empirically (Beckley and Gordon, 2010). This chapter will focus on the GST model developed for borderline personality disorder (BPD) by Farrell and Shaw (1994), which was later tested in a randomized clinical trial (Farrell, Shaw and Webber, 2009). An intensive version of this model was also developed (Farrell and Shaw, 2005) and has been tested in inpatient psychiatric settings in the US and Germany (Reiss, Lieb, Arntz, Shaw and Farrell, submitted).

In this chapter we discuss our understanding of how the group format itself impacts on ST and speculate about how group-specific curative factors may augment and catalyze schema mode change. We describe the adjustments to limited reparenting that groups require and the modifications needed in core ST techniques when used in group (e.g., imagery work), as well as the additional opportunities for creative experiential work that the group offers. Suggestions are also given about ways to handle the added challenges of groups, including their emotional intensity and complexity.

The Healing Power of the GST

One interpretation of the large treatment effect size in Farrell and colleagues' (2009) study is simply that the group augmented and even catalyzed ST techniques that target core BPD symptoms such as abandonment, emptiness, defectiveness, lack of belonging, and stormy relationships. We assume that factors not present in individual ST contribute to the group's effectiveness, foe example, mutual support and validation by group members, the possibility to safely experiment with emotion expression and new behaviors in the group, mutual attachment that might heal unsafe attachment representations, empathic confrontations that group members give each other, the expansion of limited reparenting from a dyad to two "parents" and an entire "family," and the additional options and players available for experiential techniques. GST benefits from the general curative factors of groups (Yalom, 2005), namely instillation of universality, altruism, experience of group cohesiveness, corrective recapitulation of the primary family, opportunities for emotional catharsis, additional information sources, modeling, vicarious learning, interpersonal learning, *in vivo* desensitization, and social skill practice opportunities. These curative factors are woven through GST and can be harnessed to benefit the goals and expand the techniques of ST, providing additional healing experiences in the group for patients' Abandoned/Vulnerable Child mode. Each will be discussed further in terms of the aspects of GST on which they have an impact.

Group Schema Therapy for BPD: the Beginning Stage

In general, our GST model is consistent with the phases of treatment and goals outlined for individual ST by Young, Klosko, and Weishaar (2003) and the Arntz and van Genderen (2009) publication of the treatment protocol from the successful trial in the Netherlands (Giesen-Bloo *et al.*, 2006). A therapeutic group experience for BPD patients requires that a safe and supportive family structure for the group is developed and maintained by the "parent-therapists." The patients' ability to tolerate emotional expression must be developed, along with trust in the therapists. The group therapist must be ready and able to set firm limits on modes such as the Angry Child or Punitive Parent verbally or physically attacking peers or the patient himself. The patients' Vulnerable Child mode needs to know that the therapists will protect them from such experiences and not abandon them. In addition, it must be possible for the Angry/Impulsive Child mode to vent anger in the group setting without being abandoned as a result of inappropriate behaviors. When anger expression or venting occurs, some group members will feel able to stay in the physical vicinity while others will feel the need to be behind a protective barrier of pillows or chairs. Importantly, the therapists and group members must find ways for these different needs to be met without "sacrificing" anyone. Accomplishing this provides cognitive and experiential antidotes for a variety of maladaptive schemas.

The GST approach developed by Farrell and Shaw (1994) includes an early psycho-education component focused on the diagnosis and etiology of BPD. Discussion of the origins of BPD in terms of unmet childhood and adolescent needs and experiences of trauma, allows group members to bond around similarities in their growing-up experiences, such as sexual, physical, and/or emotional abuse or deprivation or abandonment. Emotional validation and empathy, expressed by the group therapists toward the innocent children who experienced these traumas, assists bonding with the therapists. Bonding and cohesiveness provide hope and commitment for treatment. It also helps patients to restructure their thinking about personal history and current experiences in a self-compassionate manner.

> After a couple of weeks in the group Mary started seeking the therapists' attention by exaggeratedly and constantly complaining (e.g. about the temperature, the smell of the room, the topic, etc.). Growing up, Mary had learned that she would only get attention by constantly crying or complaining to her parents, who had no time for her because work was their principal focus. Her Lonely/Vulnerable Child still needed attention so she carried on complaining. When Mary had the attention of the therapist, she felt better. However, her constant need deprived other patients from getting attention from the therapists. Mary's need and the need of the other group members both required validation, so a compromise was needed ("Every single person is important to this group"). Talking about the modes her behavior triggered in others helped Mary understand the reactions (e.g., withdrawal, anger) of people in her personal surroundings to her complaints. The compromise the group worked out was that whenever Mary felt that she needed additional attention, she would, as a first step, make contact (e.g., eye contact, hold pinkies, etc.) with the person (therapist or group member) sitting next to her. This strategy helped Mary reduce her complaints and have her needs better met, thus avoiding becoming an annoyance to the group and having her "abandonment" and "isolation" schemas reinforced. At the same time, it effectively helped the other patients to get their needs for attention and support met.

Limited Reparenting Broadened: Building a "Healthy Family"

As in individual ST, limited reparenting is an essential "active ingredient" of group treatment. The initial goal is to establish an active, supportive, and genuine relationship with each patient individually and collectively with the group. ST group therapists must be able to balance individual needs and the collective needs of the group. This mirrors a parent's handling of a siblings in a family. It is imperative that the therapists model a strong, consistent, affirming, and supportive presence. The group therapist must be the "parent" who accepts and values each patient for being herself/himself and maintains a connection with all group members. A voice that conveys warmth and genuineness is an important medium for limited reparenting. Further, maintaining good eye contact and directing an accepting warm gaze at patients are also crucial. In groups, we think that non-verbal behavior can be an important way to maintain connections with all members. Our physical gestures of inclusion (e.g., open arms and leaning forward) are larger and even somewhat exaggerated in a group setting. We move around more than in individual psychotherapy, to be close enough to a patient who is distressed, to set limits, or to set up experiential work. We also amplify our nonverbal protective gestures toward group members, for example separating angry venting members from those in Vulnerable Child mode by literally standing between them. We see such adaptations in therapist style as appropriate efforts to match the larger stage that groups present.

Limited reparenting is accomplished, in part, by psychotherapists providing patients with the experience of acceptance, validation, and support to help heal patients' damaged sense of self, self-hatred, and hopelessness. In the group, these experiences are made even more powerful by the presence of a second therapist and the group members. In addition, acceptance and validation coming from peers may have slightly different effects. Patients frequently report that positive expressions from other patients seem "more believable" or "real" than those from therapists, since the therapist is perceived as a professional who "must say those things" and not a "real human" responding to them.

Because a psychotherapy group is a closer analog of the childhood family of origin or adolescent peer group than an individual psychotherapist can provide, schema mode triggering and healing opportunities are augmented. In addition, group members who can be experienced as "siblings" stimulate different associations and access different implicit memories from those therapist "parents" do. "Siblings" are particularly significant for patients whose biological siblings played key roles in the

> Rose was abandoned by her biological parents when she was a baby. She grew up in foster families, where physical, sexual, and emotional abuse occurred. When she was 16, she became homeless for a few years and worked as a prostitute. When she started ST group one of her most frequent modes was Aggressive Protector. Shortly after this mode was hostile to someone, her Punitive Parent mode would attack her mercilessly ("You are a worthless piece of shit. Nobody will ever want to be close to you, you will always be alone. It would have been better, if you were never born."). Rose told the group how she would always wait until the last minute to enter the group room in a posture signaling "don't come near me." When the group therapist told Rose that she liked having her in the room because she liked spending time with her, Rose's Aggressive Protector mode answered: "You've got to say that since you are a therapist and you earn your money when patients are in the room." Ann, another group member, who was often in Vulnerable Child mode in group, fearing that something bad might happen, responded by saying: "You know, Rose, I would also really like to have you in the room. It scares me to wait outside for the others to show up and I would feel a lot safer if you were in the room with me. You have this tough look and I always wished I had had an older sister like you to protect me." Ann's words bypassed Rose's Aggressive Protector and silenced her Punitive Parent, allowing a real connection between the two patients.

etiology and/or maintenance of their schemas. Group members also provide extra characters for role-plays and other experiential work, which can increase the salience of these techniques.

Our BPD groups tend to be very cohesive and often refer to themselves spontaneously as a "family." We strategically foster this group cohesion by referring to the group as a healthy "surrogate family" to provide patients with a safe "home" in which to fill gaps in emotional learning about self and others and the emotions that normally occur in the process of healthy development. The acceptance and feelings of belonging that accompany the healthy family experience of the group are healing to the Vulnerable Child mode of patients with BPD. This perception is even stronger in the inpatient groups who actually live together like a family. With trained psychotherapists as the "parents," many patients have their first experience of a healthy and validating family or peer group in this therapeutic setting. Patients can experience feeling valued from individual psychotherapy, but it is more difficult to feel a sense of belonging. The group curative factors of belonging and acceptance have particular significance for the schema issues of patients with BPD, including Defectiveness/Shame, Abandonment, Emotional Deprivation and Mistrust/Abuse. BPD patients frequently tell us that they were labeled "black sheep" or "losers" in their families. Experiences of acceptance, affection, and care from the group "family" provide important corrective emotional experiences that can be processed in the group, resulting in schema change. Identity is formed in part by internalizing early significant others' views of us. As we know, families of patients who develop BPD often provided very distorted "fairground" mirrors for patients to view themselves in when they were young children. A therapy group can provide new and more accurate reflections of the patient.

> An example of these healing group effects is the case of Terry, who came to her first inpatient ST group with a hood pulled down to obscure most of her face and described herself as "evil." After some time in the group, she offered that she had decided that she was "not entirely evil" because her peers did not treat her as if she was an undesirable and unworthy person.
>
> Terry grew up on a large farm and was kept socially isolated with her abusive biological father, who was also her biological grandfather. Her mother's response to her was one of discomfort and distress, since Terry reminded her of being raped by her own father. Terry's father/grandfather reacted in a similar way because she represented the reason he had spent time in jail. Terry internalized their reactions as her identity and explained their lack of love and mistreatment as due to her being "bad and evil." The therapy group was Terry's first exposure to accepting peers. She had also been made fun of, bullied, and rejected by schoolmates in her home town who knew her family background. Terry had seen individual psychotherapists, but their acceptance had much less impact than that of seven peers. She felt for the first time that she was "one of them" and belonged somewhere. Terry went on from this group experience to successfully complete a college degree in social work and is working in mental health.

Schema Mode Change

Once the group has bonded, schema mode work becomes the focus. The core elements of schema mode change apply in group work as in individual work. A group of patients, who understand the schema modes well from their experience of them, can become skillful in identifying modes operating in others and assist group therapists with this step. The descriptions of group mode work that follow are not meant as a strict order to follow, since group Schema Therapists must follow the modes that are present in the collection of group members. Groups, even more so than individual patients, are dynamic entities with a life and course of their own.

Breaking through the Detached Protector

The Detached Protector is a coping mode developed in an attempt not to be overwhelmed by painful, anxiety-provoking feelings and its final line of defense in BPD patients is often the ultimate detachment – a suicide attempt. For that reason, we think it is vital to develop healthy distress management and safety plans at the same time as work to get through the Detached Protector. The work to increase emotional awareness is in itself one way to break through the Detached Protector. We begin emotional awareness work with kinesthetic exercises, as most patients with BPD are at the sensorimotor, global level of emotional awareness (see Farrell and Shaw, 1994). These include grounding exercises that increase the ability to feel physical sensations in one's body, which is the beginning of the experience of emotion. These exercises are done with less self-consciousness in a group, and a play element can be introduced that balances the anxiety people with BPD often have about feeling their bodies. As emotional awareness increases, patients become aware of points at which they can allow the Detached Protector to remove them or stay with an uncomfortable or frightening emotion. As they are able to stay present the Vulnerable/Abandoned Child can be accessed to take in the comfort and support the group and therapists offer and begin the process of healing.

One advantage of doing emotion-focused work in a group is that affect can be amplified by the presence of more people in the therapy space, thus assisting the goal of eliciting the implicit knowledge and associational memories that accompany affect. This emotional material can then be explored to learn more about the root experiences of a patient's schema modes and will ultimately assist in trauma processing work that includes cognitive restructuring and imagery work of the meaning of memories. Often just the experience of doing imagery, even the "safe place" image, as a group creates enough energy to make a chink in the armor of the Detached Protector. Other times observing other group members doing role-play work triggers emotional responses that reach the Vulnerable/Abandoned Child. When doing role-plays with the Detached Protector, other group members can be very effective "devil's advocates" because they know all too well the responses likely to be given in that mode and which compelling counterarguments to make.

Vulnerable/Abandoned Child

For some patients, experiential work feels safer in the presence of peers. The Vulnerable/Abandoned Child's fear, elicited by imagery work, may be transferred easily to seeing the therapists as if they were the Punitive Parent of childhood. Although therapists being seen as parents is part of the healing process of ST, since it allows the therapist to take on a "good parent" role, too much fear can trigger Detached Protector and shut down the process.

> After a couple of weeks Sue declared that she was going to leave the group. Most of the members were shocked since they did not understand her decision and felt abandoned by Sue. They asked her to explain and Sue replied, "All this emotional involvement is just a waste of time since in the end, I still have to deal with all my problems by myself." She said this without feeling, as if it was just fact. We asked Sue which mode she thought she was in and she answered "Detached Protector, probably. But who cares?" One of the therapists asked if she could sit next to her and Sue agreed. We then asked the group if others had had this feeling of being overwhelmed by problems. Some answered that they did and we explored how they coped with this. One group member, Ann, answered that she cried a lot and didn't know what to do at those times; another, Diane, said that she used to detach by staying in bed all day to avoid thinking about problems. She empathized with Sue and told her, "I really know how you feel. Sometimes you just want to run away from it all." This exchange established an emotional connection between the peers and the wall of Sue's Detached Protector developed a little chink. The therapists could now validate the feeling of being overwhelmed and alone that little Sue was experiencing. Offers of support from peers such as "You can call me anytime, when you feel like that" or "Oh, I had to go through this insurance application, too – I might be able to help you with it" could now be discussed, because little Sue felt safe enough to talk about her problems and accept support. Once Sue was able to overcome the Detached Protector, she no longer wanted to leave the group and in later sessions was able to identify quitting as one of her old coping strategies when in distress.

Mode imagery work in a group. We start in groups by having all patients use their safe place image. After they have experienced the safe place we instruct them to switch to an image of their Vulnerable Child. We have them stay with that for a few minutes (longer, later in the group process) and then come back to being in the group with eyes open. We ask about their experiences. Usually there will be a member who reacts more than the others emotionally or expresses the desire to do imagery work first. We have that person go back to the Vulnerable Child image, identify what the need is, and then the therapists and the group work creatively to supply the need or help the person get the need met.

We end imagery work by processing the experience of each member during the exercise. Then we move on to do imagery work with another member. We keep the individual focus relatively brief (not more than 10 minutes), using it as a launching pad for all kinds of work that are targeted at shared issues in the group. In this way the group is always brought into any individual work. We want to avoid experiences that would feel like individual therapy with the group as spectators.

After we went through the safe place image and Vulnerable Child images, a group member, Kay, said that she had been in Vulnerable Child mode all week because it was the anniversary of a dear friend's death. This was particularly significant for her because her first suicide attempt occurred just after this friend died. Group therapist 1 had Kay close her eyes and go back to the image. She asked how old she was, where she was, how she felt, what she needed, etc. Kay said she was nine years old, alone in the playground, she felt lonely and weak, and needed support and safety. Therapist 1 asked if she could sit next to her and hold her hand. Kay said "yes." With some additional questions, Kay communicated feeling that "she mattered" with the therapist sitting by her side and saying reassuring good parent things about "little Kay's" value. Then therapist 2 talked to little Kay about the "little friends" she had around her now, referring to the other group members. Therapist 1 asked the rest of the group if their Vulnerable Child ever felt what Kay had expressed. Each of them shared some of their Vulnerable Child feelings. At that point, therapist 2 asked the group if they felt comfortable holding each other's hands as a circle of little friends for Kay and for each other. She asked them to close their eyes to connect more with their Vulnerable Child, and then open them to look around at the circle of little friends they have in the group. The therapists asked them to take in the safety, protection, warmth, and connection of the group and the therapists. Therapist 2 then asked them to move to an awareness of their strong Healthy Adult women and the strength, resources, and support of that group connection. In Vulnerable Child imagery work we move from bringing in external support and safety (the therapists, the group, memories of protective caretakers) to becoming aware of the resources of one's own Healthy Adult, followed by connecting the Healthy Adult with the Vulnerable Child. We ask patients to have eyes open or closed during different parts of the imagery work. Usually eyes are closed when the focus is on an image and open when the focus moves to the present and the group. Because eye contact is an important vehicle for emotional connection, whenever we focus on group input or connection we ask patients to look around and really take in what they are seeing. At the point when we begin individual imagery, the rest of the group members usually have their eyes open. As the imagery work progresses, if it is an experience that most share in some way, we may have the group close their eyes and join the individual patient in the imagery. If it is a trauma that most do not share, we have them keep their eyes open since there is no therapeutic value in their visiting that particular image. The example of Kay follows these general guidelines.

Another way that schema mode change occurs is the process of collecting experiential "antidotes" that counter negative core beliefs about self, others, and the world. Many mode healing experiences for the Vulnerable/Abandoned Child take place in response to emotional validation, kind treatment, and respect in the group. These experiences create feelings of being worthy that contradict schemas of defectiveness that developed from core needs for validation and acceptance not being met in childhood.

> An example of a group situation that had this potential was a patient's experience of group forgiveness for being five minutes late due to a traffic accident. Jane had been harshly punished for any fault as a child, and no explanation prevented blame and punishment from her mother. She consequently internalized a harsh Punitive Parent who punished her with self-injury whenever she made a "mistake" and developed a maladaptive coping Protector Mode that led to her avoiding any interaction with people in which a "fault" might be exposed. Jane forced herself to come to group, fearing the worst, and was shocked when the group expressed concern about her and relief that she was unharmed since she never came late. The group had no idea, until this experience was processed, that they were playing an important role in providing experiential evidence that she did not have to be perfect to be accepted and cared about, and that her life long avoidance of relationships as a way to protect herself was not necessary in her adult life.

Many opportunities for such emotional level mode change occur in GST where affect is aroused and cognitive processing is facilitated by therapists and other group members. More opportunities for creative healing activities are possible in a group because there are more people.

Issues of sibling rivalry arise naturally in group, and the resulting emotions and schema material can be explored and processed as opportunities for change. This can be an important therapy moment for patients whose Abandoned/Vulnerable Child feels like she never had her parents' attention or that her siblings were favored. The therapists' ability to balance their responses to individual members based on the mode they are in can provide the Vulnerable/Abandoned Child with healing attention. The group can feel like there is "enough for everyone to get something," unlike in their family of origin experience. The patient group can also provide siblings – healthy big brothers or sisters. These positive experiences in the group are particularly desensitizing and schema changing when abuse occurred with biological siblings.

Angry Child

The group can be a safe place for the Angry Child to vent anger safely. Role-play work is particularly useful here since there are numerous potential "actors" to call upon. To help vent the underlying rage of the child whose needs were not met, one therapist can even play the Punitive or Demanding Parent with the second therapist playing the supportive Good Parent Defender or Coach. The collective physical strength and emotional presence of a number of people can provide a sense of containment that is reassuring to other patients and the therapists. Assertiveness can be practiced in group as the Angry Child develops Healthy Adult skills to get needs met.

Group experiential exercises can be used to access the Angry Child of more repressed patients. Examples are "tug-of-war" games, contests in which, back to back, patients try to push each other across the room. With therapists monitoring, these are safe exercises to access anger in a setting where it can be worked with. Patients with BPD are so frightened of their anger that it can take years to access it in individual therapy, or after it is accessed the patient runs away in fright to take punishing action or even prematurely end therapy.

> Angry Child mode work was undertaken with Jim, a very large, strong man with a lot of Angry Child energy about his early parental abandonment, which easily flips into Angry Detached Protector mode and makes it very difficult for anyone to connect with him. Jim's abandonment sensitivity was so intense that when it was triggered he moved with lightning speed from Abandoned/Vulnerable Child to Angry Child to Angry Detached Protector. This flipping of modes occurred whenever the group focus moved away from him. He would angrily tell us that he was "being abandoned by the group, just as my parents dumped me as an infant." He would then erupt in a string of obscenities that included calling the group a "bunch of bitches" as he stormed out of the group, slamming the door so that the room shook. Fortunately, on a locked inpatient unit his safety was not in question. In all groups there are contracts about agreeing to not leave the group if at all possible, and for outpatients not to leave the building if they have left the group in distress. Depending on the circumstances and the mode a patient is in, one of the two therapists checks on them and encourages their return. Jim was eventually able to understand the intensity of his reaction in schema terms, vent his rage and pain at his parents in role-play instead of at the group, and see the other group members accurately as the accepting, caring people they were, whom he could safely let in and connect with. This example also illustrates how effectively mode reactions triggered by group interactions can provide material for schema change in contrast to less salient patient descriptions in individual therapy or outside of session events.

Happy Child

The Happy Child is an important mode to access and support in BPD patients. Elements of play are more easily introduced in the group setting than in individual therapy for a number of reasons. As the group bonds and forms the multiple overlapping attachments of a working psychotherapy group, the supportive atmosphere that is generated along with the sharing of experiences provides a comfortable mutuality that lends itself to play. During stages of therapy during which patients rely on their individual therapists for protection and nurture, it may be difficult and even disturbing to see them as playful kids. In a group, the therapists can play more than one role, one of them setting up and containing play as a parent would and the other allowing her/his playful side to be present.

A particularly imaginative play experience for the Happy Child parts occurred on an inpatient unit when the group staged a "Winter Olympics." Teams representing imaginary countries were formed with athlete participants and cheering fans. An "opening ceremony" with costumes was held to the enjoyment of all. The games emphasized fun over skill, such as the "speed-skating" down the corridors with boxes as skates. Sharing this kind of fun builds cohesiveness, provides a positive memory of an experience shared with peers, and therapist participation is "humanizing" and adds to the group's experience of group therapists as genuine people. The modeling by therapists of having fun and even being silly is supportive for the happy child and challenging to restrictive modes such as Demanding and Punitive Parent.

The Therapy Group Provides Opportunities for Identity Formation

Unstable identity is a core deficit in BPD and underlies feelings of emptiness, abandonment fears, and difficulties with interpersonal relationships. We develop our identities by internalizing feedback (reactions to us, labels, descriptions, positive and negative defining experiences with others, including acceptance or rejection) from important caretakers in early life and from our peer group in adolescence. ST addresses this BPD deficit through schema mode work in which disconnected aspects of self are healed or transformed, and ultimately integrated into a strengthened Healthy Adult mode. Early identity work for the young Vulnerable/Abandoned Child can be effectively accomplished in individual or GST. The therapist can provide information about normal childhood needs against which patients can re-evaluate their childhood experiences and the expectations and reactions of their parent/caretakers. Patients learn a lot about themselves from getting through the Detached Protector enough to explore their real wants, needs, likes, and dislikes, and understanding that these were and are healthy despite being different from those dictated by emotionally deprived or unhealthy family situations.

As the life of a GST continues, young child schema mode issues are healed and the group focus turns to issues of later childhood and adolescence – separation, individuation, and identity. ST groups can serve as a close analogue for the missing adolescent "peer group" experience of patients with BPD and thus play a healing role in unfinished identity formation. Because of invalidating or abusive childhood environments, most patients with BPD had schema issues that interfered with connecting to or developing a sense of belonging to a healthy peer group or any peer group at all. Often in abusive homes little contact with the outside world is allowed. This deprivation of potentially healthy input regarding self is particularly destructive for adolescents who do not have a solid childhood base of feeling worthy and loved. Adolescents are desperate to belong somewhere, which leads them to attempt connection almost at any cost. Defectiveness schemas may lead to alliances with negative peer groups that encourage substance abuse, criminal behavior, and running away from home. They often begin unhealthy romantic and sexual relationships in adolescence in an effort to fill their emptiness.

Adolescence is also a developmental period in which healthy separation/individuation occurs. The focus becomes exploring and reaching understanding of the larger world outside the family and contemplating what place one wants to have in it and what the meaning of one's life is. The relational need here is to have people to discuss and explore this with. In addition, it is difficult to "separate" from parents if there is no peer group to transition to. The therapy group may be able to support this needed transition to a Healthy Adult life. GST offers opportunities to explore

An example of a creative group exercise we use to impact the defectiveness schema so common in patients with BPD experientially and to strengthen the budding positive identities of our patients involves making a group multi-bead bracelet. In a group session, the therapist provides a selection of inexpensive beads and group members and therapists select a bead for each member that represents a personal characteristic that they like or value. The "identity bracelet" for each person is built by group members taking turns presenting a bead and making a statement about what it represents. This process continues until all patients have a completed bracelet. The therapist then leads an imagery exercise that includes feeling the bracelet on one's wrist, going over in visualization the experience of receiving the beads with the instruction to let the bracelet represent and anchor in memory what it felt to take that in. This experience can then be recalled with the therapist's or group's help. In a later group session, Jill, a group member, told the group that she "knew in her head" that she was not a hideous monster, but she "felt like one." She was asked to recall the bracelet experience and a smile came to her face as she extended her wrist with the bracelet on it. We had her put her other hand over it, close her eyes, and recall the experience as fully as possible. She was able to do this and the positive feelings of acceptance and value that came to mind combated her old feeling of "being bad" and even capable of "contaminating" anyone she touched. This use of the bracelet was repeated many times and the group as a whole was given the assignment of touching the bracelet and recalling the experience whenever the Punitive or Demanding Parent threatened to disconnect them from others. The group bracelet representing positive peer group feedback became a physical anchor on which to build a more stable positive identity. Before this experience, Jill left home infrequently in fear of being pointed at and called names as she had been as a teenager in a small rural town. In this example, a tangible object that represented the experience of being accepted and cared for in a peer group broke through to a patient usually locked in Detached Protector with a vicious punitive parent berating her defectiveness. Jill's dramatic facial transformation from pain and no eye contact to reflexively touching it while looking up and smiling when reminded of her bracelet is evidence of being affected at the emotional level. This reaction continued whenever she was reminded of the bracelet and she was still wearing it when discharged from hospital. This is also an example of using transitional objects from the group as part of healing. It is reminiscent of the behavior that we see with adolescents who often trade pieces of jewelry or clothing with "best friends" as part of the bonding and identification process that underlies identity formation. Group relationships can be opportunities to have the defining "best friend" relationship that is another part of adolescent identity formation. We see this acted out particularly in the inpatient BPD ST groups. We observe frequent occurrences of group members giving each other inexpensive pieces of jewelry, wearing the same T-shirts in group, even getting the same haircut, and interpret this as additional clinical evidence for the process of adolescent stage identity development being reenacted in the structure of the "sibling" psychotherapy group.

later stages of identity formation, since the group provides a peer group "surrogate" to work in. This addition may facilitate the integration of modes into Healthy Adult and be one of the reasons for the large effect sizes found in Farrell *et al.* (2009).

Punitive or Demanding Parent work: Using the "Group Army"

Banishing the Punitive (or Demanding) Parent is a goal of ST that is significantly augmented in a group. An entire group of strong adult patients can more powerfully challenge and banish the Punitive Parent than a patient who feels like a small child and their individual therapist are able to. Imagery work in which the group and co-therapists become one's "protective army" can be developed, practiced, and used to continue individual Punitive Parent work. Patients can concretize their army with drawings that they place in strategic locations to remind them of the group experience. Another exercise we use in groups is building a parent figure out of cloth that patients can write negative messages on which represent the input of their Punitive or Demanding Parent. This figure can be placed on a chair to literally represent their parent. Using such a tangible representation evokes a lot of emotion, beginning at times with fear, but moving on to anger and rejection. The parent "effigy" can later be locked in a closet or taken away by the therapists to underline its powerlessness to do harm.

One of our patients, who was inspired by the exercise, also made a literal representation of her new "good parent" who was comprised of the therapists and supportive peers whom she represented on a one-dimensional parent figure made mostly of paper and cloth that she could literally wrap around her body as if she was a small child being enfolded in a hug. This was done by a patient who had experienced severe childhood sexual abuse and had difficulty with anyone actually hugging her. Punitive Parent work is an area of mode work where vicarious learning can be particularly helpful. Group members too afraid to confront their still powerful internalized Punitive Parent even symbolically can watch the activity and see that nothing bad happens to the therapists or peers. The next time they are often brave enough to take on their Punitive Parent with the group's support.

Using Group Curative Factors to Build the Healthy Adult Mode

Another curative factor of a group is its function as a microcosm of the larger world, providing opportunities to observe others, get feedback, and practice skills in a safe environment that are not present in the same way in individual therapy. An extension of the therapy group that often occurs is that group members get together for social and supportive activities outside of group sessions. This has traditionally been discouraged in group therapy, but we see it as a learning experience and view it as a way to provide a transitional, relatively healthy adult peer group that many patients with

BPD lack. In a way, this extends the "family" aspect of limited reparenting that we believe the group provides in sessions. Problems may arise in these interactions, but they can be processed and resolved in the group more easily than when they occur completely outside therapists' view. We do, however, discourage romantic relationships between group members who do not have strong Healthy Adult modes. We think that it is too tempting for most patients without a strong identity to fill up their emptiness with a romance.

Frequently, as patients experience these positive relationships, they become aware that their frequent trips to the ER and acute or even longer hospital stays have been maladaptive solutions to loneliness at a time when schemas about defectiveness kept them from reaching out to others in a more adaptive way. In addition, in group they can learn *in vivo* to reach out to others, express needs, and receive a positive response as other BPD patients are often more tolerant and understanding of the intensely emotional schema mode experiences that are extremely difficult for people who do not have BPD to understand. Patients are often more able to risk expressing needs, including boundaries, to peers who they know understand and experience these modes.

The emotional experiences of people with BPD are arguably of a different character and intensity from those without this neurobiological sensitivity and greater reactivity. Their unique experiences in interpersonal relationships and their potential for negative distortions of the meaning of others' behavior combine to require a controlled experience with others to facilitate the healing schema change that they need. Such healing does not occur naturally in adult life or in mixed psychotherapy groups where these rejection-sensitive people may once again feel misunderstood and be ostracized due to their extreme behavior. Groups with therapists as the ever-present "good parents" feel safe enough that patients will test interpersonal relationships there. We are not suggesting that all of patients' social interactions revolve around their therapy groups, but people with BPD rarely have healthy friendships when they come to treatment, and group relationships can be stepping stones toward other healthy adult relationships. We expect that as the Healthy Adult mode is strengthened, patients will be able to expand their social networks.

Another opportunity for *in vivo* work of learning about connection can occur in the context of group relationships. Strong connections in group are often formed initially based on schema chemistry and can be opportunities for learning about connection. These relationships can be examined and renegotiated with the help of the group to grow and become healthier.

The group provides many opportunities for vicarious learning, for example, to observe cognitive distortions, impulsive actions, and the effects on others of intense emotional reactions and expressions. Vicarious learning can feel safer than the more direct learning of individual psychotherapy and can pave the way for taking risks. For example, group members observe the way peers are responded to by the therapists in situations of disagreement and conflict even when the Angry Protector is present. They also see that peers are not rejected or abandoned for being less than perfect, since the therapists and peers side with them, not the Punitive/Demanding Parent Mode. They observe as well that when a Vulnerable/Abandoned Child is present, she is nurtured and comforted safely by the therapists and group. These vicarious learning experiences make it easier for them to risk being in the Abandoned/Vulnerable Child

> One example from an inpatient group was the friendship between Sam and Ann. Sam coped with the fear, loneliness, and lack of love of his Vulnerable Child via surrender to Self-Sacrifice and Subjugation schemas and the anger and feelings of being used of his Angry Child through a Detached Protector mode. In the Detached Protector mode he made suicide attempts. He connected strongly with Ann, who was often in Vulnerable/Abandoned Child mode, expressing needs for comfort and care that were at an early developmental level and often physical. When she underwent knee surgery Sam stepped in to take care of her with attentiveness that approached catering to her "every whim." They quickly made plans to live together in a platonic relationship after hospital discharge. Sam became aware that as Ann recovered from surgery and needed him less physically, he felt less connected to her. He verbalized that he felt like the relationship was over and identified this as the usual pattern of his relationships – attracted by need, then as the need waned the relationship died. He realized that in childhood he had an enmeshed relationship with his mother who was unhappily married to his distant father. When he was a young teen, they divorced and he became her main confidant and caretaker. When he was an older teen she remarried and he was forced to leave home due to the new husband's abuse and he described feeling as if he had no meaning, purpose, or connection with his mother after that. He solved the emptiness he felt with substance abuse and occasional swallowing of foreign objects, which led to medical hospitalizations. As he came to understand the pattern of his schema modes and the role of his history, he re-examined his current "best friend" relationship and asked for a healthier connection that included his needs and some reciprocity. This caused initial conflict between Sam and Ann, followed by some maturation in their friendship as they processed it in group sessions. Ultimately, Sam decided that living with Ann was a bad idea since he was still too prone to succumb to the pull to deny his needs and care for her, and she realized that she too frequently asked him to be her Healthy Adult instead of developing and accessing her own. This is a good example of how the limited reparenting approach of not attempting to prohibit group friendships, but standing on the sidelines identifying schema issues and allowing venting, can generate significant schema mode change.

mode that is so critical to ST. Patients also report that observing and even experiencing the effects of peers' Angry/Impulsive mode behavior or their over-compensating defenses has more impact in motivating them to change their versions of those modes than getting verbal feedback about the effects of their similar behavior from psychotherapists. In addition, this vicarious learning in general seems easier for many of these rejection-sensitive patients to take in and make use of than therapist feedback.

Cognitive work is also effectively done in GST and augmented in a number of ways. Information about what is "normal," reality-testing of the "truth" of family of origin beliefs (e.g., it is weak to express feelings), and the effects of unmet childhood needs can be discussed in group with the addition of a larger pool of information on these topics. Group members sharing their experiences can provide normalizing effects similar to the effects of therapist selective self-disclosure. Members may put into words an experience the individual has had and can recognize, but had no words to express. Sometimes information from professionals seems ideal or not part of the world the patient lives in, whereas peers are seen as more realistic sources of this kind of information.

Challenges of Group Schema Therapy

Some group therapist tasks present a high level difficulty and complexity. GST requires a therapist pair to be optimally effective. A therapist team that has learned to work well together benefits the group and the therapists. For example, we are able to play different roles in vital ST experiential work. One of us can be supportive of a patient's feelings, while the other can set necessary limits. If needed we can even briefly leave the group to assess safety for a member who leaves abruptly, or step out with a patient in Angry Child mode who needs to vent, but who is scaring others. Two therapists with different styles and temperaments also provide an opportunity for patients to feel a connection with one of them. Having two therapists can help with meeting the cumulative needs of a group of patients with BPD who, at different stages in mode work, can be quite needy. GST can at times be intensely schema-triggering for therapists themselves. On those occasions, either in the session or later in peer supervision, the co-therapist's observations and support are very helpful.

Many of the group challenges with BPD patients are related to the abandonment or rejection sensitivity of this group and their propensity to distort feedback they are given along schema lines. The fact that there are more people involved translates into increased possibilities for immediate triggering effects of peers, intense "sibling" rivalry, and schema chemistry. Group members can have very variable experiences to the same situation or even therapist-initiated exercise in the group depending on their personal histories and particular mistrust or abuse issues.

In summary, we conceptualize psychotherapy for BPD as a broad process of facilitating emotional development to healthy adulthood by correcting the maladaptive schema modes that resulted from critical needs not being met in childhood and adolescence. We speculate that each of these stages is optimally impacted by a different modality of ST. The attachment needs of infants and young children may be optimally met in an individual psychotherapy relationship that can provide individual limited reparenting, which offers the emotional experiences of safety, validation, and comfort unavailable in the patient's early environment. The next stages of healthy development, late childhood, and adolescence, where the separation and individuation tasks of identity formation are critical, and adulthood, where healthy autonomy and more equal relationships are the focus, require learning experiences that go beyond relationships with an individual therapist "parent" to include "siblings" and a peer group. Groups require stability, consistency, flexibility, creativity, a loud or soft voice depending on the task, a well-developed sense of fairness, a good deal of freedom from schema issues, and a good support or supervisory group. One contribution of GST to the treatment of patients with BPD is made clear in the most frequent post-treatment evaluation comment made by 100 patients: "This is the first time in my life that I felt like I belonged, was understood, and accepted. There are actually others like me!"

The Future

Many of the issues raised in this chapter need to be investigated empirically to provide more grounded speculations and testable hypotheses, for example, the idea that the needed emotional learning and schema change of particular developmental stages may be best facilitated by a particular modality. Patients at another level of development or higher function may not need a "family" group, but a peer group. Two therapists are important for the all-BPD group, with a high level of emotional need and abandonment and emotional deprivation schemas, but a single therapist may be adequate for other patient groups, and two therapists will not be practical in many settings. The frequency of sessions needed, the optimal combination of group and individual sessions, predictors of treatment outcomes, patient retention, cost-effectiveness and cost-utility, requirements of therapist training, and the preferences of the most important stakeholders, the patients and therapists, all need additional evaluation.

Edwards and Arntz (Part I, Chapter 1) discuss GST as a third stage in the development of ST. The large effect sizes for GST in Farrell *et al.* (2009) study are compelling and there are significant economic and service delivery reasons as well to expand development and testing of the group modality. Just as individual ST is being used for many different patients and problems and has growing empirical validation, we anticipate similar expansion and validation for GST in the future. The model described in this chapter was developed specifically for patients with BPD and it is currently being tested in a large RCT at multiple international sites. A model of GST has been developed for forensic patients (Beckley and Gordon, 2010). A working group on GST has been set up within the International Society of Schema Therapy to facilitate the international development and research efforts on this modality of ST.

References

Arntz, A. and Genderen, H. van (2009) *Schema Therapy for Borderline Personality Disorder*. New York: Wiley.

Beckley. K.A. and Gordon. N.S. (2010) Schema Therapy within a high secure setting, in *Using Time Not Doing Time: Practitioner Perspectives in Personality Disorder and Risk* (eds A. Tennant and K. Howells). Chichester: Wiley-Blackwell.

Farrell, J.M. and Shaw, I.A. (1994) Emotional awareness training: a prerequisite to effective cognitive-behavioral treatment of borderline personality disorder. *Cognitive and Behavioral Practice*, 1, 71–91.

Farrell, J., Shaw, I. and Webber, M. (2009) A schema-focused approach to group psychotherapy for outpatients with borderline personality disorder: a randomized controlled trial. *Journal of Behavior Therapy and Experimental Psychiatry*, 40, 317–328.

Reiss, N., Lieb, K., Arntz, A., Shaw, I.A. and Farrell, J.M. (submitted for publication) Responding to the treatment challenge of patients with severe BPD: results of three pilot studies of inpatient schema therapy.

Yalom, I.D. (2005) *The Theory and Practice of Group Psychotherapy*, 5th edition. New York: Basic Books.

Young, J.E., Klosko, J.S. and Weishaar, M.E. (2003) *Schema Therapy: a Practitioner's Guide*. New York: Guilford Press.

6
Implementation of Schema Therapy in an Inpatient and Day Treatment Group Setting

Eelco Muste

Schema Therapy (ST) was originally developed for individual outpatient therapy (Young, 1990; Young, Klosko and Weishaar, 2003; Muste, 2006). Adaptations of ST for groups have been in development, but only recently published (outpatient groups: Farrell and Shaw, 1994; van Vreeswijk and Broersen, 2006; inpatient groups; Thunnissen and Muste, 2002, 2005; Reiss, Lieb, Arntz, Shaw and Farrell, submitted). One randomized controlled trial (RCT) has been conducted on a specific group ST (GST) model developed for borderline personality disorder (BDP) patients, which demonstrated positive effects from adding GST to individual psychotherapy (but not ST) (Farrell, Shaw and Webber, 2009).

Integrating ST into inpatient and day treatment settings required major adaptation of the individual outpatient model of ST. This task was led by Sloane, who had experience with both groups and multidisciplinary teams. Sloane provided years of training for the entire staff of the Schema Therapy unit of De Viersprong in Halsteren, an psychotherapy center for personality disorders in the Netherlands. In this training, individual outpatient therapy was changed to a group-focused inpatient and day treatment version of this therapy method.

Inpatient and day treatment ST models have not yet been investigated in a RCT. There are, however, a number of open-trial pilot studies, which suggest positive treatment effects. A small cohort within the Sceptre research (Andrea, 2008) demonstrated large effect size reductions in the Brief Symptom Inventory, pre- and post-treatment. A similar large treatment effect for a Cluster B group was found by Bartak and colleagues (2010). In addition, a significant decrease in symptoms was found at the end of the treatment, and maintained at one-year follow-up, in the report of the Standard Evaluation Project (Timman *et al.*, 2006).

In Practice

To illustrate the treatment program, we describe a typical day in the life of an inpatient.

The Wiley Blackwell Handbook of Schema Therapy: Theory, Research, and Practice, First Edition.
Edited by Michiel van Vreeswijk, Jenny Broersen, and Marjon Nadort.
© 2012 John Wiley & Sons, Ltd. Published 2015 by John Wiley & Sons, Ltd.

> On Monday morning, Steve closes himself off from the group. At the beginning of the week the group members talk to him about his stated goal, which is to open up more about his feelings and break through his Detached Protector mode. Hesitantly, he tells the group about the fight he had with his girlfriend and how he tried to detach from his feelings by smoking cannabis excessively.
>
> In an individual session with his psychotherapist, Steve examines the details of that situation. The fight was initiated by his girlfriend saying that, once in a while, she wanted to go out with her girlfriends. With the group's help, Steve identified that his Defectiveness/Shame schema was activated, and that he overcompensated by becoming very angry. Later that day, in a schema education session Steve recognizes that his Abandonment/Instability schema was also activated in the argument. He realizes that when he feels vulnerable he copes by reacting angrily (over-compensating), and smokes cannabis to disconnects from his feelings and intensify his Detached Protector mode.
>
> Later that week, in conversation with the environmental therapist, Steve once more reflects on what need he is attempting to meet with drug use. He is motivated to look for healthy alternatives and agrees with his personal coach that he should make an alert plan to increase his self-control and support his use of healthy coping.

This case describes what happens when Steve's schemas are activated in response to an argument with his girlfriend. His feelings of vulnerability become intense and he flips between the maladaptive coping modes of over-compensation and detachment.

In the group, patients can recognize the mode patterns in others and eventually learn to recognize them in themselves. This is an example of one of the learning opportunities that groups provide and the benefit of establishing a safe therapeutic ambience where underlying feelings can be examined and better understood. If Steve can resist flipping into the Detached Protector mode and stay emotionally present, he will be able to genuinely listen to others and begin to recognize other issues that he struggles with.

This case also demonstrates the limit-setting aspect of limited reparenting. In this case, the environmental therapist set a limit. Limit-setting is not punitive, but rather has a focus on the problem behavior. In Steve's case, the limit was placed in his treatment plan to foster behavior change and self-efficacy.

Approach

Characteristics of Schema Therapy: the inpatient and day treatment version

The patient population in hospital and day treatment settings has severe and entrenched maladaptive behavior patterns, which have not responded to previous treatment or have relapsed (Weertman, 2009). Many aspects of their lives are affected. They have inadequate social support networks and experience high levels of anxiety. They have an abundance of maladaptive schemas and modes and their primary schemas are in the domain of Disconnection and Rejection (Muste *et al.*, 2009).

Inpatient and day treatment ST involve a multidisciplinary team with members of the following disciplines conducting treatment.

- Environmental Therapy
- Psychotherapy
- Creative Experiential Therapy
- Socio-therapy
- Family Therapy
- Pharmacotherapy.

Environmental therapy refers to interventions in the whole treatment. It concerns the therapeutic climate in which the treatment is set. The effect of environmental therapy can be seen on many different levels (Edens and Kerstens, 2009), extending from the individual, the group, and the treatment unit to the organization and the place of the organization in society (see Figure 6.1). Specific features of environmental therapy include the treatment agreement, in which the preconditions of the treatment, the treatment plan, and the treatment schedule are drawn up, and also the composition of the team and cooperation between members of the team.

Specific to the inpatient and day treatment version of ST, and the cornerstone on which the therapeutic environment is built, is the existence of basic needs as formulated within ST (safety, connection, autonomy; competence and feelings of identity, realistic limits, self-expression; freedom to express needs, emotions, spontaneity, and games).

A prerequisite is that the environment is safe. A sense of safety is created by means of transparency and predictability. Patients know where they stand, motives involved in deciding on certain intervention are explained, and it is clear who plays which role.

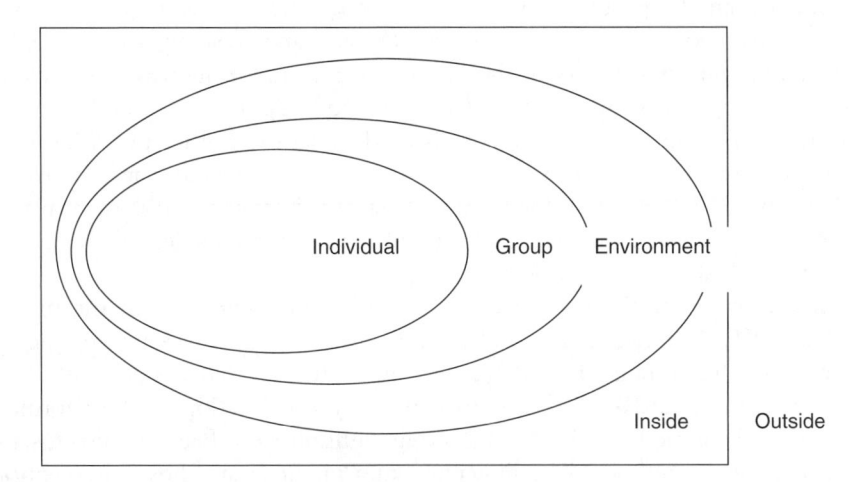

Figure 6.1 Levels in ST inpatient and day treatment

Furthermore, sufficient safety provides the chance for patients to connect with each other and gain mutual significance within this connection. An example of the way in which environmental therapy creates preconditions to connect is illustrated by the principle that all members of the therapy group have to be present before the session starts, and that, if there is an absentee, the reason for their absence must be clearly communicated.

The boundaries within which the treatment takes place is very important. The limitations of the treatment are clearly formulated and are the same for everybody (e.g., concerning confidentiality and aggression). These preconditions are set out in the treatment agreement. Furthermore, it is possible to make specific appointments in the individual treatment plan (e.g., regarding alcohol and drugs).

Accordingly, there is sufficient room for autonomy, self-expression, and spontaneity within the set frameworks. During the inpatient phase, patients can choose how to develop these in the unstructured time, for example, they can be helped to join the patient council or take advantage of sport facilities, games, and leisure-time facilities.

Maintaining the therapeutic environment is everybody's responsibility. Patients and staff have to contribute to creating the best possible atmosphere. The environment therapist is there in order to follow and monitor this process. This therapist supervises the different processes (on the previously described levels) and intervenes if necessary.

Psychotherapy plays a leading role within inpatient and day treatment ST. Interventions from different disciplines are incorporated into the psychotherapeutic framework and are made concrete by individual case conceptualization. The psychotherapy itself is implemented in different ways. Within the program, psycho-education is offered, in which patients are familiarized with the different terms used in ST. There is a cognitive behavioral-oriented group session, in which schema and mode diary forms are developed. There is also a less structured group session. In this session, the group process can be developed if necessary, or patients can receive individual input. On each occasion, all group members are involved, and the group itself is of central importance. Therapists remain directive and they make themselves responsible for the safety and connection within the group. During the sessions, different techniques are used, for example chair work, role-play, and imagery (Vinken and Westenbroek, 2009). For example, an imagery may be about the Punitive Parent mode and results in writing all punitive messages to map out this mode well, and to fight it accordingly.

Besides group psychotherapy, there is also individual psychotherapy within inpatient and day treatment ST. Depending on the treatment group, these individual sessions can be used to draw up the schema conceptualization and treatment plan at the start of the treatment, or they may continue through the clinical phase and the first part-time phase of the treatment.

Creative experiential therapy can consist of different disciplines. In the manual (day) clinical ST (Günther et al., 2009), expressive, art, and psychomotor therapy are described. The combination of ST and music therapy has also recently been described (Verburgt, 2010). In order to come to a classification of the enormous diversity of working methods, it is useful to highlight divisions between direct, semi-direct, and indirect methods. The direct working methods are those interventions that affect schemas or modes directly. On the basis of a discussion about the treatment plan, or the patient's own contribution, you can choose whether to examine a specific pattern more closely. Patients can join in during this session or they can work individually on their own patterns.

In the case of semi-direct working methods, work starts from a theme. This theme can trigger modes or schemas in group members. When creating a safe place, schemas such as Mistrust and/or Abuse, Abandonment/Instability or Dependence/Incompetence can be activated.

Indirect working methods are more about the process. Creative experiential therapies are applicable when starting a process that is a less verbal or preverbal (Smeijsters, 2000). By means of experience in, for example, offering working methods, materials or space, patterns that can be named in a later stage of the treatment become clear.

Socio-therapy is the most common discipline in the inpatient phase of the treatment. Besides being present in the structured (scheduled) time, socio-therapists are also present in the unstructured time, such as at mealtimes and in the evening. During the day treatment phase there is less unstructured time, but the socio-therapist plays an important role in opening and closing the therapy day. In this way, the socio-therapist contributes importantly to creating the therapeutic environment.

Structured interventions in socio-therapy take place in different groups and during individual counseling. Socio-therapy works with task groups, communication groups, and social skill groups (de Weerd and Oudmaijer, 2009).

In task groups, tasks are divided between the group members and commissions with a specific aim are created. Communication groups are group sessions in which teamwork comes up for discussion, weeks and weekends are discussed, and there are openings and endings to the day. Social skill groups relate to social skills training, reintegration, and work.

Socio-therapists are trained to be behavioral therapeutic assistants. In individual conversations with patients, they deal with actual problems. They draw up alert plans with patients so they can learn how to control destructive behavior, map out problems (e.g., about housing and finances), and keep a record, if necessary, of specific problem areas (e.g., anxiety and mood complaints).

Family therapy can be added to the treatment, but is not necessary for all patients. However, all patients have an intake session with the family therapist in which an assessment is made as to whether there are important people in the patient's ambit who will be involved in family therapy.

The family therapist and the family sessions are separated from the treatment team and the treatment. Family therapy forms a co-construction (Lenaerts, 2009) around the patient and his surroundings. In this way, the treatment is one aspect of these surroundings, besides family, relevant others, work environment, culture, and society. The family therapist adopts a "not knowing" position (Lenaerts, 2002) and is a link between the treatment and the surroundings of the patient. Furthermore, the patient can be helped by implementing changes that occur within the treatment outside the treatment.

Pharmacotherapy is a fixed aspect of treatment. A psychiatrist is connected to the team and meets all patients at the start of the treatment. The policy on medication is attuned to the treatment of the schema conceptualization in the patient. Besides the team, the group can be used to observe and evaluate changes in the event of alterations.

Individual within the group

The patient sets up the treatment on the basis of the treatment plan in cooperation with the team and the group. In this treatment plan, schemas and modes are appointed, as well as short and long-term aims. Furthermore, these aims are operationalized within the different disciplines. Patients work with a workbook (Muste et al., 2009) in which inpatient and day treatment ST is explained. Steps that have to be taken to achieve a change are concentrated on inpatient and day treatment ST and are described per schema. In the last part of the workbook, the therapy forms used to support the treatment are compiled (schema diary form, memory flash, registration forms, experiment forms, and so on). The workbook is part of the therapy and during a weekly session it offers concrete tools that can be used to achieve sub-goals for the next therapy week. The sub-goals of all patients are written on a big fly sheet and displayed during the therapy sessions. In this way, the weaving of an expanding web throughout the treatment is achieved and group members can talk to each other, and motivate each other to work towards these goals.

The group functions as a work group. The climate within the group has to be safe and connected so that patients can work toward their individual goals. It is possible to work around an individual patient, but there must always be a link to other group members so that broadening can occur. This improves the mutual involvement, and with this, cohesion within the group (Reijen and Haans, 2008). If patterns within the group influence the cohesion in a negative way, this must be dealt with immediately. The basis of a work group is lacking in such a case and by using group psychotherapeutic techniques (e.g., Yalom, 1981; Berk, 2005), an assessment can be made regarding what is going on in the group. In addition, this process provides a lot of information and it visualizes the investigation of the group process schemas and modes in group members very well. Repeating processes of which a person is unaware, can surface in this way.

Degrees of intervention

An essential part of treatment in an inpatient and day treatment setting is the language and communication within the team. Through daily meetings, and by exchanging data about the different groups and individual processes within these groups in a mutual language, there emerges a strong aspect of the treatment in which the patient finds himself constantly confronted with both his problems and possible ways in which to work on them. In order to obtain the best possible therapeutic climate, it is important that team members know of each other both what they do and what can be expected of them (Janzing and Lansen, 1985). In this way, a team dynamic develops in which team members know who does what, and in which a patient can easily be helped to find his way in the treatments offered.

When planning interventions, the level at which the interventions have an influence (see Figure 6.1) must be checked constantly. Discussing a patient from a group can, for example, lead to the decision to empathically confront the patient in group psychotherapy with the way in which he withholds contact out of fear of not being understood. This is an individual intervention within the group. This intervention can also have an effect on a group level, for example, if there are other patients who

	Individual	Group	Environment
Cognitive			
Behavioral			
Experiential			
Interpersonal			

Figure 6.2 Matrix of treatment strategies and intervention levels

are afraid to experience and share emotions. Should a tendency become visible that patients feel in secure in sharing their feelings (e.g., by disturbance within the treatment team), then interventions on the level of the environment are appointed (such as organizing an extra meeting between the treatment team and the patient group). On a higher level, there should perhaps be tuning of the program and its preconditions within the institution. Changes in financing provide an example of an "outside" influence on the entire institution that can also reflect on the program.

Daily interventions especially occur on the level of the individual, the group, and the environment. In Young and colleagues (2003), cognitive, experiential, behavioral, and interpersonal strategies are used to change schemas, coping styles, and modes in the changing phase. With the three intervention levels and the four groups of treatment strategy mentioned above, an imagery matrix in which interventions occur can be designed, with possible overlaps (see Figure 6.2).

It is important to check in which level, and from which discipline, interventions constantly occur.

Treatment Strategies

The effect per strategy in the program is described next.

Cognitive strategies recur in different phases of treatment. However, the focus remains on the discipline of psychotherapy. The most cognitive setting is the S-training (ST training). During the S-training, work is focused on tracking dysfunctional (core) beliefs by using schema or modes diary forms, and these beliefs are then challenged. This eventually results in a balanced, rational alternative, which can be used as the basis of a "flash card." During a session, the aim is to focus on two patients. Sometimes, the entire group makes a schema diary card but only if a specific theme is relevant for the entire group.

Group psychotherapy is very adaptable and can be used to test cognitions, and during individual sessions basic assumptions can be worked on. However, cognitive treatment strategies are not reserved for the discipline of psychotherapy. Within socio-therapy, thoughts about oneself and others are also regularly tested. Creative experiential therapies do have a more experiential character, but it is important to make a connection, where possible, to underlying core assumptions with these experience-focused therapies (Muste, 2010).

Behavioral strategies are used during all of the therapies. Behavior change often occurs directly after treatment starts. The program provides a clear day structure and schedule. The day opening and day closure demarcate working time and the unstructured time. At the day closing, a link to the evening will always be made and an explicit question about plans will be asked. The leads into the treatment are formed, as well as the evaluations, by a "Step-by-step" session or a "Homework" session. Every week, points of interest are formulated and evaluated, which (gradually) lead to formulated aims.

> During the step-by-step session, Naomi talks about her birthday, which she celebrated within the group the day before. She went shopping with a group member, but had difficulties making choices. After talking about it, the socio-therapist names the Enmeshment/Undeveloped-Self schema. Naomi feels insecure when she has to show her true colors. In this situation, she is also self-punitive. As a result, it is hard for her to develop the feeling of being someone moving on from her experiences. We agree that she will keep a "positive event diary" in which she records positive experiences of choices made by herself.

As mentioned before, all disciplines work with behavioral treatment strategies. Schemas and modes are always connected with behavior in the here and now, and the patient is challenged to experiment with new behavior every time. However, the emphasis placed on the implementation of specific behavior strategies lies with the socio-therapists. Especially in individual conversations with their personal coach, patients discuss problems in their social life and society, and more specific Axis I problems will be worked on.

Creative experiential therapies play an important role in the implementation of *experiential strategies*. These therapy methods are more focused on perception and non verbal aspects of communication because of their nature. Basic needs are often encountered here. In these experience-focused therapies, themes such as basic safety, confidence, autonomy, self-esteem, self-expression, and limitation are easily revealed. Furthermore, these themes can be translated into individual schema conceptualizations. Basic needs offer direction in terms of the attitude of the therapist. In this way, the reaction to a question of someone with the Emotional Deprivation schema can be answered with the attitude "come on," while the answer to the same question from a patient with weak autonomy might be with the attitude "go ahead" (Heijs and Vos, 2001).

Experiential techniques are also used within psychotherapy, both in a group and individually. Imagery can be used in groups when it is about more general topics, and chair work is also very applicable to groups.

> One of the schemas that fits Ellis is Mistrust and/or Abuse. During psychomotor therapy, Mark is rocked in a hammock. The therapist asks two group members to rock him; one of them is Ellis. She thinks it is exciting. When the therapist rocks Mark and hums a tune, Ellis slowly moves closer. Mark (with the Emotional Deprivation schema) begins to cry when he starts to feel how the situation matches his needs. Ellis makes the first move tentatively, by joining in the movement, and later by taking over the rocking. She is visibly touched. Later, she says that she could clearly see that Mark felt safe. This moved her. She also wants to feel safe, but hasn't had that feeling ever since her uncle abused her.

Interpersonal strategies play an important role in the treatment of patients with personality disorders and are integrated within the therapeutic environment. The concept of "limited reparenting" will have its own place within an inpatient and day treatment environment. Besides the individual psychotherapist, the group and the therapeutic environment are important components here. Living together for a long period, and working in an atmosphere where basic needs are a priority, takes over a big part of the function of limited reparenting. In the group therapy literature, other terms such as "holding," "containing," and "good mother" (Berk, 1986) are used. These concepts help to design limited reparenting within the program. In the day treatment, the same team is used and so this function continues. A patient is confronted with empathic confrontation everywhere, in contact with the staff and also within the group. Group members are often very capable of connecting emotionally with a patient, and touching the sore spot. This is one of the strengths of a group (Horvath and Luborsky, 1993; Berk, 2005). But if the group becomes insecure, the staff will play a more active role.

> Mary has just started to attend the group. She attracts attention because of her questioning way of watching. During the group session, she keeps an eye on the therapists, and as soon as she is the focus of attention, she easily bursts into tears. Tom, a group member, is her mentor. However, he often ignores her, and, in a number of ways, shows that he doesn't really want to be her mentor. The therapists point out to him that he is neglecting Mary. At first, she feels supported. However, at the same time, she is confronted with her nagging way of attracting attention. This gives Tom some space. When some space has been made for both of them to consider underlying patterns, they find recognition in the lack of shortage (Emotional Deprivation schema) and Mary realizes that another schema, Subjugation, covers this shortage in her case.

Interpersonal strategies return in group therapy and during individual sessions. The therapist can take over the role of a parent or a protector, for example, when using chair work or (individually) in an imagery with rescripting.

Ego-strength: Healthy Adult mode

In the literature, ego-strength is defined in different ways (Lake, 1985). The concept refers to the extent that someone is capable of controlling his thoughts, feelings, and actions, and to the extent that someone is capable of dealing with anxiety. Within ST, these characteristics are integrated in the Healthy Adult mode. This mode is often barely present in patients with strong personality pathology, and the therapist has to choose this position to protect and develop the Vulnerable Child (Young, 1990; Young and Klosko, 1994; Arntz and Kuipers, 1998). Within inpatient and day treatment ST, not only the therapist, but also the group can function as an external Healthy Adult. The group often corrects the biased experience of reality that an individual patient has.

The extent to which a patient controls the Healthy Adult mode determines which treatment environment is applicable. If a patient controls this mode reasonably well, and is capable of having triadic contact, offering group sessions may be advantageous. In this case, more emphasis is placed on confrontation and disorder. Patients who have less control in the Healthy Adult mode need more structure and support. These patients have more difficulties in taking advantage of triadic contacts and often benefit from a dyadic contact. In this way, an environment can be formed that fits a specific population of patients as well as possible (see Figure 6.3).

Forming a treatment environment based on the extent to which the Healthy Adult mode is present in a patient also has implications for the extent to which individual therapy is part of the treatment. It is important for "ego-weak" patients to work through dyadic contact toward triadic contact. In this case, individual psychotherapy

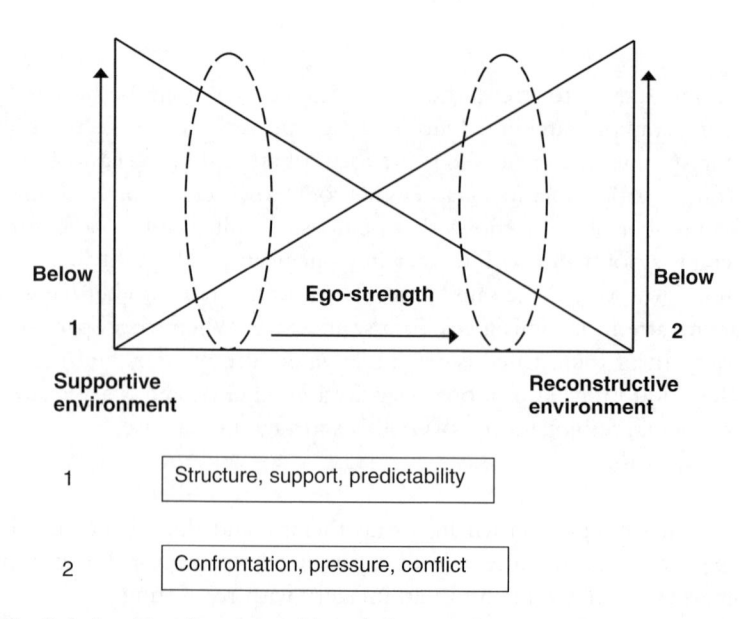

Figure 6.3 Relationship of ego-strength and therapeutic environment

is part of the program and the patient will be given support to discuss things in a safe surrounding. The experience within a step-down program is that during the treatment patients are increasingly capable of benefiting from the group, and so individual sessions can be stopped in a later phase of the treatment.

Pitfalls and Tips

In summary, ST in an inpatient and day treatment version is described above. It has become clear that the different phases of a treatment must form a whole (Multi-disciplinaire richtlijn persoonlijkheidsstoornissen, 2008). It is important for patients with severe personality disorders that the treatment is transparent and requires insight. ST provides clear tools for this.

Implementing ST within a multidisciplinary group setting is not easy. Although the ST model seems easy to understand initially, the complexity of theory and technique only becomes apparent in practice. Therefore, it is important that when a new model is implemented, the management supports this choice by setting aside time and money to gain knowledge about and implementation of this model.

The demand for training has increased enormously. This concerns training in both outpatient and inpatient and day treatment ST, and in teams. The school in which a team was trained thus far will partly determine which difficulties have to be faced. In general, psychoanalytically educated people will have difficulties with the controlled and transparent approach. They will have to train in the different cognitive behavior therapeutic techniques that will be implemented within ST. Cognitive behavior therapeutic-adjusted teams will have more difficulties with the implementation of interpersonal strategies. Working with the therapeutic alliance and the reparenting elements in the environmental treatment deserves extra attention.

Discrete from the frame of reference, and dependent on the population and the goal of the treatment, the balance between group and individual deserves attention. Furthermore, who will do what in the treatment must be discussed. Not all team members will feel the need to implement more psychotherapeutic techniques, and are, furthermore, not trained for this. Finally, the extent to which schemas and modes are actually named is often a subject of debate due to the fear that language will start to serve as a rationalization.

The Future

There are many more challenges to be met in the development of inpatient and day treatment ST. Although there is a consistency between disciplines and the implementation of different techniques within both versions of ST, the effects of specific factors are still insufficiently researched. Monitoring the therapeutic process possibly offers greater understanding of these specific factors. With this, the duration of treatment is an important variable, as well as the efficacy of step-down treatment, in which the intensity of the treatment decreases because inpatient treatment is followed by day treatment, and the treatment is gradually completed.

Although ST, and especially the inpatient and day treatment version, is a fusion of different psychotherapeutic frameworks in itself, new techniques are constantly being implemented. This suits the current belief in working in a pragmatic and integrative way instead of clinging tenaciously to one psychotherapeutic movement or psychotherapeutic framework. An example of this is the combination of (inpatient) ST with EMDR (Eye Movement Desensitization Reprocessing) which is being developed at this moment. In the past years, EMDR has been seen as a promising intervention technique for the treatment of traumas (Gersons and Olff, 2005; ten Broeke, de Jongh and Oppenheim, 2008). Young, Zangwill, and Behary (2002) describe ways to integrate EMDR in the treatment, both in the assessment phase and in the changing phase. How EMDR fits in inpatient ST and when it can offer an alternative for imagery with rescripting remain to be investigated.

Another example concerns the implementation of mindfulness or Attention-focused Cognitive Therapy. Schurink (2006) and Whitfield (2006) describe the integration of mindfulness in cognitive therapy. Van Vreeswijk, Broersen, and Schurink (2009) discuss integration of mindfulness in ST. Within inpatient and day treatment ST, it is conceivable that this form of attention-focused therapy can have a place in the treatment program (e.g., in a module concept).

Besides these examples, you can also think of implementing (parts of) DBT (Linehan, 1993) or Acceptance and Commitment Therapy (Hayes and Strosahl, 2004). Within inpatient ST, parts of this treatment (possible in module form) are a good fit, for example, with emotion regulation, dealing with a crisis, concentration techniques, and learning how to be tolerant. However, when integrating techniques from other therapy movements, you must stay alert to the consistency of the treatment program. It should not become a melting pot and the methods used have to be clear and transparent. Furthermore, the suggestion should not be made that everything can happen and that everything is "curable," as long as there is a complete scale of techniques available. Within the inpatient and day treatment version of ST, a therapist should not only be a jack-of-all-trades, but in general, the multidisciplinary team must also be at least partly trained.

References

Andrea, H. (2008) Cohort klinische schematherapie; data uit Sceptre onderzoek. Personal communication.

Arntz, A. and Kuipers, H. (1998) Cognitieve gedragstherapie bij de borderline persoonlijkheidsstoornis, in *Behandelingsstrategieën bij de Borderline Persoonlijkheidsstoornis* (eds W. van Tilburg, W. van den Brink and A. Arntz). Houten/Diegem: Bohn Stafleu Van Loghum.

Bartak, A., Andrea, H., Spreeuwenberg, M.D. *et al.* (2010) Effectiveness of outpatient, day hospital, and inpatient psychotherapeutic treatment for patients with Cluster B personality disorder. *Psychotherapy and Psychosomatics*, 80, 28–38.

Berk, T. (1986) *Groepstherapie, Theorie en Techniek*. Houten: Bohn Stafleu van Loghum.

Berk, T. (2005) *Leerboek Groepspsychotherapie*. Utrecht: De Tijdstroom.

Broeke, E. ten, Jongh, A. de and Oppenheim, H. (2008) *Praktijkboek EMDR: Casusconceptualisatie en Specifieke Patiëntengroepen*. Amsterdam: Harcourt Assesment BV.

Edens, W. and Kerstens, J. (2009) Het milieutherapeutische arrangement voor klinische schematherapie, in *Handboek Klinische Schematherapie* (eds E.H. Muste, A. Weertman and A.M. Claassen). Houten: Bohn Stafleu van Loghum, pp. 59–77.

Farrell, J.M. and Shaw, I.A. (1994) Emotional awareness training: a prerequisite to effective cognitive-behavioral treatment of borderline personality disorder. *Cognitive and Behavioral Practice, 1*, 71–91.

Farrell, J., Shaw, I. and Webber, M. (2009) A schema-focused approach to group psychotherapy for outpatients with borderline personality disorder: a randomized controlled trial. *Journal of Behavior Therapy and Experimental Psychiatry, 40*(2): 317–328.

Gersons, B.P.R. and Olff, M. (2005) *Behandelstrategieën bij Posttraumatische Stresstoornissen*. Houten: Bohn Stafleu van Loghum.

Günther, G., Blokland-Vos, J., Mook, C. van and Molenaar, J.P. (2009) Vaktherapie binnen klinische schematherapie, in *Handboek Klinische Schematherapie* (eds E.H. Muste, A. Weertman and A.M. Claassen). Houten: Bohn Stafleu van Loghum, pp. 99–130.

Hayes, S.C. and Strosahl, K.D. (2004) *A Practical Guide to Acceptance and Commitment Therapy*. New York: Springer-Verlag.

Heijs, I. and Vos, J. (2001) *Schematherapie en Non-verbale Therapie op De Kliniek*. June 11, PTC De Viersprong.

Horvath, A.O. and Luborsky, L. (1993) The role of therapeutic alliance in psychotherapy. *Journal of Consulting and Clinical Psychology, 61*, 561–573.

Janzing, C. and Lansen, J. (1985) *Milieutherapie. Het arrangement van de Klinisch-Therapeutische Zetting*. Assen and Maastricht: Van Gorcum.

Lake, B. (1985) Concept of ego strength in psychotherapy. *British Journal of Psychiatry, 147*: 471–478.

Lenaerts, P. (2002) Invloed van het postmodernisme op psychotherapie. *Tijdschrift voor Familietherapie, 8*, 21–39.

Lenaerts, P. (2009) Systeemtherapie en klinische schematherapie, in *Handboek Klinische Schematherapie* (eds E.H. Muste, A. Weertman and A.M. Claassen). Houten: Bohn Stafleu van Loghum, pp. 161–178.

Linehan, M.M. (1993) *Cognitive Behavioral Treatment for Borderline Personality Disorder*. New York: Guilford Press.

Multidisciplinaire Richtlijn Persoonlijkheidsstoornissen (2008) Richtlijn voor de diagnostiek en behandeling van volwassen patiënten met een persoonlijkheidsstoornis. Trimbos-instituut

Muste, EH (2006). Book Review - J.E. Young, J.S. Klosko and M.E. Weishaar (2005). Schema therapy. Handbook for therapists. *Journal of Psychotherapy, 32–5*, 373–378.

Muste, E.H. (2010) Schematherapie en vaktherapie, in *Muziek en schema – schema en muziek. Wat kunnen muziektherapie en schematherapie voor elkaar betekenen* (ed. J. Verburgt). Nijmegen: Creatieve Therapie Opleiding.

Muste, E.H. and Thunnissen, M.M. (2003) Klinische psychotherapie bij persoonlijkheidsstoornissen. Schematherapie in een therapeutisch milieu, in *Handboek Milieutherapie*, Vol. 2 (eds C. Janzing, A. van de Berg and F. Kruisdijk). Assen: Van Gorcum.

Muste, E.H., Weertman, A. and Claassen, A.M. (eds) (2009) *Handboek Klinische Schematherapie*. Houten: Bohn Stafleu van Loghum.

Reijen, J. van and Haans, T. (2008) *Groepsdynamica in Gedragstherapeutische en Psychodynamische Groepen*. Houten: Bohn Stafleu van Loghum.

Reiss, N., Lieb, K., Arntz, A., Shaw, I.A. and Farrell, J.M. (submitted for publication) Responding to the treatment challenge of patients with severe BPD: results of three pilot studies of inpatient schema therapy.

Schurink, G. (2006) Mindfulness: integratie in de cognitieve gedragstherapie. *Gedragstherapie*, *39*, 282–291.

Smeijsters, H. (2000) *Handboek Creatieve Therapie*. Bussum: Uitgeverij Coutinho.

Thunnissen, M.M. and Muste, E.H. (2002) Schematherapie in de klinisch-psychotherapeutische behandeling van persoonlijkheidsstoornissen. *Tijdschrift voor Psychotherapie*, *28*, 385–401.

Thunnissen, M.M. and Muste, E.H. (2005) Klinische psychotherapie bij persoonlijkheidsstoornissen: schematherapie in een therapeutisch milieu, in *Jaarboek voor psychiatrie en psychotherapie*, Vol. 9 (ed. A.H. Schene). Houten: Bohn Stafleu van Loghum, pp. 205–217.

Timman, R., Verstraten, J. and Trijsburg, R.W. (2006) *Standaard Evaluatie Project*; STEP Rapport 2006–2010, De Viersprong Kliniek, De Viersprong IOP.

Verburgt, J. (2010) *Muziek en Schema – Schema en Muziek. Wat Kunnen Muziektherapie en schematherapie voor Elkaar Betekenen*. Nijmegen: Creatieve Therapie Opleiding.

Vinken, S.M.C. and Westenbroek, M.M. (2009) Psychotherapie binnen klinische schematherapie, in *Handboek Klinische Schematherapie* (eds E.H. Muste, A. Weertman and A.M. Claassen). Houten: Bohn Stafleu van Loghum, pp. 79–98.

Vreeswijk, M.F. van and Broersen, J. (2006) *Schemagerichte Therapie in Groepen. Cognitieve Groepspsychotherapie bij Persoonlijkheidsproblematiek*. Houten: Bohn Stafleu van Loghum.

Vreeswijk, M.F., Broersen, J. and Schurink, G. (2009) *Mindfulness en Schematherapie; Praktische Training bij Persoonlijkheidsproblematiek*. Houten: Bohn Stafleu van Loghum.

Weerd, D. de and Oudmaijer, M. (2009) Sociotherapie en klinische schematherapie, in *Handboek Klinische Schematherapie* (eds E.H. Muste, A. Weertman and A.M. Claassen). Houten: Bohn Stafleu van Loghum, pp. 131–160.

Weertman, A. (2009) Doelgroepomschrijving en indicatiestelling, in *Handboek Klinische Schematherapie* (eds E.H. Muste, A. Weertman and A.M. Claassen). Houten: Bohn Stafleu van Loghum, pp. 31–40.

Whitfield, H.J. (2006) Towards case-specific applications of mindfulness-based cognitive-behavioural therapies: a mindfulness-based rational emotive behaviour therapy. *Counselling Psychology Quarterly*, *19*(2): 205–217.

Yalom, I.D. (1981) *Groepspsychotherapie in Theorie en Praktijk*. Houten: Bohn Stafleu van Loghum.

Young, J.E. (1990) *Cognitive Therapy for Personality Disorders: a Schema-focused Approach*. Sarasota, FL: Practitioner's Resource Series.

Young, J.E. and Klosko, J. (1994) *Reinventing Your Life*. New York: Plume (in Dutch: *Leven in je Leven*. Lisse: Swets & Zeitlinger, 1999).

Young J.E., Klosko, J.S. and Weishaar, M.E. (2003) *Schema Therapy: a Practitioner's Guide*. New York: Guilford Press.

Young, J., Zangwill, W. and Behary, W. (2002) Combining EMDR and schema-focused therapy: the whole may be greater than the sum of the parts, in *EMDR as an Integrative Psychotherapy Approach* (ed. F. Shapiro). New York: Guilford Press, pp. 181–209.

7

Schema Therapy in Groups: A Short-Term Schema CBT Protocol

Jenny Broersen and Michiel van Vreeswijk

The publication of the short-term protocol treatment for group schema cognitive behavior therapy (SCBT-g; van Vreeswijk and Broersen, 2006) was the first initiative in Europe to describe and further develop the implementation of this therapy method for outpatient groups. In this therapy method, the emphasis is, in particular, on the cognitive behavioral therapeutic techniques of Schema Therapy (ST). ST for outpatient groups hadn't yet been described in Europe but only for groups in an inpatient and day treatment setting (Thunnissen and Muste, 2002, 2005).

A few years later, Muste, Weertman, and Claassen (2009) published on the inpatient and day treatment group setting and small-scale studies were conducted on group ST (e.g., Zorn, Roder, Muller, Tschacher and Thommen, 2007; Farrell, Shaw and Webber, 2009).

A group working in the US were the first to develop and validate group ST in a randomized controlled trial ($N = 32$). This study compared group ST for borderline personality disorders with treatment as usual (TAU) and large effects of group ST for borderline personality disorder were reported (Farrell, Shaw and Webber, 2009; Reiss, Lieb, Arntz, Shaw and Farrell, submitted).

In 2008, a group of international researchers (Arntz, 2010; Arntz and Farrell, 2010) began a randomized study to further investigate the (cost)-effectiveness of group ST for BPD. In the ST condition, patients undertake group ST once or twice a week for two years. They are also investigating whether group ST should be combined with individual therapy sessions. Institutes in the US, Germany, Australia, and the Netherlands are participating in this study, the results of which will be published within a few years.

In 2003, SCBT-g was developed and the authors have been conducting an effect study (van Vreeswijk, Spinhoven, Broersen and Eurelings-Bontekoe, unpublished) since 2004. The first results show a significant positive change in symptoms, schemas,

> **Box 1:**
>
> Frank, aged 25 years, seems to miss a lot of the group sessions. His Self-Sacrifice schema is responsible for the fact that he has too much on his plate at home. He always puts his own needs second, as a result of which everything eventually gets on top of him. His Insufficient Self-Control/Self-Discipline schema is subsequently activated. It all becomes too much for him, he doesn't keep his appointments, and stops attending his therapy sessions. The group members wonder how the therapists will deal with his absence. They think that they will have to take action and they would like to know what the therapists are going to do. They are very annoyed by Frank's behavior, however, they don't say this to him (avoiding his and their schema triggering).

and schema modes. Study into the indication field has yet to take place. The question is, for which patients with personality problems is SCBT-g sufficient, and which patients will need additional treatment?

In Practice

More and more patients and therapists are requesting ST. Not all patients need long-term ST; they can also benefit from SCBT-g. Because the triggering of schemas and schema modes often occurs in contact with others, group ST seems to be an important alternative to individual ST. Within the safe therapeutic climate, interpersonal learning can start and be repaired.

In daily practice, it seems that there is a different group dynamic within every group. This dynamic is partly determined by the structure of present schemas and moods that the patients have. The example below describes a patient participating in SCBT-g (see Box 1).

Approach

Diagnostic, outcome measures, and assessment

Patients who are referred for SCBT-g often have relapsing Axis I symptoms for which they have had prior treatment. During the assessment, it is determined whether a personality disorder is the primary diagnosis or if there are other reasons to consider ST.

After assessment, a symptoms list, Schema Questionnaire (SQ, Dutch version; Sterk and Rijkeboer, 1997; YSQ L2, English version Young and Brown, 2003), the schema modes questionnaire (SMI-1 Dutch version; Lobbestael, van Vreeswijk, Arntz and Spinhoven, 2010; SMI-1.1 English version: Young et al., 2008) are completed. In group therapy, the list and the questionnaires are also completed by the patient at midway evaluations and at the final evaluation. It is advisable to complete a personality questionnaire as well. The test outcomes are worked up into a report and feedback is given to the patient in the next session. The report is given to the patient.

During the consultative session, whether the patient is suitable for SCBT-g, according to the test outcomes, is determined. Is it about symptoms as a result of personality problems (in which case ST is indicated), or is the patient suitable for group therapy? A contraindication for group therapy is, for example, a patient who shows too little consideration for others. Equally, a patient with (severe) hearing or stuttering problems is inappropriate for a group.

Patients with both Cluster B and Cluster C problems are included. Some of these patients have complete personality disorders; others have features of this disorder. Personality disorders are heterogeneous. In the assessment, it is important for therapists to take this into consideration.

In the consultative session, SCBT-g is explained and pitfalls, which can play a role within the group, are discussed. The patient is told that group sessions are recorded on DVD. If they are absent from a session, the patient has to watch the DVD of the missed group session before the next therapy session.

In SCBT-g, there are a few rules that need to be followed to ensure that everyone feels safe and that the group process progresses smoothly. In the consultative session, it is important to reach agreement with the patient regarding the therapy. To state explicitly that confidentiality is required for both group members and therapists is one of these agreements. In addition, it can be explained that general remarks about the group are allowed and that a patient can talk about himself. Another agreement concerns punctuality and how patients can cancel a session when necessary. The absence of a group member is always reported in SCBT-g (see Box 2). In the therapy sessions, the patient's emotions can become overwhelming. So how the patient can best deal with this, and what his needs are in such a situation, are discussed. A patient is allowed to leave the group for a short break, but must return to the group within a few minutes. Finally, the patient agrees that whatever he discusses with group

---

Box 2:

Emily was absent from the last session without giving notice, whilst during the previous session she took a vulnerable position. Amber confronts Emily carefully about the fact that she didn't like it that Emily was absent without warning. She was afraid that Emily wasn't coming back (Abandonment/Instability schema). Dave agrees and tells Emily that he was worried, but that he is also angry with her because she had let the others down (Self-Sacrifice schema, but avoiding expressing his own needs). Emily is offended and wants to leave. She doesn't have to take anyone else into consideration (Insufficient Self-Control/Discipline and Entitlement Grandiosity schemas). One of the group therapists asks Emily to stay seated and to tell them what else she feels. Then, Emily admits that she feels under attack and frustrated. She starts to cry when a group member says that she understands her pain, because she would feel the same way, but Emily also sees how the other group members and the therapists are trying to help her.

members outside the group therapy he will bring back into the group therapy. In addition, when he has had a (crisis) contact with one of the group therapists, this too will be discussed within the group. In order to keep an open and safe atmosphere in the group and to avoid the formation of subgroups, it is important that patients share with each other anything they may have discussed outside the group session. It is wise to limit discussion outside of group sessions with fellow group members about what happens within the group to a minimum.

Treatment

The group consists of 8–10 patients. This therapy involves a closed group, which means that all patients start at the same time and no new patients can join after the group has started.

The therapy consists of 18 group sessions and two follow-up sessions. There is no individual psychotherapy outside of the group sessions. However, an individual session can be held with a patient, in the event of a crisis, a risk of dropout, or repeated absences. Group therapists aren't available 24 hours a day. Patients can contact them on working days, but they have to take into consideration that what they talk about will be shared with the group.

The weekly group sessions take 1½ hours and follow a predetermined structure. At the beginning of a session, all patients hang up their flip chart on which their most important schemas are written, as well as the weekly ratings and the extent of the changes to their schemas. In the subsequent 40 minutes, there is group discussion. The subjects discussed are linked to the schemas and modes of the patients. During this time there is the opportunity for the group therapists to identify what they have noticed regarding the group dynamic. In the remaining time, the focus is on one specific schema technique. Sometimes this technique is first developed in subgroups, but it is always discussed further within the group.

Schema techniques

Each patient is given a workbook (Broersen and van Vreeswijk, 2006) in which homework forms, with explanations, are added for each group session. Information about schemas, cognitive strategies, and interventions, in order to break through behavioral patterns (e.g., role-playing), are examples of schema techniques used (Young, Klosko and Weishaar, 2003; van Vreeswijk and Broersen 2006). The experience and the emotional perception of the patient are given a lot of space. Chair work can also be implemented in this protocol. Besides the previously mentioned techniques, there is a focus on the therapeutic alliance and the relationship with group members. In addition, attention is drawn to limited reparenting and empathic confrontation.

The implemented schema techniques are, in particular, focused on situations from the present. In this treatment, links can be made with situations from the past, although, in this set up, they choose a short-term approach, and techniques focused on situations from the past (imaginary, rescripting, and historic role-playing) aren't employed (descriptions of these techniques can be found in Young *et al.*, 2003). The authors of this chapter share the opinion that these techniques are of great value for the treatment, however, they have chosen to describe the experiential techniques that focus on the past in a separate module (van Vreeswijk and Broersen, unpublished). In this way, the treatment can keep its short-term character. Furthermore, research is yet to show whether these techniques are necessary for effective treatment. Weertman and Arntz (2007) concluded that techniques such as role-playing that are focused on the present are as effective as techniques that focus on the past.

Group psychotherapeutic techniques

This group therapy shares similarities with the classic behavioral therapeutic group therapy and the interpersonal group therapy (Wilfley, MacKenzie, Welch, Ayes and Weysman, 2000, p. 33). In group therapy, consideration for the different phases that a group passes through is of importance (e.g., Burlingame, MacKenzie and Strauss, 2004). A good working relationship between the two group therapists is also important (Hubert, 1994; Maas, 1994; Berk, 2005).

Patients get to know each other during the first group sessions; however, time is still needed to build up safety within the group. Group therapists often have the task of increasing the cohesion within a group. They play an active role and connect the experiences of group members, in order to increase recognition of the problems in schemas.

In the working phase (group sessions 6–15), group members should be heading toward more interactions with each other. Interventions focused on increasing group cohesion become less necessary. There is more room for empathic confrontation and limited reparenting. Group therapists can confront a patient, respectfully, when the development of his schemas or modes, in a working alliance with group members and group therapists, comes across in a dysfunctional way. In Frank's case the following occurred during the 12th group session (see Box 3).

It is important to discuss the group dynamic. Patients who struggle with their schemas often find it difficult to make real contact and show their emotions. This can occur within the group, where they are always friendly to each other but won't discuss things that irritate them about the others. Another form of expression is that patients regularly have one-on-one contact.

Box 3:

Frank had been absent a lot during previous group sessions. He reacted from his Insufficient Self-Control/Self-discipline schema when group members and group therapists didn't ask him directly how he was doing. He reacted very violently (Angry Child mode) toward one of the group therapists. The therapist restricted Frank's anger and told him that he does his very best for him and that Frank's unpleasant behavior was hurtful. In addition, the group therapist explains, in a calm and concerned way, that Frank has treated himself badly for a long time, because he always neglects his own needs at home (Self-Sacrifice schema). This is, therefore, the likely cause of his violent reaction. Frank's anger subsides, and his vulnerability becomes more visible. The group members gain a greater understanding of his problems.

> **Box 4:**
>
> In the ST group, Mary, aged 43 years, seems to submit to the Self-Sacrifice schema all the time. She gives advice to everybody and avoids voicing irritations or conflicts (Compliant Surrender mode). She receives a lot of praise from the group members because she shows them all empathy. But nobody dares to interrupt her when she tells her story. In this way, Mary's Emotional Deprivation schema isn't activated within the group. It shows that, although group members sympathize with each other, they don't express their irritations during the first half of the therapy. Group therapists highlight the group process, and they link this to Mary's and the others' schemas. The group members all experience anxiety when it comes to criticizing each other.

In Mary's case (see Box 4), it becomes clear that group members have an intense way of making contact with each other, after she is confronted with her schema-confirming behavior by the group therapist. Within the group, there is often anxiety toward intensifying contact with each other. Exposing oneself to this anxiety (i.e., by making contact with others) can be a way of dealing with schemas in a different manner.

During the final group sessions, saying goodbye becomes the main focus. In this phase, the group therapists try to avoid confrontations and play a more active role. It is important to mention that, during the last group sessions, symptoms and schemas can temporarily increase.

Pitfalls and Tips

In this protocol treatment, a group therapist can come across many pitfalls. This chapter is restricted to a number of potential pitfalls that are related to group therapy, ST, and protocol working.

The danger of protocol treatment is the temptation to stick too rigidly to the protocol, and as a consequence pay insufficient attention to the group therapeutic process and the emotional process of the patients. Besides taking the different group phases into consideration, it is also important to start the group psychotherapeutic process. This therapy method doesn't only focus on an individual working within a group. In addition to the cognitive and behavioral therapeutic strategies, focusing on the emotional process is important.

Another potential pitfall arising from following the protocol very precisely is that the group therapists won't manage the time well. For example, discussing each group member's homework every week isn't possible. The advice is to wait and see whether the patients bring in the homework themselves. For example, there are patients who let others speak all the time, and as a result they don't get enough attention themselves. There are also patients who always take the initiative and (often) dominate the discussion. It is important that group therapists state the roles that schemas play in these situations.

A third potential pitfall is that group therapists appoint a chairperson, who divides the time equally among group members. The Emotional Deprivation schema can play a role here. It is then possible that conflict within the therapy group isn't discussed openly. The group therapists need to check, together with the patients, whether there is a conflict within the group.

In the therapy group, patients sometimes have the tendency to ask for information from or give advice to one group member during a session. Often, this has to do with anxiety. These group members don't dare to stand out themselves. They are either afraid of rejection (e.g., Defectiveness/Shame schema) or they don't dare to confront themselves or each other (e.g., Subjugation schema). Group therapists can break through this process by discussing the subject "group safety" and the role of avoidance. The fact that group members continuously ask questions can be brought up for discussion. Time can also be spent on the meaning of making some room for themselves and talking about their own vulnerability.

In group therapy, another potential pitfall can be that the patients ask the group therapists too many theoretical questions. This behavior can be displayed by a patient who struggles with the Emotional Inhibition and Emotional Deprivation schemas. Role-playing is avoided by continued discussion and by not coming up with situations that can be used in role-play. The task of group therapists is to motivate, stimulate, and explain to the patient that more can be achieved by "acting and experiencing" than just by "discussing" it.

Group therapists can also face endless criticism from patients. Patients can be dissatisfied about the short therapy time or about the fact that symptoms aren't resolved quickly enough. The Demanding Parent can play a role in this. That group therapists contain the Demanding Parent and make patients aware of the possible presence of the Demanding Parent is of importance. Furthermore, attention can be focused on the emotional inner world of the patient and therapists can ask for his real emotional needs. The group therapists can stimulate the patients to share this with each other in order to have more contact and to connect more with each other.

The fact that the group accept that a group member detaches himself and takes up a hidden and closed position can be another pitfall. Group therapists often have the task of teaching group members that they can confront each other in an open and respectful manner about how the behavior of the other affects a group member. It is possible that the Insufficient Control/Discipline schema has been triggered, and that he is so detached that he needs the group to reach out to him.

The Future

In the future, SCBT-g must be investigated in a more controlled and randomized way.

Within the next few years, the results of an international study into group ST for patients with the primary diagnosis of borderline personality disorder will be published. In this international study, group ST is given in a different manner than SCBT-g. For this protocol treatment, the study results will provide greater insight into the efficacy of group ST in general, and also, for example, whether it is necessary to combine it with individual treatment.

It is also important to investigate the effect of techniques that are more focused on childhood experiences vs. techniques that are more focused on the present. With this understanding, the current protocol can be adapted if necessary.

Not all patients end therapy following SCBT-g. Some need additional ST, in which even more focus is placed on experiential techniques. In the last few years, the authors of this chapter have developed schema-focused group modules aimed at experiential techniques (van Vreeswijk and Broersen, manuscript) and mindfulness techniques (van Vreeswijk, Broersen and Schurink, 2009). The group modules mentioned above can be given in either outpatient or inpatient and day treatment group setting. In the near future, refining and studying this technique further is of importance.

References

Arntz, A. (2010) Personal communication.
Arntz, A. and Farrell, J. (2010) International developments in schema therapy research for personality disorders, World Congress of the Association for Cognitive and Behavioral Therapy, Boston, MA, June 4.
Berk, T. (2005) *Leerboek Groepspsychotherapie*. Utrecht: De Tijdstroom.
Broersen, J. and van Vreeswijk, M.F. (2006) *Schemagerichte Therapie in Groepen (Werkboek)*. Houten: Bohn Stafleu van Loghum.
Burlingame, G.M., MacKenzie, K.R. and Strauss, B. (2004). *Bergin and Garfield's Handbook of Psychotherapy and Behavior Change*, 5th edition (ed. M.J. Lambert). New York: Wiley.
Farrell, J.M., Shaw, I.A. and Webber, M. (2009) A schema-focused approach to group psychotherapy for outpatients with borderline personality disorder: a randomized controlled trial. *Journal of Behavior Therapy and Experimental Psychiatry*, 40(2): 317–328.
Hubert, W. (1994) Co-therapie, algemene principes, in *Handboek Groepspsychotherapie* (eds T.J.C. Berk, M.P. Bolten, M. el Boushy et al.), Houten: Bohn Stafleu van Loghum.
Lobbestael, J., van Vreeswijk, M.F., Arntz, A. and Spinhoven, P. (2010) The reliability and validity of the Schema Mode Inventory (SMI). *Behavioural and Cognitive Psychotherapy*, 38, 437–458.
Maas, J. van der (1994) Co-therapie in de groepspsychotherapie; casuïstiek, in *Handboek Groepspsychotherapie* (eds T.J.C. Berk, M.P. Bolten, M. el Boushy et al.), Houten: Bohn Stafleu van Loghum.
Muste, E., Weertman, A. and Claassen, A. (2009) *Handboek Klinische Schematherapie*. Houten: Bohn Stafleu van Loghum.
Reiss, N., Lieb, K. Arntz, A., Shaw, I.A. and Farrell, J.M. (submitted for publication) Responding to the treatment challenge of patients with severe BPD: results of three pilot studies of inpatient schema therapy.
Sterk, F. and Rijkeboer, M.M. (1997) *Schema-Vragenlijst [Schema Questionnaire]*. Utrecht: Ambulatorium, Utrecht University.
Thunnissen, M.M. and Muste, E.H. (2002) Schematherapie in de klinisch-psychotherapeutische behandeling van persoonlijkheidsstoornissen. *Tijdschrift voor Psychotherapie*, 28, 385–401.
Thunnissen, M.M. and Muste, E.H. (2005) Klinische psychotherapie bij persoonlijkheidsstoornissen: schematherapie in een therapeutisch milieu, in *Jaarboek voor psychiatrie en psychotherapie*, Vol. 9 (ed. A.H. Schene). Houten: Bohn Stafleu van Loghum, pp. 205–217.

Vreeswijk, M.F. van and Broersen, J. (2006) *Schemagerichte Therapie in Groepen (Handleiding)*. Houten: Bohn Stafleu van Loghum.

Vreeswijk, M.F. van and Broersen, J. (unpublished) *Module Experiëntiële Technieken in een Groep*. GGZ Delfland.

Vreeswijk, M.F. van, Broersen, J. and Schurink, G. (2009) *Mindfulness en Schematherapie: een Praktische Training bij Persoonlijkheidsonderzoek*. Houten: Bohn Stafleu van Loghum.

Vreeswijk, M.F. van, Spinhoven, P., Broersen, J. and Eurelings-Bontekoe, E.H.M. (unpublished) Changes in symptom severity, schemas and modes in heterogeneous psychiatric patient groups following a short-term schema cognitive behavioral group therapy: a pre-post treatment naturalistic design in an outpatient clinic.

Weertman, A. and Arntz, A. (2007) Effectiveness of treatment of childhood memories in cognitive therapy for personality disorders: a controlled study contrasting methods focusing on the present and methods focusing on childhood memories. *Behaviour Research and Therapy*, 45, 2133–2143.

Wilfley, D.E., MacKenzie, K.R., Welch, R.R., Ayes, V.E. and Weysman, M.M. (2000) *Interpersonal Psychotherapy for Groups*. New York: Basic Books.

Young, J., Arntz, A., Atkinson, T. *et al.* (2008) *Schema Mode Inventory Version 1.1*. Cognitive Therapy Center of New York.

Young, J. and Brown, G. (2003) *Young Schema Questionnaire: Long Form*. Cognitive Therapy Center of New York.

Young, J.E., Klosko, J.S. and Weishaar, M.E. (2003) *Schema Therapy: a Practitioner's Guide*. New York: Guilford Press.

Zorn, P., Roder, V., Muller, D.R., Tschacher, W. and Thommen, M. (2007) Schemazentrierte emotiv-behaviorale Therapie (SET): eine randomisierte Evaluationsstudie an patienten mit persönlichkeitsstörungen aus den Clustern B und C. *Verhaltenstherapie*, *17*: 233–241.

8
Schema Therapy in a Psychodynamic Group

Helga Aalders and Janie van Dijk

Over 10 years ago the authors started to develop a psychodynamic schema-focused group for patients with personality disorders. This patients are described by Young (Young and Pijnaker, 1999) as patients with the following psychological characteristics: diffused presentation of symptoms, frequently recurring interpersonal problems, pronounced inflexibility in patterns of thinking, feeling, and behaving, and a strong cognitive and affective avoidance. Specific characteristics in analytical terms can be added to this list: splitting, leading to black-and-white thinking, or identity diffusion. Holding and containment were missing during the early stages of development, and therefore there is an enormous need for this in the present. Patients with personality disorders experience their problems particularly while interacting with others. Therefore, group therapy is meaningful. In practice, both structured behavior therapeutic groups and insight-oriented psychodynamic groups appear to offer insufficient help for this group of patients. Too much structure within the behavior therapeutic group extinguishes the dynamics that are needed to experience personality problems; too little structure, and these patients can be overwhelmed by the severity of the dynamics. A shortcoming of the psychodynamic groups is the absence of the possibility of stimulating patients to actively change behavior.

The search for treatment that would solve these problems led to the theory and practice of Schema Therapy (ST). This framework offers the possibility to combine a structured, educative approach with experience-focused learning and a focus on intra- and interpersonal dynamics.

In Practice

In this schema-focused psychodynamic group, knowledge and techniques from both schema-focused, psychodynamic, and group dynamic therapies are used. The psychodynamic character is demonstrated in the diagnostic phase through alertness to possible unconscious motives or conflicts that deflect the problems. The principles of group dynamics are is used in the open form of group therapy. Patients are invited to contribute anything that is on their minds. Because of the open nature of the therapy, tension can rise and intra-psychological and interpersonal problems may become apparent. Therapists work with a closed group with nine patients and two therapists.

There are 40 weekly sessions. Each session consists of two parts of one hour, each with a different set up. Patients are mostly referred after they have already had one or more treatments. After completing group therapy, approximately 70% of the patients continue life without further treatment. The other 30% are referred on for more treatment. Treatment continues in these cases with the aim of consolidating the results. Sometimes it is also advisable to have couples therapy or individual trauma treatment (EMDR).

Approach

The assessment criteria to assess the suitability of a patient for the schema focused psychodynamic group therapy one might look at individual aspects, but one has also to focus on how the patient will fit in the group as a whole. On an individual level, an initial assessment of the form and extent to which personality problems play a role in maintaining the symptoms is made. Also, anxiety tolerance has to be sufficient because of the unstructured character of the second part of the group. A personality assessment will always be done. In order to participate within the group, we work with the guideline that there has to be a neurotic or a "high level" borderline personality organisation. The capacity for insight at least at the cognitive level is expected, as are some development capacities on the emotional level. Sufficient education is required to rapidly learn the material needed. Motivation is another important criterion. Apart from attending the weekly group sessions, patients have to be prepared to make time for homework assignments. Finally, the usual contraindications apply: overt suicide intention, psychotic symptoms, self-injurious behavior, aggression, or drug abuse.

> Nathalie, aged 28 years, has struggled with relapsing depressive disorders and social anxiety symptoms for more than 10 years. Despite her gloominess, she has gained a university degree, has a good job, and is in a long-term relationship. She had two years of psychodynamic psychotherapy and has participated in a cognitive behavior group for social anxieties. She has also used several antidepressants. Despite these treatments, she still suffers from chronicle depression and has trouble feeling at ease in social situations. Because of previous treatments, she has come to realize that an important reason for the persistence of her complaints lies in the way she treats herself and others, which is very hard to change.

> William, aged 33 years, works as a nurse, and has lived with his partner for several years. Starting at the age of 18, he has struggled with depression and loneliness, and he uses cannabis regularly. He has received long-term individual treatment focused on dealing with traumatic experiences from the past. The patient and his partner were in couples therapy, in which his tendency to withdraw in difficult situations was addressed.

> Ryan, aged 25 years, a student, has had short-term inpatient psychotherapy for depression, feelings of emptiness, and problems with his studies. The inpatient treatment was evidently successful, but Ryan is not able to consolidate and expand this by himself.

To assess the suitability of the patient for a group therapy, a number of aspects of group dynamics have to be taken into account (Berk, 2005, p. 219). Every patient must be able to identify to some degree with one or more group members regarding problems, socioeconomic and cultural background, gender, and stage of life. Furthermore, it is important that there is a good balance within the group with regard to the dimensions of control vs. impulsiveness and tolerance vs. over-sensitivity. Based on experiences of forming groups, the following formula is used: not more than one patient with a narcissistic personality disorder, not more than two patients with borderline personality disorder, and not patients with Cluster C personality problems exclusively. Patients that seem to benefit most from this form of group therapy have both Cluster B and Cluster C personality features.

A group session is divided into two parts, each lasting one hour. Between the two a 15-minute break is allowed. The first hour is structured, and has two phases in the course of the 40 sessions: the assessment phase and the schema shifting-phase. In the second hour, the emphasis is on group dynamics and the group session is unstructured.

The Structured Hour

The assessment phase in the first hour consists of about 10 sessions. Assessment and the formulation of a case conceptualization are the main issues. From session 11 on, the focus is on schema-shifting.

Assessment phase

Patients and therapists sit round a table. There is a positive work attitude. During the first session, the principles of ST are explained with the use of the book *Reinventing Your Life* (Young and Klosko, 1994). A start is made with the assessment. Here, the same tools are used as in individual ST, which can be adapted for use in a group setting. The schema inventories are handed out to patients during the first sessions.

The results are discussed in the third plenary session. Patients start work on diaries, which they can mail to the therapists when completed from the second session on.

In a diary form, patients analyze an emotionally charged incident from the previous week. The incident is briefly described. Then the patient adds what his thoughts, feelings, behaviors, and consequences were. Next, hypotheses are formulated about the schemas that played a part in this incident. The therapists read and comment on the forms, and return them in the next session. Patients can discuss the diary forms in a plenary session if they want to. This part of the treatment is focused on identifying situations that evoke schemas and on determining the relevant schemas. Patients find mailing the diary forms between sessions valuable. It acts as a prompt to get to work. On an emotional level extra holding is experienced. In terms of ST one can consider this as an act of limited reparenting.

Patients write a brief autobiography with the assignment to trace the schemas in it. The life story is also used to retrace aspects of temperament and of cognitive and emotional development in the origin of schemas. The therapists read the autobiographies and return them with notes on the role of the schemas. The life stories are not discussed in the group, but are taken into the case conceptualization, which is presented at the end of the assessment phase. The assessment phase is concluded with a plenary presentation of the case conceptualizations. The focus for the treatment is then formulated. An important point worthy of attention in this phase is whether all patients can keep up and complete the homework assignments. Some participants experience problems with this. An example is provided below, in order to illustrate how you can deal with this.

Schema-changing process

> Kevin is 25 years old and has been studying geography for seven years. He can't complete his studies. In group therapy, the same problem quickly emerges. Despite his good intentions and strict planning, he comes to therapy empty-handed week after week. The therapists' strategy is not to react from the Unrelenting Standards/Hypercriticalness schema with regard to his inability to produce homework, and not to let it pass, thus neglecting the patient. In the group, his problem is explained in schema terms: his Unrelenting Standards/Hypercriticalness and Defectiveness/Shame schemas result in his avoiding completing the assignments. This will be his focus in the treatment.

In this phase (approximately from session 12 until the completion of the treatment), different ST techniques are used in the first hour. Patients get the opportunity to bring up their problems. A technique that fights the schema is chosen *in situ*. The means that are practiced are similar to those used in individual ST. Generally, therapists first work with cognitive techniques, followed by experiential assignments. In the last phase, the focus is on assignments related to behavior change. At the beginning of the schema change phase, patients are given an explanation of and training in a number of cognitive techniques, for example the downward arrow technique, the multidimensional evaluation (both related to the basic schemas), the Socratic dialogue, and the fight against schema-related way of thinking. There will also be practice in using the schema dialogue of a maladaptive schema vs. the healthy side. Work on fighting schemas on a cognitive level by using schema diary forms is done in small groups or plenary sessions.

The experiential techniques are applied individually within the group or in plenary sessions. Individually, imagery rescripting is done with one patient, while the rest of the group either observe or (sometimes) play an active role in the rescripting. This is a very powerful tool for all the group members, because generally all sorts of personal dilemmas and conflicts emerge. In a plenary session, each group member chooses an imagery assistant who will play a role within the imagery. Then, the imagery takes place in silence. Patients use their assistant in the imagery when they need help in the imagined situation. This way of imagery rescripting within a group is only used if all participants have enough ego-strength and when they have experience with the somewhat "easier" diagnostic imageries.

Other experiential techniques that we use are chair work, imagery dialogue, (historical) role-play, and written assignments. An example of a written assignment is writing (but not sending) a letter to someone important in the patient's life. The group is involved as much as possible (reading aloud in the group, rituals with the group).

Behavior change is gradually worked toward, both in and out of the group. Behavior experiments, flash cards, and role-play are used with this in mind.

Unstructured Hour

In the second hour of a group therapy session the focus is on psychodynamics and group dynamics. A "classic" group therapy setting is made. There is no fixed agenda. The assignment is for patients to express whatever is on their mind. This can be related to the experiences they have had with group members or therapists, it can be related to the first hour, or to something outside the group, in the present or the past. Group members are invited to react freely to each other. As described by Van Vreeswijk and Broersen (2006), therapists aim for a group environment in which the five schema domains of safety, room for autonomy and competence, expression of emotions and needs, spontaneity and expression, and realistic limits are assured. The schema therapeutic frame of reference reveals itself in the terminology that the therapists use. What happens within the group, intra- or interpersonally, is formulated in terms of schemas, schema processes, or modes. Because this ST group is limited in time, Schema Therapists will be more active than in continuous, unlimited group therapy. The case of patient William is provided as an example of the effect of the combination of both methods (first structured hour and second unstructured hour).

> In the first hour, William describes in imagery and diary form situations of abandonment and unstable relationships in his childhood, and mistrust in the present (e.g., mistrusting the motives of colleagues or strangers). The second hour shows how he experiences this within the group; the meaning he gives to where the others will sit in relation to him, how they respond to his attributes,

> and whether they criticize him. William has already worked this out in diary form several times. This eventually leads to his announcement that he doesn't want to continue with the treatment because it is clear to him that he doesn't matter to the group, since they don't take him seriously. The feedback of his group companions however, is supportive and provides a new perspective for William. His projections in the Abandonment/Instability, and Mistrust and/or Abuse schemas become clear to him. He decides to stay and to check his anxious fantasies about the group with the group members, when necessary.

In the Levine model (Hoijtink, 2004) of the process within a group therapy, you can distinguish different consecutive phases: parallel phase, inclusion phase, mutuality phase, and termination phase. Successful completion of these phases leads groups toward a climate of increasing intimacy, sincerity, and depth. Knowledge about the organization of groups is important regarding the ability to anticipate specific patterns of response in patients with certain schemas in certain stages. In other words, each phase has certain characteristics that can activate specific schemas. For example, a patient with the Abandonment/Instability schema still feels relaxed during the first phases of the group (parallel and inclusion phase). The more intimacy and sincerity grow (mutuality phase), the more the patient's tension increases. Another example is the patient with the Social Isolation/Alienation schema. In the parallel phase, in which relationships and bonds are still to be worked out, the group climate is still tolerable for this patient. As soon as the process of subgroup forming starts (inclusion phase) the schema is triggered more often.

Working toward the mutuality phase requires that the therapists are aware of the schemas that might be triggered in this phase, and take care of good therapeutical atmosphere for clients to benefit from the intimacy of this phase (limited reparenting).

The termination phase is very important and demands attention and care. This phase, in which separation plays a key role, is characterized by the approaching end of meaningful relationships that have often been built up with difficulty. For patients with personality disorders, the relationships they form in group therapy can be the first relationships in their life in which they have experienced respect, equality, and understanding. Ending these relationships can trigger the recollection of experiences of loss or deprivation from the past. Many patients have no experience of parting in a meaningful way. Patients are encouraged to experience this with their group members, since it is viewed as a corrective experience. In the termination phase the modus Healthy Adult is given full attention. It is emphasized that patients can build up their life on their own in a meaningful way.

In this schema focused group therapy patients are not offered individual treatment alongside group therapy. The focus is within the group. In this way, the issues etc, patients are concerned about won't spill over into other therapies. There are exceptions to this rule. These are carefully considered and discussed within the group. If a patient has another treatment contact outside the group, this will not be with one of the group therapists. The patient informs the group about the main topics in his individual psychotherapy. Limited contact with the group therapists outside of the group sessions is possible. The therapists can be reached by phone at appointed times. Furthermore, it is possible to email homework or other matters that trouble these patients to the therapists. These mails are generally discussed in the group. In the setting of "limited reparenting" the therapists sometimes reply to these emails.

Pitfalls and Tips

Dilemmas within the structured part of the group

The first part of the session is structured and has an agenda. Difficulties arise when a patient at the start of this hour wants to get something off his chest right away. One way to deal with this is to give the patient a moment of time to say what is bothering him and explain that the second hour will be used to talk about it. In the first hour, after all, the emphasis shouldn't be placed on group dynamics in order that sufficient attention can be given to "work" (role-play, imagery, diary forms), so that this kind of work is not avoided. Another point is that therapists cannot keep up with and adjust to to the process of each group member individually, especially not with plenary-held experiential exercises. Therefore, it is important that patients have sufficient strength or self-regulating power to carry out such an exercise in silence.

Patients can vary markedly in the way and pace in which they do their homework. Some independence is important. Not doing the homework can be an important focus in the treatment (which schemas are being activated?). Finally, the (home)work load for therapists should not be underestimated within this therapy group. Especially for therapists with an Unrelenting Standards/Hypercriticalness schema, peer supervision to keep aware of counter transference is important.

The organization should allow for sufficient indirect time for preparation and evaluation.

Dilemmas within the unstructured part of the group

The most important dilemma arises from the transition from the first to the second part of the group session. Patients might ask for more structure and advice during the second hour. A good explanation of the whys and wherefores of this working method is often enough to dispel any unease. This doesn't alter the fact that some patients experience the more hands-off attitude of the therapists as neglect. This might be difficult for therapists with Self-Sacrifice, Defectiveness/Shame, and Failure schemas.

The Future

The experience of the authors is that combining ST and working with a group dynamic approach has added value for a certain group of patients. Patients with personality disorders experience their problems especially while interacting with others. Group therapy offers room to research and alter these interactional problems in a safe environment. Research will have to show for which groups of patients ST within a group is preferable to individual therapy. Furthermore, the optimal number of sessions for this group treatment has not yet been determined, nor which type of interventions are effective and when.

References

Berk, A. (2005) *Leerboek Groepspsychotherapie*. Utrecht: De Tijdstroom.
Hoijtink, T.A.E. (2004) *Ontwikkelingsfasen in Groepen. Handboek Groepspsychotherapie*. Houten: Bohn Stafleu van Loghum.
Vreeswijk, M.F. van and Broersen, J. (2006) *Schemagerichte Therapie in Groepen. Cognitieve Groepspsychotherapie bij Persoonlijkheidsproblematiek. Handleiding voor Therapeuten.* Houten: Bohn Stafleu van Loghum.
Young, J. and Klosko, J. (1994) *Reinventing Your Life*. New York: Plume.
Young, J. and Pijnaker, H. (1999) *Cognitieve Therapie voor Persoonlijkheidsstoornissen: een Schemagerichte Benadering*. Houten: Bohn Stafleu van Loghum.

9
Schema Therapy in Adolescents

Maryke Geerdink, Erik Jongman
and Agnes Scholing

Schema Therapy (ST) was developed for adult patients, but is also used in the treatment of adolescents (16–23 years old) who develop personality problems. To date, hardly any literature exists concerning ST and adolescents. Searching for the terms "schema-focused therapy and adolescent" in several databases (e.g., Psychinfo and Pubmed, end-2007) resulted in six references, of which four were about family-focused psychotherapy, one was a book review, and one a study into cognitive schemas. In the only treatment study about ST published so far (Giesen-Bloo et al., 2006), patients aged 18 years and older participated, but there was no distinction made between adolescents within the population. Young (2005) provided a case description of a 20-year-old woman with borderline personality disorder and a post-traumatic stress disorder, yet didn't provide guidelines about specific age.

In the Netherlands, there is an interest in this type of treatment for adolescents, but it is little used in practice. An email survey of a limited number of therapists, administered by the authors in the fall of 2007, demonstrated that lack of knowledge about and experience in ST within this target group holds back many therapists from using this type of treatment.

In Practice

There are some points of interest concerning the treatment of adolescents regardless of the nature of the treatment. These result from the developmental phase in which the youngster is. Learning how to deal with autonomy vs. dependency and with his own often strong emotions and those of others are the points of attention. Adolescents have to leave the parental home and establish their own identity. Furthermore, patients who qualify for ST often have a rather tempestuous life with frequent conflicts and problems at school or at work. Their impulsiveness can be expressed in, for instance, excessive substance abuse and parasuicidal behavior.

The Wiley Blackwell Handbook of Schema Therapy: Theory, Research, and Practice, First Edition.
Edited by Michiel van Vreeswijk, Jenny Broersen, and Marjon Nadort.
© 2012 John Wiley & Sons, Ltd. Published 2015 by John Wiley & Sons, Ltd.

> Soraya is a 20-year-old woman of Syrian descent. She refers herself for the second time because of her outbursts of anger in intimate relationships. The first treatment ended after she didn't show up several times and finally broke off contact completely. In the evaluation letter, the therapist left the door open. A year later, Soraya got in contact with the therapist again. She experiences a lot of stress in her relationship with her boyfriend. She thinks he will leave her for a Dutch woman. After the reassessment, it appears that she is pregnant. Because it is inappropriate to be pregnant while not being married in her culture, her family puts pressure on her to marry him. Soraya reacts with aggressive outbursts directed at her boyfriend. Nevertheless, she decides to continue her relationship with him.

Approach

Especially at the beginning of treatment there are more hurdles to overcome than is the case with adults. After years of misery, adults mostly have a better understanding that something needs to change. In adolescents, this understanding is variable. They often report that it's not that bad. Their motivation for treatment is easily subverted because they normally suffer less from explicit or long-term dysfunctional behavior as compared to adult patients. The positive side of this picture is that, in general, their life is less wasted in terms of unfinished education, jobs, and relationships, and they still have many opportunities to develop in a positive way.

More limited reparenting from the therapist is required because of the attitude and behavior of the youngster. Furthermore, the therapist must realize that all sorts of traumatic experiences of varying intensity are still fresh in the adolescent's memory and that certain interactions may be very recent (e.g., in contact with parents).

Assessment

Patients at this age often enter treatment on their own initiative for the first time. According to the principle of stepped care but also in order to meet the wishes of the patient, who normally (still) has little motivation to enter long-term treatment, the treatment will, in principle, be short-term. If this treatment is not successful and problems are more related to impulsivity and an inability to cope with emotions, a schema-focused approach can be tried as the next step. As far as we know, in the Netherlands, ST in adolescents is especially used in forensic settings, because a binding agreement in this age group is usually required in order to complete this long-term and intensive treatment successfully.

Motivation

Motivating occurs, as with adults, throughout treatment. Garcia and Weisz (2002) note that the parents of the youth are mentioned as the main factor for dropping

> Soraya is offered ST after she ended previous behavior therapy that didn't yield any results. It seems she acts in a schema-affirmative way. The aim of the treatment is that she will start to recognize her own schemas (including Abandonment/Instability) and the way in which these schemas dictate her behavior. Following this, she has to learn to react differently in situations that activate her schemas (e.g., by discussing her anxieties with her partner).

out of the therapeutic alliance. Of course, this doesn't mean that youngsters concur with this. Unfortunately, detailed research here is missing. However Spinhoven, Giesen-Bloo, van Dyck, Kooiman, and Arntz (2005), who studied borderline patients who attended ST, showed that a negative evaluation of the therapeutic alliance (by patient and therapist) was prognostic of dropout. From the outset, there has to be a focus on creating a good, strong therapeutic alliance between the adolescent and the therapist, for example, by continuously asking about the surroundings the adolescent lives in and about the persons and activities that are important in their life.

Diagnostic and case conceptualization

The best thing would be to complete the schema inventories with the therapist during the case conceptualization. Adolescents are often reluctant to do that, or are less conscientious when they do it at home. They would rather avoid confronting their problems – a behavior in which you see the Detached Protector mode again. They will also change their mind about their parents, for example, quite often.

In general, most modes are present in young people, but they haven't yet crystallized. Throughout the day many things are going on, and modes move along in these events. This also has a positive side: modes in adolescents are usually less rigid than they are in adults and therefore easier to tackle within the treatment. An important request for help by adolescents is regarding self-control of anger and aggression. You can often see what can best be described as the Angry Protector mode in them (Bernstein, Arntz and de Vos, 2007).

The role of the parents

One of the biggest differences compared to the treatment of adults is that the therapist often has to deal with the parent(s) right away. Many patients are still living at home. Therefore, it is important to ascertain how the therapist can reach the patient without creating complicated situations with the patient's parents at the beginning of the treatment. During the diagnostic stage it is also important to make clear what role the parents play in the life of the adolescent, and how they can be available for him in a positive manner. Following this, the therapist will discuss with the patient how his parents can be involved in the treatment. Depending on the goal of the conversations and the stage of treatment, this can be done with the parents alone or with the parents and the youngster together. The content of the conversations with

> In the case conceptualization, Soraya reported that her parents often let her down as a child because they had important political careers. Later, she challenged negative comments about her parents. Twice, she asked the therapist to talk to her parents alone to explain to them about the origin of her anger and her fear of abandonment. The therapist suggested doing this together as soon as Soraya felt she was ready. Later, Soraya didn't feel the need to arrange such a conversation; she told her parents about her schemas herself.

the parents will be discussed in detail with the adolescent beforehand. The therapist must explain why it is important to discuss certain subjects with the parents, but the patient will take the final decision about what will be discussed. Furthermore, the therapist and patient will agree on how the patient can show that he doesn't want to continue talking about a certain subject.

Appointments and Absences

It is difficult for adolescents to attend therapy twice a week. This is partly because of their ambivalence, but also because they get deeply involved in their daily activities, which may make them forget the appointment or mean that it is not important for them. Therefore, it is important to negotiate the appointments on a regular basis. Care for the patient has priority with regard to this: absence stands in the way of the help that a therapist can and wants to offer. The youngster will be addressed as a Healthy Adult, who has to learn to take care of himself appropriately, as far as possible.

Imagery Exercises

Most adolescents perceive imagery exercises – and to a lesser degree chair work – as "weird" and "stupid." The therapist has to make time for this, without delaying or skipping the exercises. It helps to start the exercise without much explanation and to accept that they won't close their eyes. It is important that the adolescent does not look at the therapist during the imagery exercise; if they do, the imagery will not get enough space. The therapist can turn aside, or ask the patient to focus on a fixed spot (e.g., a table).

Pitfalls and Tips

As mentioned above, adolescents often miss their therapy sessions. A potential pitfall for the therapist is that he will take up the position of the Demanding Parent and will make high demands. It is helpful when the therapist realizes that their behavior

> Soraya stubbornly resists the imagery exercises. She refuses to close her eyes to go to her safe place. When she finally closes them briefly, she immediately and emphatically says that "nothing has happened." She is convinced that imagery will "definitely not work for her" and she often laughs and compares imagery exercises disparagingly with hypnosis. She does like the chair work techniques; she can move and walk around.

belongs to the developmental stage. Within treatment, this means discussing the absence, but accepting it and keeping the door open. It is important to keep the meetings formal and to discuss the consequences for the patient himself. Only if this doesn't have the desired effect will the therapist discuss the consequences for the therapeutic alliance: absence makes it more complicated for the therapist to remain involved with the patient. Therefore, there is a risk that the youngster will start to see the therapist as (one of) his parents and will withdraw into one of his protective modes, or he will stay away. Empathic confrontations will easily be interpreted as mothering – especially in the early stages of treatment – and this will lead to absence.

Another potential pitfall is that the therapist tries to be a better parent, especially with adolescents who have been emotionally deprived by their own parents. The way the therapist deals with this doesn't differ from the way adults are treated. Its helps to be aware of this pitfall and staying alert to situations that provoke it.

Furthermore, the therapist has to distinguish between maladaptive schemas and normal adolescent behavior. Most adolescents struggle with the theme of autonomy. When a therapist too quickly sees their attempts at independence as over-compensation for the Dependency/Incompetence schema, the youngster may easily become irritated.

When making an inventory of the problems and case conceptualization several pitfalls can be encountered. The youngster can get into a loyalty conflict by being forced to talk "badly" about his parents while he is in daily contact with them, is dependent on them, and struggles with ambivalent feelings toward them. The emphasis then has to shift so that the patient can "de-accuse" the parents. The therapist discusses the idea that although the parents have played a strong role in the origin of the schemas, it was not their intention to harm their child. They are often struggling with their own problems and pitfalls. This "de-accusing" is a delicate process. On the one hand, the youngster can feel misunderstood and detaches himself from the therapist; on the other, he can start feeling guilty about his parents. The Punitive and Demanding Parent mode can then obstruct progress. In the beginning, this can be practically solved by naming the "strong voice" entirely or partly as part of the adolescent himself, instead of placing it completely "on the outside," determined by the parents.

When the breakthrough of the negative patterns between parents and youngsters is chosen as an explicit aim of treatment, a family or systematic treatment may be necessary – for example, Functional Family Therapy (FFT; Alexander and Sexton, 2002) or Multidimensional Family Therapy (MDFT; Liddle *et al.*, 2001). A treatment such as Multisystemic Therapy (MST; Henggeler, Schoenwald, Borduin,

Rowland and Cunningham, 1998) seems less useful for this group because this treatment strongly focuses on repairing the hierarchy between the parents and youngster.

The Future

Considering the specific points outlined above, development of knowledge regarding this group is required. In this way, it may be possible that group ST can be offered to this age range. In this stage of development, one is more sensitive to the influences of one's peers and solidarity and identification with other adolescents can increase the commitment to the treatment and decrease possible absence. As a continuation of the development of protocols for ST group treatment in adults, the time seems right for the development of a specific version for adolescents.

References

Alexander, J.F. and Sexton, T.L. (2002) Functional family therapy: a model for treating high-risk, acting-out youth, in *Comprehensive Handbook of Psychotherapy*. Vol. 4: *Integrative/Eclectic* (ed. J. Lebow). New York: Wiley, pp. 111–132.

Bernstein, D., Arntz, A. and de Vos, M.E. (2007) Schemagerichte therapie in de forensische setting. *Tijdschrift voor Psychotherapie*, 33, 120–138.

Garcia, J.A. and Weisz, J.R. (2002) When youth mental healthcare stops: therapeutic relationship problems and other reasons for ending youth outpatient treatment. *Journal of Consulting and Clinical Psychology*, 70, 439–443.

Giesen-Bloo, J., van Dyck, R., Spinhoven, P. et al. (2006) Outpatient psychotherapy for borderline personality disorder: randomized trial of schema-focused therapy vs. transference-focused psychotherapy. *Archives of General Psychiatry*, 63, 649–658.

Henggeler, S., Schoenwald, S.K., Borduin, C.M., Rowland, M.D. and Cunningham, P.B. (1998) *Multisystemic Treatment of Antisocial Behavior in Children and Adolescents*. New York: Guilford Press.

Liddle, H.A., Dakof, G.A., Parker, K. et al. (2001) Multidimensional family therapy for adolescent drug abuse: results of a randomized clinical trial. *American Journal of Drug and Alcohol Abuse*, 27, 651–688.

Spinhoven, P., Giesen-Bloo, J., van Dyck, R., Kooiman, K. and Arntz, A. (2005) The therapeutic alliance in schema-focused therapy and transference-focused psychotherapy for borderline personality disorder. *Journal of Consulting and Clinical Psychology*, 75, 104–115.

Young, J. (2005) Schema-focused cognitive therapy and the case of Ms. S. *Journal of Psychotherapy Integration*, 15, 115–126.

10
Schema Therapy for Cluster C Personality Disorders

Arnoud Arntz

Introduction

Although Cluster C personality disorders (PDs) are usually seen as less severe than Cluster A and Cluster B PDs, they can be a real challenge for therapists. Patients' reliance on avoidance or control as primary safety strategies can be difficult to break through. These patients often stick to a passive patient role, demanding treatment without making the essential steps that are needed to recover. This chapter discusses a Schema Therapy (ST) approach for difficult Cluster C patients. The approach is partly based on earlier evidence that important aspects of ST are effective in this population (Weertman and Arntz, 2007) and partly on new insights into schema modes that are characteristic for these patients, and the kind of techniques they need to be successfully addressed in treatment. The order of the focus in treatment is based on preferences of patients and therapists in Weertman and Arntz (2007), but therapists and patients can choose their own order or mix.

Approach

Cluster C personality disorders and Schema Theory

Cluster C consists of three PDs: avoidant, dependent, and obsessive-compulsive. The common characteristic of these PDs is that anxiety dominates the functioning. Recent developments in ST for PDs focus more on *schema modes* than on *schemas*. Also with Cluster C PDs, the patients' complex problems are relatively easily understood in terms of schema modes and therapists can detect which modes are active during a session and apply techniques specifically developed for each one. Table 10.1 presents an overview of the most common modes in Cluster C PDs (Bamelis, Renner, Heidkamp and Arntz, 2011).

Table 10.1 Overview of the most common schema modes in Cluster C PDs

Mode	Description
Coping Modes	
Avoidant Protector	Uses situational avoidance as survival strategy. Leads to loneliness, putting off decisions and important tasks, and an empty and boring life.
Detached Protector	Detaches from inner needs, emotions, and thoughts as a survival strategy. Although there might be interpersonal contact, there is lack of connection. The person feels empty.
Compliant Surrender	Complies with other people's wishes and suppresses own wishes as a survival strategy. This slave-like strategy might create inner resentment.
Perfectionistic Over-Controller	Uses excessive control and perfectionism as strategy to avoid making mistakes and/or feeling guilty for things that go wrong.
Self-Aggrandizer	Plays superior to compensate for inner feelings of inferiority, inadequacy, or doubt.
Child Modes	
Vulnerable Child	General term for any state in which the person feels like a little child with no help from other people that can be trusted to protect, nurture, and create safety. Includes the child modes listed below.
Abandoned/Abused Child	State in which the person feels the abandonment or abuse experienced as a child again, or fears repetition of such experiences.
Lonely/Inferior Child	State in which the person feels the loneliness and/or inferiority experienced as a little child.
Dependent Child	State in which the person feels, thinks, and acts like a little child confronted with (practical) tasks the child does not know how to handle.
Internalized Parent Modes	
Punitive Parent	Internalization of punitive responses by parents/caretakers to needs, emotional expressions, assertiveness, autonomy. Usually leads to guilt feelings.
Demanding Parent	Internalization of high demands by parents/caretakers about productivity, perfectionism, social status, and moral issues. Not meeting the standards leads to feeling bad and ashamed.
Healthy Modes	
Healthy Adult	State in which the person takes care of him/herself and of other people in a healthy, mature way. Good balance between own needs and those of other people.
Happy Child	State in which the person is playful and joyful like a happy child. Is generally weak in Cluster C PDs.

Avoidant PD. In avoidant PD, anxiety is related to worries that other people find the person socially inept and inferior, but also that the patient does not have the capacity to deal with challenging situations in general. Avoidance is the dominant coping strategy – hence the name. That self-view is characterized by low self-esteem. Over the decades, the concept of avoidant PD has gradually changed from a personality characterized by fear of novelty and emotions, with the use of avoidance as a general coping strategy, to a personality characterized by these phenomena only in an interpersonal context. But arguments have been put forward that avoidant PD is characterized by avoidance not only in the social sphere and empirical findings support this (Arntz, 1999; Alden, Laposa, Taylor and Ryder, 2002; Taylor, Laposa and Alden, 2004; Bernstein, Arntz and Moll, in preparation). Thus, these people tend to avoid making decisions, experiencing negative *and* positive emotions, sharing intimate feelings, experiencing bodily sensations, experiencing sexual arousal, eating flavored and spicy food, and engaging in potentially risky activities. For ST this is an important finding, since it indicates that treatment should not only focus on social-phobic issues, but also deal with avoidance of a wide range of issues, notably emotions and risk-taking. Moreover, treatment should focus on low self-esteem, and views of the self as inadequate and inferior. Avoidant PD is associated with high levels of emotional abuse in childhood (Lobbestael *et al.*, 2010). Looking at parenting behaviors in a longitudinal study, Johnson and colleagues (2006) found evidence that lack of parental affection and nurturing was related to the development of avoidant PD (but also to six other PDs). Comorbid (recurrent) depression and dysthymia, anxiety disorders, and addiction are common.

A recent study by Bamelis and colleagues (2011) demonstrated that avoidant PD is characterized by specific modes (see Figure 10.1). Two coping modes are strongly present in avoidant PD: the Avoidant Protector and the Detached Protector. The Avoidant Protector is characterized by the use of situational avoidance; the Detached Protector mode is characterized by detaching from inner needs, feelings, and thoughts,

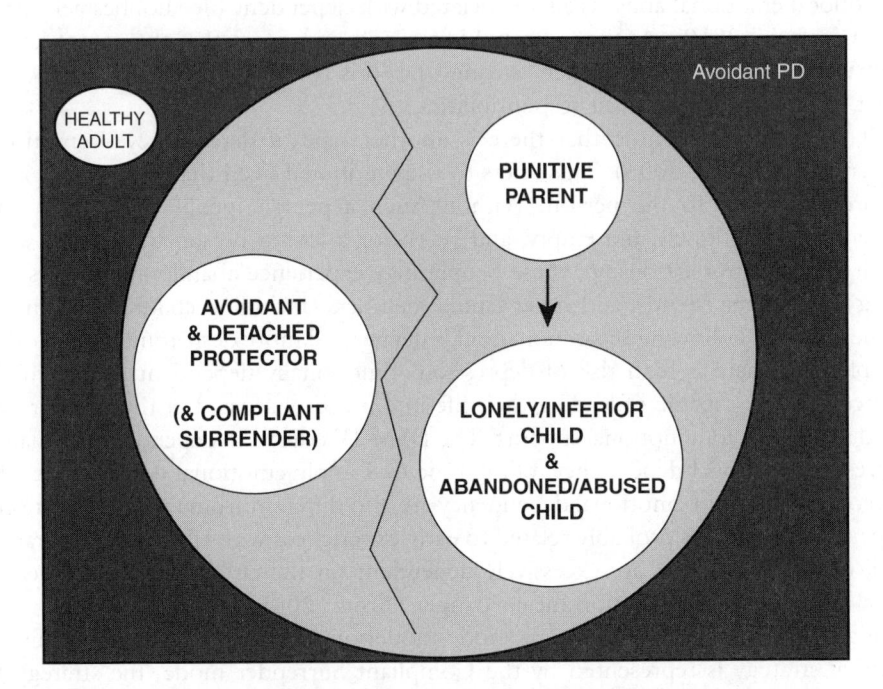

Figure 10.1 Schema mode model of avoidant personality disorder

and from emotionally connecting to other people. There might also be a Compliant Surrender coping mode, when patients tend to comply with other people's wishes. Second, a Punitive Parent mode is active, representing the internalization of emotionally abusive parenting experienced as a child. Third, at the core of the problem are the Lonely/Inferior Child and Abandoned/Abused Child modes. The Lonely/Inferior Child mode represents the emotional state these people try to avoid, in which they feel again the loneliness and inferiority they experienced as a child. The Abandoned/Abused Child mode represents the emotional state they experienced when they were abused or abandoned as a child. There is quite some overlap in modes with borderline PD (BPD), with BPD having additional Impulsive/Angry Child Modes and less Avoidant Protector mode.

Dependent PD. Dependent people worry about their capacities to lead an adult life. They feel incapable of making minor and major decisions and believe that they have to rely on a strong person to help them because they believe that they are not capable of running their life in *a practical sense*. Dependent people lack self-confidence and autonomy, have problems with taking adult responsibilities, and demand reassurance and support in practical areas from a strong helper. With a helper, they might seemingly function without problems, but problems may become very acute when this help threatens to stop or actually ceases. Because of the dependency focus on practical issues, it is helpful to label it as functional dependency (Arntz, 2005). The main specific etiological factor of dependent PD is authoritarian parenting, though overprotection may also play a role (Bornstein, 2005). Probably in interaction with a fearful makeup, children raised by authoritarian methods don't develop autonomy and trust in their own capacities to handle problems and make good choices. Childhood emotional abuse is also associated with dependent PD (Lobbestael, Arntz and Bernstein, 2010). As they were told over and over again that the parent knows best, they tend to turn to other "strong" persons to tell them what to think and what to do, and to take over responsibilities.

It is important to note that there is another type of dependency – emotional dependency (Arntz, 2005). This refers to the emotional need that somebody else is securely attached to the person. Without such a person, people with emotional dependency feel lonely and empty, and yearn for a loving person to connect with. With an intimate relationship, these people may experience abandonment fears and cling to partners, friends, and other family members (including children, leading to enmeshment). Following separation, grief is deeper and more despairing than in other people, and there is high risk of depression. Emotionally dependent people might feel completely capable of leading their life in a practical sense, but they desperately need somebody for emotional support. The DSM-IV criteria of dependent PD mainly represent functional dependency, but criteria 6–8 imply emotional dependency. The etiological factors of emotional dependency are also different from those of functional dependency: they are probably related to early experiences with (threat of) separation and/or to parents that are excessively dependent on the child. What these people have learned is that separation means danger (Arntz, 2005).

Figure 10.2 presents the schema mode model of dependent PD. The prominent survival strategy is represented by the Compliant Surrender mode, the strategy to comply with other people's opinions and requests, and to surrender to other people's

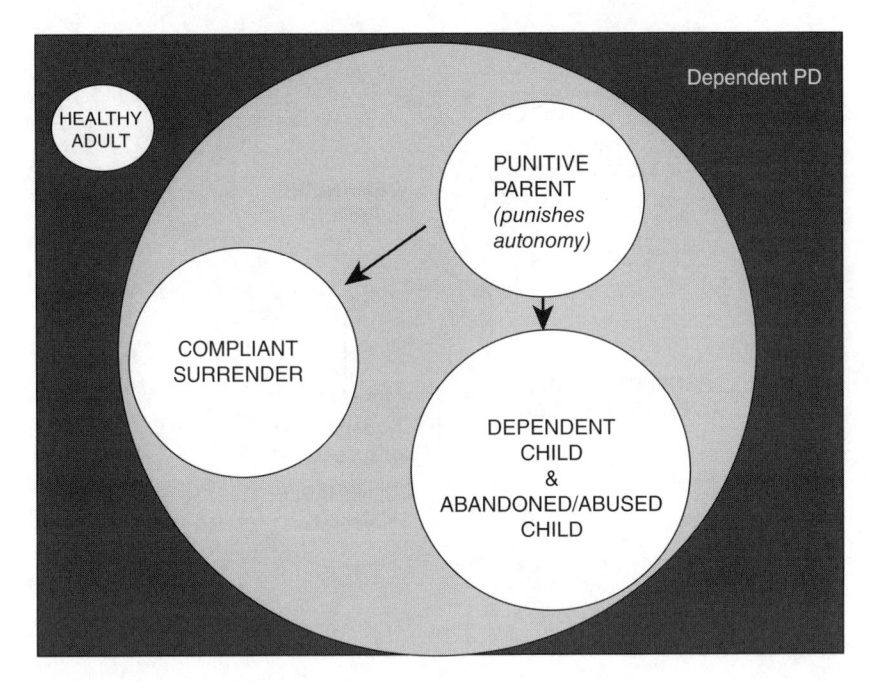

Figure 10.2 Schema mode model of dependent personality disorder

directions. There is an internalization of punitive responses by caretakers, notably those that punish autonomy, in the Punitive Parent mode. There is usually a strong Dependent Child mode, in which the patient feels overwhelmed by demands that adult life makes and will panic when others are not available or don't reassure them and take responsibility. There might also be an Abandoned/Abused Child mode, notably when there is emotional dependence (abandonment feelings and excessive fear of abandonment), or when there is re-experiencing of the emotional abuse that took place in childhood. The Healthy Adult mode is weak.

Obsessive-Compulsive PD. Obsessive-Compulsive PD (OCPD) is characterized by an excessive and compulsive devotion to productivity at the expense of other areas of life, including social relationships, love, recreation, and other basic needs. Standards are usually extremely high, with the conviction that only the person him/herself is capable of doing things correctly. Emotions are not seen as valuable. OC people often view themselves as superior to others in terms of conscientiousness, responsibility, and moral norms. Others are viewed as lazy, careless, and morally inferior. These views might be partly implicit, i.e., not directly available to introspection (Weertman, Arntz, de Jongh and Rinck, 2008). Like the other Cluster C PDs, OCPD is associated with emotional abuse in childhood. Other etiological roots, apart from genetic and other biological factors, are probably related to a cold and strict parenting with high standards in the area of achievement. Emotions had to be controlled and were considered of little worth. In their youth, these patients were often expected to accept too much responsibility for their age.

Figure 10.3 depicts the schema mode model of OCPD. Very prominent is the Perfectionistic Over-Controller mode, the survival strategy characterized by

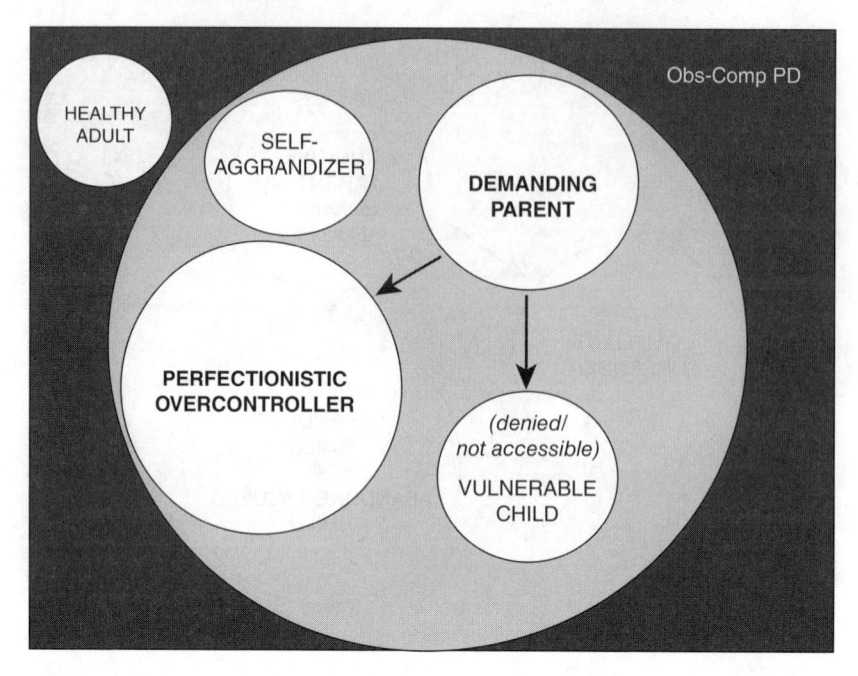

Figure 10.3 Schema mode model of obsessive-compulsive personality disorder

perfectionism and the excessive use of control. This coping mode is a direct response to the Demanding Parent. It represents the internalization of the high demands experienced as a child. Because OCPD people typically believe that others are careless and irresponsible, whereas they are capable of meeting the standards that should be met, they also have an element of the Self-Aggrandizer mode. OCPD patients usually deny (or cannot access) a Vulnerable Child mode. However, this mode usually emerges during therapy.

Case Conceptualization

Although we presented schema mode models for each Cluster C PD, for each individual patient a personalized mode model is made. Patients might differ slightly in the modes that are of importance for them. Knowledge of their PDs and PD traits can help in the formulation, but it is advisable to access other sources of information too: self-report questionnaires, clinical observations, diagnostic imagery exercises, anamnestics, and interviews. Figure 10.4 gives an example of an idiosyncratic mode model of a patient with OC and dependent PD. Two internalized parent modes, the Punitive and Demanding Parent modes, were chunked. This is recommended when modes are triggered at the same time and belong to one and the same category.

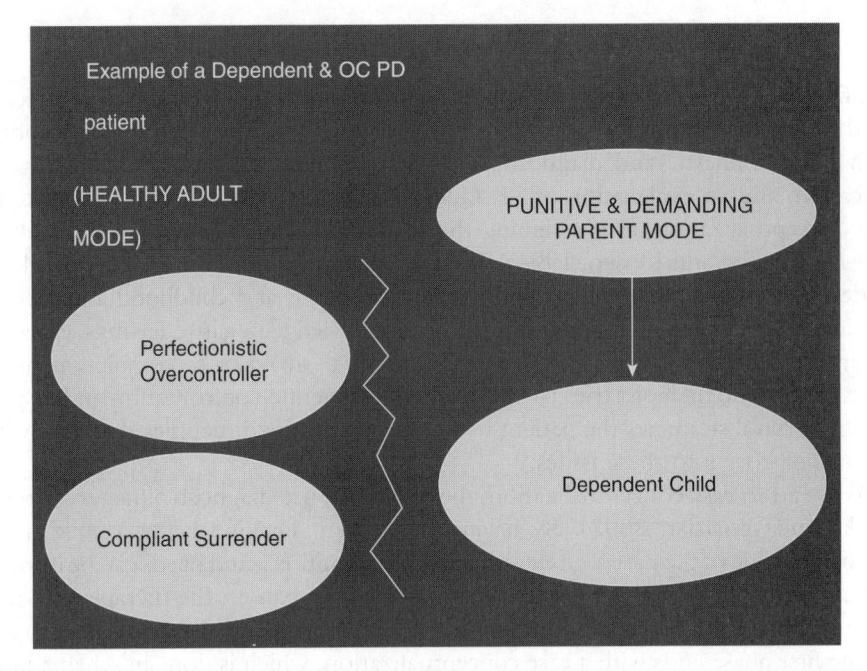

Figure 10.4 Idiosyncratic schema mode model of a patient with obsessive-compulsive and dependent personality disorder

Table 10.2 Overview of the phases in treatment

Year 1: 40 sessions
- Sessions 1–6: introduction, case conceptualization
- Sessions 7–24: focus on childhood memories
- Sessions 25-40: focus on present and behavioral change

Year 2: 10 booster sessions (± monthly)

Next, the conceptualization links modes to historical antecedents and present problems. This helps both patient and therapist understand the model, and organizes the problems to be addressed in therapy as they are now linked to modes (see Figure 10.5).

Treatment Approach

A general overview of the treatment is given in Table 10.2, describing a 50-session protocol. For educational purposes, the phases are described as more distinct than they need to be. The therapy might also be extended if necessary. The different phases will now be discussed, with the main foci and techniques of that phase.

Start of treatment: the first sessions

The first five to six sessions are devoted to getting acquainted with the patient, learning the patient's reasons for seeking therapy, learning what the patient hopes to obtain from ST, anamnestic and diagnostic interviewing, case conceptualization, psychoeducation, and an explanation of ST. Questionnaires are useful to help to make the case conceptualization, as is assigning the reading of some chapters of *Reinventing your Life* (Young and Klosko, 1994). The therapist introduces the concept of schema modes, and connects the modes with present problems and childhood antecedents.

Cluster C patients often find it difficult to acknowledge negative feelings, especially toward their parents. This might lead to attempts to avoid or to complete denial of these issues. The therapist tries to balance between gentle confrontation and respecting the survival strategies the patient uses to deal with the difficulties that arise when the patient goes into these issues.

As an aid to case conceptualization, therapists can use diagnostic imagery (Young, Klosko and Weishaar, 2003). By having the patient imagine being a child in the company of one of the parents, relevant feelings, cognitions, and needs can be clarified. If the patient has experienced severe traumas with the parent, the therapist can offer reassurance that traumatic memories should not be the topic of this diagnostic imagery.

The first phase ends with a case conceptualization, which is done in schema mode terms (see above). The therapist explains the mode concept and the origins of modes. A next step, in collaboration with the patient, is to connect the modes to the present problems. Axis I disorders are also related to modes. For instance, depression is often related to Detached and Avoidant Coping, Abandoned Child, and/or to Punitive Parent modes. The result of staying most of the time in an Avoidant/Detached Protector mode might be that life gets extremely boring, needs are not met, and depression follows as result of lack of positive experiences. Therapist and patient next try to understand how the modes developed in childhood. In other words, they relate the modes to experiences in childhood (Figure 10.5 gives an example). There is no need to strive for completeness (many aspects become clearer during treatment), but a general understanding helps patients to see their problems in perspective and prepares the ground for the treatment. Lastly, the therapist explains the general goals of therapy. In a nutshell, they are:

1. to help the child modes to develop and find safety, which is mainly achieved through emotional processing of (traumatic) childhood experiences, acknowledging needs and emotion of the little child, and corrective experiences in the treatment (limited reparenting);
2. to eliminate the punitive and demanding mode(s) as much as possible from the patient's system and replace them with healthy attitudes toward needs and emotions, and healthy standards and moral principles;
3. to let the healthy adult side develop, so that
4. the dysfunctional coping modes are less necessary.

Learning to recognize schema modes

Patients can fill out a diary to learn to recognize their schema modes in daily life. Therapist and patient discuss the diaries and can take one situation to work on further and address the problematic modes with one of the appropriate techniques.

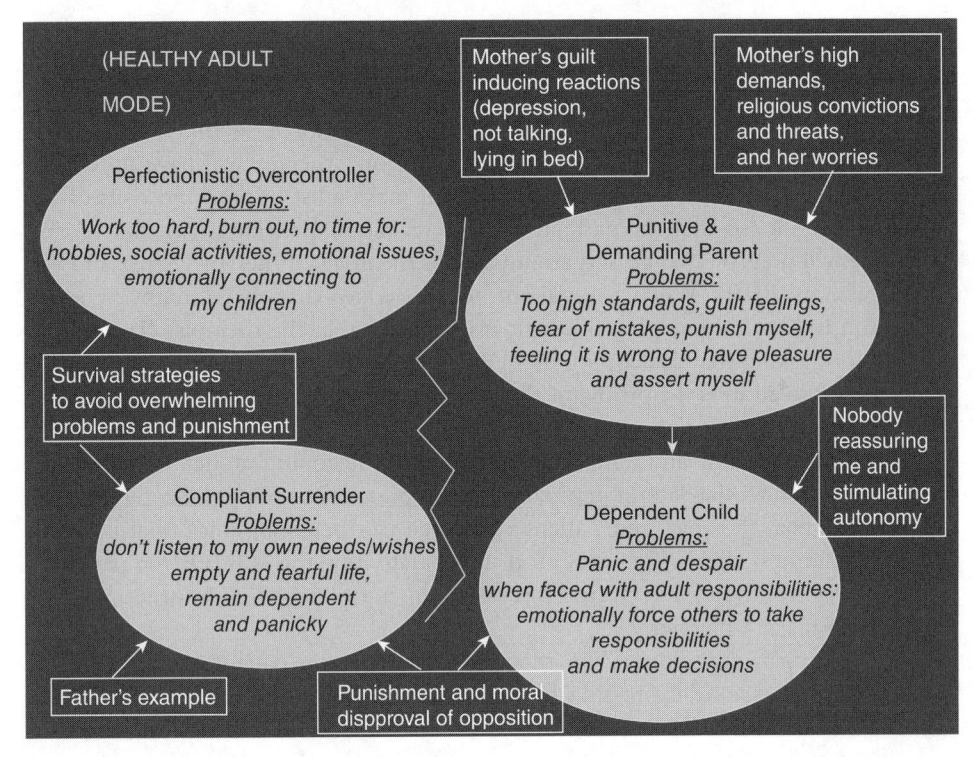

Schema Therapy for Cluster C Personality Disorders 405

Figure 10.5 Historical antecendents and present problems placed in the schema mode case conceptualization (example)

During the session, the therapist can ask about changes in emotions and attitudes, and about a possible mode change. If the patient has no idea, the therapist can make a tentative suggestion and check with the patient to see if she/he agrees.

A typical session starts by asking the patient how she/he has been doing since the last session. The way the patient responds informs the therapist about the mode the patient is in, and the discussion will inform the therapist about emotional events that have taken place since the last session and what modes played a part. The therapist can then either continue with an important experience since the last session to focus on one or more specific modes, or focus on the mode that is active at that moment.

Setting the stage for the focus on childhood experiences

If Protector or Over-Compensator modes are very strong, they might block access of emotions and childhood memories related to emotions. In Cluster C patients, the Detached Protector mode might totally detach patients from emotions and childhood memories. In this mode, patients might claim that there is no use experiencing emotions and exploring childhood memories. The Perfectionistic Over-Controller might be very dominant in sessions, for instance when patients constantly correct the therapist for not exactly paraphrasing and summarizing what the patient said. The obsession with all the factual details distracts the patient from experiencing, and is therefore quite dysfunctional in treatment. In such cases, therapists might use a number of techniques to get the patient to get round these blockades.

1. Tentatively label the mode, empathize with it, and ask about the emotions underlying it.
2. Explanation. The therapist can explain that emotional issues should be addressed and their relationship to childhood experiences explored so that change on a schema level can take place. By avoiding emotions, therapy will have no effect.
3. Listing pros and cons. Therapist and patient make a list of pros and cons of the coping mode, so that the patient starts to realize that sticking with this coping mode will prevent change and attainment of the goals of therapy (Arntz and van Genderen, 2010). When the patient acknowledges that there might be some reason to lessen the coping mode, it is important that the therapist clarifies that he is not asking that the coping mode be completely eliminated, but temporarily bypassed to address the problems the patient wants help for. Usually, this method is followed by negotiation.
4. Negotiate a gradual and temporary lessening of the coping mode. Therapist and patient can negotiate about gradually and temporarily lessening the coping mode. For instance, therapist and patient can agree to discuss an emotional issue for three minutes, after which they stop to evaluate how this was. Or the patient is given control over when to stop discussing an emotional issue. Another possibility is to make a hierarchy.
5. Multiple chair technique. The therapist can have the patient sit on different chairs, on each one expressing ideas, needs, and feelings from one mode. For instance, on one chair the patient expresses the Detached Protector: the concerns of letting down the Detached Protector. On another chair the patient expresses the Vulnerable Child, for instance the need for real contact. On another the patient expresses the views of her Healthy Adult. The therapist can interview the different modes. At the end, the therapist might discuss with the Healthy Adult what is to be done.
6. Empathic confrontation. With this technique the therapist, on the one hand, empathizes with the intentions of the coping mode, and on the other, confronts the patient about the change that is needed.
7. Imagery. Sometimes the therapist can bypass a Detached Protector or Perfectionistic Over-Controller mode by just asking the patient to close the eyes and starting an imagery exercise. Imagery is related to a higher level of affect than talking and is therefore an effective technique to bypass obstructive coping modes.

Focus on childhood experiences

Fighting the Punitive and Demanding Parent modes. When the Punitive or Demanding Parent mode is very active during the session, or has played a major role in a recent problem, the therapist combats it. The most important methods, as in ST of BPD (Arntz and van Genderen, 2010), are:

1. Empty chair technique. The therapist asks the patient to sit on another chair and to express what the mode is saying. The patient should be instructed to say "you" rather than "I," for example: *"you have failed and it is your fault; you are guilty."* Next the patient returns to the original chair. The therapist then talks to the

mode on the empty chair as if it is a person, clearly disagreeing: *"It is not true that Jane failed, and it is not her fault. She just overlooked a sentence when she typed her boss's messy notes. You cannot use such words for this. First, nobody is perfect and overlooking something is human. Second, saying that she is guilty implies that she did it on purpose. Well, it is obvious she didn't overlook the sentence on purpose. So you are not correct. You'd better stay out of this as you are not helping. You are only creating problems instead of helping Jane. What Jane needs is reassurance and somebody telling her that she did a great job making sense of the messy notes, and that it is not a problem that she overlooked something, and that she does not need to be perfect to be valued."* The therapist then asks the patient what the Punitive/ Demanding mode is saying. If it is not quiet, he either asks her what the mode is saying, or asks the patient to sit on the chair again and repeat what the mode is saying, after which the patient returns to the original chair. The therapist continues to combat the Punitive or Demanding mode until the mode is quiet. Therapists should not start a discussion with Punitive/Demanding modes, as they are irrational and unconvinced by rational arguments. Rather, determination and power are central. In some cases this mode is very persistent, in which case the therapist puts the empty chair outside the room. This is often effective in shutting down the mode. Although the therapist addresses the Punitive/ Demanding mode, the Healthy Adult and the Vulnerable Child are listening. It is therefore important to weave in validation of the child's needs and feelings, and psycho-educate about healthy and functional attitudes. Later in therapy, the patient starts to combat the Punitive/Demanding mode him/herself, either from a (Angry) Child perspective, or from the Healthy Adult mode. The therapist coaches and simulates getting angry, something that can be difficult for Cluster C PD patients.
2. Imagery rescripting. The therapist asks the patient to close their eyes, evoke an image of a recent situation where the Punitive or Demanding Parent mode was active, and experience the mode again. Next, the therapist asks the patient to let the image go but stay with the feelings, and instructs him/her to see whether an image from childhood pops up. Alternatively, the therapist asks the patient to close their eyes and directly get an image of the parent that was punitive, critical, or demanding. After the patient has experienced what the parent's behavior evoked in the Vulnerable Child, the therapist steps into the scene and intervenes by talking to the parent and telling him/her to stop, as with the empty chair technique (see Arntz and Weertman, 1999; Arntz and van Genderen, 2010; Arntz, 2011).
3. Psycho-education. Many Cluster C patients have dysfunctional views of (children's) needs, emotions, guilt, and shame. For instance, they might think that they need a Demanding mode because without it they wouldn't get anything done. Psycho-education helps to distance them from these internalized dysfunctional high and punitive standards. Special care should be taken to explain issues such as indirect guilt-induction (e.g., the mother lying depressed in bed and not talking to the child for days in reaction to the child's "bad" behavior), negative loyalty (enforcing loyalty and obedience by threatening the child, in contrast to healthy positive loyalty, where the child is loyal because it gets positive things such as love and protection from the parents), and intergenerational transmission of punitive and demanding attitudes.

4. Letter writing. Patients can write a letter to their parents, telling them what their demanding, critical, and punitive behavior meant for them when they were a child and how it still influences their lives. Don't let them send the letter until a plan has been set out of how to deal with possible negative reactions from the parents or other family members. This technique primarily aims at stimulating expression of feelings and opinions, and creating a distance from the negative parental influences.

Taking care of the Vulnerable Child modes

The Vulnerable Child modes consist of the Abandoned/Abused Child, the Dependent Child, and the Lonely Child modes. It is important that attention is given to these modes, especially during the early phases of treatment. In summary, the techniques are as follows:

1. Care and validation through limited reparenting. Through limited reparenting, therapists offer validation of the needs and feelings that patients experience from their Vulnerable Child modes. Safety to express emotions and needs during the therapy is essential to meet the core needs of the Vulnerable Child and to correct unsafe attachment and emotional abuse that is characteristic of Cluster C patients. Thus, if during a session primary emotions are accessed, the therapist is empathic and validating, and reassures the patient that it is OK to have and express these emotions. This is especially important with sadness, since many Cluster C patients are extremely afraid of sadness and are rather depressed or suffer from somatoform complaints rather than feeling sad (and angry).
2. Imagery rescripting. In this technique, an image of a childhood memory is "rescripted" by having an adult enter the scene and intervening, thus changing the script. In Cluster C patients, it is advisable that initially the therapist does the rescripting. Most Cluster C patients have not received real care as a child and they should learn, on the child level so to say, to receive and accept care. The following approach is suggested.
    a. A problem experienced during the last week is identified (or a feeling emerging during the session).
    b. The patient closes the eyes and imagines the recent problem. The patient describes in here-and-now terms, from his/her own perspective, what happens and what he/she experiences and needs.
    c. The feeling and the experienced needs are used for an "affect bridge" to retrieve a (traumatic) memory from childhood.
    d. The patient describes the scene in here-and-now terms, from the viewpoint of the Vulnerable Child, and experiences feelings and needs. If severe abuse is near, the therapist doesn't wait to intervene.
    e. The therapist tells the patient that he/she is entering the scene and describes how he/she is acting to correct what is happening. The patient might protest (patients often avoid or subordinate, and might want therapists to do the same), but therapists have to trust that what they do is OK. If there is abuse or threat of abuse, therapists stop or prevent it. The patient describes what happens next in the image, and how he/she feels then, and what he/she

needs. Rescripting continues until the threat is under control. Then the therapist takes care of the Vulnerable Child. Often the child needs to be soothed.
   f. After imagery rescripting the exercise is discussed. The patient is asked to listen to the recording and to repeat the whole exercise at home.
   g. If the patient is not satisfied, other ways of rescripting are tried. Patients are invited to develop variations that are tried out. Extended discussion and examples can be found in Arntz (2010), Arntz and van Genderen (2010), and Arntz and Weertman (1999).
3. Historical role-play. With this technique, situations from childhood are enacted rather than imagined. Usually it begins with the patient playing the child and the therapist the other person, often one of the parents. The technique can be used to elicit emotions and clarify childhood situations, but also to change perspectives and to rescript memories. Role-switching can be used, that is to say, after an initial round the patient now plays the other person and the therapist the child. Therapist and patient can discuss how the patient experienced the situation from the perspective of the parent, which sometimes leads to a change in interpretation of the parent's behavior (e.g., the patient discovers that the parent was depressed and tired, leading to neglecting the needs of the child, but not not-loving the child). Rescripting can be done by having the therapist or the patient as an adult enter the scene, address the parent, and take care of the Vulnerable Child. Historical role-play is less suitable for physical and sexual abuse, as these cannot (for obvious reasons) be played out. The technique is more fully described in Arntz and Weertman (1999) and Arntz and van Genderen (2010).
4. Stimulating and teaching the patient to get basic needs better met. During treatment therapists help patients to recognize their needs better, and encourage them to get these better met. Although some of the unmet childhood needs cannot be fully repaired in adulthood, this does not imply that related needs cannot be met on an adult level. In general this implies that patients have to change how they handle their personal relationships, work, and spare time.

Focus on change in the present

Especially in the second half of treatment, the focus is increasingly focused on the present and on behavioral change. Therapists should not expect that patients will easily change their behavior as a result of intellectual and emotional insight gained in the previous phase of therapy. Cluster C patients especially are often seemingly addicted to the short-term effects of their coping modes, the emotion-avoiding effects of avoidance, detachment, submission, or perfectionism and control. If patients avoid asserting themselves, but complain about being mistreated and feeling tired, the therapist gently but firmly motivates the patient to try out healthy assertiveness. All kinds of behavioral techniques can be used. Some of the specific ST techniques in this phase are:

1. Multiple chair technique. The therapist can ask the patient to express the different modes that play a role on different chairs. Finally, the Healthy Adult is asked

to express what he/she thinks of the whole situation and what should be done. The therapist can discuss with the Healthy Adult what are good strategies to handle the situation and what can be tried out.
2. Mode diary. The patient fills out a diary about a difficult situation in which he reports which modes were activated and what these modes felt and thought about it. He can then challenge dysfunctional views and try to formulate a healthy view (and try out healthy behavior).
3. Flash card. Patient and therapist make a flash card that can help the patient to deal in a more functional way with difficult situations. On one side, the typical trigger and the triggered mode with its feelings, thoughts, and behaviors is written. On the other side, the Healthy Adult view is written including reality testing if indicated (e.g., pointing out that triggered feelings are more related to situations from the past than to the present) and healthy behavior is described.
4. Role-plays. The patient can try out new behaviors in role-plays. The therapist can model different variants.
5. Empathic confrontation. This technique is mainly used for dysfunctional coping modes. A good empathic confrontation relates the dysfunctional behavior to a mode, empathizes with the mode's function, and relates this to its childhood origins, then clarifies what is different between the present and the childhood situation, and pushes for change in a validating way (e.g., "You, like everybody else, have the fundamental right to express your opinion").
6. Imagery rescripting. Imagery rescripting can also be used to rescript future situations. First, the patient imagines the future situation, which usually leads to uncomfortable feelings that are raised again. This is then related to a mode that is triggered. Next the therapist asks the patient to switch to the Healthy Adult mode and imagine handling the situation from that mode. When needed, the therapist enters the image and coaches the patient. Imagery rescripting with difficult situations in the present or future can be very empowering.
7. Teaching healthy attitudes. Patients might lack knowledge about healthy attitudes and behaviors. Teaching them can be important.
8. Push toward healthy choices. Some patients have become trapped in unhealthy situations because they made the wrong choices due to their PD pathology. Some need to be pushed to make healthy choices to overcome their problems. For instance, if abusive partners or bosses cannot be changed, patients would do better to leave them. Patients might find this very difficult or frightening, and the therapist should support them emotionally.
9. Focus on the therapeutic relationship. If the patient behaves in a dysfunctional way in the therapeutic relationship, the therapist should gently point this out, discuss what modes are underlying it, and help the patient to find a healthy way to relate to the therapist.

Techniques focusing on childhood situations can be combined with techniques focusing on the present. Trying to make changes in the present can trigger strong emotions related to childhood memories, and it may be appropriate to address them, for instance, with imagery rescripting. After addressing childhood memories, an explicit connection to the present is made and the need for behavioral change is discussed.

Booster sessions

At the end, booster sessions are offered. One possibility would be to offer a monthly booster session for a year, but other intervals are conceivable.

The aim is that patients try out life without intensive therapy, without abruptly breaking off the positive influence of therapy. Patients are well prepared for these booster sessions. Booster sessions are real therapy sessions, not just a chat. Thus, all techniques can be used, even imagery of childhood events (as patients might come with new, unprocessed memories). A typical approach would be to ask the patient how (s)he has been doing since the last session, and if the patient reports any problems or relapse that the patient has not successfully addressed him/herself, patient and therapist try to find what modes were related to it. Usually, more and more responsibility is given to the patient to promote the development of skills and habits to detect and correct dysfunctional modes.

In using ST techniques, patients' Healthy Adult parts are given the lead more and more. For instance, in imagery rescripting of childhood memories the Healthy Adult part of the patient rescripts.

Whilst some patients quite rapidly find this phase is therapeutic, others can resist it for quite some time. We have learned that many responded to the gradual withdrawal of the therapist with seeming relapses, complaining that they had not changed or even accusing the therapist of maltreating them. But we also learned that in the end, these patients realized that therapists cannot rescue them and that they had to make a decision: either to return to old patterns or to act on what they learned in therapy. Framing the difficulties that are often presented by these patients as if they are helpless victims as *choices* is important here. Thus, the therapist should point out, once the modes are clear, that the Healthy Adult can make a decision: to use the old coping strategies (e.g., the Avoidant Protector) or use a new functional strategy, even when it makes them fearful. Therapists gradually reduce their motivational and pushing attitude, and gently hand over the choice to the patient.

Pitfalls and Tips: Specific Issues with the Different Cluster C PDs

Boxes 10.1–10.3 give an overview of the specific issues that are relevant in the treatment of avoidant, dependent, obsessive-compulsive PD. These issues may help the therapist to treat these patients and to adapt ST to what they need.

Discussion

A ST approach for the three Cluster C PDs based on schema mode models was discussed. The reader should realize that ST for Cluster C PD has only recently been developed and the empirical evidence for its effectiveness is still limited. Weertman and Arntz (2007) suggested strong effects of the major ingredients of ST for Cluster C PDs, and high effect sizes for the total package (Cohen's d was about 1.5). But this study was not a comparison of different treatments. A large, multicenter RCT

> **Box 10.1** Specific issues with avoidant PD
>
> At start: focus on avoidance of experiencing needs and emotions
> Fight Punitive Parent and correct low self-esteem (e.g., by imagery rescripting)
> Push to less avoidance of:
>   Feeling
>   Social contacts and roles
>   Intimacy
>   Making choices
>   Having opinions and expressing them
> Be aware of alcohol, drugs, medication abuse, and addiction: many of these patients would rather abuse substances than feel emotions.
> Address how to deal with conflicts and irritation.

> **Box 10.2** Specific issues with dependent PD
>
> Correct authoritarian parenting
> Push to express own opinions and emotions
> Push autonomy
> Don't allow patient to submit to you and make you an authority (be aware of your own schemas)
> Teach how to have disagreements.
>
> Note: this reparenting is a bit different from many other PDs (don't promote dependence, but independence). Gets complicated when there is both a Dependent and an Abandoned Child mode. Try to decide for yourself whether the patient needs *emotional* connection and safety, or tries to get *practical* help, or tries to make you responsible.

> **Box 10.3** Specific issues with obsessive-compulsive PD
>
> Get rid of Demanding Parent mode
> Ask patient to reduce the Perfectionistic Over-Controller
> Explain and push for importance of emotions, intimacy, and social contacts
> Let patient experiment with imperfection.

that compared ST to treatment as usual (TAU) and to an interesting psychotherapeutic alternative, client-centered therapy according to Sachse (2001), was recently completed but final data are not yet available.

Meanwhile, clinical and empirical observations indicate that ST is not a panacea for all Cluster C patients. In the RCT mentioned above, drop out from treatment was significantly lower in ST than in TAU conditions, but was still 25% over two years. In-depth interviews with ST patients indicated that, at least in the early phases, patients found imagery very difficult and confrontational (ten Napel-Schutz et al., 2011). An extended explanation of experiential techniques might help, but fear of emotions and reliance on avoidant and controlling survival strategies probably remain a problem.

Acknowledgment

Part of the research on which this chapter is based was funded by grant 945-06-406 from ZonMW, the Netherlands Organization for Health Research and Development, awarded to Arnoud Arntz. The content is partly based on Arntz (2010). The author is greatly indebted to Jeffrey Young, who co-developed the protocol outlined in this chapter.

References

Alden, L.E., Laposa, J.M., Taylor, C.T. and Ryder, A.G. (2002) Avoidant personality disorder: current status and future directions. *Journal of Personality Disorders*, 16, 1–29.

Arntz, A. (1999) Do personality disorders exist? On the validity of the concept and its cognitive-behavioural formulation and treatment. *Behaviour Research and Therapy*, 37, S97–S134.

Arntz, A. (2005) Pathological dependency: distinguishing functional from emotional dependency. *Clinical Psychology: Science and Practice*, 12, 411–416.

Arntz. A. (2010) Schematherapie bei Cluster C Persönlichkeitsstörungen, in *Fortschritte der Schematherapie, Konzepte and Anwendungen* (eds E. Roediger and G. Jacob). Göttingen: Hogrefe-Verlag, pp. 146–182.

Arntz. A. (2011) Imagery rescripting for personality disorders. *Cognitive and Behavioral Practice*, 18, 466–481.

Arntz, A. and Genderen, H. van (2010) *Schematherapie bei Borderline-Persönlichkeitsstörung*. Weinheim: Beltz.

Arntz, A. and Weertman, A. (1999) Treatment of childhood memories; theory and practice. *Behaviour Research and Therapy*, 37, 8, 715–740.

Bamelis, L.L.M., Renner, F., Heidkamp, D. and Arntz, A. (2011) Extended schema mode conceptualizations for specific personality disorders: an empirical study. *Journal of Personality Disorders*, 25(1), 41–58.

Bornstein, R.F. (2005) *The Dependent Patient: a Practitioner's Guide*. Washington, DC: American Psychological Association.

Johnson, J.G., Cohen, P., Chen, H., Kasen, S. and Brooks, J.S. (2006) Parenting behaviors associated with the risk for offspring personality disorder during adulthood. *Archives of General Psychiatry*, 63, 579–587.

Lobbestael, J., Arntz, A. and Bernstein, D.P. (2010) Disentangling the relationship between different types of childhood maltreatment and personality disorders. *Journal of Personality Disorders*, 24, 285–295.

Napel-Schutz, M.C. ten, Abma, T.A., Bamelis, L. and Arntz, A. (2011). Personality disorder patients' perspectives on the introduction of imagery within Schema Therapy: a qualitative study of patients' experiences. *Cognitive and Behavioral Practice*, *18*, 482–490.

Sachse, R. (2001) *Psychologische Psychotherapie der Persönlichkeitsstörungen*. Göttingen: Hogrefe.

Taylor, C.T., Laposa, J.M. and Alden, L.E. (2004) Is avoidant personality disorder more than just social avoidance? *Journal of Personality Disorders*, *18*, 571–594.

Weertman, A. and Arntz, A. (2007) Effectiveness of treatment of childhood memories in cognitive therapy for personality disorders: a controlled study contrasting methods focusing on the present and methods focusing on childhood memories. *Behaviour Research and Therapy*, *45*, 2133–2143.

Weertman, A., Arntz, A., de Jong, P.J. and Rinck, M. (2008) Implicit self- and other-associations in obsessive-compulsive personality disorder traits. *Cognition and Emotion*, *22*, 1253–1275.

Young, J.E. (1999) *Cognitive Therapy for Personality Disorders: a Schema-focused Approach*, revised edition. Sarasota, Fl.: Professional Resource Press.

Young, J.E. and Klosko, J.S. (1994) *Reinventing Your Life*. New York: Plume.

Young, J.E., Klosko, J.S. and Weishaar, M.E. (2003) *Schema Therapy: a Practitioner's Guide*. New York: Guilford Press.

11
Schema Therapy in Personality Disorders and Addiction

Truus Kersten

The most common form of dual diagnosis is personality disorder and substance abuse (Verheul, van den Bosch and Ball, 2005). Antisocial and borderline personality disorders are most prevalent in substance abuse patients, followed by Cluster C (especially avoidant personality disorder) and Cluster A (especially paranoid personality disorder) (Rounsaville *et al.*, 1998).

In Dutch addiction treatment centers, the percentage of patients with a DSM-IV diagnosis of drug dependence with one or more concomitant personality disorders varies from 44% in alcoholics, 70% in cocaine addicts, and up to 79% in heroin addicts. This concerns in particular borderline and antisocial personality disorders (Verheul, van den Brink and Hartgers, 1995). Addicts often have several personality disorders. De Jong, van den Brink, Harteveld, and van der Wielen (1993) showed that alcoholics had an average of 2.3 personality disorders and drug users an average of as many as 4.4 personality disorders.

In Dutch forensic psychiatric centers, 75–80% of the patients have one or more personality disorders. This is 4.5 times the number found in general psychiatric hospitals. These are in particular Cluster B disorders.

Antisocial, borderline, narcissistic, and paranoid personality disorders occur most frequently. Furthermore, 34% of these patients have a diagnosis of substance abuse or drug dependence. If you factor in the "intensive drug use or addiction during the criminal offense," the percentage of patients is much higher: 65–70% (Emmerik and van Brouwers, 2001).

In de Rooyse Wissel, in Venray, a Dutch forensic psychiatric center (FPC), as many as 81% of the patients have a personality disorder in addition to a diagnosis of substance abuse (1/3) or drug-dependence (2/3). More than half the patients (56%) use more than one drug. Treatment of both personality problems and addiction are very important for these patients especially as addiction is a risk factor for relapse in criminal offense behavior.

The Wiley Blackwell Handbook of Schema Therapy: Theory, Research, and Practice, First Edition.
Edited by Michiel van Vreeswijk, Jenny Broersen, and Marjon Nadort.
© 2012 John Wiley & Sons, Ltd. Published 2015 by John Wiley & Sons, Ltd.

Thus far, remarkably few studies have been carried out into the treatment of these dual diagnosis problems despite the high comorbidity. Only two so-called dual focus treatments have been described and researched (Verheul, van den Bosch and Ball, 2007): *Dialectical Behavior Therapy-Substance Abuse* (Linehan, Schmidt and Dimeff, 1999) and *Dual Focus Schema Therapy* (Ball, 1998). *Dialectical Behavior Therapy-Substance Abuse* (DBT-S) has been developed for patients with substance abuse and borderline personality disorder. For this dual focus treatment there is some evidence in borderline patients in terms of dropout and decrease in substance abuse (Linehan et al., 1999).

Dual Focus Schema Therapy (DFST) is a 24-week manual-guided psychotherapy for the full range of personality disorders. It consists of a set of 16 core and 12 elective topics individualized for each patient, based on a comprehensive personality assessment and conceptualization of early maladaptive schemas and coping styles. Relapse prevention techniques are combined with coping skills training and schema-focused techniques. Ball uses schemas, and not the schema modes that were developed by Young in a later period. There is some preliminary support for DFST as a promising treatment deserving of further evaluation in a few different populations: opioid-dependent outpatients (methadone maintenance) and homeless drop-in center patients with substance abuse and personality disorders (Ball, Cobb-Richardson, Connolly, Bujosa and O'Neal, 2005; Ball, 2007).

The little research that has been done shows that it is useful to continue with the development of and research into integrated dual diagnosis treatment for personality disorders and addiction.

Ball (2007), however, following Linehan, argues that it is probably more useful to hypothesize that different personality disorders need different approaches. He also refers to the more recent study by Young, which assumes that a mode-focused approach is better for complex Cluster B patients. Furthermore, Verheul and colleagues (2007) offer a number of important guidelines, based on current scientific evidence. The most important are:

1. From the outset treatment needs to focus on both addiction and personality disorders. An integrated package of effective treatment methods for both disorders is desirable.
2. A good therapeutic alliance and intensive and long-term contact are important. The best context is long-term clinical treatment that offers sufficient structure and safety. It is desirable that such a treatment program includes training in skills and relapse-prevention.
3. Motivational interviewing is an important method within treatment. In dual diagnosis problems, often a chronic lack of motivation and difficulties with interpersonal relationships are found.

With the conclusions and guidelines mentioned above as a basic principle, a proposal is made in this chapter for a schema mode-focused, integrated treatment of Cluster B personality disorders and addiction problems (i.e., substance abuse, drug-dependence, and gambling). The basic principles for this are Young's schema mode models for borderline and narcissistic personality disorders, Bernstein, Arntz and de Vos's (2007) adjusted schema modes for antisocial personality disorders and psychopaths in forensic settings (see Part IV, Chapter 12), and evidence-based treatment for addiction, such as motivational interviewing, self-control techniques, social and problem solving skills training, relapse-prevention training, and contingency management (Emmelkamp and Vedel, 2007).

In Practice

The prevalence of personality disorders and comorbid addiction problems in maximum security psychiatric hospitals is very high. In fact, in this setting there is even the matter of triple diagnosis problems: personality disorders, substance abuse or drug-dependence (often in combination with ADHD), and one or more serious violent offenses.

There are many variations in the nature and severity of addiction problems, in the function of substance abuse in personality disorders, and in criminal offense behavior. Therefore, it is important in treatment to conduct a thorough analysis of the connection between comorbid disorders and criminal offense behavior.

In Young's schema mode model addiction (substance abuse and gambling), is seen as an avoidant coping style. A patient can, for example, use heroin or cannabis, or start to gamble, in order to avoid emotional pain and anxiety (Detached Self-Soother or Self-Stimulator). This mechanism often occurs in borderline personality disorders. In these cases, the self-medication model or stress-reducing model of addiction is applicable.

However, clinical experience shows that substance abuse and gambling can also have other kinds of functions within the schema mode model. For example, a patient can use cocaine or ecstasy out of the need for new stimuli (novelty-seeking) and a sensitivity for reward. Impulsivity and antisocial behavior lower the threshold for using drugs. Furthermore, other patients are likely to intensify their narcissistic and antisocial schema modes by using drugs. This will in turn increase their violent and criminal behavior (e.g., the Self-Aggrandizer, Bully and Attack, or Predator mode). Finally, drugs can be used as a consequence of destructive thoughts focused on the patient himself (Punitive Parent mode).

All addictive drugs can strongly intensify schema modes because of their psychotropic effects. In summary, addictive drugs can have four types of function within schema mode models as shown in Figure 11.1: intensifying over-compensating coping modes, avoidance coping modes, child modes, and Punitive Parent mode.

In 2009, a comprehensive research study was conducted in de Rooyse Wissel, with 14 patients of the Schema Therapy study (see Part VII, Chapter 3) with dual diagnoses. The purpose was to study and test the hypothesis that substance abuse can have different functions within different Cluster B personality disorders in terms of schema modes. These 14 patients completed an addiction analysis: in 4–6 sessions, substance abuse, personality disorders (including schema modes), and criminal offense behavior are mapped out and the functions of the substances are analyzed in terms of schema modes. These addiction analyses provide the material for the qualitative analysis. In addition, the psychotherapists were interviewed to test the comorbidity patterns that were found.

All 14 patients had at least one Cluster B personality disorder and most also displayed other personality disorders. The combination of antisocial personality disorder,

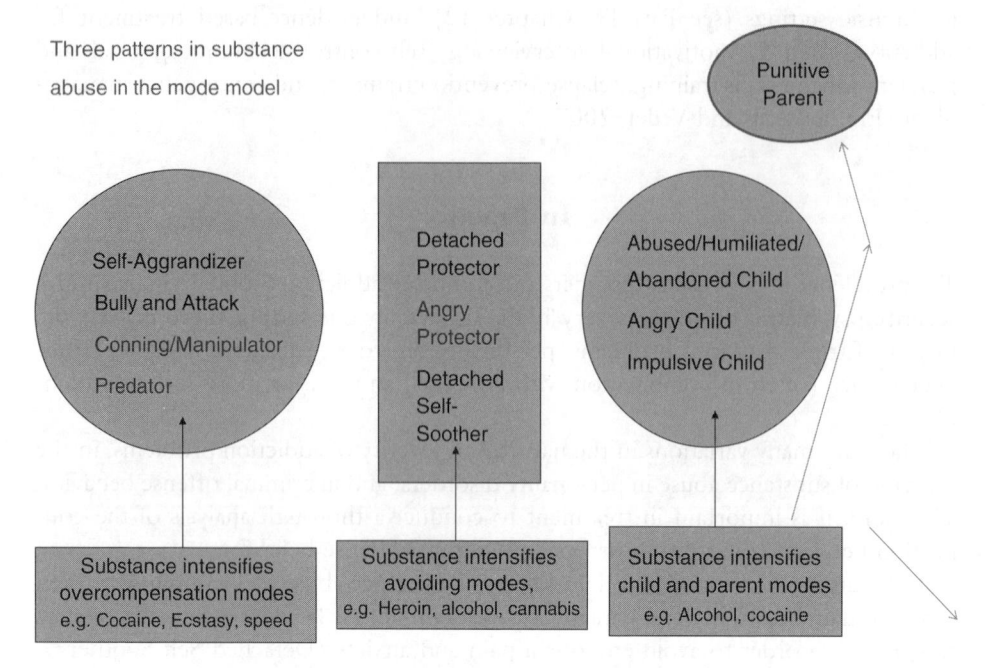

Figure 11.1 Schema modes and functions of substance abuse

Three patterns in substance abuse in the mode model:

- **Self-Aggrandizer, Bully and Attack, Conning/Manipulator, Predator** → Substance intensifies overcompensation modes, e.g. Cocaine, Ecstasy, speed
- **Detached Protector, Angry Protector, Detached Self-Soother** → Substance intensifies avoiding modes, e.g. Heroin, alcohol, cannabis
- **Abused/Humiliated/Abandoned Child, Angry Child, Impulsive Child** (with Punitive Parent) → Substance intensifies child and parent modes, e.g. Alcohol, cocaine

borderline personality disorder, and narcissistic features occurred most frequently. In four patients, paranoid features were also diagnosed. Two patients had avoidant features and one had dependent features (Cluster C). Most patients were dependent on several drugs, which often fulfilled different functions. On Hare's Psychopathic Checklist (PCL-R), six patients scored high (>26) and eight patients scored average (15–26). Research showed the following comorbidity dynamics.

In patients with (primarily) a borderline personality disorder, there was often a mainly internalized comorbidity dynamic visible. Heroin, cannabis, and alcohol were the drugs most frequently used. The following functions were exhibited:

- Avoidance of feelings of abandonment, assault, abuse, grief (Vulnerable and Angry Child). Expression in modes as Self-Soother/Self-Stimulator or increasing the Detached Protector mode.
- Emotion regulation, self-medication: the function of creating stability and rest. In this way, substances are used to stabilize fluctuating mood swings and the rapid change of different modes.
- Substance abuse by the Angry or Impulsive Child, because of immature anger and impulsiveness.
- Extreme amounts of substances or an overdose as a way of destructive, self-injurious behavior because of the Punitive Parent mode.

In patients with (primarily) antisocial personality disorders (and in a number of cases psychopathic), there was often an external comorbidity dynamic. Substances such as cocaine (often in combination with alcohol), ecstasy (3,4-methylenedioxymethamphetamine), and speed (methamphetamine) were used most frequently. The following functions were exhibited:

- The drive to feel superior and powerful: Self-Aggrandizer mode.
- Being capable of committing violent and sexual offenses in a calculating way, without emotion and conscience: Predator mode.
- Being capable of intimidation or attack without anxiety: Bully and Attack mode.
- Being capable of conning and cheating without any moral dilemma: Conning and Manipulative mode.
- Substance abuse by the Angry or Impulsive Child, because of a childish anger and impulsiveness (similar to borderline disorder).

In (primarily) narcissistic comorbidity dynamics, in which in particular heroin, cannabis, and cocaine were used, the following functions were exhibited:

- Increasing self-esteem: Self-Aggrandizer mode.
- Filling emptiness, loneliness, and feelings of inferiority by soothing or stimulating oneself: Self-Soother and Self-Stimulator modes.
- Substance abuse by the Spoilt or Undisciplined Child, because of a protest against rules, authority, or resistance.

Box 1:

Danny has been convicted of rape and had previous violent offenses. He has a history of emotional deprivation and physical abuse by his father. He has an antisocial personality disorder, with narcissistic, paranoid, and borderline characteristics, and he scores high on impulsivity in all cases and on the Psychopathic Check List (PCL-R, Hare, 2003). Furthermore, he abuses several substances (alcohol, cocaine, cannabis). Danny was under the influence of substances when he committed the offenses.

The substances Danny used performed different functions in (the development of) his personality problems. Cannabis originally had a social function (belonging to a group). Danny was a "follower," as he described himself (Compliant Surrender and also Conning and Manipulative mode). Furthermore, cannabis had a relaxing effect (Detached Self-Soother mode). He used cocaine in order "to be a man," initially, to be more powerful toward his father (his macho side, Self-Aggrandizer mode); later, "to be able to fight" in the criminal environment he was raised in (Bully and Attack mode and Predator mode). Danny only offended when he was under the influence of substances. If he hadn't used any substances, he never went beyond threatening language. Alcohol helped him to forget the pain of his maltreatment (Detached Self-Soother mode). However, it also made him lose self-control and had a strong aggressive dislocating effect on him (Impulsive Child mode). Alcohol and cocaine enhanced his macho side and predator side. He often used these substances at night so that he could fight in the gang he was a member of.

Approach

There are more factors that play a part in the development and continuation of addiction. In the analysis that is described above, the focus was mainly on the original triggers and functions of substance abuse. As soon as (excessive) substance abuse crosses over into addiction it becomes an autonomous process in which the original functions of substances become less visible.

As previously mentioned, most patients in this research study had several personality disorders, and the substances used also performed different functions. An example of a patient (see Box 1) and the functions that different substances accomplished for him.

> Danny had undergone four years ST and was monitored for three more years. Two or three times a year he had a follow-up session with the Schema Therapist. More than a year ago, the court ended his detention in a maximum security psychiatric hospital because it didn't consider Danny in danger of re-offending. Untill now Danny didn't relapse in drug abuse and agression. He found a women and became father last year. ST was a difficult therapeutic process. His motivation to undergo therapy was mainly based on external factors (parole, the need to make amends in relation to his mother, the need for a relationship with a woman). In his therapy, limited reparenting, empathic confrontation, and setting limits were the focus. At first, the Self-Aggrandizer, Bully and Attack, Paranoid Over-Controller, Angry Protector, and Angry Child modes were present during the sessions. On the ward, they often saw the Predator, the Conning and Manipulative, and Bully and Attack modes, especially when Danny felt offended. In ST, the Vulnerable Child mode gradually came to the fore, especially when discussing maltreatment by his father, feelings of guilt toward his mother, and shame and blame because of the rape.
>
> At first, Danny was not willing to do imagery exercises regarding to his past (Paranoid Over-Controller), the maltreatment by his father, or the rape. He also refused chair work and role-play. He found these techniques too mysterious, not 'genuine'. Two reasons for refusing imagery exercises became apparent. He was afraid of feeling pain and anger toward his father. Furthermore, he was afraid to be confronted with a strong craving for substances again, and as a consequence he would feel the need to start using them again. The Vulnerable Child and substance abuse as a coping mode (Detached Self-Soother) proved to be strongly linked. There was an extended focus on inclination and how to deal with this by "mindsurfing" and by training in alternative coping. Expressing emotions in conversations and undertaking employment (cleaning) proved to be good behavior alternatives. Finally, as Danny gained more confidences in the therapist, he agreed to do a few imagery exercise in relation to the maltreatment by his father. During these imageries, he was very emotional, his craving for drugs was strong, but he could stand it and could wait untill the craving diminished during the imagery. It was an important exercise in self-control.

> The rescripting also went well. However, Danny thought that the imagery was unprofitable and was determined to draw a line under his youth. He hadn't been able to cope with it since.
>
> ST was completed three years ago, because most of the maladaptive schema modes had decreased considerably and Healthy Adult behavior had increased. Mistrust, impulsivity, and antisocial behavior were markedly less significant. Danny reported that he felt calmer, he had dealt with the pain of his past, and that wasn't "triggered" so quickly. During the evaluation, he also mentioned that he had started to appreciate another kind of music: instead of aggressive, hardcore music, he now preferred calm, romantic music. The change was also clearly visible in the treatment department. Psychiatric therapists noticed that Danny was more open, less mistrustfull, and was better at waiting and frustration tolerance.
>
> For the first time in years, he no longer caused incidents, he didn't use any substances, and he was better at keeping appointments. He became more and more realistic in setting goals and taking decisions. This process continued when Danny entered a rehabilitation project, started work, and began a relationship with a woman. Danny himself reported that ST had been very useful for him.

Personality pathology (psychopathy) was Danny's most prevalent problem. The psychopath schema modes (Predator and Self-Aggrandizer modes) and Impulsive Child mode are the most important risk schema modes. Under the influence of mainly cocaine and alcohol these modes are intensified, and as a result a direct danger of offending arises.

All this shows that it is very important to make a thorough analysis of the relationship between personality pathology, addiction, and criminal offense to be able to give a personalized treatment. An analysis of the function of substances in terms of schema modes proved to be valuable. Furthermore, there is the added value of a dual focus during the treatment. Partly due to experiences in a number of dual-focus treatments, a set-up for individualized, integrated treatment of dual diagnosis problems has been developed. This consists of the following phases and parts.

1. Diagnostic phase

Through questionnaires (e.g., the YSQ), tests and observation tools such as the Mode Observation Scale (MOS; Bernstein, de Vos and van den Broek, 2009) diagnostic analysis referring to addiction and personality problems is conducted, and DSM-IV classification is determined. Schemas and modes are diagnosed.

2. Crime scene and addiction analysis

Case conceptualization. During the crime scene, the case conceptualization and mode models are set up in cooperation with the patient; addiction problems are included.

Addiction analysis. An addiction analysis is made, an analysis of the functional relations of (personality) problems, addiction, and offense (holistic theory and functional analyses) of schema modes.

3. Criminal chain group and addiction care program

All patients participate in an criminal chain group, in which cognitive, emotional, behavioral, and situational factors are mapped out preceding, during, and after the offense. Schema modes and the role of substance abuse within them are included in the offense sequence (risk schema modes and risk substances).

Dual diagnosis patients will start with two addiction modules during this phase: the substance info module (information and motivation), followed by the substances and coping modules (dealing with craving, behavior alternatives).

In the rehabilitation phase, patients participate in the Relapse Management Module (dealing with risk situations and relapse).

4. Individual dual focus treatment

Parallel to or after the completion of the offense sequence group, individual ST will start, including interventions focused on addiction problems. The treatment consists of the following phases and elements:

- building up therapeutic reparenting alliance, patient education about Schema Therapy and addiction;
- training in self-control techniques (cognitive and behavior conventions) related to craving and/or substance abuse;
- experiential techniques (imagery, chairwork) to work on internal provokers of addiction (e.g., traumatic memories), a focus on dealing with craving at the same time;
- motivational interviewing in relation to setting targets for each substance: total abstinence or controlled use;
- training relapse management techniques, especially in the rehabilitation phase;
- in addition to psychotherapy, art therapy and psychomotor therapy can also play an important role in dual focus treatment.

Pitfalls and Tips

"Addiction is no longer a problem"

Because of the 'forced remission' of alcohol and drugs in the maximum security psychiatric hospital, many patients think that they no longer have an addiction problem because they don't experience craving and they have been abstinent for years. They think they won't have any problems when they are released. However, relapse always remains a danger, as becomes clear when patients reach the rehabilitation phase. During parole outside the clinic, when patients are exposed to external provocations, they realize that their addiction is still there. Tip: keep addiction and craving on the agenda during the entire period in the maximum security hospital and pay continuous attention to it. Focus on internal triggers of craving and substance abuse (e.g., humiliation, loneliness, restlessness, grief – the Vulnerable Child modes) through experiential techniques in the inpatient phase. In the rehabilitation phase, it is important to focus on dealing with external triggers, especially relapse prevention and management techniques (behavioral and cognitive techniques).

"I don't believe in the imagery"

Several antisocial patients with a strong Paranoid Over-Controller mode (primal compensating mode for the abused/maltreated child) refuse imagery exercises and don't believe in rescripting. They think it's "fake" and only do things when they can see the point. Tip: first, use other techniques then, when time is right, try to negotiate with the patient about a few "test" sessions.

"You are the predator now"

Diagnosing schema modes can stigmatize or intensify a mode, especially in the case of an antisocial schema mode. For example, referring to the Predator mode when the patient is in that mode might increase the cold aggression, and this is therefore risky. Tip: care and especially good timing are essential when referring to and discussing behavior in terms of antisocial schema modes. Limit setting is indicated in the case of predator and bully and attack modes.

The Future

This chapter reports of the first phase in the development of a dual-focused treatment in which Schema Therapy and addiction treatment are combined. This treatment still has to be developed and described further. The intention is to describe specific methods and techniques in as much detail as possible in guidelines or protocols. The main focus is to describe how ST techniques and cognitive behavior techniques for addiction can be integrated in such a way that treatment is effective on personality disorders and addiction. Our clinical experiences with this treatment is promising. Experiential techniques appear to be have a strong effect on the internal triggers of addiction, the schema's of the vulnerable child mode. The next step will be implementation of this dual focused treatment and an effectiveness study.

References

Ball, S.A. (1998) Manualized treatment for substance abusers with personality disorders: dual focus schema therapy. *Addictive Behaviors, 23*, 883–891.
Ball, S.A. (2007) Comparing individual therapies for personality disordered opioid dependent patients. *Journal of Personality Disorders, 21*(3), 305–321.
Ball, S.A., Cobb-Richardson, P., Connolly, A.J., Bujosa, C.T. and O'Neil, T.W. (2005) Substance abuse and personality disorders in homeless drop-in center clients: symptom

severity and psychotherapy retention in a randomized clinical trial. *Comprehensive Psychiatry*, *46*, 317–379.

Bernstein, D.P., Arntz, A. and de Vos, M.E. (2007) Schemagerichte therapie in de forensische setting. Theoretisch model en voorstelen voor best clinical practice. *Tijdschrift voor psychotherapie*, *33*(2): 120–139.

Bernstein, D.P, de Vos. M.E. and den Broek, D.M. (2009) *Mode Observation Scale*. University of Maastricht.

Emmelkamp, P. and Vedel, E. (2007) Alcohol- en drugsverslaving. *Een Gids voor Effectief Gebleken Behandelingen*. Uitgeverij Nieuwezijds.

Emmerik, J.L. and van Brouwers, M. (2001) *De Terbeschikkingstelling in Maat en Getal: een Beschrijving van de TBS-Populatie in de Periode 1995–2000*. Den Haag: Ministerie van Justitie.

Hare, R.D. (2003) *Hare Psychopathy Checklist–Revised (PCL-R)*, 2nd edition. Toronto: Multi-Health Systems.

Jong, C.A.J. de, van den Brink, W., Harteveld, F.M. and van der Wielen, G.M. (1993) Personality disorders in alcoholics and drug addicts. *Comprehensive Psychiatry*, *34*: 87–94.

Linehan, M.M., Schmidt, H. and Dimeff. L.A. (1999) Dialectical behavior therapy for patients with borderline personality disorder and drug-dependence. *American Journal of Addictions*, *8*, 279–292.

Rounsaville, B.J., Kranzler, H.R., Ball, S.A. *et al.* (1998) Personality disorders in substance abusers: relation to substance abuse. *The Journal of Nervous and Mental Disease*, *186*, 87–95.

Verheul, R., van den Brink, W. and Hartgers, C. (1995) Prevalence of personality disorders among alcoholics and drug addicts. *European Addiction Research*, *1*, 166–177.

Verheul, R., van den Bosch, L.M.C. and Ball, S.A. (2005) Substance abuse, in *Textbook of Personality Disorders* (eds J.M. Oldham, A.E. Skodol and D.S. Bender). Washington, DC. American Psychiatric Publishing, pp. 463–476.

Verheul, R., van den Bosch, W. and Ball, S.A. (2007) Verslaving en persoonlijkheidspathologie, in *Handboek persoonlijkheidspathologie* (eds E.H.M. Eurelings-Bontekoe, R. Verheul and W.M. Snellen). Houten: Bohn Stafleu van Loghum.

12
Schema Therapy in Forensic Settings

David Bernstein, Marije Keulen-de Vos, Philip Jonkers, Ellen de Jonge and Arnoud Arntz

Introduction

Forensic patients pose special challenges that are uncommon in general psychiatry. These patients usually have problems with aggression, impulsivity, or anger. Some patients deceive and manipulate to achieve their goals. Many patients are very wary, which makes them difficult to engage in treatment. Patients with personality disorders represent the most prevalent diagnostic group in most forensic settings (Rasmussen, Storsaeter and Levander, 1999; Timmerman and Emmelkamp, 2001; Hildebrand and de Ruiter, 2004; Leue, Borchard and Hoyer, 2004). Cluster B personality disorders (e.g., antisocial, borderline, and narcissistic personality disorder) are especially common. Cluster B patients, and especially highly psychopathic patients, have an increased risk of recidivism (Salekin, Rogers and Sewell, 1996; Hemphill, Hare and Wong, 1998; Rosenfeld, 2003; Jamieson and Taylor, 2004). Many experts are skeptical that psychotherapy can treat these patients, though there is little empirical support for this view (D'Silva, Duggan and McCarthy, 2004). In contrast, Schema Therapy (ST) has a more optimistic perspective on change in severe personality disorders (Young, Klosko and Weishaar, 2003; Rafaeli, Bernstein and Young, 2011), a view that is supported by findings of a recently completed multicenter randomized clinical trial on borderline personality disorder (BDP) outpatients (Giesen-Bloo *et al.*, 2006). Of the patients randomized to receive ST, 50% were judged to have recovered from their BDP pathology and 70% showed clinically significant improvement after three years of therapy and a one-year follow-up (Giesen-Bloo *et al.*, 2006).

These impressive results inspired Bernstein and Arntz to adapt ST for forensic patients with personality disorders (Bernstein, Arntz and de Vos, 2007). This forensic adaptation of ST is currently being tested in a multicenter randomized clinical trial at seven Dutch forensic hospitals in the Netherlands. Our preliminary findings in the first cohort of 33 patients to complete two years of treatment are promising: over 80% of the patients randomized to receive ST were approved to begin the process of supervised re-entry into the community – a crucial phase of treatment in the Dutch forensic system – compared to 60% of patients receiving usual forensic treatment (Bernstein, 2009). Although these findings are preliminary – patients must complete three years of treatment and a three-year follow-up, and a much larger sample is being recruited and tested – they suggest that ST may be able to help some of the most challenging forensic patients with personality disorders, a population that is often considered untreatable.

In this chapter we describe the forensic adaptation of ST that is currently being tested in several Dutch forensic psychiatric settings (Bernstein, Arntz and de Vos, 2007). The forensic ST model focuses on personality characteristics that are seen as risk factors for violence and crime. In this model, these risk factors are conceptualized as schema modes (Young et al., 2003) – fluctuating emotional states that, when triggered, increase the probability of aggressive, impulsive, or other antisocial behavior. As schema modes are relatively dissociated from each other, they dominate a person and his thoughts, feelings, and behavior at a given point in time (Young et al., 2003). By reducing the severity of these maladaptive modes and enhancing a patient's Healthy Adult mode, forensic ST aims to achieve real personality change, resulting in a reduced risk of future antisocial behavior.

Clinical Practice

To understand the psychological motivations behind criminal behavior and to guide forensic ST we expanded Young and colleagues' (2003) the original schema mode model by including five "forensic schema modes": Angry Protector, Bully and Attack, Paranoid Over-Controller, Conning and Manipulative, and Predator Mode (Bernstein et al., 2007). In Angry Protector mode, a patient's hostility, irritability, or sullen withdrawal keeps others at a safe distance. In Bully and Attack mode, the patient uses threats or aggression to intimidate others. In Paranoid Over-Controller mode, the patient is hypervigilant and looks for hidden enemies who want to hurt or humiliate him. In Conning and Manipulative mode, the patient presents a "false self" by lying, cheating, or charming others to achieve a certain goal. In Predator mode, the patient eliminates a threat, rival, or obstacle in a cold, emotionless, and ruthless manner.

By using this expanded mode model, "senseless" crimes can sometimes be explained in terms of a sequence of schema modes.

> John's girlfriend ended their relationship. He became furious and, after getting high on drugs, decided to go to her house to kill her. When he could not find her house, he stopped a female stranger to ask for directions. He then pulled her into his van and raped her. During his crime he switched between apparent concern for his victim and threats and intimidation when she refused to do what he wanted.

> Edgar, a patient in a drug treatment program, was accused of selling drugs. He became convinced that another patient had betrayed him. Eventually his suspicions fell on a patient whom he suspected of wanting to take over his "territory." Although there was no solid evidence that the informant was this patient, he decided to teach him a lesson. He grabbed a knife and carved a symbol in the man's cheek to show him (and others) not to "mess with him." He expressed little emotion during the attack, while he made sure to carve the symbol so that everyone could see it.

In John's case, abandonment was the trigger (Vulnerable Child mode). The patient tried to calm himself by getting high on drugs (Detached Self-Soother mode), but when his anger became too great (Angry Child mode), he decided to take revenge. When his desired victim, his girlfriend, could not be found, he chose a victim at random. He played with his victim to demonstrate his power over her (Self-Aggrandizer mode) and used threats to ensure she cooperated with his demands (Bully and Attack mode).

In the second case, the belief that another patient had betrayed him was the trigger. He was convinced that he had found the source of his betrayal, despite the lack of evidence (Paranoid Over-Controller mode). He decided to teach his rival a lesson so that there would no doubt as to who was in charge (Self-Aggrandizer mode). Coldly and efficiently, he eliminated the (perceived) threat to his drug dealing (Predator mode).

In these case examples, which involve highly psychopathic patients, emotional states (schema modes) can trigger each other in a sequence culminating in violence. By treating these modes, ST aims to break this chain.

Approach

In our experience over the past five years, many forensic patients can benefit from ST, provided that their therapists become familiar and adept at working with the kinds of schema modes that are most common in forensic patients. The basic ST approach remains the same when working with these types of patients as it does when working with personality disorders in general. However, in forensic ST the following issues are stressed.

The reparenting relationship

The reparenting relationship is the cornerstone of forensic ST, just as it is for ST in general (Young et al., 2003). However, many forensic patients are extremely mistrustful and emotionally detached, which makes them more difficult to engage in treatment. Thus, the therapeutic relationship needs to be built up slowly. The therapist's consistency, availability, openness, and compassion toward the patient are essential in building this trust. The therapist needs to be patient and optimistic, and must not expect big changes too quickly.

Schemas and modes

Patients with less severe personality disorders can be treated with standard ST, which emphasizes early maladaptive schemas and coping responses. In contrast, for more severe personality disorders, such as those typically seen in forensic patients (e.g., antisocial, narcissistic, and BDP), ST focuses on schema modes. Because patients with severe personality disorders often switch between emotional states, a schema mode approach helps the therapist monitor and intervene with the modes that appear in the "real time" of the therapy session (Young *et al.*, 2003). Experience shows that most forensic patients understand the mode concept and learn to apply it to themselves quite quickly, so long as they are sufficiently intelligent (e.g., IQ > 80). We teach patients to label their modes, but not their schemas, because switching between schema and mode terms can become confusing for the patient. On the other hand, we do incorporate schemas as an adjunct to modes, though not explicitly. For example, when discussing the Vulnerable Child mode, we can talk about "that side of yourself that is afraid of being abandoned" (Abandonment/Instability schema).

Assessment and case conceptualization

The schema mode case conceptualization is essential in forensic ST because it determines the strategies that a therapist will use to target a patient's schema modes in treatment. The assessment combines different sources of information, including criminal records and observations of the patient's interactions with others (e.g., staff members and patients), as well as other sources traditionally used in ST assessment (e.g., schema and mode inventories, imagery for assessment). The therapist teaches the patient the schema mode model. He presents the patient with a simplified version of his case conceptualization, starting with a small number of modes that are the initial focus of the treatment.

Protector modes

Most forensic patients have particularly strong Detached Protector, Angry Protector, and/or Detached Self-Soother modes. They may seem emotionally flat or deny having emotions or problems. They can present themselves as hyper-normal by responding in a socially desirable manner or come across as detached, defiant, or uncooperative. They might use drugs, alcohol, or other compulsive behavior for blocking out painful feelings. Behind these protective modes there is usually a pervasive distrust of other people and a fear of their own emotions. This tendency to stay detached is usually reinforced by the institutional setting in which patients learn to adapt by avoiding people and situations that trigger their problematic behavior. These detached modes are often a main focus of the first two years of forensic ST. The therapist uses standard ST techniques such as empathic confrontation, role-play (e.g., two-chair method), and guided imagery, and above all, the slow building of trust through the reparenting relationship, to break through the patient's detachment and gain access to the child modes that are usually hidden underneath.

Vulnerable Child mode

Some forensic patients can easily experience and admit to inner pain. Others deny such feelings altogether. In our experience, when a patient denies having any feelings, this is due to the Detached Protector mode or other modes that block access to the Vulnerable Child mode. Evidence supporting the assumption that these patients do have a more emotional side is that they often refuse to do imagery exercises or get extremely upset because of the emotions that are released through imagery. Even patients who deny having any feelings will often acknowledge that they don't trust others or that they feel that others try to humiliate them. Thus they make external attributions (Weiner, 1990) where others are seen as the cause of their emotions ("I do not feel humiliated. *You* are trying to humiliate me!") rather than feeling that their emotions are intrinsic to themselves. Discussing with the patient which side of him feels mistrustful can be a first step in accessing the patient's vulnerability. Although we cannot be certain that all forensic patients have a vulnerable side, our experience suggests that even highly detached psychopathic patients may show vulnerable feelings under some circumstances.

How many forensic patients, especially psychopathic ones, are able to experience emotions remains unknown. Research suggests that psychopathic patients often show deficits in the ability to recognize emotions, particular fear and sadness, and that these deficits are tied to low amygdala activation in the brain (Blair, Mitchell and Blair, 2008). However, we have observed many examples where ST has been able to break through the emotional reserve of even highly psychopathic patients to reach the patient's vulnerable side. This suggests that a schema mode model, in which patients switch between detached and more vulnerable emotional states, may capture the emotional reality of many forensic patients better than a trait model that assumes that patients are the same way all the time.

> In his first therapy session, Gerry, a forensic patient, told his therapist not to bother exploring his feelings, because he was a psychopath and didn't have any emotions. The patient had a highly traumatic background, having been physically and emotionally abused by his father at a very young age and placed in foster care at the age of four. When asked about these experiences, he said that he "didn't give a damn" about them. Gerry was highly emotionally detached and self-aggrandizing, acting in an aloof, arrogant, and at times intimidating manner. He continued to deny feelings whenever he was asked about them. On one occasion, however, he needed to be hospitalized for a medical emergency. When his girlfriend visited him, he broke down in tears. Later, when his therapist asked him about this episode, he replied that he almost never experienced such feelings, and that the therapist should not expect to witness them again.

> Henry, a highly psychopathic patient, had been in ST with a female therapist for about one year when he arrived for a session appearing palpably anxious. His therapist had never before seen him in such a state. Henry had been convicted of rape and sentenced to treatment in a forensic hospital. He rarely showed his feelings and was described by many as a "classic psychopath." In his session, he told his therapist that he had suddenly realized how frightened he was of women. He revealed that he had been impotent in some of his sexual encounters. Thus, for the first time he was able to show his therapist a vulnerable side that had not previously been apparent. This breakthrough signaled the beginning of a new phase of the therapy, in which his vulnerable side could be explored and eventually integrated.

Impulsive Child mode

Many forensic patients grew up in families where few boundaries were set. These patients are not able to tolerate frustration or comply with rules, because they never learned to do this as a child. Instead, they have a strong Impulsive Child mode that "wants what he wants when he wants it," and behaves without thinking about the consequences.

Helping the patient to accept limits is a crucial part of the therapist's reparenting role. This is complicated by the fact that these patients often experience limits as punitive and arbitrary, and mistrust the intentions of those in authority. This is not surprising, given the inadequate parenting that many have experienced, which often fluctuated unpredictably between being overly permissive and overly punitive or even abusive. Thus, the therapist's providing firm but fair and consistent limits is an important aspect of reparenting – in fact, just as important as providing the nurturance that was also often missing in these patients' childhoods.

> Ron, a hospitalized forensic patient, had made a painting that he wanted to hang on the wall of his room. He was so excited by this prospect that he decided to take a hammer and nail from the workshop where he had made the artwork and bring it to his room on the inpatient ward where he lived. When he entered the ward, he encountered a staff member who asked if he had received permission from the ward chief to carry the hammer and nails onto the ward. He said that he had received the ward chief's permission, although he had not. Only later did he acknowledge having fleetingly considered the consequences of his ill-conceived actions, but had decided, "Oh, what the hell!" and gone ahead anyway.

Angry Child and Angry Protector modes

The ST therapist must learn to distinguish different modes that refer to anger or aggression, such as Angry Child, Angry Protector, Bully and Attack, and Predator modes.

Knowing which mode is present "in the room" at a given moment in time is the key to knowing how to intervene, because different modes call for different interventions. For example, Young *et al.*, (2003) have proposed three steps for dealing with the Angry Child mode: venting the emotion, empathizing with the patient, and reality testing. This strategy works well when the patient expresses his anger openly. Many forensic patients, however, express their anger indirectly, through irritation, sulking, pouting, complaining, withdrawal, and oppositional behavior – in other words, the Angry Protector mode. This behavior is self-defeating because other people are unable to empathize with the patient's feelings and instead feel irritated with or frustrated with the patient. In fact, the Angry Protector mode serves the function of erecting a "wall of anger" that keeps others at a safe distance, where they can't harm the patient. The therapist uses empathic confrontation and other techniques to explore the reasons why patients may feel unable to express their feelings directly, while at the same time emphasizing the self-defeating nature of this behavior. At the same time, in his reparenting role, he encourages the healthy, constructive expression of anger.

Over-compensatory modes

Over-compensatory modes are the hallmark of patients with antisocial personality disorder, and especially of patients who are highly psychopathic. Our research indicates that a cluster of five schema modes – the Self-Aggrandizer, Bully and Attack, Conning Manipulator, Paranoid Over-Controller, and Predator modes – are highly associated with the interpersonal features of psychopathy (Keulen-de Vos, Bernstein and Arntz, 2010). These five modes are based on an over-compensatory coping style in which the patient "turns the table" on other people and attempts to gain the upper hand. If the patient feels humiliated, he tries to humiliate others (Self-Aggrandizer mode). If he fears that others will hurt or abuse him, he goes on the offensive, bullying and intimidating them (Bully and Attack mode). If he feels that he cannot get his needs met in an open and direct way, he gets what he wants in an indirect way (Conning and Manipulative mode). If he experiences other people as dangerous, he seeks out his enemies before they can attack him (Paranoid Over-Controller). If he sees the world as consisting of victims and predators, he makes a cold, calculating decision to be a predator rather than a victim (Predator mode). Thus, each of these modes reflects a specific kind of coping response involving a tendency to over-compensate for underlying schemas of abuse, deprivation, humiliation, abandonment, and so forth.

In our experience, over-compensatory modes are almost always involved in patients' acts of crime and violence. Although patients often take pains not to show these sides of themselves to treatment providers, they are often expressed in more subtle forms of demeaning, intimidating, controlling, or manipulative behavior directed at the therapist. Moreover, in forensic settings, these sides of the patient may be more evident in patients' encounters with each other, for example, in battles over positions in dominance hierarchies on the ward, or in conflicts with staff members who attempt to set limits. These kinds of interactions are described in the forensic literature as "offense-paralleling behaviors" (Jones, 2004) – behaviors occurring in the forensic setting that parallel the patients' pattern of violent and criminal behaviors. In ST, such offense-paralleling behaviors can be conceptualized in terms of schema modes, particularly modes involving over-compensation. When these modes appear in therapy sessions or on the ward, they provide an opportunity for the therapist and other staff members to call the patient's attention to them, initiating a process whereby the patient can become aware of these sides of himself, the reasons why they exist, and their destructive and self-defeating consequences.

Pitfalls and Recommendations

Self-Aggrandizer mode

Many forensic patients, particularly narcissistic and psychopathic patients, have a Self-Aggrandizer mode. This mode can hinder treatment progress, especially if the patient denigrates the therapist. When the therapist does not respond to the deprecating attitude of the patient, the patient is inclined to see the therapist as weak and to escalate his vilifications. For this reason, the therapist must confront the patient directly and immediately, but without being judgmental. A pitfall is when a therapist over-compensates for his own schemas (e.g., Defectiveness/Shame) and tries to put the patient in his place (Self-Aggrandizer mode), or on the other hand, behaves in a submissive manner (Compliant Surrender mode), which only encourages further denigration from the patient. Instead, the therapist should be firm but compassionate, not afraid to address a patient's arrogant or deprecating behavior, but in a respectful and non-threatening manner.

Conning and Manipulative mode

Dealing with patients' lies or manipulation is one of the most difficult challenges of working in the forensic field. When a patient cries, for example, it is sometimes difficult to know whether the emotion is sincere or designed to get the therapist's sympathy. In other instances, the patient may ask the therapist for special favors or try to get the therapist on his side in a conflict. Forensic care providers have an understandable and sometimes justified tendency to be cautious about patients' manipulative behavior. Some go too far, however, if they instinctively react mistrustfully toward patients. On the one hand, the ST therapist has to be able to respond to the genuine feelings and needs of a patient (e.g., by providing limited reparenting). On the other hand, he has to confront him with his inauthentic and manipulative

> Dimitri, a patient in a forensic hospital, sued the hospital for alleged malpractice. He had previously been treated in another forensic hospital, which he had also sued, winning a sizable award. His therapist saw Dimitri as an innocent victim of circumstances. However, the therapist may have been missing another side to the story. Dimitri had been twice interviewed for psychopathic tendencies with the Psychopathy Checklist-Revised (PCL-R; Hare, 1991). On the first occasion, he had received only a moderate score, but on the second occasion, he was given a score in the psychopathic range. Such a discrepancy could have raised doubts about the patient's sincerity.

behavior (e.g., through empathic confrontation). In our experience, most therapists are aware when patients are trying to manipulate them and can discern the difference between authentic and inauthentic emotions. However, we have also come across exceptions, particularly in treating highly psychopathic patients.

A high PCL-R score does not necessary mean that the patient cannot be trusted. The schema mode model assumes that patients may switch between modes in which they show genuine emotions and other modes in which they con and manipulate. For this reason, it is essential that therapists who work with forensic patients get regular supervision or peer supervision in which they can receive feedback from colleagues. Making video recordings of therapy sessions, which can be shown to supervisors or colleagues, is an effective way to elicit colleagues' impressions of patients' schema modes. This can help therapists avoid the pitfalls that sometimes occur in working with forensic patients who may lie or manipulate.

Limit-setting and empathic confrontation

The ST therapist sets limits when a patient's behavior is threatening or insulting, when it undermines the therapy, or is a danger to the patient or others. When the therapist fails to set limits, the behavior of the patient often escalates. ST therapists set limits in a clear, decisive, but non-punitive way. They emphasize the differences between healthy expressions of anger and the patient's threatening or insulting behavior. Most forensic patients calm down quickly when they sense that a therapist is strong enough to set limits in a determined but non-punitive way. If the threatening or dangerous behavior continues, the therapist tells the patient that he will impose consequences, if the patient is unable to respond to limits. When aggressive modes such as Bully and Attack or Predator mode are present in a session, an intervention should follow immediately, either by empathic confrontation or by limit-setting. The choice of the intervention depends on the seriousness of the aggression: the more serious the threats or aggressive behavior, the more likely it is that the therapist will set limits before he can explore the reasons for the presence of this mode. Although less obvious than in cases of overt aggression, limits may also need to be set when schema modes threaten to undermine the therapy.

> In his first session, Eli, a forensic patient, told his therapist that his goal in the therapy was to have the therapist know as little about him by the end of the therapy as at the beginning. He refused to make eye contact with the therapist, and gave only one- or two-word answers to her questions. He stared at the floor, while she patiently tried to introduce new topics that the patient would respond to. After several months in which she grew more and more frustrated and angry, she finally decided to confront Eli about his Angry Protector mode, which was making therapy impossible. She told him that she had reached the end of her patience and would have to stop the therapy unless he could take some risks to open up and share more with her. The intervention worked. Although he was initially taken aback, he agreed to her conditions, which enabled the therapy to move forward.

Many therapists feel uncomfortable about setting limits, because it is a skill that most are not trained in. However, it can be very empowering for them to learn this skill and to see how limit-setting can ultimately help patients to gain greater self-control.

Experiential techniques

For many forensic patients, traditional "talking therapies" are insufficient to break through their emotional detachment. The patient may talk in a fluent but unemotional and superficial way about his problems, spend his time complaining about the forensic institution and the unfair way that he is being treated, or avoid discussing himself and his feelings altogether. In such circumstances, the therapist may feel that the therapy is going nowhere and respond to this lack of progress by becoming detached or bored himself, or by getting angry at the patient. For this reason, experiential techniques play a vital role in ST with forensic patients. Experiential techniques, such as guided imagery and role-play, are used in ST to access and reprocess patients' emotions. These techniques are particularly effective in bypassing patients' detached modes and accessing more vulnerable emotions (Holmes and Mathews, 2005).

Although some forensic patients participate quite readily in experiential exercises, others are reluctant to do them. This is understandable, given that many of these patients are quite frightened of their own emotions, which they often associate with traumatic experiences from childhood or with their own proneness to anger and violence. When forensic patients are reluctant to do experiential exercises, it is important to explore the reasons for their hesitancy and to gently persist in getting them to try them. Some patients who initially refuse to do experiential exercises will agree to do them later in the therapy, after sufficient trust in the therapist has developed. Other patients will agree to do these exercises if their purpose is explained sufficiently or when procedures are introduced that make them less threatening (e.g., beginning imagery with an image of a safe place; allowing patients to do imagery with their eyes open while focusing on a fixed point, rather than closing their eyes; letting the patient signal for a "time out" if the exercise is becoming too overwhelming). In our experience, many if not most forensic patients will eventually engage in experiential exercises, often with beneficial effects.

> Han, a psychopathic forensic patient, had developed a good relationship with his ST therapist. However, after more than a year in therapy, he still refused to try experiential techniques. Eventually, his therapist confronted him, saying that she felt that the therapy could go no further unless he was willing to give these techniques a try. After she explored the reasons for his reluctance, and again explained the purpose of the techniques, Han agreed to try guided imagery. The image that he produced was one where he was beaten as a teenager by his sadistic father. Further, at a moment when his father was off guard, Han had caught him by surprise and savagely beaten him. This image represented a turning point in the therapy, since it vividly put the patient in touch with his mistrust and fear of abuse and the over-compensatory way in which he had learned to take the role of aggressor to protect himself from victimization.

Motivating and engaging forensic patients

Forensic patients vary in their motivation for treatment. Some patients are quite willing or even eager to engage in the therapeutic process, while others are reluctant or refuse. The patient's active participation in treatment is usually considered a prerequisite for success. However, when the patient refuses to recognize that he has a problem, appears not to be suffering from his problems or to have a desire to change, or fails to engage in the basic tasks of therapy, such as forming a bond with his therapist, agreeing on the goals of treatment, or self-disclosing, we often describe him as "unmotivated," "non-compliant," or "resistant." These patients are understandably highly frustrating for the professionals who work with them. In many cases, such patients are denied further attempts at treatment, creating a self-fulfilling prophesy in which treatment is withheld from the patients who need it the most. Recent research, however, suggests that treatment motivation is a dynamic rather than a static concept (Drieschner, Lammers and van der Staak, 2004). Patients' willingness or ability to engage in therapy may change over time. Motivational interviewing methods, for example, have been shown to enhance the treatment motivation of patients with addictive disorders, as well as patients in forensic settings (McMurran, 2009).

ST is not predicated on patients being ready or motivated for psychotherapy. Instead, it views patients' motivation in terms of the schema modes that are active at any one time. Thus, patients' motivational levels fluctuate with their emotional states, which can be triggered by a number of internal and external factors, including the therapy and the forensic setting itself. Rather than being "unmotivated" or "resistant," patients are viewed in terms of the sides of themselves ("schema modes") that present obstacles to treatment. For example, the Detached Protector mode says, in effect, "Don't ask me about my feelings – I don't have any!" The Self-Aggrandizer mode says, "I don't have a problem – you do!" The Angry Protector mode says, "I can't trust you – keep away from me!" The goal is to work with these sides in order to flip or switch patients into modes that are more therapeutically productive, such as the Vulnerable Child mode, in which patients are directly in touch with their feelings, and the Healthy Adult mode, in which patients can reflect on themselves and their situation in a balanced and objective way. The therapist works with the full range of ST techniques in order to enhance the patient's motivation, although reparenting undoubtedly plays the most important role in overcoming the patient's mistrust and beginning to reach his vulnerable side. Enhancing the patient's motivation and building the therapeutic relationship via reparenting is usually the central focus in ST with forensic patients in the first year of therapy.

> Paul, a forensic patient with a high psychopathy score and a history of aggressive, impulsive, and antisocial behavior, had made no progress during four years of treatment at a previous forensic hospital. At his new hospital, his behavior alternated between friendly and cooperative and periods in which he became angry and refused to participate in treatment. At the beginning of ST, he missed many sessions, but seemed to enjoy the sessions he did attend. He was angry

with the clinic and the Ministry of Justice, and sometimes threatened to terminate his treatment, saying, "Just lock me up for life and throw away the key!" At the same time, he seemed to respond positively to the therapist's attention and grew calmer when the therapist asked him how his Healthy Adult side would respond to these statements. Nevertheless, he continued to be provocative in his behavior outside of the sessions and caused a number of incidents, receiving numerous sanctions.

After six months of ST, the hospital requested that his forensic treatment be terminated and that he be sent to a "long-stay" facility, where he would be detained indefinitely. This shocked Paul and represented a turning point in his treatment. Although the rest of his treatment activities were stopped at this point, he requested that he be allowed to continue with ST and increased his frequency of sessions from once to twice a week. He began to see that his difficulties with the hospital stemmed from his own impulsive and aggressive behavior (Impulsive Child and Angry Protector modes, respectively). Using the two-chair technique, an experiential method in which different sides of the patient are asked to sit in different chairs and dialogue with each other, the therapist explored with him the advantages and disadvantages of these modes. The patient became better able to view things from his Healthy Adult side and started to experience remorse for his actions. When Paul expressed frustration with his treatment, or asked to end a session early because "there was no point in talking," his therapist used empathic confrontation to help him see the sides of him that were blocking progress. The therapist was then able to help Paul articulate goals for the therapy that served to enhance his motivation (e.g., learning to be less impulsive so that he would receive fewer sanctions; being calmer during his daughter's visits). Paul agreed to go on medication, which he had previously refused, to help him stay calm.

At this point, his Protector modes seemed to diminish and the therapist was able to make more contact with his vulnerable, lonely, and anxious sides. The therapist introduced imagery exercises, where Paul was able to re-experience painful events from his childhood, with the therapist "stepping into" the images to provide reparenting directly to the Vulnerable Child. In this way, the therapist was able to give "little Paul," in imagery, some of the love and attention that he lacked as a child and protect him from the abusive father who had terrorized him. Paul seemed notably relieved after these imagery exercises, and his behavior in the hospital became calmer and more cooperative. After 18 months, the hospital withdrew its application for "long-stay." Although Paul's further treatment had its ups and downs, as is the case for many forensic patients, he continued to make progress. After two years of ST, the clinic requested that Paul begin the resocialization process, which involves granting the patient leave to go outside the hospital with progressively less stringent levels of supervision, with the goal of reintegrating him into the community. This indicated that the hospital no longer considered him at high risk for recidivism. In his many years of forensic treatment, he had never before reached this point, at which he could see a future outside of the hospital.

The Future

The adapted mode approach presented in this chapter is a work in progress. A multicenter randomized clinical trial on this forensic adaptation of ST is currently being conducted in several Dutch forensic psychiatric hospitals (see Part VI, Chapter 1). The results of this study will provide crucial information about the effectiveness of ST in reducing the personality disorder symptoms and recidivism risk of forensic patients. Our experiences so far and the preliminary results of this study (see above) suggest that ST is a promising approach for many forensic patients with personality disorders.

References

Bernstein, D. (2009) Effectiveness of schema-focused therapy for forensic patients with Cluster B personality disorders. Paper presented at the 9th Annual Congress of the International Association of Forensic Mental Health Services, Edinburgh, Scotland.

Bernstein, D., Arntz, A. and de Vos, M. (2007) Schema-focused therapy in forensic settings: theoretical model and recommendations for best clinical practice. *International Journal of Forensic Mental Health*, 6, 169–183.

Blair, J., Mitchell, D. and Blair, K. (2008) *The Psychopath: Emotion and the Brain*. Oxford: Blackwell.

D'Silva, K., Duggan, C. and McCarthy, L. (2004) Does treatment really make psychopaths worse? A review of the evidence. *Journal of Personality Disorders*, 18, 163–177.

Drieschner, K., Lammers, S. and Staak, D. van der (2004) Treatment motivation: an attempt for clarification of an ambiguous concept. *Clinical Psychology Review*, 23, 1115–1137.

Giesen-Bloo, J., van Dyck, R., Spinhoven, P. et al. (2006) Outpatient psychotherapy for borderline personality disorder: a randomized clinical trial of schema-focused therapy versus transference-focused psychotherapy. *Archives of General Psychiatry*, 63, 649–658.

Hare, R.D. (1991) *Manual for the Hare Psychopathy Checklist–Revised*. Toronto: Multi-Health Systems.

Hemphill, J., Hare, R. and Wong, S. (1998) Psychopathy and recidivism: a review. *Legal Criminology Psychology*, 3, 141–172.

Hildebrand, M., and De Ruiter, C. (2004) PCL-R psychopathy and its relation to DSM-IV Axis I and II disorders in a sample of male forensic psychiatric patients in the Netherlands. *International Journal of Law and Psychiatry*, 27, 233–248.

Holmes, E. and Mathews, A. (2005) Mental imagery and emotion: a special relationship? *Emotion*, 5, 489–497.

Jamieson, L. and Taylor, P. (2004) A re-conviction study of special (high security) hospital patients. *British Journal of Criminology*, 44, 783–802.

Jones, L. (2004) Offence parralleling behavior (OPB) as a framework for assessment and interventions with offenders. *Applying Psychology to Forensic Practice* (eds A. Needs and G. Towl). Malden, MA: Blackwell.

Keulen-de Vos, M., Bernstein, D. and Arntz, A. (2010) Assessing schema modes in forensic patients. Paper presented at the bi-annual meeting of the International Society for Schema Therapy, Berlin, July.

Leue, A., Borchard, B. and Hoyer, J. (2004) Mental disorders in a forensic sample of sexual offenders. *European Psychiatry*, 19, 123–130.

McMurran, M. (2009) Motivational interviewing with offenders: a systematic review. *Legal and Criminological Psychology*, 14, 83–100.

Rafaeli, E., Bernstein, D. and Young, J. (2011) *Schema Therapy: Distinctive Features*. London: Routledge.

Rasmussen, K., Storsaeter, O. and Levander, S. (1999) Personality disorders, psychopathy, and crime in a Norwegian prison population. *International Journal of Law and Psychiatry*, 22, 91–97.

Rosenfeld, B. (2003) Recidivism in stalking and obsessional harassment. *Law and Human Behavior*, 27, 251–265.

Salekin, R., Rogers, R. and Sewell, K. (1996) A review and meta-analysis of the Psychopathy Checklist and Psychopathy Checklist–Revised: predictive validity of dangerousness. *Clinical Psychology*, 3, 203–215.

Timmerman, I.G. and Emmelkamp, P.M. (2001) The prevalence and comorbidity of Axis I and Axis II pathology in a group of forensic patients. *International Journal of Offender Therapy and Comparative Criminology*, 42, 198–213.

Weiner, B. (1990) Attribution in personality psychology, in *Handbook of Personality Theory and Research* (ed. L.A. Pervin). New York: Guilford Press, pp. 465–484.

Young, J.E., Klosko, J. and Weishaar, M. (2003) *Schema Therapy: a Practitioner's Guide*. New York: Guilford Press.

Part V
The Therapist
Training, Supervision and Self-Care in Schema Therapy

1
Training for and Registrations of Schema Therapists

Marjon Nadort, Hannie van Genderen and Wendy Behary

This chapter describes the training for and registration of Schema Therapists. First, international developments and tentative guidelines, as determined by the International Society of Schema Therapy in 2010, are set out. Following this, the Dutch situation will be explained, since the Netherlands is the first country to have established a register for Schema Therapy, in 2006. Originally, Schema Therapy (ST) was developed to enable psychotherapists, (healthcare) psychologists, and psychiatrists to provide this therapy. After all, the target group for which ST was originally developed consisted of patients with personality disorders, and persistent anxiety and mood disorders. Developments over the last few years show that socio-therapists and creative experiential therapists are also starting to use ST, or at least some of its strategies. This chapter mainly focuses on the training of psychotherapists, psychologists, and psychiatrists. The implementation of Schema Therapy by other disciplines is described in Part VII, Chapters 2 and 3.

In Practice

International developments

In 2006, during the first conference, in Stockholm, a group of approximately 50 Schema Therapists from Europe and the US met to discuss international developments in ST. They proposed the formation of an International Society of Schema Therapy (ISST). During this meeting, an attempt was made to regulate international registration and training requirements. However, at the time international regulation wasn't possible, because training requirements appeared to differ greatly between countries. In September 2007, the second ISST conference was organized this time in Delft. During this two-day congress, speakers from different countries presented new developments within ST, and there was a discussion about international regulation of

The Wiley Blackwell Handbook of Schema Therapy: Theory, Research, and Practice, First Edition.
Edited by Michiel van Vreeswijk, Jenny Broersen, and Marjon Nadort.
© 2012 John Wiley & Sons, Ltd. Published 2015 by John Wiley & Sons, Ltd.

training requirements. Temporary committees were set up, which were concerned with training, registration, and scientific research. In 2008, the official foundation of the ISST took place in Coimbra, Portugal. Agreements about international registration and training requirements were made. The last ISST congress was held in Berlin in 2010. During the past years, guidelines for international certification have been drawn up.

An overview determined by the ISST follows, for which it has to be noted that all Standard and Advanced Level Schema Therapists must be licensed, certified, or registered to legally practice in their country. The guidelines can be found at www.isst-online.com. There are two levels: the Standard and the Advanced Level Certified Schema Therapist.

1. Standard International Certification: Therapists at this level are certified to practice ST, to participate in outcome studies, and to train or supervise other therapists at a basic level only. They are not qualified to run training programs, assess sessions, or offer supervision on difficult cases.
2. Advanced International Certification: Therapists are certified to treat all patients, to participate in outcome studies, to supervise/train/assess others, and to run training programs.
3. Alternative Schema Therapist: A therapist who has been recommended by a member of the Research Community of ISST for approval to assist in ongoing or forthcoming studies in ST, and has shown exemplary skill in utilizing the model with patients. While there is currently no certification being offered for Alternative Schema Therapists, the Training Committee is currently working on the details for this third level of affiliation, which would include therapists who are highly trained in ST and committed to the integrity of its application, but do not meet the criteria for certification due to non-traditional backgrounds in psychology and/or psychotherapy, such as art, music, and movement therapies, and have restrictions regarding independent practice in their country.

Each country can decide which of these levels it wants to offer (including other non-certification courses). Furthermore, any country can insist on *additional* requirements beyond the minimum guidelines set by ISST, as long as they are approved by the Training Committee of the ISST Board.

Content of approved certification training program

For individual therapy, an approved certification training program has 25 teaching hours and the curriculum needs to cover the following subjects:

- Schemas, coping styles, and modes: defined and differentiated.
- Assessment: including interviews, imagery, and inventories.
- Linking schemas with early childhood experiences.
- Temperamental factors.
- Conceptualizing a case in schema terms.
- Treatment formulation – clarifying goals and needs in schema terms.

- Schema change: including schema dialogues, emotion-focused chair work.
- Use of imagery, limited reparenting, empathic confrontation, limit-setting, flash cards, diaries, confronting maladaptive coping modes, and punitive and demanding parent modes, therapy relationship work (including the appropriate use of self-disclosure), role-plays, cognitive strategies, behavioral strategies, and homework.
- Schema mode work with BPD and NPD.
- Schema therapy for couples (optional).
- Reading: *Reinventing Your Life*; *Schema Therapy: A Practitioner's Guide*.
- Other reading materials.

For group therapy, an official work group has been formed on developing group Schema Therapy (GST). The work group consists of members who have been working for the last two years on the treatment protocol for the collaborative multi-site BPD RCT, and others who have expressed strong interest in GST. This work group will refine, and possibly expand, the GST model for a range of Axis I and II

Table 1.1 2010 ISST minimum certification training requirements

Type of Requirement	*Standard Certification*	*Advanced Certification*
Hours of training	25 hours	25 hours
Supervised role-play in pairs and groups	Minimum 15 hours	Minimum 15 hours
Individual case supervision	20 supervision sessions (50–60 minutes each) (single or converted group minutes; see www.isst-online.com)	40 supervision sessions (50–60 minutes each) (single or converted group minutes; see www.isst-online.com)
Personal therapy as part of case supervision	Recommended, optional: Max. three sessions out of 20 can be primarily personal therapy	Recommended, optional: Max. six sessions out of 40 can be primarily personal therapy
Group case supervision	Up to 25% "group converted" minutes (see www.isst-online.com)	Up to 25% "group converted" minutes (see www.isst-online).
Peer supervision	Recommended, optional	Recommended, optional
Minimum number of cases treated with ST	Min. two cases, at least 25 therapy hours each; one case must be BPD	Min. four cases, at least 25 therapy hours each; one case must be BPD and one must be other PD
Minimum number of patient sessions (at least 45 minutes each)	80 sessions	160 sessions
Duration of supervision	At least 1 year	At least 1 year
Session competency ratings of patient or realistic role-play	One session, with minimum STCRS score of 4.0, and a case conceptualization form	Two sessions, with minimum STCRS score of 4.5, and two case conceptualization forms

disorders. It will develop adherence and competency scales for rating therapists conducting groups, and will explore and reach consensus within ISST about the best way to integrate GST certification into the current certification process. If there is a consensus on GST certification, the minimum criteria for training in GST will be identified and GST will be integrated into existing training programs.

Approach

What are the necessary qualities to become a Schema Therapist?

A certification procedure was established in order to be able to maintain an official guarantee. There are several reasons why it is important that therapists already have several years' experience in working with patients with complex problems before they start to practice. First, ST is a treatment model in which many different methods and techniques are used and, second, the implementation of ST is designed for patients with personality problems and persistent anxiety and mood disorders. Aside from the formal quality guarantee, there are several other points of interest that make a person suitable to be a Schema Therapist.

A Schema Therapist must be sufficiently emotionally healthy in order to be aware of and manage his own maladaptive schemas and coping modes. It is therefore essential for a therapist to have ST supervision and to participate in peer supervision. It is also sometimes recommended that he pursues (ST) personal therapy. Furthermore, it is necessary to be familiar with and alert to interactions between the schemas of the therapist and those of the patient. According to Young (Young, Klosko and Weishaar, 2003), a good Schema Therapist must possess the following characteristics:

- The therapist must be capable of offering sufficient limited reparenting and must be able to judge whether the patient needs this.
- The therapist must be flexible.
- The therapist must be capable of partly meeting the basic emotional needs of the patient, within the restrictions of the therapeutic alliance.
- The therapist is able to correct and confront the patient in an empathic way.
- The therapist is able to react adequately when a patient shows compensating behavior during a session.
- The therapist is able to cope with expressions of strong emotions (both positive and negative) by the patient.
- The therapist has realistic expectations of both himself and the patient.
- The therapist is satisfied with himself and his life.
- The therapist is able to set limits to his own behavior and the patient's behavior.
- The therapist is able to handle crises within the therapeutic alliance in an adequate way.
- The therapist knows when to keep a proper distance and when to approach.

Sometimes schema activation occurs between therapist and patient, especially in the case of schema complementarities (if the therapist and the patient have schemas that both complement and trigger each other, see Box 1).

> **Box 1:**
>
> Janet is a borderline patient who has a very isolated life. She has only a few friends, no job, and lives on social security. Furthermore, she has an alcohol problem. She depends very much on the two sessions of psychotherapy, which she has every week. During the weekends, when she doesn't see her therapist, loneliness strikes hard. She makes a habit of calling her therapist several times during the weekend. The therapist, who sympathizes with her, allows this initially. The patient feels better for a little while following every short telephone call. However, throughout the course of the treatment, it becomes clear that the therapist starts to become reluctant to take the telephone calls at the weekend. After a discussion in the peer supervision group, the therapist discovers that he didn't indicate sufficiently, under the influence of his own schema Self-Sacrifice and the patient's Dependency/Incompetence schema, whether telephone calls outside working hours were possible and acceptable (in the case of a crisis) or not (in the case of loneliness).

> **Box 2:**
>
> The therapist asks a patient to keep a record of the situations in which she asks too much of herself. For the next session, the patient wrote down two situations. The therapist expected more and he sets to work energetically discussing every day of the past week and checking whether there are more examples to be found. The following week, the therapist receives an email from the patient every day with detailed descriptions of the specific situations mentioned. The therapist answers every email, taking up more and more of his time by doing so. It is clear that the therapist and patient are keeping each other trapped in a spiral of increasing demands and expectations.

When the therapist and the patient have the same maladaptive schemas, or a resemblance in schemas, the therapist may have a blind spot for the patient's schema, which is why he fails to confront or correct (see Box 2).

Another problem can occur within the therapeutic alliance when the therapist has schemas that make it impossible for him to offer the patient what he needs (see Box 3).

For a more extended list of examples regarding schema combinations of therapist and patient see *Schema Therapy: A Practitioner's Guide* (Young et al., 2003, chs. 6 and 7) and *Schema Therapy for Borderline Personality Disorder* (Arntz and van Genderen, 2009, ch. 4).

The Dutch situation

In 1990, ST was introduced to the Netherlands by Christine Padesky and Kathleen Mooney. Since 1995, Tim Beck, Cory Newman, and Jeffrey Young have provided

> **Box 3:**
>
> Alice is a borderline patient who was severely neglected by her father in her childhood. He regularly failed to come home on time and he often left his pre-school child waiting for hours on the doorstep. The therapist himself has the Emotional Inhibition schema, which means he isn't capable of giving the patient the love, care, and warmth she needs. Therefore, in the imagery with the patient, he can talk to the father about his irresponsible conduct, but he isn't able to comfort the little girl, reassure her, or treat her lovingly. As a result, Alice feels supported by the fact that her father is talked to by the therapist, but emotionally she is left in the cold.

workshops and training programs in Maastricht on ST as a treatment for personality disorders.

The "borderline project" for the ST condition of the randomized controlled trial (RCT) *Outpatient Psychotherapy for Borderline Personality Disorder, Randomized Trial of Schema-Focused Therapy vs Transference Focused Psychotherapy* (Giesen-Bloo et al., 2006) resulted from this, for which a large group of psychotherapists from Leiden, The Hague, Amsterdam, and Maastricht were trained and supervised by Young. In 1997, a training program for ST in groups at the Viersprong in Halsteren, conducted by Marty Sloane, began. This large group of therapists, trained in the 1990s, developed training programs, courses, and supervision courses that have been offered in the Netherlands since 1999. At this time, approximately 1,000 therapists (psychotherapists, healthcare psychologists, and psychiatrists) have attended a four-day or longer course with teachers/trainers. In the past few years, many psychotherapists have also been trained to start new studies (Bamelis et al., 2006–10; Bernstein, Arntz and de Vos, 2007; Nadort, 2005; Nadort and Giesen-Bloo, 2005).

Books on ST have been published (Arntz and Bögels, 2000; Schacht and Peeters, 2000; van Genderen and Arntz, 2005; van Vreeswijk and Broersen, 2006), and training material developed (Nadort, Arntz, et al., 2009; Nadort, van Dyck, et al., 2009). These books are mainly used during courses to train therapists, alongside Young's (Young and Klosko, 1994, 1999; Young, 2005; Young et al., 2003) publications. Although a number of people may have acquired ST techniques by reading or by attending workshops, the authors of this chapter prefer social workers to take an intensive training program in which they have the opportunity to practice the techniques with expert supervision.

The establishment of the register for Schema Therapy

As described above, ST quickly became familiar in the Netherlands. As a result, the need for a register of therapists who can offer ST arose, both from the point of view of social workers and from the point of view of potential patients. In 2006, a group of people who had been involved in the introduction of ST in the Netherlands since the beginning decided that the time was ripe to implement a register of Schema Therapists, in order to make it easier for social workers to contact each other for peer supervision and references, and for the continuation of the development and dissemination of ST. Part of the register is also made accessible to patients, so they can find a Schema Therapist themselves. The compilers of the register didn't establish a new association, but wanted to organize a platform of and for Schema Therapists. ST is not considered a new therapy method, which would justify having its own association, but is considered to be a promising model of integrative therapy that could and should be developed further.

At first, joining one of the existing psychotherapy associations, for example, the Dutch Association of Behavioral Therapy and Cognitive Therapy (VCGt), was considered, but eventually rejected, because joining a certain association with a specific reference framework would interfere with accessibility for people from different reference frameworks.

What are the qualification requirements for a Schema Therapist?

After taking legal advice, the decision was made to restrict membership to those who are registered on a professional register or are members of a specialized psychotherapist association. This registration offers the guarantee that the parties concerned are obliged to follow professional codes of practice. A separate part of the register will be made available for other professions (e.g., creative experiential therapists, who want to establish themselves within the register). Everyone who meets the criteria can register if they meet the requirements in the area of training, supervision, and peer supervision in the field of ST. The decision was made to subdivide membership into four groups.

Prospective members. Prospective members aren't yet certified to offer ST, but are training to become Schema Therapists and are registered on the professional competence register and trained to become registered members, or they are a member of a specialized psychotherapy association and they would like to be informed on the developments in the field of ST and/or have the opportunity to look for a supervisor and a peer supervisor group.

Junior Schema Therapists. Junior members are halfway through their training program to become a senior Schema Therapist (see below).

Senior Schema Therapists. Senior members have met all the training requirements to become a Schema Therapist and are working as a Schema Therapist.

Supervisors. A supervisor must be acknowledged as a supervisor by one of the professional associations or specialized associations and must meet the requirements demanded of the senior membership of the Schema Therapy register in order to be registered as a supervisor. In order to be registered as a junior or senior therapist, the following requirements (set out in Table 1.2) must be met.

Pitfalls and Tips

Short training and education of (too) complex patients

As discussed in other chapters, ST attracts a great deal of interest. This means that students participate in training programs enthusiastically, and following this they

Table 1.2 Registration requirements to become a junior or senior ST therapist

	Junior	Senior
Professional competence registration or a member of a recognized specialized psychotherapy association	Required (in training for one of these registrations is also allowed)	Required
Participation in peer supervision with Schema Therapists	Required	Required
Recognized training hours[a]	≥24 contact hours (+ working hours)	≥50 contact hours (+ working hours)
Hours of received peer supervision on Schema Therapy	≥10 hours individual or pro rata in a group[b]	≥20 hours individual or pro rata in a group[c]
Years of experience as a Schema Therapist (counted after the successful completion of the first 24 required training hours)[d]	≥1 year	≥3 years
Number of treated patients or patients in treatment	≥4 individual or 2 individual and ≥2 groups with a minimum of 20 sessions	≥8 individual or 4 individual and ≥4 groups with a minimum of 20 sessions
Number of completed sessions[e]	≥100 sessions individual or ≥50 group therapy sessions	≥200 sessions individual or ≥100 group therapy sessions

[a.] Training programs are recognized when they are given by a ST supervisor. A training program must last at least four days. A workshop lasting at least two days also counts as training. Conferences and short workshops don't count.

[b.] The supervision must be given by a recognized ST supervisor (see above), who is on the Schema Therapy register. Naturally, the supervision of ST is recognized from the moment that the supervisor is recognized as a ST supervisor. Supervision is only recognized when started two days after basic training.

[c.] As formulated in the guidelines of the VGCt: In the case of individual supervision, 45 uninterrupted minutes of contact time count as 1 hour of supervision. Supervision can also take place in groups of two or three supervisees. In a group of two, the supervision consists of sessions of at least 60 uninterrupted minutes of contact time, and in a group of three, it consists of sessions of at least 90 minutes of uninterrupted contact time.

A supervision session may be extended to a maximum of two sessions, on the condition that the uninterrupted contact time is at least twice as long as the above mentioned requirements for individual or group supervision.

[d.] Years of experience start to count following the completion of four training days in Schema Therapy and the start of a treatment of a patient with Schema Therapy, provided that the person involved receives supervision from a ST supervisor and/or is part of a ST peer supervision group consisting of at least one senior member and two or more members who have followed at least four days of ST training.

[e.] The number of sessions that are counted may only include 50% peer supervision group discussion. The other 50% must take place under supervision.

begin energetically. This is to be welcomed, but the following critical points need to be taken into account. It is important that students, after following an introductory course (24 or 25 hours) do not immediately start treating very complex patients. The advice is to start with borderline patients, narcissistic patients, or patients with antisocial personality disorders only after taking a longer course (50 hours).

Only carry out treatment when you are a member of a peer supervision group

Working with ST requires an enormous effort on the part of both patient and therapist. Especially when working with a crisis-sensitive population, participating in a peer supervision group is a *sine qua non*. The advice is to offer ST only if there is sufficient support and feedback from a peer supervision group.

Supervision is always necessary

When starting ST, supervision is essential regarding practicing several techniques, maintaining the therapeutic alliance, and contributing one's own schemas. It is advisable to have supervision periodically, even as an experienced ST therapist, in order to identify possible blind spots.

Treating many patients and variation in patients

To be able to learn how to implement ST well, it is important to treat many patients. Furthermore, having patients in therapy who have different problems is important. When a therapist begins to treat borderline patients exclusively after 50 hours training, it is likely that the therapist will be easily discouraged if a treatment doesn't seem to work. It is advisable to carry out a few "good working" treatments as well as difficult treatments. Furthermore, it is important not to have too many borderline, antisocial, and narcissistic patients in treatment at the same time, since this may be too demanding, resulting in the therapist becoming overburdened. How much an individual therapist can handle varies per person, but experience shows that it is better not to start with more than three patients (one or two sessions a week). An experienced therapist can, in addition, treat approximately another three or four patients who are more advanced in their therapy and experience fewer crises.

The Future

Schema Therapy should be offered by psychotherapists, psychologists, and psychiatrists. At the same time, there is an increasing interest in Schema Therapy from socio-therapists and creative experiential therapists. In Part VII, Chapter 3 about ST in the forensic setting, the implementation of ST in disciplines other than by psychotherapists, psychologists, and psychiatrists is reported. In the future, there must be a greater focus on training socio-therapists and creative experiential therapists within ST. A first step to this end was made within the Dutch register for Schema Therapy in 2008. (For further developments, see www.schematherapie.nl).

The ISST has also become aware of the growing number of (alternative) experiential therapists, as well as socio-therapists, who have shown an interest in ST. Many have demonstrated an impressive grasp of the material and a facility for case conceptualization, treatment formulation, and competent clinical applications. The current society standards for certification, which call for traditionally educated and independently licensed practitioners – in accordance with their jurisdiction's requirements, as determined by their specific regulating boards of examiners – are being revamped in order to provide an acceptable place for these alternative therapists to receive a certification, perhaps with limited rights. For example, the "alternative" therapist may not be allowed to supervise fellow therapists for the purpose of certification or for the purpose of quality assurance in clinical trials, but may be able to participate in treating patients within a study or clinical trial, and assist in screening and assessment of subjects, as long as they are receiving ongoing supervision from an advanced-certified ST supervisor or trainer. The rationale behind this has to do with the (typical) absence of sustained supervision in former academic training, and limited exposure to and experience with treating complex clinical populations. They often have little to no requirements for supervisory training and/or ethical training. Nonetheless, many of these therapists show impressive promise and competence in their work with patients, utilizing the ST approach. These discussions are currently underway in ISST board meetings, and among society members and workgroup members who are involved in training and certification issues.

Register and certification in the Netherlands

The register to which certificated Schema Therapists can subscribe has been established. The set up of the register is still in its infancy. This also applies to the criteria. Only after the register has been operating for some time can judgment be passed on whether the criteria were drawn up correctly or need to be revised.

References

Arntz, A. and Bögels, S. (2000) *Schemagerichte Cognitieve Therapie voor Persoonlijkheidsstoornissen. Praktijkreeks Gedragstherapie.* Houten: Bohn Stafleu van Loghum.

Arntz, A. and Genderen, H. van (2009) *Schema Therapy for Borderline Personality Disorder.* Oxford: Wiley-Blackwell.

Bamelis, L. and Arntz, A. (2006–2010) *Psychological Treatment of Personality Disorders: a Multicentered Randomized Controlled Trial on the (Cost-) Effectiveness of Schema-Focused Therapy.* Promotietraject Universiteit Maastricht.

Bernstein, D.P., Arntz, A. and de Vos, M.E. (2007) Schemagerichte therapie in de forensische setting, theoretisch model en voorstellen voor best clinical practice. *Tijdschrift voor psychotherapie, 33*(2): 120–133.

Genderen, H., van and Arntz, A. (2005) *Schemagerichte Cognitieve Therapie bij Borderline Persoonlijkheidsstoornis.* Amsterdam: Uitgeverij Nieuwezijds.

Giesen-Bloo, J., Dyck, R., Spinhoven, P. *et al.* (2006) Outpatient psychotherapy for borderline personality disorder, randomized trial of schema-focused therapy vs. transference focused psychotherapy. *Archives of General Psychiatry, 63,* 649–658.

International Society of Schema Therapy: www.isst-online.com.

Nadort, M. (2005) *Schema Therapy for Borderline Personality Disorder. Therapy Techniques*. DVD. www.schematherapie.nl.

Nadort, M., Arntz, A., Smit, J.H. *et al.* (2009) Implementation of outpatient schema therapy for borderline personality disorder with versus without crisis support by the therapist outside office hours: a randomized trial. *Behaviour Research and Therapy, 47*, 961–973.

Nadort, M., van Dyck, R., Smit, J.H. *et al.* (2009) Three preparatory studies for promoting implementation of outpatient schema therapy for borderline personality disorder in general mental healthcare. *Behaviour Research and Therapy, 47*, 938–945.

Nadort, M. and Giesen-Bloo, J., (2005) *Pilot Implementation Study of SFT for Borderline Patients*. Eindrapportage college voor Zorgverzekeraars.

Schacht, R. and Peeters. R. (2000). *Schemagerichte Therapie voor Moeilijke Mensen*. Leuven-Apeldoorn: Garant Uitgevers.

Vreeswijk, M.F., van and Broersen, J. (2006) *Schemagerichte Therapie in Groepen*. Houten: Bohn Stafleu van Loghum.

Young, J.E. (2005) *Schema Therapy Competency Rating Scale (te verkrijgen via)*. www.isst-online.com.

Young, J.E. and Klosko, J.S. (1994) *Reinventing Your Life*. New York: Plume.

Young, J.E. and Klosko, J.S. (1999) *Leven in je Leven. Leer de Valkuilen in je Leven Kennen*. Lisse: Swets & Zeitlinger.

Young, J.E., Klosko, J.S. and Weishaar, M.E. (2003) *Schema Therapy: a Practitioner's Guide*. New York: Guilford Press.

2
Training and Supervision in Schema Therapy

Marjon Nadort, Hannie van Genderen
and Wendy Behary

As described in Part V, Chapter 1, following the training curriculum, supervision, and peer supervision are necessary conditions for learning to apply Schema Therapy (ST) skillfully. Merely following a training program is an insufficient basis from which to learn to practice limited reparenting, the pace and flow of treatment, and the selection and application of relevant strategies. This is largely due to the fact that ST is an integrative form of psychotherapy in which the therapist acts as an adaptive (limited) reparenting role model for the patient in order to heal early painful experiences and help the patient get their unmet needs fulfilled. In particular, ST was developed to treat patients with personality disorders. Given the nature of Axis II pathology, with its diverse and deeply imbedded challenges, implications for effective outcomes in treatment include a wide range of strategies within a unified conceptual approach.

In Practice

In most countries, a complete training program to become a Schema Therapist takes place in one institute. This means that all the items mentioned in the 2010 guideline are offered by a small group of teachers led by one supervisor. Supervision is often also part of the package. In the Netherlands, it is possible to organize training programs supervision and peer supervision separately.

There are different kinds of training programs. A four-day training program (24 or 25 hours) is introductory in character. Once this training program is completed, the therapist is well informed about the most important aspects of ST. This training program is particularly for therapists who want to familiarize themselves with ST and who do not treat patients whose problems are too complex. The 50-hour training programs are more extensive, go into the different techniques in more detail, and have a more specialized nature. These programs are especially for therapists who want to specialize in specific disorders or settings (groups and couples). The training presented in in-company workshops varies and often specifically caters for the question of that particular institution.

Content of the curriculum

Besides the training of theoretical skills, recognizing and defining schemas and/or modes and coping strategies, and designing a case conceptualization, practical skills have to be practiced in the form of role-play. Furthermore, it is important that students gain insight into their own schemas by completing schema inventories for themselves. This is discussed in general within the training group. Contributing their own situations in the role-play, for example, when doing imagery exercises, is also important.

The role of the therapist in the therapeutic alliance should also be examined by looking at the interaction between the patients' schemas and those of the therapist.

A complete training program must consist of the following items:

1. Schema Theory and Conceptualization
   - Schemas, coping styles, and modes: defined and differentiated
   - Assessment: including interviews, imagery, and inventories
   - Linking schemas with early childhood experiences
   - Temperamental factors
   - Conceptualizing a case in schema terms and/or modes
2. Treatment Formulation
   - Clarifying goals and needs in schema terms and/or modes
2.1 Treatment–Strategies Overview
   - Confronting maladaptive coping modes
   - Confronting Punitive and Demanding Parent modes
   - Limited reparenting with child modes, especially for the Vulnerable and Angry Child modes
2.2 Therapy Relationship
   - Limited reparenting
   - Empathic confrontation
   - Limit-setting
   - Therapists' schemas: dealing with obstacles in treatment when therapists' schemas are activated by certain patients
   - Appropriate use of self-disclosure
2.3 Cognitive Techniques
   - Diaries
   - Flash cards

- Schema dialogues
- Psycho-education about the needs and rights of children

2.4 Experiential Techniques
- Emotion-focused chair work
- Imagery
- Imagery rescripting
- Role-play

2.5 Behavioral Strategies and Homework
2.6 Schema Mode Work with BPD and NPD and Other Personality Disorders
2.7 Schema Therapy for Couples (optional)
2.8 Schema Therapy in Groups (optional)
3. Literature
- *Reinventing Your Life* (Young and Klosko, 1994)
- *Schema Therapy: A Practitioner's Guide* (Young, Klosko and Weishaar, 2003)
- Other reading materials

Practical exercises (practicing skills)

For ISST certification, as well as the didactical training programs, a minimum of 15 hours of group practice in pairs is required, which must contain the following:

- Whole group or "fishbowl" exercises are encouraged and can count toward as much as two hours of the pairs group practice requirement, as long as the whole group participates. Whole group exercises can be a good way to demonstrate strategies in preparation for dyadic and triadic practice.
- Dyadic group practice: Therapists pair up and take turns (approximately 30 minutes each) in the role of patient and that of therapist. If the group is large and supervisors are few, a participant may act as the observer/coach. But the observer should only be in that role once so as to maximize practice opportunity.
- Dyadic group practice exercises must include: limited reparenting with child modes, especially with the Vulnerable and Angry Child modes, confronting the Detached Protector mode, confronting the Punitive (Demanding) Parent mode, the use of empathic confrontation, imagery, limit-setting, and therapy relationship work.
- Therapists' schemas: Dealing with obstacles in treatment when therapists' schemas are activated by certain types of patients.

While there is no standard for the didactic part of a certification program, meaning that there may be 30–40 participants in the room with only one certified trainer facilitating the practice, having a minimum of one trainer for every 20 participants (ideally one trainer for every 10 participants) in the dyadic role-play part of the program is proposed. This may be challenging in some countries where the number of advanced schema therapists is still small. In these cases offering separate consecutive dates for smaller group training to cover the dyadic role-play might be sufficient to help meet this requirement. It is one of the most important aspects of the training program for learning the model, in addition to personal and group supervision, and therefore requires that advanced schema therapy supervisors be available to guide and coach the dyadic practice exercises.

Supervision

In order to learn how to implement ST well, it is necessary that certain treatments are monitored and supported intensively by a specifically trained supervisor.

Standard certification requires 20 hours of supervision, advanced certification 40 hours of supervision. Supervision regarding ST can be offered both individually and in small groups. The advantage of individual supervision is that there is room for every patient that is brought in and that sufficient time is given to the influence of the supervisee's schemas on the problems of the patient. The advantage of supervision in small groups is that supervisees can learn from each other's cases and it is possible to practice with different techniques, in which the supervisees can alternately play the role of therapist and patient so they can observe how the supervisor plays the role of the therapist.

Elements of supervision:

- Learning to handle the therapeutic alliance well.
- Learning to handle all the items of the integrative approach that are a characteristic of ST.
- Supervisees looking at their own schema activation in the context of their work with patients.
- Personal therapy should be encouraged when needed and should be related to counter-transference issues in treatment.
- Comprehensive use of the case conceptualization forms/case summaries are recommended and are prerequisites for ST (assessing contextual road blocks, such as limited finances, limited access to patient, blending other therapies, suicidal tendencies, crisis intervention, medication evaluations) are discussed with supervisees.
- The supervisor should respectfully provide positive and negative feedback to candidates.
- The supervisor should handle obstacles related to schema activation in supervision, and confront avoidance and detached protector modes with supervisees.
- It is necessary that role-plays are implemented with candidates.
- The use of exercises from training programs can help trainees experience their own schema-triggering and maladaptive modes.
- There must be an emphasis on mode work.
- Writing reports, and listening and watching audio and video material are important.

- Being attentive to parallel processes between therapist and patient and supervisor and supervisee is important.

Regarding the parallel processes between therapist and patient and supervisor and supervisee, it is important to give the role of complementary schemas or symmetrical schemas some thought. Below are examples of a good supervisor–supervisee relationship and a poor supervisor–supervisee relationship.

An example of a successful supervision

> The supervisee brings in an example of the treatment of a patient who is a perfectionist (Unrelenting Standards/Hypercriticalness schema). The patient writes many diary entries and sends emails and articles for the therapist to read. The supervisee himself has the Failure schema with, as a coping strategy, Over-Compensation. The therapy doesn't go well. Both supervisee and patient push themselves to the limit, and the patient doesn't receive a corrective experience. The supervisor notices that the patient's schema and the therapist's coping strategy aren't constructive and act as schema-confirming for both patient and therapist. The supervisor confronts the supervisee in an empathic manner and advises her to take it a bit easier and to ask the patient to reduce the homework and in that way work toward a change in the Unrelenting Standards/Hypercriticalness schema.

An example of a non-successful supervision

> A supervisee with the Emotional Deprivation/Emotional Inhibition schema has a patient in treatment who was treated coldly and emotionally abused in her childhood. During the treatment, they work with imagery and rescripting. After the therapist has used this technique a few times, he discusses in supervision his belief that this technique isn't working. During the imagery, he manages to talk to the neglecting father, but, according to him, nothing changes within the experiences of the patient. The supervisor agrees too quickly with the supervisee and advises him to switch to the chair work technique. In this way, the Emotional Deprivation schema is maintained. It would have been better for the supervisor to have asked to listen to the audio material from the session, because then the supervisor would have heard that the supervisee wasn't able to offer the child mode the emotional warmth that the patient needed in the imagery.

An example of schema similarity in supervisor and supervisee

> A supervisee has a very busy schedule: she has just moved in with her partner, is looking for a new job, and is very busy completing her mental healthcare psychologist training. Furthermore, she must also complete 25 hours of supervision. The supervisee often reschedules appointments at the last moment, prepares little for the supervision sessions, makes a lot of ad hoc comments, and switches from one subject to another. The supervisor is also busy; is working on his doctoral research, has his own practice and training institute, and is responsible for two children. They both experience the meetings as pleasing and lively. It may be clear that the supervisor has a blind spot: he has the task of pointing out to the supervisee that she lacks structure and preparation, and displays the Insufficient Self-Control/Self-Discipline schema. In this supervision, the supervisee receives no correction.

Approach

In order to evaluate and rate the competence of therapists using ST, the *Schema Therapy Competency Rating Scale* (Young, 2005) is used. This list, developed by Young, is used to judge whether a therapist has sufficient skills in the fields of limited reparenting, mode identification, conceptualization, behavioral techniques, experiential techniques, cognitive and educational techniques, empathic confrontation, setting limits, coping skills and doing homework, focusing on acting out problems, discussing the past, and focusing on the therapeutic alliance. For each item, a score of 0 (unacceptable) to 6 (excellent) can be given. According to the ISST guidelines, a standard-level schema therapist should have an average of 4 and an advanced-level schema therapist an average of 4.5. This list should be used in supervision when listening to and judging audio- and videotapes. However, the STCRS is a pilot scale, as are the cut-off scores. It is expected that the STCRS and cut off scores will be refined over the next year or two based on research data. In addition to the required 4 (standard) and 4.5 (advanced) minimum required score a candidate must receive an individual rating of no less than 4 on items 6–9 of the STCRS (see www.isst-online.com).

Ratings on the STCRS

Session ratings will normally be provided by the site offering the training program or by the supervisor. However, to become a certified Schema Therapist, each final rating session must be rated by an Advanced Certified Schema Therapist other than the trainee's supervisor(s) and by someone who is relatively unfamiliar with the trainee personally.

Becoming an ISST Supervisor

Taking the trainers/supervisors workshop is mandatory for all advanced level certified schema therapists who wish to facilitate as supervisors and/or trainers in ISST approved training programs.

Pitfalls and Tips

When a newly graduated psychologist enthusiastically inquires about ST and registers for a short (four-day) training program, but still has little or no experience in treating patients with personality problems, he will gain a lot of theoretical knowledge from the training but will not be sufficiently prepared to apply it in practice.

In order to do justice to the content of the training programs, it is important to have sufficient knowledge, at an academic level, of cognitive-behavioral therapy. It is also necessary that students have some practical experience in treating patients with personality disorders and complex problems. Furthermore, it is important that students start practicing the skills during the training program. The advice is to offer the training over a period of several months. There are, however, four-day training programs, which means it is not always possible to practice as extensively as desired. Yet, the advantage of this uninterrupted period is that it is easier to practice with personal situations, because there is more of a group process. It is also useful for several colleagues from one institution to follow a training program together, so they can organize peer supervision.

It must be emphasized that in a training program the four foci (the past, present, and the future of the patient plus the therapeutic alliance between patient and therapist) have to be dealt with. It also needs to be made clear that ST consists of three broad techniques: cognitive, behavioral, and experiential. In keeping with the model, these strategies become integrated within the treatment process. The use of separate items, within a biased frame of reference, merely becomes eclectic therapy. It is also important for the student to realize that after following a short (four-day) training program, he is not an expert in ST; and that further training, peer supervision, and individual supervision are necessary if he is to become a competent Schema Therapist. In addition, after following a long-term training program, supervision is also necessary, as is being part of a peer supervision group of Schema Therapists. ST for complex patients is demanding. Supervision and peer supervision are necessary to be able to reflect properly on the therapist's own experience, including pitfalls and mastery, and to receive feedback from colleagues.

During supervision, it is important for the supervisor to ensure that the therapist pays attention to the concrete content of what the patient says, but also that he pays attention to the underlying schemas and coping strategies. Also of importance is that the supervisor listens to or watches audio or video material regularly. A potential pitfall here is to act only on what the supervisee says. Only by listening to or watching the material, or by demonstration, can the supervisor ascertain if the supervisee has mastered a certain technique. It is also the only way to assess the appropriate and relevant use of physical touch, self-disclosure, and other boundary issues in treatment.

> A supervisor periodically struggles with the Defectiveness/Shame schema. She says that, especially when treating narcissistic patients, this schema is activated. She provides the example of a narcissistic patient who told her: "You may be good with borderline patients, but apart from that, I think you lack depth and overview." The supervisor says that this hit her very hard and that her first reaction was "the patient is right," resulting from her Defectiveness/Shame schema. Only later was she able to get a grip on herself and see that the remark, whilst partly true, originated primarily from the patient's narcissistic problem.

If supervision takes place in a group, a safe setting is important, so that supervisees can reveal their difficulties and vulnerabilities. It is the responsibility of the supervisor to guide and monitor this process. In order to have good insight into the supervisees' own schemas, completing and scoring the schema inventories for themselves is important. In this way, they can more easily pay attention to their own schemas and the potential pitfalls they may encounter when interacting with patients. During most ST training programs supervisees will have completed the schema inventories and so will be aware of their own schemas. Exercises will have been done concerning the interaction of the schemas of the patient and of the therapist. It is important to pay attention to the supervisees' own schemas at the beginning of the supervision and not to wait until problems occur. Supervisees can also learn from and help each other during peer supervision groups. It is also helpful if the supervisor practices self-disclosure and describes his own schemas and the challenges he faced with patients in the past.

Naturally, the rules of professional confidentiality not only apply to patient records, but also to the supervisees when sharing information among each other. The process in supervision is monitored by the supervisor: he is responsible for exercising good judgment in allotting time between the different supervisees, to ensure that everyone gets an equal opportunity to share. Furthermore, it is important that patients are not only *discussed*, but that the use of role-play is a part of ongoing practice in supervision. If problems arise within the supervision group (e.g., coming late, absence, or inappropriate remarks regarding a peer), the supervisor guides the process with the use of empathic confrontation and limit-setting.

The Future

Although many ST training programs have begun in the last few years, access is still limited. The development of training programs focused on specific target groups is recommended for the future (e.g., ST for couples and ST for adolescents, young adults, and the elderly). Training programs for the treatment of patients with substance abuse and addiction, and forensic psychiatry, are also under development. Furthermore, the development of training programs for ST for creative experiential therapies is important. This process has already begun.

With regard to supervision, the Schema Therapy Competency Rating Scale must be more widely applied in order to be able to evaluate therapists' treatment competence. The list must also be adapted for the evaluation of group ST. In order to judge the quality of ST, audiovisual materials should be used more widely than they are currently. It would be interesting to conduct a study examining which factors are predictive of successful supervision, as well as looking at the role of schemas and modes in supervisor–supervisee relationships.

With regard to supervision, a new development started in 2011: creating a trainer workshop. The Trainers/Supervisors Workshop is a mandatory requirement for all advanced-level certified Schema Therapists who wish to work as supervisors and/or trainers in ISST-approved training programs. Highly effective teaching and supervising, as we know, goes beyond being well-trained, experienced, and talented. It also calls on a specifically robust, keen, and intuitive therapist to tactfully confront interpersonal obstacles and clinical challenges with a colleague, clearly communicate complex theoretical and strategic concepts, spark enthusiasm, and enhance comprehension capacities with articulate, flexible, and accessible skill.

The Trainers and Supervisors Resource Network, a recently (ISST board) appointed subcommittee, will facilitate the mandatory seminars under the leadership of its chairperson. In addition to facilitating seminars for advanced certified Schema Therapists who wish to act as supervisors and/or trainers in ISST-approved certification training programs, the mission of this workgroup is:

- To provide guidance, emotional support, recommendations, supervision, clarification, and assistance to advanced therapists who may have questions regarding roles and responsibilities; or may be dealing with clinical conflicts with supervisees or trainees, relational issues, or personal schema activation in supervision.
- To assist in troubleshooting logistic or bureaucratic challenges in designing a training program within a clinical community.
- To oversee, discuss, and consistently evaluate the content and delivery of content in the Trainers and Supervisors Seminars.
- To develop and produce access to communication via social networking, blogs, podcasts, and other resources relevant to trainers and supervisors on the ISST website.

References

Young, J.E. (2005) *Schema Therapy Rating Scale*. www.isst-online.com.
Young, J.E. and Klosko, J. (1994) *Reinventing Your Life*. New York: Plume
Young, J.E., Klosko, J. and Weishaar, M.E. (2003) *Schema Therapy: a Practitioner's Guide*. New York: Guilford Press.

3
The Schema Mode Model in Personal Therapy

Gitta Jacob

Introduction

Personal therapy is an important component of therapy training in particular for psychoanalytical therapists. In some countries, such as Germany, the psychotherapy training system requires a limited amount of personal therapy for CBT trainees too. However, the effects of personal therapy on the therapist-clients and/or their work with patients have been little studied. Therapists generally evaluate personal therapy positively and regard it as helpful with respect to their professional performance (Macaskill, 1992; Macran and Shapiro, 1998; Macran, Stiles and Smith, 1999). At least the awareness of countertransference issues seems to be correlated with the quantity and type of personal therapy (MacDevitt, 1987).

The approach and the issues handled in personal therapy may differ depending on the psychotherapy school. While in psychoanalytic personal therapy personal patterns and the biography of the therapist-client are central, CBT-oriented personal therapy may mainly focus on dysfunctional patterns of the therapist-client in professional situations. Thus, on the one hand, the overlap with supervision can be substantial, since supervision also focuses on problematic professional situations. On the other hand, since people tend to show similar dysfunctional patterns in a broad range of interpersonal situations, even a pure focus on professional situations may offer material to work intensively with central emotional issues of the therapist-client in personal therapy.

Since Schema Therapy (ST) has been developed from CBT, and the author is herself trained as a CBT therapist, personal ST as described in this chapter is typically brief and focuses on professional situations rather than on personal issues. As a result, the distinction between supervision and personal therapy may sometimes seem rather artificial, although the intensity of emotional work is usually higher in personal ST than in ST supervision. To avoid confusion, I only use the term personal therapy and therapist-client in this chapter, although sometimes supervision and supervisee might have been used. Nevertheless, it is important to be aware of the mandate of the therapist-client, to confirm whether it refers to supervision or personal therapy (see "pitfalls"). In the following I will first give an overview of typical problems of (young) therapists in therapy and the relationship with their own schema issues and offer suggestions on how to handle them in personal therapy. The focus will be mainly on emotional problems within the role as a therapist; however, the respective patterns of therapists are usually relevant in situations other than the professional role. This personal therapy approach is brief; some therapist-clients only get between one and five one- or two-hour sessions. As personal therapy is not obligatory in ST training, I only work with therapist-clients who are motivated to receive this kind of treatment and actively ask for it.

In Practice

Typical difficulties of therapist novices can be summarized as follows (Jacob, Lieb and Berger, 2009):

- *Unrealistic expectations*: Often therapists with limited experience have unrealistic expectations. The degree of change they expect in their patients can simply not be met given the resources of the patient. However, the therapist feels responsible for achieving these high goals. From a schema mode perspective, this would be a typical Demanding Parent mode in the therapist.
- *Over-involvement*: Related to their high expectations, therapists may get extremely involved and feel immense pressure and responsibility for the patient's progress. In such sessions, the therapist typically seems to be more active than the patient. This can be conceptualized as Demanding Parent and/or Compliant Surrender modes in the therapist. Sometimes it may even have the character of an Over-Controller mode, for example when a therapist wants to make detailed prevention plans with regard to problem behaviors, which are beyond the patient's range of functioning.
- *Experience of failure*: If they don't succeed as desired, feelings of insecurity and failure may occur, which are typical of the Vulnerable Child mode. The Vulnerable Child mode typically feels overstressed, helpless, deprived, and/or guilty.
- *Problems confronting patients*: Many therapists find it hard to confront patients with their dysfunctional interactional patterns. This often applies to coping mode patterns in the patient which are very persistent and interfere with treatment, such as endless complaining, avoidance of decision-making, evasion of emotionally difficult topics, or narcissistic belittling of the therapy. In such sessions, the patient typically stays in his and her coping mode and the therapist does not step in. From a schema perspective, the therapist stays in a Detached or Avoidant Protector mode when confronted with the patient's coping mode.

It is important to realize that the Demanding Parent mode of therapists often resembles the guilt-inducing Demanding Parent modes of dependent PD patients. Typical messages of this mode may be that "You are responsible for the well-being of others," "It is important that everybody feels good with you," "You must not say unkind things to others." If a therapist does not comply with the demands of the parent mode, he or she may not necessarily feel like a failure; however, they will often experience guilt because they are "not caring enough."

Studies into the psychological health of psychotherapists show that an intensive occupation with patients suffering from mental health problems can have deleterious effects on the therapist's well-being. Typical symptoms are physical and mental exhaustion, bad temper, or cynicism toward the patient (for an overview see Frank, 2000). This mostly concerns junior therapists, in whom enthusiasm and willingness to take responsibility in therapy are high.

When the coping mechanisms of therapists are explored, different coping modes can be seen, especially in the course of less successful treatments. Many therapists are over-engaged and more active than their patient (see above). They seem to be driven by their Demanding Parent mode, which tells them to strive in caring for their patient. "Others for whom I feel responsible must not be unhappy, must not cry. I must not confront them with negative facts about themselves." This may be mixed with a Compliant Surrender coping mode. Sometimes these two modes can hardly be differentiated.

Other therapists report exhaustion particularly in sessions with "difficult" patients with persisting interactional patterns. This can be conceptualized as avoidant coping or a Detached/Avoidant Protector mode.

Various forms of anger may also emerge. In direct contact with patients, anger may be experienced as mild irritation; however, colleagues in teams or supervision groups may see more open expressions. This is mostly due to the Angry Child mode, which is triggered by frustration about the lack of change in the patient or lack of therapy success. Sometimes narcissistic over-compensation appears when therapists blame their patients for lack of success or react aggressively toward them. In schema terms, such patterns may be regarded as over-compensation of self-sacrifice. Other related schemas typically are Emotional Deprivation, Subjugation, and/or Unrelenting Standards.

When we conceptualize these problems in personal therapy in terms of schemas and modes and explore the biographical background (e.g., with the help of imagery exercises), we often find an emotionally Demanding Parent figure, for whose well-being the therapist-client felt responsible as a child.

Case example

> Maria S., a CBT trainee, wants to understand in her personal ST why she finds a particular patient very difficult. The patient is an elderly woman who always complains and is full of regret. She complains about various issues including pain, but also about the injustice of fate and the mistakes of others. Maria feels under pressure to help her patient and feels guilty when the patient does not improve. However, none of her interventions and suggestions seems to reach the patient, who is stuck in her complaining Detached Protector mode. After work, Maria can hardly stop thinking about this patient.

> Her personal therapist suggests an imagery exercise. She starts from the current experience of insufficiency and guilt and goes back to childhood images. In the emerging childhood scene, "little Maria" is 10 years old and alone with her mother. Her mother cries and complains about problems in her marriage; little Maria feels responsible for her mother's well-being and tries to comfort and soothe her. However, the mother does not respond to her efforts and little Maria feels alone and helpless.

According to our experience in supervision and personal therapy of therapists, the following biographical patterns are typical:

- A parent figure (often mother) who was depressed or suffered in some other way. Related childhood images contain the suffering parent figure and the therapist as the child feeling responsible for the parent figure.
- Parent figure as a model for subjugation, self-sacrifice, or Compliant Surrender mode, Demanding Parent mode. Self-sacrifice or subjugation of the parent figure may have been shown toward another person. A typical childhood image would be the mother being subjugated by the grandmother or the father of the child, who is in some way dysregulated (e.g., drinks too much or is quick to anger).
- Sometimes the Demanding Parent mode seems to be mostly modeled by a parent figure (and not induced by the parent's own neediness or helplessness in the context of a stressful situation). Typical examples are a mother caring very much for others, or when a sibling suffered from a chronic illness or disability, and it was important to give a lot care to this sibling. Thus as a child the therapist primarily experienced that caring for others takes precedence over caring for oneself. However, this experience was not necessarily connected to the experience of anxiety or threat.

It is important to stress that some level of self-sacrifice and willingness to care for others above usual standards is probably an important characteristic for becoming a successful (schema) therapist. The respective patterns should be regarded as a problem only when the therapist feels over-stressed or when they impede the course of therapy

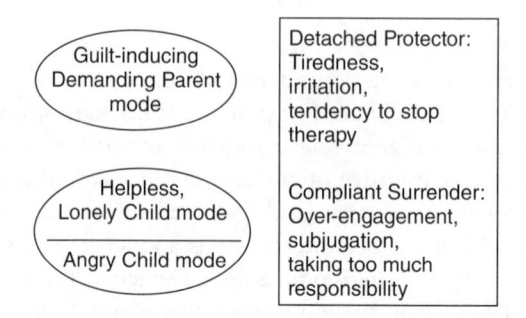

Figure 3.1 Mode model for a (junior) therapist

(e.g., when the therapist does not confront a patient with dysfunctional behavior although this is clearly indicated).

Approach

In personal therapy, this model can be used in various ways, in line with the usual therapeutic principles and procedures of ST. When a therapist-client shows avoidant or submissive behavior in therapy, or reports that he or she finds a certain patient difficult, the emotions connected to the therapy situation are explored. We discuss with the therapist-client whether the current problem is a typical, problem or whether it is due to a unique situation or to technical problems in applying therapeutic interventions correctly. If the therapist-client expresses mainly lack of skills (a "technical problem"), training or supervision is needed, and the respective skills are learned in role-plays until the therapist-client applies the intervention correctly. However, the role-play may also show that the therapist-client finds it hard to confront the patient or cease submissive behaviors due to personal emotional reasons. Then we consider the current problem as a personal dysfunctional pattern.

Only in cases of a typical pattern are the following suggestions appropriate. In this case, biographical origins can be explored with imagery techniques. Then, the Vulnerable Child mode can be soothed and strengthened and/or the Demanding Parent mode is limited by the usual emotional interventions of ST (mainly imagery rescripting and chair dialogues). Role-play (actual or imagery) can be used to implement alternative behavior patterns. The following case example illustrates this process.

Case example

Catherine is a 34-year-old CBT therapist with several years of work experience. She asks for personal therapy because of her persisting problems in confronting and limiting the over-compensating behavior of narcissistic patients. This is her self-report: "I know how important it is to confront coping behaviors, but even thinking about limiting over-compensation behaviors in patients makes me panicky. Thus I always allow the patient to dominate the session. Actually, I cannot really tell what I'm afraid of. It's a strong sense of vague fear. In my private life, I am very easily intimidated by persons with narcissistic features, too. It is very hard for me to express myself clearly toward them, but I don't know why."

The personal therapist suggests exploring Catherine's emotional problems within a chair dialogue with three chairs. The feelings of panic and threat are assigned to the "frightened Catherine" chair (Vulnerable Child mode). The avoidant behaviors (allowing the patient to dominate, not confronting him) are assigned to the Detached Protector mode chair. Her insight about the dysfunctional character of her avoidant behavior is assigned to the Healthy Adult mode chair. In the chair dialogue, Catherine first takes the position of the Healthy Adult mode. She explains why she should confront narcissistic patients with their over-compensation behavior. This triggers the vague anxiety she had characterized in her problem description. So, she moves and sits in the "frightened Catherine chair" to explore her emotions in more detail.

Through exploration, anxiety increases and becomes clearer – she reports fear of being persecuted and beaten up.

Suddenly, Catherine becomes aware of the biographical background of her emotions. When she was 14 years old, one of her fellow students (who was a little older) with repeated misbehavior in school was out to get her because she had reported one of his misdeeds to the headmaster. The boy was excluded from school and, since he blamed this on Catherine, he had threatened to beat her up. Catherine did not report his threats to anybody, since she was afraid of being labeled as a "squealer" for reporting his misbehavior. For several months she went to school full of fear, always aware of being persecuted and the risk of being attacked.

The next step in the personal therapy session is an imagery rescripting exercise of this traumatic memory. Catherine gets into an image in which her persecutor appears in the school and approaches her in a threatening way. In the rescripting, the movie character of "Terminator" shows up to help Catherine. He stops and arrests her persecutor and sends him to an adventure-based educational project far away in Canada. This image brings strong emotional relief for Catherine.

To strengthen her new position and to address transfer issues, the personal therapist suggests a role-play. She plays a narcissistic patient and asks Catherine to confront the over-compensatory behavior. Catherine is easily able to do this, still with a sense of strong relief.

The whole session took 90 minutes in all and no further personal sessions were offered. A few weeks later Catherine reports in a brief telephone follow-up that she could easily transfer these experiences to her work and in personal relationships.

The following list summarizes important aspects of personal therapy for each of the most prominent modes found in therapists:

- *Guilt-inducing Demanding Parent:* First, it is important to understand the biographical background of this mode, since this helps therapist-clients in distancing themselves from the demands of this mode. Second, the therapist-client must understand that he or she is not the only one in control of therapeutic progress. The responsibility for the therapy must always be borne by the therapist and the patient together, otherwise the therapy will not succeed. In some cases, for example in the treatment of patients with dependent personality disorder, it is a mistake in treatment not to put the patient in charge of the therapy. In personal therapy, this issue can be covered with chair dialogues between the Demanding Parent mode and the Healthy Adult mode. Sometimes the Angry Child mode is important in these chair work exercises as well.
- *Helpless Vulnerable Child:* The idea of not being fully responsible for the patient implies that therapy may fail (or not have excellent effects) due to lack of motivation, lack of resources, or bad luck, for example. This insight often leads to strong feelings of helplessness in the therapist-client, which are connected to the Vulnerable Child mode. Biographically, this reflects the helplessness of the child who has to accept that he or she cannot help the mother (or the suffering parent figure), and that a bad situation will not change. To help the therapist-client with these feelings, imagery exercises with rescripting of helpless or desperate childhood images are suitable.

- *Avoidant or Detached Protector:* In this mode, therapists typically avoid the feelings of the Vulnerable Child and are able to keep at least the façade of a caring and very responsible therapist. As with the Demanding Parent mode, it is important to clarify that a therapist in a strong Detached Protector mode is usually not able to apply meaningful therapy. It is important to work through the feelings of the Vulnerable Child; after that the Detached Protector mode will become redundant.
- *Healthy Adult:* The therapist's Healthy Adult mode has to accept that therapy can have only limited effects, and that the therapist does not have the power to heal every patient. It is important to see things realistically. When a patient shows highly dysfunctional interpersonal behaviors, it is the job of the therapist's Healthy Adult mode to confront the patient.

As compared to ST with patients, these processes can often be achieved within only one or a few sessions of personal therapy. Therapists are trained in perceiving emotional processes and usually own a lot of personal resources; thus it is usually much easier for them to benefit from emotional interventions as compared to patients.

Pitfalls and Tips

As briefly mentioned in the beginning, the personal therapy approach overlaps with supervision. A possible pitfall is the blurring of borders. It is important to clarify with the therapist-client whether he or she is willing to work with personal emotional issues on a deeper level than just understanding his or her own patterns in therapy.

In general, personal therapy seems to be much more effective than therapy with "real" patients, because therapist-clients are much more used to psychological thinking and are usually very conscious of their emotional processes. However, it may eventually happen that things do not change as quickly and successfully as expected. It is important to realize in that case that longer therapy may be indicated. This point is particularly critical when supervision is extended to personal therapy without clearly defining it as personal therapy.

Note that a major counterargument for working emotionally in personal therapy or supervision can lie in the roles of therapist-client and personal therapist – if, for example, the supervisor is also the boss of the therapist-client, or if personal therapy takes place in a group setting with colleagues from a competitive system, it may be complicated for the therapist-client to open up emotionally for reasons other than detachment. Then it would be important to look for a more appropriate setting or a more suitable personal therapist.

However, even when the setting does not inhibit opening up emotionally, therapist-clients may stay in a Detached Protector mode. The personal therapist may need to insist on this issue for some time before the therapist-client is willing to work with emotion-focused techniques on his or her patterns.

This chapter is mostly concerned with therapist-clients with problems resembling Cluster C personality symptoms. Of course, therapists' dysfunctional patterns are not restricted to Cluster C patterns; narcissistic behavior patterns can also be observed in therapists (e.g., when therapists self-aggrandize, blame the patient or other colleagues for lack of therapy success, or do not respect differing positions of patients or colleagues). However, in my experience, like narcissistic patients, these colleagues are often not motivated to reflect on their respective patterns. Maybe the positive reinforcement achieved by narcissistic behavior has simply a much stronger effect than negative consequences such as interpersonal conflicts or negative feedback from others. In cases where therapist-clients "admit" narcissistic patterns, they typically also have a very Demanding or even Punitive Parent mode and are aware of strong feelings of shame or failure (Vulnerable Child mode). Then the work as described in this chapter can be applied, since the narcissistic mode has already been weakened. My experience with narcissistic patients is similar; they are often willing to work with ST if they already feel (suffer from) dysfunctional Child and Parent modes. As long as the narcissistic compensation is to the fore, motivation for (schema) therapy is often rather low.

The Future

Two goals are connected with personal ST. First, the therapist's emotional problems in therapy can often be quickly resolved. Second, the therapist gains experience with the ST approach and gets an impression of the typical emotional processes in ST. Although ST was originally developed for the treatment of severe personality disorders, it is also possible (and often very rewarding) to address minor emotional problems, which can still cause significant problems. However, the long-term process is very different. While in the treatment of personality disorders it usually takes at least several months to bring about emotional changes, the "treatment" of emotional problems in therapist-clients as described in this chapter can mostly be done within a small number of sessions (assuming that the therapist does not have a severe personality pathology). The respective emotional changes are often stable and enduring.

This model of personal therapy relates to emotional processes and problems in the therapist-client much more than standard CBT personal therapy often does. Thus it is important to discuss this approach with the therapist-client in advance and to clarify his or her motivation to experience and change emotional processes. If a (junior) therapist is not motivated for this kind of work, although dysfunctional patterns are obvious in his or her work as a therapist, this lack of motivation is in generally treated as a Detached Protector mode in patients – the reasons for avoidance are explored and the pros and cons are discussed.

The model described in this chapter is currently only a clinical concept, which has not been the subject of empirical investigation yet. In my view, this approach helps therapists to overcome their own dysfunctional patterns in therapy and thus improve their treatments. Furthermore, therapists often report strong positive effects for their personal and emotional well-being. Although I mainly refer to "junior" therapists, sometimes even very experienced therapists find it helpful to get this kind of personal therapy. However, it would be desirable to investigate this approach to test its effects on the well-being and the performance of therapists.

References

Frank, R. (2000) Wohlbefinden von Psychotherapeutinnen und Psychotherapeuten: Evaluation von Selbsterfahrung während der Aus- und Weiterbildung, in *Selbsterfahrung in Psychotherapie und Verhaltenstherapie. Empirische Befunde* (ed. A-R. Laireiter). Tübingen: dgvt, pp. 539–571.

Jacob, G.A., Lieb, K. and Berger, M. (2009) *Schwierige Gesprächssituationen in Psychiatrie und Psychotherapie*. München: Elsevier.

Macaskill, N. (1992) Psychotherapists-in-training evaluate their personal therapy: results of a UK survey. *British Journal of Psychotherapy*, 9, 133–138.

MacDevitt, J.W. (1987) Therapists' personal therapy and professional self-awareness. *Psychotherapy: Theory/Research/Practice/Training*, 24, 693–703.

Macran, S. and Shapiro, D.A. (1998) The role of personal therapy for therapists: a review. *British Journal of Medical Psychology*, 71, 13–25.

Macran, S., Stiles, W.B. and Smith, J.A. (1999) How does personal therapy affect therapists' practice? *Journal of Counseling Psychology*, 46, 419–431.

4
Therapist Self-Care in the Context of Limited Reparenting

Poul Perris, Heather Fretwell and Ida Shaw

Definition of Self-Care: Therapist Burn-Out

Burn-out. It's a lonely term, evoking a sense of fatigue and dread, of no longer having interest in empathic listening or sometimes even in caring. For all of us entering one of the "helping professions" with hope and enthusiasm, we must attend to our own well-being and preventive maintenance of self in order keep up the demanding task of significant emotional support of wounded others. While the literature on the topic of self-care for psychotherapists is sparse, in general burn-out is associated with "emotional exhaustion, depersonalization, and reduced sense of personal accomplishment," and of having close emotional involvement without adequate support from peers, friends, or family (Boscarino, Adams and Figley, 2010). Additional risk factors include a highly empathic approach to therapy, working with patients with trauma histories, and a history of personal trauma (Boscarino et al., 2010).

For a Schema Therapist, self-care is of critical importance. Almost by definition, a ST therapist is already working with risk factors due to the high level of empathy demanded by ST, and by the high prevalence of trauma in the patient population, particularly borderline personality disorder. However, to our knowledge, nothing has been written in ST literature in terms of recommendations for such self-care. As ST has grown over the last several years, there has been an increasing level of interest in this subject.

Generally speaking, there is no formalized definition of self-care work for therapists that is required for their practice. Psychotherapists are free to decide what they consider helpful and adequate in their practice of self-care. A commonly used strategy of taking care of oneself as a therapist seems to be staying in touch with other therapists by means of regular supervision, peer supervision, working in a team, and face-to-face or telephone conversations with other team members. The practical dilemma of confidentiality in treatment and the resulting loneliness of the psychotherapist can be

The Wiley Blackwell Handbook of Schema Therapy: Theory, Research, and Practice, First Edition.
Edited by Michiel van Vreeswijk, Jenny Broersen, and Marjon Nadort.
© 2012 John Wiley & Sons, Ltd. Published 2015 by John Wiley & Sons, Ltd.

compensated for when working in a team. Social connectedness within the profession seems much more difficult when working alone in private practice, leaving this group more vulnerable. A common way of taking care of oneself as a therapist is having social activities, such as going out for dinner after work or otherwise engaging in positive individual activities, such as music, sports, or other creative pursuits.

Schema Therapy is a treatment focusing on core emotional needs through cognitive, experiential, and behavioral strategies, while relying on the process of healing within the therapeutic relationship. Therefore, to be genuine as Schema Therapists and have ongoing energy for the work involved in limited reparenting, we need to be aware of and take meeting our own emotional needs seriously. One important part of taking care of oneself as a therapist is emotional awareness and being able to take appropriate action to meet these needs.

Therapist self-care in ST involves conscientiously attending to core emotional needs as a therapist. Examples include making sure that needs such as refueling love, nurturance, and support in intimate relationships are met, and that you have someone to share difficult experiences with in order to feel guided, supported, and well-connected while retaining a sense of autonomy and independence. As is defined in ST, relationship and connectedness are core elements of healing.

In this chapter we will discuss or present: human suffering; the overall approach to human suffering in ST; an exercise designed for therapists to assess the status of their own core emotional needs; demands in ST; a practical guide on how self-care can be put into practice within the context of limited reparenting; therapist pitfalls and tips in the context of emotional distress; concluding remarks.

Definition of Human Suffering

When discussing self-care we also briefly want to discuss and define our view of human suffering. There are many ways of defining human suffering. Cassell (2004), one of the most cited authors on the subject, says that suffering is a state of severe distress associated with events that threaten the intactness of the person. From a ST vantage point one can say that *human suffering is the experience of a gap between what you need emotionally and what you get, and what you desire and what you attain*. This definition suggests two basic, interconnected levels of suffering: a primary and a secondary. The primary level is related to the frustration of core emotional needs, and the secondary level is related to obstacles in fulfilling personal inclinations (i.e., the frustration of personal values). The former ties in with common humanity, evolution, and biology, and the latter with expectations in a sociocultural context. The two levels of suffering are illustrated in the following example. All humans need love and protection to flourish; if we only receive hate and harm, then we'll suffer (a primary level of suffering). A person who values being famous but remains unknown to the broader public will suffer (a secondary level of suffering).

In ST the primary level of suffering is addressed with limited reparenting and the secondary level is addressed by helping the client establish a healthy, realistic, personal vision. Establishing a healthy personal vision involves helping the client to shape and internalize personal values that are in step with our universal core emotional needs (e.g., value spending time with loyal and caring friends, value leisure time and family time as important as work and career). Chapter 17 ("A Philosophy of Change") in *Reinventing Your Life* (Young and Klosko, 1993) addresses key aspects of how to create a healthy personal vision and can be used by Schema Therapists as a guide for self-care addressing a secondary level of suffering.

Due to limitations on the scope of this chapter we will mainly focus on the needs and means of therapist self-care in the context of providing limited reparenting when addressing a primary level of human suffering.

A ST Approach to Human Suffering and its Implications for Therapist Self-Care

Schema Therapy is an approach focused on core needs. These needs have often remained unmet in our patients since childhood (e.g., the need to have an attachment figure providing emotional needs such as nurturance, love, validation, support, and empathic limits) which has prevented them from achieving healthy emotional maturation and growth. In ST we use the concept of limited reparenting when meeting our clients' needs within the therapeutic relationship. Successful limited reparenting is thought to largely depend on the therapists' interpersonal skills, such as emotional awareness and the ability to adaptively respond to core needs in the here and now in the therapeutic process.

Like everyone else, Schema Therapists have individual limitations (e.g., issues of unrelenting standards, abandonment, self-sacrifice) which can interfere with the treatment process. Working with limited reparenting, considering its personal and intimate nature, is therefore likely to trigger the therapist's own schemas and dysfunctional coping styles. Clinical experience also suggests that this experience is inevitable and therefore therapist self-care, attending to one's own needs, gives us the possibility of preventing or lowering the occurrence of ineffective limited reparenting and also increases the therapist's professional and personal well-being. In the following section we will present an exercise that can be used as a guide when assessing your current core emotional needs status.

Therapist core emotional needs assessment exercise: "The captain on a ship"

The following exercise is centered on a metaphor of being a captain on a ship and is designed to help you as a therapist to assess the current status of your own core emotional needs. The exercise addresses four target areas clinically related to core emotional needs.

Picture yourself as a captain on a ship who needs to develop and promote:

1. healthy nurturing relationships with your crew (a stable base; connection);
2. realistic expectations of yourself as a captain (balanced efforts/self-compassion);
3. a sense of direction and appropriate navigation skills (autonomy);
4. an organized mind to handle the restrictions of weather and water conditions, and consideration and care for the needs of other sailors at sea (structure and limits).

Find a place where you can sit alone for at least 30 minutes; bring a notebook and a pen. Make yourself comfortable and read through each section (1–4) below. Each contains questions that will help you assess the status of your core needs for each target area. Start by reading a whole section, then set the book aside, reflect on the questions for a moment, return to the section and read the questions again. Try answering them aloud to yourself, and write down in your notebook any thoughts and feelings that comes to mind.

1. What people make up your ship? Who are the people closest to you? How much quality time have you spent with them lately? If you take a moment and feel your body and listen to your own Vulnerable Child, who is he/she longing for the most? What steps do you need to take in order to connect with someone you feel comfortable with? Do you feel emotionally connected with your family, friends, colleagues at work? "Is there anyone you could reach out to who could help you if needed? Do you have regular contact with a supervisor?"
2. As a captain are you taking care of yourself? Close your eyes and listen closely to the child part of yourself. Is someone listening to what he/she feels and wants? Is the adult part of you validating the needs and feelings of your Vulnerable Child? Do you have balanced standards? Do you push yourself too hard, too little? What/who are your reference points? Do you look after your physical health in a balanced way? Do you take regular breaks during the day to "recharge your batteries"? Are you satisfied with your sleep routines? How do you make sure not to see too many clients? At what time do you turn out the lights at night?
3. Where are you going and why? Do you know how to navigate and how to find your destinations? If you're not on the route you desire, what are the roadblocks? Do you have the skills you need to do your job? Do you feel like you're making a difference with your contributions in life? Are you taking on new challenges? How could you extend your comfort zone in regards of work and career? Is there anyone showing gratitude for your achievements? Do you feel that you have the proper skills to undertake your tasks? Are the people around you giving you enough freedom to speak up and be part of important decisions and issues around you? How often do you find yourself standing up for yourself? What are your ambitions for your life, family, friends, work, leisure time?
4. Are you organized, focused, and respectful? Do you evaluate your life and work on a regular basis? Do you follow through on day-to-day routines? In what ways do you show care and consideration for the people around you? How often do you write client reports or do other work-related routines? How much time do you spend wandering away from your obligations? How often do you vent your frustration on others?

After you've completed all four sections, spend a few minutes reflecting on what you've written. This exercise is likely to elicit strong emotions. Maybe you've just discovered (or put into words) that you have a lot of frustrated core needs that are crying out for your attention. But maybe you're living a busy and stressful life and finding yourself ambivalent about how to proceed. Maybe it feels that an easy way out would be to close the door you've just opened and say to yourself "I'll take care

Table 4.1 List of examples of how you, as a Schema Therapist, can attend to and nurture your own core emotional needs

	Target areas to focus on when recharging your core emotional needs			
	Connections	*Balanced efforts/ Self-compassion*	*Autonomy*	*Structure and limits*
Examples of how you can attend to your core emotional needs as a Schema Therapist:	Nurture your intimate connections (family, partner, and friends) by spending time together airing and sharing private thoughts, feelings, and concerns. Be physical e.g., give each other a massage or a manicure.	Take time off to engage in leisure activities. Do creative things that you enjoy and don't find demanding e.g., paint, play, sing, garden, sports, decorate your office. Engage in a soothing and positive inner dialogue with your Vulnerable Child.	Sign up for workshops and read books related to your professional field. Form peer supervision groups. Video a client session and watch it with a colleague and ask for feedback. Try to develop a focused area of expertise.	Be organized in your private and professional life. Set long-term goals. Follow through on "to do" lists. Evaluate your progress regularly. Reset your mind through mindfulness meditation. Vent frustrations in a reciprocal manner.

of it later." It might be helpful to remember the saying that even a small step can be a step in the right direction.

In Table 4.1 we've listed some examples of how you can start to attend to and nurture your core emotional needs.

General Demands of ST

Being present and genuine

A key feature of the therapeutic stance in ST is being open, genuine, and direct (Young, Klosko and Weishaar, 2003). Schema Therapists are trained to respond to client needs in a personal and transparent way, avoiding taking on the traditional, more distant "role of a therapist." Transparency implies revealing personal reactions to the patient, helping the patient to understand explicitly what's going on in the therapeutic relationship. Any healthy relationship involves experiencing a mixture of positive and negative emotions; sometimes it is easier to balance mind and mood than at other times. A Schema Therapist needs to allow her- or himself to make mistakes in therapy. Our philosophy is that mistakes are human and that by making mistakes we have a chance to learn and grow, and that shared efforts at problem-solving strengthen our interpersonal bonds. This also creates a healthy model for our patients, who are often taught that even small mistakes are catastrophic and end relationships. By exercising compassion for ourselves, we model what we hope patients will learn.

Empathy, validation, and acceptance

Empathy involves imagining another's inner life and experiencing that world from his or her viewpoint, in the framework of the personal history. Validation and acceptance involve acknowledging and accepting the other person's inner life. Empathy, combined with validation and acceptance in ST, helps our patients feel seen, understood, and interpersonally safe. Shared empathy, validation, and acceptance strengthen the interpersonal bond between the therapist and the patient. The energy required for empathy and emotional attunement can be considerable, particularly when working with a client whose culture or morality differs considerably from one's own, and also when a client is in high distress, exhibiting anger, or processing trauma. For therapist self-care in this regard, it is important to monitor one's energy levels before and after sessions. Whenever needed, take a few minutes of self-care in the office: meditate or do a brief muscle-relaxation exercise, eat a healthy snack, or input something positive such as looking at humorous media (e.g., a favorite cartoon strip). Listen to soothing or uplifting music while writing the session note, or briefly process the interaction with a colleague if one is available.

Limited reparenting vs. help to self-help

Limited reparenting involves meeting the patient's frustrated core emotional needs within the therapeutic relationship. This means that the therapist explicitly takes on a parent-like role. Most contemporary psychotherapies such as dialectical behavioral therapy (DBT) (Linehan, 1993) and traditional cognitive behavioral therapy (CBT) are aimed at helping the client to help him- or herself (help to self-help). In psychoanalytically oriented therapies such as mentalization-based therapy (MBT) (Bateman and Fonagy, 2004) it is even explicitly contraindicated for the therapist to gratify the client's frustrated emotional needs. From a ST perspective a help to self-help approach implies viewing the patient as essentially autonomous. Our experience is that this is not the case, especially when treating severely impaired clients, for example, with BPD. Instead, we view BPD patients as essentially needy, with an innate potential to develop a sound sense of self and autonomy *if* explicitly nurtured in their emotional needs. Therefore, ST for this patient group begins with the therapist focusing primarily on establishing a secure attachment bond with the client. This involves, among other things, offering extra session time, being available between sessions within reasonable limits, being caring and nurturing, and showing genuine, parental-like love and affection. It is later, when a secure attachment bond has been established and when the client expresses a stable sense of self, that we shift our aim in treatment and begin focusing on interventions to strengthen the client's sense of autonomy (i.e., start focusing on help to self-help strategies). This does not mean that we don't teach our patients skills to independently manage intense emotions early in treatment, such as mindfulness meditation (see Part III, Chapter 9); it's simply that those kinds of interventions are secondary to explicit nurturance and formation of a secure connection. Focusing on teaching independence strategies too early in treatment might run the risk of reinforcing the patient's detachment issues.

Limited reparenting also raises important ethical considerations. In contrast to the more technically neutral approaches such as DBT and MBT, limited reparenting calls for Schema Therapists to take responsibility for influencing their clients on a more personal level. Consequently, ST training and supervision is largely focused on identifying and coping with important pitfalls of limited reparenting (see "Pitfalls and Tips" below). Mindful attentiveness and awareness of these potential pitfalls is the first step to active problem-solving and self-care.

Demands of Group ST

In group ST (see Part IV, Chapters 4, 5, 7, and 8), working as a co-therapist team can be extremely rewarding for the therapists. It can enhance creativity and confidence. It can provide the experience of having back up in difficult situations and someone who can give you constructive feedback if your schemas have been triggered. In working with very ill patients, having a partner helps greatly in offering patients different styles of learning experiences. Some of the best teams involve pairing a therapist who has particular strengths in cognitive work with a therapist with strength and expertise in experiential work. However, just as with two well-meaning "parents," conflicts can occur and for this reason having excellent communication is vital in the team. For self-care, it is essential to increase self-awareness and to nurture oneself. For teamwork, it is vital to connect with and nurture your partner. It takes time to develop a balanced style. Pitfalls include one therapist becoming "dominant," resulting in frustration in one or both therapists (the "dominant" therapist may feel resentful that he is doing all the work, while the partner may feel undervalued) or differences in opinion on the type of intervention in the group setting. When conflicts occur, make sure you have allowed your partner to express his point of view, then assertively state your own. Sometimes it is useful to have these discussions while the group watches since it models two healthy adults reaching a compromise. If regular communication of this type does not solve the problem, obtaining supervision for your partnership is a good idea.

Approach to therapist self-care in group ST: connecting-centering exercise

Instruction: Place two chairs facing each other

1. Nonverbal phase: This phase is short (about 1 minute). In it the pair should try to find an interpersonally mindful and relaxed position.

The pair doing the exercise should be seated in front of each other with their knees touching (the exercise is more powerful with slight physical contact).

The pair start by breathing with the belly and relaxing the shoulders, finding a comfortable upright position on the chair.

Next they should seek eye contact and maintain it for a few minutes while striving for a warm and caring facial expression, tuning in to the other person and having a mimic dance.

2. *Verbal phase:* This should include both a Healthy Adult and a Vulnerable Child response; the former is cognitive and reflective and the latter is more emotional in the here and now.

One of the two starts out by pointing out something he or she likes about the other person and also expressing what that feature makes him or her feel (e.g., "I really like the way you look at me with genuine warmth when we meet, it makes me feel important and cared for").

Healthy Adult response. The same person then continues by expressing how it feels in the here and now to give this validation (e.g., "Sitting here now telling you this makes me feel a bit nervous and I wonder if you feel the way I think you do about me, but expressing this to you also feels warm and joyful since I really like having you in front of me").

Vulnerable Child response. The pair then switch and the other person starts by giving spontaneous emotional feedback on the Vulnerable Child response of the other (e.g., "Hearing you say that you feel a bit nervous makes me feel more comfortable since I too felt a bit nervous and it is good to know that you feel the same, and I too feel glad to have you in front of me".)

Then the second person starts from the beginning, giving a Healthy Adult response and pointing out something he or she likes about the other, followed by a Vulnerable Child response in the here and now.

The exercise can continue for a couple of rounds until both feel relaxed, interpersonally connected, and centered.

Therapist Self-Care in Practice

In the following section we will discuss how therapist self-care can be put into practice by providing adequate limited reparenting to our clients.

How do we perform adequate limited reparenting?

The concept of limited reparenting raises the question of how to explicitly perform adequate limited reparenting. There's not just one way to answer the question, since there are many ways of being a healthy parent. Each parent (and therapist) has his or her own unique set of personal values, temperament, and style of putting core emotional needs into action. Evolution has taught us that this diversity is important for the survival of our species, but it also implies that not all parents (or therapists) are suitable to "raise" (treat) all "children" (clients). It's important that the therapist always builds his or her reparenting skills on a genuine and authentic self. Sometimes a fundamental mismatch occurs that may cause significant distress within the relationship. Schema therapists have to accept not being able to emotionally attach to all clients; again exercising compassion with themselves for being human with human limitations.

A step-by-step guide to adequate limited reparenting; refueling needs at both ends

Although we encourage Schema Therapists to build their reparenting skills in their unique personal style we do train them in developing specific relational behaviors that are consistent with the general features of a healthy adult mode. Our experience is that meeting the clients' core emotional needs in an adaptive way reduces the risk of burn-out. Providing limited reparenting gives emotional refueling to both parties. When you fail to meet a client's needs in an adaptive way (e.g., repeatedly reaching a dead end when trying to bypass a dysfunctional mode of a client) you run the risk as a therapist of becoming emotionally drained. This can also occur if you have a "self-sacrifice" schema and your reparenting is "unlimited." Therefore, in the section below, we've outlined a step-by-step guide with specific examples of reparenting strategies promoting the target areas: Connection, Balanced Efforts/Self-Compassion, Autonomy, and Structure and Limits (these parallel the schema domains: Disconnection, Impaired Autonomy, Extreme Efforts, and Impaired Limits discussed by Lockwood and Perris in Part I, Chapter 3).We find that having a clear awareness of explicit reparenting strategies helps therapists to avoid the reparenting pitfalls discussed in the preceding sections. Approaching limited reparenting in this way will meet the client's need and reinforce the Healthy Adult on both parts in the therapeutic relationship. An accurate conceptualization of your clients' schemas and modes will allow you to identify what target area to prioritize.

Target area: connection

Connection can be defined as having a secure relationship, one that is characterized by a sense of stability, safety, trust, intimacy, love, and belonging. Below are examples of specific reparenting strategies that promote developing a secure attachment bond with your client.

Stability: Make sure to follow through on scheduled appointments. Try to schedule ahead as many sessions as possible, discuss how to arrange for vacation periods, hence providing your client with a sense of stability and continuity. If you need to make last-minute cancellations, try to give your client more than one option for scheduling a new appointment and provide them with the reason for the cancellation. You can also reinforce the client's sense of stability within the relationship in acting proactively by checking in with him or her at times (e.g., by sending an email or text message).

Availability: Make yourself available to the client as much as possible. Give him or her your email address, telephone number, or Skype address so they can reach you if needed. Remember never to offer your client more time and availability than you can continue to provide, although exceptions can be made during crises and after you've established a mutual agreement regarding how long this extra contact will be offered.

Emotionally predictable: Keep a stable and predictable mood during sessions without suppressing your emotions, i.e., express a full range of emotions within the realm of a Healthy Adult mode.

Presence: Give your full attention to your client. Sit close to him or her (within the client's and your comfortable physical boundaries). Try to have an open feeling in the space between you in the room. Maintain eye contact and stay focused. Avoid disturbing noises (e.g., a ticking clock on your office wall, or others in the office talking outside the door). Be calm and alert. If you are taking notes during sessions, try to put them away at times to keep from appearing mechanical or creating a sense of interrogation.

Protection: Help the client to foresee and/or prevent getting into destructive situations (e.g., going to parties with destructive friends that usually end badly). Show that you care for your client's safety. Help your client to break acute states of being stuck in destructive modes, such as the Punitive Parent. Have someone, such as a co-therapist when using the group modality, stand in for you during absences. Establish a detailed crisis management plan with your client.

Engaged: Try to be fully absorbed in the world of your client and in the relationship between you. Be curious, ask questions, follow up on questions, explore your client's thoughts, feelings, and ideas. Use a tone of voice that mirrors adaptive emotions in the here and now. Try to provide a deeper sense of interest by referring to what your client said in earlier sessions (e.g., "This reminds of when you told me about . . .").

Open and direct: Be responsive, share your personal thoughts and feelings in the here and now if the client asks for them (within healthy limits). Remember that empathic confrontation is helpful when responding to dysfunctional coping modes. Always show transparency and have an open agenda.

Honesty: Always speak the truth. Do not avoid stating potentially painful facts (e.g., if the client asks you if you are angry with him or her, use a Healthy Adult mode and be honest and say yes if you are).

Empathy: Take your client's perspective on a situation, mirror what you see with explicit warmth and care, and understand and experience these emotions when doing so. Reinforce your empathy and understanding by linking current painful experiences and maladaptive coping modes to his or her childhood experiences and early maladaptive schemas.

Nurturing: Show your client warmth and care by tuning into implicit needs in the here and now (e.g., offer your client water if he or she seems thirsty, or give your client a warm hug if he or she seems sad). Try to find ways to show consideration and concern (e.g., by lending your client personal belongings such as literature, films, CDs) that you believe could be helpful to the therapeutic process. Providing your client with such items can also serve the function of a "transitional object" (reinforcing a sense of connectedness).

Praise and love: Try to make your client feel unique and special (e.g., by addressing his or her Vulnerable Child in a personal and loving way (e.g., "You're such a sweet and special person," "You have such a warm-hearted soul," "I was so glad this morning knowing I would get to see you today").

Accepting: Act non-judgmentally and show acceptance for personal flaws in yourself and your client. Quirks and flaws are what make us human. Acceptance is usually the first important step when aiming for healthy change.

Loyalty: Stand up for your client, no matter what (within realistic limits). Never turn your back on him or her, even if he or she has broken agreements you might have made (or agreements your client might have made with others).

Confidentiality: Show absolute trust, unless this has been repeatedly broken over an extended period of time. Share personal secrets (within ethical boundaries) providing a sense of special connection, similar to having secrets with very close friends at school or with family members (e.g., reveal your personal opinion about a person you both know outside treatment). This serves the purpose of making your client feel a special connection in a healthy way, so it should not be spreading destructive rumors.

Target area: balanced efforts/self-compassion

We define self-compassion – a broad theoretical and clinical concept that attracts many researchers and practitioners, hence forming a school of its own – as viewing oneself as valuable and important, and of showing oneself unconditional consideration and care (see also Germer, 2009). Balanced efforts and self-compassion involves having a sense of authenticity and of mutual freedom to express core needs, dreams, desires, and demands in relationships. It also involves valuing leisure and joy and of having reasonable expectations about yourself and your achievements.

Below are examples of specific reparenting strategies that promote the development of balanced efforts and self-compassion.

Playfulness and spontaneity: Provide playfulness and spontaneity. Avoid acting rigidly. Use expressive interventions whenever appropriate, such as painting, role-play, and poetry. Prevent rigid patterns forming in the therapeutic relationship, for example, switch chairs from time to time in the session room, don't always begin every session with the same question (or if you do then make jokes about it). Use "miracle" questions such as "What would you do if you woke up tomorrow and didn't have any relational problems?" Change the session environment if possible later in treatment when the client has reached a stage of safety with you, (e.g., try having a session outside). Be intuitive and creative; use metaphors adapted to your client's life and culture.

Forgiveness: Show understanding and forgiveness if your client acts out in a dysfunctional way (always provide realistic limits). Be open-minded, respectful, and compassionate toward yourself and your client when mistakes occur. We all feel tired, exhausted, or just not in a good mood at times. It is important occasionally to allow oneself an emotional break. Try including a sense of humor in your discussions.

Optimism: Be optimistic; bring in helpful perspectives if you and the client are stuck (e.g., ask a colleague to sit in on a session). If your client has experienced traumatic life events such as the death of a close relative or friend, after expressing compassion, provide nurturance and validate the pain. It can be helpful to remember that outliving traumatic events and existential pain and sorrow can make a person grow stronger, while knowing that first we need to be validated and soothed in our current pain.

Realistic standards: Do not be too hard on your client or on yourself as a therapist, but rather act as a healthy role model for realistic standards. This may be difficult since therapists frequently have some of the "unrelenting standards" schema themselves. Never push your client toward change prematurely. Always be in agreement with each other regarding the process of change and the stage that the client is in. Discuss realistic therapeutic goals that take into consideration the circumstances your client faces on a day-to-day basis. Discuss the role of temperamental factors and their implications for overall treatment outcome.

Encourage and respect your client's emotions: Help your client to listen to and express his or her needs throughout sessions and always solicit and consider input from the Vulnerable Child when making important decisions. Help the client to express intense emotions if he or she feels suppressed (e.g., by stamping his or her foot illustrating how angry he or she feels, while you do the same in order to physically experience some of the frustration your client is feeling).

Communicate hope: Staying connected to your client's Vulnerable Child brings a sense of hope to his or her Vulnerable Child. Feelings of hopelessness are usually something we experience when feeling abandoned and all alone. If your client experiences intense feelings of hopelessness it can be helpful to conduct a connecting imagery exercise, helping your client to reconnect with his or her Vulnerable Child to nurture him or her and provide a sense of hope.

Target area: autonomy

Autonomy is characterized by a sense of confidence in managing life's challenges independently, such as dealing with school or work. Autonomy involves a sense of mastery and faith in personal skills and capacities. Below are examples of specific reparenting strategies that promote the development of autonomy.

Provide direction: Help your client find adaptive ways to handle day-to-day tasks and life situations (e.g., help finding directions on the internet for school assignments, how to deal with carpenters/repair personnel, how to make travel arrangements, and help filling out various application forms).

Emotional and practical support: Adaptive independence involves staying "well connected" and reaching out for help when needed. Don't interfere with your client's need for integrity but always provide emotional and practical support at the near-boundary of his or her knowledge and competency, e.g., if your client has a job application to fill out that he or she finds complicated, then you could say, "Try fill it out as much as you can by yourself at home and bring it to me next session and I'll go through it with you."

Role-play: Role-play new strategies, skills, and/or interpersonal behaviors with your client before he or she needs to use them in real-life situations (e.g., role-play a planned job interview).

Ask your client for advice: Let your client be part of small decisions in your life to make him or her feel important (e.g., ask your client to help choose a new carpet for your office, or suggest a good book to read).

Let the client take the lead: Let your client set the agenda (within realistic limits). Let your client design his or her own homework assignments. Ask the client to decide when he or she wants to begin thinking of ending the therapy. Let your client explore life goals (a personal vision) tailored to his or her personal interests and values.

Feedback and praise: Give constructive feedback on assignments. Recognize and praise successful achievements, and praise your client for having tried even if he or she fails. Give personal praise but always try to take your client's perspective (e.g., "What an excellent homework assignment you've done – I'm amazed, you should be proud of yourself, especially considering how little help your Vulnerable Child has had over the years").

Encourage independent actions: Encourage your client to act independently when appropriate (e.g., later in treatment, have a short break in the therapy to allow your client to practice being independent of you and relying on his or her Healthy Adult mode).

Target area: structure and limits

Having internalized adaptive structure and limits is characterized by a feeling of being in balanced control (emotionally, behaviorally, and cognitively) and of having a clear sense of how things fit together (temporal order of events). It involves being able to see the "big picture," to place situations in a larger context (meta-capacities). It involves being disciplined, organized, and focused. It involves tolerating frustrations within realistic limits and of having empathy and reciprocity in relationships. Below are some examples of specific reparenting strategies that promote the internalization of adaptive structure and limits.

Emotional distress management: Help your client to act and express strong emotions adaptively. Let the client vent frustration. As a therapist, validate the client's justified feelings, show empathy with underlying maladaptive schemas, reframe the situation correctly if distorted, help the client to see how his or her behavior might have negative consequences (e.g., anger makes people withdraw, leaving the client feeling abandoned), share your personal experience of your client's behaviors, role-play adaptive expressions of your client's current needs.

Meta-level shift: Pause during the sessions if your client is emotionally upset or aroused and practice mindful meditation in order to reset and recenter the mind, to help your client to diffuse from painful and/or destructive child modes and/or coping modes and "flip" into a Healthy Adult mode (i.e., facilitate a meta-level shift of attention).

Empathic limit-setting of an impulsive mode: Avoid trying to impose limits (unless safety is involved) when your client is emotionally distressed. Approach limit-setting by taking the perspective of the impulsive side (e.g., say "If you keep talking without letting others get a word in, they will become frustrated and stop listening to you, and I know you get upset when no one pays attention to what you have to say"). If you try to make the client see the perspective of others when in Impulsive Child mode (e.g., "If you talk all of the time, then no one else gets to say anything") it will most likely backfire and the client will feel invalidated and misunderstood.

Teaching delay strategies: Encourage your client to practice delaying sharing his or her thoughts and emotions with you until he/she has taken the time to reflect on them. For example, if your client has a pattern of asking you for advice excessively or of "dumping" things on you to reduce distress in the here and now, then you can ask your client to wait until the following session, reassuring him or her that you will respond then. You can also ask your client to write down his or her current thoughts and feelings and reflect on them at home before the next session. It is important to be transparent in your approach to this work, explaining ahead of time why you are doing this so that it can be collaborative and not experienced as invalidating.

Discipline: Help your client to establish routines and to be disciplined in his or her everyday life (e.g., by eating and sleeping at regular hours, doing laundry and house hold chores on a regular basis).

Responsibility to others: You can help your client develop a sense of responsibility for others by starting with very small things such as taking care of flowers, aquarium fish, etc.

Be organized: Be a good role model and keep organized; prevent your office from being a mess (but avoid having it pristine). Make sure that your client keeps a session notebook for homework assignments and a folder for worksheets and exercises.

Reflect collaboratively: Help your client to balance being present in the here and now with reflection and planning. Pause every once in a while during the session and let your client make short summaries, reflect together on what has been said and on current feelings and thoughts. Ask your client if there is something he or she would like to do differently before continuing with the topic of the session.

Be strong and decisive: Many clients, like young children, need a strong parent figure who is sure of him or herself and decisive, who follows through with what has been said, but not in a rigid way. Keep the therapeutic process on a steady path, show strength and endurance, but do not set unrelenting standards for yourself and expect never to falter in this. We also need to continue to be role models of being imperfect humans (which is not difficult for most of us).

Pitfalls and Tips

There are various potential pitfalls in psychotherapy – the therapist having maladaptive schemas and modes activated during sessions, sexual feelings arising within the therapeutic relationship, the therapist lacking an adaptive crisis management plan, the therapist not having guidelines for termination with difficult clients. These pitfalls are all likely to create significant emotional distress for the therapist. In the following section we have listed a few pitfalls that we have experienced and that other Schema Therapists might step into, with tips on how to either prevent each pitfall or learn from them.

Therapist schemas and modes being triggered

Unresolved maladaptive schemas and modes of the therapist might interfere negatively with the treatment process, causing emotional distress on both sides. Below are some examples of therapeutic pitfalls related to therapist maladaptive schemas and modes.

Avoidant Coping mode: If the therapist has an avoidant coping pattern it may prevent him or her from being open and direct with the client or addressing "hot topics" as they arise during sessions. Avoidance on the part of the therapist can prevent the development of a healthy therapeutic process. This can make the client openly frustrated, further reinforcing the therapist's avoidant coping. An increase in client frustration might also run the risk of activating maladaptive schemas linked to the avoidant coping, such as abandonment or failure, which will add to the emotional distress of both client and therapist.

Over-Compensating mode: A therapist that is over-compensating for various maladaptive schemas might, in contrast to an avoidant coping therapist, be too confrontational. A therapist over-compensating in response to a failure schema might be quick to point out and criticize clients for not being able to follow through on assignments. A therapist over-compensating for a defectiveness schema might make the client feel flawed when revealing private thoughts and behaviors that the therapist dislikes within him- or herself. A therapist over-compensating for emotional deprivation might start getting angry at the client for not seeing his or her needs (e.g., ending the session in order to get home on time). A therapist over-compensating a mistrust/abuse schema might fail to set healthy limits for the client, placing them both in potentially dangerous situations. A therapist with over-compensation issues that are not cared for in a healthy manner will run the risk of becoming stressed and burned-out due to ongoing schema activation during sessions.

Compliant Coping mode: A therapist with a compliant coping style, (i.e. surrendering to his or her schemas) will run the risk of burn-out due to not setting necessary limits and/or not standing up for his or her own needs. A therapist surrendering to a failure schema might put the blame on him- or herself during sessions if the client is not making progress instead of placing realistic responsibility on the client for not following through on his or her part of the work. A therapist with mistrust/abuse issues might allow clients to criticize and bully him or her instead of setting realistic limits (e.g., when working with narcissists). A therapist surrendering to a self-sacrifice schema might foster client dependency and eventually have difficulty meeting the client's level or range of needs.

Demanding Parent mode: Many professionals find a Demanding Parent to be adaptive in certain situations (e.g., at school, when working to meet deadlines, or to complete detail-oriented tasks). However, an ever-present internal Demanding Parent can rob a therapist of job satisfaction, lead to unnecessary frustration with progress or duration of therapy, and undermine therapist confidence and feelings of mastery. This dysfunctional Parent mode can also cause a therapist to have an imbalance in work vs. pleasurable and relationship activities – another route to burn-out.

Tips for the therapist on how to handle personal maladaptive schemas and modes

The best way for a Schema Therapist to overcome the risk of maladaptive coping modes interfering when conducting therapy is to seek personal therapy (see Part V, Chapter 3). Training requirements of having personal therapy to become a licensed psychotherapist vary internationally. It is therefore preferable that all Schema Therapists during training seek a certified Schema Therapist for personal therapy, or at least for a focused life history assessment of maladaptive schemas and modes. If a Schema Therapist experiences ongoing emotional distress, or shows symptoms of becoming burned out, then filling out questionnaires such as the YPI, YSQ, or SMI could be a helpful start. The therapist can discuss the results with a certified ST supervisor and receive adaptive assistance. We also suggest that practicing Schema Therapists prevent themselves from falling into dysfunctional patterns by having regular access to supervision and/or being part of a peer supervision group. Professional and peer supervision are both important ways for therapists to get needs met (e.g., validation, confidence-building, constructive feedback, reinforced competence, acceptance).

Sexual feelings within the therapeutic relationship

"How do I respond to a client falling in love with me? How do I deal with having sexual feelings toward my client?"

ST often involves forming an attachment bond with the client as part of the healing process (i.e., by providing limited reparenting). As in any close and nurturing relationship (e.g., a healthy parent–child relationship), genuine closeness will evoke intense feelings of warmth, care, and (non-sexual) love. In ST this is a desired effect when treating clients with attachment disorders. However, forming attachment bonds with adult patients also runs the risk of evoking sexual feelings. In contrast to a parent attaching to his or her infant child, the therapist attaching to an adult client involves connecting with the Vulnerable Child part of an adult with a fully developed sexuality. A client, in particular one who has experienced the sexualization of bonding from childhood sexual abuse, may only know unhealthy and sexualized ways of connecting and use these with the therapist. A client who has not experienced the nonsexual love of a parent may experience "falling in love" with the therapist or express various kinds of sexual feelings or fantasies toward the therapist. This always needs to be addressed, discussed, and understood in therapy sessions. Appropriate professional limits must be made clear in a gentle manner that acknowledges the mixture of child and adult needs. Our experience from supervision is that this is sometimes a difficult issue for the therapist and a source of emotional distress.

General guidelines on how to respond to sexual feelings directed toward the therapist

1. Let the client express his or her sexual feelings toward you openly, but without allowing them to relate detailed sexual fantasies.
2. Validate the client's feelings as understandable adult feelings in a close relationship.
3. Empathize with the client's longing for intimacy.
4. Set appropriate limits by stating that you feel for the Vulnerable Child part of the client in the way a healthy parent loves and cares for his or her child and as with a healthy parent, these feelings are not sexual. Explicitly communicate that there will never be any sexual interaction between you.
5. Show empathy with the part of the client that might feel rejected or embarrassed because of their feelings. Be alert for the Punitive Parent mode to criticize or humiliate the client and challenge that mode.
6. Reassure the client's Vulnerable Child that you will not abandon him or her. Remind your client that thoughts and feelings are not actions and need not be judged negatively.

Although rarely reported, psychotherapists do at times have sexual feelings for their clients and sometimes also act on them. If this happens, then the therapist is seriously violating ethical boundaries and existing laws and the situation has to be handled according to national regulations. Within the International Society for Schema Therapy (ISST) there is a committee, the 3C (Current Concerns and Conflicts) workgroup, that can assist Schema Therapists who are handling difficult ethical issues. In addition, patients and/or therapists can contact 3C if they are aware of any ethical violations by a certified Schema Therapist.

Vicarious traumatization

One risk in working with patients who have endured significant trauma is the experience of vicarious traumatization. This phenomenon has begun to attract more attention in recent years (Pross, 2006). The symptoms are similar to those of post-traumatic stress disorder and include feeling anxious or fearful when seeing or thinking about a particular patient and their story, wanting to avoid that client or thinking about their trauma, and intrusive thoughts and images of a client's trauma experience. They may also include sleep and concentration difficulties. In ST terms, our own Vulnerable Child mode can be activated and overwhelmed by the intensity of emotional experiences related by the patient. A Vulnerable Child state, including horror, helplessness, nausea, and the urge to avoid the histories triggering these feelings can occur. Therapists at highest risk for vicarious traumatization are those who utilize high empathy and those with personal histories of trauma.

Managing this involves much conscious self-nurturing, such as: relaxation exercises, aromatherapy, a hot drink, permission to grieve for the harm done to another, acknowledging and tolerating the helplessness of not being able to prevent the trauma, and generating hope to help that client in the present. Personal therapy or group supervision can be very helpful. Imagery work for the therapist's Vulnerable Child, having your Healthy Adult comfort and soothe your Vulnerable Child, can be helpful. It is also helpful to find and do the things that help fill your "well" of energy, creativity, and self-confidence. The use of protective imagery that allows a therapist to stay present while protecting their own heart is another option. An example would be to create an image of a cocoon that protects your emotional boundaries while allowing you to be present.

Suicidal issues

When a client expresses suicidal ideation it can trigger many emotions, schemas, or modes in the therapist. Again, self-awareness is key; take a moment and look for schemas of failure, unrelenting standards, self-sacrifice, subjugation, and dysfunctional coping modes. Contemplate the truths that many clients struggle with severe depression, tragic life histories, and insufficient resources, and their symptoms are at times beyond the direct control of themselves or their therapists. Avoid the pitfall of judging your skill as a therapist by the symptom level of severely ill clients. Most importantly, make arrangements that represent the best care for the safety of the client, yourself, and your staff. It is a fact that the suicide rate of persons with borderline personality disorder far exceeds that of the general population (10% completed suicide rate; Lieb, Zanarini, Schmahl, Linehan and Bohus, 2004). A client completing suicide is a critical moment that illustrates the need for therapist self-care. Be certain to contact a supervisor in these instances to reflect on one's own activated schemas and modes; but also to reflect on the positive moments with that client, the frustrating moments, and what you have learned from the experience of being involved in their treatment. Allow yourself time to grieve.

Terminating therapy with difficult clients

As discussed above, it is not realistic to expect every therapist to have a natural bond with every client. Sometimes a therapist may sense a difficulty in bonding from the first meeting; at other times therapy may have begun but is on a very "bumpy" course. Finding that one's own temperament and reparenting style are not suited to a particular client can be a triumph of personal awareness and refusal to surrender to a failure schema. The key is to remember that the goal is client recovery and relief from symptoms and maladaptive life patterns. If you come to the realization that transferring the client to another therapist is advisable, take action sooner rather than later. When addressing this with clients, disclose your thought process and emphasize your desire for their growth and recovery. Support the client's grief or other reactions to your decision in an empathic manner, but gently and firmly make it clear that while you can no longer see them, you will assist them in finding another therapist or treatment center. This is another area where supervision can be a useful "reality check" to ensure that other mechanisms (e.g., an avoidance coping mode) are in place, and also to validate, support, and encourage the therapist's personal growth. Remember that as therapists, we need realistic limits as well.

Conclusion

Therapist self-care is an important but underdeveloped area of investigation. Applying the therapeutic principles of Schema Therapy to ourselves as well as our clients is one way to ensure that we meet our own emotional needs, which allows us to be "healthy parents" for our clients. Using the exercises suggested here can increase self-awareness and expand feelings of competence by using realistic limits. As we model the Healthy Adult for our clients, let us also reach for the positive growth within ourselves, valuing our own relationships, our insight and understanding of ourselves, philosophical change (Linley, Joseph and Loumidis, 2005), and heightened compassion for ourselves and others. We hope that you have found this a practical guide to limited reparenting and self-care in the spirit of Schema Therapy. Remember that we must use the same warmth and empathy we utilize with our clients for ourselves, and with each other. Let us accept responsibility for our self-nurturing, and as a collective continue to learn and grow in our lives and in our practice.

References

Bateman, A. and Fonagy, P. (2004) *Psychotherapy for Borderline Personality Disorder: Mentalization-based Treatment.* New York: Oxford University Press.

Boscarino, J.A., Adams, R.E. and Figley, C.R. (2010) Secondary trauma issues for psychiatrists. *Psychiatric Times, 27*(11).

Cassell, E.J. (2004) *The Nature of Suffering and the Goals of Medicine.* New York: Oxford University Press.

Germer, C.K. (2009) *The Mindful Path to Self-Compassion: Freeing Yourself from Destructive Thoughts and Emotions.* New York: Guilford Press.

Lieb, K., Zanarini, M.C., Schmahl, C., Linehan, M.M. and Bohus, M. (2004) Borderline personality disorder. *Lancet*, *364*(9432): 453–461.

Linehan, M.M. (1993) *Cognitive Behavioral Treatment of Borderline Personality Disorder*. New York: Guilford Press.

Linley, P.A., Joseph, S. and Loumidis, K. (2005) Trauma work, sense of coherence, and positive and negative changes in therapists. *Psychotherapy and Psychosomatics*, *74*(3): 185–188.

Pross, C. (2006) Burnout, vicarious traumatization and its prevention. *Torture*, *16*(1): 1–9.

Young, J. and Klosko, J. S. (1993) *Reinventing Your Life*. New York: Penguin.

Young, J., Klosko, J.S. and Weishaar, M. (2003) *Schema Therapy: a Practitioner's Guide*. New York: Guilford Press.

Part VI
Research in Schema Therapy

1
Effectiveness Studies

Lotte Bamelis, Josephine Bloo, David Bernstein and Arnoud Arntz

Schema Therapy (ST) is a treatment method that has gained a lot of popularity in the last decade. This combination of cognitive-behavioral, interpersonal, psychodynamic, and experiential techniques, originating in the US, is also used for patients with personality disorders in the Netherlands and seems promising. However, empirical support for the efficacy of ST remains rare. Even though a randomized controlled trial (RCT) from a methodological point of view is the gold standard to study clinical effectiveness and cost-effectiveness, a search through the literature reveals that such designs are not carried out very often. There is a great demand for controlled empirical efficacy studies.

In this chapter, the authors describe the most important results of the studies that have been published thus far, with the focus on implications for clinical practice. They distinguish between studies in which the treatment is primarily focused on personality problems and studies in which the focus is on the treatment of Axis I disorders.

Schema Therapy for Personality Disorders

Thus far, the efficacy of Schema Therapy has mainly been investigated for borderline personality disorders (BPD). Study results regarding BPD are discussed first, followed by a summary of the evidence for other personality disorders.

Schema therapy for borderline personality disorders

Over the last years, several publications have been published in which an outline of the treatment methodology per schema mode for BPD were described (e.g., Young,

Table 1.1 Evidence for the efficacy of Schema Therapy for borderline personality disorder

Authors	Year of publication	Design	Outcome
Nordahl and Nysaeter	2005	Single-case series, $N = 6$ Duration of individual therapy: weekly, average 22 months	Five persons improved significantly on depression and anxiety symptoms, general psychopathology, and interpersonal dysfunction. Maladaptive schemas reduce significantly (ES = 1.6)
Giesen-Bloo, et al.	2006	RCT, $N = 86$ ST compared with TFP Duration of individual therapy, twice weekly for three years	Both treatments show significant clinical improvements, ST on all measures dominant compared with TFP. In Schema Therapy lower risk of premature dropout
Nadort, et al.	2009	Randomized two-group design, $N = 62$ ST with extra phone support compared with ST without extra phone support. Duration of therapy two years, twice weekly in year 1, and once weekly in year 2	After 18 months, 42% lost BPD diagnosis. Extra 24-hour phone support has no effect on the outcomes
Farrell, Shaw and Webber	2009	RCT, $N = 32$ women Groups ST + TAU compared with TAU only TAU weekly (individual psychotherapy, eclectic and supportive) ST + TAU 30 extra group sessions in eight months	ST + TAU group had significant lower scores on BPS symptoms and on the global odds of psychiatric symptoms, and higher GAF scores compared with TAU only. No dropout in ST + TAU group

BPD = borderline personality disorder; ES = effect size; GAF = global assessment of functioning; N = number of patients; ST = schema-focused therapy; TFP = transference-focused therapy; TAU = treatment as usual

2005; Kellogg and Young, 2006). These publications offer a clear overview about how the treatment can be carried out, but don't provide evidence as to whether the treatment is effective. Table 1.1 summarizes the scientific evidence regarding the efficacy of ST for BPD.

The outcomes of a single-case series design from Norway provide a first indication of the efficacy of ST (Nordahl and Nysaeter, 2005). Analyses showed a strong reduction in the power of maladaptive schemas and improvements in secondary outcome measures. Furthermore, progress observed directly after the therapy continued in the follow-up monitoring. However, this study does have to be interpreted with caution.

Using a single-case design in which only one therapist uses the schema model makes it impossible to generalize to a larger group. Furthermore, the post-treatment assessment and follow-up were not carried out by independent evaluators, which may have influenced the validity of the outcomes. Therefore, this study offers an indication of ST as a valid evidence-based treatment method, but it provides no concrete evidence.

This evidence is offered by an RCT into the efficacy of ST for borderline personality disorder (BPD) (Giesen-Bloo et al., 2006). In a two-group design, ST was compared with transference-focused psychotherapy (TFP). Eighty-six people with BPD were randomly assigned to one of two treatment conditions and received protocolized outpatient treatment two sessions a week for three years. Both ST and TFP resulted in significant clinical improvements in several domains, for example, a decrease of specific borderline symptoms, an improvement in the quality of life, and an improvement in the field of general psychopathologic functioning. However, ST was dominant compared to TPF for all outcome measures. Furthermore, there was a lower risk of dropout from the treatment in the ST condition. This is noteworthy for this population, because the risk of dropout is very high for borderline patients.

In Giesen-Bloo et al. (2006), some of the possible strong points of the schema model for BPD are described: 1) the transparency of the model; 2) the specific reparenting attitude of the therapist regarding attachment problems; 3) the use of techniques that are easy to implement and strategies that provide control, structure, and safety; and 4) the possibility to contact the therapist between sessions. This study also show the therapeutic alliance (which has a positive influence on the inner changing processes) is rated higher by both patients and therapists in the ST condition than in the TFP condition.

Recently, Nadort and colleagues (2009) completed an implementation study in which they investigated, alongside the implementation of the borderline protocol in daily practice, whether providing 24-hour telephone support or no 24-hour telephone support had any effect on outcome. The most important results of this study were 1) successful implementation is possible, given that more than half of the patients no longer met the criteria of a BPD after 1.5 years; and 2) telephone support additional to the ST protocol had no effect (see Part VII, Chapter 1 for more detailed outcomes of this study).

In summary, it can be said that the efficacy of ST for BPD is scientifically underpinned. However, it should be noted that results were obtained from only a small number of studies and therefore should be interpreted with caution. Furthermore, there are some critical comments on Giesen-Bloo et al.'s (2006) RCT. The trial was checked statistically regarding the use of medication, but not experimentally, and they didn't use a waiting list condition or a TAU (Treatment as Usual) condition. Even after an intensive long-term treatment, it seemed that almost one-third of the subjects were still receiving treatment. However, the intensity of treatment sessions had been reduced: after four years, more than 60% of the ST patients received less than one treatment session per week, whereas 50% received only one session every three weeks (booster sessions). The average number of sessions in the ST condition was significantly lower than in the TPF condition (Giesen-Bloo et al., 2006).

Farrell, Shaw, and Webber (2009) compared the combination of TAU and group SFT with only TAU in a group of 32 women (aged between 22 and 52 years) with

BPD. All patients had already received TAU (a weekly individual supporting therapy) previous to study enrolment, and were randomly assigned to a group SFT (30 sessions in eight months) or to a control group. The post-treatment assessment showed significantly lower scores for the severity of BPD symptoms, as well as higher global functioning in the combined condition. These scores were clinically significant and stable in the follow-up after six months. Effect sizes within the combined group were very high, and approximately zero in the TAU alone condition. It was also remarkable that not a single patient dropped out in the combined condition, whereas four patients (25%) were dropouts in the TAU condition.

An open study into the effects of clinical group ST of the same group again showed significant effects (Reiss and Farrell, 2010).

An open pilot study into residential group treatment for BPS in Mainz showed much weaker effects. However, a clear learning curve was noticeable: groups that started later in time showed better results (Reiss, Lieb and Vogel, 2010).

Schema therapy for other personality disorders

Whereas the research into the efficacy of ST for BPD is still in its infancy, there is even less evidence-based proof for other personality disorders. No scientific study with a strong design has been published so far. However, a lot is happening in this field. In the Netherlands, two ambitious studies into the efficacy of ST are currently being conducted, in which the focus is on milder personality disorders, on the one hand, and forensic psychiatry on the other.

Schema therapy for milder personality disorders

Since the middle of 2006, Bamelis and colleagues have been carrying out a large-scale effectiveness study in which both the clinical and cost-effectiveness of ST are compared with TAU for people with one or more of the six milder personality disorders (avoidant, dependent, obsessive-compulsive, paranoid, histrionic, and narcissistic). Three hundred subjects were selected in 12 Dutch healthcare institutes, and randomly assigned to either a ST protocol consisting of 50 sessions or a treatment that is common for the specific personality disorder within the respective institute.

A few schema modes that are characteristic for this population were developed (Avoiding Protector, Paranoid Over-Controller). In the first year, ST sessions are held once a week, and then booster sessions take place in the second year. The frequency and content of the TAU condition vary depending on what is common within the respective outpatient setting.

In three institutes, patients are additionally randomly assigned to a third protocol treatment: clarification-oriented psychotherapy, according to the model developed by Sachse. By adding this standardized protocol, it is possible within this design to compare two standardized protocol treatments and so thus reducing the possible effect of non-specific factors. Patients in this study have a baseline measurement, and accordingly extensive assessments every six months. Three years after the start of treatment, there is a follow-up assessment.

Table 1.2 Efficacy studies into Schema Therapy for other personality disorders

Authors	Year of publication	Design	Research population
Bamelis et al.	In progress	RCT, N = 300 Schema Therapy compared with TAU and clarification-oriented psychotherapy according to Sachse Duration: individual treatment two years, twice a year assessment, one-year follow-up	Target group = Cluster C, paranoid, histrionic, and narcissistic personality disorders Recruitment in 12 Dutch mental healthcare institutes
Bernstein et al.	In progress	RCT, N = 120 ST compared with forensic TAU Duration individual treatment three years, twice a year assessment, three-year follow-up	Target group = Cluster B personality disorder in a forensic setting Recruitment in seven Dutch high-security forensic institutions
Weertman and Arntz	2007	Cross over design, N = 21 (from mental healthcare institutes) Techniques focused on present compared with techniques focused on the past Duration individual treatment 48 sessions, one-year follow-up	Comparable outcome for focus on present and focus on past Therapists and patients prefer to start with focus on the past Effect is visible in follow-up after one year
Hahusseau and Pélissolo	2006	Naturalistic study, N = 14 patients in outpatient care Duration treatment 13 months	Target group = Cluster B and C Significant improvement in all outcome measurements
Zorn et al.	2007	RCT, N = 93 (from mental healthcare) Schema-oriented emotional-behavioral treatment (SET) compared with social skills training	Target group = Cluster B and C, mainly narcissistic PS Outcome: SET dominant on clinical outcome measurements and lower dropout

The primary outcome measures are: no longer meeting the diagnosis of personality disorder and a reduction of the symptoms. Several secondary outcome measures are studied: quality of life, general psychological functioning, social functioning, and specific schema-related concepts.

The personality disorders mentioned in the Bamelis study have not yet been approached as a primary treatment focus in scientific publications. Every now and then, they appear in studies as comorbid problems alongside certain Axis I symptoms (see below). Some exceptions are a case description by Cecero and Young (2001) and a naturalistic study by Hahusseau and Pélissolo (2006). In Cecero and Young, the treatment process of a female patient who has a dependent PD, besides depression and an anxiety disorder, is described. First, depression and anxiety were reduced by means of cognitive behavioral techniques. Following this, a schema-focused case conceptualization was made with the patient. The patient found more and more evidence for maladaptive schemas by implementing experiential techniques and by identifying schema-specific behavior during treatment sessions. The central change process consisted of four strategies: 1) cognitive schema reorganization; 2) experiential techniques; 3) breaking behavioral patterns; and 4) the use of the therapeutic alliance.

In an explorative study, Hahusseau and Pélissolo (2006) followed 14 psychiatric patients (mainly Cluster C and B), who received an average of 26 ST consultsations over a little more than a year (the most important techniques were emotional catharsis and the use of corrective emotional experiences). Outcomes showed significant improvement on the primary outcome measurement (social adaption scale), as well as improvement on outcome measurements regarding anxiety, depression, and general psychopathology.

Weertman and Arntz (2007) showed that experiential techniques that focused on the past (e.g., historic role-play and imagery rescripting) had the same positive effect as techniques that focused on the present. Exploring the background of the problems had no, or even a negative, effect. The effect size of the complete program was large, with an average of approximately 1.5.

Schema Therapy in a forensic setting

There is a high need to adapt schema therapy to forensic patients with a personality disorder.

Bernstein, Arntz, and de Vos (2007) described a schema mode model for forensic patients with Cluster B personality disorders (anti-social, narcissistic, and borderline). This model consists of forensic modes (e.g., Angry Protector, Bully and Attack, Conning and Manipulative, and Predator). Bernstein and colleagues have set up a multi-center RCT for patients with Cluster B personality disorders in several Dutch forensic psychiatric institutes.

In the study, 120 patients are randomized into two treatment conditions: ST and the usual forensic treatment. Patients receive individual treatment for three years. In the ST condition, patients have a session twice per week. In the TAU condition, the contact with social workers occurs once per week. TAU within forensic institutes is multi-modal: patients normally receive both individual and group therapy, combined with education, rehabilitation, and other services.

In this study, the primary outcome measures are change in personality disorders and risk of relapse, which is monitored every six months. General psychopathology and changes in early maladaptive schemas and schema modes are secondary outcome measures. After the treatment phase, patients are followed for another three years in order to determine current relapse (or, if applicable, violence within the institute).

Currently, seven forensic institutes are participating. Expectations are that the follow-up study will end in 2014.

Apart from the RCTs mentioned above, for which outcomes aren't yet available, there are hardly any studies into the effectiveness of ST for personality disorders other than borderline. Although scientific research into the efficacy of ST is still scarce and currently finds itself in the implementing phase, there are indications that ST can offer effective added value. Richardson (2005) shows that there are persistent maladaptive schemas present in a group of young sexually violence perpetrators: demanding/grandeur, egocentrism, social isolation, emotional inhibition, and insufficient self-control/discipline. Psycho-education and social skills training seem to produce no significant and long-term change. ST might offer a solution.

Schema Therapy in groups for personality disorders

Originally, ST was intended as an outpatient and individual approach, but it has also been modified for a group-focused approach.

A study in which schema-focused emotional-behavioral group therapy (SET) was compared with classic social skills training for 93 subjects with a Cluster B or C diagnosis (in particular narcissistic personality disorder), showed that the schema–focused group achieved more progress in the field of interpersonal behavior, emotional coping, and symptom reduction. Clinically relevant effects of the ST group were the reduced severity of and suffering from the disorder, and a significant decrease in dropout rates (Zorn, Roder, Muller, Tschacher and Thommen, 2007).

In Norway, two RCTs are currently being carried out, in which group ST in day treatment is compared with the usual treatment, for subjects with borderline personality disorder on the one hand, and subjects with an avoidant personality disorder on the other (Fosse, in progress). There are 48 subjects in each study group. The first outcomes are promising. In the Netherlands, a pilot study into group ST for borderline personality disorders is being carried out, in which there are two sessions a week – one group session and one individual session (Dickhaut and Arntz, in progress). Intermediate outcomes show large effect sizes. Positive elements in a group treatment can be: great involvement of other group members, the possibility for recognition, and actual setting for direct practice (Thunissen and Muste, 2002).

Schema Therapy for Axis I Problems

Initially, ST was developed for treatment of people with personality disorders, in which underlying schemas are very rigid, implicit, and extremely dysfunctional. Because of the success with Axis II problems, interest rose to study the relevance of this therapy method for various Axis I problems. Relatively little high quality scientific research has been conducted in this field. The publications thus far are described as complete as possible below. After a summary in Table 1.3, both strong and weak points of the studies are described.

Schema Therapy for substance dependency and abuse

A variation of ST that is implemented in substance abuse and comorbid personality disorders, is Dual Focus Schema Therapy (DFST) (Ball, 1998). This treatment

Table 1.3 Evidence for the efficacy of Schema Therapy in Axis I problems

Authors	Year	Target Group	Design	Outcome
Ball and Young	2000	Substance abuse and at least one PS	Case study, $N = 10$ Duration: 24 sessions	Reduction of substance abuse, psychiatric symptoms, and negative affect
Ball, Cobb-Richardson, Connolly, Bujosa and O'Neall	2005	Substance abuse in homeless people with personality problems	RCT, $N = 52$ DFST compared with standard group counseling Duration: 24 sessions	DFST dominant on almost all outcome measures However, more severe personality problems profit more from counseling
Ball	2007	Substance abuse with personality problems	RCT, $N = 30$ DFST compared with standard group counseling Duration: 24 sessions	Faster reduction of substance abuse in DFST condition Faster reduction in the degree of dysphoria in group counseling Stronger therapeutic alliance in DFST
Ball 2011		Substance abuse with personality problems	RCT, $N = 105$ DFST compared with individual group counseling	Equal symptom reduction in both conditions, individual drug counseling resulted in more sustained reduction in several symptoms
Morrison	2000	Depression and anxieties	Single-case design Duration individual therapy 3 years and 6 months, 73 sessions	Fluctuation in mood during the treatment Reduction of depression, anxieties, and maladaptive schemas to a normal clinical level at the end of treatment and after one-year follow-up
Hoffart, Versland and Sexton	2002	Panic disorder agoraphobia with comorbid Cluster C problems	$N = 35$ Duration: 11 weeks	Obvious change in Cluster C features, interpersonal problems, awareness of affect
Gude and Hoffart	2008	Agoraphobia with comorbid Cluster C problems	$N = 44$ Standard compared with cognitive ST Duration: 12 weeks	Strong reduction in interpersonal problems in ST condition
Ball, Mitchell, Malhi, Skillecorn and Smith 2006		Bipolar symptoms	RCT Individual CT with ST elements compared with TAU Duration: 6 months, 20 sessions	Depression scores and dysfunctional attitudes diminished more in CT condition Greater time to relapse in CT condition

Table 1.3 (*Continued*)

Authors	Year	Target Group	Design	Outcome
Cockram, Drummond and Lee	2010	PTSD	$N = 54$ PTSD with ST group compared with cognitive behavioral therapy group Duration: 190 hours, 12 weeks	Stronger reduction of anxiety, PTSD, and depression complaints in PTSD ST group Strong reduction of maladaptive schemas
De Keijser	2004	Mourning problems	$N = 1$ Duration: individual therapy: 3 years, 60 sessions	Decrease in the mourning questionnaire scores
Ohanian	2002	Bulimia nervosa	$N = 1$ Duration: individual therapy: 8 sessions CBT, 1 session rescripting	Binge-eating and purging stopped completely after imagery rescripting Results continued until follow-up
George et al.	2004	Eating disorders	$N = 8$ Motivating day treatment with SFT elements	Improved mood, increased will to change, physical improvement
Jakes and Rhodes	2003	Psychotic symptoms	$N = 5$ Single-case design, individual therapy	Significant reduction of belief in the illusion, increase of self-image

method simultaneously focuses on dealing with the Axis I symptomatology and on changing maladaptive schemas and assumptions. Schemas frequently found in substance abusers are Insufficient Self-Control, Mistrust and Abuse, Self-Sacrifice, Abandonment, and Emotional Inhibition. Although addiction is the primary focus of the treatment, schema conceptualization and mapping maladaptive coping mechanisms are considered to be essential items of therapy in order to reduce the risks of relapses.

DFST consists of two phases: 1) early relapse prevention, schema case conceptualization and training; and 2) change of maladaptive schemas and coping styles.

Ball and Young (2000) completed a case-study report of 10 patients with a substance abuse diagnosis and one or more personality disorders. In addition, patients received a 24-session during DSFT treatment, in which the focus was on standard schema work, but with the possible addition of a schema mode module. Positive results were described in the analyses (see Table 1.3). Eight of the 10 patients described DFST as the best and most useful treatment method they had ever received.

Table 1.3 also describes the results of the effectiveness of DFST in two small-scale RCTs. It is remarkable that DFST appeared to be dominant in the therapeutic alliance (Ball, 2007). This is important because substance abusers are usually characterized by a high dropout rate.

However, caution is in order: although most outcome measures provided better results in DFST, it seemed that dysphoria was strongly reduced by the other treatment method (12 step facility therapy in Ball, 2007a) and patients with more severe personality disorders gained more benefit from group counseling (Ball, Cobb-Richardson, Connolly, Bujosa and O'Neall, 2005).

An RCT for 115 adolescents and adults with substance abuse and criminal problems also produced mixed findings. Patients were assigned at random to DFST or to individual substance counseling. Although symptoms reduced in both groups, individual counseling was dominant over DFST regarding sustained reduction of psychiatric symptoms and dysphoric affect. These data suggest that PD patients with significant affect instability, impulsivity, and avoidance might have more stabilizing benefit from addiction-focused treatment than from insight- and change-oriented therapies (Ball, Maccarelli, LaPaglia & Ostrowski, 2011).

A critical comment on the outcomes of the studies mentioned above is the difficult comparison between treatment conditions: individual vs. group treatment, differences in frequency of sessions and supervision of clinicians. These are some uncontrolled nonspecific studies which may influence the outcomes.

Schema Therapy in mood and anxiety disorders

Although there is no scientific evidence, several authors have described how schema mode work can have a positive influence on depression (e.g., Young and Mattila, 2002; Bordelon, 2007).

In a single-case study by Morrison (2000), the positive outcomes for a patient who struggled with severe depression and anxieties at the beginning of the therapy are described. The treatment consisted of a combination of standardized cognitive behavioral therapy and ST.

Throughout the treatment, strong mood swings were observed, probably the result of schema activations. The positive outcomes at the end of treatment – a decrease in symptoms to a normal clinical level – were repeated at the follow-up monitoring after a year. Offering booster sessions on a regular base after an intensive treatment seemed to have a positive effect on learning how to let go of the therapeutic alliance and to take more personal responsibility.

Ball, Mitchell, Malhi, Skillecorn, and Smith (2003) propose a modified ST specifically focused on the treatment of subjects with bipolar mood disorders. By focusing on early childhood experiences, personality, and the nature of a patient, ST provides additional value to the traditional treatment method for bipolar mood disorders, which is based on the role of genetic and biological risk factors in combination with stressful life-events. In the modified ST, three phases are described:

1. *Sickness phase*, in which the focus is on reducing prominent symptoms and the experience of the diagnosis by the patient.
2. *Schema phase*, in which core schemas are detected. Frequent schemas in bipolar mood problems are: shame, failure, subjugation. After the patient learns, through emotional empathy and validation of the schemas, that his behavior and emotions are understandable, further treatment reveals whether the current schemas are adaptive or not.

3. *Sickness and schema phase*: this last phase works on assimilation of the patient with the mood disorder diagnosis (focusing on the past, and plans for the future). Building up a healthy self-concept is the main focus.

Recently, an RCT has been carried out in Sydney, Australia. In this study, the ST modification, is compared with TAU, while both treatment groups also received mood stabilizers. Outcomes are in favour of the ST modification (see Table 1.3), especially immediately after treatment, and indicate a further reduction of symptoms in the following months (Ball et al., 2006).

A recent study by Cockram, Drummond, and Lee (2010) of 54 war veterans showed the superiority of ST for treatment of subjects with post-traumatic stress disorder (PTSD). The subjects followed a PTSD group program in which ST was integrated, and were compared with 127 veterans who received a cognitive behavioral program (see Table 1.3). In addition to a stronger reduction of anxiety, PTSD, and depression measures within the ST group, a significant weakening of maladaptive schemas was seen. It is important to note that this study was not a RCT but a historical comparison between groups within the same center.

Axis I and II problems often coexist. Gude and Hoffart (2008) found that agoraphobic patients with a Cluster C personality disorder showed a larger reduction in interpersonal problems than patients who received TAU after a cognitive ST program. In a study by Hoffart, Versland, and Sexton (2002), 35 patients were treated for panic disorder and/or agoraphobia, and a comorbid Cluster C personality disorder. During the first half of the treatment, the focus was on the cognitive model of panic and agoraphobia. In the final six weeks, ST, in combination with individual and group sessions, was offered. Outcomes are summarized in Table 1.3. The effect size of the change between baseline assessment and follow-up was medium to large (0.65). However, because of the lack of an adequate control group and the exposure to other therapeutic influences between sessions, it cannot be stated that the outcomes are a result of the treatment.

This study also shows that the power of the therapeutic alliance is equally important in Axis I symptoms. The degree of intimacy and common engagement was scored by independent raters. A better therapeutic alliance during the first session predicted a larger reduction of the degree of maladaptive beliefs in later phases (Hoffart, Sexton, Nordahl and Stiles, 2005).

Schema Therapy in mourning problems

De Keijser (2004) describes a case study with positive outcomes in which ST aspects are integrated into the three phases model of psycho-trauma in the treatment of a complicated mourning process. Maladaptive schemas regarding saying goodbye and extricating oneself are detected and changed into more adequate schemas.

Schema Therapy for eating disorders

The effectiveness of cognitive behavioral therapy in certain eating disorders is often declared by the focus on negative automatic thoughts or dysfunctional assumptions regarding weight, food, and self-image (Waller, Kennerly and Ohanian, 2007).

However, it appears that not only eating-related cognitions but also cognition and emotions in general vary between women with bulimia and a healthy control group. A comparison between 50 women with bulimia and 50 women without an eating disorder showed that the groups could be divided based on four central maladaptive schemas: Defectiveness/Shame, Emotional Inhibition, Failure, and Insufficient Self-Control (Waller, Ohanian, Meyer and Osman, 2000), which were significantly more present in women with bulimia. Waller and colleagues (2001) postulated a model in which beliefs and maladaptive schemas function as mediators in the relationship between early child abuse and the development of bulimia nervosa.

In a group of 60 women with bulimia, 21 with a history of child abuse reported significantly higher maladaptive tendencies and more psychopathology. A recent study showed that women with eating disorders used more behavioral-somatic avoidance compared to a control group of women without eating disorders (Sheffield, Waller, Emanuelli, Murray and Meyer, 2009).

These studies plead for adding schema therapeutic elements to treatment, with a focus on basic cognitive and emotional factors. A six-month motivational day treatment with additional ST elements in eight women with an eating disorder showed promising results, with a low dropout rate, improved mood, physical improvement, and an increased desire to change (George, Thornton, Touyz, Waller and Beumont, 2004). There are some case descriptions in which the effect of a schema-focused approach is shown (e.g., the effect of imaginary rescripting; see Ohanian, 2002). However, these have to be looked at critically: the research population consists nearly exclusively of women and the outcomes are based on self-reports (Waller *et al.*, 2007). Waller and colleagues advise the use of traditional cognitive-behavioral techniques at the start of the treatment, and a shift to ST if the treatment doesn't achieve the desired results. ST for eating disorders is probably most effective when eating disorders are comorbid with dissociation, personality disorders, (very) low self-esteem, and/or prior trauma.

Schema Therapy for psychotic disorders

In a single-case study, a psychological treatment for subjects with delusions was divided into several phases, one of which was ST (Jakes and Rhodes, 2003). In the ST phase, they worked on identifying negative schemas and developing positive alternative schemas. Positive outcomes were described.

Other studies

Nordahl, Holthe, and Haugum (2005) examined whether change in maladaptive schemas had an influence on symptom reduction at the end of treatment, for 82 subjects in outpatient treatment. Diagnoses within the population comprised both Axis I problems and Axis II disorders. This study supported the schema model by showing that the strength of early maladaptive schemas was related to personality pathology. Furthermore, changes in all early maladaptive shemas predicted the reduction of general psychological dysfunctioning.

The possible effectiveness of ST has also been observed for less clear psychopathological domains (e.g., ST elements in problems at work, such as stress and burn-out; see Bamber, 2006).

Conclusion

This chapter describes research on the effectiveness of ST. The existing literature reveals two striking findings: an obvious faith in the effectiveness of ST, but a paucity of strong methodological scientific studies.

Several case descriptions have been published, in which the effectiveness, pitfalls, and methodologies are described. The many books regarding this treatment method that have been published recently highlight the urgent need for guidelines and research focus.

However, empirical research with strong designs remains scarce. So far, only some large-scale controlled trials into borderline personality disorder, and the few RCTs in which dual-focused ST is investigated, provide evidence for the effectiveness of Schema Therapy. Furthermore, many of the research that has been conducted is based on the original schema model, and not on the model in which the mode work is added. Evidence for effective working with schema modes is, with a few exceptions, only available for borderline disorders (Nordahl and Nysaeter, 2005; Giesen-Bloo et al., 2006; Nadort et al., 2009). The conceptualization in "modes" is nevertheless described by patients as one of the most useful elements on the way to real change. This evidence pleads for adding the schema mode work to studies in the future.

Pitfalls and Tips

The need for well-designed scientific research is clear. There are some points that researchers should take into consideration when setting up a trial on the effectiveness of ST.

When conducting scientific research, the research population is often described as specific and detailed as possible (for example, subjects with a borderline personality disorder). This can, however, be a pitfall in the study of personality disorders, because Axis II problems often occur with Axis I symptoms. This can result in problems for both the treatment itself and the interpretation of the study results.

When choosing the research design, the following factors have to be taken into account: provide an adequate control group, work with psychometrically sound instruments, and try to make generalizations as broad as possible. It is noteworthy that a number of currently running RCTs are comparing ST with TAU, but not with other protocols. When comparing standardized protocols with TAU, the influence of non-specific factors (e.g., frequency of sessions) increases. It is, however, still justifiable to compare ST with TAU because effectiveness studies into ST are still at an early stage. The typical first step, when the effectiveness of an experimental treatment is being investigated, is to make comparisons with TAU.

The Future

Despite the popularity of ST, it is too early to describe it as evidence-based. For this purpose, more randomized effectiveness studies are needed to compare ST with other protocols and TAU. Also, the natural development of psychological syndromes, should be investigated. In addition to the frequently studied borderline PD, the implementation of ST should also be studied in other target groups (both in other personality problems and Axis I symptoms) and in combination with other treatment methods (e.g., pharmacotherapy). Studies should be replicated in other countries. The area of research should be enlarged to ST for children, adolescents, and seniors.

As described in this chapter, there is a lot going on in this field. The combination of these research efforts on the one hand, and the strong belief in ST on the other, could add to the further development of this treatment method in the near future.

References

Ball, S.A. (1998) Manualized treatment for substance abusers with personality disorders: dual focus Schema Therapy. *Addictive Behaviors*, 23(6): 883–891.

Ball, S.A. (2007) Comparing individual therapies for personality disordered opioid dependent patients. *Journal of Personality Disorders*, 21(3): 305–321.

Ball, S.A., Maccarelli, L.M., LaPaglia, D.M., Ostrowski, M.J. (2011) Randomized trial of dual-focused vs. single-focused individual therapy for personality disorders and substance dependence. *Journal of Nervous and Mental Disease*, 199(5): 319–328.

Ball, S.A., Cobb-Richardson, P., Connolly, A.J., Bujosa, C.T. and O'Neall, T.W. (2005) Substance abuse and personality disorders in homeless drop-in center clients: symptom severity and psychotherapy retention in a randomized clinical trial. *Comprehensive Psychiatry*, 46: 371–379.

Ball, J.R., Mitchell, P.B., Corry, J.C., Skillecorn, A., Smith, M., & Malhi, G.S. (2006) A Randomized Controlled Trial of Cognitive Therapy for Bipolar Disorder: focus on long-term change. *Journal of Clinical Psychiatry*, 67(2): 277–286.

Ball, S.A. and Young, J.E. (2000) Dual focus Schema Therapy for personality disorders and substance dependence: case study results. *Cognitive and Behavioral Practice*, 2000(7): 270–281.

Bamber, M. (2006) A schema-focused approach to treating work dysfunctions, in *CBT for Occupational Stress in Health Professionals: Introducing a Schema-focused Approach* (ed. M.R. Bamber). New York: Routledge/Taylor & Francis, pp. 177–190.

Bernstein, D., Arntz, A. and de Vos, M. (2007) Schema focused therapy in forensic settings: theoretical model and recommendations for best clinical practice. *International Journal of Forensic Mental Health*, 6(2), 169–183.

Bordelon, S.K. (2007) Comorbidity of chronic depression and personality disorders: application of schema mode therapy, in *Cognitive Behavior Therapy in Clinical Social Work Practice* (eds T. Ronen and A. Freeman). New York: Springer, pp. 447–465.

Cecero, J.J. and Young, J.E. (2001) Case of Silvia: a schema-focused approach. *Journal of Psychotherapy Integration*, 11(2), 217–229.

Cockram, D.M., Drummond, P.D. and Lee, C.W. (2010) Role and treatment of early maladaptive schemas in Vietnam veterans with PTSD [electronic version]. *Clinical Psychology and Psychotherapy*. doi: 10.1002/cpp.690.

De Keijser, J. (2004) Gecompliceerde rouw: Diagnostiek en behandeling. *Tijdschrift voor Psychotherapie*, 30, 100–116.

Farrell, J., Shaw, I. and Webber, M. (2009) A schema-focused approach to group psychotherapy for outpatients with borderline personality disorder: a randomized controlled trial. *Journal of Behavior Therapy and Experimental Psychiatry*, 40, 317–328.

George, L., Thornton, C., Touyz, S.W., Waller, G. and Beaumont, P.J. (2004) Motivational enhancement and schema-focused cognitive behaviour therapy in the treatment of chronic eating disorders. *Clinical Psychologist*, 8(2), 81–85.

Giesen-Bloo, J., van Dyck, R., Spinhoven, P. *et al.* (2006) Outpatient psychotherapy for borderline personality disorder: randomized trial of schema-focused therapy vs. transference-focused psychotherapy. *Archives of General Psychiatry*, 63, 649–658.

Gude, T. and Hoffart, A. (2008) Health and disability: change in interpersonal problems after cognitive agoraphobia and schema-focused therapy versus psychodynamic treatment as usual of inpatients with agoraphobia and Cluster C personality disorders. *Scandinavian Journal of Psychology*, 49, 195–199.

Hahusseau, S. and Pélissolo, A. (2006) Young's schema-focused therapies in personality disorders: a pilot study. Thérapies comportementales et cognitives centrées sur les schémas de young dans les troubles de la personnalité: Etude pilote sur 14 cas. *L'Encéphale: revue de psychiatrie clinique biologique et thérapeutique*, 32(1), 298–304.

Hoffart, A., Sexton, H., Nordahl, H.M. and Stiles, T.C. (2005) Connection between patient and therapist and therapist's competence in schema-focused therapy of personality problems. *Psychotherapy Research*, 15(4), 409–419.

Hoffart, A., Versland, S. and Sexton, H. (2002) Self-understanding, empathy, guided discovery, and schema belief in schema-focused cognitive therapy of personality problems: a process–outcome study. *Cognitive Therapy and Research*, 26(2), 199–219.

Jakes, S.C. and Rhodes, J.E. (2003) The effect of different components of psychological therapy on people with delusions: five experimental single cases. *Clinical Psychology and Psychotherapy*, 10, 302–315.

Kellogg, S.H. and Young, J.E. (2006) Schema therapy for borderline personality disorder. *Journal of Clinical Psychology*, 62(4), 445–458.

Morrison, N. (2000) Schema-focused cognitive therapy for complex long-standing problems: a single case study. *Behavioural and Cognitive Psychotherapy*, 28, 269–283.

Nadort, M., Arntz, A., Smit, J.H. *et al.* (2009) Implementation of outpatient schema therapy for borderline personality disorder with versus without crisis support by the therapist outside office hours: a randomized trial. *Behaviour Research and Therapy*, 47(11), 961–973.

Nordahl, H.M., Holthe, H. and Haugum, J.A. (2005) Early maladaptive schemas in patients with or without personality disorders: does schema modification predict symptomatic relief? *Clinical Psychology and Psychotherapy*, 12, 142–149.

Nordahl, H.M. and Nysaeter, T.E. (2005) Schema Therapy for patients with borderline personality disorder: a single case series. *Journal of Behavior Therapy and Experimental Psychiatry*, 36, 254–264.

Ohanian, V. (2002) Imagery rescripting within cognitive behavior therapy for bulimia nervosa: an illustrative case report. *International Journal of Eating Disorders*, 31, 352–357.

Reiss, N. and Farrell, J. (2010) Data presented at the 1st International Congress on Borderline Personality Disorder, Berlin.

Reiss, N., Lieb, K. and Vogel, F. (2010) Results of an open study of inpatient individual plus group Schema Therapy in Germany. Paper presented at the 6th World Congress of Behavioral and Cognitive Therapies, Boston, MA.

Richardson, G. (2005) Early maladaptive schemas in a sample of British adolescent sexual abusers: implications for therapy. *Journal of Sexual Aggression*, 11(3), 259–276.

Sheffield, A., Waller, G., Emanuelli, F., Murray, J. and Meyer, C. (2009) Do schema processes mediate links between parenting and eating pathology? *European Eating Disorders Review*, 17, 290–300.

Thunissen, M.M. and Muste, E.H. (2002) Schematherapie in de klinisch-psychotherapeutische behandeling van persoonlijkheidsstoornissen. *Tijdschrift voor Psychotherapie*, 28, 385–401.

Waller, G., Kennerly, H. and Ohanian, V. (2007) Schema-focused cognitive behavioral therapy for eating disorders, in *Cognitive Schemas and Core Beliefs in Psychological Problems: a Scientist-Practitioner Guide* (eds L.P. Riso, P.L. du Toit, D.J. Stein and J.E. Young). Washington, DC: American Psychological Association, pp. 139–175.

Waller, G., Meyer, C., Ohanian, V. *et al.* (2001) The psychopathology of bulimic women who report childhood sexual abuse: the mediating role of core beliefs. *The Journal of Nervous and Mental Disease*, *189*(10), 700–708.

Waller, G., Ohanian, V., Meyer, C. and Osman, S. (2000) Cognitive content among bulimic women: the role of core beliefs. *International Journal of Eating Disorders*, *28*(2), 235–241.

Weertman, A. and Arntz, A. (2007) Effectiveness of treatment of childhood memories in cognitive therapy for personality disorders: a controlled study contrasting methods focusing on the present and methods focusing on childhood memories. *Behaviour Research and Therapy*, *45*, 2133–2143.

Young, J.E. (2005) Schema-focused cognitive therapy and the case of Ms. S. *Journal of Psychotherapy Integration*, *15*(1), 115–126.

Young, J.E. and Mattila, D.E. (2002) Schema-focused therapy for depression, in *Comparative Treatments of Depression* (eds M.A. Reinecke and M.R. Davison). New York: Springer, pp. 291–316.

Zorn, P., Roder, V., Muller, D.R., Tschacher, W. and Thommen, M. (2007) Schemazentrierte emotiv-behaviorale therapie (SET): eine randomisierte evaluationsstudie an patienten mit persönlichkeitsstörungen aus den clustern B und C. *Verhaltenstherapie*, *17*, 233–241.

2
Experimental Studies of Schema Modes

Jill Lobbestael

Most research within the framework of Schema Therapy (ST) focuses on the efficacy of treatment using this therapy method, whether or not in comparison with other therapies or treatment as usual. Until now, few studies of the theoretical foundation underlying the central constructs of schemas and schema modes in ST have been conducted. Fundamental theoretical research about ST is extremely important; the theoretical hypotheses of the therapy can be critically examined and the theoretical conceptualization of mental disorders can be developed and refined. This chapter offers an overview of experimental studies of schema modes. First, a number of studies are outlined that have investigated whether the modes that are supposed to be central to certain personality disorders are indeed more strongly present in these groups than in other groups. Following this, a number of studies that used alternative methods to map out schema modes in patients and looked at the influence of emotional induction on the presence of schema modes are discussed. Since experimental research into schema modes is still in its infancy, this chapter offers recommendations for future research in this field.

In Practice

It is important that therapists have a good theoretical understanding of which modes are central in specific Axis II pathology, in which way modes can be observed, and under which circumstances an alternation between modes can be expected. Therapists mainly obtain this from ST manuals and from their expertise and supervision. Experimental research into schema modes can contribute significantly to this knowledge; not only because the supposed connection between modes and personality disorders can be tested, but also because the theoretical conceptualization of modes

The Wiley Blackwell Handbook of Schema Therapy: Theory, Research, and Practice, First Edition.
Edited by Michiel van Vreeswijk, Jenny Broersen, and Marjon Nadort.
© 2012 John Wiley & Sons, Ltd. Published 2015 by John Wiley & Sons, Ltd.

relevant to the different personality disorders is unclear. In this way, research can contribute to the development of the theoretical framework. Adding to knowledge in this field increases the critical attitude of therapists and decreases the chance that the presence of a certain mode is overlooked.

Approach

Self-report of schema modes in personality disorders

Four studies (Arntz, Klokman and Sieswerda, 2005; Lobbestael, Arntz and Sieswerda, 2005; Lobbestael, van Vreeswijk and Arntz, 2008; Bamelis, Renner, Heidkamp and Arntz, 2011), have checked for the presence of schema modes in groups of patients with different personality disorders. Since the mode model was originally developed to explain borderline problems, two of these studies (Arntz *et al.*, 2005; Lobbestael *et al.*, 2005) are mainly focused on this population. Both studies used the same research method. By means of structured diagnostics (SCID-II interviews), a research group of borderline patients in different outpatient and clinical institutes was recruited. These patients were asked to complete a schema mode inventory. This questionnaire was also presented to pathological control groups (e.g., patients with a Cluster C personality disorder or an antisocial personality disorder) to determine whether these modes were specifically applicable to borderline personality disorders, rather than to personality disorders in general. Finally, the mode inventory was completed by a group of healthy participants (i.e., without Axis I or Axis II pathology). Because the mode conceptualization of the different personality disorders is still in development, slightly different versions of this mode inventory were used each time. In each case, items that the ST model predicted to be specifically applicable to certain personality disorders were added.

Arntz *et al.* (2005) compared the presence of schema modes in 18 borderline patients, 18 Cluster C patients (with an indirect, dependent, and/or obsessive-compulsive personality disorder), and 18 non-patient controls. This study measured the presence or absence of seven schema modes: Detached Protector, Punitive Parent, Angry Child, Abandoned/Abused Child, Compliant Surrender, Over-Compensator, and Healthy Adult.

The items that were reflected by these modes were clustered in three sections: emotions, thoughts, and behavior. All items had to be scored on a 10 cm visual analog scale. In line with Young's prediction, this study showed that borderline patients scored significantly higher than the two control groups on the Detached Protector, Punitive Parent, Angry Child, and Abandoned/Abused Child modes. It also showed that the presence of the Healthy Adult mode was, to a considerable extent, lower in borderline patients, as compared with the other groups, which emphasizes the severity of the borderline pathology. This study thus provided the first proof of the accuracy of the mode model in borderline patients.

A second study (Lobbestael *et al.*, 2005) compared the presence of schema modes between three groups: a borderline group, an antisocial group, and a non-patient control group, each comprising 16 participants. The mode inventory used in this study measured the presence of six schema modes. Unlike Arntz and colleagues' study

(2005), two modes (Compliant Surrender and Over-Compensator) were not measured because they were not considered to be central to the research groups in this study. The Bully and Attack mode was added, because it was expected to be important for the antisocial group. In accordance with Arntz and colleagues (2005), the results showed that the Detached Protector, Punitive Parent, Angry Child, and Abandoned/ Abused Child modes were specifically applicable to borderline patients. These four modes were also significantly more present in the antisocial group than in the non-patient control group, but less so in borderline patients.

Although the antisocial group scored highest on the Bully and Attack mode, this score was not significantly higher than the score of the borderline group. Therefore, it cannot be concluded that the Bully and Attack mode is particularly applicable to the antisocial group. A remarkable conclusion drawn by Lobbestael et al., (2005) was that the antisocial group showed a very intense presence of the Healthy Adult mode, and scored to a considerable extent the same as the non-patient control group. In summary, this study showed that antisocial patients didn't score very highly on one of the maladaptive modes, as compared to the other groups. However, they demonstrated a well-developed healthy mode. This finding is striking, because it seems to be in contrast with the high level of pathology that these patients show. Therefore, it is likely that these patients did not complete the questionnaire correctly. There are two possible explanations for this: either antisocial patients lack self-insight or they intentionally deny the presence of pathological modes.

A third study investigating the connection between schema modes and personality disorders (Lobbestael et al., 2008) was not specifically focused on borderline issues, but on the entire spectrum of personality disorders. In a sample of 489 participants, consisting of 390 patients with different Axis I and Axis II problems and 99 non-patient controls, SCID-inventories were administered, as well as the Schema Mode Inventory (SMI; see Part VI, Chapter 5). By means of path analysis, the correlation between 10 personality disorders and the 14 schema modes was determined. The advantage of this technique is that while determining the strength for these correlations, the presence of other personality disorders can also be tested. In this way, the strength of these correlations reports the relatively pure associations between personality disorders and modes. The results indicated that the modes that showed a significant correlation with Axis II disorders varied strongly between the personality disorders. Certain personality disorders, such as schizotypal and schizoid, showed only a strong correlation with a schema mode, while other Axis II disorders, such as borderline and avoidant personality disorders, showed strong correlations with a large number of modes (11 and 7 respectively). Nevertheless, each personality disorder loaded uniquely regarding its mode conceptualization. All strong correlations between schema modes and personality disorders found were either predicted by schema-focused therapy or through logical reasoning. Thus, this study again provided evidence of the presence of the Detached Protector, Punitive Parent, Angry Child, and Vulnerable Child modes in borderline patients, and evidence of a negative correlation with the Healthy Adult mode. This shows that these modes were more strongly present in borderline patients as compared to Cluster C and antisocial personality disorders, or in fact any of the 10 personality disorders. Furthermore, this study showed that several other modes were characteristic of borderline disorder (e.g., Enraged Child and Detached Self-Soother). The correlation between these extra modes and borderline personalities can be explained easily by the problems that these patients have. In this way, the presence of the Enraged Child can be explained by the extreme and uncontrolled aggression that sometimes turns up in borderline patients, and the Detached Self-Soother can be explained by the frequent use of drugs in borderline patients. Nevertheless, the many different modes that were found in borderline personality disorders make the mode model for these patients less specific than was originally expected.

The fourth study (Bamelis et al., 2011) was set up in the framework of a large-scale study of ST in patients with Cluster C, paranoid, histrionic, and narcissistic personality disorders (Bamelis and Arntz, 2006–12). Eighteen modes were measured, including new modes specifically formulated for this target group, by means of administering the SMI-2 (see Part VI, Chapter 5) to a sample of 444 participants, of whom 323 were patients with personality disorders and 121 non-patient controls, diagnosed by SCID II. Some, but not all, correlations in Lobbestael, van Vreeswijk, Spinhoven, and Arntz (2010) could be replicated. This can possibly be attributed to the inclusion of forensic patients in this study. Furthermore, results showed that these newly formulated modes connected to the histrionic, avoidant, dependent, and paranoid personality disorders. The question of whether expansion of the schema mode model to include these modes is desirable partly depends on the outcome of the ST efficacy study of these specific personality disorders (Bamelis and Arntz, 2006–12).

Comparison between Self-Report of Schema Modes and Reports Made by Others

In previous studies, a strong correlation between antisocial personality disorders and the Healthy Adult mode was shown. Therefore, doubts were raised about the validity and reliability of self-report tools in antisocial patients. Lying and a denying style are central features of this population, so it is essential to compare self-report to the reports made by others. In a current study by Lobbestael, Arntz, Löbbes, and Cima (2009), the self-report of schema modes in patients was compared to the mode report of the therapists of these patients. This research included 96 patients, of whom 19 were antisocial, 49 were borderline, and 28 were Cluster C patients. Both patients and their therapists filled out the SMI. In this study the possible differences or discrepancies between patient and therapist reports of schema modes were investigated. The results demonstrated that where discrepancies existed, the patients always reported a lower presence of their maladaptive modes than their therapists did. With the Cluster C and borderline patients this discrepancy was significant for three of the 14 modes. With the antisocial group, however, 11 of the 14 mode report discrepancies were significant. These results clearly show that antisocial patients under-reported the presence of their maladaptive modes more often than other Axis II groups. The implication of these findings for practice is that lower scores on maladaptive modes and higher scores on healthy modes in antisocial patients should raise alarm for clinicians. In such cases, it is highly likely that this is not an adequate reflection of the actual presence of maladaptive modes, since antisocial patients may deny the presence of this mode, or lack insight into it. Therefore, it is important to obtain information from alternative sources and not only from the self-report of antisocial patients.

The Influence of Emotional Inductions on Schema Modes

Patients with severe personality disorders are supposed to be able to switch modes very rapidly in reaction to changes in their surrounding (Young, Klosko and Weishaar, 2003). Therefore, it is important to study the impact of mode presence in reaction to mood inductions. The results of the following studies provide more insight into the temporary character and the modifiability of modes. The first research in this context was by Arntz and colleagues (2005). They showed their participants a clip of the scene "No child of mine," in which a 10-year-old child is physically, emotionally, and sexually abused. The participants completed a state version of the mode questionnaire, both before and after viewing. Results showed that all participants scored higher on the Abandoned/Abused Child, Punitive Parent, and Detached Protector modes. This means that confrontation with abuse-related material triggered a wide range of negative modes in participants; not only the Abandoned/Abused Child mode, which is considered to be directly connected to the abusive past of a person, but also the self-punitive modes and the coping style of avoidance. When looking at group differences, it appeared that the borderline group showed a significantly higher incidence of the Detached Protector mode, as compared with the Cluster C and non-patient control groups. These results demonstrated that borderline patients switched to the Detached Protector mode in extremely stressful situations.

Lobbestael, Arntz, Cima, and Chakhssi (2009) investigated the influence of anger induction on self-reported emotion and the presence of schema modes. Participants in this research were made angry by means of a stress-inducing interview (Dimsdale, Stern and Dillon, 1988; see also Lobbestael, Arntz and Wiers, 2008), in which they were asked if they wanted to talk about a situation in the past that had made them extremely angry. By means of specification and empathic confrontation from the test leader, this situation was then "relived" by the participants. Both before and after this stress-induced interview, the participants completed a self-report questionnaire regarding their current emotions and schema modes. This study consisted of 155 participants, divided into antisocial, borderline, Cluster C, and a non-patient control groups. All groups showed a significant increase in self-reported anger and in the anger-related Angry Child, Enraged Child, and Bully and Attack modes. The borderline group reported a significantly stronger increase in the Angry Child mode than the other groups. Although other schema modes also increased under influence of the anger induction, the increase in these non-anger related modes was significantly less than the increase in the anger-related modes. The results showed that when under the influence of anger induction, people switched to anger-related schema modes.

Example of an anger induction interview

R (researcher): Can you tell me about a situation in the past, in which you felt a lot of anger?

PT: Well, yesterday for instance, my boss criticized me in front of other people.

R: What was this criticism about?

PT:	There was a little mistake in the report I had made.
R:	How did your boss express this criticism?
PT:	He said: "This report is all wrong."
R:	What exactly was it that made you so angry?
PT:	Well, there was only a tiny little mistake in the report, the rest was perfectly well in order!
R:	What did you think of your boss at that moment?
PT:	That he is a bastard! And why did he have to tell me that in front of my colleagues?
R:	Imagine you could have told him exactly what you thought. What would you have told him?

Pitfalls and Tips

The research outlined above shows that it is important not to take the self-report of schema modes in antisocial patients at face value. It is important that therapists refer to alternative sources to obtain a more accurate picture of the presence of maladaptive modes in these patients.

Research shows that certain maladaptive modes only appear under extreme circumstances (e.g. when certain emotions are triggered). It is important that therapists are aware of this and that they take into account that patients are possibly unaware of these maladaptive modes in neutral situations.

The anger induction interview is easy to use in practice. However, situations that cause anger in patients often trigger other emotions. For example, when somebody reports that he was very angry because he was criticized, the criticism can also trigger feelings of sorrow or fear. Therefore, it is very important, when conducting an anger induction interview, to make sure your patient sticks to his feelings of anger. This is why you should, as a therapist, only go into the specific feelings of anger and make adjustments if other emotions become prominent. For experimental researchers, the uniformity of the anger induction interview is important. Make sure that the questions you ask are largely similar, that administering the interview takes the same amount of time, and that the research interviews are conducted by the same person if possible.

The Future

Experimental research about schema modes is still in an early stage. Although the studies outlined above give a clear description of the modes that are central to certain personality disorders, such as borderline personality disorder, the concept of modes can be refined and specified. For example, Bernstein, Arntz, and de Vos (2007) predict the presence of the Predator and Conning and Manipulative modes in psychopaths. Furthermore, the influence of other emotional inductions on mode representation should be investigated. In addition, it is important to validate the shifting of modes by means of implicit measures, such as physiological responses or implicit cognitive associations, or by changes in behavior. Because the mode-shifting concept supposes a simultaneous change of emotions, cognitions, and behaviors, it would be important to test whether these three levels do indeed change at the same time. In the future, it might be possible to use the experimental techniques in relation to modes as efficacy measures. In this way, it could be checked whether patients that are effectively treated show less extreme mode-shifting than patients who are not treated. Furthermore, it could be tested whether a decrease in personality pathology also has an impact on implicitly measured schema modes or on corresponding physiological and behavioral changes.

References

Arntz, A., Klokman, J. and Sieswerda, S. (2005) An experimental test of the schema mode model of borderline personality disorder. *Journal of Behavior Therapy and Experimental Psychology, 36*, 229–239.

Bamelis, L. and Arntz, A. (2006–2012) *Psychological Treatment of Personality Disorders: a Multicentered Randomized Controlled Trial on the (Cost-) Effectiveness Of Schema-Focused Therapy.* Promotietraject Universiteit Maastricht.

Bamelis, L.L.M., Renner, F., Heidkamp, D. and Arntz, A. (2011) Extended schema mode conceptualizations for specific personality disorders: an empirical study. *Journal of Personality Disorders. 25*(10), 41–58.

Bernstein, D.P., Arntz, A. and Vos, M.E. (2007) Schemagerichte therapie in de forensische setting. Theoretisch model en voorstellen voor best clinical practice. *Tijdschrift voor Psychotherapie, 33.*

Dimsdale, J.E., Stern, M.E. and Dillon, E. (1988) The stress interview as a tool for examining physiological reactivity. *Psychosomatic Medicine, 50*, 64–71.

Lobbestael, J., Arntz, A., Cima, M. and Chakhssi, F. (2009) Effects of induced anger in patients with antisocial personality disorder. *Psychological Medicine, 39*, 557–568.

Lobbestael, J., Arntz, A., Löbbes, A. and Cima, M. (2009) A comparative study of patients' and therapists' report of schema modes. *Journal of Behavior Therapy and Experimental Psychiatry, 40*, 571–579.

Lobbestael, J., Arntz, A. and Sieswerda, S. (2005) Schema modes and childhood abuse in borderline and antisocial patients. *Journal of Behavior Therapy and Experimental Psychology, 36*, 240–253.

Lobbestael, J., Arntz, A. and Wiers, R.W. (2008) How to push someone's buttons: a comparison of four anger induction methods. *Cognition and Emotion, 22*, 353–373.

Lobbestael, J., van Vreeswijk, M. and Arntz, A. (2008) An empirical test of schema mode conceptualizations in personality disorders. *Behaviour Research and Therapy, 46*, 854–860.

Lobbestael, J., van Vreeswijk, M., Spinhoven, P. and Arntz, A. (2010) Reliability and validity of the Dutch version of the Schema Mode Inventory (SMI). *Behavioural and Cognitive Psychotherapy, 38*, 437–458.

Young, J.E., Klosko, J. and Weishaar, M.E. (2003) *Schema Therapy: a Practitioner's Guide.* New York: Guilford Press.

3
Experimental Studies for Schemas

Simkje Sieswerda

After undergoing Schema Therapy (ST) for borderline personality disorders, according to Young (Young, Klosko and Weishaar, 2003), it seems that approximately half the patients in one study (Giesen-Bloo *et al.*, 2006; Nadort *et al.*, 2009) and 94% of the patients in another (Farrell, Shaw and Webber, 2010) no longer met the criteria for personality disorders. ST-inclusive treatment of traumatic childhood experiences in other personality disorders has also shown significant effects (Weertman and Arntz, 2007). Considering that personality disorders were understood to be nearly impossible or at least very difficult to treat for a long time, researchers justifiably claim that the outcomes are very encouraging. Conversely, most of the effects of the treatment mean that many patients still suffer from a personality disorder after ending long-term and intensive treatment. Although it is possible that parts of the personality problems are resistant to treatment, it seems likely that treatment of these problems can be improved.

One way in which therapy can be developed further is through scientific research into the illness model behind the therapy. Although therapy based on a wrong but convincing illness model can be effective, it is to be expected that therapy based on the right model is more effective and more efficient, at least if the known causes can be treated.

This chapter offers an overview of experimental studies into schemas and other factors that are thought to play a causal role in theoretical models. Research into schema modes from Young *et al.*, (2003) are described in Part VI, Chapter 2). In this chapter a number of themes and questions that emerge from the theory and practice of ST are discussed, followed by a description of the experimental studies in which these are researched. The chapter concludes with some pitfalls that may be encountered when implementing this kind of study, and directions for the future.

The Wiley Blackwell Handbook of Schema Therapy: Theory, Research, and Practice, First Edition.
Edited by Michiel van Vreeswijk, Jenny Broersen, and Marjon Nadort.
© 2012 John Wiley & Sons, Ltd. Published 2015 by John Wiley & Sons, Ltd.

In Practice

Until now, experimental studies of Beck-type schema models (Beck, Freeman and Davis, 2004) and Young's schema model for personality problems (Young *et al.*, 2003) have focused mainly on schemas, hypervigilance, and dichotomous and/or childlike thinking.

Schemas

Schema models presume that people with personality problems are characterized by maladaptive schemas regarding themselves and the (social) world, and that treatments for personality problems can best be focused on these schemas. Beck and colleagues (2004) are of the opinion that each personality disorder has a specific cognitive profile that consists of, among others, specific basic schemas. For example, the avoidant personality disorder could be characterized by the basic schemas "I'm incompetent and vulnerable" and "other people will criticize me." Below is a description of a patient with an avoidant personality disorder who fits these basic schemas well. This vignette also fits a number of schemas from Young's schema model for personality problems (e.g., the Mistrust and/or Abuse, Emotional Deprivation, Defectiveness/Shame, and Subjugation schemas). However, this model doesn't offer specific personality disorder schema sets, although some specific schema modes are described for some of the severe personality disorders.

Research can show whether schema models are applicable or whether it is better for therapies to focus on other aspects.

> A 36-year-old programmer with an avoidant personality disorder was an unwanted child. He was humiliated by his parents when he was young. He has developed such a strong self-loathing that he doesn't have any mirrors in his house and repeatedly has cosmetic surgery. He has never had a partner and his friendships have always ended in humiliation. He has always had the feeling he was entirely in the other person's hands. This has led to an increasingly secluded life since his college days. An inventory of his supposed "loser" image within the framework of cognitive therapy shows many positive opinions, but his self-image remains very negative.

Hypervigilance

Beck's schema model (Beck *et al.*, 2004) supposes there are some other pathological cognitive characteristics of personality disorders other than maladaptive schemas. One of these characteristics in patients with a borderline personality disorder is hypervigilance, or increased alertness (Pretzer, 1990). Patients with borderline personality disorders are almost constantly on the alert for signs of danger. Such hypervigilance is supposedly the result of tension between a powerless and vulnerable ego schema on the one hand, and a malicious world schema on the other.

> A 22-year-old student with a borderline personality disorder is hospitalized after several suicide attempts. The nurses notice that she becomes increasingly restless every evening and they are worried that she will injure herself again. After having refused to discuss this initially, she says later that the reason she refused is because she is supposedly a "bitch" and feels she is a bad person. She is afraid she will be threatened and overwhelmed by an evil power within her, as a consequence of which everyone who has something to do with her could be harmed. She thinks that this is the case because she has done something terrible, but she can't remember what it could be. In the evenings, she becomes more afraid because everybody is leaving, and she and others will be handed over to this evil.

Unlike, for example, patients with a dependent or paranoid personality disorder, hypervigilant patients can neither trust others nor themselves. Traumatic childhood experiences, which are often reported in patients with borderline personality disorders (Sabo, 1997), are thought, for the most part, to be the source of these schemas. The vignette (from Kroll, 1998) describes what the combination of a powerless ego schema and a malicious world schema, resulting in hypervigilance, can look like in practice.

Hypervigilance in borderline personality disorders is treated in Schema Therapy with anxiety techniques, including dealing with traumas. Research shows that hypervigilance is a characteristic of these patients and that these techniques are necessary.

Dichotomous and childlike thinking

Another specific cognitive characteristic of borderline personality disorder in Beck's schema models is dichotomous (black-and-white) and childlike thinking (Pretzer, 1990; Layden, Newman, Freeman and Morse, 1993). Dichotomous thinking, according to the cognitive model, is a common error of reasoning in mental problems. However, among people with mental problems, dichotomous thinking is especially characteristic of patients with borderline personality disorders. The standard error could be an important (contributory) cause of extreme and volatile thoughts, affects, and behavior in patients with borderline personality disorders. Some authors (e.g., Layden *et al.*, 1993) suppose that dichotomous thinking in borderline personality represents regression to a childlike way of thinking in activated schemas, comparable with splitting, found in borderline organizations in psychoanalytical models. Young's model isn't explicit on dichotomous thinking in borderline personality disorder, even though it could characterize the child modes in these patients in line with van Layden and colleagues.

Considering the important role of dichotomous thinking in Beck's cognitive models of borderline personality disorders, the correction of this standard error is considered to be essential within therapies according to these models. Whether this will prove necessary is a matter for further research.

Approach

Research into the cognitive model of personality disorders is still in its infancy. This concerns the studies into inventories (see Part VI, Chapters 4 and 5), but in particular experimental studies. First, a definition of experimental studies is given, followed by a summary of the results.

Experimental studies

"Experimental" means "establishing by experience." In an experimental study, the researcher does a "test" and "experiences" what the effect of this test is. Effects, read thoughts, affects, and behavior in this case are not estimated by the researcher or the patient, either before or afterward, but are determined as soon as they occur. In this way, many disturbing assessment errors can be prevented, which is important in a study into people with personality disorders.

A study using experimental manipulation can test causal connections. For example, the expected causal role of a schema in a personality disorder can be studied by activating this schema in a number of cases, not activating it in other cases, and then determining whether patients display more pathological behavior in the first condition than in the second. In a "pure" experiment, coincidence determines which manipulation condition is applied in order to exclude the effects of any possible other (contributory) causal factors, when the experiment has been repeated sufficiently. If a coincidental manipulation isn't possible for practical or ethical reasons, a "quasi-experiment" or "analog experiment" can be used to yield a result. In a quasi-experiment the causal factor isn't manipulated, but varied on the basis of pre-existing differences (e.g., patients with and without personality disorder). In an analog experiment the influence of an independent variable is studied by manipulation of a comparable variable (e.g., a study into students with characteristics of a personality disorder instead of patients, or hypervigilance, by using attentional exercises instead of a trauma).

Table 3.1 describes paradigms used in experimental studies of factors within the cognitive model for personality disorders. With each paradigm a description of the experimental manipulation and the measured dependent variable are given.

Attention and hypervigilance

Attention to threatening stimuli (hypervigilance or selective attention) has been studied extensively in different Axis I disorders and has been shown to play a crucial role in the etiology and maintenance of pathological anxiety in particular (Williams, Watts, MacLeod and Mathews, 1997). This isn't surprising, considering that a quick detection of danger (i.e., during the first stage of information processing) optimizes the chances of survival. The first studies into schema-related biases in attention in personality disorders have focused on borderline personality disorders.

Several emotional Stroop studies have shown that patients with borderline personality disorders are characterized by early biases in information processing of

Table 3.1 Experimental paradigms

Paradigm	Experimental Manipulation	Dependent Variable
Emotional Stroop	Offering of (schema-related) emotional words vs. (schema-unrelated emotional and) neutrally colored words for which the color has to be named	(Schema-congruent) bias in early information processing (selective attention) *Measuring:* delay in giving color of (schema-related) emotional words compared to (schema-unrelated and) neutral words
Visual (dot)-probe	Offering of (schema-related) emotional stimuli vs. (schema-unrelated) neutral stimuli followed by a signal on the same or an opposite position that has to be reacted upon	(Schema-related) attentional bias toward the stimulus or away from it *Measuring:* acceleration in reaction to the signal in the same or opposite position
Semantic Simon	Offering of schema-related words vs. schema-unrelated words with a second characteristic (for example language) that must be reacted to, as either schema-congruent or incongruent	Schema-congruent bias in information processing *Measuring:* acceleration of schema-congruent reactions to irrelevant stimulus characteristics (e.g. English vs. Dutch) compared to schema-incongruent reactions
Implicit association	Offering of object words (e.g. "I," "other") and/or schema-related vs. schema-unrelated attribute words that must be categorized	Strength of mental associations between object and attribute categories *Measuring:* acceleration of categorization of words in schema-congruent object and attribute pairs
Game of trust	1. Subject plays role of investor and is supposed to grant a loan to an imaginary person 2. Subject plays role of loan receiver, receives large vs. small amount and needs to pay it back with a random profit share	Trust and/or cooperation (interpersonal schemas) *Measuring:* size of granted loan or profit share
Pragmatic interference	Offering of schema-related vs. schema-unrelated short stories in which a conclusion must be drawn	Schema-congruent interpretation *Measuring:* schema-congruent conclusions in closed and/or open answering format
Thematic apperception	Offering of drawings of emotional vs. neutral ambiguous social situations from which a story must be made up	Schema-congruent interpretation *Measuring:* schema-congruent affects, interpersonal relations, strategies in the stories, made up from the drawings
Evaluation	1. Offering of schema-related film clips vs. schema-unrelated and neutral clips 2. Discussion with rejecting or accepting vs. neutral social worker 3. Playing frustrating vs. stimulating computer games in which film character, social worker or game must be evaluated.	Dichotomous, childlike (splitting) and negative evaluations *Measuring:* extremity, negativity and/or differentiation of schema-related, schema-unrelated and neutral evaluations

threatening stimuli (Arntz, Appels and Sieswerda, 2000; Waller and Button, 2002; Sieswerda, Arntz and Kindt, 2007; Sieswerda, Arntz, Mertens and Vertommen, 2007; Wingenfeld et al., 2009). In two of these studies, selective attention seemed to be related to schemas (Waller and Button, 2002; Sieswerda et al., 2007) and patients with borderline personality disorder named colors of, for example, schema-related emotional negative words (such as "unreliable") less quickly than schema-unrelated emotional negative words (such as "stingy"). Another emotional Stroop study showed an attentional bias for individual, personally relevant stimuli and not for generally negative emotional stimuli in patients with borderline personality disorder (Wingenfeld et al., 2009). Furthermore, one study showed personality disorder-specific selective attention in borderline patients (Sieswerda et al., 2007).

Research into *selective* attention in borderline disorders indicates an initial orientation toward general emotional stimuli, followed by a mood-dependent avoidance or approach of emotionally negative stimuli. Compared to healthy subjects, adolescents with borderline personality disorder reacted more quickly to very short presentations of neutral stimuli (500ms) that were presented at the same location as opposed to the opposite location than emotionally negative and positive faces that were presented (dot-probe task). However, when stimuli were presented for a longer period (1200–1500ms), borderline patients in a bad mood demonstrated a stronger approach to negative faces, while healthy non-patients in a bad mood and students with many self-reported borderline characteristics showed more avoidance of these faces (von Ceumern-Lindenstjerna, 2004; Berenson et al., 2009).

Two studies underpinned a hypothesized central role for hypervigilance in borderline personality disorder. In this way, a positive connection between a schema-related Stroop effect on the one hand, and sexual abuse in childhood and borderline personality disorder-related anxiety on the other, has been found in patients with borderline personality disorders, for whom tests for other comorbid disorders were carried out (Sieswerda et al., 2007). However, another study showed that a specific attentional bias is only characteristic of borderline personality disorder with comorbid post-traumatic stress disorder (Wingenfeld et al., 2009). A mood-increasing attentional bias may also be specific for borderline personality disorder and probably contributory to typical strong mood swings. Finally, patients who were cured of borderline personality disorder showed a normal level of reduced hypervigilance, while the hypervigilance of non-cured patients remained stable (Sieswerda, Arntz and Kindt, 2007).

Reactions

Some researchers are of the opinion that Stroop experiments are actually biases in *reactions*, rather than measurements of attention. However, if Stroop experiments are excluded, there remains only one study into schema-related reactions in personality disorders (Weertman, Arntz, de Jong and Rinck, 2008). This study underpinned a schema-congruent influence of reactions, as predicted by the cognitive model. In two of three Simon experiments, subjects with features of obsessive-compulsive personality disorder reacted quicker in schema-congruent stimulus reaction combinations (e.g., the English stimulus "I am a perfectionist" and the reaction "yes") than in cases of schema-incongruent combinations (e.g., the Dutch stimulus "others are irresponsible" and the reaction "no"). These effects were not present in schema-unrelated combinations or in subjects with a maximum of one feature of obsessive-compulsive personality disorder.

Furthermore, the cognitive model is indirectly supported by reactions of borderline patients in studies using the implicit association test and trust games. Consistent with the schema "I'm powerless and vulnerable" and "I'm intrinsically unacceptable," the reactions of borderline patients, with and without post-traumatic stress-disorder, indicated a strong association between self-related and anxiety or shame-related stimuli compared to patients with social phobias and healthy control subjects (Rüsch, Corrigan et al., 2007; Rüsch, Lieb et al., 2007). Two studies in which subjects played the role of investors (Unoka, Seres, Áspán, Bódi and Kéri, 2009) or loan receivers (King-Casas, Sharp, Lomax-Bream, Fonagy and Montague, 2008) showed more indirect underpinning of a malicious-other schema in borderline personality disorders. Borderline patients as both investors and loan receivers showed little trust in their negotiator; they gave smaller loans than depressive patients and healthy controls and had fewer tendencies to seduce investors into taking a larger loan with high return than healthy controls.

Interpretations and Evaluations

Most studies into interpretations and evaluations in personality pathology have shown biases congruent with schemas formulated in cognitive models for different personality disorders. Several studies examined interpretations of social situations. In these studies, it seems that subjects who are in particular associated with avoidant personality disorders drew conclusions in a pragmatic interference task more often (e.g., "the other guests preferred talking to others") than control subjects (Dreessen, Arntz, Hendriks, Keune and van den Hout, 1999). Subjects with features of independent personality disorders gave schema-congruent interpretations (Weertman, Arntz, Schouten and Dreessen, 2006) in a study using the Thematic Apperception Test (TAT). In another study, patients with an avoidant/dependent borderline or obsessive-compulsive personality disorder were asked to respond to some scenario descriptions, for example, a scenario in which the subject discovered so many mistakes in the work of a colleague that the subject took over (Weertman, Arntz, Salet and Coenen, 2006). All three patient groups seemed to be schema-congruent in the open questions and showed disorder-specific reactions. The responses to closed questions were, unexpectedly, not schema-congruent, which the researchers explained by possible limited introspective skills in these patients.

Dichotomous thinking

Most studies into dichotomous thinking in patients with borderline personality disorders found variable results. In a first evaluation experiment, in which subjects had to judge the different characteristics of film personalities from film clips, borderline patients seemed to assess these characters more dichotomously than patients with Cluster C personality disorders and non-patients (Veen and Arntz, 2000). A study in which subjects spoke with empathic, rejecting, and neutral social workers, and judged them on a number of characteristics afterward, resulted in more dichotomous evaluations from patients with borderline personality disorders (Ten Haaf and Arntz, in preparation). Spontaneous judgments, by the same patients with borderline personality disorders from the first mentioned study, were not dichotomous, but mainly negative (Arntz and Veen, 2001). A second evaluation experiment with film personalities also showed negative judgments by patients with borderline personality disorders, in which they were distinguished from negative judgments of schema-related positive personalities (e.g., a loving partner; Sieswerda, Arntz and Verheul, submitted). Patients with borderline personality disorders seemed to judge even non-social stimuli (computer games) relatively negatively (Sieswerda, Arntz and Wolfis, 2005). A general negative evaluation style also seemed a recurrent result in a sequence of studies into the affect-tone of interpretations of, among others, TAT pictures of patients with borderline personality disorders (see overview in Westen, 1990). Explanations for variable results (e.g., an inaccurate measure of dichotomous thinking) have not yet been studied successfully.

The relevance of dichotomous evaluations in personality disorders was supported in a study into dichotomous thinking in borderline personality disorders before, during, and after three years of therapy (Sieswerda and Arntz, submitted). This study showed that dichotomous evaluations decreased during therapy and that this decrease was correlated with a decrease in borderline symptoms, especially during the first half of the therapy. Negative evaluations decreased less obviously in this study. This may mean that a negative evaluation style plays no central role in borderline personality disorder or is a persistently recurrent symptom.

Childlike thinking

Research into dichotomous thinking in borderline personality disorders as a way of thinking that represents the remaining emotional cognitive development in these patients has provided more consistent results. Dichotomous thinking in patients with borderline personality disorders appears to be stronger in schema-congruent situations than in emotional and neutral control situations (Veen and Arntz, 2000). However, their evaluations seem, in general, to be multidimensional (i.e., mixed positive and negative) (Veen and Arntz, 2000; Sieswerda *et al.*, 2005; Sieswerda and Arntz, submitted; Sieswerda *et al.*, submitted; Ten Haaf and Arntz, submitted) and/or normally differentiated, even in rather strong emotional conditions (e.g., a discussion with a rejecting social worker; Ten Haaf and Arntz, submitted). Borderline patients are therefore capable of giving evaluations which, in complexity, measure up to evaluations given by patients with other personality disorders and non-patients. This means that dichotomous thinking in borderline personality disorders isn't necessarily an expression of a low cognitive emotional development.

Nor do studies into empathy point consistently in the direction of underdeveloped cognitions in borderline patients. These patients, like patients with Cluster C personality disorders, seem to explain complex social and physical situations, when intelligence level is controlled for, rather better than healthy non-patients (Arntz, Bernstein, Oorschot and Schobre, 2009). Furthermore, they recognized the emotions of others as well as, and sometimes even better than, healthy non-patients (Lynch *et al.*, 2006; Fertuck *et al.*, 2009).

Conclusion

In summary, we have demonstrated the initial findings of experimental studies into schema models of personality problems that have been carried out thus far:

- schema-related and disorder-specific hypervigilance, and selective attention in borderline personality disorders;
- schema-congruent reactions in obsessive-compulsive personality disorders;
- schema-congruent and disorder-specific interpretations in avoidant/dependent personality disorders, obsessive-compulsive personality disorders, and borderline personality disorders;
- schema-related and disorder-specific dichotomous, but not childlike evaluations in borderline personality disorders;
- disorder-specific negative evaluations in borderline personality disorders;
- relevance of hypervigilance and dichotomous social evaluations in borderline personality disorders.

Pitfalls and Tips

Conducting experimental studies into personality disorders has many pitfalls. The following are typical for experimental studies into personality disorders.

First is the inclusion of meaningless control conditions. Several experimental studies into personality disorders compare an experimental patient group with a healthy non-patient group. These studies can, at best, show how the patient group differs from healthy subjects, but they don't show how this patient group differs from other patient groups.

A second potential pitfall is lack of confidence or experimental studies in clinical institutions in which the study is carried out, especially for experimental studies with strong emotional stimuli. Due to this, the study can act as a lightning rod for dissatisfaction about other matters within the institution and the study runs the risk of ending prematurely. Methodological and ethically well-constructed research, well-informed and motivated people who are directly and indirectly involved, support for the test leaders and common sense, can help avoid this.

The last pitfall is the influence of the personality disorder on experimental manipulation. Patients with personality disorders often react differently to research situations than patients with other disorders or non-patients do. For example, several patients with borderline personality disorders refused, in a detection task of a Stroop experiment, to guess the meaning of words that were offered below the detection threshold. At the other end of the spectrum, an evaluation study using very emotional film clips was received very positively by a large number of patients with borderline personality disorders. Pilot research and debriefing the subject after conclusion of the research can bring these influences to light.

The Future

Experimental research of the ST theoretical model is still in its infancy. Future research could focus on:

- the barely studied cognitive models in histrionic, narcissistic, and Cluster A personality disorders;
- further understanding of current research methods (e.g., dichotomous thinking in borderline personality disorder);
- testing the causal role of cognitive aspects with the help of analog experiments;
- further development of paradigms in which schemas and cognitive characteristics can be measured for validity and reliability, if desired for individual (personality) diagnosis.

References

Arntz, A., Appels, C. and Sieswerda, S. (2000) Hypervigilance in borderline disorder: a test with the emotional Stroop paradigm. *Journal of Personality Disorders, 14*, 366–373.

Arntz, A., Bernstein, D., Oorschot, M. and Schobre, P. (2009) Theory of mind in borderline and Cluster C personality disorder. *Journal of Nervous and Mental Disease, 197*, 801–807.

Arntz, A. and Veen, G. (2001) Evaluation of others by borderline patients. *The Journal of Nervous and Mental Disease, 189*, 513–521.

Beck, A.T., Freeman, A. and Davis, D.D. (2004) *Cognitive Therapy of Personality Disorders*, 2nd edition. New York: Guilford Press.

Berenson, K.R., Gyurak, A., Ayduk, O. *et al.* (2009) Rejection sensitivity and disruption of attention by social threat cues. *Journal of Research in Personality, 43*, 1064–1072.

Ceumern-Lindenstjerna, I.A. von (2004) *Selektive Aufmerksamkeitsausrichtung auf emotionale Reize bei Patientinnen mit Borderline-störung (Richting van selectieve aandacht voor emotionele stimuli bij patiënten met borderline persoonlijkheidsstoornis).* Proefschrift, Ruprecht-Karls-Universität, Heidelberg.

Dreessen, L., Arntz, A., Hendriks, T., Keune, N. and van den Hout, M.A. (1999) Avoidant personality disorder and schema-congruent information processing bias: a pilot study with a pragmatic inference task. *Behaviour Research and Therapy, 37*, 619–632.

Farrell, J.M., Shaw, I.A. and Webber, M.A. (2010) A schema-focused approach to group psychotherapy for outpatients with borderline personality disorder: a randomized controlled trial. *Journal of Behavior Therapy and Experimental Psychiatry, 40*, 317–328.

Fertuck, E.A., Jekal, A., Song, I. *et al.* (2009) Enhanced "reading the mind in the eyes" in borderline personality disorder compared to healthy controls. *Psychological Medicine, 39*, 1979–1988.

Giesen-Bloo, J., van Dyck, R., Spinhoven, P. *et al.* (2006) *Archives of General Psychiatry, 63*, 649–658.

King-Casas, B., Sharp, L., Lomax-Bream, T.L., Fonagy, P. and Montague, P.R. (2008) The rupture and repair of cooperation in borderline personality disorder. *Science, 321*, 806–810.

Kroll, J. (1998) *The Challenge of the Borderline Patient.* New York and London: W.W. Norton.

Layden, M.A., Newman, C.F., Freeman, A. and Morse, S.B. (1993) *Cognitive Therapy of Borderline Personality Disorder.* Needham Heights, MA: Allyn & Bacon.

Lynch, T.R., Rosenthal, M.Z., Kosson, D.S. *et al.* (2006) Heightened sensitivity to facial expressions of emotion in borderline personality disorder. *Emotion, 6*, 547–555.

Nadort, M., Arntz, A., Smit, J.H. *et al.* (2009) Implementation of outpatient schema therapy for borderline personality disorder with versus without crisis support by the therapist outside office hours: a randomized trial. *Behaviour Research and Therapy, 47*, 961–973.

Pretzer, J. (1990) Borderline personality disorder, in *Cognitive Therapy of Personality Disorders* (eds A.T. Beck, A. Freeman and Associates). New York: Guilford Press, pp. 176–207.

Rüsch, N., Corrigan, P.W., Bohus, M. *et al*. (2007) *Journal of Nervous and Mental Disease*, *195*, 537–539.

Rüsch, N., Lieb, K., Göttler, I., *et al*. (2007) Shame and implicit self-concept in women with borderline personality disorder. *American Journal of Psychiatry*, *164*, 500–508.

Sabo, A.N. (1997) Etiological significance of associations between childhood trauma and borderline personality disorder: conceptual and clinical implications. *Journal of Personality Disorders*, *11*, 50–70.

Sieswerda, S., and Arntz, A. (submitted for publication) Change of extreme and negative interpersonal evaluations of borderline patients during psychotherapy.

Sieswerda, S., Arntz, A. and Kindt, M. (2007) Successful psychotherapy reduces hypervigilance in borderline personality disorder. *Behavioural and Cognitive Psychotherapy*, *35*, 387–402.

Sieswerda, S., Arntz, A., Mertens, I. and Vertommen, S. (2007) Hypervigilance in patients with borderline personality disorder: specificity, automaticity, and predictors. *Behaviour Research and Therapy*, *45*, 1011–1024.

Sieswerda, S., Arntz, A., and Verheul, R. (submitted for publication) Not dichotomous, but negative interpersonal evaluations characterize borderline patients.

Sieswerda, S., Arntz, A. and Wolfis, M. (2005) Evaluations of emotional non-interpersonal situations by patients with borderline personality disorder. *Journal of Behavior Therapy and Experimental Psychiatry*, *36*, 209–225.

Ten Haaf, J.E. and Arntz, A. (submitted for publication) Social cognition in borderline personality disorder: evidence for dichotomous thinking but no evidence for primitive attributions.

Unoka, Z., Seres, I., Áspán, N., Bódi, N. and Kéri, S. (2009) Trust game reveals restricted interpersonal transactions in patients with borderline personality disorder. *Journal of Personality Disorders*, *23*, 399–409.

Veen, G. and Arntz, A. (2000) Multidimensional dichotomous thinking characterizes borderline personality disorder. *Cognitive Therapy and Research*, *24*, 23–45.

Waller, G. and Button, J. (2002) Processing of threat cues in borderline personality disorder. Unpublished manuscript.

Weertman, A. and Arntz, A. (2007) Effectiveness of treatment of childhood memories in cognitive therapy for personality disorders: a controlled study contrasting methods focusing. *Behaviour Research and Therapy*, *45*, 2133–2143.

Weertman, A., Arntz, A., de Jong, P.J. and Rinck, M. (2008) Implicit self- and other-associations in obsessive-compulsive personality disorder traits. *Cognition and Emotion*, *22*, 1253–1275.

Weertman, A., Arntz, A., Salet, S. and Coenen, I. (2006) Obsessive compulsive personality disorder and interpretation of schema-related events, in *The Cognitive Model of Personality Disorders* (ed. A. Weertman). PhD Thesis, Universiteit Maastricht.

Weertman, A., Arntz, A., Schouten, E. and Dreessen, L. (2006) Dependent personality traits and information processing: assessing the interpretation of ambiguous information using the Thematic Apperception Test. *British Journal of Clinical Psychology*, *45*, 273–278.

Westen, D. (1990) Towards a revised theory of borderline object relations: contributions of empirical research. *The International Journal of Psychoanalysis*, *71*, 661–693.

Williams, J.M.G., Watts, F.N., MacLeod, C. and Mathews, A. (1997) *Cognitive Psychology and Emotional Disorders*, 2nd edition. Chichester: John Wiley & Sons.

Wingenfeld, K., Mensebach, C., Rullkoetter, N., *et al*. (2009) Attentional bias to personally relevant words in borderline personality disorder is strongly related to comorbid post-traumatic stress disorder. *Journal of Personality Disorders*, *23*, 141–155.

Young, J.E., Klosko, J. and Weishaar, M.E. (2003) *Schema Therapy: a Practitioner's Guide*. New York: Guilford Press.

4
Validation of the Young Schema Questionnaire

Marleen Rijkeboer

Based on cognitive and developmental psychological theories of psychopathology, combined with his extended clinical experience, Young identified the different so-called early maladaptive schemas, in short, schemas. He states that these schemas contain general themes that are present in everyone. However, these schemas are more extreme and rigid in nature in individuals who experience more, or more symptomatic, problems. Young's schema mode model is in Young's words a working model. His ideas about which schemas are important for personality pathology are continuously in development (see Young, Klosko and Weishaar, 2003).

All of this has affected how his model is put into practice through questionnaires. Over time, several versions of the Young Schema Questionnaire (YSQ) were developed. The best known and most commonly used is the YSQ-2, in which, in accordance with Young's original classification, 16 schemas are identified (Young and Brown, 1994). This questionnaire is used by social workers all over the world and has been translated into at least nine languages, including Dutch.

Internationally, many studies into the psychometric properties of the YSQ-2 have been published. The first studies into YSQ-2 demonstrated that the Social Undesirability schema couldn't be identified as an independent factor (Schmidt, Joiner, Young and Telch, 1995; Lee, Taylor and Dunn, 1999). Based on these outcomes, both the original long version and the short version of the YSQ-2 were used in continuation of the research, in which Social Undesirability was omitted. In subsequent studies, Young adapted his working theory and formulated a model with 18 schemas (YSQ-3; see Young *et al.*, 2003). However, research into YSQ-3 is still in its infancy.

This chapter reports on the Dutch translation and version of the YSQ-2 (Schema-Vragenlijst (SQ); Sterk and Rijkeboer, 1997). The questionnaire was investigated thoroughly for its psychometric properties in several studies (Rijkeboer, 2005).

Several new developments will also be discussed. For example, the SQ appeared to be less applicable for certain age groups, such as children and adolescents. Furthermore, the SQ seems to be less applicable in the forensic field, in which the underreporting of problems hinders interpretation of the questionnaire. Therefore, several adaptations of the SQ have been developed. These adaptations will also be described.

In Practice

Different versions of the YSQ-2 are available in each language. Not only are there several translations available, but the order of the items varies in the different questionnaires. Furthermore, regardless of the version, different scoring formats are used. This plurality of procedures has led to some confusion. This will be explained below.

Translating the YSQ-2

The translation of the SQ went through several phases, in which standard procedures were always followed (van de Vijver and Hambleton, 1996). With Young's permission, two independent professional translators separately translated the items into Dutch. In addition to this, they then translated each other's translation into English. Next, the authors chose the best translated items. Following this, the Dutch version was discussed with Arnoud Arntz and Jeffrey Young. Some items appeared to have a seemingly obvious translation that in fact did not correspond with the original content. Sometimes, this led to long discussions over the items concerned. In addition, the structure of the questionnaire was refined in close cooperation with Young, after which he gave his authorization. Finally, the order of the items was randomized. The next paragraph details this.

Order of the items

Some versions follow the original order of items, which means that the items are clustered per scale. A frequently heard argument by therapists in favor of this clustering is that this method simplifies the checking of the patient's score for each item, without needing to search for which scale the particular item belongs to. Although this argument is understandable, such an approach can result in a less reliable diagnosis (see Nunnally and Bernstein, 1994). Generally, examining the individual items provides irrelevant information, since each item itself has a low reliability. Furthermore, clustering items can provide certain response tendencies, for example, trying to answer the successive items as consistently as possible and/or trying to create a very negative image on the scales that are important for the patient. Therefore, it is preferable to randomize the order of the items.

Scoring rate of the YSQ-2

Initially, Young advised to count the most extreme scores (5 and 6) per scale only (see Cecero and Young, 2001). Waller, Shah, Ohanion, and Elliott (2001) compared the effect of this method of scoring with one in which *all* scores on items within the scale were added up and averaged. They concluded that the last scoring method is preferable, since counting only the extreme scores can lead to psychopathology remaining hidden. This influences the predictive value of the questionnaire. Therefore, it is advisable to calculate the average of all scores per scale.

Approach

Research into the SQ

The SQ has been investigated for several psychometric properties. This section offers an overview of the outcomes of five validity studies (see also Rijkeboer, 2005). The results are ordered by means of the hypotheses concerning the maladaptive schemas as represented in the questionnaire (Young *et al.*, 2003).

One of the assumptions is that the schemas identified by Young, occur in *all* people (Young and Klosko, 1994). This hypothesis is the basic principle of a study into the factor structure of the SQ (Rijkeboer and van den Bergh, 2006), in which both a clinical group, consisting of patients with personality problems, and a non-clinical group of students were investigated. For Young's hypothesis to hold out, the factor structure must be identical for both groups, since the same constructs will be measured, but the range of the scores may vary. Using confirmatory techniques (structural equation modeling) the structure for both the patient group and the student group was investigated simultaneously. Results suggest that the factor structure is invariable and that the scales have a good construct validity and reliability. This means that when using SQ, clearly defined schema constructs are measured in people with and without significant mental problems, in a precise and identical way. Furthermore, the results indicated that *all* 16 schema factors can be replicated, including Social Undesirability. Although a previous study into the English YSQ-2 didn't demonstrate this factor as a separate dimension, it appeared that Social Undesirability does have a unique contribution when using more advanced techniques. Therefore, there was no reason to delete this scale from the Dutch version of the SQ. Furthermore, the scale can be useful for the diagnosis of social anxiety (see Pinto-Gouveia, Castilho, Galhardo and Cunha, 2006), assessment, for example, in Cluster C personality disorders.

Furthermore, Young states that schema scales represent deeply entrenched, permanent structures, which are subject to little change (Young *et al.*, 2003). So the SQ should measure constructs, which are, in any case, stable over time. Therefore, in a second study the test-retest reliability was investigated in a non-clinical group of students (Rijkeboer, van den Bergh and van den Bout, 2005). The stability of the rank-order and the mean of scores was analyzed. The interval between both measures was six weeks. The test–retest correlation coefficients appeared to be satisfactory for all scales.

In this study it was investigated whether the SQ discriminates between patients and students. According to the theory, symptomatic individuals should score considerably higher on the schema scales than individuals without noticeable mental problems. Results indicated that both groups were significantly discriminated by all schema scales. The Emotional Inhibition scale appeared to have most discriminative power. Furthermore, classification analyses demonstrated that 88% of the participants could be correctly assigned to the group they belonged to using the SQ. Although a substantial proportion, it should be noted that the SQ is slightly less able to correctly classify patients compared to students. This is probably due to a larger variance in scores within the clinical group, meaning the patients show more unique profiles on the SQ. In other words, the variation of scores per scale in the clinical group is large, meaning that within a patient population the scores on the various scales are very diverse and each patient shows a personal unique pattern of scores. Therefore, it is possible for a patient to score relatively low on some scales, while scoring very high on other scales. Studying the scale scores in combination with each other is recommended in order to gain a better view of the presence and nature of the pathology.

If scale scores are checked separately, the research mentioned above (Rijkeboer et al., 2005) indicated that for most schema scales it was found that a mean score of 2,5 or higher falls mainly within the clinical range. This cut-off value for Defectiveness/Shame is at an average of 2, while the cut-off for Self-Sacrifice and Unrelenting Standards/Hypercriticalness is a mean score of around 3.

Thus far (international) research into the YSQ-2 has focused on the sum scores of items in each scale. In none of the studies the possible bias of the *separate* items was investigated. Item bias implies that an item doesn't measure a similar latent construct among the examined groups (e.g., patients and non-patients). This means that respondents from different groups infer different meanings from the item concerned. This may lead to erroneous conclusions when comparing groups. Therefore, for a valid use of the YSQ scale scores for clinical and research purposes, absence of item bias for identified groups is essential. In a third study, the possible bias of items in the SQ was therefore tested (Rijkeboer, van den Bergh and van den Bout, 2011). The results demonstrated that there is no indication that men and women interpret the questions differently. Only one item showed differential item functioning for educational level and 10 of the 205 items yielded an inconsistent response pattern for patients compared to the non-patients. These 10 items are evenly spread over the questionnaire, which means that the sum score of the scales isn't substantially influenced by the differential functions of certain items. In summary, it can be stated that the items of the SQ are generally understood in a similar way by different groups and the comparison between groups based on the sum score of the SQ scales can be readily interpreted.

Young states, in addition, that schemas are central to personality pathology (Young et al., 2003). Therefore, there must be clear and meaningful associations between the SQ and the questionnaires that measure stable personality features and which also have established relevance in the diagnosis of personality disorders. In a first study into the concurrent validity, the SQ was related to the NEO-PI-R (Costa and McCrae, 1992), an inventory that has been developed within the Five-Factor Model of personality. A second study dealt with the relationships between the SQ and the Temperament and Character Inventory (TCI; Cloninger, Pzrybeck, Svrakic and Wetzel, 1994), a tool that is frequently used within psychiatric institutes. In both studies several structural models were tested, containing a priori specified relationships between the YSQ scales and the domains and facets of the questionnaires involved (see Rijkeboer, 2005). The results from both studies support most of the hypotheses, which means that the SQ has good convergent and divergent validity. This means that the schema scales are consistent with scales that are to measure identical constructs, and significantly differ from scales that are to measure unrelated constructs. It also appears that almost all schema scales, regardless of content, are characterized by a number of specific personality aspects. The schema scales related to, for example, a tendency to desperation, loneliness, pessimism about outcomes, and demoralization. Furthermore, subjects who score highly on the SQ are characterized by a conventional attitude and compulsive behavior. They also have a limited idea of internal control and a tendency to blame others for the problems that confront them.

It is remarkable that, contrary to expectations, schema scales hardly seem to be related to aspects of anxiety. Subsequent analyses, however, indicated that many scales don't relate so much linearly as they do curvilinearly to these anxiety aspects. Up to a mean score of 3.5 on practically every schema scale there is a linear relation with anxiety. A higher score on the schema scales is associated with a higher score on the anxiety aspects. However, higher mean scores on the schema scales no longer are related with these aspects, since a ceiling effect occurs. The anxiety score has increased to such extent that higher scores are no longer possible. This means that the schema scales are indeed related to these aspects and represent a strong feeling of anxiety. Furthermore, these result indicate that a questionnaire such as the NEO-PI-R does not differentiate between the higher levels of anxiety, while the SQ clearly does. Where in the NEO-PI-R a ceiling effect occurs, higher scores are still possible in the SQ.

Finally, it should be noted that hardly any relationships were found between the scales of the SQ and aspects that are connected to sensation seeking and a cooperative attitude. However, this could be an artifact of the composition of the investigated group: relatively few patients with an antisocial or schizoid personality disorder participated. On the other hand, it is possible that the SQ mainly represents internalizing problem behavior. This implies that the schema model might need expansion with scales that reflect more externalizing tendencies.

Research into the SQ for adolescents and children

Young (1994) states that maladaptive schema develop at a very young age. In order to be able to test both this hypothesis and the predictive validity of schemas for mental problems in children and adolescents, several adjustments to the original questionnaire were made by adapting the items to the life experience and environment of children and adolescents. As a result, a short form of the SQ for adolescents was developed (van Vlierberghe, Rijkeboer, Hamers and Braet, 2004; Muris, 2006) and one specifically for children (de Boo and Rijkeboer, 2004).

Research into the SQ for youngsters (Muris, 2006; van Vlierberghe, Rijkeboer, Hamers and Braet, 2004; Rijkeboer and de Boo, 2010) and adolescents (aged respectively 12–15 years and 12–18 years) showed that the schema scales have satisfactory reliability. Based on confirmatory factor analysis, Van Vlierberghe et al. (2010) found support for Young's adapted schema model, in which all 15 schemas are distinguished. In addition, Muris (2006) found support for a higher-order factor model consisting of three dimensions, or schema domains, with adequate factor loadings for the diverse schema scales. However, in the study by Van Vlierberghe and colleagues, equal values for divers fit indices were found for higher-order factor models with three, four, or five schema domains. From a psychometrical point of view, there is no preference for a specific higher-order model. Both studies also showed that the schema scales were related to a broad spectrum of psychopathology. In a group studied by van Vlierberghe and Braet (2007), the schema model accounted for approximately 45% of the variance in the internalizing and 19% in the externalizing problem behavior. This is consistent with the results that were found in the research into adults.

The SQ for children was investigated using a large group of schoolchildren aged 8–13 years, with diverse cultural backgrounds (Rijkeboer and de Boo, 2010). Results obtained by the help of confirmatory factor analysis suggest a good fit for a model that contained, besides eight of the original 15 factors, three new factors, for each of which two or three of the remaining original factors were clustered on theoretical bases. Study into the concurrent validity suggests that most schemas were associated with the temperament dimension Negative Affectivity, which corresponds with the previously described studies into adolescents and adults. However, a remarkable difference was found for the scales Enmeshment/Undeveloped Self and Self-Sacrifice, which appeared to have no relation to Negative Affectivity, but were strongly related to Positive Affectivity and Self-Control. Although these two schemas have an obvious maladaptive character in youngsters and adults, it seems that they are not dysfunctional in children, probably because the phase of development in which they find themselves implies a dependent relationship with a focus on important others. This interesting fact is worth investigating further.

Pitfalls and Tips

The YSQ is a self-report tool. Although it has advantages, this type of assessment also has pitfalls. The fact is that a self-report can be influenced in several ways. This will be explained below.

Therapists frequently ask to what extent a patient's score on the YSQ is influenced by the mood they are in. In fact, what they are referring to is the nature of the measured constructs: are they more trait- or state-related? This is an important question concerning the validity of the YSQ. Young proposes that the schemas are fixed, permanent beliefs, that is, beliefs that aren't subject to situation-related change. Can a self-report tool measure such trait-related constructs?

Rijkeboer et al. (2005) demonstrated that the schema scales have good test–retest reliability, in other words, participants complete the questionnaire consistently at different points in time. This is a first indication of its stability. However, checking whether the YSQ scores also remain consistent after a mood change or after evoking negative memories is another matter.

Stopa and Waters (2005) demonstrated that scores on most schema scales remain similar after a mood induction. With the help of music, positive or negative moods were evoked in participants. This mood induction appeared to influence only two schemas: the score for Emotional Deprivation increased after a negative mood induction, while the score for Entitlement/Grandiosity increased as a result of a positive change of mood. Furthermore, two so-called priming studies investigated the extent to which evoking negative memories influenced the endorsement of the YSQ (Jacquin, 1998; Brandon, 2000). In both studies no evidence was found that priming affects the scores. In summary, it can be concluded that thus far, there is little reason to assume that situation-specific factors influence the way the YSQ is completed. However, more research, with perhaps stronger interventions, is required to determine whether the schemas, as represented by the YSQ, have a primarily trait-related character.

Another issue that is reported by therapists is that, because of the self-reporting, patients can easily create a favorable or unfavorable impression of themselves on the YSQ. In particular in the forensic setting, this complicates its use, especially when scales with an "undesirable" content for that setting are taken into view. In order to overcome this, an implicit measure was made for one of the most prominent schemas within the forensic field: Insufficient Self-Control/Self-Discipline (Rijkeboer and Huntjens, 2007). In this way an indirect measure is taken of the extent to which subjects associate themselves with the characteristics represented in this schema. For this purpose, a computer task was developed in which schema-congruent and incongruent words appear on the screen in capitals or in lower-case letters. The task is to respond as quickly as possible to the word format – the task-relevant feature of the words (e.g., with "yes" if the word is written in capitals and with "no" if the lower-case lettering is used), while the meaning of these words – the irrelevant characteristic – is ignored. Studies using the irrelevant feature paradigm show that participants, even when following the instructions strictly, still spontaneously process information about the meaning of the words. This influences the speed at which they react. This reaction time can then be used as a measure of the implicit personal association with the features used in the task.

The initial, and currently preliminary, results of an experimental study (Rijkeboer and Huntjens, 2007) indicate that the stimulus words that were used were representative of the corresponding YSQ scale. Furthermore, this implicit measure appeared to spontaneously (and therefore uncontrollably) predict schema-relevant behavior, whereas no link between the self-report and this behavior was found. Obviously, more research is required, but these initial results are promising, for the implicit measure could be a useful alternative for measuring the schema Insufficient Self-Control/Self-Discipline in the forensic setting.

The Future

The YSQ-2 is a long questionnaire, which requires a great deal of effort from some patients. Therefore, a shortened version in English has been developed, consisting of 75 items, divided into 15 scales. The Social Undesirability scale is not included. The short form of the YSQ-2 has been well studied and the results demonstrate that this version seems to have good psychometric properties (e.g., Stopa, Thorne, Waters and Preston, 2001). Currently, a Dutch short form of the YSQ, which does include the Social Undesirability schema, is being investigated, as well as a short form focused on senior citizens.

Furthermore, it should be noted that Young's schema model is in development and new schemas are being added to it. Therefore, the YSQ-3, which includes 18 schemas, has been in circulation for some time. These are the schemas of the YSQ-2 (without Social Undesirability) and three new schemas: Approval and Recognition Seeking, Negativity/Pessimism, and Punitiveness. The YSQ-3 is still in a experimental phase. Thus far, there has been little study into the value of this extension of the YSQ, although studies in several countries have begun. Therefore, until more results are published, use of only the validated version is recommended for clinical purposes.

It is noteworthy that the extension of the schema model is again related to the internalizing problems of anxiety, depression, and dependency. Several studies into the YSQ, in adults, and in and adolescents and children, demonstrate that this type of pathology is measured in particular. Themes referring to hate, anger, hostility, and aggression are less well represented in the YSQ. Therefore, it would be desirable to create a more balanced classification of both internalized and externalized themes for the model in the near future.

References

Boo, G.M. de and Rijkeboer, M.M. (2004) *Schema Inventory for Children*. University of Amsterdam, Department of Clinical Psychology.

Brandon, R A. (2000) Early recollections as a trigger technique for identifying early maladaptive schemas. *Dissertation Abstracts International*, 61(3), 1626B.

Cecero, J.J. and Young, J. (2001) Case of Silvia: a schema-focused approach. *Journal of Psychotherapy Integration*, 11, 217–229.

Cloninger, C.R., Pzrybeck, T.R., Svrakic, D.M. and Wetzel, R.D. (1994) *The Temperament and Character Inventory (TCI): a Guide to its Development and Use*. Washington University Center for Psychobiology of Personality, St. Louis.

Costa Jr., P.T. and McCrae, R.R. (1992) *Revised NEO Personality Inventory (NEO-PI-R) and NEO Five-Factor Inventory (NEO-FFI)*. Odessa, FL: Psychological Assessment Resources, Professional Manual.

Jacquin, K.M. (1998) The effects of maladaptive schemata on information processing. *Dissertation Abstracts International*, 59(1): 435B.

Lee, C.W., Taylor, G. and Dunn, J. (1999) Factor structure of the Schema Questionnaire in a large clinical sample. *Cognitive Therapy and Research*, 23, 441–451.

Muris, P. (2006) Maladaptive schemas in non-clinical adolescents: relations to perceived parental rearing behaviours, big five personality factors, and psychopathological symptoms. *Clinical Psychology and Psychotherapy*, 13, 405–413.

Nunnally, J.C. and Bernstein, I.H. (1994) *Psychometric Theory*, 3rd edition. New York: McGraw-Hill.

Pinto-Gouveia, J., Castilho, P., Galhardo, A. and Cunha, M. (2006) Early maladaptive schemas and social phobia. *Cognitive Therapy and Research*, 30, 571–584.

Rijkeboer, M.M. (2005) *Assessment of Early Maladaptive Schemas. On the Validity of the Dutch Young Schema Questionnaire*. Universiteit Utrecht: PhD Thesis.

Rijkeboer, M.M. and Bergh, H. van de (2006) Multiple group confirmatory factor of the Young Schema Questionnaire in a Dutch clinical versus non-clinical sample. *Cognitive Therapy and Research*, 30, 263–278.

Rijkeboer, M.M., Bergh, H. van de and Bout, J. van de (2011) Item bias analysis of the Young Schema Questionnaire for psychopathology, gender, and educational level. *European Journal of Psychological Assessment*, 27, 65–70.

Rijkeboer, M.M., Bergh, H. van de, and Bout, J. van de (2005) Stability and discriminative power of the Young Schema Questionnaire in a Dutch clinical versus non-clinical sample. *Journal of Behavior Therapy and Experimental Psychiatry*, 36, 129–144.

Rijkeboer, M.M. and Boo, G.M. de (2010) Early maladaptive schemas in children: development and validation of the Schema Inventory for Children. *Journal of Behavior Therapy and Experimental Psychiatry*, 41, 102–109.

Rijkeboer, M.M. and Huntjens, R.J.C. (2007) *EMS's in forensic settings: an implicit measure of insufficiënt self-control/self-discipline*. A pilot study. Paper presented at the World Congress of Behavioural and Cognitive Therapies, Barcelona, July 12–14.

Schmidt, N.B., Joiner, T.E., Young, J.E. and Telch, M.J. (1995) The Schema Questionnaire: investigation of psychometric properties and the hierarchical structure of a measure of maladaptive schemas. *Cognitive Therapy and Research*, 19, 295–231.

Sterk, F. and Rijkeboer, M.M. (1997) *Schema-Vragenlijst*. Utrecht: Ambulatorium Universiteit Utrecht.

Stopa, L., Thorne, P., Waters, A. and Preston, J. (2001) Are the short and long forms of the Young Schema Questionnaire comparable and how well does each version predict psychopathology scores? *Journal of Cognitive Psychotherapy*, 15, 253–272.

Stopa, L. and Waters, A. (2005) The effect of mood on responses to the Young Schema Questionnaire: short form. *Psychology and Psychotherapy: Theory, Research and Practice*, 78, 45–57.

Vijver, F.J.R. van de and Hambleton, R.K. (1996) Translating tests: some practical guidelines. *European Psychologist*, 1, 81–99.

Vlierberghe, L. van and Braet, C. (2007) Dysfunctional schemas and psychopathology in referred obese adolescents. *Clinical Psychology and Psychotherapy*, 14, 342–351.

Vlierberghe, L. van, Braet, C., Bosmans, G., Rosseel, Y. and Bögels, S. (2010) Maladaptive schemas and psychopathology in adolescence: on the utility of Young's schema theory in youth. *Cognitive Therapy and Research*, 34, 316–332.

Vlierberghe, L. van, Rijkeboer, M.M., Hamers, P. and Braet, C. (2004) *Schema Questionnaire for adolescents*. Department of Personality Development and Social Psychology. University of Gent, Gent.

Waller, G., Shah, R., Ohanian, V. and Elliott, P. (2001) Core beliefs in bulimia nervosa and depression: the discriminant validity of Young's Schema Questionnaire. *Behavior Therapy*, 32, 139–153.

Young, J.E. (1994) *Cognitive Therapy for Personality Disorders: a Schema-focused Approach*, rev. edition. Sarasota, FL: Professional Resource Press.

Young, J.E. and Brown, G. (1994) *Young Schema Questionnaire*, 2nd edition. In J.E. Young, *Cognitive Therapy for Personality Disorders: a Schema-focused Approach*, rev. edition. Sarasota, FL: Professional Resource Press, pp. 63–76.

Young, J.E. and Klosko, J.S. (1994) *Reinventing Your Life*. New York: Plume.

Young, J.E., Klosko, J.S. and Weishaar, M.E. (2003) *Schema Therapy: a Practitioner's Guide*. New York: Guilford Press.

5
Validation of the Schema Mode Inventory

Jill Lobbestael

The presence of schema modes can be determined by three methods, by: 1) mapping out problematic situations that patients experience and interpreting the behavior that they show in these situations as schema modes; 2) tracing modes using experiential techniques, in which patients are led back to the past; and 3) the most consistent method used to trace modes: self-report questionnaires. The first two methods are mainly used in therapy sessions, while the use of inventories is suitable for both therapy and research purposes. In practice, a combination of these three methods is recommended.

In this chapter, a new inventory used to determine the presence of modes is introduced: the Schema Mode Inventory (SMI; Young *et al.*, 2007). Both the precursors of this inventory and the different methods used to measure modes are discussed. The translation procedure, interpretation, and psychometric characteristics of SMI are also discussed. Finally, potential pitfalls and tips about using SMI are introduced, followed by recommendations for future research into inventory modes.

In Practice

Motivation to develop the SMI

The currently available instruments used to determine the presence of schema modes (e.g., the Young Atkinson Mode Inventory, YAMI; Young, Atkinson, Engels and Weishaar, 2004; and the Schema Mode Questionnaire; Klokman, Arntz and Sieswerda, 2005) are insufficient for three reasons. First, with these inventories, the presence of modes can only be measured by 10 central modes. Therefore, it is not possible to determine specific disorder modes. Second, there is no official Dutch translation of the YAMI inventory. Third, information about the reliability and validity of the existing mode questionnaires is limited. These limitations are an impediment to an adequate diagnosis by the use of self-report inventories, and yet this is one of the main steps taken during the initial evaluation in the mode conceptualization at the start of therapy.

Methods to measure modes

To measure modes using self-report inventories, two considerations regarding the scoring instruction of the items must be taken into account. First, the malfunctioning of modes can be determined in two ways: by assessing frequency and intensity. People can be upset by their maladaptive modes when they occur often, but also when these modes are not apparent, but are very intense. Both dimensions can be important within the therapeutic setting. A pilot study was therefore carried out to determine if it was possible to score every item of the SMI on both frequency (How often does it occur?) and intensity (How intense was this thought, emotion, or behavior for you?). However, this pilot study showed that it was very difficult for patients to distinguish between the two dimensions. Therefore, a decision was made to score every item in the SMI on frequency alone. It is nevertheless important for the therapeutic goals to map out the intensity of the modes present.

The second consideration concerning the measurement of mode items is that it is important to distinguish so-called state from trait conceptualizations of modes. Because schema modes reflect the current situation of a patient, modes are state concepts by definition. However, there are still two possible methods in which modes can be mapped out. By asking which modes are present *at the moment of completing* the inventory, only the mode or modes that are triggered at *that* moment are shown. The chance that a patient is in a relatively neutral or healthy mode when completing the questionnaire is relatively high. Therefore, the possibility exists that this isn't an adequate reflection of the severity of the patient's pathology. It is more explorative for both therapeutic and research purposes to obtain an overview of the modes that the patient in question shows most often, independent of the mode the patient is in while completing the questionnaire. Therefore, in the introduction of the SMI, the patient is asked to rate *how often* each item applies to him *in general*.

Approach

Precursors of the SMI

So far, two inventories have been used to determine the presence of schema modes. First, there is the Schema Mode Questionnaire (SMQ) developed by Klokman *et al.* (2005). The SMQ consists of 119 items, which map out the presence of seven schema modes: the Abandoned/Abused Child, the Angry Child, the Detached Protector, the Punitive Parent, the Compliant Surrender, the Over-Compensator, and the Healthy Adult. Each mode has 17 items: seven items express a thought, five express feelings, and five express behavior. These items are measured on a continuous scale (the Visual Analog Scale [VAS] scale) with a scale of 10 cm, which runs from "I don't believe this at all" to "I absolutely believe this" for thoughts, "I never feel like this" to "I always feel like this" for feelings, and "I never do this" to "I always do this" for behaviors. These SMQs were used by Arntz, Klokman, and Sieswerda (2005). Lobbestael, van Vreeswijk, Arntz, Spinhoven, and 't Hoen (2005) added the Bully and Attack mode to their SMQ, because they expected that this mode would be characteristic of patients with an anti social personality disorder, one of the central groups identified in this research. Both studies showed that the connection between the items in the mode scales was good: the Chronbach's alpha values varied in these two researches from $\alpha = 0.80$ to $\alpha = 0.94$, with an average of $\alpha = 0.91$.

The second currently used mode inventory is the Young–Atkinson Mode Inventory (YAMI) that was developed in 2004 by Young et al. This inventory contains 186 items, which measure the presence of 10 modes: the Impulsive Child, the Demanding Parent, and the Happy Child modes are added to the seven modes of the SMQ. Another difference from the SMQ is that the Abandoned/Abused Child is called the Vulnerable Child in the YAMI, which offers a somewhat broader definition. Furthermore, the items of the YAMI are not randomized or split into sections regarding thoughts, feelings, and behaviors, but are clustered into modes. The items in the YAMI are measured for frequency using a six-point scale, ranging from "never or almost never" to "all of the time." So far, no data are available on the validity or reliability of the YAMI.

Development of the SMI

Young and colleagues' Schema Mode Inventory (SMI) was published in 2007. This inventory was developed because there was a need for a mode inventory suitable for measuring the presence of all schema modes identified thus far. According to Young, Klosko, and Weishaar (2003), there is, for example, a Self-Aggrandizer mode with a narcissistic personality disorder. However, this mode cannot be measured with the SMQ or the YAMI, since these only contain the covering mode of Over-Compensator. With these earlier versions, it is not possible to check whether a certain patient or group of patients is characterized by this specific Self-Aggrandizer mode. Therefore, the SMI offers more information about the specific disorder modes, which increases the clinical relevance of the inventory. The SMI is in particular an enlargement of the SMQ and the YAMI, and it contains all items of the SMQ and YAMI (with the exception of a few items that showed insufficient relevance to their mode scales). Furthermore, the SMI was completed with items based on suggestions made by Beck, Freeman, and Davis (2004), and Young and colleagues (2003), and on clinical observation.

The translation procedures of YAMI items

The items of the YAMI were translated with Young's permission. Translation of these YAMI items appeared in the following sequence: first, the items were translated from English into Dutch by Dutch SMI authors. Then, these Dutch versions were translated back into English, by an independent bilingual translator. Next, the translated English version was compared with the original YAMI items by an independent research assistant. Finally the (often subtle) linguistic differences detected between the two versions were explained by an American. Accordingly, it was decided by the Dutch authors of the SMI, in consultation with Jeffrey Young, how the original YAMI items should be interpreted, and which Dutch terms most resembled the terms in Young's YAMI.

The set-up of the SMI

Originally, the SMI consisted of 269 items, which measured the presence of 16 modes. The acquisition of data from this questionnaire was very time-consuming and labor-intensive for both patients (time of questioning 30–45 minutes) and therapists, who had to score and interpret data from this questionnaire. Therefore, a new and final version of the SMI was published (Young et al., 2007). To compile this SMI, the authors selected items for each mode. These items fitted, statistically speaking, best to this specific mode and had the least overlap with other scales (they showed the most possible unique overtone). In search of these unique overtone items, the items of the Lonely Child mode and the Abandoned/Abused Child modes appeared to cover the overtone of both scales; not enough unique overtone items could be selected here. Therefore, the authors decided to combine these two scales, and it was renamed the Vulnerable Child. At the same time, it appeared that the items of the Over-Compensator mode were charged more in other scales, and for this scale, no unique overtone items could be defined. As a result, this scale was removed from the SMI. Therefore, the SMI finally comprised 14 scales:

1. Vulnerable Child: feels like a lonely child that is only appreciated to the extent that he pleases his parents. Because the most important emotional needs are unmet, emptiness and loneliness have developed. The feelings of immense emotional pain and fear of being abandoned are closely linked with the child's abusive past.
2. Angry Child: feels intensely angry, infuriated, enraged, or impatient because core emotional (or physical) needs are not being met.
3. Enraged Child: feels intense anger, expressed by offending or damaging actions against people or objects. These feelings of rage cannot be controlled.
4. Impulsive Child: acts on non-core desires or impulses in a selfish or uncontrolled manner to get his or her own way, and often has difficulty delaying short-term gratification.
5. Undisciplined Child: cannot force himself to finish routine or boring tasks; is easily frustrated and gives up quickly.
6. Happy Child: feels loved, contented, connected, satisfied, fulfilled, protected, accepted, praised, worthwhile, nurtured, guided, understood, validated, self-confident, competent, appropriately autonomous or self-reliant, safe, resilient, strong, in control, adaptable, included, optimistic, and spontaneous.
7. Compliant Surrender: acts in a passive, subservient, submissive, approval-seeking, or self-deprecating way around others out of fear, conflict, or rejection. Tolerates abuse and/or bad treatment.

8. Detached Protector: cuts off needs and feelings. Detaches emotionally from people and rejects their help. Feels withdrawn, spacy, distracted, disconnected, depersonalized, empty, or bored.
9. Detached Self-Soother: Aims for distraction, self-soothing, or self-stimulating activities (e.g., drug abuse, work, sleep, surfing the internet, chatting, sport, or sexual activities), in a compulsive or excessive way, to take his mind off painful feelings or in order to avoid having them in the first place.
10. Self-Aggrandizer: Behaves in an egocentric or self-interested manner in order to get his own way, without showing consideration for other people's feelings. Shows superiority and devaluation of others. Can feel super-special or believes he is entitled to special rights and privileges.
11. Bully and Attack mode: Offends, controls, deceives, or behaves in a passive–aggressive manner toward others to over-compensate in order to be able to deal with abuse, mistrust, deprivation, or shortcomings.
12. Punitive Parent: Feels that self or others deserves punishment or blame and often acts on these feelings by being blaming, punishing, or abusive toward self (e.g., self-injurious behavior) or others.
13. Demanding Parent: Feels that the "right" way to be is to be perfect or achieve at a very high level, to strive for high status, to be humble, to puts other needs before one's own, or to be efficient or avoid wasting time.
14. Healthy Adult: Nurtures, validates, and affirms the Vulnerable Child mode. Sets limits for the Angry and Impulsive Child modes. Promotes and supports the Happy Child mode. Combats and eventually replaces the maladaptive coping modes (such as the Obsessive Over-Controller and Bully and Attack modes). Neutralizes or moderates the maladaptive parent modes (Punitive Parent and Demanding Parent modes).

In total, the SMI contains 118 items. The number of items per mode varies from 4 to 10, with an average of 8.4 items. Administering the SMI takes approximately 20 minutes. All items are randomized. The items are scored using a six-point scale, which varies from "never or hardly ever" to "always." The disadvantage of using a six-point scale instead of a continuous VAS scale is that with the six-point scale, it is not possible to give a more differentiated answer. The VAS scale has many more possible response options. However, because scoring for the VAS scale is very time-consuming, the authors settled on a six-point scale.

Interpretation of the SMI

The final scores of the different SMI modes are determined by the average of all items of that scale. Table 5.1 shows the decile scores of non-patients ($N = 319$), Axis I patients ($N = 136$), and Axis II patients ($N = 236$). In this way, a check can be made regarding which decile score the individual mode score fits, in comparison to the group that the patient belongs to. For example, when a patient with an Axis I diagnosis has an average score of 4 on Vulnerable Child, the score of this patient falls within the highest 10% of the subgroup of Axis I patients. In this way, the clinician can estimate how extreme the score of an individual patient is, compared to the whole group.

Table 5.1 Psychometric characteristics of the SMI

		VC	AC	EC	UC	HC	CS	DP	DS	BA	SA	BA	PP	DP	HA
Non-patients	10	1.00	1.30	1.00	1.44	1.50	3.90	1.71	1.00	1.00	1.60	1.22	1.00	2.20	3.90
	20	1.00	1.40	1.00	1.67	1.67	4.10	2.00	1.11	1.40	1.80	1.33	1.10	2.60	4.10
	30	1.10	1.50	1.00	1.89	1.83	4.30	2.29	1.22	1.40	1.90	1.44	1.20	2.70	4.40
	40	1.20	1.60	1.00	2.00	2.17	4.40	2.43	1.33	1.60	2.20	1.56	1.30	2.90	4.50
	50	1.30	1.70	1.10	2.11	2.17	4.60	2.57	1.44	1.80	2.30	1.67	1.40	3.10	4.70
	60	1.50	1.90	1.20	2.22	2.33	4.70	2.71	1.67	2.00	2.40	1.78	1.50	3.20	4.80
	70	1.60	2.00	1.20	2.33	2.50	4.80	2.86	1.78	2.20	2.60	1.89	1.60	3.40	4.90
	80	1.90	2.20	1.30	2.56	2.83	4.90	3.00	2.00	2.40	2.80	2.11	1.70	3.60	5.10
	90	2.10	2.50	1.60	2.89	3.00	5.10	3.14	2.22	2.80	3.00	2.33	2.10	3.80	5.30
Axis I patients	10	1.47	1.50	1.00	1.56	1.50	2.20	2.00	1.22	1.80	1.57	1.22	1.17	2.47	2.90
	20	1.70	1.80	1.00	1.78	1.83	2.70	2.29	1.56	2.20	1.80	1.33	1.30	2.74	3.30
	30	1.91	2.00	1.10	2.01	2.00	2.91	2.57	1.67	2.40	2.00	1.44	1.50	2.91	3.50
	40	2.38	2.10	1.28	2.31	2.30	3.10	2.71	1.89	2.80	2.20	1.64	1.80	3.20	3.80
	50	2.65	2.30	1.30	2.44	2.67	3.40	2.86	2.33	3.00	2.30	1.78	2.05	3.50	4.00
	60	2.92	2.70	1.50	2.56	2.67	3.50	3.14	2.44	3.40	2.60	2.00	2.20	3.70	4.20
	70	3.20	2.99	1.70	2.78	2.83	3.80	3.43	2.78	3.58	2.80	2.12	2.50	3.90	4.40
	80	3.46	3.40	1.96	3.00	3.27	4.20	3.57	3.07	3.60	2.90	2.33	2.86	4.20	4.76
	90	4.10	3.80	2.30	3.44	3.67	4.70	4.19	3.67	4.20	3.53	2.78	3.40	4.53	5.10
Axis II patients	10	1.80	1.90	1.00	1.89	1.67	2.00	2.14	1.67	2.20	1.60	1.33	1.60	2.50	2.50
	20	2.30	2.20	1.20	2.11	2.17	2.20	2.43	2.11	2.60	1.90	1.56	1.90	3.00	2.84
	30	2.80	2.50	1.38	2.44	2.33	2.40	2.71	2.44	2.80	2.10	1.78	2.20	3.30	3.01
	40	3.10	2.80	1.60	2.78	2.67	2.60	3.00	2.67	3.00	2.30	1.89	2.40	3.50	3.40
	50	3.35	3.10	1.90	3.00	3.00	2.80	3.29	2.89	3.40	2.46	2.11	2.70	3.70	3.50
	60	3.70	3.30	2.20	3.22	3.17	3.00	3.57	3.16	3.60	2.70	2.22	2.90	3.90	3.90
	70	4.00	3.60	2.40	3.56	3.50	3.30	3.86	3.33	3.80	2.99	2.44	3.10	4.29	4.10
	80	4.40	3.90	2.90	3.89	3.83	3.56	4.14	3.67	4.20	3.40	2.89	3.60	4.50	4.36
	90	4.83	4.40	3.33	4.48	4.22	4.00	4.57	4.22	4.60	3.80	3.33	4.10	4.80	4.80

VC = Vulnerable Child; AC = Angry Child; EC = Enraged Child; UC = Undisciplined Child; HC = Happy Child; CS = Compliant Surrender; DP = Detached Protector; DS = Detached Self-Soother; SA = Self-Aggrandizer; BA = Bully and Attack; PP = Punitive Parent; DP = Demanding Parent; HA = Healthy Adult (Lobbestael, van Vreeswijk, Spinhoven, Schouten and Arntz, 2010).

Sample Survey

The SMI is the first mode inventory to be thoroughly checked for reliability and validity. This was carried out in a sample survey with 863 subjects. Because it is necessary to have a large research population for the validation of the inventories, it is tempting to make it relatively easy by asking healthy people to complete the survey. However, the problem with this is that scores on modes from a population that consists largely of people with little pathology are no-representative because healthy people score relatively low on pathological modes. Therefore, it is important to select a sample survey with a varying measure of pathology. The population used for the SMI validation research consisted of 319 non-patients, 136 Axis I patients, and 236 Axis II patients. Thirty-seven participants were patients who did not meet the minimum required number of traits of any of the Axis I or II diagnoses. Sixteen participants were screened as non-clinical participants, but met some criteria on Axis I or II without fulfilling the complete diagnostic criteria for a specific disorder. Due to missing values, there were no SCIDs available for 119 non-patient this way, we do a have a total of N = 863. These patients came from inpatient and outpatient mental healthcare institutes, prisons, and detention centers in the Netherlands and Belgium. Of these participants 88% were diagnosed as Axis I and Axis II by structured and clinical interviews for DSM-IV Axis I and Axis II disorders (SCID I and II, First, Spitzer, Gibbon, Williams and Benjamin, 1994; First, Spitzer, Gibbon and Williams, 1997; Weertman, Arntz and Kerkhofs, 2000).

Factor structure

As a first step, the factor structure of the SMI was determined. It is important to test whether it is best to divide the SMI into 14 scales, or whether some scales are so similar that it would be better to put them in the same factor. For example, you could test if the scales of the Punitive Parent and the Demanding Parent are differentiated by separate items, or if it would be better to include them in the Maladaptive Parent scale, because the scores on items of both scales are too alike. To determine the factor structure of an inventory, explorative factor analysis in SPSS is often used as prototype. However, explorative factor structure is only useful when there is no *a priori* assumption about the factor structure of the inventory in question. Whenever there is a theoretical framework, checks must be made as to whether the obtained data correspond to the assumed theory by confirmed factor analysis. This can be achieved by means of the statistical programs Lisrell (Jöreskog and Sörbom, 2001) or Amos (Arbuckle, 2005). Because the classification of the SMI into 14 scales is founded on the mode classification of Young, confirming factor analysis was used in this research.

The outcome of these factor analyses showed that it was best to keep 14 scales for each of the separate factors in SMI. This means that it is useful statistically to distinguish all of these scales because they do indeed measure separate constructs. This corresponds with the clinical observation, which many therapists and patients experience, that even though several modes resemble each other, they fundamentally represent separate constructs, which are also distinguishable from one another. Considerable interdependence between the different modes emerged because these modes often had a high inter-correlation. In particular, the modes that belong to the same category show this correlation. For example, the Angry Child and Enraged Child, both belong to the anger-related child modes, and the Happy Child and Healthy Adult both reflect the healthy modes within the mode theory. Parallel to that, Cronbach's alpha analyses show that the internal connection of all items of the 14 mode scales is sufficient to excellent. This means that the scoring patterns on the items of the different scales show sufficient similarities and could therefore measure the same scale.

Modes scores in subgroups

The concept of modes is especially developed to interpret the pathology of personality disorders, and in particular to explain the enormous variety of problems that people with severe personality disorders show, and explain the rapid changes in their condition. In line with this, you might expect modes to be less present in healthy people, more present in patients with Axis I disorders, and most evident in Axis II patients. This hypothesis was also tested in the study examining the validation of the SMI. Outcomes showed that the number of maladaptive modes increased from the healthy to the Axis I to the Axis II patients. Furthermore, the intensity of the modes was predicted by the severity of the personality disorder. This shows that the concept of modes is indeed specifically suited to describing personality disorders, and modes in particular give an explanation for the pathology of this category of patients.

Connection modes and schemas

In order to know more about the connection between schema modes and the early maladaptive schemas, the correlation between both concepts was ascertained. The great similarity in content between the constructs manifested itself in a moderate to high correlation between the 14 modes and the 15 schemas. Most high correlations could be explained by the large content similarity between certain modes and schemas, for example between the Compliant Surrender mode and the Functional Dependence, Subjugation, and Self-Sacrifice schemas. Furthermore, it appeared that modes that reflect more extreme behaviors (e.g., Enraged Child or Self-Aggrandizer) showed less overlap with the schemas. This might refer to the fact that the extreme behaviors, characteristic of personality disorders, are manifested more in modes than in schemas. This supports Young's rational vision that underlies the development of the mode concept.

Construct validity

To check whether the conceptualization of a mode can measure the aimed content (e.g., if the Angry Child mode actually measures anger), it is important to look at the connection between modes and other (subscales of) questionnaires, which have been shown to measure the particular construct in a reliable and valid way. This is known as construct validity. Although the construct validity of the SMI pointed in the right direction, the expected correlation between modes and items from other questionnaires of similar content were somewhat lower than expected. A possible explanation is that the constructs measured by these theoretically linked questionnaires are often more unambiguous than the modes, which mostly give a combination of different opinions, emotions, and behaviors.

Test–retest reliability

Finally, the test and retest reliability was measured in this research. Although modes reflect temporary states, it is still important that the combination of modes that patients often report remain stable over time. Results showed that this was definitely the case.

Conclusion

In conclusion, we can say that the SMI shows demonstrates reliability and validity. Therefore, it is a valuable tool to use within clinical practice, as well as for research purposes.

International development of the SMI

The SMI is currently translated into and validated for 15 languages: English, Dutch, Italian, German, Swedish, Turkish, French, Spanish, Portuguese, Greek, Korean, Norwegian, Spanish, Danish, and Urdu. An initial study of the psychometrics of the German SMI (Jacob, Dominiak, Harris, Reiss, Voderholzer and Lobbestael, submitted for publication) investigated construct validity and showed that most modes strongly correlated with different degrees of psychopathology, interpersonal problems, and feelings of guilt and shame. The over-compensation modes were correlated with narcissism and a dominant/cold interpersonal style. One interpretation is that these correlated patterns between modes and other measures mainly support the construct validity of the concept of modes, although the general psychopathology explains a great part of the variation.

SMI-2

A second version of the SMI (SMI-2; see Bamelis, Renner, Hiedkamp and Arntz, in press), was recently developed to measure, in particular, the modes for patients with Cluster C, paranoid, histrionic, and narcissistic personality disorders.

The SMI-2 measures 18 modes, has 174 items, and is distinct from the SMI in that two modes (the Happy Child and Bully and Attack) were omitted and seven modes (Lonely Child, Abandoned/Abused Child, Dependent Child, Avoiding Protector, Approval/Recognition-Seeking, Perfectionist Over-Controller, and Suspicious Over-Controller) were added. Psychometric analyses showed an adequate fit for the 18-factor model and a good internal reliability of the subscales.

In general, it is assumed that patients with an anti social personality disorder tend to deny their negative characteristics. This assumption was confirmed in a study in which self-report of the modes was compared to the report of the modes by a clinician (Lobbestael, Arntz, Löbbes and Cima, 2009). Patients with anti social personality disorders self-reported a significantly lower presence of most of the pathological modes compared to their clinician's report. Therefore, a possible underreporting of the maladaptive modes should be taken into accounts for patients with an anti social profile. Underreporting of maladaptive modes can, however, also result from a lack of self-insight on the part of patients. When the scores of the different modes are significantly lower than expected, based on the clinical image the therapist has of the particular patient, it is important not to accept this straight away, but always to ask a third party to describe the presence of the modes in this person. This can be achieved, for example, by asking them to complete a SMI regarding this patient. Another option is to measure the presence of modes in a patient indirectly, for example through Implicit Association Tasks (e.g., Greenwald, McGhee and Schwartz, 1998).

Pitfalls and Tips

A therapist who works at a detention clinic is considering starting Schema Therapy with one of her patients. This patient suddenly shows many fluctuating emotional states in his behavior, feelings, and way of thinking. The therapist suspects a strong presence of the Enraged Child mode, and also the Punitive Parent and Vulnerable Child modes. The therapist asks the patient to fill out the SMI, but she finds a completely different score from the one she had expected: the patient had a higher score for the Healthy Adult mode and lower scores for all the maladaptive modes. The therapist is in doubt. Has she assessed the patient completely wrongly? Does this mean Schema Therapy would not be useful for this patient? Did the patient complete the SMI honestly?

The Future

Without a doubt, more modes that are at the center of certain personality disorders will be specified in the future. In order to avoid compiling an inexhaustible list of modes, it is important to critically consider the unique significance of every mode. Clearly, each individual may show a slightly different variation in a specific mode. It is only useful to add more modes if they go beyond the idiosyncratic level and would be specific enough for a certain subgroup of personality disorders. If it is assumed that certain modes have sufficient additional significance to provide a better and more complete conceptualization of the mode model, the items of such modes should be added to the current SMI, whereupon all stages of the psychometric testing must be completed again.

References

Arbuckle, J.L. (2005) *Amos 5 for Windows*. Chicago: Small Waters.
Arntz, A., Klokman, J. and Sieswerda, S. (2005) An experimental test of the schema mode model of borderline personality disorder. *Journal of Behavior Therapy and Experimental Psychiatry*, 36, 226–239.

Bamelis, L.L.M., Renner, F., Heidkamp, D. and Arntz, A. (in press) Extended schema mode conceptualizations for specific personality disorders: an empirical study. *Journal of Personality Disorders.*

Beck, A., Freeman, A. and Davis, D. (2004) *Cognitive Therapy of Personality Disorders,* 2nd edition. New York: Guilford Press.

First, M.B., Spitzer, R.L., Gibbon, M. and Williams, J.B.W. (1997) *Structured Clinical Interview for DSM-IV Axis I Disorders (SCID I).* New York: Biometric Research Department.

First, M., Spitzer, R., Gibbon, M., Williams, J. and Benjamin, L. (1994) *Structured Clinical Interview for DSM-IV Axis II Personality Disorders (SCID II).* New York: Biometric Research Department.

Greenwald, A., McGhee, D. and Schwartz, J. (1998) Measuring individual differences in implicit cognition: the implicit association task. *Journal of Personality and Social Psychology, 74,* 1464–1480.

Jacob, G.A., Dominiak, P., Harris, D. *et al.* (submitted for publication) Construct validity of the schema mode concept.

Jöreskog, K.G. and Sörbom, D. (2001) *LISREL 8.54.* Chicago: Scientific Software International.

Klokman, J., Arntz, A. and Sieswerda, S. (2005) *The Schema Mode Questionnaire (State and Trait Version).* Internal document. Maastricht University.

Lobbestael, J., Arntz, A., Löbbes, A. and Cima, M. (2009) A comparative study of patients' and therapists' report of schema modes. *Journal of Behavior Therapy and Experimental Psychiatry, 40,* 571–579.

Lobbestael, J., van Vreeswijk, M., Arntz, A., Spinhoven, P. and 't Hoen, T. (2005) *The Schema Mode Inventory – revised.* Maastricht: Maastricht University.

Lobbestael, J., van Vreeswijk, M., Spinhoven, P., Schouten, E. and Arntz, A. (2010) The reliability and validity of the Schema Mode Inventory (SMI). *Behavioural and Cognitive Psychotherapy, 38*: 437–458.

Weertman, A., Arntz, A. and Kerkhofs, M.L.M. (2000) *Gestructureerd Diagnostisch Interview voor DSM-IV Persoonlijkheidsstoornissen (SCID II) [Structural and Clinical Interview for DSM-IV Personality Disorders (SCID II)].* Lisse: Swets Test.

Young, J., Arntz, A., Atkinson, T. *et al.* (2007) *The Schema Mode Inventory (version 1).* New York: Schema Therapy Institute.

Young, J.E., Atkinson, T., Engels, A.A. and Weishaar, M.E. (2004) *The Young–Atkinson Mode Inventory.* New York: Cognitive Therapy Center.

Young, J.E., Klosko, J. and Weishaar, M.E. (2003) *Schema Therapy: a Practitioner's Guide.* New York: Guilford Press.

Part VII

Implementation and Public Relations in Schema Therapy

Part VII

Implementation and Public Relations in Schema Therapy

1
Implementation of Schema Therapy in General Mental Healthcare Institutes

Marjon Nadort

This chapter will first describe briefly what implementation implies. In addition, the study into the implementation of Schema Therapy (ST) for borderline personality disorder within general mental healthcare institutions in the Netherlands will be described in detail.

Implementation

Implementation can be described as "a process and systematic implementation of innovations and/or improvements (of evidence-based values) with the aim of making it an integral part of the (professional) proceeding, the organizational functioning or the structure of mental healthcare" (Hulscher *et al.*, 2000; Grol, Wensing and Eccles, 2005). This definition consists of several important elements:

- Process and systematic implementation: strategies and activities are chosen rationally and conducted in order to achieve the implementation of certain innovations or changes. Such strategies can be focused on social workers and patients, or on the organizational or integral aspects of care.
- Innovations and/or improvements (of evidence-based values): this is about implementing procedures, techniques, or organizational forms, which are newer, better, or different from usual in a certain setting. This includes new therapies or diagnostic procedures that have demonstrated their value in well-planned patient-oriented research.
- Integral part: implementation should lead to a long-term effect of change.
- The (professional) proceeding, the organizational functioning, or the structure of mental healthcare: changes can occur at different levels. Implementation starts

from the idea that changes in the organization or the structure of healthcare should have consequences for the patient and the primary process of the healthcare, with direct effects for patients as a result (Grol and Wensing, 2006).

Based on research literature, it is recommended that particular attention is paid to the following areas (Grol, Wensing and Eccles, 2005; Grol and Wensing, 2006):

- A systematic approach to and good planning of implementation activities.
- A focus on practical issues and creating/designing incentives to change is.
- Implementation for the target group means completing every phase of the process.
- Attention to the innovation: is it a "good product"?
- Mapping out the care as usual and deviation from the proposed behavior.
- A diagnostic analysis of the target group and settings should take place before implementation.
- Subgroups of the target group can be in different phases of the change process and can have different needs: take segments within the target group into consideration.
- The target group should be involved in the development and adaption of the innovation, as well as in planning the implementation.
- The choice of implementation activities should be linked to the results of the diagnostic analysis.
- A single method of measure is mostly insufficient; looking for a cost-effective mix is better.
- To distinguish between the different phases of implementation (dissemination, implementing, integrating) different measures and strategies are effective in different phases.
- To take the right measures at different levels: national, regional, team, practice, professional.
- Continuous evaluation of both the implementation process and its results: feedback to the target group.
- Implementation should become an integral part of the existing structures and long-term effects should be the aim.

Approach

When we look at the current position regarding the implementation of ST, we find that it is provided in several ways: individual therapy, group therapy, couple therapy, as an independent therapy method, or as outpatient therapy within a (day) clinical setting. Furthermore, there is an enormous difference in the duration of the ST offered: this can vary from 240 sessions of individual outpatient psychotherapy (Giesen-Bloo et al., 2006), in which patients were offered two sessions a week for three years, to 20 sessions of schema group therapy (van Vreeswijk and Broersen, 2006).

Not only is ST provided in different ways, but also the availability within general healthcare is diverse. For example, ST is offered in several institutes of general mental healthcare institutes (outpatient clinics and regional institutes for mental welfare; RIAGGs), but also in specialized centers for personality disorders. ST is also implemented within forensic institutes and institutes for patients with substance abuse problems. Furthermore, ST is offered by independent psychologists and psychotherapists.

Literature search into long-term psychotherapy

ST is often offered to patients with personality disorders. ST in an outpatient setting is often long-term. Implementing this form of psychotherapy, with the exception of research studies, was until recently very problematic due to the Dutch government regulation of a maximum of 50 sessions of psychotherapy for patients with a personality disorder diagnosis.

Based on their literature study into long-term psychotherapy (LPT), Daenen, van Reekum, Knapen, and Verheul (2005) concluded that long-term psychotherapy is an effective treatment method for different groups of patients and should form part of the range of psychotherapeutic treatments on offer. Long-term psychotherapy is a logical step between short-term psychotherapy and outpatient treatment programs.

In another article in which different studies into long-term outpatient psychotherapy were compared, Daenen and van Reekum (2006) concluded that "in cases of a maximum duration of fifty sessions, a large number of patients with personality disorders would be undertreated. This is in particular the case for both patients with a personality disorder and patients with comorbid psychiatric disorders." Since then the government restriction to a maximum of 50 sessions of psychotherapy has been withdrawn and patients can now be treated longer within diagnosis treatment combinations (DBCs, a predefined average packet of care [treatment] with, in most cases, a fixed cost, which is applied when a specific diagnosis is made). This offers more possibilities for the implementation of long-term ST.

Effectiveness study

The (cost-)effectiveness of ST for borderline personality disorders was studied in a randomized controlled trial (RCT), *Outpatient Psychotherapy for Borderline Personality Disorder, Randomized Trial of Schema-Focused Therapy vs. Transference Focused Psychotherapy* (Giesen-Bloo *et al.*, 2006; van Asselt *et al.*, 2008). At the time of writing, a number of controlled trials are being carried out in which the efficacy and cost-effectiveness of ST is being studied. These include the implementation study of ST in borderline personality disorder within general mental healthcare (Nadort, Arntz *et al.*, 2009; Nadort, Dyck *et al.*, 2009) and a study into ST in 50 sessions (Bamelis and Arntz, 2006–10). A study into ST in a forensic setting is also being carried out (Bernstein, Arntz and de Vos, 2007). Furthermore, group therapy is being investigated (Farrell, Shaw and Webber, 2009).

Implementation study within general mental healthcare institutes

Based on the outcomes of the RCT (Giesen-Bloo *et al.*, 2006) in which ST was found to be the best method, it was decided that ST needed to be implemented. When a grant for the RCT was awarded, the Board of Healthcare Insurers, who provided the grant, included the condition that a (small) amount of the award should be used for the implementation of the most (cost-) effective treatment. With the help of this grant, the first step toward implementation of ST for borderline personality disorder was taken.

Following the implementation principles of Grol and Wensing (2006), two steps were taken: a diagnostic analysis was carried out in which promoting and hindering factors were identified (Arntz, Dirksen and Bleecke, 2005) and an implementation survey (Nadort and Giesen-Bloo, 2005). The diagnostic analysis included a written survey of therapists and managers of mental healthcare institutes and oral interviews. Based on the outcomes of the diagnostic analysis, a need for a "new, evidence-based effective" therapy for the treatment of borderline patients was identified.

Implementation trial

The implementation trial consisted of the following elements:

- Developing a ST training program for therapists in the form of a 50-hour course, specifically aimed at the treatment of borderline patients. In order to guarantee quality and also to make the implementation of the training program attractive for therapists in the future, the course was organized as a special follow-up within the norms of the Dutch Association of Behavioral and Cognitive Therapy.
- A DVD set of ST techniques was produced (Nadort, 2005). This consists of 34 segments averaging 10 minutes in length, making a total six hours of film on seven DVDs.
- A website (www.schematherapie.nl) was created that provided information about ST and a manual for the use of the DVD set was added.
- Training was carried out and evaluated. The training was offered by two trainers, Hannie van Genderen and Marjon Nadort, who have expertise in borderline research. Eight clinicians from general mental-health services and forensic psychology participated. Following the training, it was evaluated and documented in a written report by participants and trainers. The participants evaluated the training on the five-point Likert scoring format and rated it 5 (very good). After completion, the skills of the therapists were examined by three short role-plays with actors. These role-plays were videoed and rated by three independent evaluators using the Young Therapy Adherence and Competence Scale (Young, Klosko and Weishaar, 2005). The average rate by the independent evaluators showed that the training program of 50 hours was judged sufficient to good in providing the participants with the competence to offer ST. Based on written evaluation reports by the participants, the evaluation of the role-playing by independent evaluators and the general evaluation by the two trainers, it was concluded that the training could be used for implementation on a larger scale.
- In order to implement ST on a broader scale than just within the general Dutch mental healthcare institutes, a grant application was written for the program Efficacy of The Netherlands Organization for Health Research and Development (ZonMw) in 2005: Implementation of outpatient schema therapy for borderline

personality disorder in three settings: general psychiatry, forensic psychiatry and addiction treatment (Nadort *et al.*, 2005). It was necessary for several general Dutch mental healthcare institutes, the addiction treatment and the forensic psychiatry to commit to participation in order to apply for a grant. To achieve this, several institutes were approached. Finally, five agreed to participate in the implementation study. In each of the five institutes, a minimum of six clinicians would be trained. Every clinician would treat two patients, resulting in a minimum of 60 patients.

- However, at the beginning of 2006, it became clear that four out of the five institutes, particularly the addiction treatment and the forensic psychiatry, had decided not to be involved for different reasons (see below). Only one of the institutes of the general mental healthcare institutes now wanted to take part in the implementation study.
- In addition to this and in consultation with ZonMw, the grant application was revised to: Implementation of schema-focused therapy for the borderline personality disorder in regular psychiatry. However, ZonMw stated as a condition that a more thorough analysis would be conducted in order to investigate the promoting and hindering factors for implementation.
- Next, more institutes within general mental healthcare were approached. Eight institutes agreed to participate. The overview of the participating institutes follows.

Implementation study

Following completion of the implementation trial in 2005, the implementation study itself started in 2006.

Research issues

The main aim of the study was to examine whether implementation of ST for borderline personality disorders within the general Dutch mental healthcare institutes was possible, and if implementation was possible, what the consequences for the efficacy of the treatment and the cost-effectiveness would be. In the RCT, ST was mainly implemented within an academic setting and the long-term psychotherapy was financed with the help of grants. The treatment consisted of two sessions a week for a period of three years. Therapists were also trained by international experts (J. Young, C. Newman, and A.T. Beck). In the implementation study, treatments were mainly carried out within the general mental healthcare institutes (outpatient clinics and RIAGGs) and treatments were financed under the Exceptional Medical Expenses Act (AWBZ). The treatment was less intense: two sessions a week during the first year, one a week in the second year, and one a week or one a fortnight in the third year. Therapists received less intensive training by Dutch experts.

The second aim was to examine the importance of phone support outside office hours. Extra phone support had already been described in the RCT (Giesen-Bloo *et al.*, 2006), by Young, Arntz and Giessen-Bloo (2005) and by van Genderen and Arntz (2005) as an important element of ST treatment for borderline patients. However, there was no systematic research done to examine whether this was necessary and extra phone support appeared to be a hindering factor for several therapists in the RCT to carrying out the treatment. Therefore, it was important for the implementation of ST to examine this factor in detail. This was carried out in the following way: all the therapists were asked whether they would agree to provide the extra phone support before participating in the study. Therapists who didn't agree were excluded. Following this, half of the therapists were by random stratification allocated to the condition with extra phone support. Each therapist treated two patients, either with or without extra phone support. Therapists with and without the condition of extra phone support participated in the same peer supervision group and had similar training and the same supervision. The therapists registered the number of telephone contacts on standardized forms, which were developed specifically for this purpose. The therapists could specify whether the contact was during a crisis or an administrative or therapeutic contact. The aim of the implementation study was to examine whether a difference in effect between the condition with and the condition without extra phone support outside office hours could be shown. Which condition was most cost-effective was also examined.

Study design

The study was designed as a multicenter trial, in eight Dutch institutes: GGZ Friesland (in Heerenveen and Leeuwarden), BAVO RNO Groep (in Brainpark and Capelle a/d Ijssel), GGZ Dijk and Duin (in Purmerend and Zaandam), GGZ Buitenamstel (in A.J. Ernststraat and Hogguerstraat), AMC/de Meren (in Domselaerstraat and Nienoord), Altrecht (in Zeist), and Riagg Amersfoort and the Bascule (in Lauriergracht).

Training of therapists: treatment and measurements of patients

In spring 2006, 31 therapists were trained for eight days by three experienced trainers. Each therapist was allocated two patients so that 62 patients in total were treated. This was the minimum number of patients necessary to compare the two conditions, according to the power calculation. At all times the crisis services of general practitioners and the emergency services of hospitals were available to all patients.

All therapists participated in a peer supervision group for one hour a week. Each peer supervision group had three hours of supervision from the researcher once a month. All patients received a first assessment after inclusion, and assessments after six months, a year and 18 months. After three years, they received a final assessment.

In Practice

Implementing long-term psychotherapy in an outpatient setting is a tricky business. Prior to the implementation trial, the previously mentioned diagnostic analysis was conducted into the promoting and hindering factors (Arntz et al., 2005), such as that described in Grol and Wensing (2006). This diagnostic analysis yielded a positive image: cognitive behavioral therapist Holland wanted a new evidence-based treatment for borderline patients. However, practice showed otherwise. It appeared there were several bottlenecks.

Figure 1.1 Geographical distribution of the eight institutes

Maximum number of psychotherapy sessions

During the implementation of the diagnostic analysis, the maximum number of sessions of psychotherapy that could be offered hadn't yet been introduced. Therefore, this wasn't reported as a benchmark. However, during the implementation trial, long-term psychotherapy was limited by government regulation to a maximum of 50 sessions. Since then, this regulation has been rescinded, nevertheless doubts regarding the implementation of such long-term treatment was expressed by the institutes.

Personal financial contribution psychotherapy

The personal financial contribution to psychotherapy was another problem. The population that requires long-term psychotherapy (i.e., borderline patients) is a financially marginal group. The personal contribution per psychotherapy session amounted to €15, or €120 a month, for two sessions a week. Fortunately, the maximum amount that could be charged by law was €684 a year, but even so this proved an insurmountable sum for many patients.

Exemption could be obtained from various institutes via so-called "special welfare," but applying for this was hard for both the therapist and the patient. Furthermore, exemption wasn't always granted. Although an institute could waive the personal contribution not all institutes were willing to do so, because it would reduce their income. In the implementation study, special welfare was applied for and granted to several patients and a number of institutes did waive personal contribution, but others did not and in these cases the patient had to pay the personal contribution in full. If ST is implemented nationally in the future, a solution for this problem will have to be found.

Implementation in addiction treatment and forensic psychiatry

Although a number of institutes agreed to participate in the implementation study, problems arose that were not foreseen in time: it appeared there were only a few patients with a primary diagnosis of BPD within the outpatient forensic setting, but mainly patients with antisocial personality problems; within forensic psychiatry, the therapists weren't willing to provide extra phone support outside offers hours; the primary aim within the addiction treatment was working on the addiction problem and not working on the personality problem, and there were too few cognitive behavioral therapists working within the addiction treatment.

Extra phone support outside office hours

A number of therapists decided not to participate in the study because they feared that offering phone support outside office hours would become too burdensome. One institute from the general mental healthcare institutes described this as follows:

> "Within the team of psychotherapists, psychiatrics, and mental healthcare psychologists with experience and affinity with the treatment of patients with a borderline personality disorder, there are no therapists prepared to offer extra phone support."

> A therapist from another institute explained her refusal to participate in these terms:

> "I am ambivalent concerning the extra phone support. I think that a possible crisis intervention in my private time is too much to ask, along with the care for two small children."

Three-year commitment

Several therapists had other reasons for not participating. It was hard for them to commit themselves to the study for three years because of oncoming retirement or for personal reasons:

> "I would have loved to participate in this project, but at the moment, my partner is looking for a job in America, so it might be that I have to move next year. That's why I must decide not to participate, unfortunately."
>
> "I'm very interested in this project, but I don't have a permanent contract from my current employer. Therefore, it might be that I will be searching for a new job somewhere else in the country soon, and I can't commit myself for three years."

Peer supervision meetings for therapists who work at different institutes

In the implementation study, many therapists worked at different institutes. Some had to travel several hours a week for an hour of peer supervision. This raised problems in terms of production and cost-effectiveness.

All factors (both promoting and hindering) were mapped out and described (Nadort, Arntz *et al.*, 2009). Interim solutions and changes were also described. At the end of the implementation study, an evaluation was carried out, and recommendations made for the future. In the implementation study, the possibilities for future implementation were also investigated through questionnaires and interviews with clinicians, managers, and healthcare insurers.

Screening for the implementation study was carried out by trained screeners at different locations. They were trained on location to apply the following treatment outcome measures: M.I.N.I., SCID II, a part of borderline personality disorder, BPDSI-IV, and healthcare cost interview. They were also given information on the written questionnaires the patients had to complete themselves.

To diagnose the Axis I problems, the M.I.N.I. was used. The choice of administering the M.I.N.I. was made from an implementation point of view, because it was easier to train screeners for this and because it took less time to administer with the patients.

The inclusion criteria were:

- primary diagnosis of borderline personality disorder according to the SCID II;
- age 18–60 years;
- a BPDSI score above 20;
- adequate knowledge of Dutch.

The exclusion criteria were:

- BPD not the primary diagnosis;
- BPDSI score below 20;
- a psychotic disorder;
- bipolar disorder, ADHD, or DIS;
- substance abuse of such a nature that clinical detoxification is necessary;
- insufficient knowledge of Dutch.

```
                    ┌─────────────────────┐
                    │ 92 patients screened for │
                    │ eligibility             │
                    └─────────────────────┘
                              │         ┌─────────────────────────────────┐
                              │         │ Excluded (n = 28)               │
                              ├─────────│ (some double-diagnosed)         │
                              │         │ Did not meet inclusion criteria │
                              │         │ (n = 16)                        │
                              │         │ Met exclusion criteria          │
                              │         │ (n = 11)                        │
                              │         │ Other reasons (n = 2))          │
                              │         └─────────────────────────────────┘
                    ┌─────────────────────┐
                    │ Randomized: (n = 62)│
                    └─────────────────────┘
                      /                  \
     ┌──────────────────┐          ┌──────────────────┐
     │ Condition with   │          │ Condition        │
     │ extra phone      │          │ without extra    │
     │ support          │          │ phone support    │
     │ (n = 32)         │          │ (n = 30)         │
     └──────────────────┘          └──────────────────┘
              │                              │
     ┌──────────────────┐          ┌──────────────────┐
     │ Dropout          │          │ Dropout          │
     │ 12               │          │ 10               │
     └──────────────────┘          └──────────────────┘
```

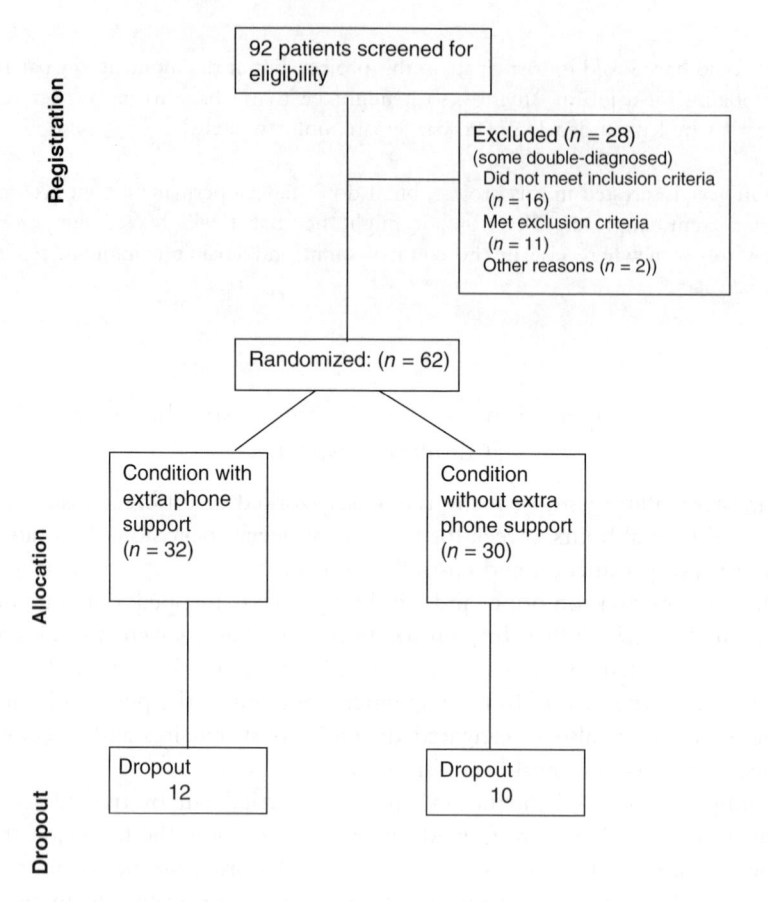

Figure 1.2 Consort diagram

Patients were seen for a screening/assessment after six months, a year, 18 months, and three years. The following tools were used: BPDSI, BPD-47 symptom checklist, healthcare cost interview, EuroQol, WHOQol, Young schema inventories, and SCL-90. Furthermore, the WAI therapist and WAI patient were administered for the therapeutic alliance, as well as the DDPQR (see Nadort, Arntz *et al.*, 2009; Nadort, Dyck *et al.*, 2009).

Ninety-two patients in different institutes were screened for eligibility of whom 28 were excluded for the following reasons:

- BPS < 5 ($N = 14$)
- BPDSI < 20 ($N = 16$)
- Psychotic disorder ($N = 9$)
- ADHD ($N = 1$)
- Bipolar disorder ($N = 1$)

This left 64 patients. Two were not included for logistical problems, because of the waiting list and because of removal.

The remaining group consisted of 62 patients – 60 women and two men. The average age was 31.97 years (SD 9.06). The percentage of this group that used psychotropic medication was 58.1% ($N = 36$). The average number of diagnoses for Axis I was 2.27 (SD 1.42). The average on the BPDSI baseline was 30.91 (SD 20.22–52.55).

Of these 62 patients, 32 were allocated to the condition with extra phone support outside office hours. The first treatments started in July 2006.

Outcomes

Although the elaborate outcomes after three years of treatment will now be known, in terms of efficacy, cost-effectiveness, and the therapeutic alliance, this chapter can provide only a summary since the three-year findings have not yet been published. These will be published in the course of 2011 in several journals. The outcomes after 18 months of treatment are described in Nadort, Arntz, and colleagues (2009) and Nadort, Dyck, and colleagues (2009).

Data on 62 DSM-IV-defined BPD patients were analyzed. Using an intention-to-treat approach, statistically and clinically significant improvements in both conditions were found on all measures. After three years of ST, 48.4% of the patients had recovered from BPD and 62.9% of the patients were reliably changed. The mean number of sessions was 94. The dropout rate was 35.5%. There were no significant differences in dropout or number of sessions between the two conditions.

Overall results were comparable to a previous RCT undertaken in academic settings.

No added value of therapist telephone availability was found on the BPDSI score or on any other measure after three years of ST.

ST for BPD can be successfully implemented in regular mental healthcare. Treatment results and dropout rates were comparable to a previous clinical trial. Because it could not be shown that extra phone support by the therapist outside office hours was of additional value, this telephone availability will not be recommended for national implementation.

Pitfalls and Tips

Extra phone support

As mentioned above, half of the therapists and patients had extra phone support outside office hours and the other half did not. The way the patients used this varied. Some patients called a lot, including in the evening and during the weekend; some called regularly (once a week or once a fortnight); and some never called, even though they were entitled to. Analysis of the latest results with the help of predictors' research is yet to show whether the use of the extra phone support is connected to different factors, such as the severity of the BPDSI symptoms, comorbid symptoms on Axis I, the duration of the problems, or the extent to which a person someone has had prior treatment, in order to learn to deal with these symptoms in case of crisis (Linehan training or VERS training).

The way in which the telephone availability was experienced by the therapists also varied: a number of therapists were pleased that they were assigned to this group and felt that because of the extra phone support they could offer good treatment. Others agreed, but sometimes felt overburdened by the extra phone support. There were also therapists that simply found it too problematic and taxing. Furthermore, therapists reported that the support by means of the weekly peer supervision sessions were a *sine qua non* to keep up the treatment and the extra phone support. All telephone calls were registered using special registration forms in order to ascertain how each patient used this support.

Peer supervision and supervision

All therapist evaluations clearly showed that weekly peer supervision was essential in order to carry out this treatment. Supervision was also paramount. In the implementation study, the frequency of the supervision during the first year was once a month. The supervision time was three hours per institute/peer supervision group. In the second year, the frequency was reduced to once every two or three months. In the third year, the frequency was once every four months. The general finding, however, was that both peer supervision and supervision were necessary for the good implementation of the treatments and for the good implementation of this therapy method. Therefore, this condition should be made clear to policy-makers and heads of departments.

Minimum number of ST therapists per location within an institute

In the implementation study, the number of therapists per institute varied. The minimum number of therapists per institute was two (the Bascule) and the maximum eight (GGZ Buitenamstel). Therapists worked at different locations. In this study, there were some locations in which the ST therapists worked alone. Their experiences showed that it is difficult to work alone with this method, because little inter-collegial support and feedback was received, and the crisis center for their patients was not always well organized. If there were a larger number of ST therapists at one location, support and crisis services could be provided more easily.

Support by management and crisis services

Based on the recommendations in Grol and colleagues (2005) and Grol and Wensing (2006) on effective implementation, consultation with managers and heads of departments took place during the implementation trial and preparation of the implementations in all institutes. In a number of institutes, presentations on the implementation projects were also given.

Nevertheless, during the implementation, it appeared that, in practice, clinicians weren't always supported by their heads of department. For instance, owing to the heavy pressure of work within the mental healthcare institutes, which are mainly focused on generating productivity, insufficient consideration had been taken of the hours dedicated to the project. Clinicians had difficulty finding time for the treatment hours, for the extra phone support within office hours, and for peer supervision and supervision. It is possible that the hours budgeted for the study were too few, considering the amount of work that calling back patients, setting up crisis services, and preparing the sessions, reading literature, producing session reports, recording sessions, and completing questionnaires cost the therapists at the beginning of the treatment. Later in the treatment, the time investment was reduced because the treatment had become more familiar, the number of telephone calls was reduced, and there were fewer sessions. Furthermore, it was notable that within some institutes cooperation with the crisis services was excellent while in others it was difficult, because some crisis centers found the idea of "limited reparenting" and the availability of the therapist unclear or exaggerated. It is possible that during the preparation this was given too little thought. More attention will have to be paid to this in the future.

Indications for references/predictors

The outcomes of the study showed that it was difficult for patients who were happy with the treatment of a prior clinician (non-ST) to make the switch to a new therapist for ST treatment. We therefore recommend not interrupting well-functioning treatments, but to refer patients for ST when they are not yet in treatment or when a treatment is not satisfactory.

Another outcome was that the young adult group (18–23 years old) that participated in the study had difficulties keeping to the therapy frequency of twice a week in the first year. It is possible that the distress level wasn't high enough or that they found two sessions a week too much. Furthermore, this group was characterized by multiple cancellations or no shows. These outcomes match the findings described in Part IV, Chapter 9 on adolescents and may be attributed to the phase of life. In this project, the clinicians tried to motivate the young adults as much as possible to attend and they were allowed to come less often than twice a week. The number of young adults in the study was too small to be able to come to definite conclusions, however.

The Future

Based on the outcomes of the implementation study, it became clear that ST for borderline personality disorder can be implemented within general mental healthcare settings. It also showed that extra phone support outside office hours wasn't necessary for the efficacy or cost-effectiveness of the treatment. Therefore, a national implementation of extra phone support isn't recommended. Preliminary findings indicate that it is necessary to carry out a thorough consultation with heads of departments and crisis centers prior to implementation. Furthermore, it is important for the implementation of ST for borderline patients that the costs are financed through healthcare insurance.

References

Arntz, A., Dirksen, C. and Bleecke, J. (2005) *Promoting and Interfering Factors Related to Implementation of Schema Focused Therapy for Borderline Personality Disorder in Dutch Mental Healthcare Institutes*. Eindrapportage college voor Zorgverzekeraars.

Asselt, A.D.I. van, Dirksen, C.D., Arntz, A. et al. (2008) Outpatient psychotherapy for borderline personality disorder: cost effectiveness of schema-focused therapy versus transference focused psychotherapy. *British Journal of Psychiatry*, 192: 450–457.

Bamelis, L. and Arntz, A. (2006–2010) *Psychological Treatment of Personality Disorders: a Multicentered Randomized Controlled Trial on the (Cost-) Effectiveness of Schema-focused Therapy*. Promotietraject, Universiteit Maastricht.

Bernstein, D.P., Arntz, A. and de Vos, M.E. (2007) Schemagerichte therapie in de forensische setting, theoretisch model en voorstellen voor best clinical practice. *Tijdschrift voor psychotherapie*, 33(2), 120–133.

Daenen, E.W.P.M. and Reekum, A.C. van (2006) Ambulante langerdurende psychotherapie bij patiënten met een persoonlijkheidsstoornis. *Tijdschrift voor Psychotherapie*, 32(I), 20–32.

Daenen, E.W.P.M., Reekum, A.C. van, Knapen, P.M.F.J.J. and Verheul, R. (2005) Langerdurende ambulante psychotherapie is effectief. Een kritisch literatuuroverzicht per stoornis. *Tijdschrift voor Psychiatrie*, 47(9), 603–612.

Farrell, J.M., Shaw, I.A. and Webber, M.A. (2009) A schema-focused approach to group psychotherapy for outpatients with borderline personality disorder: a randomized controlled trial. *Journal of Behavior Therapy and Experimental Psychiatry*, June, 40(2), 317–328.

Genderen, H., van and Arntz, A. (2005) *Schemagerichte Cognitieve Therapie bij Borderline Persoonlijkheidsstoornis*. Amsterdam: Uitgeverij Nieuwezijds.

Giesen-Bloo, J., Dyck, R. van, Spinhoven, P. *et al.* (2006) Outpatient psychotherapy for borderline personality disorder, randomized trial of schema-focused therapy vs transference focused psychotherapy. *Archives of General Psychiatry*, 63: 649–658.

Grol, R. and Wensing, M. (2006) *Implementatie: Effectieve Verbetering van de Patiëntenzorg*. Maarssen: Elsevier.

Grol, R., Wensing, M. and Eccles, M. (2005) *Improving Patient Care: The Implementation of Change in Clinical Practice*. Maarssen: Elsevier.

Hulscher, M., Wensing, M. and Grol, R. (2000) *Effectieve Implementatie: Theorieën en Strategieën*. Den Haag: ZON.

Nadort, M. (2005) *Schematherapie voor de Borderline Persoonlijkheidsstoornis. Therapietechnieken*. DVD.

Nadort, M., Arntz, A., Smit, J.H. *et al.* (unpublished) Implementation of outpatient schema therapy for borderline personality disorder with versus without crisis support by the therapist outside office hours: results after three years of treatment.

Nadort, M., Arntz, A., Smit, J.H. *et al.* (2009) Implementation of outpatient schema therapy for borderline personality disorder with versus without crisis support by the therapist outside office hours: a randomized trial. *Behaviour Research and Therapy*, 961–973.

Nadort, M., Dyck, R., Smit, J.H. *et al.* (2005) *Implementation of Out-patient Schema-focused Therapy for Borderline Personality Disorder in Three Settings: General Psychiatry, Forensic Psychiatry and Addiction Treatment*. Subsidieaanvraag voor het programma Doelmatigheid/deelprogramma Implementatie van ZonMw, aanvraagnummer 4197.

Nadort, M., Dyck, R., Smit, J.H. *et al.* (2006) *Implementation of Out-patient Schema-focused Therapy for Borderline Personality Disorder in General Psychiatry*. Subsidieaanvraag voor het programma Doelmatigheid/deelprogramma Implementatie van ZonMw, aanvraagnummer 945-16-313.

Nadort, M., Dyck, R., Smit, J.H. *et al.* (2009) Three preparatory studies for promoting implementation of outpatient schema therapy for borderline personality disorder in general mental healthcare. *Behaviour Research and Therapy*, 47: 938–945.

Nadort, M. and Giesen-Bloo, J. (2005) *Pilot Implementation Study of SFT for Borderline Patients*. Eindrapportage college voor Zorgverzekeraars.

Vreeswijk, M.F. van and Broersen, J. (2006) *Schemagerichte Therapie in Groepen*. Houten: Bohn Stafleu van Loghum.

www.schematherapie.nl.

Young, J.E., Arntz, A. and Giesen-Bloo, J. (2005) *Young Therapy Adherence and Competence Scale*, aangepaste versie.

Young, J.E., Klosko, J.S. and Weishaar, M.E. (2005) *Schemagerichte Therapie: Handboek voor Therapeuten*. Houten: Bohn Stafleu van Loghum.

2

Using ST Principles to Increase the Therapeutic Efficacy of the Forensic Care Team's Interactions with Personality Disordered Clients

Naomi Murphy, Des McVey and Geoff Hopping

Introduction

Many clients within the remit of forensic services, whether within the criminal justice system or the mental health system, meet diagnostic criteria for personality disorder (e.g., Taylor *et al.*, 1998; Eastern Specialized Mental Health Commissioning Group, 2005). People with this disorder manage their schemas with various dysfunctional coping strategies, such as addictions, violence, self-harm, and interpersonal rejection, which impact directly on those around them who are attempting to provide them with a service. Indeed, the behavior of some clients is such that when services are able to avoid their obligation with an apparently legitimate reason to discharge the individual (e.g., the client refuses to engage in treatment) some are quick to do so. When services retain the client, either because discharge is not an option or because they recognize the individual needs treatment, it is often difficult to ensure he receives a cohesive treatment approach because individual members of the team may have very different interpretations of the underlying motives for the client's challenging behavior. This chapter is concerned with using schema-focused therapy (ST) principles to improve the accessibility of services for personality disordered clients, to enhance the efficacy of treatment, and to strengthen cohesion across the team in relation to individual clients.

Murphy (2010) argues that transdisciplinary teamwork is essential when treating people with personality disorders since teams can meet multiple needs of the client, enhance communication, use resources more efficiently, make higher-quality decisions, offer higher-quality services, have improved processes, and be more innovative and more emotionally supportive; thus the treatment is ultimately safer for the client and practitioner. Treatment delivered by a transdisciplinary team is arguably more effective than that offered by a psychological therapist working alone. However, significant work is needed to ensure effective team functioning. Failure to transform into a transdisciplinary team, defined as a "complex approach to team working where team members perform unique roles and integrate their approaches to assessment, formulation, and delivery of treatment in order to achieve mutually dependent goals" (Murphy, 2010, p. 158), will undermine treatment efficacy. We would argue that the ST model offers the team significant advantages in establishing transdisciplinary working since each discipline can modify its role to incorporate ST's principles.

In Practice

Common forensic team practices

Nursing contribution to treatment. Unfortunately, services charged with the care of people diagnosed with personality disorder are often established with philosophies and practices that collude with psychopathology, thus perpetuating the existence of maladaptive schemas (Murphy and McVey, 2001). Staff frequently provide schema-confirming responses to individuals who are experiencing schema-triggering episodes.

The situation is complicated further when the patient presents with different schema modes toward staff (e.g., presenting as Critical Parent to female staff, as Detached Self-Soother to young male staff, and as Vulnerable Child to older staff). This can result in teams having different interpersonal experiences of the patient, thus leading to team splits. Again, this can leave patients exposed to schema-perpetuating experiences because they are exposed to inconsistent responses from the team.

> John was admitted to hospital, diagnosed with anti social personality disorder, and presented with behaviors driven by an abandonment schema. The clinical team decided that his burdensome behavior should be shared out and decided to change his named nurse on a monthly basis, thus exposing John to frequent experiences of abandonment.

Nursing has struggled to develop a professional identity that incorporates a role in treatment. Some nursing practices are difficult to differentiate from psychological therapy (Tennant, Davies and Tennant, 2000). Other approaches tend toward management (Melia, Moran and Mason, 1999) or game-playing strategies (Moran and Mason, 1996). In general, nursing approaches to treatment and management of people with personality disorder are defensively responsive and reactive, and interventions may be delivered in the absence of any theoretical rationale or clinical formulation, thus risking the reinforcement of maladaptive schemas.

> When John's brother failed to arrive for a scheduled visit John told his named nurse that he felt like smashing the unit and "doing drugs." This resulted in John (who also has an emotional deprivation schema) being coerced into taking sedative medication, leaving him emotionally numb, detached, and again failing to receive emotional support.

This response is consistent with the traditional disease model in which nurses are indoctrinated. The disease model dictates that if symptoms are alleviated, then success has been demonstrated. However, while John's anger dissipated and he did not smash up the unit, his pathology was perpetuated since there was no intervention based on long-term goals and a formulation unique to John.

Nursing "treatment" planning usually involves developing care plans in which symptoms are identified and interventions prescribed. When extended to people with personality disorder, who do not present with "symptoms" as such, nurses can struggle to develop a cogent treatment plan and often resort to developing collaborative contracts in which maladaptive behaviors are viewed as the problem areas. Traditionally, the behaviors identified as requiring amelioration are those manifested when the patient is in a cognitive and emotional crisis.

In Table 2.1, should John be found under the influence of cannabis or become hostile toward staff, it is likely he would be discharged. If John's cannabis use were the consequence of a schema (e.g., abandonment or emotional deprivation) being triggered, the response of the staff team would perpetuate rather than challenge the schema.

Prison officers' approach. In the UK, significant numbers of people with personality disorder whose distress is manifest through offending behavior are processed within the criminal justice system and given custodial sentences. The prison population, whose behavior is clearly governed by maladaptive schemas, is continually exposed to experiences that are likely to confirm the maladaptive templates they have constructed to make sense of themselves, their relationships, and their experiences.

> After using cannabis, John was discharged from hospital. He moved in with his partner and became very controlling of her: he refused to let her go out without him and monitored her movements. She decided to end the relationship. John went into a rage and, using a kitchen knife, stabbed her 45 times until she was dead. John was convicted of murder and sentenced to imprisonment. In prison, John was demanding of staff time and hypervigilant to unprofessional staff conduct, constantly challenging the integrity of the system. He continued to use illicit drugs and threatened violence if anyone came into his cell. John would often end up in segregation, isolated in a cell.

Table 2.1 Example of nursing care plan

Problem	Goal	Intervention
John uses cannabis and violence to cope when distressed	John to refrain from using cannabis and violence	John should approach his named nurse should he feel violent or crave drugs

The prison service attempts to manage the population with one set of rules that are applied uniformly. In general, good behavior is rewarded and bad behavior punished. When applied to those with schema-driven behavior, these rules are often ineffective. Intended punishments may be highly reinforcing to those whose behavior is motivated by dysfunctional schemas. This generates considerable distress for staff who attempt to assert control by becoming increasingly restrictive but merely perpetuate the schema, often arriving at a "Mexican stand-off." These prisoners are typically moved around the prison system at great cost, eliciting schema-confirming responses from each prison they are accommodated within.

Generally, prison staff believe they control their relationships with prisoners, although reality could be perceived differently. John behaved in a manner that elicited verbal, emotional, and behavioral responses from the prison staff and, as such, he was in control of the emotions experienced by prison officers. Ultimately, John's behavior with staff galvanized his schemas, thus maintaining his long-term risk and making interactions with John very stressful. This dynamic, therefore, merely maintained John's psychopathology since it prevented him accessing alternative interpersonal experiences that would have supported him in challenging his maladaptive schemas.

Another aspect of the UK prison system supports the maintenance of maladaptive schemas via the use of modes. Prison culture is such that functioning within three distinct modes is reinforced. Historically, prisoners were referred to by their surname; then prisoners tended to have nicknames and also use first names within some key relationships. Not uncommonly, prisoners utilize different operational modes depending on the name they are responding to. With regards to John; Smith represented the Self-Aggrandizer, Jonno represented the Detached Self-Soother, and John represented the Vulnerable Child. Staff had different experiences of John, depending on which mode they had developed a relationship with. This potentially had a detrimental effect on staff relations: those who saw the vulnerable John, those who saw the music-playing, gym-going, jocular Jonno, and those who experienced the hostile, integrity-challenging Smith found it hard to integrate their perspectives.

Psychological therapists in teams

Too often, psychological therapists perceive their role in treatment as being to provide individual psychotherapeutic interventions with a clear rationale. Frequently, these are provided as a separate, distinct activity within wider psychiatric or custodial settings. Considerable challenges confront individual therapists in settings where the overall aims, values, and techniques of psychotherapy are neither shared nor understood by the wider staff team. In such an absence, the client and therapist have to hold the integrity of the psychotherapy between them. This is difficult enough when therapy is going well. However, when schema-reinforcing or sabotaging behavior inevitably becomes

> John's therapist used psychotherapy to understand, experience, and restructure her client's interpersonal style in relation to his abandonment schema. The relationship became difficult as John grew increasingly hostile in subconscious attempts to elicit rejection from the therapist. John failed to attend sessions and requested a change of therapist and more medication, leaving the care team concerned that he was unable to cope and putting pressure on the therapist to terminate therapy.

manifest in therapy, treatment effectiveness can be seriously compromised if staff do not have a shared understanding of the therapeutic task or the desired outcomes.

In an environment where there is no awareness that appropriate management of this type of enactment is integral to the ultimate success of the therapeutic task, these requests may be acceded to and treatment compromised. Similarly, problems arise when nursing staff and prison officers find it difficult to identify their own role in treatment. Perceiving that one's professional training has been inadequate preparation for the task of treating people with personality disorder is one of several powerful dynamics to be overcome in attempting to engage the broader care team in this work (Murphy and McVey, 2010). Typically, staff who are unable to identify their own role in treatment locate entire responsibility for change with the individual therapist. For example, a client who presents the wider staff group with schema-coping behavior in respect of, say, a Mistrust and Abuse schema by being excessively hostile and demanding of staff time (e.g., by threatening to harm himself or others), may exhaust resources and engender negative, punitive, blaming attitudes toward not only the client but also his therapist for failing to "sort it out." Further difficulties that may arise when some staff do not have an active role in treatment include: impoverished formulations that are not accepted by the entire team and do not encapsulate all modes that the client operates within; homework tasks being misconstrued and sabotaged by the team; therapists and clients employing safety behaviors in an attempt to manage therapy without upsetting the other staff. Therefore, a failure to facilitate an active treatment-oriented role for all staff within a service for people with personality disorder can impact on both the team and its ability to contain difficult patients.

When psychotherapy with individual patients is taking place in residential settings, there needs to be a shared philosophical understanding of the problem, a clear, agreed strategy for managing pathological relationship styles, and a supportive environment in which staff can work through their differences, since people with personality disorders are almost certain to engender splitting within a staff team (Saradjian, Murphy and McVey, 2010). The role of the psychological therapist is more useful when incorporating an emphasis on sharing psychological theory to enable other disciplines to develop a shared understanding of the problem, and practices that are formulation-driven and treatment-focused, rather than assisting them in adopting the role of psychological therapist, which undermines the unique contribution of each discipline. The SFT model readily lends itself to this purpose and has been used by the first two authors to achieve this aim in both prison and hospital settings (Murphy and McVey, 2001, 2010).

Approach

Schema-focused treatment plans

Schema-focused treatment plans (STP) were developed with the aims of: reducing clients' challenging behavior by reducing staff behavior that colludes with client psychopathology; assisting staff in providing consistent care across the team; and increasing the "likability" of the client, thereby reducing hostility to him.

People with personality disorder often behave in ways that elicit complementary, schema-perpetuating responses from those around them. For example, the person who expects abandonment may present as clingy and demanding and thus be avoided. The primary aim of STPs is to reduce the likelihood of staff providing the client with responses that confirm his schema. Consequently, the plan needs to enable staff to identify responses they give that reinforce maladaptive schemas, and are therefore unhelpful, whilst selecting responses that may assist in the development of a healthier schema.

Sample STP for John Smith

Schema of focus: abandonment. This schema causes individuals to anticipate that others will be unreliable or inconsistent in the support and connection that they offer. They tend to believe that others will not be able to continue providing emotional support, connection, or protection because they are emotionally unstable and unpredictable (e.g., the other will have angry outbursts), unreliable, or erratically present; or because they will abandon the individual in favor of someone better. This schema usually arises when an individual was separated for long periods of their childhood from their caregiver, they lost the attention of a caregiver in a significant way, or the relationship between the individual and their caregiver was characterized by instability.

> John is the eldest of seven children. His father was often imprisoned during John's childhood and his mother had an alcohol addiction that left John having to care for his siblings with the help of his maternal grandmother, who lived in the family home until she died when John was 10 years old. His mother had two short-term extramarital relationships with men to whom John grew attached. When John was 16, his mother died and he tried to support all his siblings, but they were all placed in children's homes within six months. John moved to London where he met a man who was initially kind but subsequently prostituted him. John began using drugs and alcohol to cope.

Strategies adopted to manage schema

a) Avoidance. Strategies used by John to avoid his abandonment schema being activated are:

- Avoiding interacting with male staff who are firm and direct.
- Avoiding interacting with other prisoners.

- Sleeping for prolonged periods.
- Excessive engagement in solitary activities.
- Using drugs and alcohol.

These strategies ultimately perpetuate John's schema since he fails to develop any good-quality relationships with others and thus receives no challenges to his belief that all relationships will end in abandonment.

b) Over-compensation. John over-compensates for his schema being triggered in the following ways:

- Constantly demanding female attention especially at the end of a shift.
- Constantly asking others for advice or support.
- Underrating his competence and asking others to do things on his behalf.
- Challenging the integrity of others with formal complaints requiring much paperwork and constantly enquiring how this is progressing.
- Aggressive outbursts when personal officer and therapist are absent.
- Threatening prisoners who seek support from his personal officer.
- Threatening to kill himself when his therapist discusses her leave.

These strategies ultimately perpetuate John's schema since staff feel overwhelmed by his demands on their time and coerced into meeting his needs, and thus try to keep their distance. Prisoners are repulsed and irritated by the monopolization of staff time and ultimately reject him.

c) Surrender. John maintains his schema in the following ways:

- Neglecting personal hygiene.
- Staring at women's breasts and invading their personal space.
- Telling tall stories.
- Making loud, disparaging comments about those who engage with him to staff.
- Being critical and punitive toward others in groups.
- Criticizing staff for being "unprofessional."

These strategies make it difficult for others to like John. Those who choose to engage with him often feel hurt by his behavior so relationships are short-lived. Thus, John's belief that all relationships will soon end tends to be confirmed.

Staff interventions to combat schema. In order to reduce the strength of his schema, it is important that staff resist giving responses to John that continue to reinforce the presence of his schema. Within all interactions with John, staff should be thinking; "Is this an attempt by John to maintain his belief that he will be abandoned or rejected by others?" If so, a schema-disconfirming response should be selected. A disconfirming response is an alternative response to one that John's behavior is designed to elicit, thus they challenge the presence of the schema.

- Male staff should be proactive in initiating interactions with John, particularly when he is sleeping. Staff should remember that John usually isolates himself and may resist encouragement to interact but initial rebuffs should be downplayed.
- Encourage John to participate in group activities, reminding him that he often enjoys the company of others when he allows himself to participate.
- When John demands attention at the end of a shift, staff should point out that his abandonment schema has been triggered and assure him they will be returning.
- When John is demanding staff time and attention or submits formal complaints, it should be pointed out to him that he often behaves like this when he feel disliked and fears rejection. Staff who can authentically reassure him he is liked should do so and let him know the times that he is most likable.
- When John has an aggressive outburst or threatens others, staff should suggest to him that his abandonment schema may have been triggered and he is using hostility to avoid feeling vulnerable. Normal sanctions apply.
- When John makes threats to himself, staff should remind him that his abandonment schema may make him frightened, but reassure him that they are able to support him in the absence of key relationships.
- When John is being critical or disparaging of others, staff should point out that John often tries to mask his vulnerability to abandonment by rejecting others first and suggest he gives others the chance to know the more likable, vulnerable John.
- When John is neglecting his hygiene, telling tall stories, or staring at women's breasts, he should be reminded that his abandonment schema causes him to expect rejection and suggest that maybe he is engaging in this behavior to ensure rejection comes sooner rather than later.

Pitfalls and Tips

Plans need to be accessible to the entire team. Staff reading the plan may have little knowledge of the individual's history, little psychological knowledge, and limited time. Plans therefore need to be brief so that staff are not deterred from reading them. Equally, they need to be self-explanatory so that neither detailed knowledge of the client nor psychological theory is required. Challenging behavior poses an obstacle to relationships forming, or being maintained, so STPs need to convey the client's vulnerability in order to elicit understanding of the client and warmth toward him.

Developing STPs

Engaging other team members in developing the plan can create greater team ownership and ensure that all challenging aspects of the client's behavior are incorporated. Before choosing a schema to focus on, listing all the prisoner's challenging behaviors and identifying the functions they serve within interpersonal relationships can be useful. If it is difficult to identify the function, consider the impact on those they interact with. Analysing the function of the challenging behaviors should point to one key schema to be addressed. Typically with forensic clients, this would be from the domain of disconnection and rejection. Sometimes another schema may be selected, but this would be inappropriate if the schema is being used to defend against mistrust/abuse or abandonment, etc., as when narcissistic entitlement is used to defend against defectiveness or emotional deprivation. Forensic clients often have multiple schemas to be addressed, but in the interest of clarity, one should be selected as a way in to enhance staff treatment of the client. Which one is chosen may be less significant.

STPs should:

- include brief descriptions of the schema and how it developed;
- describe how the challenging behaviors perpetuate the schema;
- suggest alternative, anti-complementary responses.

Schema-disconfirming responses need to be simple and, wherever possible, provide statements that could be made by less imaginative staff who need support to resist providing an intuitive, perpetuating response.

Preparing environments for the introduction of STPs

Considerable preparation is needed when introducing psychological models to non-psychological therapists. Initially, training in the model combining both didactic and experiential opportunities is crucial. Staff recognize that everyone has schemas that impact on their behavior and that this has a protective but also limiting impact on the way we experience life and relationships. However, without an experiential focus, the material can remain "outside" the individual rather than be owned and recognized as a felt experience. Training needs to be handled sensitively and offer opportunities for accessing support and supervision since staff become more aware of their own schema with experiential learning and this can destabilize some staff. Staff in forensic settings are particularly vulnerable due to the disturbed nature of the clients and their tendency to amplify splits in the staff group. Supervisors should pay attention to the schemas of the supervisee, since this will be instrumental in how they manage themselves and their interventions. Not uncommonly, staff share the same schema as their client, particularly unrelenting standards and defectiveness. This may result in over-collusive or punitive relationships if left unattended.

ST language also needs to be incorporated into team meetings and briefings with information pertaining to client schemas, modes, and formulations forming a specific focus. It is essential that the transdisciplinary team explore behaviors and traits that are displayed by the client and how these are received and responded to by staff, thus allowing staff to conceptualize ways in which they may be colluding with schema perpetuation and identify new ways of working.

Summary

Applying ST within a therapeutic milieu and employing STP can enhance work undertaken within structured individual sessions and groups. Such an approach permits all staff in contact with the client to act as a therapeutic agent, working within a shared formulation that attempts to disconfirm the maladaptive schemas whilst role-modeling healthy interpersonal modes. It allows staff to understand the function of maladaptive behavior within the context of the client's life and thus reduces interpersonal tension since staff are able to be more objective while treating the distress and risk of this population. In response, the clients are continually faced with new, positive interpersonal experiences that force them to re-evaluate the authenticity of their core schemas, management strategies, and maladaptive modes, encouraging change at a core level that is not situation-specific.

References

Eastern Specialized Mental Health Commissioning Group (ESMHCG)(2005) *Personality Disorder Services Framework.* www.esmhcg.nhs.uk/PD_Capacity_Plan_June_05.pdf.

Melia, P., Moran, T. and Mason, T. (1999) Psychiatric nursing for PD patients: crossing the boundaries safely. *Journal of Psychiatric and Mental Health Nursing,* 6: 15–20.

Moran, T. and Mason, T. (1996) Revisiting the nursing management of the psychopath. *Journal of Psychiatric and Mental Health Nursing,* 3(3), 189–194.

Murphy, N. (2010) Effective transdisciplinary teamworking, in *Treating Personality Disorder* (eds N. Murphy and D. McVey). London: Routledge.

Murphy, N. and McVey, D. (2001) Nursing personality disordered inpatients: a schema-focused approach. *British Journal of Forensic Practice,* 13(4), 8–15.

Murphy, N. and McVey, D. (2010) The difficulties that staff experience in treating people with personality disorder, in *Treating Personality Disorder* (eds N. Murphy and D. McVey). London: Routledge.

Saradjian, J., Murphy, N. and McVey, D. (2010) Delivering integrated treatment to people with personality disorder, in *Treating Personality Disorder* (eds N. Murphy and D. McVey). London: Routledge.

Taylor, P.J., Leese, M., Williams, D. *et al.* (1998) Mental disorder and violence: a special (high security) hospital study. *British Journal of Psychiatry, 172*: 218–226.

Tennant, A., Davies, C. and Tennant, I. (2000) Working with the personality disordered offender, in *Forensic Mental Health: Current Approaches* (eds C. Chaloner and M. Coffey). Oxford: Blackwell.

3
Implementation of Schema Therapy in de Rooyse Wissel Forensic Psychiatric Center

Truus Kersten and Lieda van de Vis

In Dutch maximum security psychiatric hospitals, 75–80% of patients struggle with personality disorders, mainly Cluster B types (van Emmerik and Brouwers, 2001). Most of the clinicians' time and attention is focused on these patients. In recent years, implementing an effective way of treating personality disorders has been a top priority within this sector. Two treatment models were adapted for the forensic sector and have been implemented in recent years: dialectical behavior therapy (DBT) in the Dutch forensic psychiatric center of Oldenkotte (Blondelle, Williams and van den Bosch, 2007), and Schema Therapy (ST) (Bernstein, Arntz and de Vos, 2007) in the Dutch forensic psychiatric centers of de Rooyse Wissel, Oostvaarderskliniek, and Van der Hoevenkliniek, and more recently in several other forensic clinics in the Netherlands.

This chapter describes how ST has been implemented in de Rooyse Wissel, in Venray, over the past few years. The chosen methods used and the pitfalls in treatment encountered are explained. A description of the implementation of ST within the treatment wards, especially in psychiatric treatment, is the focus of this chapter.

In Practice

De Rooyse Wissel consists of a maximum security psychiatric hospital and an outpatients' department, both situated in two locations. The clinic consists of 13 wards, in which, in total, 239 male patients are hospitalized: 140 patients with personality disorders (mainly Cluster B), 65 patients with primary psychotic disorders, and 34 patients with a mental disability. Each ward has a mixed population of patients in terms of the problems they present. However, there are separate wards for hospitalization and rehabilitation of the more (psychotic) vulnerable patients and for the less mentally disabled patients. The treatment is offered in three care programs aimed at patients with personality disorders, with psychotic disorders, and with less mentally disabled patients respectively. Each ward has a Treatment Manager, a Psychiatric Manager, a ward psychologist, and a team of psychiatric therapists. The ward psychologist plays an important role both in the treatment content and in the support of the psychiatric therapists. The wards use the Therapeutic Service, which consists of diagnosticians, psychotherapists, art and psychomotor therapists, psychiatrists, trainers, and social workers. These professionals conduct (among other tasks) diagnostics, crime scene analysis, and treatments, and are guided by the Managers of treatment in the different wards. They are part of the multidisciplinary teams that are created around patients.

In 2003, de Rooyse Wissel adopted ST as the main treatment model within its personality disorders care program and, moreover, uses it as a common language within the entire institute. In the same year, a pilot study was conducted and psychiatric therapists were trained in the basic principles of ST.

Following this, a large-scale training project was set up. It started with a two-day basic training course for the managers of treatment and of the psychiatric environment. The professionals of the Therapeutic Service also received this basic training. Psychotherapists and art and psychomotor therapists received additional training in ST and attended ST workshops. All psychiatric therapists and ward psychologists followed a six-session ST training course in 2005–6. This was run by psychotherapists and art and psychomotor therapists at de Rooyse Wissel, all of whom were trained for this purpose. This training project is run for new employees every other year.

Approach

Within the psychotherapy and art psychomotor therapy, ST has been implemented satisfactorily. Four ST psychotherapists participated in the study run by Bernstein (see Part VI, Chapter 1). In parallel to ST psychotherapy, patients also attend art and psychomotor therapy sessions, in which the principles of ST are integrated. These professionals hold alternating supervision and peer supervision meetings every week.

A schema-focused case conceptualization is implemented in the crime scene analysis. This is developed further in offense sequence groups led by psychotherapists in de Rooyse Wissel. The method used is the offense schema procedure. This consists of a series of semi-structured sessions used to map out cognitive, emotional, behavioral, and situational aspects prior to, during, and after the offense was committed (van Beek, 1999). Schema modes that play a role in a criminal offense (schema modes as risk factors) are analysed within the offense sequence.

Because the implementation of ST stagnated in the treatment wards, a new implementation plan was written (Kersten, 2007), partly based on literature about effective implementation (Grol and Wensing, 2006). The plan focused on what needed to be implemented in the divers disciplines. In this plan, the tasks of psychiatric therapists are described as: observing a patient's problematic behavior in the ward, mapping out this problematic behavior with the help of functional analysis of modes, recognizing and designating the involved schema modes, and discussing healthier behavior alternatives.

Furthermore, attention must be given to the question of how the language and the ST treatment can be implemented in psychiatric therapists on the ward, for example, by improving expertise, coaching during transference sessions, and developing a protocol for psychiatric therapists. An important basic principle is that psychotherapists and art and psychomotor therapists who are trained in ST, and the psychologists in the ward, must play a leading role, since they have the most expertise in the field. A second basic principle is that "implementation" can be interpreted as a process of setting goals, development, implementation, guaranteeing, and evaluation, according to the model devised by Grol and Wensing (2006). When considering implementation, it is important to distinguish between: 1) development, implementation, and evaluation in a smaller pilot phase; and 2) adjustment and implementation on a broader scale.

In 2008 and 2009, a ST implementation pilot took place in the de Nijl ward, one of the treatment wards for patients with personality disorders. Ten patients were accommodated in this ward and 13 psychiatric therapists were working there. The main goals of this pilot were to develop and implement a methodology and a ST protocol for the psychiatric therapists. The working method started with four training sessions in cognitive behavioral therapy and schema-focused therapy. In addition, the schemas and modes in patients who received ST were discussed by a ST therapist during the monthly team days at de Nijl. In the daily treatment evaluation and handover by the psychiatric therapists at the end of their shifts on the ward sessions in the ward, a ST therapist and a ward psychologist were present at the same time, approximately once a fortnight. During these transference sessions, the most important schema modes in 10 patients (modes that were most visible in the ward) were explained. A ST case conceptualization was available for most of the patients, and for a few patients a mode model, which had been drawn up in psychotherapy/art and psychomotor therapy sessions, was also available. Following this, ST treatment plans (goals and interventions the psychiatric therapist can use) were developed with regard to different dysfunctional schema modes. Psychiatric therapists were coached accordingly to implement these ST interventions by the ward psychologist.

The implementation process was difficult. We list here the four most important bottlenecks:

1. In de Nijl ward, only two patients had prior experience of ST in psychotherapy and art and psychomotor therapy; these patients had participated in Bernstein's study. The other patients were not familiar with ST and the ST terminology, yet three took part in the treatment as usual (TAU) condition. Difficulties arose for these patients in particular because their treatment plan was formulated in ST terminology. Patients were confused and TAU psycho therapists were (understandably) critical of the ST treatment plan of psychiatric therapists, because there was no consistency in therapeutic language with regard to TAU patients.

2. Many changes of staff (both Treatment Managers and psychiatric therapists), a mainly young and inexperienced team, and (as a consequence) an initial lack of commitment to the goals of the pilot were the reasons that the pilot lasted longer and demanded more time and energy from the ST therapist and ward psychologist. At the evaluation stage, the team stated that they were willing to actively continue with ST implementation.
3. A lack of cooperation between different disciplines and insufficient understanding of ST as shown by the ward psychologist were the reasons that it was not (yet) possible to maintain a consistent treatment plan around a patient.
4. Practical problems related to rosters and changes in meeting schedules led to instances, for example, where the personal coach of a patient could not be present when the goals and interventions were drawn up, that transference sessions could not take place, or that the contact person in socio-therapy could not attend the group meetings.

These and other bottlenecks have led to a change in direction regarding further ST implementation. It has been decided that this will take place exclusively in a so-called case course, in other words, solely around patients who are already receiving ST from psychotherapy. With these patients, it is of the greatest importance that a common language is employed and it is more effective to organize the implementation of this common language with the patients as the focus.

The end-result of the pilot is a manual for the implementation of ST in the other treatment wards (Kersten, 2009). An additional protocol has been developed, in which examples of psychiatric goals and interventions are prescribed for each schema mode.

The implementation procedure, as described in the manual, consists of the following steps:

1. A basic course cognitive behavioral therapy and ST in four sessions.
2. Schema mode meetings. Focused professional development about a specific ST patient in psychotherapy/art and psychomotor therapy during a team day; presentation of case conceptualization and mode model and fine-tuning with socio-therapy.
3. Determining and implementing ST aims and interventions in socio-therapy. ST psychotherapists provide a supporting role.
4. Coaching and training of psychiatric therapists is assisted by ST psychotherapists of the appointed ST patient, both during transference sessions and on request during psychiatric therapist team days.

Pitfalls and Tips

The implementation process at de Rooyse Wissel highlighted a number of potential pitfalls. The three most important are discussed here:

1. Over ambition. The initial plan for implementing ST in the whole institution proved too ambitious. De Rooyse Wissel is a dynamic institution that was forced

to contract recently after years of forced expansion. Furthermore, high psychiatric therapists turnover became a chronic problem. Tip: start with a small pilot in one stable ward that is ready to gain more insight with respect to ST content, and develop protocols there that can be implemented on a broader scale at a later date.
2. Insufficient use of ST expertise by professionals. Psychotherapists and art and psychomotor therapists were extensively trained and supervised in ST. However, they used their expertise only for the treatment of their own patients and not (or seldom) for the implementation taking place within the institute. Tip: Use professionals with ST expertise in the implementation of ST in other disciplines such as psychiatric therapists and choose a patient-oriented approach.
3. A ST course alone is insufficient. The ST knowledge that psychiatric therapists acquired soon faded away because knowledge was not established in structures. Research shows that several implementation strategies are necessary to bring about behavioral change (Grol and Wensing, 2006). Tip: Make sure that, following a course, the ST principles are secured in coachng, supervision and real protocols that support the treatment and are integrated in both the treatment process and professional development concerning individual patients.

The Future

In 2010, de Rooyse Wissel was forced to downsize as a result of cutbacks. This is an ongoing process. The project group that focused on ST implementation has been temporarily suspended because there are other priorities. At present, there are few possibilities to continue further implementation of ST in psychiatric therapists. However, the manual is on standby for active implementation when the situation improves.

Nevertheless, there are also positive developments. The need and enthusiasm for professional development of ST in socio-therapy has increased. This is illustrated by the need for professional development and coaching concerning ST patients in psychiatric therapists. Cooperation between these disciplines has also improved. Furthermore, a good multidisciplinary consultation process exists concerning a number of patients that have received ST for several years. This has resulted in a much better fine-tuning of ST.

References

Beek, D.J. van (1999) *De Delictscenarioprocedure bij Seksueel Agressieve Delinquenten*. Gouda: Gouda Quint.
Bernstein, D.P., Arntz, A. and de Vos, M. (2007) Schemagerichte therapie in de forensische setting. Theoretisch model and voorstellen voor best clinical practice. *Tijdschrift voor Psychotherapie*, 33(2), 120–139.
Blondelle, G., Williams, G. and van den Bosch, W. (2007) "Operant milieu" in een TBS-kliniek. *Maandblad Geestelijke Volksgezondheid*, 62(7/8), 634–639.

Emmerik, J.L. van and Brouwers, M. (2001) *De Terbeschikkingstelling in Maat and Getal: een Beschrijving van de TBS-Populatie in de Periode 1995–2000.* Den Haag: Ministerie van Justitie.

Grol, R. and Wensing, M. (2006) *Implementatie: Effectieve Verbetering van Patiëntenzorg.* Maarssen: Elsevier Gezondheidszorg.

Kersten, G.C.M. (2007) *Implementatieplan Schemagerichte Cognitieve Therapie ten Behoeve van de Rooyse Wissel.* Interne notitie.

Kersten, G.C.M. (2009) *Handleiding Implementatie Schematherapie in het Sociotherapeutisch Handelen in het Casuistiektraject.* Interne notitie de Rooyse Wissel.

4
Cost-Effectiveness of Schema Therapy

Thea van Asselt and Josephine Bloo

Introduction

How much does a mental illness cost?

Research into the costs of psychotherapy is a relatively under investigated area. The costs of psychotherapy might appear at first glance to be lower than, for example, those of major surgery, in which a lot of expensive equipment and many employees are involved. But besides the costs of the intervention itself, one should also think about the costs of the illness that can be "cured" with it, and these costs are, in most cases, considerable. Smit *et al.*, (2006) found that the costs of nine frequently occurring mental illnesses (alcohol abuse and dependence, and some mood and anxiety disorders) were compared in the Dutch situation. The average additional costs (i.e., other than basic consumption for non-related, minor health problems) for an average psychiatric patient were €3,200 p.a. This was slightly more than the average costs for a physical disease, which were estimated at €3,020 p.a. The costs of dysthymia and panic disorders especially were considerably high: €10,322 and €8,390 respectively. The costs of patients with a borderline personality disorder weren't calculated in this study. A cost-of-illness study in the Netherlands (van Asselt *et al.*, 2007) estimated these to be €16,852.

Although these figures are difficult to compare because different research methods were used, it can be assumed that the costs of borderline personality disorders are relatively high compared to other mental disorders, and certainly when compared to physical diseases. Much of the cost of a borderline personality disorder does not occur within healthcare, but for almost 80% in so-called productivity losses in particular and strain on the surroundings. Someone experiences productivity losses when he is incapable, or not fully capable, of undertaking paid (or unpaid) work. As a considerable number of borderline patients receive a disability benefit or are on social welfare, productivity losses are very high in this group.

The Wiley Blackwell Handbook of Schema Therapy: Theory, Research, and Practice, First Edition.
Edited by Michiel van Vreeswijk, Jenny Broersen, and Marjon Nadort.
© 2012 John Wiley & Sons, Ltd. Published 2015 by John Wiley & Sons, Ltd.

"Strain on the surroundings" refers to the degree to which a borderline patient takes up the time of a family member, neighbor, or friend because he can't manage being alone or can't organize his household himself. In a cost-effectiveness analysis, this time is estimated in financial terms because the patient isn't in a position to carry out other activities. Therefore, it can be argued that when therapy helps a patient to function better, many costs will be saved, both in and outside healthcare.

Cost-effectiveness analysis

Cost-effectiveness plays an increasingly important role within the healthcare system, which is restricted by budgets. In fact, calculating the cost-effectiveness of a therapy is about checking whether the therapy in question offers "value for money." After all, if there is another therapy that offers the same benefit for less cost, or offers something better at the same price, switching from one therapy to the other should occur because for every euro spent as many people as possible should be helped. In practice, this isn't always easy. It's often the case that one therapy is slightly better, but also slightly more expensive than another. The question that arises is whether the small extra effect is worth the extra investment. A cost-effectiveness analysis is one of the four ways an economic evaluation can be carried out (Drummond, O'Brien, Stoddart and Torrance, 1997) and provides information to support such a decision. The outcome is put in terms of extra costs per unit effect – for example, therapy A cures one patient more than therapy B and costs €10 more. This amount per unit effect is called the incremental cost-effectiveness ratio (ICER), and it is calculated as follows:

$$\frac{\text{cost of experimental treatment} - \text{cost of care as usual}}{\text{effectiveness of experimental treatment} - \text{effectiveness of care as usual}}$$

The ICER doesn't reveal all the details. An experimental treatment that is better and more expensive than the treatment as usual (TAU) can produce the same ratio as a treatment that is less effective and cheaper than TAU. The ratio of two negative numbers is, after all, positive. In order to interpret the ICER correctly, it is important to look at the incremental costs and effects (the nominator and the denominator of the ICER) separately. When comparing the incremental costs and effects, there are four possible combinations. These are shown in Table 4.1.

When the experimental treatment is cheaper and has a better effect than TAU (bottom right in Table 4.1), the choice is simple: the experimental treatment is, as it were, dominant and TAU should undoubtedly be replaced by the experimental treatment. If the situation is the other way round (top right in Table 4.1), then the

Table 4.1 The combinations of incremental costs and effects in a comparison between two treatments

	Less effect	More effect
Higher costs	Inferior	Assess ICER
Lower costs	Assess ICER?	Dominant

choice is also simple: when the experimental treatment generates less effect and is more expensive, than TAU is a better choice and the experimental treatment is inferior. In the other two cases, it becomes more complicated. If the experimental treatment is more expensive but better (top right in Table 4.1), which often occurs in practice, the ICER comes into the picture, and in this case, the ratio of incremental costs compared to incremental effects becomes important. Referring to the calculation above: is the cost for curing one extra patient acceptable? In principle, this question should be answered by policy-makers, and their decision depends on a number of factors, among which is the severity of the disorder. Finally, there is a situation in which the experimental treatment is indeed cheaper, but results in fewer good effects than TAU (bottom left in Table 4.1). Theoretically, this situation is similar to the previous situation, and the question would be whether there is an acceptable balance between the loss of effect and the cost of savings. But is a loss of effect acceptable? And if so, is the expected acceptable ratio of costs and effects similar to the one in the top right of the quadrant? In other words, if €10 or more per cured patient is designated as cost-effective, is a saving of €10 or more enough compensation for the fact that one fewer patient is cured? This is a sensitive issue and a consensus within the efficacy literature about this (Dowie, 2005; Severens et al., 2005) is yet to be reached.

In summary, a cost-effectiveness analysis implies that the incremental costs of a new intervention are most often judged, in connection with the incremental effects of this intervention, with regard to current practice. This principle is represented in Figure 4.1. For a very extended and clear explanation of cost-effectiveness analyses, Drummond et al., (1997) is recommended.

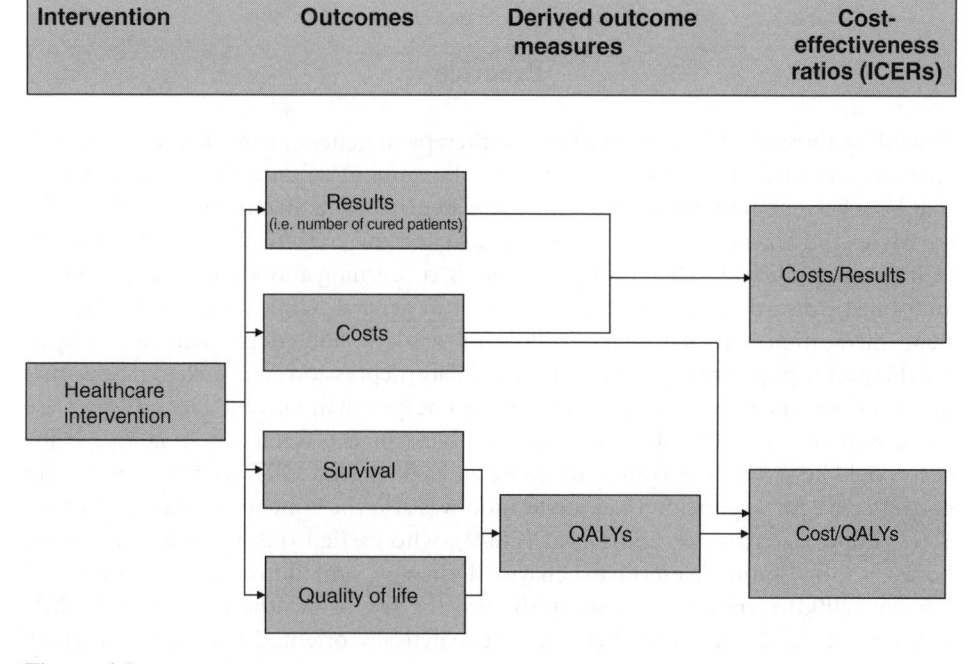

Figure 4.1

Quality adjusted life years

From a societal point of view, the costs and effects of any therapy must be considered, taking into account the costs and effects of interventions across the whole medical sphere. For example, a comparison of psychotherapy and blind gut surgery can be made. In general, the outcome of a cost-effectiveness analysis is monitored in terms of extra costs (or savings) per unit effect. Effectiveness can be expressed in natural units, for example, loss of weight in pounds [for US market], number of occurring infections, or number of "cured" patients. All these examples are illness-specific and applicable when reporting the relative cost-effectiveness of one intervention compared with another intervention for the same illness. However, effectiveness can also be expressed in Quality Adjusted Life Years (QALY). Because a QALY isn't illness-specific, but only contains an appreciation for the state of health that an illness brings, cost-effectiveness can be compared for different illnesses.

How is a QALY measured? QALY means that the life expectancy of a patient is corrected for the health-related quality of life that the patient experiences. The quality of life is reported in a so-called utility – a number between 0 and 1 – in which 0 is the worst possible state of health and 1 the best possible state of health. In addition, this utility is multiplied by the period for which the patient has lived with this quality of life, which results in the QALY of this period. In a year, the maximum number of QALYs is 1 (1*1) and the minimum number of QALYs is 0 (1*0). The utility can be assessed using several measures, of which the EuroQoL-5D (EQ-5D), (EuroQol Group, 1990) is the most widely used. The EQ-5D consists of five questions covering mobility, self-care, daily activities, pain/discomfort, and anxiety/depression. All of the questions can be answered in three possible ways, in the form no problem/ some problems/severe problems.

Practice

Regarding the cost-effectiveness of psychotherapy in general, some literature is available, even though this doesn't compare to the amount of cost-effectiveness studies that have been carried out in physical healthcare. In 2006, an annotated bibliography by Myhr and Payne about the cost-effectiveness of cognitive behavioral therapy (CBT) was published. They found 22 studies concerning mood, anxiety, psychotic, and somatic disorders. The findings were that in general, CBT is more cost-effective than medication. In particular, CBT for anxiety and depression is cheaper. Furthermore, population studies that modulate depression and anxiety show that interventions, including CBT, are in general cheaper than current care and increase social welfare. The general conclusion was that (for the Canadian situation) many costs could be saved by making CBT more accessible. That CBT is cheaper and more cost-effective for depression than medication was also the conclusion reached by Sava Yates, Lupu, Szentagotai, and David (2009), who carried out a comparative study between CBT, rational emotive behavioral therapy, and fluoxetine. Bateman and Fonagy (2003) carried out a cost study into the use of healthcare services by BPS patients before, during, and after a psychoanalytically oriented day treatment (now better known as mentalization-based therapy) "psychoanalytically oriented partial hospitalization," and found that the treated patients' own costs were lower during and after treatment. The costs of the treatment were compensated by this reduction. In 2006, a cost-effectiveness study of the BOSCOT trial (Palmer et al., 2006) was published. In this study, BPS patients were treated with CBT, with the outcome in costs per QALY. Here, the conclusion was that CBT wasn't clearly more cost-effective than TAU, since CBT was slightly cheaper, but at the same time provided slightly fewer QALYs. So, regarding the costs per QALY, the outcomes of the BOSCOT trial were comparable with the cost-effectiveness results of the Borderline Treatment Study (van Asselt et al., 2008), although this concerns a different type of therapy. Soeteman et al., (2010) conclude that psychotherapy, offered as inpatient or outpatient care, is the most cost-effective treatment strategy for patients with Cluster B personality disorders, regarding both costs per QALY and costs per recovered patient year. Byford and colleagues (2003) discovered that CBT for self-injurious behavior is, with more than 90% certainty, a more cost-effective strategy compared to TAU. The only publication in which psychotherapy wasn't deemed to be the most cost-effective strategy was Berghout, Zevalkink, and Hakkaart-van Roijen's study (2010). They compared psychoanalysis with psychoanalytical psychotherapy for patients with diverse Axis I and Axis II diagnoses. Psychoanalysis appeared to be the most effective in terms of QALYs, but also a lot more expensive than psychotherapy: the ICER resulted in €52,384. Although there are a number of studies that show psychotherapy to be cost-effective, there is little concrete evidence for ST. The cost-effectiveness analysis that was linked to the Borderline Treatment Study (van Asselt et al., 2008) showed that ST for BPD was definitely cost-effective when looked at from the number of cured patients, but from the point of view of QALYs, the situation is indeterminate. An implementation study by Nadort et al., (2009) investigated the efficacy and cost-effectiveness of ST in regular mental healthcare institutes in eight locations. The outcomes of the cost-effectiveness were completed in 2010 but not published at the time of writing. The University of Maastricht also ran a randomized multi center study (Bamelis et al., 2006–10) into the efficacy and cost-effectiveness of ST in six personality disorders (paranoia, histrionic, narcissistic, avoiding, dependent, and obsessive-compulsive). Hopefully, a broader scientific basis regarding the cost-effectiveness of ST will be available in the near future.

This chapter describes which debits, and with them the underlying behavior, are relevant in determining cost-effectiveness. According to the literature, starting from a societal perspective is recommended (Drummond et al., 1997). In the case of BPD, this implies that all costs related to the disorder have to be taken into account in the analysis. Besides the costs of the treatment itself and the costs of healthcare, there are also costs for productivity losses and strain on the surroundings. Furthermore, the patient's own costs have to be added. These will be described below.

Therapy

The costs of the therapy itself must be mapped out when investigating the cost-effectiveness of a certain psychotherapy method. In theory, this could merely be a matter of determining a cost price per session and multiplying it by the number of sessions that will take place during the research period according to the protocol. However, in practice a patient canceling a session, or not showing up, is a regular occurrence. If a patient cancels a session promptly, the therapist still has time to schedule another session for the period in question, so in principle, there are no costs incurred. If the patient doesn't cancel promptly, or doesn't show up, the therapist doesn't have a session for that particular period, and this missed session will count in the costs. When comparing different forms of psychotherapy, if patients are more likely to be absent for one therapy than for another, this can have consequences for the cost-effectiveness of the treatment. Even the quality of the relationship between patient and therapist can affect the costs. When this relationship is bad, it's possible that a patient will be less conscientious about attendance.

An important aspect of ST is telephone support offered by the therapist. Telephone support in itself doesn't involve any extra costs, but in order to make a good estimation of the costs, it is necessary to register very precisely any calls that do occur. Attention should be paid to the duration, the nature of the conversation, and the day and the time at which the call is made. When the nature of the call is administrative, it doesn't have to be calculated in the costs. This, after all, is not the essence of telephone support of ST and isn't any different from therapy without telephone support. If it concerns a crisis or therapeutic call, then the conversation does count. The costs of telephone calls vary according to the day of the week and the time of day. The implementation study by Nadort *et al.*, (2009), which investigated the cost-effectiveness of ST in regular mental healthcare, explicitly considered extra phone support in a comparison. Because it appeared to be very difficult to map out extra phone support well during the cost-effectiveness analysis, the implementation study designed a form on which contacts were recorded.

Care consumption

Besides psychotherapy, a borderline patient often uses a whole range of healthcare services, for which healthcare must be read in the broadest sense of the word. A number of patients use the crisis service, crisis center, and/or services such as short stays (usually one night) in a clinic on indication of symptoms. Sometimes, a patient has a regular check up at the general practitioner, to enable the doctor to keep track of the patient's situation. There can also be the matter of outpatient clinic appointments, day treatment, ER visits, or hospitalization in both psychiatric and general hospitals. Furthermore, there is often contact with social workers, clinics for alcohol and drug abuse, and potential home help and youth welfare work. All these costs are relevant from a societal perspective and have to be mapped out. Sometimes, it is assumed that such data are available for each individual within the databases of insurers or in national healthcare registers, but this is not the case. Care, which is covered by the Dutch law that protects people against excessive medical expenses (which is the case for most of these items), isn't registered per consultation, nor is it reducible to the individual. Interviewing the patient himself periodically by a so-called cost journal or cost interview seems to be the best option. As long as the periods between interviews aren't long (maximum three months), structural recall bias will be avoided (Severens, Mulder, Laheij and Verbeek, 2000; van den Brink *et al.*, 2005); this occurs when the patient's answers are unreliable because he doesn't remember accurately. Naturally, extra attention will have to be paid to reliability among the borderline population. It is advisable that patients don't complete the diaries/interviews themselves (which is what happens in other research populations), but that they are administered and completed by trained research assistants. The above mentioned refers to all debits that are discussed below (with the exception of judicial costs).

Medication

The majority of the borderline patients who receive treatment also receive prescribed medication. To take into account the costs of this, it is necessary to document it thoroughly. This means that the name of the medication, the period during which the medication was taken, the number of times per day, and the doses have to be known. Since a central register of medication is not normally available (because a patient might use more than one pharmacy), it is advisable to require that patients supply this information themselves.

Productivity losses

Productivity losses are an important part of the total costs of BPD. A productivity loss occurs when a patient isn't or is not fully capable of doing paid work. Unpaid work (housework, voluntary work, study) can also be calculated as a productivity loss. In Giesen-Bloo *et al.*, (2006) borderline treatment study 43% of the patients were unable to work at the beginning of the study. Nearly 13% had been on sick leave for so long that they would soon be eligible for disability allowance. A number of the disabled patients had never had a paid job since they were classified as disabled before they could enter the labor market. During the first year of the study (2000) 8.8% of the general population (15–64-year-olds) were receiving benefit under the Disabled Insurance Act (Centraal Bureau voor de Statistiek, 2004), which shows that borderline patients are severely affected by their disorder. Some patients can still function well in a full-time job, but most are regularly absent, or they are almost continuously (whether partly or not) on sick leave, which again counts as a productivity loss. Borderline disorders also pose a major obstacle regarding unpaid productivity. Patients have difficulties in organizing their household and keeping their domestic affairs running smoothly, with all the consequences that this entails. Many patients are unable to complete their studies or hold down a voluntary job for even a few hours a week.

In summary, the problem of productivity losses in BPD can be assumed to be that patients have difficulties in completing their education, and, if they aren't classified as disabled, are often absent from work. They also neglect household chores and voluntary work.

Besides productivity losses because of morbidity, productivity losses due to mortality also occur in BPD and other psychiatric disorders, as a result of suicide. When a patient dies, their future productivity capacity is reduced to zero.

Strain on the surroundings

One of the greatest debits of the cost-of-illness study into BPD (van Asselt *et al.*, 2007) was informal care, that is the strain that the patient puts on his surroundings. This strain means that patients make heavy demand on people in their immediate milieu, for example, because they can't or are too frightened be alone, they are scared to go to appointments by themselves, or go shopping alone, or they need help in their daily routine or in the care and education of their children.

Legal costs

Borderline patients can come into conflict with the law as a result of their disorder. Personality disorders are very prevalent in maximum security psychiatric hospitals and prisons. Although the outcomes of treatment studies often don't give an accurate account of the legal costs associated with BPD, because there aren't normally any institutionalized patients in the research sample, an estimation of the total costs by means of a top-down calculation (legal costs multiplied by the prevalence of borderline disorder in the study population) is possible. Timmerman and Emmelkamp (2001) found that 23.1% of the prisoners and 21.6% of the patients in maximum security psychiatric hospitals had BPD and incurs substantial expenses.

Other costs

There are also the direct costs the patient himself incurs as a result of his disorder. For example, the costs of non prescription medication (e.g., analgesics), visits to an alternative therapist who isn't funded by the health insurer, excessive consumption of substances buying wound dressings as a result of self-injurious behavior, purchases for food addictions, and smoking. Although it is often very difficult to quantify these debits and to separate the borderline-related part from the non-borderline-related part, these costs are an essential part of the societal costs, and therefore must not be ignored.

Approach

The current approach is based on the cost-effectiveness analysis (van Asselt *et al.*, 2008) which was carried out by Giesen-Bloo *et al.*, (2006) the borderline treatment study. This study compared ST with transference-focused psychotherapy (TFP) and lasted four years, in which treatment took place over three years twice a week. During these three years, the diverse research tools were monitored every three months. The last measure, the follow-up monitoring, took place one year after the end of the treatment. The ICERs that are calculated in the cost-effectiveness analysis (see Figure 4.1) are: costs per "cured" patient, in which cure was defined as a score on the Borderline Personality Disorder Severity Index-IV (BPDSI-IV) (Arntz *et al.*, 2003) of less than 15 at follow-up, and the costs per QALY.

Calculation of costs

Costs were calculated using a standardized cost-interview, administered by research assistants. This interview covered paid and voluntary work (including housework) and non-attendance at these, use of healthcare services (e.g., general practitioner, outpatient mental healthcare institute, hospital, crisis centers), use of medication, substance abuse, strain on the surroundings, and other expenses, as reported by the patient. Maximum security psychiatric hospital and suicide were not included in this interview. In Figure 4.2, the three month costs (which are derived from one monitoring) of the two groups are reported for baseline and follow-up. The cost level decreased considerably for both groups. What is also remarkable is that there is a difference between ST and TFP, both on baseline and follow-up. The difference isn't significant, but is nevertheless substantial, and persists more or less throughout the whole trial. The total costs (exclusive of baseline) for the entire four years were €37,994 for ST and €47,009 for TFP.

> ### Cost profile of a random patient from the study
>
> A 49-year-old female patient has a part-time job (20 hours per week). Before the start of the study, she has a high absence rate due to illness. She attends a therapy session with a psychiatrist/psychotherapist once a week and, in addition, visits a psychologist at a clinic for alcohol and drug abuse because of her heavy drinking (approximately 25 glasses per week). Furthermore, she uses antidepressants and anxiolytics. In total, this patient incurs expenses of approximately €1,770 in the three months prior to the start of the therapy. After the start of ST, the patient quits her job and the regular therapy appointments are canceled. She still uses some social-work services every now and then, because she hasn't yet got over her past. Her alcohol abuse remains unrelenting, but the use of medication slowly decreases. After more than two years of treatment, the patient stops the therapy (drops out). At this time, she has a new job for some time, with little or no borderline-related absence. After two years, the three-monthly costs are about €1,000.

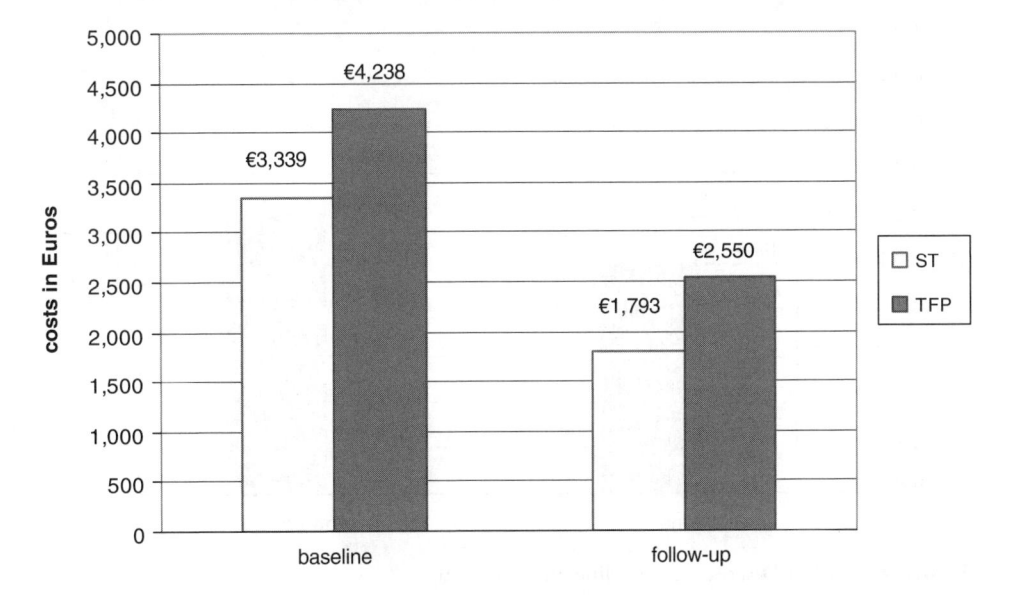

Figure 4.2 Costs on baseline and follow-up

Calculation of QALYs

QALYs are calculated with the help of EQ-5D utilities, and then multiplied by the period in which the patient remained in this condition.

Figure 4.3 shows the utilities of the two groups on baseline (prior to treatment) and on follow-up. It is clear that quality of life increases considerably after the start of the treatment. The total number of QALYs was 2.15 for ST and 2.27 for TFP. The small (non significant) difference is caused by the patients in the TFP group showing a rapid increase of the EQ-5D immediately after the start of the research. This levels off later, while the patients in the ST group increase more slowly, but eventually catch up.

Calculation of ICERs

To calculate ICERs, the total costs, the total QALYs, and the percentage of cured patients according to the BPDSI-IV (as calculated in the treatment study), which was 29% for TFP and 52% for ST, are used. As costs per cured patient are unequivocal (ST is cheaper and more effective than TFP; bottom right in Table 4.1), ICER isn't calculated here, because it isn't necessary to make a comparative assessment. The costs per QALY are more complicated. ST provides slightly fewer QALYs than TFP, as seen in the bottom left of Table 4.1. The ICER is €90,457, which means that for every QALY that is not provided for less by ST there is saving of €90,457, calculated as follows: (€47,009.92 − €36,629.95)/(2.2663 − 2.1516). The costs of ST are lower than previously discussed, because for calculation of the costs per QALY one patient was excluded from the analysis owing to of a lack of complete EQ-5D data. For ST, €37,994 was used for the calculation of the costs per recovered patient.

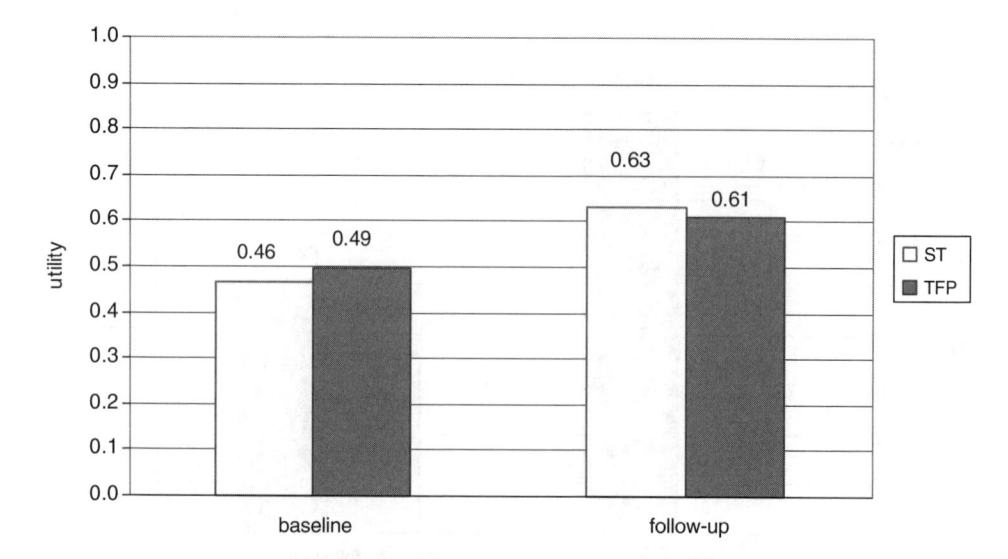

Figure 4.3 EQ-5D scores on baseline and follow-up

Pitfalls and Tips

In the study into the cost-effectiveness of ST vs. TFP discussed above, the difficulty in accessing data for care consumption was one of the biggest obstacles in gathering and verifying the data. Verification of the data regarding care consumption provided by patients is very difficult (e.g., contacts with general practitioners, specialists, psychiatrics, and psychotherapists, hospitalization and outpatient clinic visits) because of the way in which registration takes place. All care that falls under the Exceptional Medical Expenses Act (AWBZ) is registered by care centers, but checking the exact care consumption for a specific patient in a certain period is impossible. Of course, it is possible to check at a hospital whether the patient concerned was hospitalized for a certain period or whether he had outpatient clinic visits, but the patient could have been to another hospital or could even have been hospitalized abroad. It is impossible to check for each patient every possible institute where he could have attended, regardless of the privacy issues that could also play a role.

Information on the number of borderline-related cases under the Disablement Insurance Act, or, for example, the number of borderline-related suicides, is also very hard to access. To highlight the example of the Disablement Insurance Act: on inquiry at the Lisv (the insurance institute for the Dutch Disablement Insurance Act) it appeared that, in 1999, in total 717 people received benefits through the Disablement Insurance Act, for which the official cause was BPD. When this is compared to our study, in which almost 50% of the patients received disability allowance as a result of borderline problems, the number of people receiving borderline-related Disablement Insurance Act benefits in the Netherlands would be 43% of 131,900 people (calculated for an adult population of 11,990,942 and with a prevalence of 1.1%), i.e., more than 56,000. This is probably a considerable overestimation, partly due to the fact that the population in our trial isn't completely representative of the entire borderline population in the Netherlands, but it makes very clear that registration isn't comprehensive. The differences that were found between the data based on the treatment study and the data based on national registration were evident in the same order of magnitude for almost all levels (i.e., for psychiatric hospitals, general hospitals, outpatient mental healthcare institutes, general practitioners, and medication). In addition, there are cost categories that aren't recorded by a central register (e.g., strain on the family, substance abuse, use of non prescription medication, and other expenses paid by the patient). In summary, it is very difficult to verify the incoming data in a cost study into borderline patients. Although the method can be criticized, the patient is still the only person who is best informed of all the relevant events, and therefore he is the most reliable source for a cost study. In our study, the patients were asked, after the pre-measurement, to keep a record of how often they visited their general practitioner, if they had any contact with a crisis center, and whether there were any changes in their use of medication. By structuring the gathering of data in this way, and mainly because the research assistants administered the interviews personally, the reliability of the data can be considered acceptable.

The Future

In 2006, the Dutch Council of Public Health and Care published a report entitled "Sensible and sustainable care." The report expounds on why financial evaluations will become increasingly important in the future. On the one hand, costs are soaring as a result of a doubling in the aging population and advancing technology; more is possible, so more will be done, for an increasingly large number of people. On the other hand, there is, as in almost all countries, a limit to the collective means that can be spent on healthcare. These two aspects lead to the fact that in the end some limits will have to be set in meeting the expenses of care from collective means. A choice has to be made. The criteria on which selection has occurred thus far were in general not very transparent and had too little focus on hard evidence, such as cost-effectiveness. The Council advises the development of an unambiguous and transparent system of criteria for the right to qualify for funding for treatment. The Council also indicates that limits have to be determined democratically, but suggests no longer paying for the treatment of illnesses with a burden of less than 0.1. (The burden of illness is determined as the relative amount of health a person loses during his normal life expectancy when the illness isn't treated. For example, fungal nails have a burden of illness of 0.02, osteoporosis 0.08, high cholesterol 0.28, and pulmonary hypertension 0.96; Brouwer and Rutten, 2006.)

The Council also suggests a limit of €80,000 per QALY as a maximum for an intervention for a burden of illness of 1.0. The limits for the maximum "price" of a QALY, discussed in the literature thus far, when it remains cost-effective, were lower, at around €20,000–30,000 (Laupacis, Feeny, Detsky and Tugwell, 1992; Gyrd-Hansen 2003; King, Tsevat, Lave and Roberts, 2005). In the cost-effectiveness analysis of the borderline treatment study, the savings per lost QALY for ST vs. TFP was €90,457, which would mean that ST is cost-effective from the point of view of QALY. However, whether a loss of effectiveness is acceptable at all is the question, and if so, whether the usual thresholds count in this situation. In determining a threshold the more expensive and effective scenario is generally used as a starting point (top right in Table 4.1).

This is not yet current practice, however, the report offers a good indication of the direction in which healthcare is going. The more disorders and treatments have to "compete" in order to be included in the compensation package, the more important it is that there are good statistics available concerning the burden of illness and the cost-effectiveness of a treatment. It is therefore to be expected that cost-effectiveness analyses will take a more prominent place alongside clinical studies. Particularly in the field of psychiatry, where few thorough economic evaluations have been done, a large catch up effort needs to be made.

References

Arntz, A., Hoorn, M. van den, Cornelis, J. *et al.* (2003) Reliability and validity of the borderline personality disorder severity index. *Journal of Personality Disorders*, *17*: 45–59.

Asselt, A.D.I. van, Dirksen, C.D., Arntz, A. and Severens J.L. (2007) The cost of borderline personality disorder: societal cost of illness in BPD patients. *Eur Psychiatry*, 22: 354–361.

Asselt, A.D. van, Dirksen, C.D., Arntz, A. *et al.* (2008) Out-patient psychotherapy for borderline personality disorder: cost-effectiveness of schema-focused therapy v. transference-focused psychotherapy. *Br J Psychiatry*, 192(6), 450–457.

Bamelis, L., Arntz, A., Bernstein, D. *et al.* (2006–2010) Psychological treatment of personality disorders: a multi-centered randomized controlled trial on the (cost-) effectiveness of schema-focused therapy. *ZonMW Doelmatigheidsonderzoek, Subsidie Toegekend Ronde 2006*, projectnr. 945-06-406.

Bateman, A. and Fonagy, P. (2003) Health service utilization costs for borderline personality disorder patients treated with psychoanalytically oriented partial hospitalization versus general psychiatric care. *Am J Psychiatry*, 160(1), 169–171.

Berghout, C.C., Zevalkink, J. and Hakkaart-van Roijen, L. (2010) A cost-utility analysis of psychoanalysis versus psychoanalytic psychotherapy. *Int J Technol Assess HealthCare*, 26(1), 3–10.

Brink, M. van den, Hout, W.B. van den, Stiggelbout, A.M. *et al.* (2005) Self-reports of healthcare utilization: diary or questionnaire? *Int J Technol Assess HealthCare*, 21(3), 298–304.

Brouwer, W.B.F. and Rutten, F.F.H. (2006) *Afbakening van het Basispakket. I: Zicht op Zinnige en Duurzame Zorg*. Raad voor de Volksgezondheid en Zorg (Council for Public Health and Healthcare). Zoetermeer.

Byford, S., Knapp, M., Greenshields, J. *et al.* (2003) Cost-effectiveness of brief cognitive behaviour therapy versus treatment as usual in recurrent deliberate self-harm: a decision-making approach. *Psychol Med*, 33(6), 977–86.

Centraal Bureau voor de Statistiek, www.cbs.nl, statline. Geraadpleegd in 2004.

Dowie, J. (2005) No room for kinkiness in a public healthcare system. *Pharmacoeconomics*, 23(12), 1203–1205.

Drummond, M.F., O'Brien, B., Stoddart, G. and Torrance, G.W. (1997) *Methods for the Economic Evaluation of HealthCare Programmes*, 2nd edition. Oxford: Oxford University Press.

EuroQoL Group (1990). EuroQol – a new facility for the measurement of health-related quality of life. *Health Policy*, 16(3), 199–208.

Giesen-Bloo, J., Dyck, R. van, Spinhoven, P. *et al.* (2006) Outpatient psychotherapy for borderline personality disorder: randomized trial of schema-focused therapy vs. transference-focused psychotherapy. *Arch Gen Psychiatry*, 63(6), 649–658.

Gyrd-Hansen, D. (2003) Willingness to pay for a QALY. *Health Econ*, 12(12), 1049–1060.

King, J.T. Jr, Tsevat, J., Lave, J.R. and Roberts, M.S. (2005) Willingness to pay for a quality-adjusted life year: implications for societal healthcare resource allocation. *Med Decision Making*, 25(6), 667–77.

Laupacis, A., Feeny, D., Detsky, A.S. and Tugwell, P.X. (1992) How attractive does a new technology have to be to warrant adoption and utilization? Tentative guidelines for using clinical and economic evaluations. *Cmaj*, 146(4), 473–481.

Myhr, G. and Payne, K. (2006) Cost-effectiveness of cognitive-behavioural therapy for mental disorders: implications for public healthcare funding policy in Canada. *Can J Psychiatry*, 51(10), 662–670.

Nadort, M., Arntz, A., Smit, J.H. *et al.* (2009) Implementation of outpatient schema therapy for borderline personality disorder with versus without crisis support by the therapist outside office hours: a randomized trial. *Behav Res Ther*, 47(11), 961–973.

Palmer, S., Davidson, K., Tyrer, P. *et al.* (2006) The cost-effectiveness of cognitive behavior therapy for borderline personality disorder: results from the BOSCOT trial. *J Personal Disord*, 20(5), 466–481.

Raad voor de Volksgezondheid and Zorg [Council for Public Health and HealthCare] (2006) *Zinnige en Duurzame Zorg [Sensible and Sustainable Care]*. Den Haag.

Sava, F.A., Yates, B.T., Lupu, V., Szentagotai, A. and David, D. (2009) Cost-effectiveness and cost-utility of cognitive therapy, rational emotive behavioral therapy, and fluoxetine (Prozac) in treating depression: a randomized clinical trial. *J Clin Psychol*, 65(1), 36–52.

Severens, J.L., Brunenberg, D.E., Fenwick, E.A., O'Brien, B. and Joore, M.A. (2005) Cost-effectiveness acceptability curves and a reluctance to lose. *Pharmacoeconomics*, 23(12), 1207–1214.

Severens, J.L., Mulder, J., Laheij, R.J. and Verbeek, A.L. (2000) Precision and accuracy in measuring absence from work as a basis for calculating productivity costs in the Netherlands. *Soc Sci Med*, 51(2), 243–249.

Smit, F., Cuijpers, P., Oostenbrink, J. *et al.* (2006) Costs of nine common mental disorders: implications for curative and preventive psychiatry. *J Ment Health Policy Econ*, 9(4), 193–200.

Soeteman, D.I., Verheul, R., Delimon, J. *et al.* (2010) Cost-effectiveness of psychotherapy for Cluster B personality disorders. *Br J Psychiatry*, 196(5), 396–403.

Timmerman, I.G. and Emmelkamp, P.M. (2001) The relationship between traumatic experiences, dissociation, and borderline personality pathology among male forensic patients and prisoners. *J Personal Disord*, 15(2), 136–149.

5
Public Relations for Schema Therapy

Michiel van Vreeswijk, Marjon Nadort and Jenny Broersen

There is an increasing interest in Schema Therapy (ST). During the last few years, several books on ST for therapists have been published internationally. In some cases, these books focus on the treatment of a specific patient population or working method, for example, individual (e.g., Young, Klosko and Weishaar, 2003; Rafaeli, Bernstein and Young, 2010) vs. group therapy. This list would be even longer if books in all languages were mentioned. A ST self-help book for patients has also been published (Young and Klosko, 1994). Interest has increased among scientists and research-oriented clinicians (see Chapters in Part VI).

Coinciding with the publication of an article about the randomized research study into ST in borderline patients (Giesen-Bloo *et al.*, 2006), there were a number of publications in Dutch newspapers and a lot of attention was paid to ST on Dutch television. The Dutch website www.schematherapie.nl had 17,000 new visitors between April 2007 and February 2008. Outside of the Netherlands, interest in ST also grew. Between October 2008 and November 2009, the International Society of Schema Therapy (ISST) website (www.isst-online.com) had 5,981 new visitors. This number will increase as more colleagues become familiar with the website. Since 2006, the ISST has organized four international conferences; more than 330 participants attended the ISST conference in Berlin in 2010.

This chapter describes the way in which ST can be brought to the attention of clinicians/non-mental healthcare specialized referrers, patients/patients' organizations, managers of mental healthcare institutes, health insurers, and society in general (family/employers, social security administration, and the government). It should be mentioned that the situation described here relates to the Netherlands. The authors realize that healthcare systems elsewhere can be very different. Nevertheless, they hope this chapter will offer ideas about how ST can be brought (further) to attention in other countries.

The Wiley Blackwell Handbook of Schema Therapy: Theory, Research, and Practice, First Edition.
Edited by Michiel van Vreeswijk, Jenny Broersen, and Marjon Nadort.
© 2012 John Wiley & Sons, Ltd. Published 2015 by John Wiley & Sons, Ltd.

In Practice

The number of therapists who want to implement ST is increasing as a result of publicity, among others factors. However, ST hasn't yet been implemented in every Dutch mental healthcare institute. At the same time, there are institutes with a waiting list for ST. Questions are regularly asked through the Dutch website www.schematherapie.nl and also to ST supervisors about when workshops are available and if it is possible for them to organise an ST workshop within their mental healthcare institute. Patients and referrers are also looking for therapists who offer ST. This increasing demand led to the foundation of the Dutch Schema Therapy register in 2007. In addition, developments are underway internationally. In 2006, the International Society of Schema Therapy was founded. To be included on either register therapists have to meet certain ST educational criteria (see Part V, Chapter 1). The Dutch Schema Therapy register (www.schematherapie.nl) and the ISST (www.isst-online.com) are avenues for receiving more information about ST. But for whom, and how, is more information on ST supplied?

Public relations on ST training and certification

Professional associations and websites such as www.schematherapie.nl announce workshops for Dutch educational institutes in mental healthcare (e.g., RINO), as well as through the training brochures and newsletters that these organizations send to their members. The information provided consists of: the name of the instructor, target group, prior knowledge, aims, training content, working approach, literature, accreditation, data, and costs. The amount of information in this material varies. In some, it says that the training is intended for social workers who work with personality problems and/or inflexible mood/anxiety disorders, while others state explicitly that the training is intended for psychologists. In these cases, the eventual aim of the training must be adapted to the target group, taking into consideration the guidelines as drawn up in the Schema Therapy register and the ISST. The extent to which prior knowledge is necessary and in particular to the follow-up training required for ST isn't always clear to participants. Is reading a manual about ST sufficient preparation for participation in ST training? A potential participant can become preoccupied by this question. Or in cases of training for group ST, is having participated in a Rational Emotive Therapy group or assertiveness training sufficient prior knowledge and experience for group therapeutic work?

Referrers

It is often thought that colleagues, general practitioners, psychologists, psychiatrics, and social psychiatric graduate nurses know about the available treatment for a certain disorder. Because of all the publicity about ST, it may seem that referrers know when they can register a patient for ST. However, even within healthcare programs for personality disorders, it is not clear which treatment options are available or what the criteria are for deciding upon a particular course of treatment (see Box 1). Sometimes, the *couleur locale* seems to determine the choice of treatment to which the patient

> **Box 1:**
>
> For a significant period, Alexandra has problems with aggression, she has difficulties in studying, and problems with her parents. When her boyfriend ended their relationship, she injured herself and drank three bottles of wine.
>
> The next day, Alexandra was sent to the doctor by her mother. He doesn't know what to do with her. She has previously had short-term treatment for fluctuating emotional states and he realizes that another treatment focusing on her personality is necessary. But where can he send her? The local mental healthcare institute has a long waiting list and he doesn't know whether, if, and how they treat personality disorder problems at this institute. He is also not familiar with the treatment offered by other institutes.

is referred. Specific information for both internal and external referrers is often not available. Internal referrers in a mental healthcare institute sometimes hear about ST during a lecture, a treatment plan discussion, or in peer supervision. In some situations, Schema Therapists can give them a patient brochure or refer them to the Schema Therapy website.

Management of a mental healthcare institute

Changes within the Dutch health insurance system pose a challenge for ST. Long-term treatment is less attractive for mental healthcare institutes because the costs (salaries, overheads) no longer counterbalance the yields achieved by the diagnostic treatment. In addition, it is possible that institutes will start to refuse long-term (schema) therapies. Patients who miss appointments several times are told that their treatment will end earlier than scheduled. Mental healthcare institutes also have to compete with each other and therefore must prove to health insurers that they can offer good-quality care. One way to do this is by providing result indicators, but who will determine these? Who will analyze them? To whom and how will these data be presented? Will they be shown to the health insurers, or also to the patient and the clinician, or maybe anonymized to a larger audience? Again, this is an important task for Schema Therapists, because the managers of the healthcare institutes must be informed about the research outcomes of ST and about the exact content of the treatment. If the Schema Therapist doesn't inform the manager properly, it isn't surprising if the manager only agrees to short-term diagnostic treatments with a health insurer and that the result indicators lead him to choose what kind of treatment will be offered on the spur of the moment or to select the most cost-effective treatment.

Health insurers

Changes within the Dutch healthcare system mean that health insurers are becoming more critical about who provides treatment and what the costs are. Furthermore, they have to focus more on what patients want because patients are now more likely to switch health insurer if their current insurer doesn't offer what they want (see Box

2). This means that health insurers will impose demands on healthcare providers. They attach increasing importance to a quality check of treatments by means of result indicators (e.g., patient satisfaction, changes in GAF scores, and other indicators). With this, the implementation of preferred partnership has begun. Healthcare providers who meet certain quality criteria receive a higher allowance and more patients are referred to them than to healthcare providers who do not meet these criteria. The health insurers will also have to begin to inform their customers/patients about the treatment purchased and the healthcare providers they can turn to for this. Care mediation for patients who are looking for ST, but are faced with waiting lists, is not unknown. There is no information about ST on any of the websites of the five largest Dutch health insurers. Furthermore, the authors of this chapter emailed 15 health insurers' associations and Healthcare Nederland (a Dutch organization of mental healthcare institutes) and asked the following questions:

1. What information do you need from an institute in order to purchase a product such as, a long-term, Schema Therapy from them?
2. What would determine your choice if you had to choose between purchasing Schema Therapy from two institutes in the same region?
3. How do you judge quality? What kind of information do you expect an institute to provide in order to determine whether their product is of a good quality?
4. What are your preferred terms for a contract?

Thirteen health insurers (81%) replied with (often) an automatically generated answer stating that they would respond to the questions soon (of which 31% reported that they would answer in 3–7 days); 19% replied to the first mail concerning the content. This shows that health insurers aren't familiar with ST and don't necessarily know whether ST is a short-term first-line treatment (of eight sessions) or a long-term treatment in more specialized units. Thirty percent of the health insurers indicated that the overriding criterion in the choice of purchasing care is the need of the patient. They all indicated that evidence-based or best practice is also taken into account when reaching a decision. In addition, national result indicators as outcome indicators specifically aimed at the complaints, and the form of treatment, are named as grounds on the basis of which health insurers will purchase care. Institutes that have a high

Box 2:

An employee at a health insurance company calls a mental healthcare institute. They are looking for ST for one of their patients. This patient had approached several healthcare providers and heard that there is a waiting list for ST everywhere. She then called her health insurer, in order to look at institutes where ST is offered and if they can help her to find a Schema Therapist. The secretary of the mental healthcare institute gives the health insurer's assistant information about the waiting list for ST at her institute. She explains their way of working and offers to call one of the Schema Therapists for more information if necessary.

> **Box 3:**
> Casey has struggled with starting new relationships. She mostly breaks off the relationship after a few weeks, because she thinks her partner is boring or that he isn't there for her in the way she wants him to be. She also has problems with her studies. She has been a law student for eight years and she has been working on her thesis for three years. In a discussion with the student counselor in the faculty, she is advised to consider psychological help. She searches the Internet to see which therapy method would be most applicable to her and where she can get this therapy. However, she is confronted with a mass of data.

score on the national result indicators will be in a better negotiating position than institutes with lower scores. Cheaper treatments with comparable results will be increasingly considered.

Patients and patients' association

Where is the patient and his immediate environment in all this? More and more it is being said that an institute has to become demand-focused rather than offer-focused (see Box 3). What does the patient want and what does the patient know?

Interviews with Dutch patients undergoing ST show that many patients feel the need for information about the treatment in the form of data on a website and in a brochure for patients. They believe that data about this treatment method are limited and hard to find on the Internet. They also report that many referrers aren't, or are insufficiently, informed about ST. Some patients, therefore, sense that their referral was a matter of pure luck. Patients prefer the following data:

1. Which symptoms is ST applicable for?
2. How does ST work within individual treatment and group treatment (therapy rules, therapy process)?
3. What are the experiences of patients who have completed ST?
4. What is the role of the therapist in the therapy process and what is expected of the patient?
5. Which therapy techniques are used?
6. What is the (average) end result that can be expected?

The authors of this chapter carried out a random check ($N = 33$) on the Internet of well-known national and regional mental healthcare institutes throughout the Netherlands. They checked whether ST was offered within the institute and, if so, whether the questions above were answered. For this, they used the Google browser and the website www.ggzbeleid.nl/cijfers/aanbieders to search for mental healthcare institutes. In each region, the websites of at least two mental healthcare institutes were examined. The following keywords were used: Schema Therapy, schema-oriented therapy, schema-oriented cognitive therapy, and healthcare program personality disorders. Because not all mental healthcare institutes have a separate search function on their webpage but, for instance, do name their different locations, information was also searched per location. Some offer a link for available healthcare or treatment options. These links were also used to see whether there was information available on ST.

One-third of the 33 mental healthcare institutes in this study include some information on ST. This varies from the brief statement that ST is available in the treatment options, to a short explanation of ST. Only one institute answers the six questions listed above, but offers no patient experiences. Furthermore, it is surprising that the majority of the institutes that give a description of ST only describe it in the context of treatment for borderline personality disorders, which is especially highlighted on the websites, with less attention paid to other personality disorders. On 18% of the websites, there was no search function available, which made searching for ST harder, especially when there was no separate link for treatments offered. No alternative suggestions for search words for ST were given when searching the different websites. All this is surprising in light of the increasing interest in ST. The authors expected to find more information on ST on the websites, especially those belonging to institutes where they knew that Schema Therapists were active.

Interviews with patients show that it is important to them to know how they will be treated during an intake or assessment. Patients don't appreciate undergoing another assessment that looks similar to ones they have already undergone at several other institutes. However, they can understand the fact that social workers use information (from a file) of prior treatments, and that social workers can ask additional questions on the basis of this information. Patients report that these discussions can be illuminating. Furthermore, patients appreciate it when the therapist treats them as an equal, as fits with the ST model, and during the interview the problems are translated into schemas and modes. They are told that everyone has their own schemas and modes, and that it is only the severity and rigidity in reacting to them that can make the difference between someone who needs treatment and someone who can deal with their sensitivities adequately. The theoretical model of ST is readily understood by many patients, and they are often very capable of explaining the model to friends and family based on the explanation they have received. As one patient said:

> "To people who are less close to me, I sometimes explain that I attend a personal development course in order to be able to deal better with my sensitivities. I also tell them that more people would profit from this."

When patients are asked whether they are aware of the changes within the healthcare system in the Netherlands, and what the (future) consequences of this might be for their treatment, it becomes clear that only a very few know what these changes entail. Most of them pay their contribution and expect to receive as much therapy as indicated. They are unaware that the duration of treatment and no-show percentage will play a more important role in the future. And even though they disagree with possible cuts to the proposed duration of treatment by health insurers and the management of mental healthcare institutes, patients seem to agree with a stricter policy regarding the no-show rate.

Approach

So far, publicity has been primarily offered to patients and colleagues who are interested in ST. Colleagues are informed through professional literature, workshops at conferences, presentations within institutes, and through websites and mailings from mental healthcare organizations and postdoctoral education institutes. They can also order the DVD box-set "Schematherapie voor de borderline persoonlijkheidsstoornis" [Schema Therapy for borderline personality disorders] (Nadort, 2005) through www.schematherapie.nl. This DVD has English subtitles. Wijngaart and Bernstein (2010) have made an English DVD. On both DVDs, parts of the treatment are shown in the form of role-plays and dialogues. Through www.schematherapie.nl, inventories can be downloaded, there is a summary of training courses and publications, and the option to look for ST practitioners on the register. On the ISST website and on www.schematherapie.com a lot of information on the content of ST, as well as several publications and certifications, can be found.

Patients can find (limited) information on the Internet, and institutes often hand out a patient brochure with a short explanation of schemas and modes. Some patient brochures contain a fictitious vignette of a patient who has certain schemas and modes, and how these influence his life, sometimes with the addition of a case conceptualization for this fictional patient. The patient brochure often offers information about the organization of ST in terms of frequency, setting, and expected duration of the treatment. In some cases, a patient is advised to read self-help books. Extended patient information about the precise ST techniques, the expected treatment outcome, patient satisfaction and experiences of patients that have followed the treatment, are not offered.

Specific information for referrers, health insurers, the implementing body for employee insurance schemes in the Netherlands employers, managers of mental healthcare institutes and partners/families is limited or nonexistent. When questions are asked by members of these groups, a patient brochure or a referral to the ST books and scientific articles can be offered. Although this material is relevant, it is not written specifically for them, and therefore it is questionable whether it will be read. A Schema Therapist, therefore, usually offers verbal information (asked for by the people indicated in brackets) on subjects such as:

- For which group is ST indicated? *(referrer)*
- What are the inclusion and exclusion criteria? *(referrer)*
- Is this ST evidence-based and efficient? *(health insurer)*
- Is there a waiting list, and if so, how long is it? *(health insurer)*
- What is the influence of ST to the extent that the employer can be charged? *(body for employee insurance schemes/employer)*
- Can the employee be declared fully competent again after receiving ST? *(body for employee insurance schemes/employer)*
- To what extent is an (expensive) clinical psychologist/psychotherapist necessary to implement ST? *(managers of mental healthcare institutes)*
- How is ST cost-effective (time/costs/quality ratio)? *(managers of mental healthcare institutes)*

- What can I expect from my partner/relative and what is my role in therapy? *(relative/partner of patient)*
- How do I deal with the changes that I experience and by which I'm affected? *(relatives/partner of patient)*

These questions illustrate that there is also a need for information on ST for people other than the patient himself.

Pitfalls and Tips

Information on the website of mental healthcare institutes is very limited and incomplete, with the result that patients must search longer than necessary for suitable treatment. When developing the publicity material for ST, it is important to ask, among other things:

1. What is the goal?
2. Who is the target group?
3. What kind of information would the target group like to have and in which format?
4. How can I involve the target group in developing information material?
5. What is the best way/tool to reach the target group?

In addition, it is important to guarantee that evaluations of whether the information provided meets the conditions are carried out at set periods. It is important to actively involve the target group for whom the information is developed. Too often, it is developed without the active participation of the target group, and it is taken for granted that it is obvious to them and that the information they have meets their needs.

It should be said that for health insurers' information on ST should also be a focal point. Some health insurers now indicate that they are less interested in the form of therapy, and more in the cost-effectiveness of the treatment. But what if the customer is interested in this and, for example, asks for care mediation from the health insurer?

Schema Therapists and researchers will have to pay close attention to effective measurement, patient satisfaction, and cost-effectiveness. Thinking that everything will turn out well or that one investigation into ST is sufficient is not appropriate in the context of current developments within the healthcare system. Therapists can approach healthcare managers with the abovementioned measurements and supply them with information about the quality and (cost-)effectiveness of the treatment. They will also have to promote their presence in discussions with health insurers when regarding purchasing products such as ST, a development that has already begun in somatic healthcare.

When developing a website on the ST offered in a mental healthcare institute, there needs to be a search function on the website, where different search words are offered. Research into the websites of the 33 Dutch mental healthcare institutes described in this chapter shows that some do not have a search function or do not always have relevant search words. Another potential pitfall in developing websites is that many institutes offer treatment information based on the problem, expecting the patient to be aware of his diagnosis and also to know which care program this belongs to. References to relevant websites from other healthcare providers or patient associations can make the maze that visitors encounter on some websites easier to negotiate.

The Future

In the future, the Dutch Schema Therapy register will show therapists, patients, as well as health insurances and management a geographic breakdown of places where ST is offered. Websites such as www.schematherapie.nl and from mental healthcare institutes can improve their public relations by offering information specifically designed for the different target groups (referrers, health insurers, the implementing body for employee insurance schemes in the Netherlands/employers, relatives/partners, patients). For example, in the case of patient groups, anonymized stories of patients who have had ST could be offered, but also the placing of a weblog/secure chat room at the disposal of patients in order to give them the opportunity to exchange their experiences. Research outcomes of ST (and possible outcomes per institute) need to be made accessible for the different target groups. Mental healthcare institutes will have to become more client- and demand-focused in this regard.

References

Giesen-Bloo, J., Van Dyck, R., Spinhoven, P. *et al.* (2006) Outpatient psychotherapy for borderline personality disorder, randomized trial of schema-focused therapy vs. transference focused psychotherapy. *Archives of General Psychiatry, 63:* 64–65.
Nadort, M. (2005) *Schematherapie voor de Borderline Persoonlijkheidsstoornis. Therapietechnieken.* DVD box set with English subtitles. www.schematherapie.nl.
Rafaeli, E., Bernstein, D. and Young, J. (2010) *Schema Therapy: Distinctive Features.* London: Routledge.
Wijngaart, R. van der and Bernstein. D. (2010) Five DVDs available with dialogue examples for treating borderline, narcissistic, and Cluster-C personality disorders together with mode examples. www.schematherapy.nl.
Young, J.E. and Klosko, J.S. (1994) *Reinventing Your Life.* New York: Plume.
Young, J.E., Klosko, J.S. and Weishaar, M.E. (2003) *Schema Therapy: a Practitioner's Guide.* New York: Guilford Press.

6
Concluding Thoughts

Michiel van Vreeswijk, Jenny Broersen
and Marjon Nadort

With great pleasure, we edited the *Dutch Handbook of Schema Therapy*, which was published in the Netherlands in 2008. Meetings took place through Skype, since all three of us were working at different locations. The proofs were mainly read at Travis Atkinson's house (an expert in couples therapy and Schema Therapy), in the warm and forested Brattleboro, VT (US). Nothing wrong with that, the reader might think. Indeed, no argument there. Travis, once more, our heartfelt thanks for your hospitality!

Soon after publication of the book, we were asked whether it could be published abroad. This lead to a meeting with Wiley, and on a sun-drenched roof terrace in Delft (the Netherlands) the first draft of the new international handbook was written. It soon became apparent that it wasn't going to be a translation of the 2008 handbook as such, but a whole new book. Contact with many international Schema Therapists was made because in the meantime new developments in Schema Therapy had occurred, which would naturally have to find their place in this new book. In the Foreword by Jeffrey Young you have read what these new developments consist of. In front of you, you find a great collaborative project, which demonstrates the global integrated style of Schema Therapy.

We would like to thank all the authors for their generous input, enthusiasm, punctuality, excellent suggestions, and fantastic contributions. We would like to thank Wiley for the enjoyable cooperation, and, last but not least, we would like to thank our patients, who allowed us a look into their souls.

> We are cradlers of secrets. Every day patients grace us with their secrets, often never before shared. Receiving such secrets is a privilege given to very few. The secrets provide a backstage view of the human condition without social frills, role playing, bravado, or stage posturing. Sometimes the secrets scorch us; other secrets pulsate within us and

arouse our own fugitive, long forgotten memories and impulses. Those who are cradlers of secrets are granted a clarifying lens through which to view the world; a view with less distortion, denial, and illusion, a view of the way things really are. Our work provides us the opportunity to transcend ourselves, to evolve and to grow, and to be blessed by a clarity of vision into the true and tragic knowledge of the human condition.
Yalom, *The Gift of Therapy*, 2002

Michiel van Vreeswijk, Jenny Broersen, and Marjon Nadort
Amsterdam, Fall 2011

Author Index

Aalders, H 338, 383–90
Abma, TA 413
Aboud, F 47
Abramowitz, JS 173, 174
Abrams, J 14
Ackerman, D 173
Adams, RE 473
Adler, A 5, 14, 18
Adler, G 10
Agras, S 145
Akkerhuis, GW 96
Alden, L 399
Alexander, F 6, 8, 9, 324, 331
Alexander, J 396
American Psychiatric Association 3, 91, 95, 153
Andersen, B 174
Anderson, JE 48
Andrea, H 97, 337, 359
Ansbacher, HL 18
Ansbacher, RR 18
Antypa, N 45
Appels, C 524
Arbuckle, JL 547
Arnkoff, DB 8, 11
Arntz, A 52, 532
  addiction 416, 421
  adolescents 393

assessment 91, 93, 96
BPD 301
case conceptualization 125, 132, 135
Cluster C 397–414
cost-effectiveness 585, 589, 590, 592, 593, 597
eating disorders 157
efficacy and effectiveness 495–510
experiential techniques 101, 102, 104, 106
experimental studies 512–13, 514, 515, 516, 519, 524, 525, 526
forensic settings 425–38, 579, 580, 581
group ST 337–8, 339, 341, 342, 359, 361, 368, 373, 374, 377
historical perspective 3–26, 357
implementation of ST 557, 558, 559, 560, 563, 565
individual ST 311, 314
inventories 112, 113, 117, 118, 121
measuring 285, 288, 289
mindfulness and ACT 250
OCD 174, 175
SMI 541, 542, 543, 544, 546, 547, 549
techniques 185, 186, 187
theoretic model 27–40
training 446

Arrindell, WA 97
Áspán, N 525
Assagioli, R 14
Asselt, A, van 585–98, 301
Astin, JA 245
Astor-Stetson, E 239
Atalay, F 175, 182
Atalay, H 175, 182
Atkinson, T 157, 323–35, 374
　inventories 112, 113, 118
　SMI 541, 543, 544
AuBuchon, G 174
Ayduk, O 524
Ayes, VE 377

Bachner-Melman, R 46
Baer, L 173, 174
Baer, R 271
Bagby, M 146
Balaci, L 44
Baldwin, M 45
Balint, M 9
Ball, J 15, 502, 504, 505
Ball, SA 15, 16, 415, 416, 495–510
Bamber, M 506
Bamelis, L 311, 446, 495–510, 512, 514, 557, 589
　Cluster C disorders 398, 399, 413
Bandura, A 243
Banon, E 288
Baranoff, J 53, 115
Barnes-Holmes, D 250
Bartak, A 359
Bartels, A 50
Bartlett, FC 18
Bateman, A 191, 290, 478, 588
Bauer, S 283, 296
Beaudry, M 251
Beaumont, PJ 503, 506
Beck, AT 4–9, 11, 27, 559, 446
　Cognitive therapy 4–6, 7–8, 11, 14, 18
　inventories 111, 113, 114, 117, 119, 122
Beck, JS 111, 113, 119
Beckley, KA 341, 357
Beek, DJ van 580
Begley, S 324
Beglin, S 168
Behary, WT 81–90, 370, 441–51, 453–61

Belsky, J 45
Bengel, D 44
Benjamin, LS 91, 96, 547
Bennet-Goleman, T 192, 243
Bennett-Levy, J 19
Benson, H 259
Berenson, K 524
Berger, M 464
Bergh, H van den 53, 58, 116, 533–4, 536
Berghout, C 97, 589
Berk, T 364, 367, 377
Berkman, N 145
Berne, E 6, 12, 13, 14
Bernstein, D 16, 17, 175, 495–510, 516, 557
　addiction 416, 421
　Cluster C disorders 399, 400
　cost-effectiveness 589
　experimental studies 526
　forensic settings 425–38, 579
　individual ST 311
　PR for ST 599, 605
　theoretical model 33
　training 446
Beurs, E de 97, 283
Beutler, LE 98, 201
Bhar, SS 117
Bieling, PJ 126
Bishop, FM 202
Bizeul, C 146
Blackburn, IM 27
Blackmore, E 145
Blair, J 429
Blair, K 429
Blais, M 251
Blake, WD 146
Bleecke, J 558, 560
Blesky, J 43
Blinder, B 145
Blokland-Vos, J 362
Blondelle, G 579
Bloo, J 185–95, 495–510, 559, 585–98
Bódi, N 525
Bőgels, S 115, 135, 311, 446, 535–6
　techniques 186, 187
Bohlmeijer, E 271

Bohus, M 489
Boisvert, J-M 251
Bonkale, W 44
Boo, GM de 42, 535, 536
Boom, D van den 42
Borchard, B 425
Bordelon, SK 504
Borduin, C 396
Bornstein, RF 400
Boscarino, JA 473
Bosch, LMC van den 415, 416
Bosch, W van den 579
Bosmans, G 115, 535–6
Bourker, MP 146
Bout, J van den 116, 533–4, 536
Bouvard, M 53
Bowlby, J 7–8, 28, 47, 230, 323
Bradley, B 329
Bradshaw, J 14
Braet, C 115, 535–6
Brandon, RA 536
Braun, D 145–6
Brennan, KA 7
Bricker, D 15, 259–70
Brink, M van den 590
Brink, W van den 415
Broek, van der, DM 421
Broeke, E ten 316, 370
Broersen, J 271–81, 446, 556, 609–10
　group ST 337, 338, 339, 359, 370, 373–81
　measuring 293–98
　PR for ST 599–607
　techniques 185–95
Brooks, J 28, 399
Brouwer, W 596
Brouwers, M van 415, 579
Brown, GK 29, 41, 41, 77, 117, 128, 156, 285, 374, 531
Brown, LB 118, 120
Brown, P 12
Brownley, K 145
Bruce, K 146
Brunenberg, D 587
Bujosa, CT 416, 502, 504
Bulik, C 145
Burlingame, GM 283, 296, 377
Burrell-Hodgson, G 117
Butler, AC 113, 117

Button, J 524
Byford, S 589

Cahn, B 239
Cakir, Z 53, 58, 59
Calistan, M 175, 182
Canli, T 44
Capacchione, L 14
Cape, J 98
Carlson, LE 245
Carpenter, L 28
Carrasco, JL 146
Carroll, R 50, 209, 212
Carter, J 145, 146
Cashdan, S 7, 10
Casper, R 146
Cassell, EJ 474
Cassin, S 146
Castilho, P 533
Cecero, J 53, 58, 59, 499, 532
Centraal Bureau voor de Statistiek 591
Ceumern-Lindenstjerna, IA von 524
Chadwick, P 126
Chakhssi, F 515
Chang, II 205
Chen, H 399
Cho, SH 115
Chu, JA 10
Cicchetti, D 28
Cima, M 121, 514, 515, 519
Claassen, A 185, 337, 338, 361, 364, 373
Clark, D 6, 69, 70, 73, 78, 245
Clarkin, JF 44
Clarkson, P 198
Cloninger, CR 534
Cobb-Richardson, P 416, 502, 504
Cockram, DM 503, 505
Coenen, I 525
Cohen, LC 113, 117
Cohen, P 28, 399
Cohen-Tovée, E 111, 13, 119
Cohen, P 28
Coleman, RE 11
Collard, P 197
Concept Dutch Multidisciplinary Guideline Personality Disorders 284
Connolly, AJ 416, 502, 504
Conway, MA 27–8, 76, 77
Cooper, M 111, 113, 119

Cooper, Z 146
Coristine, M 53, 115
Cornelis, J 593, 597
Cornelissen, CLM 96
Corstorphine, E 118, 120
Costa, PT 44, 534
Cottrauz, J 53
Cousineau, P 249–57
Crawford, Th 28
Crişan, L 44
Critchfield, KL 91
Crow, S 145
Cuijpers, P 271, 585
Cumella, V 145
Cunha, M 533
Cunningham, P 396
Cuthbert, B 174

Daenen, E 557
Dagg, P 53, 115
Dakof, GA 396
Dalrup, R 201
Dancu, VC 11
Daniels, V 205
Dattilio, FM 4
David, D 588
Davidson, K 589
Davidson, R 239
Davies, C 570
Davis, D 19, 101, 125, 185, 315, 543
  experimental studies 520, 521
  measuring 288, 289, 290
Davis, MK 288
De Keijser, J 503, 505
Deci, EL 51, 52, 54, 61
DeClaire, J 334
Delimon, J 589
Dennis, A 146
Derksen, JL 97
Derogatis, L 120
Detsky, AS 92, 596
Diaz-Marsa, M 146
Dickhaut, V 501
Dickson, C 146
Dijk, J van 338, 383–90
Dillon, E 515
Dimeff, LA 416
Dimsdale, JE 515
Dina, C 46

Dionne, F 251
Dirksen, C 301, 557, 558, 560
  cost-effectiveness 585, 592
Dissanayake, E 50
Does, W van der 45
Dolan, B 119
Dominiak, P 549
Dorer, D 145
Dowie, J 587
Dreessen, L 113, 117, 524, 525
Drieschner, K 435
Drummond, M 586, 587, 589
Drummond, PD 503, 505
D'Silva, K 425
Duggan, C 425
Dunn, J 53, 58, 59, 531
Dutch Work Council 94, 95, 98, 290, 292, 312, 313

Eastern Specialized Mental Health Commissioning Group 569
Eccles, M 555, 556, 566
Edens, W 361
Edwards, D 3–26, 199, 202, 357
Ehlers, A 19, 174
Eisen, J 173, 174
Ekman, P 332
Ellenberg, HF 13
Elliott, P 532–3
Elliott, R 199
Ellis, A 5
Emanuelli, F 113, 118, 120, 506
Emery, G 4, 5, 6, 11, 73
Emmelkamp, P 417, 425, 592
Emmerik, J 415, 579
Engels, A 541, 543
England, E 246
Engle, D 201
Erskine, R 13
Ettema, J 97
Eurelings-Bontekoe, EHM 337, 338, 339, 373
EuroQol Group 588
Evans, C 119

Fabry, J 203
Fairburn, C 145, 146, 156, 168
Farrell, J 3, 17, 18, 496, 498, 519
  BPD 301–10, 341–58
  group ST 337–9, 341–9, 359, 373

Favaro, A 146
Feeny, D 92, 596
Fenwick, EA 587
Ferenczi, S 8–9, 12–13, 14
Fertuck, EA 526
Figley, CR 473
First, M 96, 547
Fishman, D 4
Flanagan, CM 15, 51–2, 54, 61, 251
Foa, E 11, 173
Follette, VM 249
Fonagy, P 191, 253, 290, 325, 478, 525, 588
Forman, E 284
Forman, J 240, 246
Fosse, G 501
Foster, F 146
Fothergill, CD 126
Fountoulakis, K 44
Frances, A 44
Frank, J 6
Frank, R 465
Franklin, M 173
Freedman, B 245
Freeman, A 101, 125, 185, 315, 543
  experimental studies 520, 521
  historical perspective 5, 11, 19
  measuring 288, 289, 290
Freimer, NB 44, 45
French, T 324, 331
Fretwell, H 53, 54, 473–91
Freud, S 5, 12, 14, 226
Fricke, S 174
Friederici, S 146
Friedman, B 12
Frisch, M 209
From, I 198
Fruyt, F de 96–7
Fulton, PR 249
Furrow, J 329

Gagne, GG 28
Gaines, J 198
Galhardo, A 533
Gallagher, KC 29
Garcia, J 393
Garnefski, N 315
Garske, JP 288
Geerdink, M 391–6

Gelder, MG 245
Genderen, H van 93, 174, 311, 558
  case conceptualization 125–41
  experiential techniques 102, 104, 106
  group ST 337, 342
  historical perspective 20, 28, 33
  mindfulness and ACT 250
  techniques 185, 186, 187
  theoretic model 27–40
  training 441–51, 453–62
Gendlin, ET 253
George, L 503, 506
Gergley, G 253
Germer, CK 249, 483
Gershuny, B 174
Gersons, B 370
Geus, E de 44
Gibbon, M 96, 547
Gielen, D 33
Giesen-Bloo, J 33, 301, 311, 342, 393, 425, 519
  adolescents 391
  assessment 91
  core emotional needs 43, 52
  cost-effectiveness 591, 592, 599
  efficacy and effectiveness 496, 497, 507
  historical perspective 16, 19–20
  implementation 556, 557, 558, 559
  measuring 288, 289
  techniques 185
  training 446
Gilbert, P 18, 270
Gillberg, C 146
Gillberg, I 146
Gillie, JM 53, 58, 59
Gilmore, M 44
Goldberg, W 48
Goldfried, M 4, 199, 202
Goleman, D 259, 325
Gonda, X 44
Goodman, J 243
Goodman, P 198, 199, 202
Goodwin, D 173, 174
Gordon, J 202
Gordon, NS 341, 357
Gőtestam, KG 173
Gőttler, I 525
Gottman, JM 324, 326, 327, 329, 334
Goulding, MM 13, 198, 199, 200

Goulding, R 13, 198, 199, 200
Graham, J 259
Grawe, K 209, 245, 250
Greenberg, LS 10, 12, 19, 199, 251
Greenberger, D 245
Greenland, S 173
Greenshields, J 589
Greenwald, A 550
Greenwald, S 173
Gregg, R 185
Greischar, LL 239
Grey, N 19
Grilo, CM 146
Grisham, JR 117
Griskevicius, V 51
Groenestijn, MAC van 96
Grol, R 555, 556, 558, 560, 566, 581, 583
Grover, KE 28
Gude, T 16, 70, 502, 505
Guido, VF 8
Gunderson, J 44
Günther, G 362
Guze, S 173, 174
Gyrd-Hansen, D 596
Gyurat, A 524

Haaf, JE ten 526
Haans, T 364
Haas, E 284
Hackmann, A 19, 78, 174, 245
Haeyen, S 107, 185–95
Hahusseau, S 499, 500
Hakkaart-van Roijen, L 589
Halmi, KA 145–6
Hambleton, RK 532
Hamers, P 535
Hand, I 173, 174
Hanna, GL 173
Hannah, B 1
Hannan, C 284
Hansen, B 173
Hansen, NB 283, 284, 296
Hare, RD 418, 419, 425, 432
Harmon, C 284, 287, 291–3, 295–6, 297
Harris, D 549
Harris, R 252
Hart, O van der 12
Harteveld, FM 415
Hartgers, C 415

Hartzell, M 253
Hassenpflug, K 174
Haugum, JA 115, 506
Havens L 76
Hawkins, EJ 287, 291–3, 295–6, 297
Hawton, K 6, 69, 76
Hayes, AM 288
Hayes, S 229–30, 240, 246, 249, 250, 252, 370
Hedley, LM 53, 58, 59, 77, 115
Hefferline, RF 198, 199, 202
Heidkamp, D 398, 399, 413, 512, 514
Heijs, I 366
Heils, A 44
Hellenbosch, G 97
Helzer, JE 173
Hemphill, J 425
Hendriks, T 525
Henggeler, S 396
Henriqies, GR 185
Henry, LA 125
Herbert, J 240, 246
Herrell, R 44
Herzog, D 145, 146
Hildebrand, M 425
Hill, R 284
Hinrichsen, H 146
Hobara, M 47
Hocksma, J 42
Hoekstra, HA 96–7
Hoffart, A 16, 53, 58, 59, 115, 288
  case formulation 69–80
  efficacy and effectiveness 502, 505
Hoffmann, N 174
Hofmann, B 174
Hofmann, SG 271
Hohagen, F 173
Holbrey, A 146
Holcomb, L 44
Holland, S 201
Hollander, E 173
Holmes, E 19, 174, 4334
Holte, C 115
Holthe, H 115, 506
Homberg, JR 45
Hoogduin, CA 174
Hoorn, MA van den 525, 593, 597
Hopping, G 569–78
Horney, K 5

Horowitz, M 18
Horst, R 12
Horvath, A 367
Hout, WB van den 590
Hovland, OJ 115
Hoyer, J 425
Hubert, W 377
Hulscher, M 555
Huntjens, R 537
Hurt, SW 44
Hyler, SE 146

Ianni, F 288
Ingerman, S 14
Italian Group for the Study of Dissociation 7

Jacob, G 173–84, 301–9, 463–71, 549
Jacobs, A 12
Jacobs, MD 13, 14
Jacquin, KM 536
Jakes, SC 503, 506
James, IA 27
James, M 9
Jamieson, L 425
Janet, P 12
Janzing, C 364
Jekal, A 526
Jenike, MA 174
Johnson, JG 28, 399
Johnson, RJ 14
Johnson, SL 288
Johnson, SM 323, 324, 329–30, 332, 325
Joiner, TE 53, 58, 59, 531
Jones, L 431
Jones, R 145
Jones, SH 117
Jong, CA de 415
Jong, N de 191
Jong, PJ de 401, 524
Jonge, E de 425–38, 580, 581
Jongh, A de 316, 370
Jongman, E 391–6
Jonker, D 311–22
Jonkers, P 425–38, 580, 581
Joore, MA 587
Jordan, S 53, 115
Jöreskog, KG 547
Joseph, S 490

Juhasz, G 44
Jung, CG 11, 12, 14, 203
Jurist, E 253

Kabat-Zinn, J 229, 239, 240, 249, 259, 269, 315
Kamphuis, JH 98
Kanfer, F 241
Kaplan, AS 146
Kaplan, H 173
Karahan, D 175, 182
Karaosmanoglu, A 53, 58, 59
Kasen, S 28, 399
Keel, P 145
Keijsers, GR 174
Keller, J 146
Keller, K 48
Keller, M 48
Kellog, S 15, 83, 197–207, 240, 496
Kelly, G 5
Kennerley, H 15, 16, 115, 119, 146, 505, 506
Kenrick, D 51
Kéri, S 525
Kerkhofs, M 96, 547
Kerr, I 18
Kersten, T 415–24, 579–84
Kerstens, J 361
Keulen-de Vos, M 425–38, 580, 581
Keune, N 525
Kieboom, P van den 311–22
Kilpatrick, DG 174
Kindt, M 524
King, J 596
King-Casas, B 525
Kirk, J 6, 69, 73
Klaghofer, R 146
Klokman, J 541, 542, 543
Klosko, J
  BPD 303
  case conceptualization 69, 71, 77, 125
  chair work 197, 199, 201, 202
  Cluster C disorders 404
  couples 324, 325, 326, 329, 330, 331, 333
  eating disorders 146, 147, 148, 163
  experiential techniques 102, 104
  flashcards 249, 250
  forensic settings 425, 426, 427, 428, 431

Klosko, J (cont'd)
  group ST 337, 342, 359, 365, 368, 376
  implementation of ST 558
  individual ST 311, 314, 314, 318
  inventories 116
  measuring 288, 290
  mindfulness 229, 240, 241, 249, 250, 252
  OCD 174–5
  PR for ST 599
  techniques 185, 186
  theoretical model 27–9, 33
  therapist self-care 475, 477
  training 443, 444, 446, 455
  YSG 531, 533–4
Kloss, M 174
Knapen, P 557
Knapp, M 589
Knauss, E 173–84
Kőhler, S 174
Konner, M 49, 51
Kooiman, K 288, 289, 393
Koran, L 173
Kordy, H 284
Kosson, DS 526
Kozak, M 173
Kramer, M 47
Kramer, R 6
Kranzler, HR 415
Kroll, J 521
Kűbler-Ross, E 245
Kuelz, A 174
Kuipers, H 314, 368
Kupka, RW 96
Kuyken, W 126
Kwon, SM 115

Labin, M 259–70
Lacey, H 113, 114, 117
Lachenal-Chavallet, K 53
Laheij, RJ 590
Lake, B 368
Lamb, ME 47
Lambert, M 283, 284, 287, 291–3, 295–6, 297
Lammers, S 435
Lansen, J 364
Laposa, JM 399
Laupacis, A 92, 596

Lave, JR 596
Lavori, P 146
Layden, MA 11, 521
Lazarus, A 11–12, 198
Leahy, R 18, 201
Leaman, DR 10
Leary, M 51
Lederhendler, I 145
Lee, CW 53, 58, 59, 503, 505, 531
Leese, M 569
Lehner, T 44
Leichsenring, F 288
Lenaerts, P 363
Lesch, K 44, 45
Leue, A 425
Leung, N 118, 146
Levander, S 425
Leveton, E 198
Levitt, JL 146
Lewis, C 47
Lieb, K 301, 464, 489, 498, 525
  group ST 337, 339, 341, 359, 373
Liebing, E 288
Liebowitz, M 173
Liddle, HA 396
Lindemann, MD 15
Lindorff, D 13
Linehan, M 315, 370, 416, 478, 489
  mindfulness 229, 231, 239, 240, 249, 259
Linley, PA 490
Liotti, G 7, 8
Lipovsky, JA 174
Lobbestael, J 15, 132, 175, 285, 311, 374
  Cluster C disorders 399, 400
  experimental studies 511–17
  inventories 121
  SMI 541–51
  theoretic model 33, 38
Lőbbes, A 121, 514, 549
Lockwood, G 41–66, 209–26, 481
Lohr, K 145
Lomax-Bream, TL 525
London, P 5
Loumidis, K 490
Lowen, A 12
Luborsky, L 367
Luck, A 113, 114, 117
Luoma, JB 249, 252

Lupu, V 588
Lutz, A 239
Lynch, T 526
Lyons-Ruth, K 44

Ma, S 271
Maas, J van der 377
Macaskill, N 463
MacDevitt, JW 463
MacKenzie, KR 283, 377
Mackewn, J 198
MacLeod, C 27, 522
Macran, S 463
Madewell, J 12
Mahoney, MJ 5
Maier, S 174
Malatesta, V 174
Malhi, G 15, 502, 504, 505
Malvea, B 259
Mancebo, MA 173
Manen, JG van 98
Marcus, MD 147
Marlatt, A 202, 239
Martin, DJ 288
Martin, R 53
Mason, T 570
Mathews, A 19, 27, 434, 522
Matsunagaa, M 45
Mattila, DE 504
Mauchand, P 53
Maughan, A 28
McCarthy, L 425
McCrae, R 44, 534
McCullough, J 240
McDade, T 48
McGhee, D 550
McKay, D 173
McKenna, J 48
McManus, F 78
McMurran, M 435
McVey, D 569–78
Meichenbaum, D 243
Melia, P 570
Mello, PLLC 28
Mensebach, C 524
Mertens, I 524
Mesman, J 46
Messer, S 198
Mey, H de 97

Meyer, C 146, 506
  inventories 112, 113, 114, 115, 117,
    118, 119, 120
Michael, T 19
Middeldorp, CM 44
Mikulincer, M 324
Miller, A 14
Milos, G 146
Ming, XY 204–5
Minichiello, W 173
Mironova, E 47
Mitchell, D 429
Mitchell, P 15, 502, 504, 505
Moleiro, C 98
Molenaar, JP 362
Moll, M 399
Montagne, PRR 525
Mook, C van 362
Mooney, K 446
Moran, T 570
Moreno, J 12, 198
Moritz, S 174
Morrell, B 284
Morrison, N 502, 504
Morrow, E 146
Morse, SB 11, 521
Moser, J 173
Mountford, V 118, 120, 146
Moursund, J 13
Mulder, J 590
Muller, DR 373, 499, 501
Munafo, M 44, 45
Murakami, H 45
Muran, JC 8
Muris, P 42, 535–6
Murphy, N 569–78
Murray, J 113, 118, 120, 506
Musa, M 126
Muste, E 185, 191, 337, 338, 359–72,
    373, 501
Myers, J 173
Myerson, PG 10
Myhr, G 588

Nadort, M 17, 20, 52, 519, 589, 590,
    609–10
  efficacy and effectiveness 496, 497, 507
  implementation of ST 555–68
  individual ST 311, 321

Nadort, M (cont'd)
  PR for ST 599–607
  training 441–51, 453–61
Napel-Schutz, MC ten 413
Naranjo, C 198, 199
National Institute for Health and Clinical Excellence 173
Neimeyer, R 250
Nelson, JD 53, 58, 59
Nestadt, G 173
Neuberg, S 51
Neville, D 173
Newman, CF 11, 446, 521
Ng, W 44, 45
Niederee, LJ 11
Nissen, L 311–12
Nolen, WA 96
Norcross, JC 4, 284
Nordahl, HM 115, 288, 496, 505, 506, 507
Nunnally, JC 532
Nysaeter, TE 496, 507

O'Brien, B 586, 587, 589
Oei, T 53, 115
Ogles, B 284
Oh, D 271
Ohanian, V 15, 16, 146, 503, 505, 506, 532–3
  inventories 112, 115, 119
Oldham, JM 146
Olff, M 370
Olmsted, MP 146
O'Neal, TW 416, 502, 504
Oorschot, M 526
Oostenbrink, J 585
Oppenheim, H 370
Orlinsky, DE 288
Ornel, J 96–7
Osman, S 146, 506
Oudmaijer, M 363
Oulahabib, LS 12

Padesky, C 16, 188, 245, 446
Pagano, M 146
Paivio, SC 19
Palmer, S 589
Pană, S 44
Panksepp, J 210

Parfy, E 229–37
Park, N 209
Parker, G 114, 118, 120
Parker, H 174
Parker, JDA 146
Parker, K 396
Parry, G 98
Parsons, R 71
Pascual-Leone, A 19
Pasquini, P 7
Patole, S 48
Payne, K 588
Peeters, R 311, 446
Pélissolo, A 499, 500
Percevic, R 284
Perls, FS 12–13, 198, 199, 202, 203, 204, 205
Perris, P 7, 41–66, 125, 473–91
Perry, J 288
Peterson, C 209
Peveler, RC 145
Piaget, J 8, 18
Piaget, M 245
Pigott, T 173
Pijnaker, H 311, 337
Pinto, A 173
Pinto-Gouveia, J 533
Pizzagalli, D 239
Pleydell-Pearce, CW 27–8, 76, 77
Pluess, M 43, 45
Polich, J 239
Polster, E 198, 204
Polster, M 203, 204
Pontefract, A 53, 115
Pope, KS 11
Poppinger, M 311–12
Prenger, R 271
Preston, J 112, 115, 537
Pretzer, J 521
Price, LH 28
Pross, C 489
Pruett, K 47
Pzrybeck, TR 534
Psychinfo and Pubmed 391

Rachman, S 174
Radomsky, AS 119, 174
Rafaeli, E 425, 599
Ramos, D 48

Rank, O 6
Ranson, K von 146
Raskin, J 250
Rasmussen, K 173, 174, 425
Råstam, M 146
Rawlings, NB 239
Redfearn, JW 14
Reekum, A van 557
Reich, W 12
Reid, C 146
Reijen, J van 364
Reik, T 14
Reiss, N 17, 498, 549
   BPD 301–10, 341–58, 359, 373
   group ST 337, 339, 341–58
Reiss, S 51
Renner, F 398, 399, 413, 512, 514
Reyna, LJ 5
Rheinhart, M 12
Rhodes, JE 503, 506
Ricard, M 239
Rice, LN 199
Richardson, G 501
Riemann, D 174
Rigaud, D 146
Rijkeboer, M 27–40, 42, 53, 58, 128, 285, 374
   inventories 115, 116
   YSQ 531–9
Rinck, M 401, 524
Ringham, RM 147
Risch, N 44
Riso, LP 111, 112
Roach, E 239
Roberts, MS 596
Robins, E 173, 174
Robins, L 173
Roche, B 250
Roder, V 373, 499, 501
Roediger, E 11, 19, 239–47
Rogers, C 5, 6, 10
Rogers, R 425
Ronnestad, MH 288
Ronningstam, E 81
Rosenfeld, B 425
Rosenthal, M 526
Rosseel, Y 115, 535–6
Roth, G 15
Rounsaville, B 415

Rowland, M 396
Rufer, M 174
Ruggiero, G 146
Ruiter, C de 425
Rullkoetter, N 524
Růsch, N 525
Rush, AJ 4, 5, 6, 73
Rutter, F 596
Ryan, RM 51, 52, 54, 61
Ryder, AG 399
Rygh, JL 113, 130
Ryle, A 18

Sabo, N 521
Sachse, R 413
Sacks, N 146
Saddock, B 173
Sadowsky, N 146
Saeger, H de 91–9
Safran, JD 8, 10, 12
Saiz, J 146
Salekin, R 425
Salet, S 525
Salkovskis, P 6, 69, 70, 73, 240, 245
Salter, A 5
Samoilove, A 199
Samstag, LW 8
Samuels, M 11
Samuels, N 11
Sanislow, C 146
Sansone, LA 146
Sansone, R 146
Santonastaso, P 146
Santucci, A 239
Saradjian, J 573
Saunders, B 174
Sava, FA 588
Sawyer, AT 271
Schaap, CP 174
Schacht, R 311, 446
Schäfer, I 174
Schaller, M 51
Schefft, B 241
Schiff, JL 9
Schmahl, C 489
Schmidt, H 416
Schmidt, N 53, 58, 59, 531
Schmidt, V 146
Schneider, N 96

Schnyder, U 146
Schobre, P 526
Schoenwald, S 396
Scholing, A 391–6
Schore, AN 209, 210, 241
Schouten, E 113, 117, 285, 524
Schumacher, J 239
Schurink, G 192, 281, 370, 380
Schwartz, G 259
Schwartz, HL 10
Schwartz, J 550
Searle, Y 119Seay, S 173
Sedway, J 145
Segal, Z 27, 229, 249, 259, 271
Seligman, M 209
Seok-man, K 53
Seong, HC 53
Seres, I 525
Severens, JL 585, 587, 590, 592
Sewell, K 425
Sexton, H 53, 58, 59, 70, 77, 115, 288, 502, 505
Sexton, T 396
Shackman, A 239
Shafran, R 146
Shah, R 532–3
Shapiro, D 259, 463
Shapiro, J 145
Sharp, IR 185
Sharp, L 525
Shaughnessy, MF 12
Shaver, PR 7, 324
Shaw, BF 4, 5, 6, 73
Shaw, I 17, 209–26, 301, 473–91, 557
  core emotional needs 50–1, 52, 53, 54
  efficacy and effectiveness 496, 498
  group ST 337, 339, 341–58, 359, 373
  historical perspective 3, 16, 17, 20
Sheffield, A 11–24
Sheikh, A 11
Shepard, M 198
Shorr, JE 11
Siegel, DJ 249, 250, 251, 252, 253, 325, 326
Siegel, RD 249
Sieswerda, S 512–13, 519–29, 541, 542, 543
Silver, N 331
Simmer, K 48

Simmons, J 116
Simpson, S 145–71
Sines, J 146
Singer, JL 11
Skelton, A 146
Skillecorn, A 15, 502, 504, 505
Skodol, A 146
Slade, K 287, 291–3, 295–6, 297
Slee, N 313, 315
Sletzer, MH 91
Sloane, M 359, 446
Sloor, H 97
Slowey, L 146
Smaby, MH 10
Smailes, E 28
Smart, DW 284
Smeijsters, H 192, 363
Smit, F 585
Smit, JH 17, 20, 52, 446, 519, 589, 590
  efficacy and effectiveness 496, 497, 507
  implementation of ST 557, 559, 563, 565
  individual ST 311, 321
Smith, JA 463
Smith, M 15, 502, 504, 505
Smucker, MR 11, 19
Soeteman, D 589
Song, I 526
Sörbom, D 547
Southam, L 27
Soygut, G 53, 58, 59
Speckens, AE 174
Spindler, A 146
Spinhoven, P 33, 132, 175, 301, 425, 546
  adolescents 391, 393
  assessment 91
  core emotional needs 43, 52
  cost-effectiveness 591, 592, 599
  efficacy and effectiveness 496, 497, 507
  experimental studies 514, 519
  group ST 337, 338, 339, 342, 373, 374
  historical perspective 16, 19–20
  implementation 556, 557, 559
  individual ST 311, 315
  measuring 283–97
  techniques 185
  training 446
Spitzer, RL 96, 547
Spreeuwenberg, MD 359

Sprey, A 320
Staak, D van der 435
Stanley, M 173
Steen, T 209
Steiger, H 146
Stein, DJ 111, 112
Steiner, CM 13
Steketer, G 173
Stelzer, N 173–84
Sterk, F 29, 128, 285, 374, 531
Stern, ME 515
Stevens, B 200
Stiggelbout, KM 590
Stiles, TC 91, 173, 288, 505
Stiles, WB 202, 463
Stoddart, G 586, 587, 589
Stolk, M 46
Stone, H 14
Stopa, L 112, 115, 118, 120, 536, 537
Storsaeter, O 425
Strauss, B 283, 377
Strauss, JL 288
Strosahl, K 229–30, 249, 370
Stumpf, R 145
Sullivan, HS 6, 7, 8
Sunathara, V 145
Sunday, SR 145–6
Suomi, S 42, 48
Sutander-Pinnock, K 145, 146
Sutton-Smith, B 210
Svartberg, M 91
Svrakic, DM 534
Szentagotai, A 588

Taal, E 271
Taesdale, J 271
Talebi, H 98
Tamminen, AW 10
Target, M 253, 325
Tate, G 117
Taylor, CT 399
Taylor, G 53, 58, 59, 146, 531
Taylor, P 425, 569
Taylor, S 45, 173
Teasdale, JD 19, 229, 240, 249, 259
Telch, MJ 53, 58, 59, 531
Tennant, A 570
Tennant, I 570
Terracciano, A 44

Thayer, J 44
Thera, N 239
Thimm, JC 42, 115
Thomas, GV 118, 146
Thommen, M 373, 499, 501
Thompson, E 239
Thordarson, DS 119
Thorne, P 112, 115, 537
Thornton, C 503, 506
Thunnissen, M 191, 359, 373, 501
Timman, R 359
Timmerman, IG 425, 592
Tirch, D 270
Tischler, G 173
Tlocynski, J 239
Tobin, SA 199–200
Todd, G 111, 113, 119
Toit, PL de 111, 112
Toman, S 198
Tomlinson, S 118, 120
Tőrneke, N 250
Torrance, G 586, 587, 589
Touyz, SW 503, 506
Tovée, E 111, 113, 119
Treasure, J 146
Trijsburg, RW 359
Trimbos 285
Troop, NA 146
Tschacher, W 373, 499, 501
Tsevat, J 596
Tsuang, M 173
Tugwell, PX 92, 596
Tupling, H 118, 120
Turner, S 173
Turri, MG 44
Tyrer, P 589
Tyrka, AR 28

Umphress, V 296
Unoka, Z 525

Vaihinger, H 18
Van Dyck, R 33, 301, 311, 342, 425, 519
  adolescents 391, 393
  assessment 91
  core emotional needs 43, 52
  cost-effectiveness 591, 592, 599
  efficacy and effectiveness 496, 497, 507
  historical perspective 16, 19–20

Van Dyck, R (cont'd)
    implementation 556, 557, 559, 563, 565
    measuring 288, 289
    techniques 185
    training 446
Varela, F 239
Vedel, E 417
Veen, G 525, 526
Verbeek, AL 590
Verburgt, J 362
Verheul, R 415, 416, 526, 557, 589
    assessment 91, 95, 97
Vermeersch, D 284
Vermote, R 91
Veronen, LJ 174
Versland, S 70, 502, 505
Verstraten, J 359
Vertommen, S 524
Vijver, FJ van de 532
Villeponteaux, L 174
Vinken, S 362
Vis, L van de 579–84
Visbach, GT 98
Vitiello, B 145
Vitousek, K 145, 147
Vlierberghe, L 115, 535–6
Voderholzer, U 173, 174, 549
Vogel, F 498
Vogel, P 173
Volk, BA van der 12
Vonk, R 27
Vos, J 366
Vos, M de 33, 175, 311, 416, 425, 426, 446
    historical perspective 16, 17
Vreeswijk, M van 15, 132, 146, 175, 556, 609–10
    experimental studies 512, 513, 514, 515
    group ST 337, 338, 339, 359, 370, 373–81
    individual ST 311
    measuring 283–98
    mindfulness 271–81
    PR for ST 599–607
    SMI 546
    techniques 185–95
    theoretic model 33, 38
    training 446
Vulturar, R 44

Waddington, L 288
Wallace, RK 259
Wallas, L 9
Waller, G 15, 16, 111–24, 146, 524, 532–3
    efficacy and effectiveness 503, 505, 506
Wallerstein, RS 9, 18
Walser, RD 249, 252
Walsh, R 239
Wang, PS 115
Waters, A 112, 115, 118, 120, 536, 537
Watkins, J 14
Watson, S 145, 147
Watts, FN 27, 522
Way, B 45
Webber, M 52, 223, 301, 519, 557
    efficacy and effectiveness 496, 498
    group ST 337, 339, 341, 342, 353, 357, 359, 373
    historical perspective 16, 17, 20
Weerd, D de 363
Weertman, A 101–9, 185, 377, 401, 547
    assessment 91–9
    Cluster C disorders 397, 401, 411
    efficacy and effectiveness 499, 500
    experimental studies 519, 524, 525
    group ST 337, 338, 361, 364, 373
    historical perspective 12, 16, 17, 19
    inventories 113, 117
Weiner, B 429
Weishaar, ME
    BPD 303
    case conceptualization 69, 71, 77, 125
    chair work 197, 199, 201, 202
    Cluster C disorders 404
    couples 324, 325, 326, 329, 331, 333
    eating disorders 146, 147, 148, 163
    experiential techniques 102, 104
    experimental studies 515, 519–21
    flash cards 249, 250
    forensic settings 425, 426, 427, 428, 431
    group ST 337, 342, 359, 365, 376
    implementation of ST 558
    individual ST 311, 314, 318
    inventories 112
    measuring 288, 290
    mindfulness 229, 240, 241, 249, 250
    OCD 174–5
    PR for ST 599

SMI 541, 543
  theoretical model 27–9, 33
  therapist self-care 477
  training 444, 446, 455
  YSG 531, 533–4
Weiss, L 10
Weiss, V 10
Weissmann, M 173
Weisz, J 393
Welburn, K 53, 115
Welch, RR 377
Wells, A 111, 113, 119, 240, 245
Welpton, DF 10
Wensing, M 555, 556, 558, 560, 566, 581, 583
Werkgroep (Dutch Work Council) 94, 95, 98, 290, 292, 312, 313
Westen, D 526
Westenbroek, M 362
Wetzel, RD 534
Weysman, MM 377
Whelton, W 251
Whipple, JL 284, 287, 291–3, 295–6, 297
Whitfield, H 370
Widiger, TA 44
Wielen, GM van der 415
Wiers, RW 515
Wijngaart, R 605
Wijts, P 28
Wildes, JE 147
Wilfley, D 377
Willemsen, G 44
Williams, D 569
Williams, G 579
Williams, J 96, 547
Williams, JMG 27, 229, 240, 249, 259, 271, 522
Williams, R 125
Willis-Owen, AG 44
Willutzki, U 288
Wilson, GT 145, 147, 156
Wilson, K 174, 229–30, 249, 251
Wingenfeld, K 524
Winkelman, S 14
Winnicott, D 9, 47
Winston, A 8
Witt, AA 271
Woldt, A 198
Wolfis, M 526

Wolpe, J 5, 201
Wong, S 425
Woodside, D 145
Woollams, SJ 9
Wysong, J 198

Yalom, ID 17, 338, 342, 364, 610
Yamakawac, K 45
Yates, BT 588
Yeh, C 146
Yogi, GMM 259
Young, J
  adolescents 391
  BPD 303
  case conceptualization 69, 71, 77, 125, 128, 130, 132
  chair work 197, 199, 201, 202
  Cluster C disorders 404
  core emotional needs 41, 44, 53, 54, 57, 58, 59, 60
  couples 324, 325, 326, 329, 330, 331, 332, 333
  eating disorders 146, 147, 148, 156, 157, 163
  efficacy and effectiveness 496, 499, 502, 503, 504
  experiential techniques 102, 104
  experimental studies 512, 515, 519–21
  flash cards 249, 250, 251
  forensic settings 425, 426, 427, 428, 431
  gestalt therapy 11, 13
  group ST 337, 342, 359, 365, 368, 370, 374, 376
  historical perspective 4–5, 8, 10, 11, 13–14, 15, 16, 19
  implementation of ST 558, 559
  individual ST 311, 313, 314, 318
  integration of ST 19–20
  inventories 111, 112, 113, 116, 117, 118, 119
  measuring 285, 288, 290
  mindfulness 229, 240, 241, 249, 250, 252
  narcissism case study 81, 83
  OCD 174–5
  PR for ST 599, 609
  SMI 541–50
  techniques 185, 186

Young, J (*cont'd*)
 theoretical model 27–9, 33
 therapist self-care 475, 477
 three phases of development 15–18
 training 443, 444, 446, 455, 458
 YSG 531, 532, 533–4, 535
Young, K 19
Youngclarke, D 48

Zajonc, RB 10
Zanarini, MC 489
Zangwill, W 370
Zeijl, J van 46
Zeki, S 50
Zevalkink, J 589
Zohar, A 46
Zorn, P 373, 499, 501

Subject Index – Schema Therapy

ST – schema therapy

Abandoned/Abused Child 215, 542, 543, 544, 549
   Cluster C disorders 398–401, 404, 408, 412
   experimental studies 512–13, 515
   group ST 342, 346
Abandonment/Instability 30, 32, 38, 266, 289, 291–2, 574–6
   addiction 503
   adolescents 392
   Cluster C disorders 400–1
   core emotional needs 55, 58, 59
   couples 324, 333
   eating disorders 154
   four cluster model 60
   forensic settings 426–8, 570–1, 573, 574–6, 577
   group ST 342, 343, 345, 360, 363, 375
   OCD 176, 178
   SCBT-g 375
   schema inventories 114–16, 117
abuse 7–8, 10, 45, 108, 188, 457, 506
   chair work 200–1, 204–5
   Cluster C disorders 399–400, 401, 408–9
   eating disorders 506
   experimental studies 515, 524
   joy and play 211, 225

forensic settings 429, 434
group ST 343, 344, 345, 351, 356
OCD 174
see also Mistrust/Abuse
Abused/Humiliated/Abandoned Child 418
acceptance 229–37, 239–46, 249–56
   therapist self-care 478, 482
Acceptance and Commitment Therapy (ACT) 229–37, 240, 249–56, 338, 370
accepting your thoughts 268
Adaptive Behavioral Disposition (ABD) 41–2, 54, 55–7, 62
Adaptive Behavioral Dispositions Inventory 54
addiction 415–23, 460, 501–4, 559, 562, 569
   Cluster C disorders 399, 412, 415, 418
   see also substance abuse
adequate limits 60, 61
adolescents 391–6, 504, 508, 524, 535–6, 567
   parents 393–4
   YSQ 532, 535–6, 538
Advanced International Certification 442, 443, 450, 456, 458, 461

The Wiley Blackwell Handbook of Schema Therapy: Theory, Research, and Practice, First Edition.
Edited by Michiel van Vreeswijk, Jenny Broersen, and Marjon Nadort.
© 2012 John Wiley & Sons, Ltd. Published 2015 by John Wiley & Sons, Ltd.

advice from clients 484
affective/anxiety disorders 69–80, 145
    see also anxiety and anxiety disorders
Aggressive Protector 343
agoraphobia 8, 11, 70, 73, 502, 505
alcohol 9, 36, 445
    addiction 415, 418–19, 420
    cost-effectiveness of ST 585, 590, 594
    forensic settings 428, 574–5
alloplastic change 245
alternatives to ST 94–5
anger 44, 225, 262, 320, 515–16
Angry Child 34, 35, 107, 162–3, 305, 307, 544
    addiction 418, 419, 420
    BPD 36–7, 400
    Cluster C disorders 407
    couples 324, 332, 333
    eating disorders 148, 155, 162–3
    experimental studies 542, 544–6, 547, 548
    forensic settings 427, 430–1
    group ST 342, 349–50, 355, 356, 377
    joy and play 210, 225
    mindfulness and acceptance 233, 241–2, 243, 251
    mindfulness protocol 272, 280
    OCD 178–9, 181
    personal therapy 465, 466, 468
    SCBT-g 377
    SMQ 542
    training and supervision 454, 455
Angry Detached Protector 214–15
Angry/Impulsive mode 355
Angry Protector 35, 214–15, 313, 430–1, 500
    addiction 418, 420
    adolescents 393
    BPD 354
    eating disorders 148, 165–6
    forensic settings 426, 428, 430–1, 433, 435, 436, 500
    OCD 176–7, 180
anorexia nervosa 145, 146
anti-depressants 70
anti-social personality disorders 17, 44, 449, 500, 562
    addiction 415–19, 421–3
    experimental studies 512–13, 514–15

forensic settings 425–6, 428, 431, 570
SMI 543
SMI-2 549
SMQ 543
YSQ 535
anxiety and anxiety disorders 4, 11, 44, 69–80, 188, 361, 368
    addiction 417
    BPD 346
    case conceptualization 69–80, 127
    chair work 199, 203
    Cluster C disorders 397, 398
    cost-effectiveness of ST 588
    couples 330
    eating disorders 145, 152, 159, 163
    efficacy and effectiveness of ST 499–500, 502–3, 504–5
    experimental studies 521, 522, 524, 525
    generalized 153
    individual ST 314, 317–18, 319, 320
    measurements 287, 288, 293, 294, 295
    meditation 263, 265
    mindfulness and acceptance 235, 236, 239
    mindfulness protocol 280
    personal therapy 467–8
    SCBT-g 378, 379
    schema inventories 115, 120
    training for therapists 441, 444
    YSQ 533, 535, 538
appointments and absences for adolescents 394, 395
approach to ST 95–7
Approval and Recognition Seeking 30, 53–4, 59, 30, 291
    narcissism case study 82
    SMI-2 549
    YSQ 537
art therapy 192, 193, 307, 308, 362, 442
Assertiveness/Self-expression 56, 60
assessment 91–9, 285, 313, 428, 604
    adolescents 392
    contraindications for ST 92–3
    couples 325–30
    eating disorders 155–6, 157
    experiential techniques 104, 105, 106, 109
    forensic settings 428

implementation of ST 560, 563
joy and play 211
schema inventories 112, 113
SCBT-g 374–6
training 442, 450, 454
YSQ 536
assumptions 74, 75
attachment theory 6–10, 28, 186, 230, 232
joy and play 210, 212, 213, 222
attention 522–4, 527
attention deficit hyperactivity disorder (ADHD) 417, 563–4
Attention-focused Cognitive Therapy 370
Attention-Seeker 35
audio flash cards 83, 88–9, 161
authorities, dealing with 319
automatic thoughts 74, 75
autonomy 475–7, 478, 481, 484–5
and performance 60, 61
Autonomy/Independence 61
autoplastic change 245
availability 481
Avoidance 29, 31–2, 114, 191, 515, 524, 574–5
addiction 417
case conceptualization 129–32, 136–7, 139, 140
couples 324
eating disorders 146, 147, 153
personal therapy 464, 565, 467, 470
SCBT-g 374
therapist self-care 486
avoidant personality disorder 288, 289, 312, 412, 415
case formulation 73
Cluster C disorders 397, 398–400, 411, 412
cost-effectiveness of ST 589
eating disorders 146, 152, 153
efficacy and effectiveness 498, 501
experimental studies 513, 514, 520, 525, 527
group ST 501
OCD 175
Avoidant Protector 456, 498, 549
Cluster C disorders 398, 399, 400, 404, 411
personal therapy 464, 465, 469

awareness 260–1
Axis I disorders 18, 19, 69–80, 192, 366, 443–4
assessment 92, 93, 95, 96
chair work 197
Custer C disorders 404
cost-effectiveness of ST 589
eating disorders 145, 153
efficacy and effectiveness 495, 499, 501–2, 503, 505–8
experimental studies 513, 522
group ST 341, 374
implementation of ST 564, 565
SCBT-g 374
schema inventories 114, 120
SMI 545–6, 547–8
Axis II disorders 284, 296, 443–4, 453
assessment 95, 96
case formulation 70
chair work 197
cost-effectiveness of ST 589
eating disorders 153
efficacy and effectiveness 501, 505, 506, 507
experimental studies 511, 513, 514
OCD 173
SMI 545–6, 547–8

Beck Anxiety Inventory (BAI) 326
Beck Depression Inventory (BDI-II) 326
bed-sharing/co-sleeping 48
behavior therapy 5, 11, 392
behavioral exposure 11
behavioral pattern-breaking 333–4, 338–9
behavioral techniques 186, 190–1, 271, 365, 366, 474
SCBT-g 377, 378
training 443, 455, 458
Behavioristic Psychodrama 201
Belonging and Affinity 60
Big Five 92, 97
binge-eating and purging 146–8, 150, 153, 156–9, 165–9, 503
bipedality 50
bipolar disorder 15, 502, 504, 563–4
body image work 161, 167–8
bonding 71, 271
booster sessions 411

borderline personality disorder (BPD)
15–18, 81, 185, 341–57, 604
  addiction 415, 416, 417–18, 419
  adolescents 391, 393
  assessment 92, 93, 94
  case conceptualizations 132, 137, 303–8
  chair work 106, 304, 306
  Cluster C disorders 400, 406
  core emotional needs 43, 44, 52–3, 61–2
  cost-effectiveness of ST 585–6, 588–9, 590–3, 594–6
  couples 324, 330
  eating disorders 146
  efficacy and effectiveness 557
  forensic settings 425, 428
  gestalt therapy 11
  group ST 301–9, 337–8, 341–57, 359, 373, 379
  implementation of ST 555, 557–67
  individual ST 311, 312, 314, 321
  joy and play 212, 213, 219, 223
  measurement 288–9
  mode models 33, 36–7, 38
  OCD 175
  outcome 565
  SCBT-g 373, 379
  schema inventories 120
  schema modes 33, 36–7, 38, 303
  therapist self-care 473, 478
  training 443, 445, 446, 449, 455, 460
Borderline Personality Disorder -47 Symptom Checklist 563
Borderline Personality Disorder Severity Index (CPDSI) 563–5
Borderline Personality Disorder Severity Index – IV (BPDSI-IV) 563, 593, 595
Borderline Treatment Study 589
BOSCOT trial 589
breastfeeding 47–8, 49
Brief Symptom Inventory (BSI) 97, 120, 359
brochures 605
Buddhism 229, 234, 239, 240–1, 243, 245, 246
building a safe house 224
bulimia nervosa 145–7, 153, 503, 505–6
  schema inventories 115–16, 120

Bully and Attack 35, 38, 500, 513, 515, 545
  addiction 417–18, 419, 420
  couples 324
  eating disorders 155, 158, 163–4, 165
  forensic settings 426, 427, 430, 431, 433, 500
  SMI 543, 545, 546
  SMI-2 549
  SMQ 543
burden of illness 596
burn-out 473–4, 481, 487

cannabis 417–19, 571, 572
care consumption 590–1
case conceptualization and formulation 7, 69–80, 125–40, 605
  addiction 421
  adolescents 393, 394
  Axis I disorders 69–80
  BPD 132, 137, 303–8
  Cluster C disorders 70, 402–3, 404, 405
  eating disorders 153
  forensic setting 428, 580–2
  form 126–36, 140
  individual ST 314
  schema inventories 112, 118, 121
  schema mode model 137–8
  training 442, 443, 454, 456, 458
central beliefs 115–16, 117, 118, 119, 121
certification see registration and certification of ST therapists
chair work 106–7, 108, 187, 189, 197–206, 315
  adolescents 394, 395
  BPD 106, 304, 306
  Cluster C disorders 406–7, 409–10
  eating disorders 163, 164, 168
  empty chair technique 11, 13–14
  forensic settings 436
  group ST 362, 366, 367, 376
  mindfulness 236, 240–1, 243, 271
  narcissistic PD 83, 87–8
  OCD 177, 178, 179–81
  personal therapy 467, 468
  SCBT-g 376
  training 443, 455, 457
challenging dysfunctional assumptions or thoughts 312, 315–16

character armor 12
childlike thinking 520–1, 523, 526, 527
children and YSQ 532, 535–6, 538
choice and intention 260, 261–3
client-focused therapy 5, 6, 17, 498–9
clinical interview 118, 121, 122
Cluster A personality disorders 91, 397, 415, 528
Cluster B personality disorders 91, 359, 397, 579
  addiction 415, 416, 417
  cost-effectiveness of ST 589
  efficacy and effectiveness 499, 500, 501
  forensic settings 425
  group ST 338, 375, 501
  SCBT-g 375
Cluster C personality disorders 17, 33, 397–413, 533, 549
  addiction 399, 412, 415, 418
  assessment 91
  case conceptualization 70, 402–3, 404, 405
  efficacy and effectiveness 499, 500, 501, 502, 505
  experimental studies 512–15, 525–6
  group ST 338, 375, 501
  measurement 288
  personal therapy 469
  SCBT-g 375
  treatment approach 403–11
cocaine 415, 417, 418–19, 420
Cognitive Analytic Therapy 18
cognitive-behavioral analysis system of psychotherapy (CBASP) 240
cognitive behavioral therapy (CBT) 3, 4–6, 16–17, 459, 588–9
  assessment 92
  case conceptualization 135
  chair work 197, 199, 201, 202
  eating disorders 145, 146, 152, 156, 166, 505–6
  efficacy and effectiveness 500, 503–4, 505–6
  experiential techniques 10, 101
  forensic settings 581–2
  group ST 338, 369, 373–80
  implementation of ST 560, 562, 581–2
  individual ST 315, 318
  integration of ST 18, 19

joy and play 209
measurement 288
meditation 265
mindfulness 229, 249, 271
narcissistic PD 83
OCD 173–5, 177, 178, 179–81
personal therapy 463, 466, 467, 470
SCBT-g 373–80
ST techniques 185–6, 191, 194
therapist self-care 478
cognitive behavioral therapy – BN (CBT-BN) 156–7
cognitive techniques 186, 188–9, 194, 271, 288, 365–6
  couples 330–1
  group ST 338–9, 378
  therapist self-care 474
  training 443, 454–5, 458
cognitive therapy (CT) 3, 4–6, 7–8, 15–16, 240, 289–90
  affective/anxiety disorder 69, 71
  experiential techniques 10–11, 13
  group ST 338
  integration of ST 18, 19
cohesiveness 17
collaborative relationship 6–8, 9
comorbidity 192, 319, 524, 557, 565
  addiction 415–16, 417–18, 419
  Cluster C disorders 399
  eating disorders 145
  efficacy and effectiveness 499, 506
  OCD 174
compassion-focused therapy 18
compensatory beliefs 115–16, 117, 118, 119, 121
compensatory mode 176
Competence/Self-Reliance 56
complementary diagnostics 97
Compliant Surrender 34, 38, 487, 512–13, 544
  addiction 419
  case conceptualization 132, 137, 138
  Cluster C disorders 398, 399, 400, 401, 403, 405
  couples 324, 325
  eating disorders 147, 148, 151, 155, 158, 167
  forensic settings 432
  personal therapy 464, 465, 466

Compliant Surrender (*cont'd*)
  SCBT-g 378
  SMI 542, 544, 546, 548
  SMQ 542
confidence regarding harm and illness 60
confidentiality 375, 460, 473, 482–3
  couples 328, 334
confirming factor analysis 547
congruence (genuineness) 6
connecting-centering exercise 479–80
Connection 58, 61, 481–3
connection and acceptance 60, 61
Conning and Manipulative 35, 432–3, 500, 516
  addiction 418, 419, 420
  forensic settings 426, 431, 432–3, 500
constructivism 27, 186, 250, 271
Contented Child 210, 325, 330
contraindications for ST 92–3
  couples 326, 329, 334
coping strategies and styles 29–32, 58, 81, 515
  addiction 416, 417, 420, 422
  BPD 36, 304, 347, 349
  case conceptualization 70–1, 73–7, 79, 126–7, 129–32, 135–6, 139–40
  Cluster C disorders 404, 406, 409–10, 411
  couples 323–4, 328, 333
  eating disorders 147–8, 151, 158, 159, 165
  efficacy and effectiveness 569, 573, 574–5
  experiential techniques 102–3, 104, 108
  forensic settings 428, 431–2, 569, 573, 574–5, 581
  group ST 347, 349, 360, 365
  identification 73–6
  individual ST 311
  joy and play 223
  mindfulness and acceptance 233, 241, 242, 245, 249, 251–2
  mindfulness protocol 274
  narcissism PD 81
  personal therapy 464, 465, 467
  schema inventories 111, 114, 115, 117–18
  social support interventions 295
  theoretical models 27–8, 29–32, 33, 38

  therapist self-care 482, 489
  training 442–4, 454, 457–9
core beliefs 115, 186, 223, 241
  eating disorders 146, 156
  schema inventories 111–12, 114–21
core emotional needs 41–62, 474, 475–7, 478, 481
core emotional needs model (CNM) 53–61, 62
core unmet needs 153
corrective recapitulation of the primary family experience 17
cost-effectiveness 585–97, 605, 606
  efficacy and effectiveness 495, 498
  implementation of ST 557–8, 559, 560, 563, 565, 567
countertransference 456, 463
counting breaths 262
couples 323–35, 443, 454, 455
  contraindications 326, 329, 334
  eating disorders 167
creative experiential therapy 107–8, 109, 191–2, 362–3
  addiction 422
  BPD 341, 352
  forensic settings 580–3
  group ST 341, 352, 361, 362–3, 365, 366
  training 441, 447, 449
criminality 4225–37, 569–78
  addiction 415, 417, 419–21
  see also forensic settings
crisis and extra phone support 318–19
Critical and Demanding Parent 147, 158, 163, 168
Critical Parent 147, 148, 150, 151, 155, 268, 570
Critical/Punitive Parent 16, 80
Cronbach's alpha analysis 548
culture and core emotional needs 46–9, 50, 51

day treatment 359–70
Decisional Balance 202–3
Defectiveness/Shame 29, 30, 33, 77, 120, 188, 520
  affective/anxiety disorder 69
  BPD 342, 345, 351, 352
  core emotional needs 55, 58, 59

couples 324
eating disorders 147, 154, 156, 506
four cluster model 60
forensic settings 432, 577
group ST 342, 345, 351, 352, 360, 379
measurement 293, 294, 295
meditation 263
mindfulness and acceptance 250, 251, 253, 254–5
mindfulness protocol 275
narcissism PD 81, 82
OCD 176, 178
SCBT-g 379
therapist self-care 475, 477
training 460
YSQ 534
defusion strategy 231, 254
Demanding Adult 150
Demanding Parent 35, 189, 192, 304–5, 487, 545
　adolescents 395
　BPD 304–5, 308
　case conceptualization 132, 137
　chair work 202
　Cluster C disorders 398, 402–3, 405, 406–7, 412
　couples 324, 333
　eating disorders 147, 152, 158, 163, 168
　Guilt-Inducing 464, 466, 468
　measurement 292, 296
　mindfulness 231, 233, 240, 243–4, 279–80
　OCD 175, 176, 177, 181
　personal therapy 464–70
　SMI 543, 545, 546, 547
　training 454, 455–6
　YAMI 543
Dependence/Incompetence 30, 363, 395, 445
　core emotional needs 56, 58, 59
　four cluster model 60
Dependent Child 398, 401, 403, 405, 408, 412, 549
dependent personality disorder 312, 400–1, 412, 498, 589
　Cluster C disorders 397, 400–1, 402–3, 411, 412
　experimental studies 512, 514, 521, 525, 527

OCD 175
personal therapy 464–5, 468
depression 8, 19, 29, 62, 312
　assessment 92, 93
　case conceptualization 69–73, 126, 127
　chair work 203
　Cluster C disorders 399, 400, 404
　core emotional needs 44, 45
　cost-effectiveness of ST 588
　couples 330
　efficacy and effectiveness 499–500, 502–3, 504, 505
　meditation 263
　mindfulness 229, 239, 271
　OCD 174, 178
　schema inventories 115–16, 120
　YSQ 538
Detached and Avoidant Coping 404
Detached Imaginative World mode 211
Detached Protector 34, 189, 303–4, 346, 545
　addiction 418
　adolescents 393
　BPD 36–7, 303–4, 306–9, 346, 347, 349–52, 355
　chair work 202
　Cluster C disorders 398–9, 404–6
　couples 324, 327, 329, 332, 333
　eating disorders 148, 151, 155, 157–61, 168
　experiential techniques 107–8
　experimental studies 512–13, 546
　group ST 346, 347, 349–52, 355, 360
　joy and play 216, 219–20, 225
　forensic settings 428, 429, 435
　individual ST 313, 318, 319
　measurement 290, 292, 296
　meditation 262
　mindfulness 233, 279
　OCD 175–7, 178–80
　personal therapy 464–7, 469, 470
　schema inventories 118, 120
　SMI 542, 545, 546
　SMQ 542
　training 455, 456
Detached Self-Soother 34, 189, 513–14, 545, 546
　addiction 417, 418, 419, 420
　couples 324

Detached Self-Soother (cont'd)
  eating disorders 147, 148, 151, 155, 158–9
  experimental studies 513–14
  forensic settings 427, 428, 570, 572
  joy and play 211, 225
  mindfulness 241
  narcissistic PD 82
Detached Self-Stimulator 82, 417, 418, 419
developmental analysis 6
diagnostics 73, 91, 97, 112, 393, 421
  addiction 421, 422
  adolescents 393, 394
  Cluster C disorders 402, 404
  complementary 91
  couples 326, 374–6
  eating disorders 145, 153
  experiential techniques 101–9
  experimental studies 512
  forensic settings 569–70, 580
  implementation of ST 555–8, 560–1, 563
  individual ST 312, 313
  measurement 294
  SCBT-g 374–6
  SMI validation 542, 545
  structural 91
  YSQ 532, 534
dialectical behavior therapy (DBT) 17, 94, 315, 579
  BPD 303
  group ST 338, 370
  meditation 259
  mindfulness 229, 231, 239, 240, 243, 272
  therapist self-care 478, 479
dialectical behavior therapy – substance abuse (DBT-S) 416
diaries and journals 187, 188–9, 443, 454
  Cluster C disorders 404, 410
  eating disorders 157, 158
  group ST 338
  positive 315, 364, 365, 366
dichotomous thinking 520, 521, 523, 525–6, 527–8
Differential Susceptibility 43, 44
differentiation and developed self 60
direction 484

DIS 563
Disablement Insurance Act 595
Disconnection 481
Disconnection/Rejection 58, 59, 60, 61
discipline 485
dissociation 108, 118, 120, 180, 215
dissociative personality 10
dopaminergic system 46
downward arrow technique 126, 129, 186
dramatic personality disorder 499
dreams 215–16
drugs see substance abuse
DSM-IV 36, 132, 400, 547, 565
  addiction 415, 421
  affective/anxiety disorder 73
  assessment 91–3, 95–7
  eating disorders 153
Dual Focus Schema Therapy (DFST) 422
  Addiction 416, 421, 422, 423
  efficacy and effectiveness 501–2, 503–4, 507
Dyadic Adjustment Scale (DAS) 326
dyadic group practice 455–6
Dysfunctional Parent 147, 304–6
dysphoria 502, 504
dysthymia 153, 399, 585

Early Adaptive Schemas (EASs) 41–2, 45, 54, 55–7, 61–2
  four cluster model 60
early maladaptive schemas (EMSs) 27–9, 240, 500, 531
  affective/anxiety disorder 69–71, 74–5, 77, 79
  core emotional needs 41–2, 44, 45, 53–4, 55–7, 58, 61–2
  couples 323–4
  forensic settings 500
  four cluster model 60
  joy and play 210
  narcissistic PD 81
eating disorders 8, 15, 19, 145–69, 503, 505–6
  SMI 117, 120, 157
  see also bulimia nervosa
Eating Disorders Belief Questionnaire-Negative Self-Beliefs scale 111, 113, 117, 119

eating disorder Examination Questionnaire (EDE-Q) 16
eating disorders not otherwise specified (EDNOS) 146
ecstasy 417, 419
educational group model 17
efficacy and effectiveness studies 495–508, 557, 559, 565, 567
   forensic settings 498–9, 500–1, 504, 557, 569–78
ego-strength 108, 368–9
Emotion-Focused Therapy 19
emotion predictability 481
emotional coldness 7
Emotional Core Needs Inventory 53–4
emotional dependency 400, 401
Emotional Deprivation 30, 33, 38, 188, 316, 520
   case conceptualization 77, 129–32, 135, 137, 139, 140
   core emotional needs 55, 58, 59
   couples 324
   eating disorders 147, 154
   forensic settings 571
   four cluster model 60
   group ST 345, 366, 367, 378–9
   joy and play 210
   measurement 287, 290, 292, 295
   modes 30, 33, 38
   narcissistic PD 81
   OCD 178
   personal therapy 465
   SCBT-g 378–9
   therapist self-care 487
   training 457
   YSQ 536
emotional distress management 485
Emotional Fulfilment/Intimacy 55, 60
Emotional Inhibition 30, 55, 58, 59, 445, 534
   addiction 503
   eating disorders 506
   efficacy and effectiveness 501, 503, 506
   forensic settings 501
   four cluster model 60
   mindfulness 233, 242
   personal therapy 465
   SCBT-g 379
   schema inventories 115–16, 120

therapist self-care 487
training 457
emotional and practical support 484
Emotional Spontaneity and expressiveness 55, 60
emotional Stroop studies 522–3, 524, 527
empathic confrontation 9–10, 46, 187, 433–4
   addiction 420
   adolescents 395
   Cluster C disorders 406, 410
   eating disorders 164–7, 168
   experimental studies 515
   forensic settings 428, 431, 433–4, 436
   group ST 367, 376–7
   individual ST 313, 314
   narcissistic PD 83, 84, 85–7
   OCD 180
   personal therapy 464, 467, 468
   SCBT-g 376–7
   therapeutic alliance 102
   therapist self-care 482
   training 443, 444, 454, 455, 457, 458, 460
empathy 6–8, 526
   therapist self-care 473, 478, 482, 485, 488–90
encoding meaning 10–11
encouragement and respect 484
engagement 482
enhanced cognitive behavioral therapy (CBT-E) 146
Enmeshment/Undeveloped Self 30, 77, 366, 536
   core emotional needs 56, 58, 59
   four cluster model 60
Enraged Child 34, 35, 324, 544
   experimental studies 513–14, 515
   SMI 544, 546, 547, 548, 550
Entitlement/Grandiosity 31, 81, 128, 375, 536
   core emotional needs 42, 57, 58, 59
   four cluster model 60
environmental therapy 361–2, 369
EuroQoL 563
EuroQoL-5D 588, 593–5
ethics 522, 527
   therapist self-care 479, 482, 488–9

evaluation 312, 313, 317, 523, 525–6
　flowchart 286
　implementation of ST 556, 558, 563, 582
Exaggerated Expectations 60
Exaggerated Standards 58, 59, 481
Exceptional Medical Expenses Act 559, 595
experiential interview 338–9
experiential techniques 101–9, 186, 189, 191, 194, 366, 434
　BPD 342, 344–5, 349
　chair work 197, 201, 205
　Cluster C disorders 413
　couples 331–3
　efficacy and effectiveness 500
　forensic settings 434
　group ST 342, 344–5, 349, 365, 366
　mindfulness protocol 271
　SMI validation 541
　therapist self-care 474
　training 455, 458
experiential therapies 4, 10–15, 18–19
experimental studies 522
　modes 511–17
　schemas 519–28
explorative factor analysis 547
Exposure and Response Prevention (ERP) 173, 176, 177, 179–81
external dialogues 199–201
externalizing problems 38, 46
Eye Movement Desensitization Reprocessing (EMDR) 316, 317, 370

face game 223
factor analysis 53
Failure 30, 77, 457, 464, 489, 506
　core emotional needs 56, 58, 59, 61
　eating disorders 147, 149, 154, 506
　measurement 287, 291–2
　mindfulness 235, 250, 275
　narcissistic PD 81
　OCD 176
family therapy 361, 363
Fathers/Paternal mode 46–9
Fear of Losing Control 59
feedback 308, 330, 375, 449
　BPD 351–3, 355–6
　forensic settings 433
　measurement 283–5, 291–2, 294, 297

personal therapy 470
therapist self-care 479, 484
training 456, 459
financial contribution 561–2
Five Factor Model 534
flash cards 187, 189, 315, 365, 443, 454
　Cluster C disorders 410
　couples 331, 334
　eating disorders 162, 164, 165
　joy and play 214
　mindfulness 235, 249, 251–5
floating leaves on a stream 265–6
flowchart evaluation 286
fluoxetine 588
focused life history 75–7, 79–80
follow-up therapy 278
forensic settings 33, 38, 425–37, 500–1, 562, 579–83
　cost-effectiveness of ST 592–3
　efficacy and effectiveness 498–9, 500–1, 504, 557, 569–78
　implementation of ST 556, 557, 559, 562, 579–83
　legal costs 592
　training 449, 577, 580–3
　YSQ 532, 537
forgiveness 483
formulation *see* case conceptualization and formulation
Functional Dependence 548
Functional Family Therapy (FFT) 396

gambling 82, 416, 417
game of trust 523, 525
generalized anxiety disorder 153
genes 43–6, 49
gestalt therapy 9, 11–12, 13–14, 186, 271
　chair work 197–9, 202
goals 70–1, 77–8
Good Parent Defender or Coach 349
grief 199–200, 201, 204–5
group schema therapy (GST) 9, 13, 17–18, 337–9, 359–70, 557
　affective/anxiety disorder 70
　assessment 91, 94
　BPD 301–9, 337–8, 341–57, 359, 373, 379
　challenges 356–7

efficacy and effectiveness 500, 501, 505, 557
forensic settings 500
healing power 342
joy and play 223–5
measurement 292–6
motivational interventions 293
PR 599, 600, 603
SCBT-g 373–80
therapeutic alliance 292, 369, 376
therapist self-care 479–80
training 443, 454, 455
group schema cognitive behavior therapy (SCBT-g) 338, 373–80
guided body scan meditation 261, 262
guided imagery 104, 108
see also imagery
guilt 44, 464, 465, 466, 468
Guilt-Inducing Demanding Parent 464, 466, 468

Happy Child 34, 107, 189–90, 225, 350–1, 544
  BPD 307, 309
  Cluster C disorders 398
  couples 334
  eating disorders 148, 151
  measurement 293
  mindfulness 253, 254, 276
  SMI 543, 544–5, 546, 547
  SMI-2 549
  YAMI 543
health insurers 601–3, 605, 606, 607
Healthy Adult 8–9, 16–17, 35, 189–90, 317, 545
  addiction 421
  adolescents 394
  BPD 37, 304–5, 307–8, 309, 349, 351, 353–6
  case conceptualization 138
  chair work 202
  Cluster C disorders 398–9, 401–7, 409–10, 411
  core emotional needs 43, 54
  couples 325, 330–1, 332, 333, 334
  eating disorders 150–1, 159, 160–4, 168
  experiential techniques 108
  experimental studies 512–13, 514

forensic settings 426, 435, 436
group ST 349, 351, 353–6, 368–9
joy and play 215, 216, 225
measurement 287, 293, 295, 296
mindfulness 233, 236, 240, 241–3, 249–56, 275–6, 280
narcissistic PD 83, 87–8
OCD 174, 177, 178–81
personal therapy 467, 468, 469
SMI 542, 545, 546, 547, 550
SMQ 542
therapist self-care 480, 481, 485, 489, 490
Healthy Boundaries/Developed Self 56
healthy choices 410, 411
Healthy vs Schema voice dialogue 157
Helpless/Lonely Child 466
Helpless/Vulnerable Child 468
here and now orientation 260, 266–7
heroin 415, 417–19
High-Dimensional Factor model 535
histrionic personality disorder 17, 175, 498, 589
  experimental studies 514, 528
  SMI-2 549
homework 88–9, 260, 274, 290, 366
  case conceptualization 69, 76
  couples 327, 331
  eating disorders 158, 162
  SCBT-g 376, 378
  training 443, 455, 457, 458
hominid parenting 49–51
honesty 482
hope 71, 484
hostility 7
human potential movement 13
human suffering 474–5, 476–7
humanistic movement 4, 13–15, 203
hypervigilance 520–1, 522, 524, 527
hypnotherapy 11, 12, 13, 14

idealization 114
identity formation 351–3
imagery 16, 17, 19, 78, 187, 189–90, 192
  addiction 420–1, 422–3
  adolescents 394, 395
  BPD 305–6, 346, 347–8, 353
  case conceptualization 77–9, 126, 129
  chair work 197, 202, 205

imagery (cont'd)
  Cluster C disorders 402, 404, 406, 407, 408–13
  core emotional needs 46
  couples 328–9, 332, 334
  eating disorders 157–9, 161–3, 168
  experiential techniques 11–14
  forensic settings 428, 429, 434, 436
  group ST 337–8, 346, 347–8, 353, 362, 365–7
  individual ST 315–17
  joy and play 211, 213, 215–23
  meditation 269
  mindfulness and acceptance 230, 231, 233, 243, 254
  mindfulness protocol 271, 272, 277
  narcissistic PD 83, 85–9
  OCD 177, 178, 179–81
  personal therapy 466, 467, 468
  social support interventions 295
  therapist self-care 489
  training 442, 443, 445, 454, 455, 457
imagery rescripting 11–12, 19, 187, 189–90, 367, 503
  addiction 420, 423
  Cluster C disorders 407, 408–12
  eating disorders 161–3, 168
  group ST 338
  individual ST 316–17
  mindfulness 253
  personal therapy 467, 468
  phases of ST development 16, 17
  training 455, 457
Impaired Autonomy 481
Impaired Autonomy and Performance 58, 59, 60, 61
Impaired Limits 59, 60, 94, 481
implementation of ST 555–67, 579–83
Implicit Association 523, 525, 550
Impulsive Child 34, 236, 485, 544
  addiction 418, 419, 420
  BPD 342, 400
  chair work 202
  couples 324
  forensic settings 430, 436
  joy and play 210
  SMI 543, 544–5
  YAMI 543
impulsivity 46

incremental and cost-effectiveness ratio (ICER) 586–7, 589, 592–3, 595
independence 47–8, 49, 50–1, 485
  and competence 60
indicators for ST 92
individual ST 311–21, 337, 556, 599, 603
  couples 328–9
inpatient treatment 18, 70, 301–9, 359–70, 498
  assessment 91, 93–4, 97
  group ST 341, 345, 350, 352, 355, 359–70, 373
Insufficient Self-Control/Self-Discipline 31, 38, 128, 290–1, 458
  core emotional needs 57, 59
  eating disorders 506
  efficacy and effectiveness 501, 503, 506
  forensic settings 501, 537
  four cluster model 60
  mindfulness 273–5
  narcissistic PD 81
  SCBT-g 374, 375, 377, 379
  substance abuse 503
  YSQ 537
intelligence 97, 428
Interacting Cognitive Subsystems (ICS) model 11
Internal Child and Parent 241
internal dialogues 199, 201–4, 206
internalizing problems 38, 41
International Society of Schema Therapy (ISST) 16, 20, 357, 459, 599–600
  therapist self-care 488–9
  training 441–4, 450, 455, 458, 459, 461
interpersonal theory 6–10, 17
interpersonal techniques 365, 366–7, 377
interpretation of experimental studies 525–6
intrinsic motivation 52
Invalidating Childhood Experiences Scale 120
Isolation 343

joint understanding of formulation 71
joy and play 209–26, 307, 350–1, 483
  deprivation 211–12
Junior Schema Therapists 447–8

keepsakes, memories and connection boxes 224

leading by client 484
legal costs 592
letter writing 187, 189, 332, 408
letting go 260, 265–6
leverage 83, 84–7
limit-setting 57, 61, 187, 190, 360
　addiction 420
　forensic settings 433–4
　joy and play 209
　narcissistic PD 83, 84–8
　OCD 175
　therapist self-care 485
　training 444, 454, 455, 458, 460
limited reparenting 8–9, 187, 192, 290, 343–5, 427–8, 566
　addiction 420, 422
　adolescents 392
　BPD 341–2, 343–5, 354
　Cluster C disorders 404, 408
　eating disorders 160, 163, 168
　efficacy and effectiveness 497
　forensic settings 427–8, 429, 430–1, 432, 435
　group ST 338, 341–2, 343–5, 354, 360, 367, 376–7
　individual ST 314, 316, 320
　joy and play 209
　mindfulness 231, 279
　narcissistic PD 83, 84, 88
　OCD 175, 177, 178
　SCBT-g 376–7
　therapeutic alliance 102–3
　therapist self-care 473–90
　training 443, 444, 453–5, 458
Limited Reparenting Inventory 54
Linehan training 313, 565
Lisrell program 547
Lonely Child 82–3, 306, 343, 544, 549
Lonely/Inferior Child 398, 399, 400, 408
long (L) alleles 44–5
long-term psychotherapy (LTP) 557, 559–61, 562–3
loyalty 482

magic tricks 213–14
major depressive disorder (MDD) 174
Maladaptive Child 304, 306–7
maladaptive coping modes 33, 34, 38, 216

Maladaptive Parent 176, 216, 547
mapping of resources 71
Mastery/Success 56, 60, 61
measurement 283–97, 556, 560, 588, 606
　SMI validation 541–50
　YSQ 531–8
medication 361, 363, 502, 505, 591, 594
meditation 259–70, 272
　mindfulness 229, 233, 234, 239–40, 243, 259–70
memory 250, 251
mental disability 579–80
mentalization-based therapy (MBT) 94, 290, 478, 479, 589
meta-cognitive therapy (MCT) 240–1
meta-level shift 485
metaphors 231, 233, 234, 237
methadone 416
middle childhood 50–1
mindfulness 185, 191, 192–4, 229–37, 239–46, 315
　acceptance 249–56
　eating disorders 159, 162–3, 167
　eight-session protocol 271–81
　group ST 338, 370, 380
　meditation 229, 233, 234, 239–40, 243, 259–70
　therapist self-care 478–9
mindfulness-based cognitive therapy (MBCT) 192–4, 229–30, 231–2, 234, 240
mindfulness-based stress reduction (MBSR) 229, 240
M. I. N. I. 563
Minnesota Multiphasic Personality Inventory (MMPI) 97
Mistrust/Abuse 30, 38, 104, 115–16, 119, 520
　addiction 503
　core emotional needs 55, 58, 59
　couples 324, 326
　eating disorders 154, 156
　efficacy and effectiveness 503, 573, 577
　four cluster model 60
　measurement 289, 291, 295
　mindfulness 233
　narcissistic PD 81
　therapist self-care 487

mode cycles 324–5, 326–8, 330–5
Mode Observation Scale (MOS) 421
molecular biology 43–6
motherese 50
Mothers/Maternal mode 46–9, 50
motivation 292, 293, 464, 470
  addiction 416–17, 420, 422
  adolescents 392, 393
  forensic settings 435, 436
mourning problems 503, 505
movement therapy 442
Multidimensional Family Therapy (MDFT) 396
multidisciplinary teams 361, 369, 370
  forensic settings 569–78, 580–3
Multi-Impulsivity Scale 119
Multimodal Therapy 198
Multisystemic Therapy (MST) 396
music therapy 362, 442
Mutuality/Self-Care 57

narcissistic personality disorder 15, 17, 33, 38, 81–9, 311
  addiction 415, 416, 417–18, 419
  case conceptualization 132
  cost-effectiveness of ST 589
  couples 324, 330
  eating disorders 146
  efficacy and effectiveness 499, 500, 501
  experimental studies 514, 528
  forensic settings 425, 428, 432
  group ST 338, 501
  OCD 175
  personal therapy 465, 467, 468, 469–70
  SMI 543, 549
  SMI-2 549
  training 443, 449, 455, 460
Needy Child 147–8, 151, 155, 162–3, 165, 168
negative affectivity 42–3, 44, 46, 536
Negative Self-Beliefs Scale – Eating Disorder Beliefs Questionnaire (EDBQ-NSB) 111, 113, 117, 119
Negativity/Pessimism 30, 53–4, 175, 178, 254–5, 537
NEO Personality Inventory – Revised (NEO-PI-R) 96–7, 534–5
neuroticism 42–3, 44–6
non-judgmental acceptance 260, 267–8

nurses 570–1, 573, 600
nurturing 482

object relations theory 6–10, 14, 186, 271
obsessive-compulsive disorder (OCD) 19, 115–16, 173–82
  assessment 97
  Cluster C disorders 397, 401–3, 411, 412
  cost-effectiveness of ST 589
  couples 330
  eating disorders 146
  efficacy and effectiveness 498
  experimental studies 512, 524–5, 527
  measurement 288, 289
  mindfulness and acceptance 236, 240, 254
Obsessive Over-Controller 35, 545
offense-paralleling behaviors 431–2
openness and directness 482
optimism 483
Organism-Variable 241–2
organization 486
other-joy 50
other-soothing 43, 50
outcome 112, 113–14, 374–6, 565, 603, 607
  cost-effectiveness of ST 586–7, 589
  eating disorders 168
  efficacy and effectiveness 495–508
  measurement 283, 284, 285–94
  OCD 174, 179
  routine monitoring 283–4, 294
Outcome Questionnaire-45 296
Over-Compensation 29, 31–2, 35, 106, 457, 575
  case conceptualization 129–32, 136–7, 139
  personal therapy 465, 467, 468
  therapist self-care 486–7
Over-Compensator 233, 405, 512–13
  SMI 542, 543, 544
  SMQ 542, 543
Over-Controller 16, 132, 137, 138, 464
over-involvement 464

panic disorder 69–70, 73, 585
Paranoid Over-Controller 420, 422, 498
  forensic settings 426, 427, 431

paranoid personality disorders 17, 35, 175, 549, 589
   efficacy and effectiveness 498, 499
   experimental studies 514, 521
   substance abuse 415, 418
Parental Bonding Inventory 120
parenting 28, 42–3, 393–4
patient motivation inventories 292, 293
past major depression 73
patients and patient associations 603–4
peer supervision 194, 356, 449, 601
   case conceptualization 126, 135, 139
   forensic settings 433, 580
   implementation of ST 560, 563, 566, 580
   individual ST 320, 321
   measurement 284, 294
   therapist self-care 473, 487
   training 443–8, 449, 453, 459–60
perceptions of reality 114
perfectionism 119, 138, 401–2
   eating disorders 146, 147, 152, 154
Perfectionist Controller 147, 149, 151, 158–60, 164–6, 168
Perfectionist Over-Controller 549
   Cluster C disorders 398, 401–3, 405, 406, 412
   OCD 175–7, 178–9, 181
persistence 84–5
Personal Construct Theory 5
personal therapy 463–70, 487, 489
Personality Beliefs Questionnaire (PBQ) 111, 113, 117, 119
   Short Version (PBQ-SF) 113, 117
personality disorders (PDs) 7, 14, 27–8, 33, 38, 397–414, 495–500
   addiction 415–23
   adolescents 391
   assessment 91–8
   case conceptualization 70, 127, 132
   childhood trauma 174
   cost-effectiveness of ST 585, 588, 589
   couples 330
   eating disorders 145, 146
   efficacy and effectiveness 494–508, 569–78
   experimental studies 511–17, 519–28
   forensic settings 425–8, 437, 500–1, 569–78, 579–83

   group ST 341, 366, 369, 374–5, 501
   implementation of ST 556, 557, 562, 579–83
   individual ST 311–13
   measurement 284, 288, 290
   mindfulness protocol 271–3, 280
   personal therapy 470
   phases of ST development 15, 17, 18
   PR 600–1, 604
   SCBT-g 374–5
   schema inventories 111, 117, 119
   SMI 543, 548, 549–50
   SMI-2 549
   training 441, 444, 446, 453, 455, 459
   YSQ 533–4
Personality Disorders Beliefs Questionnaire (PDBQ) 113, 117, 119
personality disorder not otherwise specified 312
Pessimism/Negativity 175, 178
pharmacotherapy *see* medication
Physical Safety/Resilience 56
Plasticity Hypothesis 44, 45–6
play 209–26, 307, 350–1, 483
   deprivation 211–12
Playful/Exuberant Child 210, 213, 215–16, 226
playful little self 211, 212–13, 215, 219–21, 225–6
polypsychism 13–14
pornography 82
Positive Affectivity 536
post-imagery discussion 78–9
post-traumatic stress disorder (PTSD) 11, 19
   adolescents 391
   efficacy and effectiveness 503, 505
   experimental studies 524, 525
   OCD 174
   vicarious 489
pragmatic interference 523
praise and love 482, 484
Predator 35, 423, 516
   addiction 417–18, 419, 420, 423
   forensic settings 426–7, 430, 431, 433, 500
pregnancy 392
presence 481–2
primary caretakers 7–8

prison officers 571–2, 573
problem integration 73, 79
problem list 71–2
Process-Experiential/Emotion-Focused Therapy 199
productivity loss 585, 589, 591
progressive muscle relaxation (PMR) 263, 264–5
prospective members 447
protection 482
Protector 16, 405
psychiatry 559, 562, 600
   cost-effectiveness 585, 590, 592, 594, 597
   forensic settings 572, 580
   training 441, 446, 449
psychoanalysis 4–9, 12, 186, 463, 478–9
   cost-effectiveness 588–9
psychodrama 9, 11–13, 16
   chair work 198, 199, 201, 202, 204
psychodynamics 4–5, 7, 10–11, 16, 18, 185
   affective/anxiety disorder 70
   chair work 197, 203
   experiential techniques 102
   group ST 338–9
   measurement 288, 290
   mindfulness 271
psychogenic blindness 12
psychologists 557, 562, 600, 605
   forensic settings 572–3, 580–2
   training 441–2, 446, 449
psychomotor therapy (PMT) 107, 362, 367
psychopathy 516
   addiction 416–17, 418, 419, 420
   forensic settings 425, 427, 429–32, 434–6
Psychopathy Checklist – Revised (PCL-R) 418, 419, 432–3
psychosynthesis 14
psychotherapy 362, 463, 465, 605
   cost-effectiveness 585, 588–90, 594
   forensic settings 572–3, 580–3
   group ST 361, 362, 365, 366
   implementation of ST 557, 559, 560–2
   therapist self-care 473, 486
   training 441–2, 446, 447, 449, 453
psychotic decompensation 108
psychotic disorders 503, 506, 563–4, 588
   forensic settings 579–80

public relations (PR) 599–607
pulvinar neurons 44
Punitive Parent 16, 35, 80, 189, 192, 305–6, 353
   addiction 417, 418
   adolescents 395
   BPD 36–7, 304–9, 342, 344, 347, 349, 351–4
   chair work 202
   Cluster C disorders 398–407, 412
   couples 324, 325, 331, 333
   experimental studies 512–13, 515
   group ST 342, 344, 347, 349, 351–4, 362
   individual ST 318
   joy and play 219, 223, 225
   measurement 292
   mindfulness 231, 240–3
   OCD 177, 178–80
   personal therapy 470
   schema inventories 118
   SMI 542, 545, 546, 547, 550
   SMQ 542
   therapist self-care 482, 488
   training 454, 455
Punitiveness 31, 53, 54, 82, 178, 537

quality adjusted life years (QALYs) 587, 588, 589, 593, 594–6
questionnaires 96–7, 374–5, 404, 531–8
   assessment 95, 96–7, 98
   couples 326, 328, 330, 334
   experimental studies 512–13, 515
   measurement 285, 287, 296
   mindfulness 230, 235, 273–4
   SMI validation 541–50

randomized controlled trials (RCTs) 3–4, 16, 17, 311
   BPD 301, 341, 357, 359
   Cluster C disorders 411, 413
   efficacy and effectiveness 495–7, 499–505, 507
   forensic settings 425–6, 437
   group ST 337–8, 341, 357, 359, 373
   implementation of ST 557–8, 559–60, 565
   training 443, 446
rational emotive behavioral therapy 5, 588

rational emotive therapy 5, 600
rational therapy 5
reactions 524–5
reasonable/realistic expectations 60, 61
Realistic Standards 60, 483
Realistic Standards/Acceptance of Imperfections 57
reality testing 287
recall bias 114, 121
Reciprocity/Equality 57, 60
Redecision Therapy 198, 200
referrers 600–1, 605, 607
reflect collaboratively 486
reflective distance 71
registration and certification of ST therapists 441–50, 600
    Advanced International 442, 443, 450, 456, 458, 461
    Dutch situation 446–8, 450
    training 455–6, 458, 459
rehabilitation 421, 422
Relapse Management Module 422
Relational Frame Theory (RFT) 250
Relational Therapy 556
relaxation 190, 236, 260, 263–5, 271
reparenting 8–9, 12–13, 17, 20
    see also limited reparenting
Reparenting Inventory 54
resolution sessions 334
responsibility to others 486
Reviewing the Evidence 157
Revised Conflict Tactics Scale (RCTS) 326
role-playing 17, 187, 189, 192, 558, 605
    addiction 420
    BPD 306, 345–6, 349–50
    Cluster C disorders 409, 410
    couples 332
    experiential techniques 104–6, 108
    forensic settings 428, 434
    group ST 337, 338, 345–6, 349–50, 362, 377, 379
    individual ST 316, 317, 319
    measurement 289, 295
    mindfulness 243, 254, 271
    personal therapy 467, 468
    SCBT-g 377, 379
    therapist self-care 484
    training 443, 454, 455–6, 460, 467

Routine Outcome Monitoring (ROM) 283–4, 294

safety 361–2, 377, 379
SCBT-g (group schema cognitive behavior therapy) 338, 373–80
schema change/trauma process 313, 316–17
schema complementarities 444–5, 458
schema dialogues 187, 315, 387, 443, 455
schema flipping 118
Schema-Focused Cognitive Therapy (SFCT) 156–7
schema-focused emotional-behavioral group therapy (SET) 501
schema-focused treatment plan (SFTP) 574–7
schema inventories 77, 111–22
Schema Mode Inventory (SMI) 112–13, 118, 120, 541–50
    BPD 303
    case conceptualization 132
    couples 326, 327, 334
    eating disorders 117, 120, 157
    experimental studies 513, 514
    measurement 285, 297
    therapist self-care 487
Schema Mode Inventory-2 (SMI-2) 549–50, 514
schema mode models 14, 16, 27, 33–5, 36–8, 531
    addiction 416, 417
    BPD 33, 36–7, 38
    case conceptualization 132, 135–6, 137–8, 403, 428
    chair work 197
    Cluster C disorders 399, 400–3, 405, 411
    dependent PD 400–1, 403
    eating disorders 146, 168
    forensic settings 426, 428, 429, 433
    mindfulness 241
    OCD 173–82, 401–2, 403
    personal therapy 463–70
schema mode questionnaire (SMQ) 374, 541, 542–3
schema questionnaire (SQ) 374
Schema Therapy Competency Rating Scale (STCRS) 458, 461

schizoid personality disorder 513, 535
schizotypal personality disorder 513
scoring 119, 532–3, 534–6
   SMI 542, 545–50
script analysis 12–13
security and stability 60, 481
self-acceptance and openness 60
Self-Acceptance/Pride 55
Self-Aggrandizer 35, 234, 236, 432, 545
   addiction 417–18, 419, 420
   Cluster C disorders 398, 402
   couples 324
   forensic settings 427, 431, 432, 435, 572
   narcissistic PD 82
   SMI 543, 545, 546, 548
self-compassion 71, 77, 78, 475–7, 481, 483–4
Self-Control/Self Discipline 7, 57, 60, 536
Self-Determination Theory (SDT) 52
self-disclosure 482–3
   narcissistic PD 83, 84, 85, 88
   training 443, 454, 459, 460
self-harm/self-injury 93, 190, 241, 338, 569, 589
   BPD 303, 304, 305
   eating disorders 148, 158, 162, 163
   individual ST 313, 314–15, 318
   OCD 176, 178
self-in-context strategy 254
Self-Punitiveness 235
self-reflection 236, 239, 242, 244, 245
self-reparenting 9
Self-Sacrifice 30, 32, 291, 445, 503, 548
   case conceptualization 129–31, 137, 139–40
   chair work 202
   core emotional needs 42, 57, 58, 59
   eating disorders 155
   group ST 355, 374, 375, 377, 378
   personal therapy 465, 466
   substance abuse 503
   therapist self-care 481, 489
   YSQ 534, 536
self-soothing 43, 46–7
self-verbalization 242
Semantic Simon 523
Senior Schema Therapists 447–8
semi-structured interviews 95, 96
serotonergic system 44, 45

setting indicators 93–4
Severity Index for Personality Pathology (SIPP) 97
sexual abuse 36, 174, 214, 215
Shame/Defectiveness 210
Shamed/Deprived Child 147–8, 151, 155, 157–63, 165, 168
short (S) alleles 44–6, 49
short-term group 338
siblings 343–4, 349, 352, 356, 466
Simon experiments 523, 524
situational analysis 73–5
sleeping problems 72, 73, 93, 105, 244
slow deep breathing 263, 264
social anxiety 72, 73, 79
Social Inclusion/Affinity with Others 55
Social Isolation/Alienation 30, 55, 58–9, 115–16, 275
   case conceptualization 129–31, 137, 140
   eating disorders 154
   four cluster model 60
   measurement 290, 294, 295
   narcissistic PD 81
   OCD 175, 176
social phobia 19, 73, 126, 127
social skills training 499, 501
social smile 50
social support interventions 292–3, 295–6
Social Undesirability 29, 30, 53, 531, 533, 537
socialization to ST 71
socio-therapy 441, 449, 450
   forensic settings 579–83
   group ST 361, 363, 365, 366
Socratic dialogue 9, 185, 187
somatic disorders 588
speed 418, 419
Spoilt or Undisciplined Child 419
Spontaneous/Joyful Child 350–1
stability 60, 481
Stable Attachment 55
Stand Evaluation Project 359
step-by-step 366
strain on the surroundings 592
strength and decisiveness 486
stress 259, 263, 273
Stroop experiments 522–3, 524, 527
structural equation modeling 533
structure and limits 475–7, 481, 485–6

structured clinical interview (SCID-I) 96, 513, 547
structured clinical interview (SCID-II) 96, 512, 547, 563
Subjugation 30, 38, 115–16, 119, 188, 548
  affective/anxiety disorder 69, 77
  core emotional needs 56, 58, 59
  eating disorders 147, 154
  experiential techniques 106
  experimental studies 520
  four cluster model 60
  group ST 355, 367, 379
  joy and play 211, 217
  measurement 291
  mindfulness 275
  narcissistic PD 82
  OCD 176
  personal therapy 465
  therapist self-care 489
substance abuse 15, 16, 120, 415–23, 501–4, 514
  adolescents 392
  assessment 93, 95, 96
  BPD 302, 303, 304, 355, 514
  Cluster C disorders 412
  cost-effectiveness of ST 585, 590, 594
  couples 326, 329, 334
  eating disorders 145, 158, 159
  forensic settings 426–7, 428, 569, 571, 572, 574–5
  group ST 338, 355, 360
  implementation of ST 557, 563
  measurement 290
  narcissistic PD 82
  training 460
  see also addiction
suicide and suicidal ideation 93, 489, 521
  BPD 302–3, 304–7, 346, 348, 355
  cost-effectiveness of ST 593, 595
  group ST 338, 346, 348, 355
  individual ST 312, 315
  OCD 178
  productivity loss 591
supervision of implementation of ST 566
supervisor-supervisee relationship 457, 458, 461
Surrender 29, 31, 32, 29 575
  case conceptualization 131–2, 136–7, 139, 140

Suspicious Over-Controller 549
sustained mutual gaze 50
symptom checklist (SCL-90) 97, 563
symptom management 312, 314–15
systematic desensitization 5
Systems Training for Emotional Predictability and Problem-Solving (STEPP) 94–5, 313
  VERS training 565

teaching delay strategies 485
teaching healthy attitudes 410
telephone support 17, 318–19, 468, 562, 565
  cost-effectiveness of ST 590
  efficacy and effectiveness 497
  individual ST 315, 319, 321
  implementation of ST 559–60, 562, 564–7
  therapist self-care 473, 481
  training 445
temperament 28–9, 42–6, 49
Temperament and Character Inventory (TCI) 534
terminating therapy 490
test-retest reliability 533, 536, 549
thematic apperception test (TAT) 523, 525, 526
therapeutic alliance/relationship 18, 186, 288–90, 291–2
  addiction 416, 422
  adolescents 393, 395
  assessment 96
  BPD 303–4, 309
  case conceptualization 71, 75–6, 79, 125–6, 128, 134–5, 141
  Cluster C disorders 410
  cost-effectiveness of ST 590
  couples 325, 328, 331, 333, 334
  eating disorders 146
  efficacy and effectiveness 497, 500, 502–5
  experiential techniques 102–4, 108
  forensic settings 427, 435
  group ST 292, 369, 376
  implementation of ST 563, 565
  individual ST 312–13, 314, 320
  joy and play 211–12, 213–15, 216
  measurement 283–97

therapeutic alliance/relationship (cont'd)
  mindfulness 271
  narcissistic PD 83
  OCD 174–5, 176–7, 178, 179
  SCBT-g 376
  sexual feelings 486, 488–9
  techniques of ST 186, 187–8, 191–2, 194
  therapist self-care 474, 475, 478, 480–3, 486, 488
  training 443–6, 449, 454–6, 458–60
therapist self-care 473–90
third-wave therapies 240, 249
tic disorder 174, 177–9
tracking your thoughts in time 266–7
Trainees and Supervisors Resource Network 461
training 441–50, 453–61, 560, 600, 606
  content of program 442–4
  Dutch situation 446–8
  forensic settings 449, 577, 580–3
  implementation of ST 558–9, 560, 565
  schema mode model 463, 467
  therapist self-care 487
Transactional Analysis (TA) 6, 9, 10, 13, 14
Transference Focused Psychotherapy (TFP) 43, 290, 496–7
  cost-effectiveness 592, 593, 594–6
transitional objects 47
transparency 477, 482
trauma 28–9, 343, 473, 521
  chair work 199, 200, 204–6
  joy and play 215, 225
  vicarious 489
treatment plans 70, 112, 442, 454, 601
  case conceptualization 70, 79, 125, 126, 135
  Cluster C disorders 403–11
  eating disorders 146
  group ST 361–3, 364
  schema-focused (SFTP) 574–7
triggers 31, 486–7, 516
  couples 328, 329, 333, 334
  forensic settings 427, 428
  group ST 344, 346, 347, 356
  mindfulness 233–5, 272–3, 275–7, 279, 280

trust 234, 482, 523
  core emotional needs 54, 55
  forensic settings 428–30, 433–5
  four cluster model 60
  joy and play 212, 218
trusted adviser imagery 269

unconditional positive regard 6
Undisciplined Child 34, 410, 544, 546
universality 17
unpredictability 7–8
unrealistic expectations 464
Unrelenting Standards/Hypercriticalness 30, 119, 274, 457
  case conceptualization 129–31, 135, 137, 140
  core emotional needs 57, 58, 59
  eating disorders 147, 149, 154
  forensic settings 577
  four cluster model 60
  measurement 291
  mindfulness 233
  narcissistic PD 81
  personal therapy 465
  therapist self-care 483, 489
  YSQ 534
unstructured clinical interview 95–6
urge surfing 163

values 260, 269
Vancouver Obsessional Compulsive Inventory 119
vicarious traumatization 489
Visual Analog Scale (VAS) 188, 542–3, 545
visual (dot)-probe 523, 524
Vulnerable Child 9, 16–17, 33, 34, 43, 189, 544
  addiction 418, 420, 422, 423
  BPD 36–7, 306–7, 309, 342–5, 348, 351, 356
  case conceptualization 132, 137, 138
  chair work 202
  Cluster C disorders 398, 402, 406–7, 408–9
  couples 325, 330–1, 332–4
  experiential techniques 107
  experimental studies 513
  forensic settings 427–8, 429–30, 435–6

group ST 342–5, 348, 351, 356, 368, 570, 572
individual ST 318
joy and play 210, 211, 213, 215, 224–5
mindfulness 232–3, 236, 240, 251, 272
narcissistic PD 82
OCD 174, 175, 176–7, 178–81
personal therapy 464, 467, 468–70
SMI 543–6, 550
therapist self-care 476, 480, 482, 484, 488–9
training 454, 455
YAMI 543
Vulnerable/Abandoned Child 215, 346–9
group ST 342, 346–9, 350–1, 354–5
Vulnerability to Harm or Illness 30, 56, 58–9, 60, 235
meditation 265
mindfulness 233, 242
OCD 175
panic disorder 69

Wechsler Abbreviated Scales of Intelligence 47
Weiss-Correto Marital Status Inventory (MSI) 326
whole group ("fishbowl") exercises 455
WHOQol 563
workbooks 364

Y-BOCS 173
yoga 159, 162

Young Atkinson Mode Inventory (YAMI) 112–13, 118–19, 132
SMI 541, 543–4
Young Compensation Inventory (YCI) 113, 117, 119, 130
Revised (YCI-R) 113, 114
Young Parenting Inventory (YPI) 113, 118, 119–20
case conceptualization 130
core emotional needs 41
couples 326
Revised (YPI-R) 113
therapist self-care 487
Young-Rygh Avoidance Inventory (YRAI) 113, 117, 119, 130
Revised (YRAI-R) 113
Young Schema Inventories (YSI) 168, 563
Young Schema Questionnaire (YSQ) 29, 31, 111–17, 119–21, 531–8
BPD 303
case conceptualizations 77, 128, 130, 139
core emotional needs 41–2, 52, 53, 58, 61
couples 326
eating disorders 156
group ST 374
measurement 285, 296–7
scoring 532–6
Short (YSQ-S) 113, 115, 116
therapist self-care 487
Young Therapy Adherence and Competence Scale 558